—BRITISH—
LITERATURE

Prepared Exclusively for the American School®

Introductions taken from:

The Longman Anthology of British Literature: The Middle Ages,
The Early Modern Period, and The Restoration and The Eighteenth Century
Volume A, Second Compact Edition
Edited by: David Damrosch, Christopher Baswell, Clare Carroll,
Constance Jordan, Anne Howland Schotter and Stuart Sherman

and

The Longman Anthology of British Literature: Romantics and Their Contemporaries,
The Victorian Age, and the Twentieth Century
Volume B, Second Compact Edition
Edited by: David Damrosch, Kevin J. H. Dettmar, Heather Henderson,
Peter J. Manning, William Chapman Sharpe, Jennifer Wicke and Susan J. Wolfson

Cover image courtesy of Photodisc/Getty

Introductions taken from:

The Longman Anthology of British Literature: The Middle Ages, The Early Modern Period, and The Restoration and The Eighteenth Century, Volume A, Second Compact Edition
Edited by: David Damrosch, Christopher Baswell, Clare Carroll, Constance Jordan, Anne Howland Schotter and Stuart Sherman
Copyright © 2004 by Pearson Education, Inc.
Published by Longman
New York, New York 10036

The Longman Anthology of British Literature: Romantics and Their Contemporaries, The Victorian Age, and the Twentieth Century, Volume B, Second Compact Edition
Edited by: David Damrosch, Kevin J. H. Dettmar, Heather Henderson, Peter J. Manning, William Chapman Sharpe, Jennifer Wicke and Susan J. Wolfson
Copyright © 2004 by Pearson Education, Inc.
Published by Longman

Printed in the United States of America

10 9 8 7 6

ISBN 0-536-30907-8

2006240417

SB/HA

Please visit our web site at *www.pearsoncustom.com*

PEARSON CUSTOM PUBLISHING
75 Arlington Street, Suite 300, Boston, MA 02116
A Pearson Education Company

COPYRIGHT ACKNOWLEDGMENTS

CONTENTS

List of Illustrations   xii

The Middle Ages

Introduction to BEOWULF   1
from BEOWULF   5

Introduction to BEDE   20
    from An Ecclesiastical History of the English People   20

Introduction to THE WANDERER   22
THE WANDERER   23

ARTHURIAN MYTH IN THE HISTORY OF BRITAIN   26

GEOFFREY OF MONMOUTH
    from History of the Kings of Britain   27

Introduction to Sir Gawain and the Green Knight   28
from SIR GAWAIN AND THE GREEN KNIGHT   29

GEOFFREY CHAUCER
    Chaucer's Middle English   41
    Introduction to THE CANTERBURY TALES   43
    from The General Prologue   44
    from The Nun's Priest's Tale   45

The Early Modern Period

EDMUND SPENSER
    Introduction to THE FAERIE QUEENE   51
    from The First Booke of the Faerie Queene   52

ELIZABETH I
    Psalm 13 ("Fools that true faith yet never had")   58
    from The Metres of Boethius's *Consolation of Philosophy*
        Book 1, No. 7 ("Dim Clouds")   59

CHRISTOPHER MARLOWE
    The Passionate Shepherd to His Love   60
    from The Tragical History of Dr. Faustus   60

SIR WALTER RALEIGH
    The Nymph's Reply to the Shepherd   63

WILLIAM SHAKESPEARE
    Sonnets
        18 ("Shall I compare thee to a summer's day")   65
        29 ("When, in disgrace with fortune and men's eyes")   65
        73 ("That time of year thou mayst in me behold")   65
        116 ("Let me not to the marriage of true minds")   66
        130 ("My mistress' eyes are nothing like the sun")   66
    Twelfth Night; or, What You Will   66

BEN JONSON
    On Something, That Walks Somewhere   122
    On My First Son   122
    Song to Celia   122

JOHN DONNE
    The Good Morrow   123
    A Valediction: Forbidding Mourning   123
    from Holy Sonnets 6   124

LADY MARY WROTH
    from A Crown of Sonnets Dedicated to Love
        ("In this strange labyrinth how shall I turn?")   125

ROBERT HERRICK
    from Hesperides
        The Argument of His Book   126
        Delight in Disorder   126
        To the Virgins, to Make Much of Time   126

ANDREW MARVELL
>   To His Coy Mistress   127

JOHN MILTON
>   How Soon Hath Time   128
>   When I Consider How My Light Is Spent   129
>   *from* Paradise Lost   129

The Restoration and the Eighteenth Century

SAMUEL PEPYS
>   *from* The Diary [The Fire of London]   138

MARY, LADY CHUDLEIGH
>   To the Ladies   142

JONATHAN SWIFT
>   Introduction to GULLIVER'S TRAVELS   143
>   *from* Gulliver's Travels Part 4. A Voyage to the Country
>   of the Houyhnhnms   144

ALEXANDER POPE
>   *from* An Essay on Criticism   164
>   Introduction to THE RAPE OF THE LOCK   165
>   *from* The Rape of the Lock   166

THOMAS GRAY
>   Elegy Written in a Country Churchyard   168

SAMUEL JOHNSON
>   *from* A Dictionary of the English
>   Language [Some Entries]   172

JAMES BOSWELL
>   *from* The Life of Samuel Johnson, LL.D.
>   [Introduction; Boswell's Method]   176

The Romantics and Their Contemporaries

ANNA LETITIA BARBAULD
>   The Mouse's Petition to Dr. Priestley   178

WILLIAM BLAKE

Introduction to SONGS OF INNOCENCE AND OF EXPERIENCE   179
from Songs of Innocence
    The Lamb   180
    The Chimney Sweeper   181
from Songs of Experience
    The Fly   182
    The Tyger   183
    A Poison Tree   184

OLAUDAH EQUIANO

from The Interesting Narrative of the Life of
    Olaudah Equiano [The Slave Ship and Its Cargo]   185

MARY WOLLSTONECRAFT

from A Vindication of the Rights of Woman   187

ROBERT BURNS

To a Mouse   188
A Red, Red Rose   189

WILLIAM WORDSWORTH

Lines Written in Early Spring   190
Lines Written a Few Miles above Tintern Abbey   190
Song ("She dwelt among th' untrodden ways")   194
The world is too much with us   194
Composed upon Westminster Bridge, Sept. 3, 1802   195
It is a beauteous Evening   195
I wandered lonely as a cloud   195
My heart leaps up   196

DOROTHY WORDSWORTH

from The Grasmere Journals   196

SAMUEL TAYLOR COLERIDGE

from The Rime of the Ancient Mariner   198
Kubla Khan   205

GEORGE GORDON, LORD BYRON

She walks in beauty   206

from Childe Harold's Pilgrimage, Canto the Third   207
from Don Juan, Canto 1   209

PERCY BYSSHE SHELLEY
    Ozymandias   212
    Ode to the West Wind   213
    To a Sky-Lark   215

JOHN KEATS
    On First Looking into Chapman's Homer   218
    Sonnet: When I have fears   218
    Ode to a Nightingale   219

The Victorian Age

CHARLES DICKENS
    from Dombey and Son   221
    from Hard Times   222

ELIZABETH BARRETT BROWNING
    from Sonnets from the Portuguese
      38("First time he kissed me, he but only kissed")   224
      43 ("How do I love thee? Let me count the ways")   224
    from Aurora Leigh, Book 5 [Epic Art and Modern Life]   225

ALFRED, LORD TENNYSON
    The Lady of Shalott   227
    from In Memoriam A. H. H.   232
    The Charge of the Light Brigade   233

ROBERT BROWNING
    My Last Duchess   235
    Love Among the Ruins   236
    from Childe Roland to the Dark Tower Came   238

ELIZABETH GASKELL
    Our Society at Cranford   242

SIR ARTHUR CONAN DOYLE
    A Scandal in Bohemia   257

MATTHEW ARNOLD
    Dover Beach   272

CHRISTINA ROSSETTI
    Song ("When I am dead, my dearest")   273
    "No, Thank You, John"   273
    Promises Like Pie-Crust   274

GERARD MANLEY HOPKINS
    God's Grandeur   275
    The Windhover   275
    Pied Beauty   276

LEWIS CARROLL
    from Through the Looking-Glass (Jabberwocky)   276
    [Humpty Dumpty on Jabberwocky]   277

OSCAR WILDE
    The Importance of Being Earnest   278

The Twentieth Century

JOSEPH CONRAD
    from Heart of Darkness   317

BERNARD SHAW
    Pygmalion   321

THOMAS HARDY
    On the Departure Platform   388
    The Convergence of the Twain   388

WILLIAM BUTLER YEATS
    The Lake Isle of Innisfree   390
    The Wild Swans at Coole   390
    Sailing to Byzantium   391

JAMES JOYCE
    The Dead   392

T. S. ELIOT
    The Love Song of J. Alfred Prufrock   418

VIRGINIA WOOLF
   from A Room of One's Own   422

KATHERINE MANSFIELD
   The Daughters of the Late Colonel   426

D. H. LAWRENCE
   Odour of Chrysanthemums   439

W. H. AUDEN
   Musée des Beaux Arts   452

GEORGE ORWELL
   Shooting an Elephant   453

DYLAN THOMAS
   The Force That Through the Green Fuse
      Drives the Flower   458
   Do Not Go Gentle into That Good Night   458

PHILIP LARKIN
   MCMXIV   459

SEAMUS HEANEY
   The Singer's House   460
   Postscript   461

TED HUGHES
   Hawk Roosting   461

EAVAN BOLAND
   The Pomegranate   462

DEREK WALCOTT
   A Far Cry from Africa   463
   52   464

Index   465

LIST OF ILLUSTRATIONS

Color Plates

 1 First page of the Gospel of Matthew, from the Lindisfarne Gospels
 2 Gold buckle, from the Sutton Hoo ship-burial
 3 The Ardagh Chalice
 4 Map of England, from Historia Major
 5 Passion Scenes, from the Winchester Psalter
 6 King Arthur and His Knights, from a manuscript of the Prose Lancelot
 7 Two scenes from The Holkham Bible Picture Book
 8 Richard II with His Regalia
 9 Page of The Wife of Bath's Tale, from the Ellesmere Chaucer
10 Anne, Duchess of Bedford, Kneeling Before the Virgin Mary and Saint Anne, from the Bedford Hours
11 John Martin, The Bard
12 Thomas Gainsborough, Mary Robinson
13 Thomas Phillips, Lord Byron
14 Anonymous, Portrait of Olaudah Equiano
15 J. M. W. Turner, Slavers Throwing the Dead and Dying Overboard, Typhoon Coming On
16 William Blake, The Little Black Boy
17 William Blake, The Little Black Boy (another version of #16)
18 William Blake, The Tyger
19 William Blake, The Sick Rose
20 Joseph Wright, An Iron Forge Viewed from Without

Black-and-White Images

Saint John, from *The Book of Kells*	xiii
Peoples and places in *Beowulf*	2
Boar, from a bas-relief carving on St. Nicholas Church, Ipswich	8
The Swan Theatre	64
William Blake, *The Fly*	182
William Blake, *A Poison Tree*	184

Saint John, from *The Book of Kells.* Late 8th century. Courtesy of
Bridgeman Art Library. © The Board of Trinity College, Dublin, Ireland.

Introduction to Beowulf

Beowulf has come down to us as if by chance, for it is preserved only in a single manuscript now in the British Library, Cotton Vitellius A.xv, which almost perished in a fire in 1731. An anonymous poem in the West Saxon dialect of Old English, it may stretch back as early as the late eighth century, although recent scholars think the version we now have was composed within one hundred years of its transcription in the late tenth century. If the later date is correct, this first "English epic" could have appealed to one of the Viking kings who ruled in northern and eastern England. This would help explain a king's burial at sea, a Viking practice, that occurs early in the poem, and the setting of most of the poem's action in Scandinavia (see map, page 2). Although it was studied by a few antiquarians during the early modern period, *Beowulf* remained virtually unknown until its first printing in 1815, and it was only in the twentieth century that it achieved a place in the canon, not just as a cultural artifact or a good adventure story but as a philosophical epic of great complexity and power.

Several features of *Beowulf* make its genre problematic: the vivid accounts of battles with monsters link it to the folktale, and the sense of sorrow for the passing of worldly things mark it as elegiac. Nevertheless, it is generally agreed to be the first postclassical European epic. Like the *Iliad* and the *Odyssey*, it is a primary epic, originating in oral tradition and recounting the legendary wars and exploits of its audience's tribal ancestors from the heroic age.

The values of Germanic tribal society are indeed central to *Beowulf*. The tribal lord was held to ideals of extraordinary martial valor. More practically, he rewarded his successful followers with treasure that symbolized their mutual obligations. A member of the lord's *comitatus*—his band of warriors—was expected to follow a rigid code of heroic behavior stressing bravery, loyalty, and willingness to avenge lord and comrades at any cost. He would suffer the shame of exile if he should survive his lord in battle; the speaker of *The Wanderer* (pages 22–25) may be such a man. Such values are explicitly invoked at the end of *Beowulf*, when Wiglaf, the hero's only loyal retainer, upbraids his comrades for having abandoned Beowulf to the dragon: he says that their prince wasted his war gear on them, and predicts the demise of their people, the Geats, once their ancient enemies, the Swedes, hear that Beowulf is dead.

Beowulf offers an extraordinary double perspective, however. First, for all its acceptance of the values of pagan heroic code, it also refers to Christian concepts that in many cases conflict with them. Although all characters in the poem—Danes, Swedes, and Geats, as well as the monsters—are pagan, the monster Grendel is described as descended from Cain and destined for hell. It is the joyous song of creation at Hrothgar's banquet, reminiscent of Genesis 1, that inspires Grendel to attack. Furthermore, while violence in the service of revenge is presented as the proper way for Beowulf to respond to inhuman assailants such as Grendel's mother, the narrator expresses a regretful view, perhaps influenced by Christianity, of the unending chain of violence engaged in by feuding tribes. And although the Danish king Hrothgar uses wealth as a kind of social sacrament when he lavishly rewards Beowulf for his military aid, he simultaneously invokes God in a "sermon" warning him against excessive pride in his youthful strength. This rich division of emotional loyalty probably arises from a poet and audience of Christians who look back at their pagan ancestors with both pride and grief, stressing the intersection of pagan and Christian values in an effort to reconcile the two. By restricting his biblical references to events in the Old Testament, the poet shows the Germanic revenge ethic as consistent with the Old Law of retribution, and leaves implicit its conflict with the New Testament injunction to forgive one's enemies.

Peoples and places in *Beowulf,* after F. Klaeber.

The style *of Beowulf* is simultaneously a challenge and a reward to the modern reader. Some of its features, such as the variation of an idea in different words—which would have been welcomed by a listening, and often illiterate, audience—can seem repetitious to a literate audience. The poem's somewhat archaic diction can make it seem difficult as well, although the translators of the version included here have adopted a more straightforward and colloquial style than was often used in the past. By rendering the opening word "Hwaet!" as "So!" rather than "Hark!" or "Lo!" they have avoided the stuffiness of earlier versions. They have also tried to reduce the confusion arising from the poem's use of patronymics—phrases identifying a character by his father's name. Though they generally retain the designations of Beowulf as "Ecgtheow's son," they often substitute the name of a minor character for the poem's patronymic, rendering "Ecglaf's son" as "Unferth," for instance.

Two other stylistic features that are indebted to the poem's oral origin are highly admired today. First, like other Old English poems, *Beowulf* uses alliteration as a structural principle, beginning three of the four stressed words in a line with the same letter. The translators have sought the same effect, even when departing considerably from the original language, as when they render the line, "waes se grimma gaest Grendel haten" in the passage below as "a horror from hell, hideous Grendel." The poet also uses compound words, such as *mearcstapa* ("borderland-prowler") and *fifelcynnes* ("of monsterkind"), with unusual inventiveness and force. A specific type of compound used for powerful stylistic effects is the "kenning," a kind of compressed metaphor, such as "swan-road" for "ocean" or "wave-courser" for "ship." The kennings resemble the Old English riddles in their teasing, enigmatic quality.

On a larger narrative level is another stylistic feature, also traceable to the poem's oral roots: the tendency to digress into stories tangential to the action of the main plot. The poet's digressions, however, actually contribute to his artistry of broad contrasts—youth and age, joy and sorrow, good and bad kingship. For instance, Hrothgar, while urging humility and generosity on the victorious Beowulf, tells the story of the proud and parsimonious King Heremod. Similarly, when Beowulf returns home in glory to the kingdom of the Geats, the poet praises his uncle Hygelac's young Queen Hygd by contrasting her with the bad Queen Modthryth, who lost her temper and sent her suitors to death.

These episodes also return to prominent themes like nobility, heroic glory, and the distribution of treasure. Such return to key themes, as well as the poem's formulaic repetition and stylistic variation, all bear comparison to insular art of its time. As seen in the page from the *Book of Kells* illustrated on page xiii, the dense repetition of lines and intertwined curves, even zoomorphic shapes (often called interlace), competes for attention with the central image of Saint John. This intricately crafted biblical image, like the royal treasure from Sutton Hoo ship burial (Color Plate 2), helps remind us that the extraordinary artistic accomplishments of Anglo-Saxon culture went hand-in-hand with its nostalgia for heroic violence.

The poet uses digression and repetition in an especially subtle way to foreshadow dark events to come. To celebrate Beowulf's victory over Grendel, the scop at Hrothgar's hall sings of events of generations earlier, in which a feud caused the deaths of a Danish princess's brother and son. Although this story has nothing to do with the main plot of the poem, there is an implied parallel a few lines later, when, ominously, Hrothgar's queen Wealtheow hints that her husband's nephew Hrothulf should treat her young sons honorably, remembering the favors Hrothgar has shown him, and soon after, she urges Beowulf also to be kind to them. The original audience would have known that after Hrothgar's death, his queen will suffer a disaster like that of the princess in the song. The poet thus applies his broad principle of comparison and contrast to complex narrative situations as well as to simpler concepts such as good and bad kings. It is the often tragic tenor of these digressions that evokes much of the dark mood that suffuses *Beowulf*, even in its moments of heroic triumph.

The following passage from the original Old English, which has been translated literally, illustrates some of the stylistic features of *Beowulf* discussed above.*

      Swā ðā drihtguman   drēamum lifdon,

100   ēadiglīce,   oð ðæt ān ongan

      fyrene fre(m)man   fēond on helle;

      wæs se grimma gǣst   Grendel hāten,

      mǣre mearcstapa,   sē þe mōras hēold,

      fen ond fæsten;   fīfelcynnes eard

105   wonsǣlī wer   weardode hwīle,

      siþðan him Scyppend   forscrifen haefde

      in Cāines cynne—   þone cwealm gewraec

      ēce Drihten,   þaes þe hē Abel slōg;

      ne gefeah hē þǣre fǣðe,   ac hē hine feor forwraec,

110   Metod for þȳ māne   mancynne fram.

      And so the warriors   lived in joy

100   happily   until one began

      the commit crimes,   a fiend from hell

      the grim demon   was called Grendel,

      notorious borderland-prowler   who dwelt in the moors

      fen and stronghold;   the home of monsterkind

105   this cursed creature   occupied for a long while

      since the Creator   had condemned him

      as the kin of Cain—   he punished the killing,

      the Eternal Lord,   because he slew Abel;

      He did not rejoice in that evil deed,   but He banished him far

110   from mankind,   God, in return for the crime.

*The passage is taken from *Beowulf and the Fight at Finnsburg,* 3rd ed., ed. Frederick Klaeber (Boston: D. C. Heath, 1950). The translation is by Anne Schotter.

from **Beowulf**[1]

I. Grendel

Hrothgar was granted
swiftness for battle   and staunchness in strife,[2]
60   so friends and kinfolk   followed him freely.
His band of young soldiers   swelled to a swarm.
In his mind he mulled   commanding a meadhall
higher than humankind   ever had heard of,
and offering everyone,   young and old,
65   all he could give   that God had granted,
save common land   and commoners' lives.
Then, I am told,   he tackled that task,
raising the rafters   with craftsmen summoned
from many kingdoms   across Middle-Earth.
70   They covered it quickly   as men count the time,
and he whose word   held the land whole
named it Heorot,[3]   highest of houses.
The prince did not fail   to fulfill his pledge:
feasts were given,   favor and fortune.
75   The roof reared up;   the gables were great,
awaiting the flames   which would flare fiercely
when oaths were broken,   anger awakened;
but Heorot's ruin   was not yet at hand.[4]

Each day, one evil   dweller in darkness
80   spitefully suffered   the din from that hall
where Hrothgar's men   made merry with mead.
Harp-strings would sound,   and the song of the scop
would recount the tales   told of time past:
whence mankind had come,   and how the Almighty
85   had fashioned the world   with its fair fields
set in wide waters,   with sun and moon
lifted on high   and lighting the lands
for Earth's first dwellers,   with forests everywhere
branching and blooming,   with life breathing
90   in all kinds of creatures.
So the king's thanes
gathered in gladness;   then crime came calling,
a horror from hell,   hideous Grendel,
wrathful rover   of borders and moors,
holder of hollows,   haunter of fens.
95   He had lived long   in the land of the loathsome,
born to the band   whom God had banished
as kindred of Cain,   thereby requiting

1. The modern English translation is by Alan Sullivan and Timothy Murphy (2002).
2. Significantly, Hrothgar is not the first-born of his generation. Leadership of the tribe was customarily conferred by acclamation upon the royal candidate who showed the greatest promise and ability.
3. The name of Hrothgar's hall in Anglo-Saxon literally means "hart" or "stag," a male deer. The epithet "adorned with horns," which is applied to Heorot later, may further suggest its function as a hunting lodge.
4. The peace concluded between the Danes and the Heathobards through intermarriage is already doomed before it has taken place. The events foreshadowed here will occur long after the time of the poem.

the slayer of Abel.[5]   Many such sprang
from the first murderer: monsters and misfits,
100   elves and ill-spirits,   also those giants
whose wars with the Lord   earned them exile.

After nightfall   he nosed around Heorot,
saw how swordsmen   slept in the hall,
unwary and weary   with wine and feasting,
105   numb to the sorrows   suffered by men.
The cursed creature,   cruel and remorseless,
swiftly slipped in.   He seized thirty thanes
asleep after supper,   shouldered away
what trophies he would,   and took to his lair
110   pleased with the plunder,   proud of his murders.

When daylight dawned   on the spoils of slaughter,
the strength of the fiend   was readily seen.
The feast was followed   by fits of weeping,
and cries of outrage   rose in the morning.
115   Hrothgar the strong   sank on his throne,
helpless and hopeless,   beholding the carnage,
the trail of the terror,   a trouble too wrathful,
a foe too ferocious,   too steadfast in rage,
ancient and evil.   The evening after
120   he murdered again   with no more remorse,
so fixed was his will   on that wicked feud.
Henceforth the fearful   were easily found
elsewhere, anywhere   far from the fiend,
bedding in barns,   for the brutal hall-thane
125   was truly betokened   by terrible signs,
and those who escaped   stayed safer afar.

So wrath fought alone   against rule and right;
one routed many;   the mead-hall stood empty.
Strongest of Spear-Danes,   Hrothgar suffered
130   this fell affliction   for twelve winters' time.
As his woes became known   widely and well,
sad songs were sung   by the sons of men:
how season on season,   with ceaseless strife,
Grendel assailed   the Scyldings' sovereign.
135   The monster craved   no kinship with any,
no end to the evil   with wergeld[6] owed;
nor might a king's   council have reckoned
on quittance come   from the killer's hand.
The dark death-shadow   daunted them all,
140   lying in ambush   for old and young,
secretly slinking   and stalking by night.

5. See Genesis 4.3–16.
6. A cash payment for someone's death. *Wergeld* was regarded as an advance over violent revenge, and Grendel is marked as uncivilized because he refuses to acknowledge this practice.

No man knows where   on the misty moor
the heathen keepers   of hell-runes[7] wander.

So over and over   the loathsome ogre
145   mortally menaced   mankind with his crimes.
Raiding by night,   he reigned in the hall,
and Heorot's high   adornments were his,
but God would not grant   throne-gifts to gladden
a scourge who spurned   the Sovereign of Heaven.

150   Stricken in spirit,   Hrothgar would often
closet his council   to ponder what plan
might be deemed best   by strong-minded men.
Sometimes the elders   swore before altars
of old war-idols,   offering prayers
155   for the soul-slayer   to succor their people.[8]
Such was their habit,   the hope of heathens:
with hell in their hearts,   they were lost to the Lord.
Their inmost minds   knew not the Almighty;
they never would worship   the world's true protector.
160   Sorry is he   who sears his soul,
afflicted by flames   he freely embraced.
No cheer for the chastened!   No change for the better!
But happy is he   who trusts in heaven
and lives to his last   in the Lord's keeping.

165   So in his sorrow   the son of Healfdene[9]
endlessly weighed   how a wise warrior
might fend off harm.   The hardship this foe
of his folk inflicted   was fierce and long-lasting,
most ruinous wrath   and wracking night-evil.

170   A thane[10] of Hygelac   heard in his homeland
of Grendel's deeds.   Great among Geats,[11]
this man was more mighty   than any then living.
He summoned and stocked   a swift wave-courser,
and swore to sail   over the swan-road
175   as one warrior should   for another in need.
His elders could find   no fault with his offer,
and awed by the omens,   they urged him on.
He gathered the bravest   of Geatish guardsmen.
One of fifteen,   the skilled sailor
180   strode to his ship   at the ocean's edge.

He was keen to embark: his keel was beached
under the cliff   where sea-currents curled

7. By rendering the Old English *helrunan*, which means "those adept in the mysteries of hell," as "heathen keepers of hell-runes," the translators are taking the liberty of suggesting that "demons" such as Grendel are familiar with runes—the letters of the early Germanic alphabet.
8. In their fear, the Danes resume heathen practices. In Christian belief, the pagan gods were transformed into devils.

9. Hrothgar. He is referred to by his patronymic, his father's name, as is frequent with male characters in the poem.
10. One of the king's principal retainers, chief among these being the earls.
11. A Germanic tribe who lived along the southwestern coast of what is now Sweden.

Boar, from a bas-relief carving on Saint Nicholas Church, Ipswich, England. Although this large and vigorous boar dates from the 12th century, it retains stylistic elements of earlier Anglo-Saxon and Viking art. An ancient totem of power, boars were often depicted on early medieval weapons and helmets. © Conway Library/Courtauld Institute of Art.

        surf against sand;   his soldiers were ready.
        Over the longboat's   bow they boarded,
185   bearing below   their burnished weapons
        and gilded gear   to hoard in the hull.
        Other men shoved   the ship from the shore,
        and off went the band,   their wood-braced vessel
        bound for the venture   with wind on the waves
190   and foam under bow,   like a fulmar in flight.[12] * * *

        A stone-paved street   steered the men hence.
        They strode on together,   garbed in glinting
        jackets of chain-mail   whose jingling rings,
        hard and hand-linked,   sang on harnesses
290   borne toward the hall   by that battle-armed band.
        Still sea-weary,   they set their broad-shields
        of well-seasoned wood   against Heorot's wall.
        Their byrnies clanged   as they bent to a bench
        and stood their sturdy   spears in a row,
295   gray from the ash grove,   ground to sharp points.
        This was a war party   worthy of weapons.

        Then a proud prince   questioned their purpose:
        "Where are you bringing   these burnished bosses,
        these gray mail-shirts,   grimly-masked helms

12. Gull-like sea bird of the far north Atlantic.

300 and serried spears?   I am Hrothgar's
herald and door-ward.   I have never beheld
a band of wanderers   with bearings so brave.
I believe that boldness   has brought you to Hrothgar,
not banishment's shame."
The eldest answered,
305 hard and hardy   under his helmet,
a warlike prince   of the Weder[13] people:
"We are Hygelac's   hearth-companions.
My name is Beowulf;   my purpose, to bear
unto Healfdene's son,   your lordly leader,
310 a message meant   for that noblest of men,
if he will allow us   leave to approach."

Wise Wulfgar,   man of the Wendels,
known to many   for boldness in battle,
stoutly spoke out: "I shall ask our sovereign,
315 well-wisher of Danes   and awarder of wealth,
about this boon   you have come to request
and bear you back,   as soon as may be,
whatever answer   the great man offers."

He went straightaway   where Hrothgar waited,
320 old and gray-haired,   with earls gathered round.
Squarely he stood   for his king to assess him.
Such was the Scylding   custom at court,
and so Wulfgar spoke   to his sovereign and friend:
"Far-sailing Geats   have come to our kingdom
325 across the wide water.   These warriors call
their leader *Beowulf*   and bid me bring
their plea to our prince,   if it pleases him
to allow them entrance   and offer them audience.
I implore you to hear them,   princely Hrothgar,
330 for I deem them worthy   of wearing their armor
and treating with earls.   Truly the elder
who led them hither   is a lord of some stature."

Helm of the Scyldings,   Hrothgar held forth:
"I knew him once.   He was only a lad.
335 His honored father,   old Ecgtheow,
was dowered the daughter   of the Geat, Hrethel.
The son now seeks us   solely from friendship.
Seamen have said,   after sailing hence
with gifts for the Geats,   that his hand-grip would match
340 the might and main   of thirty strong men.
The West-Danes[14] have long   awaited God's grace.
Here is our hope   against Grendel's dread,

---

13. An alternate name for Geat.
14. Hrothgar is, in fact, king of all the Danes: North, South, East, and West. The different terms merely con- form to the Anglo-Saxon alliterative pattern established in each line.

if I reckon rightly   the cause of his coming.
I shall give this brave man   boons for boldness.
345   Bring him in quickly.   The band of my kinsmen
is gathered together.   Welcome our guest
to the dwelling of Danes."
                                        Then Wulfgar went
through the hall's entry   with word from within:
"I am ordered to answer   that the lord of East-Danes
350   honors your father   and offers you welcome,
sailors who sought us   over the sea-waves,
bravely bent   on embarking hither.
Now you may march   in your mail and masks
to behold Hrothgar.   Here you must leave
355   war-shields and spears   sharpened for strife.
Your weapons can wait   for words to be spoken."

The mighty one rose   with many a man
marshaled about him,   though some were bidden
to stay with the weapons   and stand on watch.
360   Under Heorot's roof   the rest hastened
when Beowulf brought them   boldly before
the hearth of Hrothgar.   Helmed and hardy,
the war-chief shone   as he stood in skillfully
smithed chain-mail   and spoke to his host:

365   "Hail to you, Hrothgar!   I am Hygelac's
kinsman and comrade,   esteemed by the king
for deeds I have done   in the years of youth.
I heard in my homeland   how Grendel grieves you.
Seafarers say   that your splendid hall
370   stands idle and useless   after the sun
sinks each evening   from Heaven's height.
The most honored among us,   earls and elders,
have urged me to seek you,   certain my strength
would serve in your struggle.   They have seen me return
375   bloody from binding   brutish giants,
a family of five   destroyed in our strife;
by night in the sea   I have slain monsters.
Hardship I had,   but our harms were avenged,
our enemies mastered.   Now I shall match
380   my grip against Grendel's   and get you an end
to this feud with the fiend.   Therefore one favor
I ask from you, Hrothgar,   sovereign of Spear-Danes,
shelter of shield-bearers,   friend to your folk:
that I and my officers,   we and no others,
385   be offered the honor   of purging your hall.
I have also heard   that the rash thing reckons
the thrust of a weapon   no threat to his thews,[15]

15. Well-developed sinew or muscle.

so I shall grab   and grapple with Grendel.
Let my lord Hygelac   hear and be glad
390   I foreswore   my sword and strong shield
when I fought for life   with that fearsome foe.
Whomever death takes,   his doom is doubtless
decreed by the Lord.   If I let the creature
best me when battle   begins in this building,
395   he will freely feast   as he often has fed
on men of much mettle.   My corpse will require
no covering cloth.   He will carry away
a crushed carcass   clotted with gore,
the fiend's fodder   gleefully eaten,
400   smearing his lonesome   lair on the moor.
No need to worry   who buries my body
if battle takes me.   Send back to my sovereign
this best of shirts   which has shielded my breast,
this choice chain-mail,   Hrethel's heirloom
405   and Weland's work.[16]   Fate goes as it will." * * *

630   Cunningly creeping,   a spectral stalker
slunk through the gloom.   The bowmen were sleeping
who ought to have held   the high-horned house,
all except one,   for the Lord's will
now became known: no more would the murderer
635   drag under darkness   whomever he wished.
Wrath was wakeful,   watching in hatred;
hot-hearted Beowulf   was bent upon battle.

Then from the moor   under misty hillsides,
Grendel came gliding,   girt with God's anger.
640   The man-scather sought   someone to snatch
from the high hall.   He crept under clouds
until he caught sight   of the king's court
whose gilded gables   he knew at a glance.
He often had haunted   Hrothgar's house;
645   but he never found,   before or after,
hardier hall-thanes   or harder luck.
The joyless giant   drew near the door,
which swiftly swung back   at the touch of his hand
though bound and fastened   with forge-bent bars.
650   The building's mouth   had been broken open,
and Grendel entered   with ill intent.
Swollen with fury,   he stalked over flagstones
and looked round the manse   where many men lay.
An unlovely light   most like a flame
655   flashed from his eyes,   flared through the hall
at young soldiers dozing   shoulder to shoulder,
comradely kindred.   The cruel creature laughed
in his murderous mind,   thinking how many

16. Legendary blacksmith of the Norse gods.

now living would die   before the day dawned,
660   how glutted with gore   he would guzzle his fill.
It was not his fate   to finish the feast
he foresaw that night.
                                Soon the Stalwart,
Hygelac's kinsman,   beheld how the horror,
not one to be idle,   went about evil.
665   For his first feat   he suddenly seized
a sleeping soldier,   slashed at the flesh,
bit through bones   and lapped up the blood
that gushed from veins   as he gorged on gobbets.
Swiftly he swallowed   those lifeless limbs,
670   hands and feet whole;   then he headed forward
with open palm   to plunder the prone.
One man angled   up on his elbow:
the fiend soon found   he was facing a foe
whose hand-grip was harder   than any other
675   he ever had met   in all Middle-Earth.
Cravenly cringing,   coward at heart,
he longed for a swift   escape to his lair,
his bevy of devils.   He never had known
from his earliest days   such awful anguish.

680   The captain, recalling   his speech to the king,
straightaway stood   and hardened his hold.
Fingers fractured.   The fiend spun round;
the soldier stepped closer.   Grendel sought
somehow to slip   that grasp and escape,
685   flee to the fens;   but his fingers were caught
in too fierce a grip.   His foray had failed;
the harm-wreaker rued   his raid on Heorot.
From the hall of the Danes   a hellish din
beset every soldier   outside the stronghold,
690   louder than laughter   of ale-sodden earls.
A wonder it was   the wine-hall withstood
this forceful affray   without falling to earth.
That beautiful building   was firmly bonded
by iron bands   forged with forethought
695   inside and out.   As some have told it,
the struggle swept on   and slammed to the floor
many mead-benches   massive with gold.
No Scylding elders   ever imagined
that any would harm   their elk-horned hall,
700   raze what they wrought,   unless flames arose
to enfold and consume it.   Frightful new sounds
burst from the building,   unnerved the North-Danes,
each one and all   who heard those outcries
outside the walls.   Wailing in anguish,
705   the hellish horror,   hateful to God,
sang his despair,   seized by the grip

of a man more mighty   than any then living.

That shielder of men   meant by no means
to let the death-dealer   leave with his life,
710 a life worthless   to anyone elsewhere.
Then the young soldiers   swung their old swords
again and again   to save their guardian,
their kingly comrade,   however they could.
Engaging with Grendel   and hoping to hew him
715 from every side,   they scarcely suspected
that blades wielded   by worthy warriors
never would cut   to the criminal's quick.
The spell was spun   so strongly about him
that the finest iron   of any on earth,
720 the sharpest sword-edge   left him unscathed.
Still he was soon   to be stripped of his life
and sent on a sore   sojourn to Hell.
The strength of his sinews   would serve him no more;
no more would he menace   mankind with his crimes,
725 his grudge against God,   for the high-hearted kinsman
of King Hygelac   had hold of his hand.
Each found the other   loathsome while living;
but the murderous man-bane   got a great wound
as tendons were torn,   shoulder shorn open,
730 and bone-locks broken.   Beowulf gained
glory in war;   and Grendel went off
bloody and bent   to the boggy hills,
sorrowfully seeking   his dreary dwelling.
Surely he sensed   his life-span was spent,
735 his days upon days;   but the Danes were grateful:
their wish was fulfilled   after fearsome warfare.

Wise and strong-willed,   the one from afar
had cleansed Heorot,   hall of Hrothgar.
Great among Geats,   he was glad of his night-work
740 ending the evil,   his fame-winning feat,
fulfilling his oath   to aid the East-Danes,
easing their anguish,   healing the horror
they suffered so long,   no small distress.
As token of triumph,   the troop-leader hung
745 the shorn-off shoulder   and arm by its hand:
the grip of Grendel   swung from the gable! * * *

II. Grendel's Mother

Then Hrothgar awarded   horses and weapons
both to Beowulf,   bade that he keep them
920 and wield them well.   So from his hoard
he paid the hero   a princely reward

of heirlooms and arms   for braving the battle;
no man could fairly   or truthfully fault them.

That lord also lavished   gifts on the Geats
925   whom Beowulf brought   over broad seas,
and wergeld he gave   for the one Grendel
had wickedly killed,   though the creature would surely
have murdered more   had God in his wisdom,
man in his strength   failed to forestall it.
930   So the Almighty   has always moved men;
yet man must consistently   strive to discern
good from evil,   evil from good
while drunk with days   he dwells in this world. * * *

The hall applauded   the princely prize
bestowed by the queen,   and Wealtheow spoke
for the host to hear: "Keep this collar,
1075   beloved Beowulf;   and bear this byrnie,
wealth of our realm;   may it ward you well.
Swear that your strength   and kindly counsel
will aid these youngsters,   and I shall reward you.
Now your renown   will range near and far;
1080   your fame will wax wide,   as wide as the water
hemming our hills,   homes of the wind.
Be blessed, Beowulf,   with abundant treasures
as long as you live;   and be mild to my sons,
a model admired.   Here men are courtly,
1085   honest and true,   each to the other,
all to their ruler;   and after the revels,
well-bolstered with beer,   they do as I bid."

The lady left him   and sat on her seat.
The feast went on;   wine was flowing.
1090   Men could not know   what fate would befall them,
what evil of old   was decreed to come
for the earls that evening.   As always, Hrothgar
headed for home,   where the ruler rested.
A great many others   remained in the hall,
1095   bearing bright benches   and rolling out beds
while one drunkard,   doomed and death-ripened,
sprawled into sleep.   They set at their heads
round war-shields,   well-adorned wood.
Above them on boards,   their battle-helms rested,
1100   ringed mail-shirts   and mighty spear-shafts
waiting for strife.   Such was their wont
at home or afield,   wherever they fared,
in case their king   should call them to arms.
That was a fine folk.
                         They sank into slumber,
1105   but one paid sorely   for sleep that evening,

as often had happened   when grim Grendel
held the gold-hall,   wreaking his wrongs
straight to the end: death after sins.
It would soon be perceived   plainly by all
1110   that one ill-wisher   still was alive,
maddened by grief: Grendel's mother,
a fearsome female   bitterly brooding
alone in her lair   deep in dread waters
and cold currents   since Cain had killed
1115   the only brother   born of his father.
Marked by murder,   he fled from mankind
and went to the wastes.   Doomed evil-doers
issued from him.   Grendel was one,
but the hateful Hell-walker   found a warrior
1120   wakefully watching   for combat in Heorot.
The monster met there   a man who remembered
strength would serve him,   the great gift of God,
faith in the All-Wielder's   favor and aid.
By that he mastered   the ghastly ghoul;
1125   routed, wretched,   the hell-fiend fled,
forlornly drew near   his dreary death-place.
Enraged and ravenous,   Grendel's mother
swiftly set out   on a sorrowful journey
to settle the score   for her son's demise.

1130   She slipped into Heorot,   hall of the Ring-Danes,
where sleeping earls   soon would suffer
an awful reversal.   Her onslaught was less
by as much as a woman's   mettle in war
is less than a man's   wielding his weapon:
1135   the banded blade   hammered to hardness,
a blood-stained sword   whose bitter stroke
slashes a boar-helm   borne into battle.
In the hall, sword-edge   sprang from scabbard;
broadshield was swung   swiftly off bench,
1140   held firmly in hand.   None thought of helmet
or sturdy mail-shirt   when terror assailed him.

Out she hastened,   out and away,
keen to keep living   when caught in the act.
She fastened on one,   then fled to her fen.
1145   He was Hrothgar's   highest counselor,
boon companion   and brave shield-bearer,
slain in his bed.   Beowulf slept
elsewhere that evening,   for after the feast
the Geat had been given   a different dwelling.
1150   A din of dismay   mounted in Heorot:
the gory hand   was gone from the gable.
Dread had retaken   the Danes' dwelling.
That bargain was bad   for both barterers,
costing each one   a close comrade. * * *

1225 Beowulf spoke,   son of Ecgtheow:
      "Grieve not, good man.   It is better to go
      and avenge your friend   than mourn overmuch.
      We all must abide   an end on this earth,
      but a warrior's works   may win him renown
1230 as long as he lives   and after life leaves him.
      Rise now, ruler;   let us ride together
      and seek out the spoor   of Grendel's mother.
      I swear to you this: she shall not escape
      in chasm or cave,   in cliff-climbing thicket
1235 or bog's bottom,   wherever she bides.
      Suffer your sorrow   this one day only;
      I wish you to wait,   wait and be patient."

      The elder leapt up and   offered his thanks
      to God Almighty,   Master of all,
1240 for such hopeful speech.   Then Hrothgar's horse,
      a steed with mane braided,   was brought on its bridle.
      The sage sovereign   set out in splendor
      with shield-bearing soldiers   striding beside him.
      Tracks on the trail   were easy to trace:
1245 they went from woodland   out to the open,
      heading through heather   and murky moors
      where the best of thanes   was borne off unbreathing.
      He would live no longer   in Hrothgar's house.
      Crossing the moorland,   the king mounted
1250 a stony path   up steepening slopes.
      With a squad of scouts   in single file,
      he rode through regions   none of them knew,
      mountains and hollows   that hid many monsters.
      The sovereign himself,   son of great forebears,
1255 suddenly spotted   a forest of fir-trees
      rooted on rock,   their trunks tipping
      over a tarn   of turbulent eddies.
      Danes were downcast,   and Geats, grim;
      every soldier   was stricken at heart
1260 to behold on that height   Aeschere's head.

      As they looked on the lake,   blood still lingered,
      welled to the surface.   A war-horn sounded
      its bold battle-cry,   and the band halted.
      Strange sea-dragons   swam in the depths;
1265 sinuous serpents   slid to and fro.
      At the base of the bluff   water-beasts lay,
      much like monsters   that rise in the morning
      when seafarers sail   on strenuous journeys.
      Hearing the horn's   high-pitched challenge,
1270 they puffed up with rage   and plunged in the pool. * * *

Beowulf spoke,   son of Ecgtheow:
"Hail, Hrothgar,   Healfdene's son.
Look on this token   we took from the lake,
1460   this glorious booty   we bring you gladly.
The struggle was stark;   the danger, dreadful.
My foe would have won   our war underwater
had the Lord not looked   after my life.
Hrunting failed me,   though finely fashioned;
1465   but God vouchsafed me   a glimpse of a great-sword,
ancient and huge,   hung from the wall.
All-Father often   fosters the friendless.
Wielding this weapon,   I struck down and slew
the cavern's keeper   as soon as I could.
1470   My banded war-blade   was burned away
when blood burst forth   in the heat of battle.
I bore the hilt here,   wrested from raiders.
Thus I avenged   the deaths among Danes
as it was fitting,   and this I assure you:
1475   henceforth in Heorot   heroes shall sleep
untroubled by terror.   Your warrior troop,
all of your thanes,   young men and old,
need fear no further   evil befalling,
not from that quarter,   king of the Scyldings."

1480   He gave the gold hilt   to the good old man;
the hoary war-chief   held in his hand
an ancient artifact   forged by giants.
At the devils' downfall,   this wondrous work
went to the Danes.   The dark-hearted demon,
1485   hater of humans,   Heaven's enemy,
committer of murders,   and likewise his mother,
departed this Earth.   Their power passed
to the wisest world-king   who ever awarded
treasure in Denmark   between the two seas.

1490   Hrothgar spoke   as he studied the hilt,
that aged heirloom   inscribed long ago
with a story of strife: how the Flood swallowed
the race of giants   with onrushing ocean.
Defiant kindred,   they fared cruelly,
1495   condemned for their deeds   to death by water.
Such were the staves   graven in gold-plate,
runes rightly set,   saying for whom
the serpent-ribbed sword   and raddled hilt[17]
were once fashioned   of finest iron.
1500   When the wise one spoke,   all were silent:

---

17. On the sword hilt is the story of the flood, written in runes (letters of the early Germanic alphabet), and a decorative pattern of twisted serpent shapes. A similar pattern can be seen on the great buckle of the Sutton Hoo ship burial, Color Plate 2.

"Truth may be told   by the homeland's holder
and keeper of kinfolk,   who rightly recalls
the past for his people: this prince was born
bravest of fighters.   My friend, Beowulf,
1505   your fame shall flourish   in far countries,
everywhere honored.   Your strength is sustained
by patience and judgment.   Just as I promised,
our friendship is firmed,   a lasting alliance.
So you shall be   a boon to your brethren,
1510   unlike Heremod   who ought to have helped
Ecgwela's sons,   the Honor-Scyldings.
He grew up to grief   and grim slaughter,
doling out death   to the Danish people.
Hot-tempered at table,   he cut down comrades,
1515   slew his own soldiers   and spurned humankind,
alone and unloved,   an infamous prince,
though mighty God   had given him greatness
and raised him in rank   over all other men.
Hidden wrath   took root in his heart,
1520   bloodthirsty thoughts.   He would give no gifts
to honor others.   Loveless, he lived,
a lasting affliction   endured by the Danes
in sorrow and strife.   Consider him well,
his life and lesson.
                              "Wise with winters,
1525   I tell you this tale   as I mull and marvel
how the Almighty   metes to mankind
the blessings of reason,   rule and realm.
He arranges it all.   For a time He allows
the mind of a man   to linger in love
1530   with earthly honors.   He offers him homeland
to hold and enjoy,   a fort full of folk,
men to command   and might in the world,
wide kingdoms   won to his will.
In his folly, the fool   imagines no ending.
1535   He dwells in delight   without thought of his lot.
Illness, old age,   anguish or envy:
none of these gnaw   by night at his mind.
Nowhere are swords   brandished in anger;
for him the whole world   wends as he wishes.
1540   He knows nothing worse   till his portion of pride
waxes within him.   His soul is asleep;
his gate, unguarded.   He slumbers too soundly,
sunk in small cares.   The slayer creeps close
and shoots a shaft   from the baneful bow.
1545   The bitter arrow   bites through his armor,
piercing the heart   he neglected to guard
from crooked counsel   and evil impulse.

Too little seems all   he has long possessed.
Suspicious and stingy,   withholding his hoard
1550   of gold-plated gifts,   he forgets or ignores
what fate awaits him,   for the world's Wielder
surely has granted   his share of glory.
But the end-rune   is already written:
the loaned life-home   collapses in ruin;
1555   some other usurps   and openly offers
the hoarded wealth,   heedless of worry.

"Beloved Beowulf,   best of defenders,
guard against anger   and gain for yourself
perpetual profit.   Put aside pride,
1560   worthiest warrior.   Now for awhile
your force flowers,   yet soon it shall fail.
Sickness or age   will strip you of strength,
or the fangs of flame,   or flood-surges,
the sword's bite   or the spear's flight,
1565   or fearful frailty   as bright eyes fade,
dimming to darkness.   Afterward death
will sweep you away,   strongest of war-chiefs. * * *

III. The Dragon

High on the headland   they heaped his grave-mound
which seafaring sailors   would spy from afar.
Ten days they toiled   on the scorched hilltop,
2785   the cleverest men   skillfully crafting
a long-home built   for the bold in battle.
They walled with timbers   the trove they had taken,
sealing in stone   the circlets and gems,
wealth of the worm-hoard   gotten with grief,
2790   gold from the ground   gone back to Earth
as worthless to men   as when it was won.
Then sorrowing swordsmen   circled the barrow,
twelve of his earls   telling their tales,
the sons of nobles   sadly saluting
2795   deeds of the dead.   So dutiful thanes
in liege to their lord   mourn him with lays
praising his peerless   prowess in battle
as it is fitting   when life leaves the flesh.
Heavy-hearted   his hearth-companions
2800   grieved for Beowulf,   great among kings,
mild in his mien,   most gentle of men,
kindest to kinfolk   yet keenest for fame.

Introduction to Bede
672–735

Bede was born on lands belonging to the abbey of Wearmouth-Jarrow. He entered that monastery at the age of seven and never traveled more than seventy-five miles away. Bede is the most enduring product of the golden age of Northumbrian monasticism. In the generations just preceding his, a series of learned abbots had brought Roman liturgical practices and monastic habits to Wearmouth-Jarrow, as well as establishing there the best library in England. Out of this settled life and disciplined religious culture Bede created a diverse body of writings that are learned both in scholarly research and in the purity of their Latin. They include biblical commentaries, school texts from spelling to metrics, treatises on the liturgical calendar, hymns, and lives of saints.

Bede's *An Ecclesiastical History of the English People*, completed in 731, marks the apex of his achievement. Given the localism of his life, Bede's grasp of English history is extraordinary, not just in terms of his eager pursuit of information, but equally in his balanced and complex sense of the broad movement of history. Bede registers a persistent concern about his sources and their reliability. He prefers written and especially documentary evidence, but he will use oral reports if they come from several sources and are close enough to the original event.

The *Ecclesiastical History* suggests the contours of a national history, even a providential history, in the arrival of the Angles and Saxons, and in the island's uneven conversion to Christianity. Despite his frequent stories of battles among the Germanic peoples in Britain, Bede speaks of the English people emphatically in the singular. Nevertheless, Bede is delicately aware of the historical layering brought about by colonization and the ongoing resistance of earlier inhabitants. Further, he is always alert to profoundly transformative influences, aside from ethnicity, that color his time: the process of conversion to Christianity, and the variable coexistence of Christian and pagan instincts in individual minds; the interplay of oral and written culture; the status in religious and official life of Latin and the Anglo-Saxon vernaculars.

from An Ecclesiastical History of the English People[1]
[The Conversion of King Edwin][2]

King Edwin hesitated to accept the word of God which Paulinus[3] preached but, as we have said, used to sit alone for hours at a time, earnestly debating within himself what he ought to do and what religion he should follow. One day Paulinus came to him and, placing his right hand on the king's head, asked him if he recognized this sign. The king began to tremble and would have thrown himself at the bishop's feet but Paulinus raised him up and said in a voice that seemed familiar, "First you have escaped with God's help from the hands of the foes you feared; secondly you have acquired by His gift the kingdom you desired; now, in the third place, remember your own promise; do not delay in fulfilling it but receive the faith and keep the commandments of Him who rescued you from your earthly foes and raised you to the honor of an earthly kingdom. If from henceforth you are willing to follow His will which is made known to you through me, He will also rescue you from the everlasting torments of the wicked and make you a partaker with Him of His eternal kingdom in heaven."

1. Edited and translated by Bertram Colgrave and R. A. B. Mynors.
2. From bk. 2, chs. 12–14. Edwin became king of Northumbria in 616, aided by Raedwald, king of the East Angles. Exiled at Raedwald's court, Edwin had a vision wherein he promised a shadowy visitor he would convert if he achieved the crown. The visitor laid his right hand on Edwin's head as a sign to remember that promise when the gesture was repeated.
3. Later archbishop of York, Paulinus had been sent to Northumbria from Kent with Edwin's Christian wife after Edwin had promised tolerance of Christian worship.

When the king had heard his words, he answered that he was both willing and bound to accept the faith which Paulinus taught. He said, however, that he would confer about this with his loyal chief men and his counselors so that, if they agreed with him, they might all be consecrated together in the waters of life. Paulinus agreed and the king did as he had said. A meeting of his council was held and each one was asked in turn what he thought of this doctrine hitherto unknown to them and this new worship of God which was being proclaimed.

Coifi, the chief of the priests, answered at once, "Notice carefully, King, this doctrine which is now being expounded to us. I frankly admit that, for my part, I have found that the religion which we have hitherto held has no virtue nor profit in it. None of your followers has devoted himself more earnestly than I have to the worship of our gods, but nevertheless there are many who receive greater benefits and greater honor from you than I do and are more successful in all their undertakings. If the gods had any power they would have helped me more readily, seeing that I have always served them with greater zeal. So it follows that if, on examination, these new doctrines which have now been explained to us are found to be better and more effectual, let us accept them at once without any delay."

Another of the king's chief men agreed with this advice and with these wise words and then added, "This is how the present life of man on earth, King, appears to me in comparison with that time which is unknown to us. You are sitting feasting with your ealdormen and thegns[4] in winter time; the fire is burning on the hearth in the middle of the hall and all inside is warm, while outside the wintry storms of rain and snow are raging; and a sparrow flies swiftly through the hall. It enters in at one door and quickly flies out through the other. For the few moments it is inside, the storm and wintry tempest cannot touch it, but after the briefest moment of calm, it flits from your sight, out of the wintry storm and into it again. So this life of man appears but for a moment; what follows or indeed what went before, we know not at all. If this new doctrine brings us more certain information, it seems right that we should accept it."[5] Other elders and counselors of the king continued in the same manner, being divinely prompted to do so.

Coifi added that he would like to listen still more carefully to what Paulinus himself had to say about God. The king ordered Paulinus to speak, and when he had said his say, Coifi exclaimed, "For a long time now I have realized that our religion is worthless; for the more diligently I sought the truth in our cult, the less I found it. Now I confess openly that the truth shines out clearly in this teaching which can bestow on us the gift of life, salvation, and eternal happiness. Therefore I advise your Majesty that we should promptly abandon and commit to the flames the temples and the altars which we have held sacred without reaping any benefit." Why need I say more? The king publicly accepted the gospel which Paulinus preached, renounced idolatry, and confessed his faith in Christ. When he asked the high priest of their religion which of them should be the first to profane the altars and the shrines of the idols, together with their precincts, Coifi answered, "I will; for through the wisdom the true God has given me no one can more suitably destroy those things which I once foolishly worshiped, and so set an example to all." And at once, casting aside his vain superstitions, he asked the king to provide him with arms and a stallion; and

---

4. Ealdorman: the highest Anglo-Saxon rank below king; thegn: a noble warrior still serving within the king's household.

5. This famous simile is put in the mouth of a lay nobleman, not the pagan priest Coifi whose argument for conversion was based on disappointed self-interest.

mounting it he set out to destroy the idols. Now a high priest of their religion was not allowed to carry arms or to ride except on a mare. So, girded with a sword, he took a spear in his hand and mounting the king's stallion he set off to where the idols were. The common people who saw him thought he was mad. But as soon as he approached the shrine, without any hesitation he profaned it by casting the spear which he held into it; and greatly rejoicing in the knowledge of the worship of the true God, he ordered his companions to destroy and set fire to the shrine and all the enclosures. The place where the idols once stood is still shown, not far from York, to the east, over the river Derwent. Today it is called Goodmanham, the place where the high priest, through the inspiration of the true God, profaned and destroyed the altars which he himself had consecrated.[6]

So King Edwin, with all the nobles of his race and a vast number of the common people, received the faith and regeneration by holy baptism in the eleventh year of his reign, that is in the year of our Lord 627 and about 180 years after the coming of the English to Britain. He was baptized at York on Easter Day, 12 April, in the church of Saint Peter the Apostle, which he had hastily built of wood while he was a catechumen and under instruction before he received baptism. He established an episcopal see for Paulinus, his instructor and bishop, in the same city.

Introduction to The Wanderer

In the Exeter Book, a manuscript copied about 975 and donated to the Bishop of Exeter, are preserved some of the greatest short poems in Old English, including a number of poems referred to as elegies—laments that contrast past happiness with present sorrow and remark on how fleeting is the former. Along with *The Wanderer*, the elegies include its companion piece *The Seafarer*; *The Ruin*; *The Husband's Message*; *The Wife's Lament*; and *Wulf and Eadwacer*. While the last two are exceptional in dealing with female experience, elegies for the most part focus on male bonds and companionship, particularly the joys of the mead hall. Old English poetry as a whole is almost entirely devoid of interest in romantic love between men and women and focuses instead on the bond between lord and retainer; elegiac poems such as *The Wanderer* have in fact been called "the love poetry of a heroic society."

The Wanderer opens with an appeal to a Christian concept, as the third-person narrator speaks of the wanderer's request for God's mercy. The body of the poem, however—primarily a first-person account in the wanderer's voice—reflects more pagan values in its regret for the loss of earthly joys. Though the poem's structure is somewhat confusing, one can discern two major parts. In the first, the wanderer laments his personal situation: he was once a member of a warrior band, but his lord—his beloved "gold-friend"—has died, leaving him a homeless exile. He dreams that he "clasps and kisses" his lord, but he then wakes to see only the dark waves, the snow, and the sea birds.

The second part of the poem turns from personal narrative to a more general statement of the transitoriness of all earthly things. The speaker (possibly someone other than the wanderer at this point), looking at the ruin of ancient buildings, is moved to express the ancient Roman motif known as "*ubi sunt*" (Latin for "where are"): "Where has the horse gone? Where the man? Where the giver of gold? / Where is the feasting place? And where the pleasures of the hall?" In the concluding five lines, the reader is urged to seek comfort in heaven.

There has been much debate about the degrees of Christianity and paganism in this tenth-century poem. The positions range from the view that the Christian opening and closing are totally extraneous to the poem and have been tacked on by a monkish copyist, to the

---

6. This detail is typical of Bede's liking for textual or archaeological authentication.

view that the poem is a Christian allegory about a soul exiled from his heavenly home, longing for his lord Jesus Christ. It is now generally held that the poem is authentically Christian, in a literal rather than an allegorical way, but that the values of pagan society still exert a powerful pull in it.

The Wanderer[1]

Often the wanderer pleads for pity
and mercy from the Lord; but for a long time,
sad in mind, he must dip his oars
into icy waters, the lanes of the sea;
5   he must follow the paths of exile: fate is inflexible.

Mindful of hardships, grievous slaughter,
the ruin of kinsmen, the wanderer said:
"Time and again at the day's dawning
I must mourn all my afflictions alone.
10   There is no one still living to whom I dare open
the doors of my heart. I have no doubt
that it is a noble habit for a man
to bind fast all his heart's feelings,
guard his thoughts, whatever he is thinking.
15   The weary in spirit cannot withstand fate,
a troubled mind finds no relief:
wherefore those eager for glory often
hold some ache imprisoned in their hearts.
Thus I had to bind my feelings in fetters,
20   often sad at heart, cut off from my country,
far from my kinsmen, after, long ago,
dark clods of earth covered my gold-friend;
I left that place in wretchedness,
plowed the icy waves with winter in my heart;
25   in sadness I sought far and wide
for a treasure-giver, for a man
who would welcome me into his mead-hall,
give me good cheer (for I boasted no friends),
entertain me with delights. He who has experienced it
30   knows how cruel a comrade sorrow can be
to any man who has few loyal friends:
for him are the ways of exile, in no wise twisted gold;
for him is a frozen body, in no wise the fruits of the earth.
He remembers hall-retainers and treasure
35   and how, in his youth, his gold-friend
entertained him. Those joys have all vanished.
A man who lacks advice for a long while
from his loved lord understands this,
that when sorrow and sleep together
40   hold the wretched wanderer in their grip,
it seems that he clasps and kisses

1. Translated by Kevin Crossley-Holland.

his lord, and lays hands and head
upon his lord's knee as he had sometimes done
when he enjoyed the gift-throne in earlier days.
45   Then the friendless man wakes again
and sees the dark waves surging around him,
the sea-birds bathing, spreading their feathers,
frost and snow falling mingled with hail.

"Then his wounds lie more heavy in his heart,
50   aching for his lord. His sorrow is renewed;
the memory of kinsmen sweeps through his mind;
joyfully he welcomes them, eagerly scans
his comrade warriors. Then they swim away again.
Their drifting spirits do not bring many old songs
55   to his lips. Sorrow upon sorrow attend
the man who must send time and again
his weary heart over the frozen waves.

"And thus I cannot think why in the world
my mind does not darken when I brood on the fate
60   of brave warriors, how they have suddenly
had to leave the mead-hall, the bold followers.
So this world dwindles day by day,
and passes away; for a man will not be wise
before he has weathered his share of winters
65   in the world. A wise man must be patient,
neither too passionate nor too hasty of speech,
neither too irresolute nor too rash in battle;
not too anxious, too content, nor too grasping,
and never too eager to boast before he knows himself.
70   When he boasts a man must bide his time
until he has no doubt in his brave heart
that he has fully made up his mind.
A wise man must fathom how eerie it will be
when all the riches of the world stand waste,
75   as now in diverse places in this middle-earth
old walls stand, tugged at by winds
and hung with hoar-frost, buildings in decay.
The wine-halls crumble, lords lie dead,
deprived of joy, all the proud followers
80   have fallen by the wall: battle carried off some,
led them on journeys; the bird carried one
over the welling waters; one the gray wolf
devoured; a warrior with downcast face
hid one in an earth-cave.
85   Thus the Maker of Men laid this world waste
until the ancient works of the giants stood idle,
hushed without the hubbub of inhabitants.
Then he who has brooded over these noble ruins,
and who deeply ponders this dark life,

90   wise in his mind, often remembers
      the many slaughters of the past and speaks these words:
      Where has the horse gone? Where the man? Where the giver of gold?
      Where is the feasting-place? And where the pleasures of the hall?
      I mourn the gleaming cup, the warrior in his corselet,
95   the glory of the prince. How that time has passed away,
      darkened under the shadow of night as if it had never been.
      Where the loved warriors were, there now stands a wall
      of wondrous height, carved with serpent forms.
      The savage ash-spears, avid for slaughter,
100   have claimed all the warriors—a glorious fate!
      Storms crash against these rocky slopes,
      sleet and snow fall and fetter the world,
      winter howls, then darkness draws on,
      the night-shadow casts gloom and brings
105   fierce hailstorms from the north to frighten men.
      Nothing is ever easy in the kingdom of earth,
      the world beneath the heavens is in the hands of fate.
      Here possessions are fleeting, here friends are fleeting,
      here man is fleeting, here kinsman is fleeting,
110   the whole world becomes a wilderness."
      So spoke the wise man in his heart as he sat apart in thought.
      Brave is the man who holds to his beliefs; nor shall he ever
      show the sorrow in his heart before he knows how he
      can hope to heal it. It is best for a man to seek
115   mercy and comfort from the Father in heaven, the safe home that awaits us all.

Arthurian Myth in the History of Britain

Almost since it first appeared, the story of King Arthur has occupied a contested zone between myth and history. Far from diminishing the Arthurian tradition, though, this ambiguity has lent it a tremendous and protean impact on the political and cultural imagination of Europe, from the Middle Ages to the present. Probably no other body of medieval legend remains today as widely known and as often revisited as the Arthurian story.

One measure of Arthur's undiminished importance is the eager debate, eight centuries old and going strong, about his historical status. Whether or not a specific "Arthur" ever existed, legends and attributes gathered around his name from a very early date, mostly in texts of Welsh background. Around 600 a Welsh poem refers briefly to Arthur's armed might, and by about 1000, the story *Culhwch and Olwen,* from the Mabinogion, assumes knowledge of Arthur as a royal warlord. Other early Welsh texts begin to give him more-than-mortal attributes, associating Arthur with such marvels as an underworld quest and a mysterious tomb. In the ninth century, the Latin *History of the Britons* by the Welshman Nennius confidently speaks of Arthur as a great leader and lists his twelve victories ending with that at Mount Badon.

Some of this at least fits with better-documented history and with less-shadowy commanders who might have been models for an Arthurian figure, even if they were not "Arthur." When the Romans withdrew in 410, the romanized Britons soon faced territorial aggression from the Saxons and Picts. In the decades after midcentury, the Britons mounted a successful defense, led in part by Aurelius Ambrosius and culminating, it appears, with the battle of Badon in roughly 500, after which Saxon incursions paused for a time. In those same years of territorial threat, some Britons had emigrated to what is now Brittany, and in the 460s or 470s a warlord named Riothamus led an army, probably from Britain, and fought successfully in Gaul in alliance with local rulers sympathetic to Rome. His name was latinized from a British title meaning "supreme king." Both Riothamus and Aurelius Ambrosius correspond to parts of the later narratives of Arthur: his role as high king, his triumphs against the Saxons, his links to Rome (both friendly and hostile), and his campaigns on the Continent.

Whether the origins of Arthur's story lie in fact or in an urge among the Welsh to imagine a great leader who once restored their power against the ever-expanding Anglo-Saxons, he was clearly an established figure in Welsh oral and written literature by the ninth century. Arthur, however, also held a broader appeal for other peoples of England. The British Isles were felt to lie at the outer edge of world geography, but the story of Arthur and his ancestor Brutus served to create a Britain with other kinds of centrality. The legend of Brutus made Britain the end point of an inexorable westward movement of Trojan imperial power, the *translatio imperii,* and Arthur's forebears became linked to Roman imperial dynasties. Finally, the general movement of Arthur's continental campaigns neatly reversed the patterns of Roman and then Norman colonization.

In the later Middle Ages and after, Arthur and his court are most often encountered in works that lay little claim to historical accuracy. Rather, they exploit the very uncertainty of Arthurian narrative to explore the highest (if sometimes self-deceiving) yearnings of private emotion and social order. These Arthurian romances also probe, often in tragic terms, the limits and taboos that both define and subvert such ideals, including the mutual threats posed by private emotion and social order.

Nevertheless, the Arthurian tradition has also been pulled persistently into the realm of the real. It was presented as serious historical writing from the twelfth century through the end of the Middle Ages. Political agents have used Arthur's kingship as a model or precedent for their own aspirations, as seen in the Kennedy administration's portrayal as a version of Camelot. Even elements of the Christian church wrote their doctrines into Arthurian narrative or claimed Arthur as a patron.

Geoffrey of Monmouth's *History of the Kings of Britain*, finished around 1138, was the fullest version yet of Arthur's origin and career. Geoffrey was the first to make Arthur such a central figure in British history, and it was largely through Geoffrey's Latin "history" that Arthur became so widespread a feature of cultural imagination in the Middle Ages and beyond.

Geoffrey of Monmouth
c. 1100–1155

from History of the Kings of Britain[1]

[ARTHUR OF BRITAIN][2]

After the death of Utherpendragon, the leaders of the Britons assembled from their various provinces in the town of Silchester and there suggested to Dubricius, the Archbishop of the City of the Legions, that as their King he should crown Arthur, the son of Uther. Necessity urged them on, for as soon as the Saxons heard of the death of King Uther, they invited their own countrymen over from Germany, appointed Colgrin as their leader and began to do their utmost to exterminate the Britons. They had already over-run all that section of the island which stretches from the River Humber to the sea named Caithness.[3]

Dubricius lamented the sad state of his country. He called the other bishops to him and bestowed the crown of the kingdom upon Arthur. Arthur was a young man only fifteen years old; but he was of outstanding courage and generosity, and his inborn goodness gave him such grace that he was loved by almost all the people. Once he had been invested with the royal insignia, he observed the normal custom of giving gifts freely to everyone. Such a great crown of soldiers flocked to him that he came to an end of what he had to distribute. However, the man to whom open-handedness and bravery both come naturally may indeed find himself momentarily in need, but poverty will never harass him for long. In Arthur courage was closely linked with generosity, and he made up his mind to harry the Saxons, so that with their wealth he might reward the retainers who served his own household. The just-ness of his cause encouraged him, for he had a claim by rightful inheritance to the kingship of the whole island. He therefore called together all the young men whom I have just mentioned and marched on York. * * *[4]

[*Arthur and his followers attack Colgrin and ultimately subdue the Saxons; then they repel armies of Scots, Picts, and Irish. Arthur restores Briton dynasties throughout England, marries Guinevere, and establishes a stable peace.*]

Arthur then began to increase his personal entourage by inviting very distin-guished men from far-distant kingdoms to join it. In this way he developed such a code of courtliness in his household that he inspired peoples living far away to

1. Translated by Lewis Thorpe (1966).
2. From bk. 9, chs. 1–11.
3. That is, Northumberland and Scotland.
4. Geoffrey links the ancient practice of a king's largesse

to his warrior band together with the claim of dynastic genealogy. Arthur will again use the latter claim when he decides to invade Gaul and then march toward Rome.

imitate him. The result was that even the man of noblest birth, once he was roused to rivalry, thought nothing at all of himself unless he wore his arms and dressed in the same way as Arthur's knights. At last the fame of Arthur's generosity and bravery spread to the very ends of the earth; and the kings of countries far across the sea trembled at the thought that they might be attacked and invaded by him, and so lose control of the lands under their dominion. They were so harassed by these torment-ing anxieties that they rebuilt their towns and the towers in their towns, and then went so far as to construct castles on carefully chosen sites, so that, if invasion should bring Arthur against them, they might have a refuge in their time of need.

All this was reported to Arthur. The fact that he was dreaded by all encouraged him to conceive the idea of conquering the whole of Europe.

Introduction to Sir Gawain and the Green Knight

As a subject of literary romance, Arthurian tradition never had the centrality in later medieval England it had gained in France. It was only one of a wide range of popular topics like Havelok the Dane, King Horn, and the Troy story. Nevertheless Arthur and his court played an ongo-ing role in English society, written into histories and emulated by aristocrats and kings. And in the later fourteenth or early fifteenth century, several very distinguished Arthurian poems appeared, such as the alliterative Morte Arthure and the Awntyrs (Adventures) off Arthure.

Sir Gawain and the Green Knight is the greatest of the Arthurian romances produced in England. The poem embraces the highest aspirations of the late medieval aristocratic world, both courtly and religious, even while it eloquently admits the human failings that threaten those values. A knight's troth and word, a Christian's election and covenant, the breaking point of a person's or a society's virtues, all come in for celebration and painful scrutiny during Gawain's adventure.

Like Beowulf, Sir Gawain and the Green Knight comes down to us by the thread of a single copy. Its manuscript contains a group of poems (Sir Gawain, Pearl, Purity, and Patience) that mark their anonymous author as a poet whose range approaches that of his contemporary Chaucer, and whose formal craft is in some ways more ambitious than Chaucer's.

Gawain is the work of a highly sophisticated provincial court poet (likely in the north-west Midlands), working in a form and narrative tradition that is conservative in comparison with Chaucer's. The poet uses the alliterative long line, a meter with its roots in Anglo-Saxon poetry; the unrhymed alliterative stanzas, of irregular length, each end with five shorter rhymed lines often called a "bob-and-wheel" stanza. Within these traditional constraints, however, the poem achieves an apex of medieval courtly literature, as a superlatively crafted and stylized version of quest romance.

The romance never aims to detach itself from society or history, though. It opens and closes by referring to Troy, the ancient, fallen empire whose survivors were legendary founders of Britain, a connection well known through Geoffrey of Monmouth. Arthur, their ultimate heir, went on later in his myth to pursue imperial ambitions that, like those of Troy, were foiled by adulterous desire and political infidelity. Sir Gawain also echoes its contemporary world in the technical language of architecture, crafts, and arms. This helps draw in the kind of conservative, aristocratic court for which the poem seems to have been written, probably in Cheshire or Lancashire, a somewhat backward region whose nobles remained loyal to Richard II. Along with the pleasure it takes in fine armor and courtly ritual, the poem seems to enfold anxieties about the economic pressures of maintaining chivalric display in a period of costly new technology, inflation, and declining income from land.

By the time this poem was written, toward the close of the fourteenth century, Gawain was a famous Arthurian hero. His reputation was ambiguous, though; he was both Arthur's faithful retainer and nephew, but also a suave seducer. Which side of Gawain would dominate in this particular poem? Would he stand for a civilization of Christian chivalry or one of cynical sophistication?

The test that begins to answer this question occurs during Arthur's ritual celebrations of Christmas and the New Year, and within the civilized practices of Eucharist and secular feast. A gigantic green knight interrupts Arthur's banquet to offer a deadly game of exchanged ax-blows, to be resolved in one year's time. Although the Green Knight, with his ball of holly leaves, seems at first to come from the tradition of the Wild Man—a giant force of nature itself—he is also a sophisticated knight, gorgeously attired. He knows, too, just how to taunt a young king without quite overstepping the bounds of courtly behavior. Gawain takes up the challenge, but a still greater marvel ensues.

from **Sir Gawain and the Green Knight**[1]
Part 1

When the siege and the assault had ceased at Troy,
and the fortress fell in flame to firebrands and ashes,
the traitor who the contrivance of treason there fashioned
was tried for his treachery, the most true upon earth—
5   it was Aeneas[2] the noble and his renowned kindred
who then laid under them lands, and lords became
of well-nigh all the wealth in the Western Isles.[3]
When royal Romulus to Rome his road had taken,
in great pomp and pride he peopled it first,
10   and named it with his own name that yet now it bears;
Tirius[4] went to Tuscany and towns founded,
Langaberde[5] in Lombardy uplifted halls,
and far over the French flood Felix Brutus
on many a broad bank and brae[6] Britain established
15   full fair,
    where strange things, strife and sadness,
    at whiles in the land did fare,
    and each other grief and gladness
    oft fast have followed there.

20   And when fair Britain was founded by this famous lord,[7]
bold men were bred there who in battle rejoiced,
and many a time that betid they troubles aroused.
In this domain more marvels have by men been seen
than in any other that I know of since that olden time;
25   but of all that here abode in Britain as kinds
ever was Arthur most honoured, as I have heard men tell.
Wherefore a marvel among men I mean to recall,
a sight strange to see some men have held it,
one of the wildest adventures of the wonders of Arthur.

---

1. This translation, remarkably faithful to the original alliterative meter and stanza form, is by J.R.R. Tolkien. 2. Aeneas led the survivors of Troy to Italy, after a series of ambiguous omens and misadventures. In medieval tradition, he was also said to have plotted to betray his own city. "The traitor" in line 3, though, may refer to the Trojan Antenor, also said to have betrayed Troy.

3. Perhaps Europe, or just the British Isles. Many royal houses traced their ancestry to Rome and Troy. 4. Possibly Titus Tatius, ancient king of the Sabines. 5. Ancestor of the Lombards, and a nephew of Brutus. 6. The steep bank bounding a river valley. 7. According to Geoffrey of Monmouth and others, a great-grandson of Aeneas, exiled after accidentally killing his father and later the founder of Britain.

30   If you will listen to this lay but a little while now,
         I will tell it at once as in town I have heard
                          it told,
             as it is fixed and fettered
             in story brave and bold,
35   thus linked and truly lettered,
             as was loved in this land of old.

      This king lay at Camelot[8] at Christmas-tide
      with many a lovely lord, lieges most noble,
      indeed of the Table Round[9] all those tried brethren,
40   amid merriment unmatched and mirth without care.
      There tourneyed many a time the trusty knights,
      and jousted full joyously these gentle lords;
      then to the court they came at carols to play.
      For there the feast was unfailing full fifteen days,
45   with all meats and all mirth that men could devise,
      such gladness and gaiety as was glorious to hear,
      din of voices by day, and dancing by night;
      all happiness at the highest in halls and in bowers
      had the lords and the ladies, such as they loved most dearly.
50   With all the bliss of this world they abode together,
      the knights most renowned after the name of Christ,
      and the ladies most lovely that ever life enjoyed,
      and he, king most courteous, who that court possessed.
      For all that folk so fair did in their first estate[10]
55   abide,
             Under heaven the first in fame,
             their king most high in pride;
             it would now be hard to name
             a troop in war so tried.

60   While New Year was yet young that yestereve had arrived,
      that day double dainties on the dais were served,
      when the king was there come with his courtiers to the hall,
      and the chanting of the choir in the chapel had ended.
      With loud clamour and cries both clerks and laymen
65   Noel announced anew, and named it full often;
      then nobles ran anon with New Year gifts,
      Handsels,° handsels they shouted, and handed them out,   *gifts*
      Competed for those presents in playful debate;
      ladies laughed loudly, though they lost the game,
70   and he that won was not woeful, as may well be believed.[11]

All this merriment they made, till their meat was served;
then they washed, and mannerly went to their seats,
ever the highest for the worthiest, as well held to be best.
Queen Guinevere the gay was with grace in the midst
75   of the adorned dais¹² set. Dearly was it arrayed:
finest sendal° at her sides, a ceiling above her   *thin silk garment*
of true tissue of Tolouse, and tapestries of Tharsia
that were embroidered and bound with the brightest gems
one might prove and appraise to purchase for coin
80   any day.
             That loveliest lady there
             on them glanced with eyes of grey;
             that he found ever one more fair
             in sooth might no man say.

85   But Arthur would not eat until all were served;
his youth made him so merry with the moods of a boy,
he liked lighthearted life, so loved he the less
either long to be lying or long to be seated:
so worked on him his young blood and wayward brain.
90   And another rule moreover was his reason besides
that in pride he had appointed: it pleased him not to eat
upon festival so fair, ere he first were apprised
of some strange story or stirring adventure,
or some moving marvel that he might believe in
95   of noble men, knighthood, or new adventures;
or a challenger should come a champion seeking
to join with him in jousting, in jeopardy to set
his life against life, each allowing the other
the favour of fortune, were she fairer to him.
100   This was the king's custom, wherever his court was holden,
at each famous feast among his fair company
                              in hall.
             So his face doth proud appear,
             and he stands up stout and tall,
105   all young in the New Year;
             much mirth he makes with all. * * *

Another noise that was new drew near on a sudden,
so that their lord might have leave at least to take food.
For hardly had the music but a moment ended,
135   and the first course in the court as was custom been served,
when there passed through the portals a perilous horseman,
the mightiest on middle-earth in measure of height,
from his gorge to his girdle so great and so square,
and his loins and his limbs so long and so huge,
140   that half a troll upon earth I trow° that he was,   *trust; believe*
but the largest man alive at least I declare him;
and yet the seemliest for his size that could sit on a horse,

12. A medieval nobleman's hall typically had a raised platform at one end, on which the "high table" stood.

for though in back and in breast his body was grim,
both his paunch and his waist were properly slight,
145   and all his features followed his fashion so gay
                    in mode;
          for at the hue men gaped aghast
          in his face and form that showed;
          as a fay-man fell he passed,
150   and green all over glowed. * * *

250   Then Arthur before the high dais beheld this wonder,
and freely with fair words, for fearless was he ever,
saluted him, saying: 'Lord, to this lodging thou'rt welcome!
The head of this household Arthur my name is.
Alight, as thou lovest me, and linger, I pray thee;
255   and what may thy wish be in a while we shall learn.'
'Nay, so help me,' quoth the horseman, 'He that on high is throned,
to pass any time in this place was no part of my errand.
But since thy praises, prince, so proud are uplisted,
and thy castle and courtiers are accounted the best,
260   the stoutest in steel-gear that on steeds may ride,
most eager and honourable of the earth's people,
valiant to vie with in other virtuous sports,
and here is knighthood renowned, as is noised in my ears:
'tis that has fetched me hither, by my faith, at this time.
265   You may believe by this branch that I am bearing here
that I pass as one in peace,[13] no peril seeking.
For had I set forth to fight in fashion of war,
I have a hauberk at home, and a helm also,
a shield, and a sharp spear shining brightly,
270   and other weapons to wield too, as well I believe;
but since I crave for no combat, my clothes are softer.
Yet if thou be so bold, as abroad is published,
thou wilt grant of thy goodness the game that I ask for
                    by right.'
275   Then Arthur answered there,
          and said: 'Sir, noble knight,
          if battle thou seek thus bare,
          thou'lt fail not here to fight.'

'Nay, I wish for no warfare, on my word I tell thee!
280   Here about on these benches are but beardless children.
Were I hasped in armour on a high charger,
there is no man here to match me—their might is so feeble.
And so I crave in this court only a Christmas pastime,
since it is Yule and New Year, and you are young here and merry.
285   If any so hardy in this house here holds that he is,
if so bold be his blood or his brain be so wild,
that he stoutly dare strike one stroke for another,

13. A holly branch could symbolize peace and was used in games of the Christmas season.

then I will give him as my gift this guisarm[14] costly,
this axe—'tis heavy enough—to handle as he pleases;
290   and I will abide the first brunt, here bare as I sit.
If any fellow be so fierce as my faith to test,
hither let him haste to me and lay hold of this weapon—
I hand it over for ever, he can have it as his own—
and I will stand a stroke from him, stock-still on this floor,
295   provided thou'lt lay down this law: that I may deliver him another.
                        Claim I!
              And yet a respite I'll allow,
              till a year and a day go by.
              Come quick, and let's see now
300   if any here dare reply!' * * *

'Would you, my worthy lord,' said Gawain to the king,
'bid me abandon this bench and stand by you there,
345   so that I without discourtesy might be excused from the table,
and my liege lady were not loth to permit me,
I would come to your counsel before your courtiers fair.
For I find it unfitting, as in fact it is held,
when a challenge in your chamber makes choices so exalted,
350   though you yourself be desirous to accept it in person,
while many bold men about you on bench are seated:
on earth there are, I hold, none more honest of purpose,
no figures fairer on field where fighting is waged.
I am the weakest, I am aware, and in wit feeblest,
355   and the least loss, if I live not, if one would learn the truth.
Only because you are my uncle is honour given me:
save your blood in my body I boast of no virtue;
and since this affair is so foolish that it nowise befits you,
and I have requested it first, accord it then to me!
360   If my claim is uncalled-for without cavil shall judge
                        this court.'
              To consult the knights draw near,
              and this plan they all support;
              the king with crown to clear,
365   and give Gawain the sport. * * *

The Green Knight on the ground now gets himself ready,
leaning a little with the head he lays bare the flesh,
and his locks long and lovely he lifts over his crown,
420   letting the naked neck as was needed appear.
His left foot on the floor before him placing,
Gawain gripped on his axe, gathered and raised it,
from aloft let it swiftly land where 'twas naked,
so that the sharp of his blade shivered the bones,
425   and sank clean through the clear fat and clove it asunder,
and the blade of the bright steel then bit into the ground.

14. A long-handled ax with a spike at the end.

The fair head to the floor fell from the shoulders,
and folk fended it with their feet as forth it went rolling;
the blood burst from the body, bright on the greenness,
430   and yet neither faltered nor fell the fierce man at all,
but stoutly he strode forth, still strong on his shanks,
and roughly he reached out among the rows that stood there,
caught up his comely head and quickly upraised it,
and then hastened to his horse, laid hold of the bridle,
435   stepped into stirrup-iron, and strode up aloft,
his head by the hair in his hand holding;
and he settled himself then in the saddle as firmly
as if unharmed by mishap, though in the hall he might wear
                    no head.
440   His trunk he twisted round,
            that gruesome body that bled,
            and many fear then found,
            as soon as his speech was sped.

For the head in his hand he held it up straight,
445   towards the fairest at the table he twisted the face,
and it lifted up its eyelids and looked at them broadly,
and made such words with its mouth as may be recounted.
'See thou get ready, Gawain, to go as thou vowedst,
and as faithfully seek till thou find me, good sir,
450   as thou hast promised in this place in the presence of these knights.
To the Green Chapel go thou, and get thee, I charge thee,
such a dint as thou hast dealt—indeed thou hast earned
a nimble knock in return on New Year's morning!
The Knight of the Green Chapel I am known to many,
455   so if to find me thou endeavour, thou'lt fail not to do so.
Therefore come! Or to be called a craven thou deservest.'
With a rude roar and rush his reins he turned then,
and hastened out through the hall-door with his head in his hand,
and fire of the flint flew from the feet of his charger.
460   To what country he came in that court no man knew,
no more than they had learned from what land he had journeyed.
                    Meanwhile,
            the king and Sir Gawain
            at the Green Man laugh and smile;
465   yet to men had appeared, 'twas plain,
            a marvel beyond denial. * * *

For after their meal mournfully he reminded his uncle
that his departure was near, and plainly he said:
545   'Now liege-lord of my life, for leave I beg you.
You know the quest and the compact; I care not further
to trouble you with tale of it, save a trifling point:
I must set forth to my fate without fail in the morning,
as God will me guide, the Green Man to seek.'

550 Those most accounted in the castle came then together,[15]
    Iwain and Erric and others not a few,
    Sir Doddinel le Savae, the Duke of Clarence,
    Lancelot, and Lionel, and Lucan the Good,
    Sir Bors and Sir Bedivere that were both men of might,
555 and many others of mark with Mador de la Porte.
    All this company of the court the king now approached
    to comfort the knight with care in their hearts.
    Much mournful lament was made in the hall
    that one so worthy as Gawain should went on that errand,
560 to endure a deadly dint and deal no more
                    with blade.
        The knight ever made good cheer,
        saying, 'Why should I be dismayed?
        Of doom the fair or drear
565   by a man must be assayed.'

    He remained there that day, and in the morning got ready,
    asked early for his arms, and they all were brought him.
    First a carpet of red silk was arrayed on the floor,
    and the gilded gear in plenty there glittered upon it.
570 The stern man stepped thereon and the steel things handled,
    dressed in a doublet of damask of Tharsia,
    and over it a cunning capadoce that was closed at the throat
    and with fair ermine was furred all within.
    Then sabatons[16] first they set on his feet,
575 his legs lapped in steel in his lordly greaves,
    on which the polains they placed, polished and shining
    and knit upon his knees with knots all of gold;
    then the comely cuisses that cunningly clasped
    the thick thews of his thighs they with thongs on him tied;
580 and next the byrnie,° woven of bright steel rings   *coat of mail*
    upon costly quilting, enclosed him about;
    and armlets well burnished upon both of his arms,
    with gay elbow-pieces and gloves of plate,
    and all the goodly gear to guard him whatever
585   betide;
        coat-armour richly made,
        gold spurs on heel in pride;
        girt with a trusty blade,
        silk belt about his side.

590 When he was hasped in his armour his harness was splendid:
    the least latchet or loop was all lit with gold.
    Thus harnessed as he was he heard now his Mass,
    that was offered and honoured at the high altar;

---

15. The following list would have recalled, especially to readers of French romances, other great quests and challenges encountered by Arthur's knights. The list's order may also suggest later and more tragic episodes in the Arthurian narrative, ending with Bedivere who throws Excalibur into a lake after Arthur is mortally wounded.
16. A broad-toed armed foot-covering worn by warriors in armor.

595   and then he came to the king and his court-companions,
        and with love he took leave of lords and of ladies;
        and they kissed him and escorted him, and to Christ him commended.
        And now Gringolet stood groomed, and girt with a saddle
        gleaming right gaily with many gold fringes,
        and all newly for the nonce nailed at all points;
600   adorned with bars was the bridle, with bright gold banded;
        that apparelling proud of poitrel and of skirts,
        and the crupper and caparison[17] accorded with the saddlebows:
        all was arrayed in red with rich gold studded,
        so that it glittered and glinted as a gleam of the sun.
605   Then he in hand took the helm and in haste kissed it:
        strongly was it stapled and stuffed within;
        it sat high upon his head and was hasped at the back,
        and a light kerchief was laid o'er the beaver,
        all braided and bound[18] with the brightest gems
610   upon broad silken broidery, with birds on the seams
        like popinjays depainted, here preening and there,
        turtles and true-loves, entwined as thickly
        as if many sempstresses had the sewing full seven winters
                                in hand.
615   A circlet of greater price
                his crown about did band;
                The diamonds point-device
                there blazing bright did stand.

        Then they brought him his blazon that was of brilliant gules
620   with the pentangle[19] depicted in pure hue of gold.
        By the baldric he caught it and about his neck cast it:
        right well and worthily it went with the knight.
        And why the pentangle is proper to that prince so noble
        I intend now to tell you, though it may tarry my story.
625   It is a sign that Solomon once set on a time
        to betoken Troth, as it is entitled to do;
        for it is a figure that in it five points holdeth,
        and each line overlaps and is linked with another,
        and every way it is endless; and the English, I hear,
630   everywhere name it the Endless Knot.
        So it suits well this knight and his unsullied arms;
        for ever faithful in five points, and five times under each,
        Gawain as good was acknowledged and as gold refined,
        devoid of every vice and with virtues adorned.
635   So there
                the pentangle painted new
                he on shield and coat did wear,
                as one of word most true
                and knight of bearing fair.

17. A cloth or covering spread over the saddle or harness
of a horse, often gaily ornamented.
18. The preceding technical language of armor is now
joined by an equally technical description of needlework,
for which English women were famous.

19. A five-pointed star and symbol of perfection and eternity, since it can be drawn with an uninterrupted line
ending at the point of the star where it begins. Inscribed
within a circle, it was called Solomon's seal.

640   First faultless was he found in his five senses,
        and next in his five fingers he failed at no time,
        and firmly on the Five Wounds, all his faith was set
        that Christ received on the cross, as the Creed tells us;
        and wherever the brave man into battle was come,
645   on this beyond all things was his earnest thought:
        that ever from the Five Joys all his valour he gained
        that to Heaven's courteous Queen once came from her Child.[20]
        For which cause the knight had in comely wise
        on the inner side of his shield her image depainted,
650   that when he cast his eyes thither his courage never failed.
        The fifth five that was used, as I find, by this knight
        was free-giving and friendliness first before all,
        and chastity and chivalry ever changeless and straight,
        and piety surpassing all points: these perfect five
655   were hasped upon him harder than on any man else.
        Now these five series, in sooth, were fastened on this knight,
        and each was knit with another and had no ending,
        but were fixed at five points that failed not at all,
        coincided in no line nor sundered either,
660   not ending in any angle anywhere, as I discover,
        wherever the process was put in play or passed to an end.
        Therefore on his shining shield was shaped now this knot,
        royally with red gules upon red gold set:
        this is the pure pentangle as people of learning
665   have taught.
                Now Gawain in brave array
                his lance at last hath caught.
                He gave them all good day,
                for evermore as he thought.

670   He spurned his steed with the spurs and sprang on his way
        so fiercely that the flint-sparks flashed out behind him.
        All who beheld him so honourable in their hearts were sighing,
        and assenting in sooth one said to another,
        grieving for that good man: 'Before God, 'tis a shame
675   that thou, lord, must be lost, who art in life so noble!
        To meet his match among men, Marry, 'tis not easy!
        To behave with more heed would have behoved one of sense,
        and that dear lord duly a duke to have made,
        illustrious leader of liegemen in this land as befits him;
680   and that would better have been than to be butchered to death,
        beheaded by an elvish man for an arrogant vaunt.
        Who can recall any king that such a course ever took
        as knights quibbling at court at their Christmas games!'
        Many warm tears outwelling there watered their eyes,
685   when that lord so beloved left the castle
                        that day.

20. Poems and meditations on the Virgin's joys and sorrows were widespread. Her five joys were the Annunciation, Nativity, Resurrection, Ascension, and Assumption.

No longer he abode,
but swiftly went his way;
bewildering ways he rode,
690   as the book I heard doth say.

Now he rides thus arrayed through the realm of Logres,[21]
Sir Gawain in God's care, though no game now he found it.
Oft forlorn and alone he lodged of a night
where he found not afforded him such fare as pleased him.
695   He had no friend but his horse in the forests and hills,
no man on his march to commune with but God,
till anon he drew near unto Northern Wales.
All the isles of Anglesey he held on his left,
and over the fords he fared by the flats near the sea,
700   and then over by the Holy Head to high land again
in the wilderness of Wirral: there wandered but few
who with good will regarded either God or mortal.
And ever he asked as he went on of all whom he met
if they had heard any news of a knight that was green
705   in any ground thereabouts, or of the Green Chapel.
And all denied it, saying nay, and that never in their lives
a single man had they seen that of such a colour
                              could be.
The knight took pathways strange
710   by many a lonesome lea,
and oft his view did change
that chapel ere he could see.

Many a cliff he climbed o'er in countries unknown,
far fled from his friends without fellowship he rode.
715   At every wading or water on the way that he passed
he found a foe before him, save at few for a wonder;
and so foul were they and fell that fight he must needs.
So many a marvel in the mountains he met in those lands
that 'twould be tedious the tenth part to tell you thereof.
720   At whiles with worms he wars, and with wolves also,
at whiles with wood-trolls that wandered in the crags,
and with bulls and with bears and boards, too, at times;
and with ogres that hounded him from the heights of the fells.
Had he not been stalwart and staunch and steadfast in God,
725   he doubtless would have died and death had met often;
for though war wearied him much, the winter was worse,
when the cold clear water from the clouds spilling
froze ere it had fallen upon the faded earth.
Wellnigh slain by the sleet he slept ironclad
730   more nights than enow in the naked rocks,
where clattering from the crest the cold brook tumbled,

---

21. Identified with England in Geoffrey of Monmouth, elsewhere a vaguer term for Arthur's kingdom. Here, Gawain is heading northward through Wales, then along the coast of the Irish Sea and into the forest of Wirral in Cheshire—a wild area and resort of outlaws in the 14th century. Gawain thus moves into the area around Chester, where the poem may well have been written.

and hung high o'er his head in hard icicles.
Thus in peril and pain and in passes grievous
till Christmas-eve that country he crossed all alone
735   in need.
               The knight did at that tide
               his plaint to Mary plead,
               her rider's road to guide
               and to some lodging lead. * * *

Then the great man in green gladly prepared him,
2260 gathered up his grim tool there Gawain to smite;
with all the lust in his limbs aloft he heaved it,
shaped as mighty a stroke as if he meant to destroy him.
Had it driving come down as dour as he aimed it,
under his dint would have died the most doughty man ever.
2265 But Gawain on that guisarm then glanced to one side,
as down it came gliding on the green there to end him,
and he shrank a little with his shoulders at the sharp iron.
With a jolt the other man jerked back the blade,
and reproved then the prince, proudly him taunting.
2270 'Thou'rt not Gawain,' said the green man, 'who is so good reported,
who never flinched from any foes on fell or in dale;
and now thou fleest in fear, ere thou feelest a hurt!
Of such cowardice that knight I ne'er heard accused.
Neither blenched I nor backed, when thy blow, sir, thou aimedst,
2275 nor uttered any cavil in the court of King Arthur.
My head flew to my feet, and yet fled I never;
but thou, ere thou hast any hurt, in thy heart quailest,
and so the nobler knight to be named I deserve
                         therefore.'
2280   'I blenched once,' Gawain said,
               'and I will do so no more.
               But if on floor now falls my head,
               I cannot it restore. * * *

Wild ways in the world Gawain now rideth
2480 on Gringolet: by the grace of God he still lived.
Oft in house he was harboured and lay oft in the open,
oft vanquished his foe in adventures as he fared
which I intend not this time in my tale to recount.
The hurt was healed that he had in his neck,
2485 and the bright-hued belt he bore now about it
obliquely like a baldric bound at his side,
under his left arm with a knot that lace was fastened
to betoken he had been detected in the taint of a fault;
and so at last he came to the Court again safely.
2490 Delight there was awakened, when the lords were aware
that good Gawain had returned: glad news they thought it.
The king kissed the knight, and the queen also,
and then in turn many a true knight that attended to greet him.
About his quest they enquire, and he recounts all the marvels,

2495 declares all the hardships and care that he had,
what chanced at the Chapel, what cheer made the knight,
the love of the lady, and the lace at the last.
The notch in his neck naked he showed them
that he had for his dishonesty from the hands of the knight
2500   in blame.
              It was torment to tell the truth:
              in his face the blood did flame;
              he groaned for grief and ruth
              when he showed it, to his shame.

2505 'Lo! Lord,' he said at last, and the lace handled,
'This is the band! For this a rebuke I bear in my neck!
This is the grief and disgrace I have got for myself
from the covetousness and cowardice that o'ercame me there!
This is the token of the troth-breach that I am detected in,
2510 and needs must I wear it while in the world I remain;
for a man may cover his blemish, but unbind it he cannot,
for where once 'tis applied, thence part will it never.'
The king comforted the knight, and all the Court also
laughed loudly thereat, and this law made in mirth
2515 the lords and the ladies that whoso belonged to the Table,
every knight of the Brotherhood, a baldric should have,
a band of bright green obliquely about him,
and this for love of that knight as a livery should wear.
For that was reckoned the distinction of the Round Table,
2520 and honour was his that had it evermore after,
as it is written in the best of the books of romance.
Thus in Arthur his days happened this marvel,
as the Book of the Brut beareth us witness;
since Brutus the bold knight to Britain came first,
2525 after the siege and the assault had ceased at Troy,
                          I trow,
              many a marvel such before,
              has happened here ere now.
              To His bliss us bring Who bore
2530   the Crown of Thorns on brow!   AMEN

Geoffrey Chaucer
c. 1340–1400

Chaucer's Middle English
Grammar

The English of Chaucer's London, and particularly the English of government bureaucracy, became the source for the more standardized vernacular that emerged in the era of print at the close of the Middle Ages. As a result, Chaucer's English is easier to understand today than the dialect of many of his great contemporaries such as the *Gawain* poet, who worked far to the north. The text that follows preserves Chaucer's language, with some spellings slightly modernized and regularized by its editor, E. Talbot Donaldson.

The marginal glosses in the readings are intended to help the nonspecialist reader through Chaucer's language without elaborate prior study. It will be helpful, though, to explain a few key differences from Modern English.

Nouns: The possessive is sometimes formed without a final *-s*.

Pronouns: Readers will recognize the archaic *thou, thine, thee* of second-person singular, and *ye* of the plural. Occasional confusion can arise from the form *hir*, which can mean "her" or "their." *Hem* is Chaucer's spelling for "them," and *tho* for "those." Chaucer uses *who* to mean "whoever."

Adverbs: Formed, as today, with *-ly*, but also with *-liche*. Sometimes an adverb is unchanged from its adjective form: *fairly, fairliche, faire* can all be adverbs.

Verbs: Second-person singular is formed with *-est* (*thou lovest*, past tense *thou lovedest*); third-person singular often with *-eth* (*he loveth*); plurals often with *-n* (*we loven*); and infinitive with *-n* (*loven*).

Strong verbs/impersonal verbs: Middle English has many "strong verbs," which form the past and perfect by changing a vowel in their stem; these are usually recognizable by analogy with surviving forms in Modern English (*go, went, gone; sing, sang, sung*; etc.). Middle English also often uses "impersonal verbs" (*liketh*, "it pleases"; *as me thinketh*, "as I think"), in which case sometimes no obvious subject noun or pronoun occurs.

Pronunciation

A few guidelines will help approximate the sound of Chaucer's English and the richness of his versification. For fuller discussion, consult sources listed in the bibliography.

Pronounce all consonants: *knight* is "k/neecht" with a guttural *ch*, not "nite"; *gnaw* is "g/naw." Middle English consonants preserve many of the sounds of the language's Germanic roots: guttural *gh*; sounded *l* and *w* in words like *folk* or *write*. (Exceptions occur in some words that derive from French, like *honour* whose *h* is silent.)

Final *-e* was sounded in early Middle English. Such pronunciation was becoming archaic by Chaucer's time, but was available to aid meter in the stylized context of poetry.

The distinction between short and long vowels was greater in Middle English than today. Middle English short vowels have mostly remained short in Modern English, with some shift in pronunciation: short *a* sounds like the *o* in *hot*, short *o* like a quick version of the *aw* in *law*, short *u* like the *u* in *full*.

Long vowels in Middle English (here usually indicated by doubling, when vowel length is unclear by analogy to modern spelling) are close to long vowels in modern Romance languages. The chart shows some differences in Middle English long vowels.

Middle English	pronounced as in	Modern English
a (as in *name*)		*father*
open *e* (*deel*)		*swear, bread*
close *e* (*sweet*)		*fame*
i (*whit*)		*feet*
open *o* (*holy*)		*law*
close *o* (*roote*)		*note*
u (as in *town, aboute*)		*root*
u (*vertu*)		*few*

Open and close long vowels are a challenge for modern readers. Generally, open long *e* in Middle English (*deel*) has become Modern English spelling with *ea* (*deal*); close long *e* (*sweet*) has become Modern English spelling with *ee* (*sweet*). Open long *o* in Middle English has come to be pronounced as in *note*; close long *o* in Middle English has come to be pronounced *root*. This latter case illustrates the idea of "vowel shift" across the centuries, in which some long vowels have moved forward in the throat and palate.

Versification

All of Chaucer's poetry presented here is in a loosely iambic pentameter line, which Chaucer was greatly responsible for bringing into prominence in England. He is a fluid versifier, though, and often shifts stress, producing metrical effects that have come to be called trochees and spondees. Final -*e* is often pronounced within lines to provide an unstressed syllable and is typically pronounced at the end of each line. Yet final -*e* may also elide with a following word that begins with a vowel. The following lines from *The Nun's Priest's Tale* have a proposed scansion, but the reader will see that alternate scansions are possible at several places.

> "Avoi," quod she, "fy on you, hertelees!
> Allas," quod she, "for by that God above,
> Now han ye lost myn herte and al my love!
> I can nat love a coward, by my faith.
> For certes, what so any womman saith,
> We alle desiren, if it mighte be,
> To han housbondes hardy, wise, and free,
> And secree, and no nigard, ne no fool,
> Ne him that is agast of every tool,
> Ne noon avauntour. By that God above,
> How dorste ye sayn for shame unto youre love
> That any thing mighte make you aferd?
> Have ye no mannes herte and han a beerd?

Introduction to The Canterbury Tales

THE GENERAL PROLOGUE   The twenty-nine "sondry folke" of the Canterbury company gather at the Tabard Inn, ostensibly with the pious intent of making a pilgrimage to England's holiest shrine, the tomb of Saint Thomas Becket at Canterbury. From the start in the raffish and worldly London suburb of Southwerk, though, the pilgrims' attentions and energy veer wildly between the sacred and the profane. The mild story-telling competition proposed by the Host also slides swiftly into a contest among social classes. Set in Chaucer's own time and place, *The Canterbury Tales* reflect both the dynamism and the uncertainties of a society still nostalgic for archaic models of church and state, yet riven by such crises as plague, economic disruption, and the new claims of peasants and mercantile bourgeois—claims expressed and repressed most violently in the recent Rising, or "Peasants' Revolt," of 1381.

Chaucer's *Prologue* has roots in the genre known as "estates satire." Such writings criticized the failure of the members of the three traditional "estates" of medieval society—the aristocracy, the clergy, and the commons—to fulfill their ordained function of fighting, praying, and working the land, respectively. From the beginning the pilgrims' portraits are couched in language fraught with class connotations. The Knight, the idealized (if archaic) representative of the aristocracy, is called *gentil* (that is, "noble, aristocratic") and is said never to have uttered any *vileynye*—speech characteristic of peasants or *villeyns*. Many of the pilgrims in the other two estates display aristocratic manners, among the clergy notably the Prioress, with her "cheere of court," and the Monk, who lives like a country gentleman, hunting with greyhounds and a stable full of fine horses. Both pilgrims contrast with the ideal of their estate, the Parson, who, though "*povre*" is "rich" in holy works.

The commons are traditionally the last of the "three estates," yet they bulk largest in the Canterbury company and fit least well in that model of social order. There are old-fashioned laborers on the pilgrimage, but many more characters from the emerging and disruptive world of small industry and commerce. They are commoners, but have ambitions that lead them both to envy and to mock the powers held by their aristocratic and clerical companions.

Among the group that traditionally comprised the commons, the peasants, Chaucer singles out one ideal, the Plowman, who is, significantly, the Parson's brother. He is characterized as a diligent *swynkere* (worker), in implicit contrast to the lazy peasants castigated in estates satire. Most of the rest of the commons, however, such as the Miller and the Cook, are presented as "churlish," and their tales have a coarse vigor that Chaucer clearly relishes even as he disassociates himself from their vulgarity.

In theory, women were treated as a separate category, defined by their sexual nature and marital role rather than by their class. Nevertheless, the Prioress and the Wife of Bath are both satirized as much for their social ambition as for the failings of their gender. The Prioress prides herself on her courtesy, and the commoner Wife of Bath aspires to the same social recognition as the guildsmen's upwardly mobile wives. Her portrait is complex, however, for she is simultaneously satirized and admired for challenging the expected roles of women at the time, with her economic independence (as a rich widow and a cloth-maker) and her resultant freedom to travel. The narrator's suggestion that she goes on many pilgrimages in order to find a sixth husband bears out the stereotype of unbridled female sexuality familiar from estates satire, as her fondness of talking and laughing bears out the stereotype of female garrulousness.

Chaucer's satire is pointed but also exceptionally subtle, largely because of the irony achieved through his use of the narrator, seemingly naive and a little dense. His deadpan narration leaves the readers themselves to supply the judgment.

from **The Canterbury Tales**

from **The General Prologue**

Whan that April with his showres soote°	*sweet*
The droughte of March hath perced to the roote,	
And bathed every veine in swich licour,°	*such liquid*
Of which vertu° engendred is the flowr;	*by whose strength*
5 Whan Zephyrus[1] eek° with his sweete breeth	*also*
Inspired hath in every holt and heeth°	*wood and field*
The tendre croppes, and the yonge sonne	
Hath in the Ram° his halve cours yronne,	*the zodiac sign Aries*
And smale fowles maken melodye	
10 That sleepen al the night with open yë°—	*eye*
So priketh hem Nature in hir corages°—	*hearts, spirits*
Thanne longen folk to goon on pilgrimages,	
And palmeres[2] for to seeken straunge strondes°	*shores*
To ferne halwes,° couthe° in sondry londes;	*far-off shrines / known*
15 And specially from every shires ende	
Of Engelond to Canterbury they wende,°	*go*
The holy blisful martyr[3] for to seeke	
That hem hath holpen° whan that they were seke.°	*helped / sick*
Bifel that in that seson on a day,	
20 In Southwerk[4] at the Tabard as I lay,	
Redy to wenden on my pilgrimage	
To Canterbury with ful devout corage,	
At night was come into that hostelrye	
Wel nine and twenty in a compaignye	
25 Of sondry folk, by aventure yfalle	
In felaweshipe, and pilgrimes were they alle	
That toward Canterbury wolden ride.	
The chambres° and the stables weren wide,	*guestrooms*
And wel we weren esed° at the beste.	*accommodated*
30 And shortly, whan the sonne was to reste,	
So hadde I spoken with hem everichoon	
That I was of hir felaweshipe anoon,	
And made forward° erly for to rise,	*agreed*
To take oure way ther as I you devise.°	*relate*

1. In Roman mythology Zephyrus was the demigod of the west wind, herald of warmer weather.
2. Pilgrims who had traveled to the Holy Land.
3. St. Thomas Becket, murdered in Canterbury Cathedral in 1170.
4. Southwark, a suburb of London south of the Thames and the traditional starting point for the pilgrimage to

Canterbury in Kent, was notorious as a center of gambling and prostitution. The Tabard Inn was an actual public house at the time, named for the shape of its sign which resembled the coarse, sleeveless outer garment worn by members of the lower classes, monks, and foot soldiers alike.

from The Nun's Priest's Tale

Whan that the month in which the world bigan,
That highte March, whan God first maked man,
Was compleet, and passed were also,
Sin March biran,° thritty days and two,[1]   *finished*
425   Bifel that Chauntecleer in al his pride,
His sevene wives walking him biside,
Caste up his yën to the brighte sonne,
That in the signe of Taurus hadde yronne
Twenty degrees and oon and somwhat more,
430   And knew by kinde,° and by noon other lore,   *nature*
That it was prime, and crew with blisful stevene.°   *voice*
"The sonne," he saide, "is clomben up on hevene
Fourty degrees and oon and more, ywis.°   *indeed*
Madame Pertelote, my worldes blis,
435   Herkneth thise blisful briddes° how they singe,   *birds*
And see the fresshe flowres how they springe:
Ful is myn herte of revel and solas."
But sodeinly him fil a sorweful cas,°   *event*
For evere the latter ende of joye is wo—
440   God woot that worldly joye is soone ago,
And if a rethor° coude faire endite,°   *rhetorician / compose*
He in a cronicle saufly° mighte it write,   *safely*
As for a soverein notabilitee.
Now every wis man lat him herkne me:
445   This storye is also° trewe, I undertake,   *as*
As is the book of Launcelot de Lake,[2]
That wommen holde in ful greet reverence.
Now wol I turne again to my sentence.°   *topic*
    A colfox° ful of sly iniquitee,   *black fox*
450   That in the grove° hadde woned° yeres three,   *woods / lived*
By heigh imaginacion forncast,[3]
The same night thurghout the hegges brast°   *burst*
Into the yeerd ther Chauntecleer the faire
Was wont, and eek his wives, to repaire;
455   And in a bed of wortes° stille he lay   *cabbages*
Til it was passed undren° of the day,   *midmorning*
Waiting his time on Chauntecleer to falle,
As gladly doon thise homicides alle,
That in await liggen to mordre men.
460   O false mordrour, lurking in thy den!
O newe Scariot! Newe Geniloun![4]
False dissimilour!° O Greek Sinoun,[5]   *dissembler*
That broughtest Troye al outrely° to sorwe!   *entirely*
O Chauntecleer, accursed be that morwe
465   That thou into the yeerd flaugh fro the bemes!
Thou were ful wel ywarned by thy dremes

1. The date is thus 3 May.
2. The adventures of the Arthurian knight.
3. Predicted (in Chauntecleer's dream).
4. Judas Iscariot, who handed Jesus over to the Roman

authorities for execution; Ganelon, a medieval traitor who betrayed the hero Roland to his Saracen enemies.
5. The Greek who tricked the Trojans into accepting the Trojan horse behind the city walls.

That thilke day was perilous to thee;
But what that God forwoot moot° needes be,   *foreknew must*
After the opinion of certain clerkes:
470   Witnesse on him that any parfit° clerk is   *accomplished*
That in scole is greet altercacioun
In this matere, and greet disputisoun,
And hath been of an hundred thousand men.
But I ne can nat bulte it to the bren,[6]
475   As can the holy doctour Augustin,
Or Boece, or the bisshop Bradwardin[7]—
Wheither that Goddes worthy forwiting°   *foreknowledge*
Straineth° me nedely for to doon a thing   *compels*
("Nedely" clepe I simple necessitee),
480   Or elles if free chois be graunted me
To do that same thing or do it nought,
Though God forwoot it er that I was wrought;°   *made*
Or if his witing straineth neveradeel,
But by necessitee condicionel[8]—
485   I wol nat han to do of swich matere:
My tale is of a cok, as ye may heere,
That took his conseil of his wif with sorwe,
To walken in the yeerd upon that morwe
That he hadde met the dreem that I you tolde.
490   Wommenes conseils been ful ofte colde,°   *disastrous*
Wommanes conseil broughte us first to wo,
And made Adam fro Paradis to go,
Ther as he was ful merye and wel at ese.
But for I noot° to whom it mighte displese   *do not know*
495   If I conseil of wommen wolde blame,
Passe over, for I saide it in my game—
Rede auctours° where they trete of swich matere,   *authors*
And what they sayn of wommen ye may heere—
Thise been the cokkes wordes and nat mine:
500   I can noon harm of no womman divine.°   *guess at*
      Faire in the sond° to bathe hire merily   *sand*
Lith° Pertelote, and alle hir sustres by,   *lies*
Again the sonne, and Chauntecleer so free
Soong merier than the mermaide in the see—
505   For Physiologus[9] saith sikerly
How that they singen wel and merily.
      And so bifel that as he caste his yë
Among the wortes on a boterflye,°   *butterfly*
He was war of this fox that lay ful lowe.
510   No thing ne liste him° thanne for to crowe,   *he wanted*
But cride anoon "Cok cok!" and up he sterte,

6. Sift it from the husks (i.e., discriminate).
7. St. Augustine, the ancient writer Boethius, and the 14th-century Archbishop of Canterbury Thomas Bradwardine attempted to explain how God's predestination of events still allowed for humans to have free will.
8. Boethius argued only for conditional necessity, which still permitted for much exercise of free will.
9. Said to have written a bestiary.

As man that was affrayed in his herte—
For naturelly a beest desireth flee
Fro his contrarye° if he may it see,   *natural enemy*
515   Though he nevere erst° hadde seen it with his yë.   *before*
This Chauntecleer, whan he gan him espye,
He wolde han fled, but that the fox anoon
Saide, "Gentil sire, allas, wher wol ye goon?
Be ye afraid of me that am youre freend?
520   Now certes, I were worse than a feend°   *devil*
If I to you wolde harm or vilainye.
I am nat come youre conseil for t'espye,
But trewely the cause of my cominge
Was only for to herkne how that ye singe:
525   For trewely, ye han as merye a stevene°   *voice*
As any angel hath that is in hevene.
Therwith ye han in musik more feelinge
Than hadde Boece,[10] or any that can singe.
My lord your fader—God his soule blesse!—
530   And eek youre moder, of hir gentilesse,°   *gentility*
Han in myn hous ybeen, to my grete ese.
And certes sire, ful fain° wolde I you plese.   *gladly*
    But for men speke of singing, I wol saye,
So mote I brouke° wel mine yën twaye,   *use*
535   Save ye, I herde nevere man so singe
As dide youre fader in the morweninge.
Certes, it was of herte° al that he soong.   *heartfelt*
And for to make his vois the more strong,
He wolde so paine him that with bothe his yën
540   He moste winke,° so loude wolde he cryen;   *shut his eyes*
And stonden on his tiptoon therwithal,
And strecche forth his nekke long and smal;
And eek he was of swich discrecioun
That ther nas no man in no regioun
545   That him in song or wisdom mighte passe.°   *surpass*
I have wel rad in Daun Burnel the Asse.[11]
Among his vers how that ther was a cok,
For° a preestes sone yaf him a knok   *because*
Upon his leg whil he was yong and nice,°   *foolish*
550   He made him for to lese his benefice.[12]
But certain, ther nis no comparisoun
Bitwixe the wisdom and discrecioun
Of youre fader and of his subtiltee.
Now singeth, sire, for sainte° charitee!   *holy*
555   Lat see, conne ye youre fader countrefete?"°   *imitate*
    This Chauntecleer his winges gan to bete,
As man that coude his traison nat espye,

---

10. In addition to theology, Boethius also wrote a music   12. Lose his commission (because he overslept).
textbook.
11. The hero of a 12th-century satirical poem, *Speculum
Stultorum*, by Nigel Wirecker, Brunellus was a donkey
who traveled around Europe trying to educate himself.

So was he ravisshed with his flaterye.

    Allas, ye lordes, many a fals flatour

560 Is in youre court, and many a losengeour,°   *deceiver*

That plesen you wel more, by my faith,

Than he that soothfastnesse° unto you saith!   *truth*

Redeth Ecclesiaste[13] of flaterye.

Beeth war, ye lordes, of hir trecherye.

565   This Chauntecleer stood hye upon his toos,

Strecching his nekke, and heeld his yën cloos,

And gan to crowe loude for the nones;°   *for the purpose*

And daun Russel the fox sterte up atones,°   *at once*

And by the gargat° hente° Chauntecleer,   *throat / seized*

570 And on his bak toward the wode him beer,

For yit ne was ther no man that him sued.

    O destinee that maist nat been eschued!°   *avoided*

Allas that Chauntecleer fleigh fro the bemes!

Allas his wif ne roughte° nat of dremes!   *cared*

575 And on a Friday[14] fil al this meschaunce!

    O Venus that art goddesse of plesaunce,

Sin that thy servant was this Chauntecleer,

And in thy service dide al his power—

More for delit than world° to multiplye—   *population*

580 Why woldestou suffre him on thy day to die?

    O Gaufred,[15] dere maister soverein,

That, whan thy worthy king Richard was slain

With shot,° complainedest his deeth so sore,   *(of an arrow)*

Why ne hadde I now thy sentence and thy lore,

585 The Friday for to chide as diden ye?

For on a Friday soothly° slain was he.   *truly*

Thanne wolde I shewe you how that I coude plaine°   *lament*

For Chauntecleres drede and for his paine.

    Certes, swich cry ne lamentacioun

590 Was nevere of ladies maad whan Ilioun°   *Troy*

Was wonne, and Pyrrus[16] with his straite° swerd,   *drawn*

Whan he hadde hent King Priam by the beerd

And slain him, as saith us Eneidos,°   *Virgil's Aeneid*

As maden alle the hennes in the cloos,°   *yard*

595 Whan they hadde seen of Chauntecleer the sighte.

But sovereinly Dame Pertelote shrighte°   *shrieked*

Ful louder than dide Hasdrubales wif[17]

Whan that hir housbonde hadde lost his lif,

And that the Romains hadden brend Cartage:

600 She was so ful of torment and of rage

That wilfully unto the fir she sterte,

And brende hirselven with a stedefast herte.

    O woful hennes, right so criden ye

---

13. The Book of Ecclesiasticus.
14. Venus's day, but also an ominous day of the week.
15. Geoffrey of Vinsauf, who wrote a poem when King Richard the Lion-Hearted died, cursing the day of the week on which he died, a Friday.

16. Pyrrhus, the son of Achilles, who slew Troy's King Priam.
17. Hasdrubal was King of Carthage when it was defeated by the Romans during the Punic Wars.

As, whan that Nero[18] brende the citee
605 Of Rome, criden senatoures wives
For that hir housbondes losten alle hir lives:
Withouten gilt this Nero hath hem slain.
Now wol I turne to my tale again.
　　The sely° widwe and eek hir doughtres two   *innocent*
610 Herden thise hennes crye and maken wo,
And out at dores sterten they anoon,
And sien° the fox toward the grove goon,   *saw*
And bar upon his bak the cok away,
And criden, "Out, harrow, and wailaway,
615 Ha, ha, the fox," and after him they ran,
And eek with staves many another man;
Ran Colle oure dogge, and Talbot and Gerland,[19]
And Malkin with a distaf in hir hand,
Ran cow and calf, and eek the verray hogges,
620 Sore aferd for berking of the dogges
And shouting of the men and wommen eke.
They ronne so hem thoughte hir herte breke;
They yelleden as feendes doon in helle;
The dokes° criden as men wolde hem quelle;°   *ducks / kill*
625 The gees for fere flowen over the trees;
Out of the hive cam the swarm of bees;
So hidous was the noise a, benedicite,
Certes, he Jakke Straw[20] and his meinee
Ne made nevere shoutes half so shrille
630 Whan that they wolden any Fleming kille,
As thilke day was maad upon the fox:
Of bras they broughten bemes° and of box,°   *trumpets / boxwood*
Of horn, of boon, in whiche they blewe and pouped,°   *puffed*
And therwithal they skriked and they houped—
635 It seemed as that hevene sholde falle.
　　Now goode men, I praye you herkneth alle:
Lo, how Fortune turneth sodeinly
The hope and pride eek of hir enemy.
This cok that lay upon the foxes bak,
640 In al his drede unto the fox he spak,
And saide, "Sire, if that I were as ye,
Yit sholde I sayn, as wis° God helpe me,   *certainly*
'Turneth ayain, ye proude cherles° alle!   *ruffians*
A verray pestilence upon you falle!
645 Now am I come unto this wodes side,
Maugree° your heed,° the cok shal here abide.   *despite / planning*
I wol him ete, in faith, and that anoon.'"
　　The fox answerde, "In faith, it shal be doon."
And as he spak that word, al sodeinly
650 The cok brak from his mouth deliverly,°   *nimbly*

18. The Emperor Nero set fire to Rome, killing many of his senators.
19. Common names for dogs.
20. Jack Straw was one of the leaders of the Peasants' Revolt of 1381, which was directed in part against the Flemish traders in London.

And hye upon a tree he fleigh anoon.
    And whan the fox sawgh that he was agoon,
"Allas," quod he, "O Chauntecleer, allas!
I have to you," quod he, "ydoon trespas,
In as muche as I maked you aferd
When I you hente and broughte out of the yeerd.
But sire, I dide it in no wikke° entente: *wicked*
Come down, and I shal telle you what I mente.
I shal saye sooth to you, God help me so."
    "Nay thanne," quod he, "I shrewe° us bothe two: *curse*
But first I shrewe myself, bothe blood and bones,
If thou bigile me ofter than ones;
Thou shalt namore thurgh thy flaterye
Do° me to singe and winken with myn yë.   *make*
For he that winketh whan he sholde see,
Al wilfully, God lat him nevere thee."°   *prosper*
    "Nay," quod the fox, "but God yive him meschaunce
That is so undiscreet of governaunce
That jangleth° whan he sholde holde his pees."   *chatters*
    Lo, swich it is for to be recchelees°   *careless*
And necligent and truste on flaterye.
But ye that holden this tale a folye
As of a fox, or of a cok and hen,
Taketh the moralitee, goode men.
For Saint Paul saith that al that writen is
To oure doctrine° it is ywrit, ywis:°   *instruction / indeed*
Taketh the fruit, and lat the chaf be stille.
Now goode God, if that it be thy wille,
As saith my lord, so make us alle goode men,
And bringe us to his hye blisse. Amen.

655
660
665
670
675
680

Edmund Spenser
1552?–1599

Introduction to The Faerie Queene

THE FAERIE QUEENE   In 1583 Spenser told guests at a dinner he was attending that he proposed to write a poem in which he would "represent all the moral virtues, assigning to every
virtue a knight in whose actions and chivalry the operations of that virtue are to be expressed,
and the vices and unruly appetites that oppose themselves to be beaten down." The project,
obviously ambitious, recalls the great epics of classical antiquity: the twenty-four books of
Homer's *Iliad*, the twelve books of Virgil's *Aeneid*. Spenser must have believed he was prepared
for such an undertaking; like Virgil, he had served his apprenticeship by writing pastoral poetry. But whatever his intention, he realized his great work only in part. He depicted the first
six virtues in the "legends" of Holiness, Temperance, Chastity, Friendship, Justice, and Courtesy, in which each virtue is perfected by the trials of a particular knight fighting the evil that
most threatens his character. He published the first three books in 1590, adding the next three
in a second edition in 1596. His plan for a second set of six books resulted in only two cantos—on the virtue of Constancy.

Spenser's moral chivalry is sponsored and sustained by the court of Gloriana, the Faerie
Queene, in whom is reflected the imposing figure of Queen Elizabeth. Gloriana's story is illustrated by the actions of a character called Prince Arthur, who intervenes at crucial moments to assist
Gloriana's knights and is otherwise bent on seeking out Gloriana herself, the bride he has chosen
in a dream. In the mythical genealogy of the Tudors, King Arthur (known to Spenser's readers
through Sir Thomas Malory's *Morte Darthur*) was identified as the dynasty's progenitor; thus, in
the allegorical schema of the poem, the prospective marriage of the Faerie Queene and Prince
Arthur, also the champion of Magnificence, signifies the perfect union of monarch and state.

Book 1 relates the adventures of the knight of Holiness, known as the Redcrosse Knight
from the sign on his shield and identified as Saint George, England's patron saint. His mission
is to overcome the machinations of spiritual error menacing the English church and to deliver
the parents of Una, his lady, who is the Truth, from the demons of false faith. The foes of the
Redcrosse Knight are many: the fiendish wizard Archimago, who stands for corrupt doctrine;
the cunning queen Duessa, who, as the embodiment of duplicity, is never what she seems; the
bloated giant Orgoglio, or Pride; and the loathsome many-headed dragon who is supposed to
wield the institutional power of the Catholic Church. The Redcrosse Knight kills Pride and
the dragon but, although he at last understands that they are thoroughly sinister, fails to capture Duessa and Archimago. They return in later books to trouble Gloriana's other knights.

Book 2 tells of the adventures of the knight of Temperance, Sir Guyon, who must destroy a
garden of surpassing beauty, known as the Bower of Bliss, presided over by a brilliantly seductive
witch called Acrasia. He is accompanied on his quest by the Palmer, who, as the embodiment of
reason, informs and guides him in achieving the perfection of his virtue. In Canto 12, perhaps the
best-known canto in the entire poem, Guyon sails to Acrasia's island garden in the company of the
Palmer, is tempted by the illusionistic pleasures Acrasia provides her suitors, but finally rejects her
in a massive act of defiance, tearing down all the beguiling structures of her island in a salutary rage.

The verse form of *The Faerie Queene* is virtually unique to Spenser. It features a sequence
of stanzas each comprising nine lines (known to later readers as "Spenserian"), of which the
first eight contain five feet or accented syllables and the last contains six feet. They are rhymed
in a pattern—*ababbcbcc*—particularly difficult for poets writing in English. Unlike the
Romance languages (French, Italian, and Spanish), English has relatively few words ending in
vowel sounds, which are easily rhymed. Spenser's ear for the sound of English allowed him to

compose verse of a musicality comparable to what was possible in the Romance languages, itself an extraordinary accomplishment. The narrative units of Spenser's epic poem achieve a dramatic coherence by his constructive use of imagery in particular story lines that continuously develop new contexts for their subjects. In other words, a character signifying a special quality in one canto will not signify precisely that quality in another canto: Spenser will change his or her role with the setting the story demands. This gives the reader an active role in the poem's interpretation; in a sense, the reader finds the meaning of the poem in the process of reading it.

from The Faerie Queene
Canto 1

The Patron of true Holinesse,
Foule Errour doth defeate:
Hypocrisie him to entrapp;
Doth to his home entreate.

1

A Gentle Knight[1] was pricking° on the plaine,   *riding*
   Y cladd in mightie armes and silver shielde,
   Wherein old dints of deepe wounds did remaine,
   The cruell markes of many a bloudy fielde;
5   Yet armes till that time did he never wield:
   His angry steede did chide his foming bitt,
   As much disdayning to the curbe to yield:
   Full jolly knight he seemd, and faire did sitt,
As one for knightly giusts° and fierce encounters fitt.   *joust*

2

10   But on his brest a bloudie Crosse[2] he bore,
   The deare remembrance of his dying Lord,
   For whose sweete sake that glorious badge he wore,
   And dead as living ever him ador'd:
   Upon his shield the like was also scor'd,°   *represented*
15   For soveraine hope, which in his° helpe he had: *his Lord's*
   Right faithfull true he was in deede and word,
   But of his cheere° did seeme too solemne sad;   *demeanor*
Yet nothing did he dread,° but ever was ydrad.°   *fear / feared*

3

Upon a great adventure he was bond,
20   That greatest Gloriana[3] to him gave,
   That greatest Glorious Queene of Faerie lond,
   To winne him worship, and her grace to have,
   Which of all earthly things he most did crave;
   And ever as he rode, his hart did earne
25   To prove his puissance° in battell brave   *power*

1. This gentle or well-born knight, identified as the Redcrosse Knight from the sign on his shield and introduced to the poem in Spenser's prefatory letter, wears the armor of Christianity. The armor itself has been worn by many who fought for the faith, but the Redcrosse Knight is new to the spiritual battlefield and will have to prove himself.
2. The red cross is Spenser's figure for the salvation offered by Christ to humankind through his death on the cross, the sacrifice of his blood, and his resurrection. It was also the badge traditionally worn by St. George, the patron saint of England.
3. The character Spenser most frequently invokes when he alludes to Elizabeth I. Gloriana presides over the action of the poem, although she does not take part in it herself.

Upon his foe, and his new force to learne;
Upon his foe, a Dragon horrible and stearne.

4

A lovely Ladie rode him faire beside,
Upon a lowly Asse more white then snow,[4]
30 Yet she much whiter, but the same did hide
Under a vele, that wimpled° was full low,   *gathered*
And over all a blacke stole she did throw,
As one that inly mournd: so was she sad,
And heavie sat upon her palfrey[5] slow:
35 Seemed in heart some hidden care she had,
And by her in a line a milke white lambe she lad.

5

So pure an innocent, as that same lambe,
She was in life and every vertuous lore,
And by descent from Royall lynage came
40 Of ancient Kings and Queenes, that had of yore
Their scepters stretcht from East to Westerne shore,
And all the world in their subjection held;[6]
Till that infernall feend with foule uprore
Forwasted all their land, and them expeld:
45 Whom to avenge, she had this Knight from far compeld. * * *

Canto 11

The knight with that old Dragon fights
two dayes incessantly:
The third him overthrowes, and gayns
most glorious victory.

1

High time now gan it wex° for Una faire,   *grow*
To thinke of those her captive Parents deare,
And their forwasted° kingdome to repaire: *desolated*
Whereto whenas they now approched neare,
5 With hartie words her knight she gan to cheare,
And in her modest manner thus bespake;°   *said*
Deare knight, as deare, as ever knight was deare,
That all these sorrowes suffer for my sake,
High heaven behold the tedious toyle, ye for me take.[7]

2

10 Now are we come unto my native soyle,
And to the place, where all our perils dwell;
Here haunts° that feend, and does his dayly spoyle,°   *lurks / evil*

---

4. This imagery suggests the role the Lady will play: the ass signifies her humility, the veil her modesty, and the lamb her innocence.
5. A horse suitable for a woman.
6. The Lady traces her lineage to Adam and Eve, who held dominion over Eden before the Fall. The "infernall feend," or Satan, is represented as the destroyer of their realm, which stretched from East to West and was therefore truly universal, unlike the regions dominated by Rome or by the Catholic Church. By designating the Knight as the avenger of Adam and Eve, Spenser identifies him with Christ.
7. Una asks the heavens to witness the difficult task that the Redcrosse Knight undertakes for her.

Therefore henceforth be at your keeping well,°   *on your guard*
And ever ready for your foeman fell.°   *dangerous enemy*
15   The sparke of noble courage now awake,
And strive your excellent selfe to excell;°   *outdo yourself*
That shall ye evermore renowmed make,
Above all knights on earth, that batteill undertake.

3

And pointing forth, lo yonder is (said she)
20   The brasen towre in which my parents deare
For dread of that huge feend emprisond be,
Whom I from far see on the walles appeare,
Whose sight my feeble soule doth greatly cheare:
And on the top of all I do espye
25   The watchman wayting tydings glad to heare,[8]
That O my parents might I happily
Unto you bring, to ease you of your misery.

4

With that they heard a roaring hideous sound,
That all the ayre with terrour filled wide,
30   And seemd uneath° to shake the stedfast ground.   *almost*
Eftsoones that dreadfull Dragon they espide,
Where stretcht he lay upon the sunny side
Of a great hill, himselfe like a great hill.
But all so soone, as he from far descride°   *saw*
35   Those glistring armes, that heaven with light did fill,
He rousd himselfe full blith,° and hastned them untill.° * * *   *joyfully / toward*
them

8

By this the dreadful Beast drew nigh to hand,°   *near*
65   Halfe flying, and halfe footing in his hast,
That with his largenesse measured much land,
And made wide shadow under his huge wast;°   *bulk*
As mountaine doth the valley overcast.
Approching nigh, he reared high afore
70   His body monstrous, horrible, and vast,
Which to increase his wondrous greatnesse more,
Was swolne with wrath, and poyson, and with bloudy gore.

9

And over, all with brasen scales was armd,
Like plated coate of steele, so couched neare,°   *closely set*
75   That nought mote perce, ne might his corse be harmd
With dint of sword, nor push of pointed speare;
Which as an Eagle, seeing pray appeare,
His aery plumes doth rouze, full rudely dight,°   *violently arranged*
So shaked he, that horrour was to heare,

8. Waiting to hear good news. In the next line, Una addresses her parents, expressing her wish to bring them the good news of their rescue herself.

80   For as the clashing of an Armour bright,
           Such noyse his rouzed scales did send unto the knight.

10

        His flaggy° wings when forth he did display,   *drooping*
           Were like two sayles, in which the hollow wynd
           Is gathered full,[9] and worketh speedy way:
85   And eke the pennes,[10] that did his pineons° bynd,   *feathers*
           Were like mayne-yards,° with flying canvas lynd, *mainsail ropes*
           With which whenas him list the ayre to beat,
           And there by force unwonted passage find,[11]
           The cloudes before him fled for terrour great,
90   And all the heavens stood still amazed with his threat.

11

        His huge long tayle wound up in hundred foldes,
           Does overspred his long bras-scaly backe,
           Whose wreathed boughts° when ever he unfoldes, *wound-up coils*
           And thicke entangled knots adown does slacke,
95   Bespotted as with shields of red and blacke,
           It sweepeth all the land behind him farre,
           And of three furlongs does but litle lacke;[12]
           And at the point two stings in-fixed arre,
         Both deadly sharpe, that sharpest steele exceeden farre.

12

100   But stings and sharpest steele did far exceed
           The sharpnesse of his cruell rending clawes;
           Dead was it sure, as sure as death in deed,
           What ever thing does touch his ravenous pawes,
           Or what within his reach he ever drawes.
105   But his most hideous head my toung to tell
           Does tremble: for his deepe devouring jawes
           Wide gaped, like the griesly mouth of hell,
         Through which into his darke abisse° all ravin° fell.   *pit / prey*

13

        And that more wondrous was, in either jaw
110   Threeranckes of yron teeth enraunged were,
           In which yet trickling bloud and gobbets° raw   *chunks*
           Of late devoured bodies did appeare,
           That sight thereof bred cold congealed feare:
           Which to increase, and all atonce° to kill,   *suddenly*
115   A cloud of smoothering smoke and sulphur seare° *burning*
           Out of his stinking gorge forth steemed still,
         That all the ayre about with smoke and stench did fill.

---

9. The force of the wind fills the sails and makes them billow out.
10. The bones in the Dragon's wings.

11. Although the Dragon cannot fly normally, he does so through the sheer force with which he beats his wings.
12. The Dragon's tail measures nearly three furlongs, 660 yards, a third of a mile.

14
His blazing eyes, like two bright shining shields,
    Did burne with wrath, and sparkled living fyre;
120   As two broad Beacons, set in open fields,
    Send forth their flames farre off to every shyre,°   *district*
    And warning give, that enemies conspyre,
    With fire and sword the region to invade;
    So flam'd his eyne with rage and rancorous yre:
125   But farre within, as in a hollow glade,
Those glaring lampes were set, that made a dreadfull shade. * * *

16
The knight gan fairely couch his steadie speare,
    And fiercely ran at him with rigorous might:
    The pointed steele arriving rudely theare,
    His harder hide would neither perce, nor bight,
140   But glauncing by forth passed forward right;
    Yet sore amoved with so puissant push,
    The wrathfull beast about him turned light,°   *quickly*
    And him so rudely passing by, did brush
With his long tayle, that° horse and man to ground did rush.°   *so that / fall*

17
145 Both horse and man up lightly rose againe,
    And fresh encounter towards him addrest:
    But th'idle stroke° yet backe recoyld in vaine,   *futile swordstroke*
    And found no place his deadly point to rest.
    Exceeding rage enflam'd the furious beast,
150   To be avenged of so great despight;
    For never felt his imperceable brest
    So wondrous force, from hand of living wight;
Yet had he prov'd° the powre of many a puissant knight.   *tested*

18
Then with his waving wings displayed wyde,
155   Himselfe up high he lifted from the ground,
    And with strong flight did forcibly divide
    The yielding aire, which nigh° too feeble found   *almost*
    Her flitting partes, and element unsound,
    To beare so great a weight[13] he cutting way
160   With his broad sayles, about him soared round:
    At last low stouping with unweldie sway,°   *awkward force*
Snatcht up both horse and man, to beare them quite away.

19
Long he them bore above the subject plaine,
    So farre as Ewghen° bow a shaft may send,   *made of yew*
165   Till struggling strong did him at last constraine,
    To let them downe before his flightes end:

13. The air is almost too weak to support the Dragon; in other words, the Dragon is almost too heavy to fly, given the strength of his wings in relation to his overall weight.

As hagard hauke° presuming to contend   *untamed hawk*
With hardie fowle, above his hable° might,   *natural*
His wearie pounces° all in vaine doth spend,   *claws*
170   To trusse° the pray too heavie for his flight;   *carry off*
Which comming downe to ground, does free it selfe by fight. * * *

                    50
When gentle Una saw the second fall
    Of her deare knight, who wearie of long fight,
    And faint through losse of bloud, mov'd not at all,
445   But lay as in a dreame of deepe delight,
    Besmeard with pretious Balme, whose vertuous might
    Did heale his wounds, and scorching heat alay,
    Againe she stricken was with sore affright,
    And for his safetie gan devoutly pray;
450   And watch the noyous° night, and wait for joyous day.   *sorrowful*

                    51
The joyous day gan early to appeare,
    And faire Aurora[14] from the deawy bed
    Of aged Tithone gan her selfe to reare,
    With rosie cheekes, for shame as blushing red;
455   Her golden lockes for haste were loosely shed
    About her eares, when Una her did marke
    Clymbe to her charet, all with flowers spred,
    From heaven high to chase the chearelesse darke;
With merry note her° loud salutes the mounting larke.   *Una*

                    52
460   Then freshly up arose the doughtie knight,
    All healed of his hurts and woundes wide,
    And did himselfe to battell readie dight;
    Whose early foe awaiting him beside
    To have devourd, so soone as day he spyde,
465   When now he saw himselfe so freshly reare,
    As if late fight had nought him damnifyde,°   *harmed*
    He woxe° dismayd, and gan his fate to feare;   *grew*
Nathlesse° with wonted rage he him advaunced neare.   *nonetheless*

                    53
And in his first encounter, gaping wide,
470   He thought attonce° him to have swallowd quight,   *at once*
    And rusht upon him with outragious pride;
    Who him r'encountring fierce, as hauke in flight,
    Perforce° rebutted° backe. The weapon bright   *necessarily / attacked*
    Taking advantage of his open jaw,
475   Ran through his mouth with so importune° might,   *violent*
    That deepe emperst his darksome hollow maw,°   *mouth*
And back retyrd,° his life bloud forth with all did draw.   *retracted*

14. The goddess of the dawn, married to Tithone or Tithonus.

54

So downe he fell, and forth his life did breath,[15]
   That vanisht into smoke and cloudes swift;
480   So downe he fell, that th'earth him underneath
   Did grone, as feeble so great load to lift;
   So downe he fell, as an huge rockie clift,
   Whose false foundation waves have washt away,
   With dreadfull poyse° is from the mayneland rift,   *force*
485   And rolling downe, great Neptune doth dismay;
So downe he fell, and like an heaped mountaine lay.

55

The knight himselfe even trembled at his fall,
   So huge and horrible a masse it seem'd;
   And his deare Ladie, that beheld it all,
490   Durst not approch for dread, which she misdeem'd,
   But yet at last, when as the direfull feend
   She saw not stirre, off-shaking vaine affright,°   *empty fear*
   She nigher drew, and saw that joyous end:
   Then God she praysd, and thankt her faithfull knight,
495   That had atchiev'd so great a conquest by his might.

Elizabeth I
1533–1603

Psalm 13

Fools that true faith yet never had
Saith in their hearts, there is no God.
Filthy they are in their practice,
Of them not one is godly wise.
5   From heaven the Lord on man did look
To know what ways he undertook.
All they were vain and went astray,
Not one he found in the right way.
In heart and tongue have they deceit,
10   Their lips throw forth a poisoned bait.
Their minds are mad, their mouths° are wode,°   *speech / empty*
And swift they be in shedding blood.
So blind they are, no truth they know,
No fear of God in them will grow.
15   How can that cruel sort be good,
Of God's dear flock which suck the blood?
On him rightly shall they not call,
Despair will so their hearts appall.
At all times God is with the just,

---

15. The blood that flows from the Dragon takes his life with it.

20   Because they put in him their trust.
      Who shall therefore from Sion give
      That health which hangeth in our belief?
      When God shall take from his the smart,
      Then will Jacob rejoice in heart.
25   Praise to God

from The Metres of Boethius's *Consolation of Philosophy*
Book 1, No. 7

Dim clouds,
Sky close
Light none
Can afford.
5   If roiling seas
Boisterous soweth,°   *scatters*
Mix his° foam,   *its*
Greeny° once   *greenish*
Like the clearest
10   Days, the water—
Straight mud,
Stirred up all foul—
The sight gainsays.°   *prevents*
Running stream
15   That pours
From highest hills,
Oft is stayed
By slaked°   *cool*
Stone of rock.
20   Thou, if thou wilt
In clearest light
The truth behold,
By straight line
Hit in the path.[1]
25   Chase joys,
Repulse fear,
Thrust out hope,
Woe not retain.
Cloudy is the mind
30   With snaffle° bound   *bridle-bit*
Where they reign.

---

1. I. e., Keep to the path in a straight line.

Christopher Marlowe
1564–1593

The Passionate Shepherd to His Love

Come live with me, and be my love,
And we will all the pleasures prove,
That valleys, groves, hills, and fields,
Woods, or steepy mountain yields.

5   And we will sit upon the rocks,
Seeing the shepherds feed their flocks,
By shallow rivers, to whose falls,
Melodious birds sing madrigals.

And I will make thee beds of roses,
10   And a thousand fragrant poesies,
A cap of flowers, and a kirtle,
Embroidered all with leaves of myrtle.

A gown made of the finest wool,
Which from our pretty lambs we pull,
15   Fair lined slippers for the cold,
With buckles of the purest gold.

A belt of straw, and ivy buds,
With coral clasps and amber studs,
And if these pleasures may thee move,
20   Come live with me, and be my love.

The shepherd swains shall dance and sing,
For thy delight each May morning,
If these delights thy mind may move,
Then live with me and be my love.

from The Tragical History of Dr. Faustus

from ACT 1

from Scene 3

[*Enter Mephostophilis.*]
MEPHOSTOPHILIS: Now, Faustus, what wouldst thou have me do?
FAUSTUS: I charge thee wait upon me whilst I live,
    To do whatever Faustus shall command,
    Be it to make the moon drop from her sphere,
    Or the ocean to overwhelm the world.
MEPHOSTOPHILIS: I am a servant to great Lucifer,
40   And may not follow thee without his leave.
    No more than he commands must we perform.
FAUSTUS: Did not he charge thee to appear to me?
MEPHOSTOPHILIS: No, I came now hither of mine own accord.

FAUSTUS: Did not my conjuring speeches raise thee? Speak.
MEPHOSTOPHILIS: That was the cause, but yet *per accidens;*°   *by accident*
    For when we hear one rack the name of God,
    Abjure the scriptures and his saviour Christ,
    We fly in hope to get his glorious soul.
    Nor will we come unless he use such means
50   Whereby he is in danger to be damned.
    Therefore the shortest cut for conjuring
    Is stoutly to abjure all godliness
    And pray devoutly to the prince of hell.
FAUSTUS: So Faustus hath already done, and holds this principle:
55   There is no chief but only Belzebub,
    To whom Faustus doth dedicate himself.
    This word "damnation" terrifies not me,
    For I confound hell in elysium.°   *heaven*
    My ghost be with the old philosophers.
60   But leaving these vain trifles of men's souls,
    Tell me, what is that Lucifer, thy lord?
MEPHOSTOPHILIS: Arch-regent and commander of all spirits.
FAUSTUS: Was not that Lucifer an angel once?
MEPHOSTOPHILIS: Yes, Faustus, and most dearly loved of God.
FAUSTUS: How comes it then that he is prince of devils?
MEPHOSTOPHILIS: Oh, by aspiring pride and insolence,
    For which God threw him from the face of heaven.
FAUSTUS: And what are you that live with Lucifer?
MEPHOSTOPHILIS: Unhappy spirits that fell with Lucifer,
70   Conspired against our God with Lucifer,
    And are for ever damned with Lucifer.
FAUSTUS: Where are you damned?
MEPHOSTOPHILIS: In hell.
FAUSTUS: How comes it then that thou art out of hell?
MEPHOSTOPHILIS: Why, this is hell, nor am I out of it.
    Think'st thou that I that saw the face of God
    And tasted the eternal joys of heaven,
    Am not tormented with ten thousand hells
    In being deprived of everlasting bliss?
80   Oh, Faustus, leave these frivolous demands,
    Which strike a terror to my fainting soul.
FAUSTUS: What, is great Mephostophilis so passionate
    For being deprived of the joys of heaven?
    Learn thou of Faustus manly fortitude,
85   And scorn those joys thou never shalt possess.
    Go, bear these tidings to great Lucifer,
    Seeing Faustus hath incurred eternal death
    By desperate thoughts against Jove's deity.
    Say he surrenders up to him his soul,
90   So he will spare him four and twenty years,
    Letting him live in all voluptuousness,
    Having thee ever to attend on me,
    To give me whatsoever I shall ask,

         To tell me whatsoever I demand,
95   To slay mine enemies and to aid my friends
         And always be obedient to my will.
         Go, and return to mighty Lucifer,
         And meet me in my study at midnight,
         And then resolve me of thy master's mind.
MEPHOSTOPHILIS: I will, Faustus.   [*Exit.*]
FAUSTUS: Had I as many souls as there be stars,
         I'd give them all for Mephostophilis.
         By him I'll be great emperor of the world,
         And make a bridge through the air
105   To pass the ocean. With a band of men
         I'll join the hills that bind the Affrick shore,
         And make that country continent to Spain,
         And both contributory to my crown.
         The Emperor shall not live but by my leave,
110   Nor any potentate of Germany.
         Now that I have obtained what I desired,
         I'll live in speculation of this art
         Till Mephostophilis return again.   [*Exit.*]

from ACT 5

Scene 3

[*Enter the Scholars.*]
FIRST SCHOLAR: Come, gentlemen, let us go visit Faustus,
         For such a dreadful night was never seen
         Since first the world's creation did begin.
         Such fearful shrieks and cries were never heard.
5   Pray heaven the Doctor have escaped the danger.
SECOND SCHOLAR: Oh help us, heaven! See, here are Faustus' limbs,
         All torn asunder by the hand of death.
THIRD SCHOLAR: The devils whom Faustus served have torn him thus:
         For twixt the hours of twelve and one, methought
10   I heard him shriek and call aloud for help,
         At which self time the house seemed all on fire
         With dreadful horror of these damned fiends.
SECOND SCHOLAR: Well, gentlemen, though Faustus' end be such.
         As every Christian heart laments to think on,
15   Yet, for he was a scholar once admired
         For wondrous knowledge in our German schools,
         We'll give his mangled limbs due burial,
         And all the students clothed in mourning black
         Shall wait upon his heavy funeral.   [*Exeunt.*]

Sir Walter Raleigh
1552?–1618

The Nymph's Reply to the Shepherd[1]

If all the world and love were young,
And truth in every shepherd's tongue,
These pretty pleasures might me move,
To live with thee, and be thy love.

5   Time drives the flocks from field to fold,
When rivers rage, and rocks grow cold,
And Philomel° becometh dumb,   *the nightingale*
The rest complain of cares to come.

The flowers do fade, and wanton fields,
10   To wayward winter reckoning yields,
A honey tongue, a heart of gall,
Is fancy's spring, but sorrow's fall.

Thy gowns, thy shoes, thy beds of roses,
Thy cap, thy kirtle, and thy poesies,
15   Soon break, soon wither, soon forgotten;
In folly ripe, in reason rotten.

Thy belt of straw and ivy buds,
Thy coral clasps and amber studs,
All these in me no means can move,
20   To come to thee, and be thy love.

But could youth last, and love still breed,
Had joys no date, nor age no need,
Then these delights my mind might move,
To live with thee, and be thy love.

---

1. Raleigh's *Reply* was published together with Marlowe's poem in Jaggard's collection.

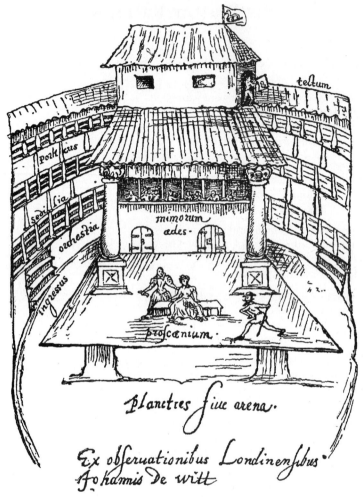

Arend von Buchell, *The Swan Theatre,* after Johannes de Witt, c. 1596. The only extant drawing of a public theater in 1590s London, this sketch shows what Shakespeare's Globe must have looked like. The round playhouse centered on the curtainless platform of the stage (*proscenium*), which projected into the yard (*planities sive arena*). Raised above the stage by two pillars, the roof (*tectum*) stored machinery. At the back of the stage, the tiring house (*mimorum aedes*), where the actors dressed, contained two doors for entrances and exits. There were no stage sets and only movable props such as thrones, tables, beds, and benches, like the one shown here. Other documents on the early modern stage are the contract of the Fortune Theatre and stage directions in the plays themselves. Modeled on the Globe, although square in shape, the Fortune featured a stage forty-three feet broad and twenty-seven and a half feet deep. Stage directions include further clues: sometimes a curtained booth made "discovery" scenes possible; trapdoors allowed descents; and a space "aloft," such as the gallery above the stage doors, represented a room above the street. Eyewitness accounts fill out the picture. In the yard stood the groundlings who paid a penny for standing room, exposed to the sky, which provided natural lighting. For those willing to pay a penny or two more, three galleries (*orchestra, sedilia,* and *porticulus*) provided seats—the most expensive of which were cushioned. Spectators could buy food and drink during the performance. The early modern theater held an audience of roughly eight hundred standing in the yard, and fifteen hundred more seated in the galleries. According to Thomas Platter, who had seen Shakespeare's *Julius Caesar* in 1599, "everyone has a good view." Courtesy of Stock Montage, Inc./Historical Pictures Collection.

William Shakespeare
1564–1616

Sonnets
18

Shall I compare thee to a summer's day?
Thou art more lovely and more temperate.
Rough winds do shake the darling buds of May,
And summer's lease hath all too short a date.°   *duration*
5   Sometimes too hot the eye of heaven shines,
And often is his gold complexion dimmed;
And every fair from fair sometimes declines,
By chance or nature's changing course untrimmed.°   *stripped bare*
But thy eternal summer shall not fade
10 Nor lose possession of that fair thou ow'st;°   *own*
Nor shall Death brag thou wanderest in his shade,
When in eternal lines° to time thou grow'st.   *of verse*
   So long as men can breathe or eyes can see,
   So long lives this, and this gives life to thee.

29

When, in disgrace with fortune and men's eyes,
I all alone beweep my outcast state,
And trouble deaf heaven with my bootless° cries,   *unavailing*
And look upon myself and curse my fate,
5   Wishing me like to one more rich in hope,
Featured like him, like him with friends possessed,
Desiring this man's art and that man's scope,°   *powers*
With what I most enjoy contented least;
Yet in these thoughts myself almost despising,
10 Haply° I think on thee, and then my state,   *perhaps*
Like to the lark at break of day arising
From sullen earth, sings hymns at heaven's gate;
   For thy sweet love remembered such wealth brings
   That then I scorn to change° my state with kings.   *exchange*

73

That time of year thou mayst in me behold
When yellow leaves, or none, or few, do hang
Upon those boughs which shake against the cold,
Bare ruined choirs[1] where late the sweet birds sang.
5   In me thou seest the twilight of such day
As after sunset fadeth in the west,
Which by and by black night doth take away,

---

1. The choir is the section of a church reserved for the singers in the choir. "Choir" puns on "quire," the gathering of pages in a book, and thus recalls the "leaves" in line 2.

Death's second self, that seals up all in rest.
In me thou seest the glowing of such fire
10	That on the ashes of his youth doth lie
As the deathbed whereon it must expire,
Consumed with that which it was nourished by.
This thou perceiv'st, which makes thy love more strong,
To love that well which thou must leave ere long.

116

Let me not to the marriage of true minds
Admit impediments. Love is not love
Which alters when it alteration finds,°	*in the beloved*
Or bends with the remover to remove.
5	O, no, it is an ever-fixèd mark°	*landmark*
That looks on tempests and is never shaken;
It is the star to every wandering bark,
Whose worth's unknown, although his height be taken.[1]
Love's not Time's fool, though rosy lips and cheeks
10	Within his bending sickle's compass° come;	*range*
Love alters not with his brief hours and weeks,
But bears it out even to the edge of doom.°	*judgment day*
If this be error and upon me proved,
I never writ, nor no man ever loved.

130

My mistress' eyes are nothing like the sun;
Coral is far more red than her lips' red;
If snow be white, why then her breasts are dun;°	*brown*
If hairs be wires, black wires grow on her head.
5	I have seen roses damasked,° red and white,	*mingled*
But no such roses see I in her cheeks;
And in some perfumes is there more delight
Than in the breath that from my mistress reeks.
I love to hear her speak, yet well I know
10	That music hath a far more pleasing sound.
I grant I never saw a goddess go;
My mistress, when she walks, treads on the ground.
And yet, by heaven, I think my love as rare
As any she belied with false compare.

Twelfth Night; or, What You Will

The Names of the Actors

ORSINO, *Duke (or Count) of Illyria*
VALENTINE, *gentleman attending on Orsino*
CURIO, *gentleman attending on Orsino*

VIOLA, *a shipwrecked lady, later disguised as Cesario*
SEBASTIAN, *twin brother of Viola*

---

1. The star by which ships navigate by measuring its altitude from the horizon (known values) is itself beyond valuation.

ANTONIO, *a sea captain, friend to Sebastian*
CAPTAIN *of the shipwrecked vessel*

OLIVIA, *a rich countess of Illyria*
MARIA, *gentlewoman in Olivia's household*
SIR TOBY BELCH, *Olivia's uncle*
SIR ANDREW AGUECHEEK, *a companion of Sir Toby*
MALVOLIO, *steward of Olivia's household*
FABIAN, *a member of Olivia's household*
FESTE, *a clown, also called* FOOL, *Olivia's jester*

A PRIEST
FIRST OFFICER
SECOND OFFICER

LORDS, SAILORS, MUSICIANS, and OTHER ATTENDANTS

Scene: *A city in Illyria, and the seacoast near it*

ACT 1

Scene 1[1]

[*Enter Orsino Duke of Illyria, Curio, and other lords (with musicians).*]

ORSINO: If music be the food of love, play on;
    Give me excess of it, that surfeiting,
    The appetite may sicken and so die.
    That strain again! It had a dying fall;°   *cadence*
5   O, it came o'er my ear like the sweet sound
    That breathes upon a bank of violets,
    Stealing and giving odor. Enough, no more.
    'Tis not so sweet now as it was before.
    O spirit of love, how quick° and fresh art thou,   *alive*
10   That, notwithstanding thy capacity
    Receiveth as the sea, naught enters there,
    Of what validity° and pitch° soe'er,   *value / worth*
    But falls into abatement° and low price   *depreciation*
    Even in a minute! So full of shapes° is fancy°   *imagined forms / love*
15   That it alone is high fantastical.°   *highly imaginative*
CURIO: Will you go hunt, my lord?
ORSINO: What, Curio?
CURIO: The hart.
ORSINO: Why, so I do, the noblest that I have.°   *pun on "heart"*
    O, when mine eyes did see Olivia first,
    Methought she purged the air of pestilence.
20   That instant was I turned into a hart,
    And my desires, like fell° and cruel hounds,   *fierce*
    E'er since pursue me.[2]
    [*Enter Valentine.*]
           How now, what news from her?

1. Location: Orsino's court.

2. Allusion to Ovid: Actaeon was turned into a stag by Diana and killed by his own hounds.

VALENTINE: So please my lord, I might not be admitted,
　　　But from her handmaid do return this answer:
25　　The element° itself, till seven years' heat,°　　　　　　　*sky / seven summers*
　　　Shall not behold her face at ample view;
　　　But like a cloistress° she will veilèd walk,　　　　　　　　　　　*nun*
　　　And water once a day her chamber round
　　　With eye-offending brine—all this to season°　　　　　　　　*preserve*
30　　A brother's dead love, which she would keep fresh
　　　And lasting in her sad remembrance.
ORSINO: O, she that hath a heart of that fine frame°　　　　*construction*
　　　To pay this debt of love but to a brother,
　　　How will she love, when the rich golden shaft°　　　　　*Cupid's arrow*
35　　Hath killed the flock of all affections else°　　　　　　　*other feelings*
　　　That live in her; when liver, brain, and heart,[3]
　　　These sovereign thrones, are all supplied, and filled
　　　Her sweet perfections,[4] with one self king!°　　　　　　　*single lord*
　　　Away before me to sweet beds of flowers.
40　　Love-thoughts lie rich when canopied with bowers.　　　*[Exeunt.]*

Scene 2[5]

[Enter Viola, a Captain, and sailors.]
VIOLA: What country, friends, is this?
CAPTAIN: This is Illyria, lady.
VIOLA: And what should I do in Illyria?
　　　My brother he is in Elysium.[6]
5　　Perchance° he is not drowned. What think you, sailors?　　*perhaps*
CAPTAIN: It is perchance° that you yourself were saved.　　　*by chance*
VIOLA: O, my poor brother! And so perchance may he be.
CAPTAIN: True, madam, and to comfort you with chance,°　　*possibilities*
　　　Assure yourself, after our ship did split,
10　　When you and those poor number saved with you
　　　Hung on our driving° boat, I saw your brother,　　　　　　*drifting*
　　　Most provident in peril, bind himself,
　　　Courage and hope both teaching him the practice,
　　　To a strong mast that lived° upon the sea;　　　　　　　　*floated*
15　　Where, like Arion[7] on the dolphin's back,
　　　I saw him hold acquaintance with the waves
　　　So long as I could see.
VIOLA: For saying so, there's gold. *[She gives money.]*
　　　Mine own escape unfoldeth to my hope,°　　　　　　　　*gives me hope*
20　　Whereto thy speech serves for authority,
　　　The like of him. Know'st thou this country?
CAPTAIN: Ay, madam, well, for I was bred and born
　　　Not three hours' travel from this very place.

---

3. Seats of the passions.
4. I.e., her sweet perfections are filled.
5. Location: The coast of the Adriatic.
6. Home of the blessed dead.

7. Greek poet who jumped overboard to escape murderous sailors and charmed dolphins with his lyre, so that they carried him to shore.

VIOLA: Who governs here?
CAPTAIN: A noble duke, in nature as in name.
VIOLA: What is his name?
CAPTAIN: Orsino.
VIOLA: Orsino! I have heard my father name him.
    He was a bachelor then.
CAPTAIN: And so is now, or was so very late;
    For but a month ago I went from hence,
    And then 'twas fresh in murmur°—as, you know,   *rumor*
    What great ones do the less° will prattle of—   *social inferiors*
    That he did seek the love of fair Olivia.
VIOLA: What's she?
CAPTAIN: A virtuous maid, the daughter of a count
    That died some twelvemonth since, then leaving her
    In the protection of his son, her brother,
    Who shortly also died; for whose dear love,
40   They say, she hath abjured the sight
    And company of men.
VIOLA: O, that I served that lady,
    And might not be delivered° to the world   *revealed*
    Till I had made mine own occasion mellow,°   *ready*
    What my estate° is!   *social position*
CAPTAIN: That were hard to compass,°   *bring about*
45   Because she will admit no kind of suit,
    No, not° the Duke's.   *not even*
VIOLA: There is a fair behavior° in thee, Captain,   *conduct; appearance*
    And though that nature with a beauteous wall
    Doth oft close in pollution, yet of thee
50   I will believe thou hast a mind that suits
    With this thy fair and outward character.°   *appearance*
    I prithee, and I'll pay thee bounteously,
    Conceal me what I am, and be my aid
    For such disguise as haply shall become
55   The form of my intent.° I'll serve this duke.   *my outward purpose*
    Thou shalt present me as an eunuch[8] to him.
    It may be worth thy pains, for I can sing
    And speak to him in many sorts of music
    That will allow° me very worth his service.   *prove*
60   What else may hap, to time I will commit;
    Only shape thou thy silence to my wit.°   *plan*
CAPTAIN: Be you his eunuch, and your mute° I'll be; *silent attendant*
    When my tongue blabs, then let mine eyes not see.
VIOLA: I thank thee. Lead me on.   *[Exeunt.]*

8. Castrato, or male soprano singer, which would explain her high-pitched voice.

Scene 3[9]

[Enter Sir Toby [Belch] and Maria.]

SIR TOBY: What a plague means my niece to take the death of her brother thus? I am sure care's an enemy to life.

MARIA: By my troth, Sir Toby, you must come in earlier o'nights. Your cousin,[10] my lady, takes great exceptions to your ill hours.

SIR TOBY: Why, let her except before excepted.[11]

MARIA: Ay, but you must confine yourself within the modest limits of order.

SIR TOBY: Confine? I'll confine myself no finer[12] than I am. These clothes are good enough to drink in, and so be these boots too. An[13] they be not, let them hang themselves in their own straps.

MARIA: That quaffing and drinking will undo you. I heard my lady talk of it yesterday, and of a foolish knight that you brought in one night here to be her wooer.

SIR TOBY: Who, Sir Andrew Aguecheek?

MARIA: Ay, he.

SIR TOBY: He's as tall[14] a man as any's in Illyria.

MARIA: What's that to the purpose?

SIR TOBY: Why, he has three thousand ducats a year.

MARIA: Ay, but he'll have but a year in all these ducats.[15] He's a very fool and a prodigal.

SIR TOBY: Fie, that you'll say so! He plays o' the viol-degamboys,[16] and speaks three or four languages word for word without book, and hath all the good gifts of nature.

MARIA: He hath indeed, almost natural,[17] for, besides that he's a fool, he's a great quarreler, and but that he hath the gift of a coward to allay the gust[18] he hath
25 in quarreling, 'tis thought among the prudent he would quickly have the gift of a grave.

SIR TOBY: By this hand, they are scoundrels and substractors[19] that say so of him. Who are they?

MARIA: They that add, moreover, he's drunk nightly in your company.

SIR TOBY: With drinking healths to my niece. I'll drink to her as long as there is a passage in my throat and drink in Illyria. He's a coward and a coistrel[20] that will not drink to my niece till his brains turn o' the toe like a parish top.[21] What, wench? *Castiliano vulgo!*[22] For here comes Sir Andrew Agueface.[23]

[Enter Sir Andrew (Aguecheek).]

SIR ANDREW: Sir Toby Belch! How now, Sir Toby Belch?

SIR TOBY: Sweet Sir Andrew!

SIR ANDREW *[to Maria]*: Bless you, fair shrew.[24]

MARIA: And you too, sir.

9. Location: Olivia's house.
10. Kinswoman.
11. I.e., let her take exception all she wants; I don't care (plays on the cant legal phrase, *exceptis excipiendis*, "with the exceptions before named").
12. Tighter; better.
13. If.
14. Brave; tall.
15. He'll spend all his money in a year.
16. Predecessor to the violincello.
17. Play on the sense "born idiot."
18. Taste.
19. Detractors.
20. Horse groom (base fellow).
21. Large top, spun by whipping, provided by the parish as a form of exercise.
22. Uncertain meaning. Possibly a call for politeness, or else a form of "speak of the devil."
23. With the thin, pale countenance of someone suffering from ague, a fever marked by chills.
24. Small creature (connotation of shrewishness probably unintended).

SIR TOBY: Accost,[25] Sir Andrew, accost.

SIR ANDREW: What's that?

SIR TOBY: My niece's chambermaid.[26]

SIR ANDREW: Good Mistress Accost, I desire better acquaintance.

MARIA: My name is Mary, sir.

SIR ANDREW: Good Mistress Mary Accost—

SIR TOBY: You mistake, knight. "Accost" is front her,[27] board her,[28] woo her, assail her.

SIR ANDREW: By my troth, I would not undertake her in this company. Is that the meaning of "accost"?

MARIA: Fare you well, gentlemen. [*Going.*]

SIR TOBY: An thou let part[29] so, Sir Andrew, would thou mightst never draw sword again.

SIR ANDREW: An you part so, mistress, I would I might never draw sword again. Fair lady, do you think you have fools in hand?[30]

MARIA: Sir, I have not you by the hand.

SIR ANDREW: Marry,[31] but you shall have, and here's my hand. [*He gives her his hand.*]

MARIA: Now, sir, thought is free. I pray you, bring your hand to the buttery-bar,[32]
55   and let it drink.

SIR ANDREW: Wherefore, sweetheart? What's your metaphor?

MARIA: It's dry,[33] sir.

SIR ANDREW: Why, I think so. I am not such an ass but I can keep my hand dry. But what's your jest?

MARIA: A dry[34] jest, sir.

SIR ANDREW: Are you full of them?

MARIA: Ay, sir, I have them at my fingers' ends.[35] Marry, now I let go your hand, I am barren. [*She lets go his hand.*]   [*Exit Maria.*]

SIR TOBY: O knight, thou lack'st a cup of canary![36] When did I see thee so put
65   down?[37]

SIR ANDREW: Never in your life, I think, unless you see canary put me down.[38] Methinks sometimes I have no more wit than a Christian or an ordinary man has. But I am a great eater of beef, and I believe that does harm to my wit.

SIR TOBY: No question.

SIR ANDREW: An I thought that, I'd forswear it. I'll ride home tomorrow, Sir Toby.

SIR TOBY: *Pourquoi,*[39] my dear knight?

SIR ANDREW: What is "*pourquoi*"? Do or not do? I would I had bestowed that time in the tongues[40] that I have in fencing, dancing, and bearbaiting. O, had I but followed the arts![41]

SIR TOBY: Then hadst thou had an excellent head of hair.

SIR ANDREW: Why, would that have mended my hair?

SIR TOBY: Past question, for thou seest it will not curl by nature.

SIR ANDREW: But it becomes me well enough, does't not?

---

25. Greet her.
26. A lady-in-waiting, not a servant.
27. Come alongside her.
28. As in a naval encounter.
29. If you let her leave.
30. Have fools to deal with (Mary chooses to take it literally).
31. Indeed.
32. Door of the wine-cellar.
33. Thirsty; aged and sexually weak.
34. Ironic; barren (referring to Sir Andrew).
35. At my disposal; in my hand.
36. Sweet wine from the Canary Islands.
37. Discomfited.
38. Knocked flat.
39. Why.
40. Languages, perhaps with a pun on curling-tongs.
41. Liberal arts (but Sir Toby plays on arts as "artifice").

SIR TOBY: Excellent. It hangs like flax on a distaff;[42] and I hope to see a huswife
80   take thee between her legs and spin it off.[43]

SIR ANDREW: Faith, I'll home tomorrow, Sir Toby. Your niece will not be seen,
or if she be, it's four to one she'll none of me. The Count himself here hard
by[44] woos her.

SIR TOBY: She'll none o' the Count. She'll not match above her degree,[45] neither
85   in estate,[46] years, nor wit; I have heard her swear 't. Tut; there's life in 't,[47]
man.

SIR ANDREW: I'll stay a month longer. I am a fellow o' the strangest mind i' the
world; I delight in masques and revels sometimes altogether.[48]

SIR TOBY: Art thou good at these kickshawses,[49] knight?

SIR ANDREW: As any man in Illyria, whatsoever he be, under the degree of my
90   betters,[50] and yet I will not compare with an old man.[51]

SIR TOBY: What is thy excellence in a galliard,[52] knight?

SIR ANDREW: Faith, I can cut a caper.[53]

SIR TOBY: And I can cut the mutton to 't.

SIR ANDREW: And I think I have the back-trick[54] simply as strong as any man in
95   Illyria.

SIR TOBY: Wherefore are these things hid? Wherefore have these gifts a curtain
before 'em? Are they like to take[55] dust, like Mistress Mall's picture?[56] Why
dost thou not go to church in a galliard and come home in a coranto?[57] My
very walk should be a jig; I would not so much as make water but in a sink-a-
100   pace.[58] What dost thou mean? Is it a world to hide virtues[59] in? I did think,
by the excellent constitution of thy leg, it was formed under the star of a
galliard.[60]

SIR ANDREW: Ay, 'tis strong, and it does indifferent well[61] in a dun-colored
stock.[62] Shall we set about some revels?

SIR TOBY: What shall we do else? Were we not born under Taurus?[63]

SIR ANDREW: Taurus? That's sides and heart.

SIR TOBY: No, sir, it is legs and thighs. Let me see thee caper. [*Sir Andrew capers.*]
Ha, higher! Ha, ha, excellent!   [*Exeunt.*]

Scene 4[64]

[*Enter Valentine, and Viola in man's attire.*]

VALENTINE: If the Duke continue these favors towards you, Cesario, you are like
to be much advanced. He hath known you but three days, and already you
are no stranger.

---

42. Staff for holding flax during spinning.
43. Treat your hair like flax to be spun; cause you to lose it through venereal disease ("huswife" may be a pun on "hussy").
44. Nearby.
45. Rank.
46. Fortune.
47. There's hope left.
48. In all respects.
49. Trifles (from the French *quelque chose*).
50. Excepting my social superiors.
51. Experienced person.
52. Lively dance in triple-time.
53. Lively leap; spice used with mutton (mutton suggests "whore").
54. Backward step in the galliard.
55. Likely to collect.
56. Any woman's portrait (usually kept under protective glass).
57. Running dance.
58. Dance like the galliard (French *cinquepace*).
59. Talents.
60. Under a star favorable to dancing.
61. Well enough.
62. Stocking.
63. Zodiacal sign said to govern legs and thighs (Sir Andrew is mistaken).
64. Location: Orsino's court.

VIOLA: You either fear his humor[65] or my negligence, that you call in question the
5   continuance of his love. Is he inconstant, sir, in his favors?
VALENTINE: No, believe me.
    [*Enter Duke (Orsino), Curio, and attendants.*]
VIOLA: I thank you. Here comes the Count.
ORSINO: Who saw Cesario, ho?
VIOLA: On your attendance,° my lord, here.   *at your service*
ORSINO: Stand you awhile aloof. [*The others stand aside.*] Cesario,
      Thou know'st no less but all.° I have unclasped   *everything*
      To thee the book even of my secret soul.
      Therefore, good youth, address thy gait° unto her;   *go*
      Be not denied access, stand at her doors,
15   And tell them, there thy fixèd foot shall grow
      Till thou have audience.
VIOLA: Sure, my noble lord,
      If she be so abandoned to her sorrow
      As it is spoke, she never will admit me.
ORSINO: Be clamorous and leap all civil bounds°   *bounds of civility*
20   Rather than make unprofited return.
VIOLA: Say I do speak with her, my lord, what then?
ORSINO: O, then unfold the passion of my love;
      Surprise° her with discourse of my dear faith.   *take her by storm*
      It shall become° thee well to act my woes;   *suit*
25   She will attend it better in thy youth
      Than in a nuncio's° of more grave aspect.   *messenger's*
VIOLA: I think not so, my lord.
ORSINO: Dear lad, believe it;
      For they shall yet belie thy happy years
      That say thou art a man. Diana's lip
30   Is not more smooth and rubious;° thy small pipe°   *ruby red / voice*
      Is as the maiden's organ, shrill and sound,°   *high and clear*
      And all is semblative° a woman's part.   *resembling*
      I know thy constellation° is right apt   *predestined nature*
      For this affair.—Some four or five attend him.
35   All, if you will, for I myself am best
      When least in company.—Prosper well in this,
      And thou shalt live as freely as thy lord,
      To call his fortunes thine.
VIOLA: I'll do my best
      To woo your lady. [*Aside.*] Yet a barful strife!°   *conflict full of impediments*
40   Whoe'er I woo, myself would be his wife.   [*Exeunt.*]

Scene 5[66]

[*Enter Maria and Clown (Feste).*]
MARIA: Nay, either tell me where thou hast been, or I will not open my lips so wide
    as a bristle may enter in way of thy excuse. My lady will hang thee for thy
    absence.

---

65. Changeableness.   66. Location: Olivia's house.

FESTE: Let her hang me. He that is well hanged in this world needs to fear no
5   colors.[67]
MARIA: Make that good.[68]
FESTE: He shall see none to fear.[69]
MARIA: A good Lenten[70] answer. I can tell thee where that saying was born, of "I
         fear no colors."
FESTE: Where, good Mistress Mary?
MARIA: In the wars,[71] and that may you be bold to say in your foolery.
FESTE: Well, God give them wisdom that have it; and those that are fools, let them
         use their talents.[72]
MARIA: Yet you will be hanged for being so long absent; or to be turned away,[73] is
15   not that as good as a hanging to you?
FESTE: Many a good hanging prevents a bad marriage; and for turning away, let
         summer bear it out.[74]
MARIA: You are resolute, then?
FESTE: Not so, neither, but I am resolved on two points.[75]
MARIA: That if one break, the other will hold; or if both break, your gaskins[76] fall.
FESTE: Apt, in good faith, very apt. Well, go thy way. If Sir Toby would leave
         drinking, thou wert as witty a piece of Eve's flesh as any in Illyria.
MARIA: Peace, you rogue, no more o' that. Here comes my lady. Make your excuse
         wisely, you were best.[77]   [Exit.]
    [Enter Lady Olivia with Malvolio (and attendants).]
FESTE [aside]: Wit, an 't be thy will, put me into good fooling! Those wits that
         think they have thee do very oft prove fools, and I that am sure I lack thee
         may pass for a wise man. For what says Quinapalus?[78] "Better a witty fool
         than a foolish wit."—God bless thee, lady!
OLIVIA [to attendants]: Take the fool away.
FESTE: Do you not hear, fellows? Take away the lady.
OLIVIA: Go to,[79] you're a dry[80] fool. I'll no more of you.
         Besides, you grow dishonest.[81]
FESTE: Two faults, madonna,[82] that drink and good counsel will amend. For give
         the dry[83] fool drink, then is the fool not dry. Bid the dishonest man mend him-
35   self; if he mend, he is no longer dishonest; if he cannot, let the botcher[84]
         mend him. Anything that's mended is but patched; virtue that transgresses
         is but patched with sin, and sin that amends is but patched with virtue. If
         that this simple syllogism will serve, so; if it will not, what remedy? As there
         is no true cuckold but calamity, so beauty's a flower.[85] The lady bade take
40   away the fool; therefore I say again, take her away.
OLIVIA: Sir, I bade them take away you.

67. Fear nothing.
68. Explain that.
69. He'll be dead and, therefore, fear no one.
70. Meager, like Lenten fare.
71. In war, "colors" would be enemy flags.
72. Abilities (reference to the parable of the talents, Matthew 25.14–29).
73. Dismissed.
74. Let mild weather make homelessness endurable.
75. Maria plays on points as "laces used to hold up breeches."
76. Wide breeches.
77. It would be best for you.
78. Feste's invention.
79. Stop.
80. Dull.
81. Unreliable.
82. My lady.
83. Thirsty.
84. Mender of old clothes.
85. I.e., Olivia has wedded calamity but will be unfaithful to it, for it is natural to seize the moment of youth and beauty.

FESTE: Misprision[86] in the highest degree! Lady, *cucullus non facit monachum;*[87] that's as much to say as I wear not motley[88] in my brain. Good madonna, give me leave to prove you a fool.

OLIVIA: Can you do it?

FESTE: Dexterously, good madonna.

OLIVIA: Make your proof.

FESTE: I must catechize you for it, madonna. Good my mouse of virtue,[89] answer me.

OLIVIA: Well, sir, for want of other idleness,[90] I'll bide[91] your proof.

FESTE: Good madonna, why mourn'st thou?

OLIVIA: Good fool, for my brother's death.

FESTE: I think his soul is in hell, madonna.

OLIVIA: I know his soul is in heaven, fool.

FESTE: The more fool, madonna, to mourn for your brother's soul, being in heaven.
55   Take away the fool, gentlemen.

OLIVIA: What think you of this fool, Malvolio? Doth he not mend?[92]

MALVOLIO: Yes, and shall do till the pangs of death shake him. Infirmity, that decays the wise, doth ever make the better fool.

FESTE: God send you, sir, a speedy infirmity for the better increasing your folly! Sir
60   Toby will be sworn that I am no fox, but he will not pass[93] his word for twopence that you are no fool.

OLIVIA: How say you to that, Malvolio?

MALVOLIO: I marvel your ladyship takes delight in such a barren rascal. I saw him put down the other day with[94] an ordinary fool that has no more brain than
65   a stone. Look you now, he's out of his guard[95] already. Unless you laugh and minister occasion[96] to him, he is gagged. I protest I take these wise men that crow so at these set[97] kind of fools no better than the fools' zanies.[98]

OLIVIA: O, you are sick of self-love, Malvolio, and taste with a distempered[99] appetite. To be generous, guiltless, and of free disposition is to take those
70   things for bird-bolts[100] that you deem cannon bullets. There is no slander in an allowed[101] fool, though he do nothing but rail; nor no railing in a known discreet man, though he do nothing but reprove.

FESTE: Now Mercury[102] endue thee with leasing,[103] for thou speak'st well of fools!
    [*Enter Maria.*]

MARIA: Madam, there is at the gate a young gentleman much desires to speak with
75   you.

OLIVIA: From the Count Orsino, is it?

MARIA: I know not, madam. 'Tis a fair young man, and well attended.

OLIVIA: Who of my people hold him in delay?

MARIA: Sir Toby, madam, your kinsman.

86. Mistake.
87. The cowl does not make the monk.
88. The multicolored fool's garment.
89. Virtuous mouse (term of endearment).
90. Pastime.
91. Endure.
92. Improve.
93. Give.
94. By.
95. Defenseless.
96. Provide occasion for wit.
97. Artificial.
98. Fools' assistants.
99. Diseased.
100. Blunt arrows for shooting birds.
101. Licensed.
102. God of trickery.
103. Make you a skillful liar.

OLIVIA: Fetch him off, I pray you. He speaks nothing but madman.[104] Fie on him!
[*Exit Maria.*] Go you, Malvolio. If it be a suit from the Count, I am sick, or
not at home; what you will, to dismiss it. [*Exit Malvolio.*] Now you see, sir,
how your fooling grows old, and people dislike it.

FESTE: Thou hast spoke for us, madonna, as if thy eldest son should be a fool; whose
85   skull Jove cram with brains, for—here he comes—
[*Enter Sir Toby.*]
one of thy kin has a most weak *pia mater*.[105]

OLIVIA: By mine honor, half drunk. What is he at the gate, cousin?

SIR TOBY: A gentleman.

OLIVIA: A gentleman? What gentleman?

SIR TOBY: 'Tis a gentleman here—[*He belches.*] A plague o' these pickle-herring!
[*To Feste.*] How now, sot?[106]

FESTE: Good Sir Toby.

OLIVIA: Cousin,[107] cousin, how have you come so early by this lethargy?

SIR TOBY: Lechery? I defy lechery. There's one at the gate.

OLIVIA: Ay, marry, what is he?

SIR TOBY: Let him be the devil an he will, I care not.
Give me faith,[108] say I. Well, it's all one.[109]   [*Exit.*]

OLIVIA: What's a drunken man like, Fool?

FESTE: Like a drowned man, a fool, and a madman. One draft above heat[110] makes
100   him a fool, the second mads him, and a third drowns him.

OLIVIA: Go thou and seek the crowner,[111] and let him sit o' my coz;[112] for he's in
the third degree of drink, he's drowned. Go, look after him.

FESTE: He is but mad yet, madonna; and the fool shall look to the madman. [*Exit.*]
[*Enter Malvolio.*]

MALVOLIO: Madam, yond young fellow swears he will speak with you. I told him
105   you were sick; he takes on him to understand so much, and therefore comes
to speak with you. I told him you were asleep; he seems to have a foreknowledge of that too, and therefore comes to speak with you. What is to be said
to him, lady? He's fortified against any denial.

OLIVIA: Tell him he shall not speak with me.

MALVOLIO: He's been told so; and he says he'll stand at your door like a sheriff's
post,[113] and be the supporter to a bench, but he'll speak with you.

OLIVIA: What kind o' man is he?

MALVOLIO: Why, of mankind.

OLIVIA: What manner of man?

MALVOLIO: Of very ill manner. He'll speak with you, will you or no.

OLIVIA: Of what personage and years is he?

MALVOLIO: Not yet old enough for a man, nor young enough for a boy; as a
squash[114] is before 'tis a peascod,[115] or a codling[116] when 'tis almost an apple.

104. The words of madness.
105. Brain.
106. Fool; drunkard.
107. Kinsman.
108. I.e., to resist the devil.
109. It doesn't matter.
110. Drink more than would make him warm.

111. Coroner.
112. Hold an inquest on my kinsman (Sir Toby).
113. Post before the sheriff's door to mark a residence of authority.
114. Unripe pea-pod.
115. Pea-pod.
116. Unripe apple.

'Tis with him in standing water[117] between boy and man. He is very well-
favored,[118] and he speaks very shrewishly.[119] One would think his mother's
120   milk were scarce out of him.
OLIVIA: Let him approach. Call in my gentlewoman.
MALVOLIO: Gentlewoman, my lady calls.   [Exit.]
         [Enter Maria.]
OLIVIA: Give me my veil. Come, throw it o'er my face.
125   We'll once more hear Orsino's embassy. [Olivia veils.]
         [Enter Viola.]
VIOLA: The honorable lady of the house, which is she?
OLIVIA: Speak to me; I shall answer for her. Your will?
VIOLA: Most radiant, exquisite, and unmatchable beauty—I pray you, tell me if
         this be the lady of the house, for I never saw her. I would be loath to cast
130   away my speech; for besides that it is excellently well penned, I have taken
         great pains to con[120] it. Good beauties, let me sustain[121] no scorn; I am very
         comptible,[122] even to the least sinister usage.[123]
OLIVIA: Whence came you, sir?
VIOLA: I can say little more than I have studied, and that question's out of my part.
135   Good gentle one, give me modest[124] assurance if you be the lady of the
         house, that I may proceed in my speech.
OLIVIA: Are you a comedian?[125]
VIOLA: No, my profound heart; and yet, by the very fangs of malice, I swear I am
         not that I play. Are you the lady of the house?
OLIVIA: If I do not usurp[126] myself, I am.
VIOLA: Most certain, if you are she, you do usurp yourself; for what is yours to
         bestow is not yours to reserve. But this is from[127] my commission. I will on
         with my speech in your praise, and then show you the heart of my message.
OLIVIA: Come to what is important in 't. I forgive[128] you the praise.
VIOLA: Alas, I took great pains to study it, and 'tis poetical.
OLIVIA: It is the more like to be feigned. I pray you, keep it in. I heard you were
         saucy at my gates, and allowed your approach rather to wonder at you than
         to hear you. If you be not mad,[129] begone; if you have reason,[130] be brief. 'Tis
         not that time of moon with me[131] to make one[132] in so skipping[133] a dia-
         logue.
MARIA: Will you hoist sail, sir? Here lies your way.
VIOLA: No, good swabber,[134] I am to hull[135] here a little longer.—Some mollifica-
         tion for your giant,[136] sweet lady. Tell me your mind; I am a messenger.
OLIVIA: Sure you have some hideous matter to deliver, when the courtesy[137] of it is
         so fearful. Speak your office.[138]

117. At the turn of the tide.
118. Good-looking.
119. Sharply.
120. Learn by heart.
121. Endure.
122. Sensitive.
123. Slightest rude treatment.
124. Reasonable.
125. Actor.
126. Supplant.
127. Outside.
128. Excuse.

129. Altogether mad? But mad?
130. Sanity.
131. I'm not in the mood.
132. Take part.
133. Sprightly.
134. One who swabs the deck.
135. Float without sails.
136. Small Maria, who guards her lady like a medieval
giant.
137. Formal beginning.
138. Business.

VIOLA: It alone concerns your ear. I bring no overture of war, no taxation[139] of homage. I hold the olive[140] in my hand; my words are as full of peace as matter.

OLIVIA: Yet you began rudely. What are you? What would you?

VIOLA: The rudeness that hath appeared in me have I learned from my entertainment.[141] What I am and what I would are as secret as maidenhead—to your
160   ears, divinity;[142] to any other's, profanation.

OLIVIA: Give us the place alone. We will hear this divinity. [Exeunt Maria and attendants.] Now, sir, what is your text?

VIOLA: Most sweet lady—

OLIVIA: A comfortable[143] doctrine, and much may be said of it. Where lies your text?

VIOLA: In Orsino's bosom.

OLIVIA: In his bosom? In what chapter of his bosom?

VIOLA: To answer by the method,[144] in the first of his heart.

OLIVIA: O, I have read it. It is heresy. Have you no more to say?

VIOLA: Good madam, let me see your face.

OLIVIA: Have you any commission from your lord to negotiate with my face? You are now out of your text. But we will draw the curtain and show you the picture. [Unveiling.] Look you, sir, such a one I was this present.[145] Is 't not well done?

VIOLA: Excellently done, if God did all.

OLIVIA: 'Tis in grain,[146] sir; 'twill endure wind and weather.

VIOLA: 'Tis beauty truly blent,[147] whose red and white
Nature's own sweet and cunning[148] hand laid on.
Lady, you are the cruel'st she alive
If you will lead these graces to the grave
180   And leave the world no copy.

OLIVIA: O, sir, I will not be so hardhearted. I will give out divers schedules[149] of my beauty. It shall be inventoried, and every particle and utensil[150] labeled to[151] my will: as, item, two lips, indifferent[152] red; item, two gray eyes, with lids to them; item, one neck, one chin, and so forth. Were you sent hither to
185   praise[153] me?

VIOLA: I see you what you are: you are too proud.
But, if° you were the devil, you are fair.   *even if*
My lord and master loves you. O, such love
Could be but recompensed,° though you were crowned   *could only be repaid*
190   The nonpareil of beauty!

OLIVIA: How does he love me?

VIOLA: With adorations, fertile° tears,   *abundant*
With groans that thunder love, with sighs of fire.

OLIVIA: Your lord does know my mind; I cannot love him.

139. Demand.
140. Olive-branch.
141. Reception.
142. Holy discourse.
143. Comforting.
144. To continue the metaphor.
145. A minute ago.
146. Fast dyed.

147. Blended.
148. Skillful.
149. Lists.
150. Article.
151. Added to.
152. Somewhat.
153. Pun on "appraise."

Yet I suppose him virtuous, know him noble,
195 Of great estate, of fresh and stainless youth,
In voices well divulged,° free,° learned, and valiant,   *well spoken of / generous*
And in dimension and the shape of nature°   *physical form*
A gracious° person. But yet I cannot love him.   *graceful*
He might have took his answer long ago.
VIOLA: If I did love you in my master's flame,°   *passion*
With such a suffering, 'such a deadly° life,   *death-like*
In your denial I would find no sense;
I would not understand it.
OLIVIA: Why, what would you?
VIOLA: Make me a willow[154] cabin at your gate
205 And call upon my soul° within the house;   *Olivia*
Write loyal cantons° of contemnèd° love   *songs / rejected*
And sing them loud even in the dead of night;
Hallow° your name to the reverberate hills,   *call; bless*
And make the babbling gossip° of the air   *echo*
210 Cry out "Olivia!" O, you should not rest
Between the elements of air and earth
But you should pity me!
OLIVIA: You might do much.
                          What is your parentage?
VIOLA: Above my fortunes, yet my state° is well.   *social standing*
I am a gentleman.
OLIVIA: Get you to your lord.
I cannot love him. Let him send no more—
Unless, perchance, you come to me again
To tell me how he takes it. Fare you well.
I thank you for your pains. Spend this for me. [*She offers a purse.*]
VIOLA: I am no fee'd post,° lady. Keep your purse.   *paid messenger*
My master, not myself, lacks recompense.
Love make his heart of flint that you shall love,
And let your fervor, like my master's, be
Placed in contempt! Farewell, fair cruelty.   [*Exit.*]
OLIVIA: "What is your parentage?"
"Above my fortunes, yet my state is well:
I am a gentleman." I'll be sworn thou art!
Thy tongue, thy face, thy limbs, actions, and spirit
Do give thee fivefold blazon.° Not too fast! Soft,° soft!   *coat of arms / wait*
230 Unless the master were the man.[155] How now?
Even so quickly may one catch the plague?
Methinks I feel this youth's perfections
With an invisible and subtle stealth
To creep in at mine eyes. Well, let it be.
235 What ho, Malvolio!
[*Enter Malvolio.*]
MALVOLIO: Here, madam, at your service.

---

154. Willow was the symbol of unrequited love.   155. Unless Cesario and Orsino changed places.

OLIVIA: Run after that same peevish messenger,
     The County's° man. He left this ring behind him, [*giving a ring*]   *Count's*
     Would I or not.[156] Tell him I'll none of it.
     Desire him not to flatter with° his lord,   *encourage*
240   Nor hold him up with hopes; I am not for him.
     If that the youth will come this way tomorrow,
     I'll give him reasons for 't. Hie thee, Malvolio.
MALVOLIO: Madam, I will.   [*Exit*]
OLIVIA: I do I know not what, and fear to find
245   Mine eye too great a flatterer for my mind.
     Fate, show thy force. Ourselves we do not owe.°   *own*
     What is decreed must be; and be this so.   [*Exit.*]

ACT 2

Scene 1[1]

[*Enter Antonio and Sebastian.*]

ANTONIO: Will you stay no longer? Nor will you not[2] that I go with you?
SEBASTIAN: By your patience,[3] no. My stars shine darkly over me. The malignancy
     of my fate might perhaps distemper yours; therefore I shall crave of you your
     leave that I may bear my evils alone. It were a bad recompense for your love
5   to lay any of them on you.
ANTONIO: Let me yet know of you whither you are bound.
SEBASTIAN: No, sooth,[4] sir; my determinate[5] voyage is mere extravagancy.[6] But I
     perceive in you so excellent a touch of modesty that you will not extort from
     me what I am willing to keep in; therefore it charges me in manners the
10   rather to express myself.[7] You must know of me then, Antonio, my name is
     Sebastian, which I called Roderigo. My father was that Sebastian of Mes-
     saline whom I know you have heard of. He left behind him myself and a sis-
     ter, both born in an hour.[8] If the heavens had been pleased, would we had so
     ended! But you, sir, altered that, for some hour[9] before you took me from the
15   breach of the sea[10] was my sister drowned.
ANTONIO: Alas the day!
SEBASTIAN: A lady, sir, though it was said she much resembled me, was yet of
     many accounted beautiful. But though I could not with such estimable won-
     der[11] over-far believe that, yet thus far I will boldly publish[12] her: she bore a
20   mind that envy[13] could not but call fair. She is drowned already, sir, with
     salt water, though I seem to drown her remembrance again with more.
ANTONIO: Pardon me, sir, your bad entertainment.[14]
SEBASTIAN: O good Antonio, forgive me your trouble.[15]
ANTONIO: If you will not murder me for[16] my love, let me be your servant.
SEBASTIAN: If you will not undo what you have done, that is, kill him whom you
     have recovered,[17] desire it not. Fare ye well at once. My bosom is full of

156. Whether I wanted it or not.
1. Location: Somewhere in Illyria.
2. Do you not wish.
3. Leave.
4. Truly.
5. Determined upon.
6. Wandering.
7. Courtesy demands that I reveal myself.
8. In the same hour.
9. About an hour.
10. The surf.
11. Admiring judgment.
12. Proclaim.
13. Even malice.
14. Reception.
15. The trouble I put you to.
16. Be the death of me in return for.
17. Saved.

kindness,[18] and I am yet so near the manners of my mother[19] that upon the
least occasion more mine eyes will tell tales of me. I am bound to the Count
Orsino's court. Farewell.   [*Exit.*]
ANTONIO: The gentleness of all the gods go with thee!
    I have many enemies in Orsino's court,
    Else would I very shortly see thee there.
    But come what may, I do adore thee so
    That danger shall seem sport, and I will go.   [*Exit.*]

Scene 2[20]

[*Enter Viola and Malvolio, at several[21] doors.*]

MALVOLIO: Were not you even now with the Countess Olivia?
VIOLA: Even now, sir. On a moderate pace I have since arrived but hither.
MALVOLIO: She returns this ring to you, sir. You might have saved me my pains, to
    have taken[22] it away yourself. She adds, moreover, that you should put your
5   lord into a desperate[23] assurance she will none of him. And one thing more:
    that you be never so hardy to come[24] again in his affairs, unless it be to
    report your lord's taking of this. Receive it so.
VIOLA: She took the ring of me. I'll none of it.
MALVOLIO: Come, sir, you peevishly threw it to her, and her will is it should be so
10   returned. [*He throws down the ring.*] If it be worth stooping for, there it lies,
    in your eye; if not, be it his that finds it.   [*Exit.*]
VIOLA [*picking up the ring*]: I left no ring with her. What means this lady?
    Fortune forbid my outside have not charmed her!

She made good view of° me, indeed so much	looked closely at
15 That sure methought her eyes had lost° her tongue,	caused her to lose
For she did speak in starts, distractedly.	
She loves me, sure! The cunning of her passion	
Invites me in° this churlish messenger.	in the person of
None of my lord's ring? Why, he sent her none.	
20 I am the man.° If it be so—as 'tis—	man of her choice
Poor lady, she were better love a dream.	
Disguise, I see, thou art a wickedness	
Wherein the pregnant enemy° does much.	resourceful Satan
How easy is it for the proper false°	handsome deceivers
25 In women's waxen° hearts to set their forms!°	malleable / impressions
Alas, our frailty is the cause, not we,	
For such as we are made of, such we be.	
How will this fadge?° My master loves her dearly,	turn out
And I, poor monster,[25] fond° as much on him;	dote
30 And she, mistaken, seems to dote on me.	
What will become of this? As I am man,	
My state is desperate° for my master's love;	hopeless
As I am woman—now, alas the day!—	
What thriftless° sighs shall poor Olivia breathe!	unprofitable

---

18. Tenderness.
19. Womanly inclination to weep.
20. Location: Outside Olivia's house.
21. Different.
22. By taking.

23. Without hope.
24. Bold as to come.
25. Because both man and woman.

35   O Time, thou must untangle this, not I;
      It is too hard a knot for me t' untie.   [*Exit.*]

Scene 3[26]

[*Enter Sir Toby and Sir Andrew.*]

SIR TOBY: Approach, Sir Andrew. Not to be abed after midnight is to be up
      betimes;[27] and *diluculo surgere*,[28] thou know'st—

SIR ANDREW: Nay, by my troth, I know not, but I know to be up late is to be up
      late.

SIR TOBY: A false conclusion. I hate it as an unfilled can.[29] To be up after mid-
      night and to go to bed then, is early; so that to go to bed after midnight is to
      go to bed betimes. Does not our lives consist of the four elements?[30]

SIR ANDREW: Faith, so they say, but I think it rather consists of eating and drinking.

SIR TOBY: Thou'rt a scholar; let us therefore eat and drink. Marian, I say, a stoup[31]
10   of wine!

[*Enter Clown (Feste).*]

SIR ANDREW: Here comes the Fool, i' faith.

FESTE: How now, my hearts! Did you never see the picture of "we three"?[32]

SIR TOBY: Welcome, ass. Now let's have a catch.[33]

SIR ANDREW: By my troth, the Fool has an excellent breast.[34] I had rather than
15   forty shillings I had such a leg, and so sweet a breath to sing, as the fool has.
      In sooth, thou wast in very gracious[35] fooling last night, when thou spok'st
      of Pigrogromitus, of the Vapians passing the equinoctial of Queubus.[36]
      'Twas very good, i' faith. I sent thee sixpence for thy leman.[37] Hadst it?

FESTE: I did impeticos thy gratillity;[38] for Malvolio's nose is no whipstock.[39] My
20   lady has a white hand, and the Myrmidons[40] are no bottle-ale houses.

SIR ANDREW: Excellent! Why, this is the best fooling, when all is done. Now, a
      song.

SIR TOBY: Come on, there is sixpence for you. [*He gives money.*] Let's have a song.

SIR ANDREW: There's a testril[41] of me too. [*He gives money.*] If one knight give a—

FESTE: Would you have a love song, or a song of good life?[42]

SIR TOBY: A love song, a love song.

SIR ANDREW: Ay, ay, I care not for good life.

FESTE [*sings*]:   O mistress mine, where are you roaming?
                        O, stay and hear, your true love 's coming.
30   That can sing both high and low.
                        Trip no further, pretty sweeting
                        Journeys end in lovers' meeting,
                            Every wise man's son doth know.

SIR ANDREW: Excellent good, i' faith.

---

26. Location: Olivia's house.
27. Early.
28. *Diluculo surgere (saluberrimum est)*—to rise early is most healthful (from Lilly's *Latin Grammar*).
29. Tankard.
30. Fire, water, earth, air.
31. Goblet.
32. Picture of two fools or asses, the onlooker being the third.
33. Round-song.
34. Voice.
35. Elegant.
36. Mock erudition.
37. Sweetheart.
38. Impetticoat (pocket up) thy gratuity.
39. Whip-handle.
40. Followers of Achilles.
41. Coin worth sixpence.
42. Virtuous living.

SIR TOBY: Good, good.

FESTE [*sings*]:   What is love? 'tis not hereafter;
                Present mirth hath present laughter;
                    What's to come is still unsure.
                In delay there lies no plenty.

40   Then come kiss me, sweet and twenty;
                    Youth's a stuff will not endure.

SIR ANDREW: A mellifluous voice, as I am true knight.

SIR TOBY: A contagious[43] breath.

SIR ANDREW: Very sweet and contagious, i' faith.

SIR TOBY: To hear by the nose, it is dulcet in contagion. But shall we make the welkin[44] dance indeed? Shall we rouse the night owl in a catch that will draw three souls out of one weaver?[45] Shall we do that?

SIR ANDREW: An you love me, let's do't. I am dog at a catch.

FESTE: By'r Lady, sir, and some dogs will catch well.

SIR ANDREW: Most certain. Let our catch be "Thou knave."

FESTE: "Hold thy peace, thou knave," knight? I shall be constrained in 't to call thee knave, knight.

SIR ANDREW: 'Tis not the first time I have constrained one to call me knave. Begin, Fool. It begins, "Hold thy peace."

FESTE: I shall never begin if I hold my peace.

SIR ANDREW: Good, i' faith. Come, begin. [*Catch sung.*]

[*Enter Maria.*]

MARIA: What a caterwauling do you keep here! If my lady have not called up her steward Malvolio and bid him turn you out of doors, never trust me.

SIR TOBY: My lady's a Cataian,[46] we are politicians,[47] Malvolio's a Peg-o'-Ramsey,[48]
60   and [*He sings*] "Three merry men be we." Am not I consanguineous?[49] Am I not of her blood? Tillyvally![50] Lady! [*He sings.*] "There dwelt a man in Babylon, lady, lady."[51]

FESTE: Beshrew me, the knight's in admirable fooling.

SIR ANDREW: Ay, he does well enough if he be disposed, and so do I too. He does
65   it with a better grace, but I do it more natural.[52]

SIR TOBY [*sings*]: "O' the twelfth day of December"—

MARIA: For the love o' God, peace!

[*Enter Malvolio.*]

MALVOLIO: My masters, are you mad? Or what are you? Have you no wit,[53] manners, nor honesty[54] but to gabble like tinkers at this time of night? Do ye
70   make an alehouse of my lady's house, that ye squeak out your coziers'[55] catches without any mitigation or remorse[56] of voice? Is there no respect of place, persons, nor time in you?

SIR TOBY: We did keep time, sir, in our catches. Sneck up![57]

---

43. Catchy; infected.
44. Sky.
45. Weavers were associated with the singing of psalms.
46. Native of Cathay; trickster.
47. Schemers.
48. Character in a popular song (here used contemptuously).
49. Related.

50. Nonsense.
51. From an old song, *The Constancy of Suzanna*.
52. Naturally (unconsciously suggesting idiocy).
53. Common sense.
54. Decency.
55. Cobblers'.
56. Considerate lowering.
57. Go hang.

MALVOLIO: Sir Toby, I must be round[58] with you. My lady bade me tell you that
75   though she harbors you as her kinsman, she's nothing allied to your dis-
orders. If you can separate yourself and your misdemeanors, you are welcome
to the house; if not, an it would please you to take leave of her, she is very
willing to bid you farewell.

SIR TOBY [sings]: "Farewell, dear heart, since I must needs be gone."[59]

MARIA: Nay, good Sir Toby.

FESTE [sings]: "His eyes do show his days are almost done."

MALVOLIO: Is't even so?

SIR TOBY [sings]: "But I will never die."

FESTE: "Sir Toby, there you lie."

MALVOLIO: This is much credit to you.

SIR TOBY [sings]: "Shall I bid him go?"

FESTE [sings]: "What an if you do?"

SIR TOBY [sings]: "Shall I bid him go, and spare not?"

FESTE [sings]: "O, no, no, no, no, you dare not."

SIR TOBY: Out o' tune, sir? Ye lie. Art any more than a steward? Dost thou think,
because thou art virtuous, there shall be no more cakes and ale?

FESTE: Yes, by Saint Anne,[60] and ginger[61] shall be hot i' the mouth, too.

SIR TOBY: Thou'rt i' the right.—Go, sir, rub your chain with crumbs.[62]—A stoup
of wine, Maria!

MALVOLIO: Mistress Mary, if you prized my lady's favor at anything more than
contempt, you would not give means[63] for this uncivil rule.[64] She shall know
of it, by this hand.   [Exit.]

MARIA: Go shake your ears.[65]

SIR ANDREW: Twere as good a deed as to drink when a man's a-hungry to chal-
100   lenge him the field[66] and then to break promise with him and make a fool of
him.

SIR TOBY: Do 't, knight. I'll write thee a challenge, or I'll deliver thy indignation
to him by word of mouth.

MARIA: Sweet Sir Toby, be patient for tonight. Since the youth of the Count's was
105   today with my lady, she is much out of quiet. For[67] Monsieur Malvolio, let
me alone with him. If I do not gull[68] him into a nayword[69] and make him a
common recreation,[70] do not think I have wit enough to lie straight in my
bed. I know I can do it.

SIR TOBY: Possess us,[71] possess us. Tell us something of him.

MARIA: Marry, sir, sometimes he is a kind of puritan.

SIR ANDREW: O, if I thought that, I'd beat him like a dog.

SIR TOBY: What, for being a puritan? Thy exquisite reason, dear knight?

SIR ANDREW: I have no exquisite reason for 't, but I have reason good enough.

---

58. Blunt.
59. From the ballad *Corydon's Farewell to Phyllis*.
60. Mother of the Virgin Mary. (Her cult was derided in the Reformation, as were cakes and ale at church feasts.)
61. Used to spice ale.
62. Remember your position.
63. I.e., provide wine.
64. Behavior.
65. I.e., your ass's ears.
66. To a duel.
67. As for.
68. Trick.
69. Byword (for dupe).
70. Sport.
71. Inform.

MARIA: The devil a puritan that he is, or anything constantly,[72] but a time-pleaser;[73]
115   an affectioned[74] ass, that cons state without book[75] and utters it by great
         swaths; the best persuaded of himself, so crammed, as he thinks, with excel-
         lencies, that it is his grounds of faith that all that look on him love him; and
         on that vice in him will my revenge find notable cause to work.

SIR TOBY: What wilt thou do?

MARIA: I will drop in his way some obscure epistles of love, wherein by the color of
        his beard, the shape of his leg, the manner of his gait, the expressure[76] of his
        eye, forehead, and complexion, he shall find himself most feelingly person-
        ated.[77] I can write very like my lady your niece; on a forgotten matter[78] we
        can hardly make distinction of our hands.

SIR TOBY: Excellent! I smell a device.

SIR ANDREW: I have't in my nose too.

SIR TOBY: He shall think, by the letters that thou wilt drop, that they come from
          my niece, and that she's in love with him.

MARIA: My purpose is indeed a horse of that color.

SIR ANDREW: And your horse now would make him an ass.

MARIA: Ass, I doubt not.

SIR ANDREW: O, 'twill be admirable!

MARIA: Sport royal, I warrant you. I know my physic[79] will work with him. I will
        plant you two, and let the Fool make a third, where he shall find the letter.
135   Observe his construction[80] of it. For this night, to bed, and dream on the
        event.[81] Farewell.   [Exit.]

SIR TOBY: Good night, Penthesilea.[82]

SIR ANDREW: Before me,[83] she's a good wench.

SIR TOBY: She's a beagle[84] true-bred and one that adores me. What o' that?

SIR ANDREW: I was adored once, too.

SIR TOBY: Let's to bed, knight. Thou hadst need send for more money.

SIR ANDREW: If I cannot recover[85] your niece, I am a foul way out.[86]

SIR TOBY: Send for money, knight. If thou hast her not i' the end, call me cut.[87]

SIR ANDREW: If I do not, never trust me, take it how you will.

SIR TOBY: Come, come, I'll go burn some sack.[88] 'Tis too late to go to bed now.
          Come, knight; come, knight.   [Exeunt.]

Scene 4[89]

[Enter Duke (Orsino) Viola, Curio, and others.]

ORSINO: Give me some music. Now, good morrow,° friends.   morning
         Now, good Cesario, but° that piece of song,   I ask only
         That old and antique° song we heard last night.   quaint
         Methought it did relieve my passion much,
5   More than light airs and recollected° terms   studied

72. Consistently.
73. Sychophant.
74. Affected.
75. Learns a stately manner by heart.
76. Expression.
77. Represented.
78. When we have forgotten who wrote something.
79. Medicine.
80. Interpretation.

81. Outcome.
82. Queen of the Amazons.
83. I swear.
84. Small, intelligent hunting dog.
85. Win.
86. Out of money.
87. Horse with a docked tail or, perhaps, a gelding.
88. Warm some Spanish wine.
89. Location: Orsino's court.

Of these most brisk and giddy-pacèd times.
Come, but one verse.

CURIO: He is not here, so please your lordship, that should sing it.

ORSINO: Who was it?

CURIO: Feste the jester, my lord, a fool that the Lady Olivia's father took much
delight in. He is about the house.

ORSINO: Seek him out, and play the tune the while.

[*Exit Curio.*]

[*Music plays.*]
[*To Viola.*] Come hither, boy. If ever thou shalt love
In the sweet pangs of it remember me;
15   For such as I am, all true lovers are,
Unstaid and skittish in all motions else°   *other emotions*
Save in the constant image of the creature
That is beloved. How dost thou like this tune?

VIOLA: It gives a very echo to the seat
Where Love is throned.°   *i.e., the heart*

ORSINO: Thou dost speak masterly.
My life upon 't, young though thou art, thine eye
Hath stayed upon some favor° that it loves.   *face*
Hath it not, boy?

VIOLA: A little, by your favor.

ORSINO: What kind of woman is 't?

VIOLA: Of your complexion.

ORSINO: She is not worth thee, then. What years, i' faith?

VIOLA: About your years, my lord.

ORSINO: Too old, by heaven. Let still° the woman take   *always*
An elder than herself. So wears° she to him;   *adapts herself*
So sways she level° in her husband's heart.   *she keeps constant*
30   For, boy, however we do praise ourselves,
Our fancies° are more giddy and unfirm,   *loves*
More longing, wavering, sooner lost and worn,
Than women's are.

VIOLA: I think it well, my lord.

ORSINO: Then let thy love be younger than thyself,
35   Or thy affection cannot hold the bent;°   *hold steady*
For women are as roses, whose fair flower
Being once displayed,° doth fall that very hour.   *full blown*

VIOLA: And so they are. Alas that they are so,
To die even when° they to perfection grow!   *just as*

[*Enter Curio and Clown (Feste).*]

ORSINO: O fellow, come, the song we had last night.
Mark it, Cesario, it is old and plain;
The spinsters° and the knitters in the sun,   *spinners*
And the free° maids that weave their thread with bones,° *innocent / bobbins*
Do use° to chant it. It is silly sooth,°   *are used / simple truth*
45   And dallies with the innocence of love,
Like the old age.°   *good old days*

FESTE: Are you ready, sir?

ORSINO: Ay, prithee, sing. [*Music.*]
    [*The Song.*]

FESTE [*sings*]:   Come away, come away, death,
50   And in sad cypress° let me be laid.   *coffin*
           Fly away, fly away, breath;
                I am slain by a fair cruel maid.
           My shroud of white, stuck all with yew,°   *yew-sprigs*
                O, prepare it!
55   My part° of death, no one so true   *portion*
                Did share it.

           Not a flower, not a flower sweet
                On my black coffin let there be strown;°   *strewn*
           Not a friend, not a friend greet
60   My poor corpse, where my bones shall be thrown.
           A thousand thousand sighs to save,
                Lay me, O, where
           Sad true lover never find my grave,
                To weep there!

ORSINO [*offering money*]: There's for thy pains.

FESTE: No pains, sir. I take pleasure in singing, sir.

ORSINO: I'll pay thy pleasure then.

FESTE: Truly, sir, and pleasure will be paid,[90] one time or another.

ORSINO: Give me now leave to leave thee.

FESTE: Now, the melancholy god[91] protect thee, and the tailor make thy doublet[92] of changeable taffeta, for thy mind is a very opal. I would have men of such constancy put to sea, that their business might be everything and their intent[93] everywhere, for that's it that always makes a good voyage of nothing.[94] Farewell.   [*Exit.*]

ORSINO: Let all the rest give place.[95] [*Curio and attendants withdraw.*]
    Once more, Cesario,
  Get thee to yond same sovereign cruelty.°   *cruel person*
  Tell her, my love, more noble than the world,
  Prizes not quantity of dirty lands;
80   The parts° that fortune hath bestowed upon her,   *possessions*
  Tell her, I hold as giddily as fortune;
  But 'tis that miracle and queen of gems
  That nature pranks° her in attracts my soul.   *adorns*

VIOLA: But if she cannot love you, sir?

ORSINO: I cannot be so answered.

VIOLA: Sooth,° but you must.   *In truth*
  Say that some lady, as perhaps there is,
  Hath for your love as great a pang of heart
  As you have for Olivia. You cannot love her;
  You tell her so; Must she not then be answered?°   *accept your answer*

---

90. Indulgence must be paid for.
91. Saturn, said to control the melancholy temperament.
92. Jacket.
93. Destination.
94. Come to nothing.
95. Leave.

ORSINO: There is no woman's sides
    Can bide° the beating of so strong a passion   *withstand*
    As love doth give my heart; no woman's heart
    So big, to hold so much. They lack retention.
    Alas, their love may be called appetite,
95   No motion° of the liver,[96] but the palate,   *emotion*
    That suffer surfeit, cloyment,° and revolt;°   *satiety / revulsion*
    But mine is all as hungry as the sea,
    And can digest as much. Make no compare
    Between that love a woman can bear me
    And that I owe° Olivia.   *have for*
VIOLA: Ay, but I know—
ORSINO: What dost thou know?
VIOLA: Too well what love women to men may owe.
    In faith, they are as true of heart as we.
    My father had a daughter loved a man
105   As it might be, perhaps, were I a woman,
    I should your lordship.
ORSINO: And what's her history?
VIOLA: A blank, my lord. She never told her love,
    But let concealment, like a worm i' the bud,
    Feed on her damask° cheek. She pined in thought,   *pink and white*
110   And with a green and yellow° melancholy   *pale and sallow*
    She sat like Patience on a monument,°   *tomb*
    Smiling at grief. Was not this love indeed?
    We men may say more, swear more, but indeed
    Our shows° are more than will;° for still we prove   *displays / our passions*
115   Much in our vows, but little in our love.
ORSINO: But died thy sister of her love, my boy?
VIOLA: I am all the daughters of my father's house,
    And all the brothers too—and yet I know not.
    Sir, shall I to this lady?
ORSINO: Ay, that's the theme.
    To her in haste; give her this jewel. [*He gives a jewel.*] Say
    My love can give no place, bide no denay.°   *cannot endure denial*
                                [*Exeunt (separately).*]

Scene 5[97]

[*Enter Sir Toby, Sir Andrew, and Fabian.*]
SIR TOBY: Come thy ways,[98] Signor Fabian.
FABIAN: Nay, I'll come. If I lose a scruple[99] of this sport, let me be boiled to death
    with melancholy.
SIR TOBY: Wouldst thou not be glad to have the niggardly rascally sheep-biter[100]
5   come by some notable shame?

96. Seat of the emotion of love.   99. A bit.
97. Location: Olivia's garden.   100. Dog that bites sheep; i.e., a sneak.
98. Come along.

FABIAN: I would exult, man. You know he brought me out o' favor with my lady about a bearbaiting[101] here.

SIR TOBY: To anger him we'll have the bear again, and we will fool him black and blue. Shall we not, Sir Andrew?

SIR ANDREW: An we do not, it is pity of our lives.

[Enter Maria (with a letter).]

SIR TOBY: Here comes the little villain.—How now, my metal of India![102]

MARIA: Get ye all three into the boxtree.[103] Malvolio's coming down this walk. He has been yonder i' the sun practicing behavior[104] to his own shadow this half hour. Observe him, for the love of mockery, for I know this letter will make
15   a contemplative[105] idiot of him. Close,[106] in the name of jesting! [The others hide.] Lie thou there [throwing down a letter]; for here comes the trout that must be caught with tickling.[107]   [Exit.]

[Enter Malvolio.]

MALVOLIO: 'Tis but fortune; all is fortune. Maria once told me she did affect me;[108] and I have heard herself come thus near, that should she fancy,[109] it
20   should be one of my complexion.[110] Besides, she uses me with a more exalted respect than anyone else that follows[111] her. What should I think on 't?

SIR TOBY: Here's an overweening rogue!

FABIAN: O, peace! Contemplation makes a rare turkey-cock of him. How he jets[112] under his advanced[113] plumes!

SIR ANDREW: 'Slight,[114] I could so beat the rogue!

SIR TOBY: Peace, I say.

MALVOLIO: To be Count Malvolio.

SIR TOBY: Ah, rogue!

SIR ANDREW: Pistol him, pistol him.

SIR TOBY: Peace, peace!

MALVOLIO: There is example[115] for 't. The lady of the Strachy[116] married the yeoman of the wardrobe.

SIR ANDREW: Fie on him, Jezebel![117]

FABIAN: O, peace! Now he's deeply in. Look how imagination blows him.[118]

MALVOLIO: Having been three months married to her, sitting in my state[119]—

SIR TOBY: O, for a stone-bow,[120] to hit him in the eye!

MALVOLIO: Calling my officers about me, in my branched[121] velvet gown; having come from a daybed,[122] where I have left Olivia sleeping—

SIR TOBY: Fire and brimstone!

FABIAN: O, peace, peace!

MALVOLIO: And then to have the humor of state;[123] and after a demure travel of regard,[124] telling them I know my place as I would they should do theirs, to ask for my kinsman Toby.

101. Target of Puritan disapproval.
102. Gold; i.e., priceless one.
103. Shrub.
104. Elegant conduct.
105. I.e., from his musings.
106. Hide.
107. Stroking about the gills.
108. Olivia liked me.
109. Fall in love.
110. Personality.
111. Serves.
112. Struts.
113. Raised.
114. By God's light.
115. Precedent.
116. Unknown reference; lady who married below her station.
117. Wicked queen of Israel.
118. Puffs him up.
119. Chair of state.
120. Crossbow.
121. Embroidered.
122. Sofa.
123. Manner of authority.
124. Grave survey of the company.

SIR TOBY: Bolts and shackles!

FABIAN: O, peace, peace, peace! Now, now.

MALVOLIO: Seven of my people, with an obedient start, make out for him. I frown the while, and perchance wind up my watch, or play with my[125]—some rich jewel. Toby approaches; curtsies[126] there to me—

SIR TOBY: Shall this fellow live?

FABIAN: Though our silence be drawn from us with cars,[127] yet peace.

MALVOLIO: I extend my hand to him thus, quenching my familiar smile with an austere regard of control[128]—

SIR TOBY: And does not Toby take[129] you a blow o' the lips then?

MALVOLIO: Saying, "Cousin Toby, my fortunes having cast me on your niece give
55   me this prerogative of speech—"

SIR TOBY: What, what?

MALVOLIO: "You must amend your drunkenness."

SIR TOBY: Out, scab!

FABIAN: Nay, patience, or we break the sinews of our plot.

MALVOLIO: "Besides, you waste the treasure of your time with a foolish knight—"

SIR ANDREW: That's me, I warrant you.

MALVOLIO: "One Sir Andrew."

SIR ANDREW: I knew 'twas I, for many do call me fool.

MALVOLIO: What employment have we here? [*Taking up the letter.*]

FABIAN: Now is the woodcock[130] near the gin.[131]

SIR TOBY: O, peace, and the spint of humors[132] intimate reading aloud to him!

MALVOLIO: By my life, this is my lady's hand. These be her very c's, her u's, and her t's; and thus makes she her great[133] P's. It is in contempt of[134] question her hand.

SIR ANDREW: Her c's, her u's, and her t's. Why that?

MALVOLIO [*reads*]: "To the unknown beloved, this, and my good wishes."—Her very phrases! By your leave, wax.[135] Soft![136] And the impressure her Lucrece,[137] with which she uses to seal. 'Tis my lady. To whom should this be? [*He opens the letter.*]

FABIAN: This wins him, liver[138] and all.

MALVOLIO [*reads*]: "Jove knows I love,
But who?
Lips, do not move;
No man must know."

"No man must know." What follows? The numbers[139] altered! "No man must
80   know." If this should be thee, Malvolio?

SIR TOBY: Marry, hang thee, brock![140]

MALVOLIO [*reads*]: "I may command where I adore,
But silence, like a Lucrece knife,

---

125. Malvolio recalls that, as a Count, he would not be wearing his steward's chain.
126. Bows.
127. With chariots; i.e., by force.
128. Look of authority.
129. Give.
130. Proverbially stupid bird.
131. Snare.
132. Whim.
133. Uppercase; copious (implying "pee").
134. Beyond.
135. Conventional apology for breaking a seal.
136. Softly.
137. Lucretia; chaste matron.
138. Seat of passion.
139. Verses.
140. Badger.

                With bloodless stroke my heart doth gore;

85   M.O.A.I. doth sway my life."

FABIAN: A fustian[141] riddle!

SIR TOBY: Excellent wench,[142] say I.

MALVOLIO: "M.O.A.I. doth sway my life." Nay, but first, let me see, let me see, let me see.

FABIAN: What dish o' poison has she dressed[143] him!

SIR TOBY: And with what wing[144] the staniel[145] checks at it![146]

MALVOLIO: "I may command where I adore." Why, she may command me; I serve her, she is my lady. Why, this is evident to any formal capacity.[147] There is no obstruction[148] in this. And the end—what should that alphabetical position

95   portend? If I could make that resemble something in me! Softly! M.O.A.I.—

SIR TOBY: O, ay, make up that. He is now at a cold scent.[149]

FABIAN: Sowter will cry upon 't[150] for all this, though it be as rank as a fox.

MALVOLIO: M—Malvolio. M! Why, that begins my name!

FABIAN: Did not I say he would work it out? The cur is excellent at faults.[151]

MALVOLIO: M—But then there is no consonancy in the sequel that suffers under probation:[152] A should follow, but O does.

FABIAN: And O shall end,[153] I hope.

SIR TOBY: Ay, or I'll cudgel him, and make him cry "O!"

MALVOLIO: And then I comes behind.

FABIAN: Ay, an you had any eye behind you, you might see more detraction[154] at your heels than fortunes before you.

MALVOLIO: M.O.A.I. This simulation[155] is not as the former. And yet, to crush[156] this a little, it would bow to me, for every one of these letters are in my name. Soft! Here follows prose.

110   [*He reads.*] "If this fall into thy hand, revolve.[157] In my stars[158] I am above thee, but be not afraid of greatness. Some are born great, some achieve greatness, and some have greatness thrust upon 'em. Thy Fates open their hands; let thy blood and spirit embrace them; and, to inure[159] thyself to what thou art like to be, cast thy humble slough[160] and appear fresh. Be opposite[161] with a

115   kinsman, surly with servants. Let thy tongue tang[162] arguments of state; put thyself into the trick of singularity.[163] She thus advises thee that sighs for thee. Remember who commended thy yellow stockings, and wished to see thee ever cross-gartered.[164] I say, remember. Go to, thou art made, if thou desir'st tobe so. If not, let me see thee a steward still, the fellow of servants,

---

141. Pompous.
142. Clever girl (Maria).
143. Prepared.
144. Speed.
145. Inferior hawk.
146. Turns to fly at it.
147. Normal understanding.
148. Difficulty.
149. Difficult trail.
150. The hound will pick up the scent.
151. Breaks in the scent.
152. Pattern in the letters that stands up under examination.
153. O ends Malvolio's name; a noose shall end his life; *omega* ends the Greek alphabet.

154. Defamation.
155. Disguise.
156. Force.
157. Consider.
158. Fate.
159. Accustom.
160. Outer skin.
161. Contradictory.
162. Sound with.
163. Eccentricity.
164. Wearing hose garters crossed above and below the knee.

120   and not worthy to touch Fortune's fingers. Farewell. She that would alter
        services[165] with thee,

                                        The Fortunate-Unhappy."[166]
            Daylight and champaign[167] discovers[168] not more! This is open. I will be
        proud, I will read politic authors,[169] I will baffle[170] Sir Toby, I will wash off
125   gross acquaintance, I will be point-devise[171] the very man. I do not now fool
        myself, to let imagination jade[172] me; for every reason excites to this, that
        my lady loves me. She did commend my yellow stockings of late, she did
        praise my leg being cross-gartered; and in this[173] she manifests herself to my
        love, and with a kind of injunction drives me to these habits[174] of her liking.
130   I thank mystars, I am happy.[175] I will be strange,[176] stout,[177] in yellow stock-
        ings and cross-gartered, even with the swiftness of putting on. Jove and my
        stars be praised! Here is yet a post-script. [He reads.] "Thou canst not choose
        but know who I am. If thou entertain'st[178] my love, let it appear in thy smil-
        ing; thy smiles become thee well. Therefore in my presence still[179] smile,
135   dear my sweet, I prithee."
            Jove, I thank thee. I will smile; I will do everything that thou wilt have
        me.   [Exit.]
    [Sir Toby, Sir Andrew, and Fabian come from hiding.]
FABIAN: I will not give my part of this sport for a pension of thousands to be paid
140   from the Sophy.[180]
SIR TOBY: I could marry this wench for this device.
SIR ANDREW: So could I too.
SIR TOBY: And ask no other dowry with her but such another jest.
    [Enter Maria.]
SIR ANDREW: Nor I neither.
FABIAN: Here comes my noble gull-catcher.[181]
SIR TOBY: Wilt thou set thy foot o' my neck?
SIR ANDREW: Or o' mine either?
SIR TOBY: Shall I play[182] my freedom at tray-trip,[183] and become thy bondslave?
SIR ANDREW: I' faith, or I either?
SIR TOBY: Why, thou hast put him in such a dream that when the image of it
150   leaves him he must run mad.
MARIA: Nay, but say true, does it work upon him?
SIR TOBY: Like aqua vitae[184] with a midwife.
MARIA: If you will then see the fruits of the sport, mark his first approach before my
        lady. He will come to her in yellow stockings, and 'tis a color she abhors,
155   and cross-gartered, a fashion she detests; and he will smile upon her, which
        will now be so unsuitable to her disposition, being addicted to a melancholy
        as she is, that it cannot but turn him into a notable contempt.[185] If you will
        see it, follow me.

165. Change places.   176. Aloof.
166. Unfortunate.   177. Haughty.
167. Open country.   178. You accept.
168. Discloses.   179. Always.
169. Political writers.   180. Shah of Persia.
170. Disgrace.   181. Fool-catcher.
171. Correct to the letter.   182. Gamble.
172. Trick.   183. Game of dice.
173. This letter.   184. Distilled liquor.
174. Attire.   185. Notorious object of contempt.
175. Fortunate.

SIR TOBY: To the gates of Tartar,[186] thou most excellent devil of wit!
SIR ANDREW: I'll make one[187] too.   [*Exeunt.*]

ACT 3

Scene 1[1]

[*Enter Viola, and Clown (Feste, playing his pipe and tabor).*]

VIOLA: Save thee,[2] friend, and thy music. Dost thou live by[3] thy tabor?[4]
FESTE: No, sir, I live by the church.
VIOLA: Art thou a churchman?
FESTE: No such matter, sir. I do live by the church, for I do live at my house, and
5   my house doth stand by the church.
VIOLA: So thou mayst say the king lies[5] by a beggar if a beggar dwell near him, or
         the church stands by thy tabor if thy tabor stand by the church.
FESTE: You have said, sir. To see this age! A sentence is but a cheveril[6] glove to a
         good wit. How quickly the wrong side may be turned outward!
VIOLA: Nay, that's certain. They that dally nicely[7] with words may quickly make
         them wanton.[8]
FESTE: I would therefore my sister had had no name, sir.
VIOLA: Why, man?
FESTE: Why, sir, her name's a word, and to dally with that word might make my
15   sister wanton.[9] But indeed, words are very rascals since bonds disgraced them.[10]
VIOLA: Thy reason, man?
FESTE: Troth, sir, I can yield you none without words, and words are grown so false
         I am loath to prove reason with them.
VIOLA: I warrant thou art a merry fellow and car'st for nothing.
FESTE: Not so, sir, I do care for something; but in my conscience, sir, I do not
         care for you. If that be to care for nothing, sir, I would it would make you
         invisible.
VIOLA: Art not thou the Lady Olivia's fool?
FESTE: No indeed, sir. The Lady Olivia has no folly. She will keep no fool, sir, till
25   she be married, and fools are as like husbands as pilchers[11] are to herrings—
         the husband's the bigger. I am indeed not her fool but her corrupter of
         words.
VIOLA: I saw thee late[12] at the Count Orsino's.
FESTE: Foolery, sir, does walk about the orb[13] like the sun; it shines everywhere. I
30   would be sorry, sir, but[14] the fool should be as oft with your master as with
         my mistress. I think I saw your wisdom there.
VIOLA: Nay, an thou pass upon[15] me, I'll no more with thee. Hold, there's expenses
         for thee. [*She gives a coin.*]
FESTE: Now Jove, in his next commodity[16] of hair, send thee a beard!

---

186. Tartarus, the section of hell for the most evil.
187. Tag along.
1. Location: Olivia's garden.
2. God save.
3. Earn your living with.
4. Drum.
5. Dwells.
6. Kid.
7. Play subtly; toy amorously.
8. Equivocal.

9. Licentious.
10. Since sworn statements have been needed to make
them good.
11. Pitchers, a kind of small fish.
12. Recently.
13. Earth.
14. Unless.
15. Fence verbally with me.
16. Shipment.

VIOLA: By my troth, I'll tell thee, I am almost sick for one—[*aside*] though I would
not have it grow on my chin.—Is thy lady within?

FESTE: Would not a pair of these have bred, sir?

VIOLA: Yes, being kept together and put to use.[17]

FESTE: I would play Lord Pandarus[18] of Phrygia, sir, to bring a Cressida to this
40   Troilus.

VIOLA: I understand you, sir. 'Tis well begged. [*She gives another coin.*]

FESTE: The matter, I hope, is not great, sir, begging but a beggar; Cressida was a
beggar.[19] My lady is within, sir. I will conster[20] to them whence you come.
Who you are and what you would are out of my welkin[21]—I might say
45   "element," but the word is overworn.   [*Exit.*]

VIOLA: This fellow is wise enough to play the fool,
And to do that well craves° a kind of wit.   *requires*
He must observe their mood on whom he jests,
The quality of persons, and the time,
50   And, like the haggard,° check° at every feather   *untrained hawk / turn*
That comes before his eye. This is a practice°   *skill*
As full of labor as a wise man's art;
For folly that he wisely shows is fit,
But wise men, folly-fall'n,° quite taint their wit.[22]   *fallen into folly*
[*Enter Sir Toby and (Sir) Andrew.*]

SIR TOBY: Save you, gentleman.

VIOLA: And you, sir.

SIR ANDREW: *Dieu vous garde, monsieur.*[23]

VIOLA: *Et vous aussi; votre serviteur.*[24]

SIR ANDREW: I hope, sir, you are, and I am yours.

SIR TOBY: Will you encounter[25] the house? My niece is desirous you should enter,
if your trade[26] be to her.

VIOLA: I am bound to[27] your niece, sir; I mean, she is the list[28] of my voyage.

SIR TOBY: Taste[29] your legs, sir. Put them to motion.

VIOLA: My legs do better understand[30] me, sir, than I understand what you mean by
65   bidding me taste my legs.

SIR TOBY: I mean, to go, sir, to enter.

VIOLA: I will answer you with gait and entrance.—But we are prevented.[31]
[*Enter Olivia and gentlewoman (Maria).*]
Most excellent accomplished lady, the heavens rain odors on you!

SIR ANDREW: That youth's a rare courtier. "Rain odors"—well.

VIOLA: My matter hath no voice,[32] lady, but to your own most pregnant[33] and
vouchsafed[34] ear.

SIR ANDREW: "Odors," "pregnant," and "vouchsafed." I'll get 'em all three all
ready.[35]

17. Put out at interest.
18. Go-between in the story of Troilus and Cressida.
19. She became a leprous beggar in Henrsyon's continuation of Chaucer's story.
20. Explain.
21. Sky.
22. Ruin their reputation for intelligence.
23. God protect you, sir.
24. You, too; your servant.
25. Enter.

26. Business.
27. Bound for; obliged to.
28. Destination.
29. Try.
30. Comprehend; stand under.
31. Anticipated.
32. Cannot be uttered.
33. Receptive.
34. Attentive.
35. Memorized for future use.

OLIVIA: Let the garden door be shut, and leave me to my hearing. [*Exeunt Sir*
75   *Toby, Sir Andrew, and Maria.*] Give me your hand, sir.
VIOLA: My duty, madam, and most humble service.
OLIVIA: What is your name?
VIOLA: Cesario is your servant's name, fair princess.
OLIVIA: My servant, sir? 'Twas never merry world
80   Since lowly feigning° was called compliment.   *false humility*
        You're servant to the Count Orsino, youth.
VIOLA: And he is yours, and his must needs be yours;
        Your servant's servant is your servant, madam.
OLIVIA: For him, I think not on him. For his thoughts,
85   Would they were blanks, rather than filled with me!
VIOLA: Madam, I come to whet your gentle thoughts
        On his behalf.
OLIVIA: O, by your leave,° I pray you.   *please*
        I bade you never speak again of him.
        But, would you undertake another suit,
90   I had rather hear you to solicit that
        Than music from the spheres.°   *heavenly harmony*
VIOLA: ·   Dear lady—
OLIVIA: Give me leave, beseech you. I did send,
        After the last enchantment you did here,
        A ring in chase of you; so did I abuse°   *deceive*
95   Myself, my servant, and, I fear me, you.
        Under your hard construction° must I sit,   *interpretation*
        To force° that on you in a shameful cunning   *for forcing*
        Which you knew none of yours. What might you think?
        Have you not set mine honor at the stake
100   And baited° it with all th' unmuzzled thoughts   *harassed*
        That tyrannous heart can think? To one of your receiving°   *intelligence*
        Enough is shown; a cypress,° not a bosom,   *thin black cloth*
        Hides my heart. So, let me hear you speak.
VIOLA: I pity you.
OLIVIA: That's a degree to love.
VIOLA: No, not a grece;° for 'tis a vulgar proof°   *step / common experience*
        That very oft we pity enemies.
OLIVIA: Why then, methinks 'tis time to smile again.
        O world, how apt° the poor are to be proud!   *ready*
        If one should be a prey, how much the better
110   To fall before the lion than the wolf!
        [*Clock strikes.*]
        The clock upbraids me with the waste of time.
        Be not afraid, good youth, I will not have you;
        And yet, when wit and youth is come to harvest
        Your wife is like° to reap a proper° man.   *likely / handsome*
        There lies your way, due west.
VIOLA: Then westward ho!³⁶

---

36. The cry of Thames watermen to attract westward-bound passengers from London to Westminster.

Grace and good disposition attend your ladyship.
You'll nothing, madam, to my lord by me?
OLIVIA: Stay.
I prithee, tell me what thou think'st of me.
VIOLA: That you do think you are not what you are.
OLIVIA: If I think so, I think the same of you.
VIOLA: Then think you right. I am not what I am.
OLIVIA: I would you were as I would have you be!
VIOLA: Would it be better, madam, than I am?
125   I wish it might, for now I am your fool.
OLIVIA [aside]: O, what a deal of scorn looks beautiful
In the contempt and anger of his lip!
A murderous guilt shows not itself more soon
Than love that would seem hid; love's night is noon.[37]—
130   Cesario, by the roses of the spring,
By maidhood, honor, truth, and everything,
I love thee so that, maugre° all thy pride,   *despite*
Nor wit nor reason can my passion hide.
Do not extort thy reasons from this clause,
135   For that I woo, thou therefore hast no cause.
But rather reason thus with reason fetter.
Love sought is good, but given unsought is better.
VIOLA: By innocence I swear, and by my youth,
I have one heart, one bosom, and one truth,
140   And that no woman has, nor never none
Shall mistress be of it save I alone.
And so adieu, good madam. Nevermore
Will I my master's tears to you deplore.°   *beweep*
OLIVIA: Yet come again, for thou perhaps mayst move
145   That heart, which now abhors, to like his love.

[*Exeunt (separately).*]

Scene 2[38]

[*Enter Sir Toby, Sir Andrew, and Fabian.*]
SIR ANDREW: No, faith, I'll not stay a jot longer.
SIR TOBY: Thy reason, dear venom,[39] give thy reason.
FABIAN: You must needs yield your reason, Sir Andrew.
SIR ANDREW: Marry, I saw your niece do more favors to the Count's servingman
5   than ever she bestowed upon me. I saw't i' the orchard.[40]
SIR TOBY: Did she see thee the while, old boy? Tell me that.
SIR ANDREW: As plain as I see you now.
FABIAN: This was a great argument[41] of love in her toward you.
SIR ANDREW: 'Slight,[42] will you make an ass o' me?
FABIAN: I will prove it legitimate,[43] sir, upon the oaths[44] of judgment and reason.
SIR TOBY: And they have been grand-jurymen since before Noah was a sailor.

37. Love cannot hide itself.   41. Proof.
38. Location: Olivia's house.   42. God's light.
39. Venomous person.   43. True.
40. Garden.   44. Testimony.

FABIAN: She did show favor to the youth in your sight only to exasperate you, to awake your dormouse[45] valor, to put fire in your heart and brimstone in your liver. You should then have accosted her, and with some excellent jests,
15 fire-new from the mint, you should have banged the youth into dumbness. This was looked for at your hand, and this was balked.[46] The double gilt of this opportunity you let time wash off, and you are now sailed into the north[47] of my lady's opinion, where you will hang like an icicle on a Dutchman's beard[48] unless you do redeem it by some laudable attempt either of
20 valor or policy.[49]
SIR ANDREW: An't be any way, it must be with valor, for policy I hate. I had as lief be a Brownist[50] as a politician.[51]
SIR TOBY: Why, then, build me thy fortunes upon the basis of valor. Challenge me the Count's youth to fight with him; hurt him in eleven places. My niece
25 shall take note of it; and assure thyself, there is no love-broker in the world can more prevail in man's commendation with woman than report of valor.
FABIAN: There is no way but this, Sir Andrew.
SIR ANDREW: Will either of you bear me a challenge to him?
SIR TOBY: Go, write it in a martial hand. Be curst[52] and brief; it is no matter how
30 witty, so it be eloquent and full of invention. Taunt him with the license of ink.[53] If thou "thou"-est[54] him some thrice, it shall not be amiss; and as many lies[55] as will lie in thy sheet of paper, although the sheet were big enough for the bed of Ware[56] in England, set 'em down. Go, about it. Let there be gall[57] enough in thy ink, though thou write with a goose pen,[58] no matter. About it.
SIR ANDREW: Where shall I find you?
SIR TOBY: We'll call thee at the cubiculo.[59] Go.

[Exit Sir Andrew.]

FABIAN: This is a dear manikin[60] to you, Sir Toby.
SIR TOBY: I have been dear to him, lad, some two thousand strong or so.
FABIAN: We shall have a rare letter from him; but you'll not deliver 't?
SIR TOBY: Never trust me, then; and by all means stir on the youth to an answer. I think oxen and wainropes[61] cannot hale[62] them together. For Andrew, if he were opened and you find so much blood in his liver[63] as will clog the foot of a flea, I'll eat the rest of th' anatomy.
FABIAN: And his opposite,[64] the youth, bears in his visage no great presage of cruelty.
[Enter Maria.]
SIR TOBY: Look where the youngest wren[65] of nine comes.
MARIA: If you desire the spleen,[66] and will laugh yourselves into stitches, follow me. Yond gull[67] Malvolio is turned heathen, a very renegado; for there is no

---

45. Sleepy.
46. Missed.
47. Out of the warmth.
48. Alludes to the arctic voyage of William Berentz in 1596–1597.
49. Stratagem.
50. Early name for the Congregationalists, after founder Robert Browne.
51. Schemer.
52. Fierce.
53. Freedom of writing.
54. Call him "thou" (informal).
55. Charges of lying.

56. Famous bed, more than ten feet wide.
57. Bitterness; ingredient in ink.
58. Goose quill; foolish style.
59. Small chamber.
60. Puppet.
61. Wagon ropes.
62. Haul.
63. A pale and bloodless liver was a sign of cowardice.
64. Adversary.
65. Smallest of small birds.
66. Laughing fit.
67. Fool.

Christian that means to be saved by believing rightly can ever believe such impossible passages of grossness.[68] He's in yellow stockings.

SIR TOBY: And cross-gartered?

MARIA: Most villainously, like a pedant that keeps a school i', the church. I have dogged him like his murderer. He does obey every point of the letter that I dropped to betray him. He does smile his face into more lines than is in the new map with the augmentation of the Indies.[69] You have not seen such a
55   thing as 'tis. I can hardly forbear hurling things at him. I know my lady will strike him. If she do, he'll smile and take't for a great favor.

SIR TOBY: Come, bring us, bring us where he is.

[Exeunt omnes.]

Scene 3[70]

[Enter Sebastian and Antonio.]

SEBASTIAN: I would not by my will have troubled you,
    But since you make your pleasure of your pains,
    I will no further chide you.

ANTONIO: I could not stay behind you. My desire,
5   More sharp than filèd steel, did spur me forth,
    And not all° love to see you—though so much   only
    As might have drawn one to a longer voyage—
    But jealousy° what might befall your travel,   solicitude
    Being skilless in° these parts, which to a stranger,   unacquainted with
10   Unguided and unfriended, often prove
    Rough and unhospitable. My willing love,
    The rather by these arguments of fear,
    Set forth in your pursuit.

SEBASTIAN: My kind Antonio,
    I can no other answer make but thanks,
15   And thanks; and ever oft good turns
    Are shuffled off with such uncurrent° pay.   valueless
    But were my worth,° as is my conscience,° firm,   wealth / inclination
    You should find better dealing.° What's to do?   treatment
    Shall we go see the relics° of this town?   monuments

ANTONIO: Tomorrow, sir. Best first go see your lodging.

SEBASTIAN: I am not weary, and 'tis long to night.
    I pray you, let us satisfy our eyes
    With the memorials and the things of fame
    That do renown° this city.   make famous

ANTONIO: Would you'd pardon me.
25   I do not without danger walk these streets.
    Once in a sea fight 'gainst the Count his° galleys   Count's
    I did some service, of such note indeed
    That were I ta'en here it would scarce be answered.°   atoned for

SEBASTIAN: Belike° you slew great number of his people?   Perhaps

ANTONIO: Th' offense is not of such a bloody nature,

68. Gross impossibilities.
69. Emerie Molyneux's map, c. 1599, which showed more of the East Indies than had ever been mapped before.
70. Location: A street.

Albeit the quality of the time and quarrel
Might well have given us bloody argument.°   *cause for bloodshed*
It might have since been answered° in repaying   *atoned for*
What we took from them, which for traffic's° sake   *trade's*
35   Most of our city did. Only myself stood out,
For which, if I be lapsèd° in this place,   *surprised*
I shall pay dear.
SEBASTIAN: Do not then walk too open.
ANTONIO: It doth not fit me. Hold, sir, here's my purse. [*He gives his purse.*]
In the south suburbs, at the Elephant,°   *an inn*
40   Is best to lodge. I will bespeak our diet,°   *order our food*
Whiles you beguile the time and feed your knowledge
With viewing of the town. There shall you have me.
SEBASTIAN: Why I your purse?
ANTONIO: Haply° your eye shall light upon some toy°   *perhaps / trifle*
45   You have desire to purchase; and your store°   *store of money*
I think is not for idle markets,° sir.   *useless purchases*
SEBASTIAN: I'll be your purse-bearer and leave you
For an hour.
ANTONIO: To th' Elephant.
SEBASTIAN: I do remember.

[*Exeunt (separately).*]

Scene 4[71]

[*Enter Olivia and Maria.*]
OLIVIA [*aside*]: I have sent after him; he says he'll come.
How shall I feast him? What bestow of him?
For youth is bought more oft than begged or borrowed.
I speak too loud.—
5   Where's Malvolio? He is sad and civil,[72]
And suits well for a servant with my fortunes.
Where is Malvolio?
MARIA: He's coming, madam, but in very strange manner. He is, sure, possessed,
madam.
OLIVIA: Why, what's the matter? Does he rave?
MARIA: No, madam, he does nothing but smile. Your ladyship were best to have
some guard about you if he come, for sure the man is tainted in 's wits.
OLIVIA: Go call him hither. [*Maria summons Malvolio.*] I am as mad as he,
If sad and merry madness equal be.
[*Enter Malvolio, (cross-gartered and in yellow stockings).*]
15   How now, Malvolio?
MALVOLIO: Sweet lady, ho, ho!
OLIVIA: Smil'st thou? I sent for thee upon a sad occasion.
MALVOLIO: Sad, lady? I could be sad. This does make some obstruction in the
blood, this cross-gartering, but what of that? If it please the eye of one, it is
20   with me as the very true sonnet[73] is, "Please one and please all."

71. Location: Olivia's garden.   73. Song.
72. Serious and sedate.

OLIVIA: Why, how dost thou, man? What is the matter with thee?

MALVOLIO: Not black in my mind, though yellow in my legs. It did come to his hands, and commands shall be executed. I think we do know the sweet roman hand.[74]

OLIVIA: Wilt thou go to bed, Malvolio?

MALVOLIO: To bed! "Ay, sweetheart, and I'll come to thee."[75]

OLIVIA: God comfort thee! Why dost thou smile so and kiss thy hand so oft?

MARIA: How do you, Malvolio?

MALVOLIO: At your request? Yes, nightingales answer daws.[76]

MARIA: Why appear you with this ridiculous boldness before my lady?

MALVOLIO: "Be not afraid of greatness." 'Twas well writ.

OLIVIA: What mean'st thou by that, Malvolio?

MALVOLIO: "Some are born great—"

OLIVIA: Ha?

MALVOLIO: "Some achieve greatness—"

OLIVIA: What sayst thou?

MALVOLIO: "And some have greatness thrust upon them."

OLIVIA: Heaven restore thee!

MALVOLIO: "Remember who commended thy yellow stockings—"

OLIVIA: Thy yellow stockings?

MALVOLIO: "And wished to see thee cross-gartered."

OLIVIA: Cross-gartered?

MALVOLIO: "Go to, thou art made, if thou desir'st to be so—"

OLIVIA: Am I made?

MALVOLIO: "If not, let me see thee a servant still."

OLIVIA: Why, this is very midsummer madness.

[Enter Servant.]

SERVANT: Madam, the young gentleman of the Count Orsino's is returned. I could hardly, entreat him back. He attends your ladyship's pleasure.

OLIVIA: I'll come to him. [Exit Servant.] Good Maria, let this fellow be looked to.
50   Where's my cousin Toby? Let some of my people have a special care of him. I would not have him miscarry[77] for the half of my dowry.

[Exeunt (Olivia and Maria, different ways).]

MALVOLIO: Oho, do you come near[78] me now? No worse man than Sir Toby to look to me! This concurs directly with the letter. She sends him on purpose that I may appear stubborn to him, for she incites me to that in the letter.
55   "Cast thy humble slough," says she; "be opposite with a kinsman, surly with servants; let thy tongue tang with arguments of state; put thyself into the trick of singularity." And consequently sets down the manner how: as, a sad[79] face, a reverend carriage, a slow tongue, in the habit[80] of some sir of note, and so forth. I have limed[81] her, but it is Jove's doing, and Jove make
60   me thankful! And when she went away now, "Let this fellow be looked to." "Fellow!"[82] Not "Malvolio," nor after my degree,[83] but "fellow." Why, every-

---

74. Italian style of handwriting.
75. Quotation from a popular song.
76. I.e., why should a fine fellow like me answer a daw (crow) like you.
77. Come to harm.
78. Appreciate.

79. Serious.
80. Attire.
81. Caught.
82. Companion.
83. According to my position.

thing adheres together, that no dram[84] of a scruple,[85] no scruple of a scruple, no obstacle, no incredulous[86] or unsafe circumstance—what can be said?—nothing that can be can come between me and the full prospect of my
65   hopes. Well, Jove, not I, is the doer of this, and he is to be thanked.

[*Enter (Sir) Toby, Fabian, and Maria.*]

SIR TOBY: Which way is he, in the name of sanctity? If all the devils of hell be drawn in little,[87] and Legion[88] himself possessed him, yet I'll speak to him.

FABIAN: Here he is, here he is.—How is't with you, sir? How is't with you, man?

MALVOLIO: Go off. I discard you. Let me enjoy my private. Go off.

MARIA: Lo, how hollow the fiend speaks within him! Did not I tell you? Sir Toby, my lady prays you to have a care of him.

MALVOLIO: Aha, does she so?

SIR TOBY: Go to, go to! Peace, peace, we must deal gently with him. Let me alone.—How do you, Malvolio? How is 't with you? What, man, defy the
75   devil! Consider, he's an enemy to mankind.

MALVOLIO: Do you know what you say?

MARIA: La you,[89] an you speak ill of the devil, how he takes it at heart! Pray God he be not bewitched!

FABIAN: Carry his water[90] to the wisewoman.

MARIA: Marry, and it shall be done tomorrow morning, if I live. My lady would not lose him for more than I'll say.

MALVOLIO: How now, mistress?

MARIA: O Lord!

SIR TOBY: Prithee, hold thy peace; this is not the way. Do you not see you move[91]
85   him? Let me alone with him.

FABIAN: No way but gentleness, gently, gently. The fiend is rough, and will not be roughly used.

SIR TOBY: Why, how now, my bawcock![92] How dost thou, chuck?[93]

MALVOLIO: Sir!

SIR TOBY: Ay, biddy,[94] come with me. What man, tis not for gravity[95] to play at cherry-pit[96] with Satan. Hang him, foul collier![97]

MARIA: Get him to say his prayers, good Sir Toby, get him to pray.

MALVOLIO: My prayers, minx?

MARIA: No, I warrant you, he will not hear of godliness.

MALVOLIO: Go hang yourselves all! You are idle,[98] shallow things; I am not of your element. You shall know more hereafter.   [*Exit.*]

SIR TOBY: Is 't possible?

FABIAN: If this were played upon a stage, now, I could condemn it as an improbable fiction.

SIR TOBY: His very genius[99] hath taken the infection of the device, man.

MARIA: Nay, pursue him now, lest the device take air and taint.[100]

FABIAN: Why, we shall make him mad indeed.

---

84. Small amount; one-eighth of a fluid ounce.
85. Doubt; one-third of a dram.
86. Incredible.
87. Brought together in a small space.
88. An unclean spirit ("My name is Legion, for we are many," Mark 5.9).
89. Look you.
90. Urine.
91. Upset.

92. Fine fellow (from French *beau-coq*).
93. Chick.
94. Chicken.
95. Dignity.
96. A child's game.
97. Coal-peddler.
98. Foolish.
99. Spirit.
100. Become exposed to air and, thus, to spoil.

MARIA: The house will be the quieter.

SIR TOBY: Come, we'll have him in a dark room and bound. My niece is already in
105   the belief that he's mad. We may carry it[101] thus for our pleasure and his
penance till our very pastime, tired out of breath, prompt us to have mercy
on him, at which time we will bring the device to the bar[102] and crown thee
for a finder of madmen. But see, but see!

[*Enter Sir Andrew (with a letter).*]

FABIAN: More matter for a May morning.[103]

SIR ANDREW: Here's the challenge. Read it. I warrant there's vinegar and pepper in 't.

FABIAN: Is 't so saucy?[104]

SIR ANDREW: Ay, is 't, I warrant him. Do but read.

SIR TOBY: Give me. [*He reads.*] "Youth, whatsoever thou art, thou art but a scurvy
fellow."

FABIAN: Good, and valiant.

SIR TOBY [*reads*]: "Wonder not, nor admire[105] not in thy mind, why I do call thee
so, for I will show thee no reason for 't."

FABIAN: A good note, that keeps you from the blow of the law.

SIR TOBY [*reads*]: "Thou com'st to the Lady Olivia, and in my sight she uses thee
120   kindly. But thou liest in thy throat; that is not the matter I challenge thee
for."

FABIAN: Very brief, and to exceeding good sense—less.

SIR TOBY [*reads*]: "I will waylay thee going home, where if it be thy chance to kill
me—"

FABIAN: Good.

SIR TOBY [*reads*]: "Thou kill'st me like a rogue and a villain."

FABIAN: Still you keep o' the windy[106] side of the law. Good.

SIR TOBY [*reads*]: "Fare thee well, and God have mercy upon one of our souls! He
may have mercy upon mine, but my hope is better, and so look to thyself.
130   Thy friend, as thou usest him, and thy sworn enemy,

Andrew Aguecheek."

If this letter move him not, his legs cannot. I'll give 't him.

MARIA: You may have very fit occasion for 't. He is now in some commerce with
my lady, and will by and by depart.

SIR TOBY: Go, Sir Andrew. Scout me[107] for him at the corner of the orchard like a
bum-baily.[108] So soon as ever thou seest him, draw, and as thou draw'st,
swear horrible; for it comes to pass oft that a terrible oath, with a swaggering
accent sharply twanged off, gives manhood more approbation[109] than ever
proof[110] itself would have earned him. Away!

SIR ANDREW: Nay, let me alone for swearing.[111]   [*Exit.*]

SIR TOBY: Now will not I deliver his letter, for the behavior of the young gentleman gives him out to be of good capacity and breeding; his employment
between his lord and my niece confirms no less. Therefore this letter, being
so excellently ignorant, will breed no terror in the youth. He will find it
145   comes from a clodpoll.[112] But, sir, I will deliver his challenge by word of

101. Carry the trick on.
102. To court.
103. Material for a Mayday comedy.
104. Spicy; insolent.
105. Marvel.
106. Windward; i.e., safe.
107. Keep watch.
108. Agent who makes arrests.
109. Reputation.
110. Testing.
111. Leave swearing to me.
112. Blockhead.

mouth, set upon Aguecheek a notable report of valor, and drive the gentleman—as I know his youth will aptly receive it—into a most hideous opinion of his rage, skill, fury, and impetuosity. This will so fright them both
that they will kill one another by the look, like cockatrices.[113]

[*Enter Olivia and Viola.*]

FABIAN: Here he comes with your niece. Give them way till he take leave, and
presently after him.

SIR TOBY: I will meditate the while upon some horrid message for a challenge.

[*Exeunt Sir Toby, Fabian, and Maria.*]

OLIVIA: I have said too much unto a heart of stone
And laid mine honor too unchary° on 't.   *carelessly*
155   There's something in me that reproves my fault,
But such a headstrong potent fault it is
That it but mocks reproof.

VIOLA: With the same havior° that your passion bears   *behavior*
Goes on my master's griefs.

OLIVIA [*giving a locket*]: Here, wear this jewel for me. 'Tis my picture.
Refuse it not; it hath no tongue to vex you.
And I beseech you come again tomorrow.
What shall you ask of me that I'll deny,
That honor, saved, may upon asking give?

VIOLA: Nothing but this; your true love for my master.

OLIVIA: How with mine honor may I give him that
Which I have given to you?

VIOLA: I will acquit° you.   *release*

OLIVIA: Well, come again tomorrow. Fare thee well.
A fiend like° thee might bear my soul to hell.   [*Exit.*]   *resembling*

[*Enter (Sir) Toby and Fabian.*]

SIR TOBY: Gentleman, God save thee.

VIOLA: And you, sir.

SIR TOBY: That defense thou hast, betake thee to 't. Of what nature the wrongs
are thou hast done him, I know not, but thy intercepter,[114] full of despite,[115]
bloody as the hunter, attends thee at the orchard end. Dismount thy tuck,[116]
175   be yare[117] in thy preparation, for thy assailant is quick, skillful, and deadly.

VIOLA: You mistake sir. I am sure no man hath any quarrel to me. My remembrance is very free and clear from any image of offense done to any man.

SIR TOBY: You'll find it otherwise, I assure you. Therefore, if you hold your life at
any price, betake you to your guard, for your opposite[118] hath in him what
180   youth, strength, skill, and wrath can furnish man withal.

VIOLA: I pray you, sir, what is he?

SIR TOBY: He is knight, dubbed with unhatched[119] rapier and on carpet consideration,[120] but he is a devil in private brawl. Souls and bodies hath he divorced
three, and his incensement at this moment is so implacable that satisfaction
185   can be none but by pangs of death and sepulcher. Hob, nob[121] is his word;[122]
give 't or take 't.

113. Basilisks, or reptiles able to kill with a glance.
114. He who lies in wait.
115. Defiance.
116. Draw your rapier.
117. Quick.
118. Opponent.
119. Unhacked; unused in battle.
120. Through court favor.
121. Have or have not.
122. Motto.

VIOLA: I will return again into the house and desire some conduct[123] of the lady. I am no fighter. I have heard of some kind of men that put quarrels purposely on others, to taste[124] their valor. Belike[125] this is a man of that quirk.[126]

SIR TOBY: Sir, no. His indignation derives itself out of a very competent[127] injury; therefore, get you on and give him his desire. Back you shall not to the house unless you undertake that with me which with as much safety you might answer him. Therefore, on, or strip your sword stark naked; for meddle[128] you must, that's certain, or forswear to wear iron[129] about you.

VIOLA: This is as uncivil as strange. I beseech you, do me this courteous office, as to know of the knight what my offense to him is. It is something of my negligence, nothing of my purpose.

SIR TOBY: I will do so.—Signor Fabian, stay you by this gentleman till my return.

[Exit (Sir) Toby.]

VIOLA: Pray you, sir, do you know of this matter?

FABIAN: I know the knight is incensed against you, even to a mortal arbitrament,[130] but nothing of the circumstance more.

VIOLA: I beseech you, what manner of man is he?

FABIAN: Nothing of that wonderful promise, to read him by his form, as you are like to find him in the proof of his valor. He is, indeed, sir, the most skillful,
205   bloody, and fatal opposite that you could possibly have found in any part of Illyria. Will you walk towards him, I will make your peace with him if I can.

VIOLA: I shall be much bound to you for 't. I am one that had rather go with Sir Priest than Sir Knight. I care not who knows so much of my mettle. [Exeunt.]

[Enter (Sir) Toby and (Sir) Andrew.]

SIR TOBY: Why, man, he's a very devil; I have not seen such a firago.[131] I had a pass[132]
210   with him, rapier, scabbard, and all, and he gives me the stuck in[133] with such a mortal motion that it is inevitable; and on the answer,[134] he pays you as surely as your feet hits the ground they step on. They say he has been fencer to the Sophy.

SIR ANDREW: Pox on 't, I'll not meddle with him.

SIR TOBY: Ay, but he will not now be pacified. Fabian can scarce hold him younder.

SIR ANDREW: Plague on 't, an I thought he had been valiant and so cunning in fence, I'd have seen him damned ere I'd have challenged him. Let him let the matter slip and I'll give him my horse, gray Capilet.

SIR TOBY: I'll make the motion.[135] Stand here, make a good show on 't. This shall end without the perdition of souls.[136] [Aside, as he crosses to meet Fabian.] Marry, I'll ride your horse as well as I ride you.

[Enter Fabian and Viola.]

---

123. Escort.
124. Test.
125. Probably.
126. Peculiarity.
127. Sufficient.
128. Engage in combat.
129. Give up your right to wear a sword.

130. Trial to the death.
131. Virago (overbearing woman).
132. Bout.
133. Thrust.
134. Return.
135. Offer.
136. I.e., killing.

[*Aside to Fabian.*] I have his horse to take up[137] the quarrel. I have persuaded
him the youth's a devil.

FABIAN: He is as horribly conceited of him,[138] and pants and looks pale as if a bear
were at his heels.

SIR TOBY [*to Viola*]: There's no remedy, sir, he will fight with you for 's oath's sake.
Marry, he hath better bethought him of his quarrel, and he finds that
now scarce to be worth talking of. Therefore draw, for the supportance of his
230   vow; he protests he will not hurt you.

VIOLA [*aside*]: Pray God defend me! A little thing would make me tell them how
much I lack of a man.

FABIAN: Give ground, if you see him furious.

SIR TOBY [*crossing to Sir Andrew*]: Come, Sir Andrew, there's no remedy. The
gentleman will, for his honor's sake, have one bout with you. He cannot by
the *duello*[139] avoid it. But he has promised me, as he is a gentleman and a
soldier, he will not hurt you. Come on, to 't.

SIR ANDREW: Pray God he keep his oath!
    [*Enter Antonio.*]

VIOLA: I do assure you, 'tis against my will.
    [*They draw.*]

ANTONIO [*drawing, to Sir Andrew*]: Put up your sword. If this young gentleman
    Have done offense, I take the fault on me;
    If you offend him, I for him defy you.

SIR TOBY: You, sir? Why, what are you?

ANTONIO: One, sir, that for his love dares yet do more
245   Than you have heard him brag to you he will.

SIR TOBY [*drawing*]: Nay, if you be an undertaker,° I am for° you.   *challenger / ready for*
    [*Enter Officers.*]

FABIAN: O good Sir Toby, hold! Here come the officers.

SIR TOBY [*to Antonio*]: I'll be with you anon.

VIOLA [*to Sir Andrew*]: Pray, sir, put your sword up, if you please.

SIR ANDREW: Marry, will I, sir; and for that I promised you, I'll be as good as my word.
    He will bear you easily, and reins well.

FIRST OFFICER: This is the man. Do thy office.

SECOND OFFICER: Antonio, I arrest thee at the suit
    Of Count Orsino.

ANTONIO: You do mistake me, sir.

FIRST OFFICER: No, sir, no jot. I know your favor° well,   *face*
    Though now you have no sea-cap on your head.—
    Take him away. He knows I know him well.

ANTONIO: I must obey. [*To Viola.*] This comes with seeking you.
    But there's no remedy; I shall answer it.
260   What will you do, now my necessity
    Makes me to ask you for my purse? It grieves me
    Much more for what I cannot do for you

---

137. Settle.   139. Dueling code.
138. I.e., Cesario has as horrible a conception of Sir
Andrew.

Than what befalls myself. You stand amazed,
But be of comfort.
SECOND OFFICER: Come, sir, away.
ANTONIO [*to Viola*]: I must entreat of you some of that money.
VIOLA: What money, sir?
For the fair kindness you have showed me here,
And part° being prompted by your present trouble,   *partly*
Out of my lean and low ability
270   I'll lend you something. My having° is not much;   *wealth*
I'll make division of my present° with you.   *what I have now*
Hold, there's half my coffer.° [*She offers money.*]   *purse*
ANTONIO: Will you deny me now?
Is 't possible that my deserts to° you   *claims on*
Can lack persuasion? Do not tempt my misery,
275   Lest that it make me so unsound a man
As to upbraid you with those kindnesses
That I have done for you.
VIOLA: I know of none,
Nor know I you by voice or any feature.
I hate ingratitude more in a man
280   Than lying, vainness, babbling drunkenness,
Or any taint of vice whose strong corruption
Inhabits our frail blood.
ANTONIO: O heavens themselves!
SECOND OFFICER: Come, sir, I pray you, go.
ANTONIO: Let me speak a little. This youth that you see here
I snatched one half out of the jaws of death,
Relieved him with such° sanctity of love,   *much*
And to his image, which methought did promise
Most venerable worth,° did I devotion.   *worthiness*
FIRST OFFICER: What's that to us? The time goes by. Away!
ANTONIO: But, O, how vile an idol proves this god!
Thou hast, Sebastian, done good feature shame.
In nature there's no blemish but the mind;
None can be called deformed but the unkind.°   *unnatural*
Virtue is beauty, but the beauteous evil
295   Are empty trunks o'erflourished° by the devil.   *ornamented*
FIRST OFFICER: The man grows mad. Away with him! Come, come, sir.
ANTONIO: Lead me on.   [*Exit (with Officers).*]
VIOLA [*aside*]: Methinks his words do from such passion fly
That he believes himself. So do not I.
Prove true, imagination, O, prove true,
That I, dear brother, be now ta'en for you!
SIR TOBY: Come hither, knight. Come hither, Fabian.
We'll whisper o'er a couplet or two of most sage saws.°   *wise sayings*
[*They gather apart from Viola.*]
VIOLA: He named Sebastian. I my brother know

305   Yet living in my glass;° even such and so   *mirror*
       In favor was my brother, and he went
       Still° in this fashion, color, ornament,   *always*
       For him I imitate. O, if it prove,°   *prove true*
       Tempests are kind, and salt waves fresh in love!   [*Exit.*]
SIR TOBY: A very dishonest[140] paltry boy, and more a coward than a hare. His dishonesty appears in leaving his friend here in necessity and denying him; and for his cowardship, ask Fabian.
FABIAN: A coward, a most devout coward, religious° in it.   *confirmed*
SIR ANDREW: 'Slid,° I'll after him again and beat him.   *God's eyelid*
SIR TOBY: Do, cuff him soundly, but never draw thy sword.
SIR ANDREW: An I do not—   [*Exit.*]
FABIAN: Come, let's see the event.°   *result*
SIR TOBY: I dare lay any money 'twill be nothing yet.°   *nevertheless*
                                                                 [*Exeunt.*]

ACT 4

Scene 1[1]

[*Enter Sebastian and Clown (Feste).*]

FESTE: Will you make me believe that I am not sent for you?
SEBASTIAN: Go to, go to, thou art a foolish fellow. Let me be clear of thee.
FESTE: Well held out,[2] i' faith! No, I do not know you, nor I am not sent to you by my lady to bid you come speak with her, nor your name is not Master
5   Cesario, nor this is not my nose, neither. Nothing that is so is so.
SEBASTIAN: I prithee, vent thy folly somewhere else. Thou know'st not me.
FESTE: Vent my folly! He has heard that word of some great man, and now applies it to a fool. Vent my folly! I am afraid this great lubber,[3] the world, will prove a cockney.[4] I prithee now, ungird thy strangeness[5] and tell me what I
10   shall vent to my lady. Shall I vent to her that thou art coming?
SEBASTIAN: I prithee, foolish Greek,[6] depart from me. There's money for thee. [*He gives money.*] If you tarry longer, I shall give worse payment.
FESTE: By my troth, thou hast an open hand. These wise men that give fools money get themselves a good report—after fourteen years' purchase.[7]
       [*Enter (Sir) Andrew, (Sir) Toby, and Fabian.*]
SIR ANDREW: Now, sir, have I met you again? There's for you! [*He strikes Sebastian.*]
SEBASTIAN: Why, there's for thee, and there, and there! [*He beats Sir Andrew with the hilt of his dagger.*]
       Are all the people mad?
SIR TOBY: Hold, sir, or I'll throw your dagger o'er the house.
FESTE: This will I tell my lady straight. I would not be in some of your coats for twopence.   [*Exit.*]

---

140. Dishonorable.
1. Location: Before Olivia's house.
2. Kept up.
3. Lout.
4. Affected person.
5. Abandon your strange manner.
6. Buffoon.
7. At great expense.

SIR TOBY: Come on, sir, hold! [*He grips Sebastian.*]
SIR ANDREW: Nay, let him alone. I'll go another way to work with him. I'll have
        an action of battery[8] against him, if there be any law in Illyria. Though I
25   struck him first, yet it's no matter for that.
SEBASTIAN: Let go thy hand!
SIR TOBY: Come, sir, I will not let you go. Come, my young soldier, put up your
        iron. You are well fleshed.[9] Come on.
SEBASTIAN: I will be free from thee. [*He breaks free and draws his sword.*] What
30   wouldst thou now?
        If thou dar'st tempt me further, draw thy sword.
SIR TOBY: What, what? Nay, then I must have an ounce or two of this malapert[10]
        blood from you. [*He draws.*]
    [*Enter Olivia.*]
OLIVIA: Hold, Toby! On thy life I charge thee, hold!
SIR TOBY: Madam—
OLIVIA: Will it be ever thus? Ungracious wretch,
        Fit for the mountains and the barbarous caves,
        Where manners ne'er were preached! Out of my sight!—
        Be not offended, dear Cesario.—
40   Rudesby,° begone!   *rude fellow*
                                [*Exeunt Sir Toby, Sir Andrew, and Fabian.*]
                        I prithee, gentle friend,
        Let thy fair wisdom, not thy passion, sway
        In this uncivil and unjust extent°   *attack*
        Against thy peace. Go with me to my house,
        And hear thou there how many fruitless pranks
45   This ruffian hath botched up,° that thou thereby   *contrived*
        Mayst smile at this. Thou shalt not choose but go.
        Do not deny.° Beshrew° his soul for me!   *refuse / curse*
        He started° one poor heart of mine, in thee.   *startled*
SEBASTIAN [*aside*]: What relish° is in this? How runs the stream?   *taste*
50   Or I am mad, or else this is a dream.
        Let fancy° still my sense in Lethe[11] steep;   *imagination*
        If it be thus to dream, still let me sleep!
OLIVIA: Nay, come, I prithee. Would thou'dst be ruled by me!
SEBASTIAN: Madam, I will.
OLIVIA: O, say so, and so be!   [*Exeunt.*]

Scene 2[12]

[*Enter Maria (with a gown and a false beard), and Clown (Feste).*]
MARIA: Nay, I prithee, put on this gown and this beard; make him believe thou art
        Sir[13] Topas[14] the curate. Do it quickly. I'll call Sir Toby the whilst.   [*Exit.*]

---

8. Assault charge.
9. Initiated into battle.
10. Impudent.
11. River of forgetfulness in the Underworld.

12. Location: Olivia's house.
13. Title for priests.
14. Comic knight in Chaucer. (The topaz stone was
believed to cure lunacy.)

FESTE: Well, I'll put it on, and I will dissemble[15] myself in 't, and I would I were the
first that ever dissembled in such a gown. [*He disguises himself in gown and*
5   *beard*.] I am not tall enough to become the function[16] well, nor lean[17]
enough to be thought a good student; but to be said an honest man and a
good housekeeper[18] goes as fairly as to say a careful man and a great scholar.
The competitors[19] enter.

[*Enter (Sir) Toby (and Maria).*]

SIR TOBY: Jove bless thee, Master Parson.

FESTE: *Bonos dies,*[20] Sir Toby. For, as the old hermit of Prague,[21] that never saw pen
and ink, very wittily said to a niece of King Gorboduc,[22] "That that is, is"; so
I, being Master Parson, am Master Parson; for what is "that" but "that," and
"is" but "is"?

SIR TOBY: To him, Sir Topas.

FESTE: What, ho, I say! Peace in this prison! [*He approaches the door behind which
Malvolio is confined.*]

SIR TOBY: The knave[23] counterfeits well; a good knave.

MALVOLIO [*within*]: Who calls there?

FESTE: Sir Topas the curate, who comes to visit Malvolio the lunatic.

MALVOLIO: Sir Topas, Sir Topas, good Sir Topas, go to my lady—

FESTE: Out, hyperbolical[24] fiend! How vexest thou this man! Talkest thou nothing
but of ladies?

SIR TOBY: Well said, Master Parson.

MALVOLIO: Sir Topas, never was man thus wronged. Good Sir Topas, do not
25   think I am mad. They have laid me here in hideous darkness.

FESTE: Fie, thou dishonest Satan! I call thee by the most modest terms, for I am one
of those gentle ones that will use the devil himself with courtesy. Sayst thou
that house[25] is dark?

MALVOLIO: As hell, Sir Topas.

FESTE: Why, it hath bay windows transparent as barricadoes,[26] and the cleresto-
ries[27] toward the south north are as lustrous as ebony; and yet complainest
thou of obstruction?

MALVOLIO: I am not mad, Sir Topas. I say to you this house is dark.

FESTE: Madman, thou errest. I say there is no darkness but ignorance, in which
35   thou art more puzzled than the Egyptians in their fog.[28]

MALVOLIO: I say this house is as dark as ignorance, though ignorance were as dark
as hell; and I say there was never man thus abused. I am no more mad than
you are. Make the trial of it in any constant question.[29]

FESTE: What is the opinion of Pythagoras[30] concerning wildfowl?

MALVOLIO: That the soul of our grandam might haply, inhabit a bird.

15. Disguise.
16. Priestly office.
17. Scholars were supposed to be poor and, therefore,
thin.
18. Neighbor.
19. Associates.
20. Good day.
21. Invented authority.
22. Legendary British king in the tragedy *Gorbobuc* (1562).
23. Fellow.

24. Boisterous.
25. Room.
26. Barricades.
27. Upper windows.
28. Allusion to the darkness Moses brought upon Egypt
(Exodus 10.21–23).
29. Consistent discussion.
30. Philosopher who originated the doctrine of the trans-
migration of souls.

FESTE: What think'st thou of his opinion?

MALVOLIO: I think nobly of the soul, and no way approve his opinion.

FESTE: Fare thee well. Remain thou still in darkness. Thou shalt hold th' opinion of Pythagoras ere I will allow of thy wits,[31] and fear to kill a woodcock[32] lest
45   thou dispossess the soul of thy grandam. Fare thee well.
      [He moves away from Malvolio's prison.]

MALVOLIO: Sir Topas, Sir Topas!

SIR TOBY: My most exquisite Sir Topas!

FESTE: Nay, I am for all waters.[33]

MARIA: Thou mightst have done this without thy beard and gown. He sees thee not.

SIR TOBY: To him in thine own voice, and bring me word how thou find'st him. I would we were well rid of this knavery. If he may be conveniently delivered,[34] I would he were, for I am now so far in offense with my niece that I cannot pursue with any safety this sport to the upshot.[35] Come by and by to my chamber.

                                                                [Exit (with Maria).]

FESTE [*singing as he approaches Malvolio's prison*]:
            "Hey, Robin, jolly Robin,
55   Tell me how thy lady does."[36]

MALVOLIO: Fool!

FESTE: "My lady is unkind, pardie."[37]

MALVOLIO: Fool!

FESTE: "Alas, why is she so?"

MALVOLIO: Fool, I say!

FESTE: "She loves another—" Who calls, ha?

MALVOLIO: Good Fool, as ever thou wilt deserve well at my hand, help me to a candle, and pen, ink, and paper. As I am a gentleman, I will live to be thankful to thee for 't.

FESTE: Master Malvolio?

MALVOLIO: Ay, good Fool.

FESTE: Alas, sir, how fell you beside your five wits?[38]

MALVOLIO: Fool, there was never man so notoriously abused. I am as well in my wits, Fool, as thou art.

FESTE: But[39] as well? Then you are mad indeed, if you be no better in your wits than a fool.

MALVOLIO: They have here propertied me,[40] keep me in darkness, send ministers to me—asses—and do all they can to face me[41] out of my wits.

FESTE: Advise you[42] what you say. The minister is here. [*He speaks as Sir Topas.*]
75   Malvolio, Malvolio, thy wits the heavens restore! Endeavor thyself to sleep; and leave thy vain bibble-babble.

---

31. Acknowledge your sanity.
32. Proverbially stupid bird.
33. Good for any trade.
34. Delivered from prison.
35. Conclusion.
36. Fragment of a song attributed to Thomas Wyatt.

37. By God (French: *par Dieu*).
38. Out of your mind.
39. Only.
40. Treated me as property.
41. Brazen me.
42. Take care.

MALVOLIO: Sir Topas!

FESTE [*in Sir Topas' voice*]: Maintain no words with him, good fellow. [*In his own voice.*] Who, I, sir? Not I, sir. God b' wi' you, good Sir Topas. [*In Sir Topas'*
80   *voice.*] Marry, amen. [*In his own voice.*] I will, sir, I will.

MALVOLIO: Fool! Fool! Fool, I say!

FESTE: Alas, sir, be patient. What say you, sir? I am shent[43] for speaking to you.

MALVOLIO: Good Fool, help me to some light and some paper. I tell thee I am as well in my wits as any man in Illyria.

FESTE: Welladay[44] that you were, sir!

MALVOLIO: By this hand, I am. Good Fool, some ink, paper, and light; and convey what I will set down to my lady. It shall advantage thee more than ever the bearing of letter did.

FESTE: I will help you to 't. But tell me true, are you not mad indeed, or do you but
90   counterfeit?

MALVOLIO: Believe me, I am not. I tell thee true.

FESTE: Nay, I'll ne'er believe a madman till I see his brains. I will fetch you light and paper and ink.

MALVOLIO: Fool, I'll requite it in the highest degree. I prithee, begone.

FESTE [*sings*]:   I am gone, sir,
                                        And anon, sir,
                                 I'll be with you again,
                                        In a trice,
                                 Like to the old Vice,[45]
100   Your need to sustain;

                                 Who, with dagger of lath,°   *Vice's weapon*
                                 In his rage and his wrath,
                              Cries, "Aha!" to the devil;
                                        Like a mad lad,
105   "Pare thy nails, dad?
                              Adieu, goodman devil!"   [*Exit.*]

Scene 3[46]

[*Enter Sebastian (with a pearl).*]

SEBASTIAN: This is the air; that is the glorious sun;
                     This pearl she gave me, I do feel 't and see 't;
                     And though 'tis wonder that enwraps me thus,
                     Yet 'tis not madness. Where's Antonio, then?
5   I could not find him at the Elephant;
                     Yet there he was,° and there I found this credit,°   *had been / belief*
                     That he did range the town to seek me out.
                     His counsel now might do me golden service;
                     For though my soul disputes well with my sense

---

43. Rebuked.
44. Alas.

45. Comic character of old morality plays.
46. Location: Olivia's garden.

10   That this may be some error, but no madness,
      Yet doth this accident° and flood of fortune   *surprise*
      So far exceed all instance,° all discourse,°   *precedent / logic*
      That I am ready to distrust mine eyes
      And wrangle° with my reason that persuades me   *dispute*
15   To any other trust° but that I am mad,   *belief*
      Or else the lady's mad. Yet if 'twere so,
      She could not sway° her house, command her followers,   *rule*
      Take and give back affairs and their dispatch°   *management*
      With such a smooth, discreet, and stable bearing
20   As I perceive she does. There's something in 't
      That is deceivable.° But here the lady comes.   *deceptive*
  [*Enter Olivia and Priest.*]
OLIVIA: Blame not this haste of mine. If you mean well,
      Now go with me and with this holy man
      Into the chantry° by. There, before him,   *chapel nearby*
25   And underneath that consecrated roof,
      Plight me the full assurance of your faith,
      That my most jealous° and too doubtful soul   *anxious*
      May live at peace. He shall conceal it
      Whiles° you are willing it shall come to note,°   *until / become known*
30   What time° we will our celebration keep   *at which time*
      According to my birth.° What do you say?   *social position*
SEBASTIAN: I'll follow this good man, and go with you,
      And having sworn truth, ever will be true.
OLIVIA: Then lead the way, good Father, and heavens so shine
35   That they may fairly note° this act of mine!   *look well upon*
                                                                   [*Exeunt.*]

                         ACT 5

                        Scene 1[1]

  [*Enter Clown (Feste) and Fabian.*]
FABIAN: Now, as thou lov'st me, let me see his letter.
FESTE: Good Master Fabian, grant me another request.
FABIAN: Anything.
FESTE: Do not desire to see this letter.
FABIAN: This is to give a dog and in recompense desire my dog again.[2]
  [*Enter Duke (Orsino), Viola, Curio, and lords.*]
ORSINO: Belong you to the Lady Olivia, friends?
FESTE: Ay, sir, we are some of her trappings.[3]
ORSINO: I know thee well. How dost thou, my good fellow?
FESTE: Truly, sir, the better for[4] my foes and the worse for my friends.

---

1. Location: Before Olivia's house.
2. Famously, Queen Elizabeth once asked Dr. Bulleyn for his dog and promised a gift of his choosing in exchange; he asked to have his dog back.
3. Ornaments.
4. Because of.

ORSINO: Just the contrary—the better for thy friends.

FESTE: No, sir, the worse.

ORSINO: How can that be?

FESTE: Marry, sir, they praise me, and make an ass of me. Now my foes tell me plainly I am an ass, so that by my foes, sir, I profit in the knowledge of
15   myself, and by my friends I am abused;[5] so that, conclusions to be as kisses, if your four negatives make your two affirmatives, why then the worse for my friends and the better for my foes.

ORSINO: Why, this is excellent.

FESTE: By my troth, sir, no, though it please you to be one of my friends.

ORSINO: Thou shalt not be the worse for me. There's gold. [*He gives a coin.*]

FESTE: But that it would be double-dealing,[6] sir, I would you could make it another.

ORSINO: O, you give me ill counsel.

FESTE: Put your grace in your pocket,[7] sir, for this once, and let your flesh and blood obey it.[8]

ORSINO: Well, I will be so much a sinner to be a double-dealer. There's another. [*He gives another coin.*]

FESTE: *Primo, secundo, tertio,* is a good play,[9] and the old saying is, the third pays for all.[10] The triplex,[11] sir, is a good tripping measure; or the bells of Saint Bennet,[12] sir, may put you in mind—one, two, three.

ORSINO: You can fool no more money out of me at this throw.[13] If you will let your lady know I am here to speak with her, and bring her along with you, it may awake my bounty further.

FESTE: Marry, sir, lullaby to your bounty till I come again. I go, sir, but I would not have you to think that my desire of having is the sin of covetousness. But as
35   you say, sir, let your bounty take a nap. I will awake it anon.   [*Exit.*]
        [*Enter Antonio and Officers.*]

VIOLA: Here comes the man, sir, that did rescue me.

ORSINO: That face of his I do remember well,
        Yet when I saw it last it was besmeared
        As black as Vulcan[14] in the smoke of war.
40   A baubling° vessel was he captain of,   *trifling*
        For shallow draft[15] and bulk unprizable,[16]
        With which such scatheful° grapple did he make   *harmful*
        With the most noble bottom° of our fleet   *ship*
        That very envy° and the tongue of loss°   *even malice / the losers*
45   Cried fame and honor on him. What's the matter?

FIRST OFFICER: Orsino, this is that Antonio
        That took the *Phoenix* and her freight from Candy,°   *Crete*
        And this is he that did the *Tiger* board

---

5. Deceived.
6. Giving twice; deceit.
7. Pocket your virtue; be generous.
8. I.e., my ill counsel.
9. Game.
10. I.e., the third time is lucky.

11. Triple-time in music.
12. Church of St. Benedict.
13. Throw of the dice.
14. Roman god of fire, smith to the other gods.
15. Depth of water a ship draws.
16. Of slight value.

When your young nephew Titus lost his leg.
50   Here in the streets, desperate° of shame and state,   reckless
In private brabble° did we apprehend him.   brawl
VIOLA: He did me kindness, sir, drew on my side,
But in conclusion put strange speech upon me.
I know not what 'twas but distraction.°   madness
ORSINO: Notable° pirate, thou saltwater thief,   notorious
What foolish boldness brought thee to their mercies
Whom thou in terms so bloody and so dear°   costly
Hast made thine enemies?
ANTONIO: Orsino, noble sir,
60   Be pleased that I° shake off these names you give me.   allow me to
Antonio never yet was thief or pirate,
Though, I confess, on base and ground° enough   solid grounds
Orsino's enemy. A witchcraft drew me hither.
That most ingrateful boy there by your side
65   From the rude sea's enraged and foamy mouth
Did I redeem; a wreck past hope he was.
His life I gave him, and did thereto add
My love, without retention° or restraint,   reservation
All his in dedication. For his sake
70   Did I expose myself—pure° for his love—   purely
Into° the danger of this adverse° town,   unto / hostile
Drew to defend him when he was beset;
Where being apprehended, his false cunning,
Not meaning to partake with me in danger,
75   Taught him to face me out of his acquaintance°   deny knowing me
And grew a twenty years' removed° thing   estranged
While one would wink; denied me mine own purse,
Which I had recommended° to his use   entrusted
Not half an hour before.
VIOLA: How can this be?
ORSINO: When came he to this town?
ANTONIO: Today, my lord; and for three months before,
No interim, not a minute's vacancy,
Both day and night did we keep company.
[Enter Olivia and attendants.]
ORSINO: Here comes the Countess. Now heaven walks on earth.
85   But for thee, fellow—fellow, thy words are madness.
Three months this youth hath tended upon me;
But more of that anon. Take him aside.
OLIVIA [to Orsino]: What would my lord—but that° he may not have—   except what
Wherein Olivia may seem serviceable?—
90   Cesario, you do not keep promise with me.
VIOLA: Madam?
ORSINO: Gracious Olivia—
OLIVIA: What do you say, Cesario?—Good my lord—
VIOLA: My lord would speak. My duty hushes me.

OLIVIA: If it be aught to the old tune, my lord,
   It is as fat° and fulsome° to mine ear   *gross / offensive*
   As howling after music.
ORSINO: Still so cruel?
OLIVIA: Still so constant, lord.
ORSINO: What, to perverseness? You uncivil lady,
100 To whose ingrate° and unauspicious° altars   *ungrateful / unpromising*
   My soul the faithfull'st offerings have breathed out
   That e'er devotion tendered! What shall I do?
OLIVIA: Even what it please my lord that shall become° him.   *suit*
ORSINO: Why should I not, had I the heart to do it,
105 Like to th' Egyptian thief[17] at point of death
   Kill what I love?—a savage jealousy
   That sometimes savors nobly. But hear me this:
   Since you to nonregardance° cast my faith,   *neglect*
   And that° I partly know the instrument   *since*
110 That screws° me from my true place in your favor,   *pries*
   Live you the marble-breasted tyrant still.
   But this your minion,° whom I know you love,   *favorite*
   And whom, by heaven I swear, I tender° dearly,   *hold*
   Him will I tear out of that cruel eye
115 Where he sits crownèd in his master's spite.°—   *despite his master*
   Come, boy, with me. My thoughts are ripe in mischief.
   I'll sacrifice the lamb that I do love,
   To spite a raven's heart within a dove. [*Going.*]
VIOLA: And I, most jocund, apt,° and willingly,   *readily*
120 To do you rest,° a thousand deaths would die. [*Going.*] *give you peace*
OLIVIA: Where goes Cesario?
VIOLA: After him I love
   More than I love these eyes, more than my life,
   More by all mores° than e'er I shall love wife.   *all comparisons*
   If I do feign, you witnesses above
125 Punish my life for tainting of my love!
OLIVIA: Ay me, detested! How am I beguiled!
VIOLA: Who does beguile you? Who does do you wrong?
OLIVIA: Hast thou forgot thyself? Is it so long?
   Call forth the holy father.
                   [*Exit an attendant.*]
ORSINO [*to Viola*]:   Come, away!
OLIVIA: Whither, my lord? Cesario, husband, stay.
ORSINO: Husband?
OLIVIA: Ay, husband. Can he that deny?
ORSINO [*to Viola*]: Her husband, sirrah?[18]

17. Allusion to the *Ethiopica* by Heliodorus, in which the   18. Address to an inferior.
robber captain Thyamis kidnaps and falls in love with
Chariclea. Threatened with death, he tries to kill her
first.

VIOLA: No, my lord, not I.
OLIVIA: Alas, it is the baseness of thy fear
        That makes thee strangle thy propriety.°   *identity*
135   Fear not, Cesario, take thy fortunes up;
        Be that thou know'st thou art, and then thou art
        As great as that thou fear'st.°   *Orsino*
    [*Enter Priest.*]
                                    O, welcome, Father!
        Father, I charge thee by thy reverence
        Here to unfold—though lately we intended
140   To keep in darkness what occasion now
        Reveals before 'tis ripe—what thou dost know
        Hath newly passed between this youth and me.
PRIEST: A contract of eternal bond of love,
        Confirmed by mutual joinder° of your hands,   *joining*
145   Attested by the holy close° of lips,   *meeting*
        Strengthened by interchangement of your rings,
        And all the ceremony of this compact
        Sealed in my function, by my testimony;
        Since when, my watch hath told me, toward my grave
150   I have traveled but two hours.
ORSINO [*to Viola*]: O thou dissembling cub! What wilt thou be
        When time hath sowed a grizzle° on thy case?°   *gray hair / skin*
        Or will not else thy craft so quickly grow
        That thine own trip° shall be thine overthrow?   *trickery*
155   Farewell, and take her, but direct thy feet
        Where thou and I henceforth may never meet.
VIOLA: My Lord, I do protest—
OLIVIA: O, do not swear!
                    Hold little° faith, though thou hast too much fear.   *a little*
    [*Enter Sir Andrew.*]
SIR ANDREW: For the love of God, a surgeon! Send one presently[19] to Sir Toby.
OLIVIA: What's the matter?
SIR ANDREW: He's broke my head across, and has given Sir Toby a bloody cox-
        comb[20] too. For the love of God, your help! I had rather than forty pound I
        were at home.
OLIVIA: Who has done this, Sir Andrew?
SIR ANDREW: The Count's gentleman, one Cesario. We took him for a coward,
        but he's the very devil incardinate.[21]
ORSINO: My gentleman, Cesario?
SIR ANDREW: 'Od's lifelings,[22] here he is!—You broke my head for nothing, and
        that that I did I was set on to do 't by Sir Toby.
VIOLA: Why do you speak to me? I never hurt you.
        You drew your sword upon me without cause,

19. Immediately.   21. Incarnate.
20. Fool's cap (here, head).   22. By God's little lives.

But I bespake you fair, and hurt you not.

SIR ANDREW: If a bloody coxcomb be a hurt, you have hurt me. I think you set
nothing by a bloody coxcomb.

[Enter (Sir) Toby and Clown (Feste).]

175   Here comes Sir Toby, halting.[23] You shall hear more. But if he had not
been in drink, he would have tickled you othergates[24] than he did.

ORSINO: How now, gentleman? How is 't with you?

SIR TOBY: That's all one.[25] He's hurt me, and there's th' end on 't.—Sot,[26] didst
see Dick surgeon, sot?

FESTE: O, he's drunk, Sir Toby, an hour agone; his eyes were set[27] at eight i' the
morning.

SIR TOBY: Then he's a rogue, and a passy measures pavane.[28] I hate a drunken rogue.

OLIVIA: Away with him! Who hath made this havoc with them?

SIR ANDREW: I'll help you, Sir Toby, because we'll be dressed[29] together.

SIR TOBY: Will you help? An ass-head and a coxcomb and a knave, a thin-faced
knave, a gull!

OLIVIA: Get him to bed, and let his hurt be looked to.

                          [Exeunt Feste, Fabian, Sir Toby, and Sir Andrew.]

    [Enter Sebastian.]

SEBASTIAN: I am sorry, madam, I have hurt your kinsman;
But, had it been the brother of my blood,

190   I must have done no less with wit and safety.[30]—
You throw a strange regard° upon me, and by that   *estranged look*
I do perceive it hath offended you.
Pardon me, sweet one, even for the vows
We made each other but so late ago.

ORSINO: One face, one voice, one habit°, and two persons,   *dress*
A natural perspective,[31] that is and is not!

SEBASTIAN: Antonio, O my dear Antonio!
How have the hours racked and tortured me
Since I have lost thee!

ANTONIO: Sebastian are you?

SEBASTIAN: Fear'st thou° that, Antonio?   *do you doubt*

ANTONIO: How have you made division of yourself?
An apple cleft in two is not more twin
Than these two creatures. Which is Sebastian?

OLIVIA: Most wonderful!

SEBASTIAN [seeing Viola]: Do I stand there? I never had a brother;
Nor can there be that deity in my nature
Of here and everywhere.° I had a sister,   *omnipresence*
Whom the blind° waves and surges have devoured.   *heedless*
Of charity,° what kin are you to me?   *tell me in kindness*

210   What countryman? What name? What parentage?

---

23. Limping.
24. Otherwise.
25. It doesn't matter.
26. Drunkard.
27. Closed.

28. Slow dance.
29. Have our wounds dressed.
30. With an intelligent regard for my safety.
31. Optical illusion.

VIOLA: Of Messaline. Sebastian was my father.
        Such a Sebastian was my brother, too.
        So went he suited° to his watery tomb.   *dressed*
        If spirits can assume both form and suit,
        You come to fright us.
SEBASTIAN: A spirit I am indeed,
        But am in that dimension grossly clad°   *clothed in the flesh*
        Which from the womb I did participate.°   *inherit*
        Were you a woman, as the rest goes even,°   *circumstances allow*
        I should my tears let fall upon your cheek
220   And say, "Thrice welcome, drownèd Viola!"
VIOLA: My father had a mole upon his brow.
SEBASTIAN: And so had mine.
VIOLA: And died that day when Viola from her birth
        Had numbered thirteen years.
SEBASTIAN: O, that record° is lively in my soul!   *memory*
        He finishèd indeed his mortal act
        That day that made my sister thirteen years.
VIOLA: If nothing lets° to make us happy both   *hinders*
        But this my masculine usurped attire,
230   Do not embrace me till each circumstance
        Of place, time, fortune, do cohere and jump°   *agree completely*
        That I am Viola—which to confirm
        I'll bring you to a captain in this town
        Where lie my maiden weeds,° by whose gentle help   *clothes*
235   I was preserved to serve this noble count.
        All the occurrence of my fortune since
        Hath been between this lady and this lord.
SEBASTIAN [*to Olivia*]: So comes it, lady, you have been mistook.
        But nature to her bias drew° in that.   *followed her bent*
240   You would have been contracted to a maid,°   *virgin man*
        Nor are you therein, by my life, deceived.
        You are betrothed both to a maid and man.
ORSINO [*to Olivia*]: Be not amazed; right noble is his blood.
        If this be so, as yet the glass° seems true,   *natural perspective*
245   I shall have share in this most happy wreck.
        [*To Viola.*] Boy, thou hast said to me a thousand times
        Thou never shouldst love woman like to° me.   *as much as*
VIOLA: And all those sayings will I over swear,°   *swear again*
        And all those swearings keep as true in soul
250   As doth that orbèd continent° the fire   *the Sun*
        That severs day from night.
ORSINO: Give me thy hand,
        And let me see thee in thy woman's weeds.
VIOLA: The captain that did bring me first on shore
        Hath my maid's garments. He upon some action°   *legal charge*
255   Is now in durance,° at Malvolio's suit,   *imprisonment*
        A gentleman and follower of my lady's.

OLIVIA: He shall enlarge° him. Fetch Malvolio hither.   *release*
      And yet, alas, now I remember me,
      They say, poor gentleman, he's much distract.
    [*Enter Clown (Feste) with a letter, and Fabian.*]
260   A most extracting° frenzy of mine own   *distracting*
      From my remembrance clearly banished his.
      How does he, sirrah?

FESTE: Truly, madam, he holds Beelzebub at the stave's end[32] as well as a man in
      his case may do. He's here writ a letter to you; I should have given 't you today
265   morning. But as a madman's epistles are no gospels, so it skills[33] not much
      when they are delivered.

OLIVIA: Open 't and read it.

FESTE: Look then to be well edified when the fool delivers[34] the madman. [*He reads
      loudly.*] "By the Lord, madam—"

OLIVIA: How now, art thou mad?

FESTE: No, madam, I do but read madness. An your ladyship will have it as it ought
      to be, you must allow *vox*.[35]

OLIVIA: Prithee, read i' thy right wits.[36]

FESTE: So I do, madonna; but to read his right wits is to read thus. Therefore per-
275   pend,[37] my princess, and give ear.

OLIVIA [*to Fabian*]: Read it you, sirrah.

FABIAN [*reads*]: "By the Lord, madam, you wrong me, and the world shall know it.
      Though you have put me into darkness and given your drunken cousin rule
      over me, yet have I the benefit of my senses as well as your ladyship. I have
280   your own letter that induced me to the semblance I put on, with the which I
      doubt not but to do myself much right or you much shame. Think of me as
      you please. I leave my duty a little unthought of, and speak out of my injury.
                                        The madly used Malvolio."

OLIVIA: Did he write this?

FESTE: Ay, madam.

ORSINO: This savors not much of distraction.

OLIVIA: See him delivered,° Fabian. Bring him hither.   *released*
                                                    [*Exit Fabian.*]

      My lord, so please you, these things further thought on,
      To think me as well a sister as a wife,
290   One day shall crown th' alliance on 't, so please you,
      Here at my house and at my proper° cost.   *own*

ORSINO: Madam, I am most apt° t' embrace your offer.   *ready*
      [*To Viola.*] Your master quits° you; and for your service done him,   *releases*
      So much against the mettle° of your sex,   *disposition*
295   So far beneath your soft and tender breeding,
      And since you called me master for so long,
      Here is my hand. You shall from this time be
      Your master's mistress.

---

32. Holds the devil off.   35. Loud voice.
33. Matters.   36. I.e., express his true state of mind.
34. Speaks the words of.   37. Consider.

OLIVIA: A sister! You are she.
    [*Enter (Fabian with) Malvolio.*]
ORSINO: Is this the madman?
OLIVIA: Ay, my lord, this same.
    How now, Malvolio?
MALVOLIO: Madam, you have done me wrong
    Notorious wrong.
OLIVIA: Have I, Malvolio? No.
MALVOLIO [*showing a letter*]: Lady, you have. Pray you, peruse that letter.
    You must not now deny it is your hand.
    Write from it,° if you can, in hand or phrase,   *differently*
305   Or say 'tis not your seal, not your invention.°   *composition*
    You can say none of this. Well, grant it then,
    And tell me, in the modesty of honor,
    Why you have given me such clear lights° of favor,   *signs*
    Bade me come smiling and cross-gartered to you,
310   To put on yellow stockings, and to frown
    Upon Sir Toby and the lighter° people?   *lesser*
    And, acting this in an obedient hope,
    Why have you suffered me to be imprisoned,
    Kept in a dark house, visited by the priest,°   *Feste*
315   And made the most notorious geck° and gull   *dupe*
    That e'er invention played on? Tell me why?
OLIVIA: Alas, Malvolio, this is not my writing,
    Though, I confess, much like the character;°   *my handwriting*
    But out of° question 'tis Maria's hand.   *beyond*
320   And now I do bethink me, it was she
    First told me thou wast mad; then cam'st in smiling,
    And in such forms which here were presupposed°   *pre-imposed*
    Upon thee in the letter. Prithee, be content.
    This practice° hath most shrewdly° passed upon thee;   *plot / mischievously*
325   But when we know the grounds and authors of it,
    Thou shalt be both the plaintiff and the judge
    Of thine own cause.
FABIAN: Good madam, hear me speak,
    And let no quarrel nor no brawl to come
    Taint the condition of this present hour,
330   Which I have wondered at. In hope it shall not,
    Most freely I confess, myself and Toby
    Set this device against Malvolio here,
    Upon° some stubborn and uncourteous parts°   *because of / qualities*
    We had conceived against him. Maria writ
335   The letter at Sir Toby's great importance,°   *importunity*
    In recompense whereof he hath married her.
    How with a sportful malice it was followed°   *carried out*
    May rather pluck on° laughter than revenge,   *induce*
    If that the injuries be justly weighed
340   That have on both sides passed.

OLIVIA [*to Malvolio*]: Alas, poor fool, how have they baffled° thee!   *disgraced*

FESTE: Why, "Some are born great, some achieve greatness, and some have greatness thrown upon them." I was one, sir, in this interlude,[38] one Sir Topas, sir,
but that's all one. "By the Lord, fool, I am not mad." But do you remember?
345   "Madam, why laugh you at such a barren rascal? An you smile not, he's
gagged." And thus the whirligig[39] of time brings in his revenges.

MALVOLIO: I'll be revenged on the whole pack of you!   [*Exit.*]

OLIVIA: He hath been most notoriously abused.

ORSINO: Pursue him, and entreat him to a peace.
350   He hath not told us of the captain yet.
When that is known, and golden time convents,°   *is convenient*
A solemn combination shall be made
Of our dear souls. Meantime, sweet sister,
We will not part from hence. Cesario, come—
355   For so you shall be, while you are a man;
But when in other habits° you are seen,   *attire*
Orsino's mistress and his fancy's° queen.   *love's*

[*Exeunt (all, except Feste).*]

FESTE [*sings*]:   When that I was and a little tiny boy,
With hey, ho, the wind and the rain,
360   A foolish thing was but a toy,°   *trifle*
For the rain it raineth every day.

But when I came to man's estate,
With hey, ho, the wind and the rain,
'Gainst knaves and thieves men shut their gate,
365   For the rain it raineth every day.

But when I came, alas, to wive,
With hey, ho, the wind and the rain,
By swaggering could I never thrive,
For the rain it raineth every day.

370   But when I came unto my beds,
With hey, ho, the wind and the rain,
With tosspots° still had drunken heads,   *drunkards*
For the rain it raineth every day.

A great while ago the world begun,
375   With hey, ho, the wind and the rain,
But that's all one, our play is done,
And we'll strive to please you every day.

[*Exit.*]

---

38. Little play.   39. Spinning top.

Ben Jonson
1572–1637

On Something, That Walks Somewhere

At court I met it, in clothes brave° enough   *showy*
    To be a courtier, and looks grave enough
To seem a statesman. As I near it came,
    It made me a great face; I asked the name.
5 "A lord," it cried, "buried in flesh, and blood,
    And such from whom let no man hope least good,
For I will do none; and as little ill,
    For I will dare none." Good lord, walk dead still.

On My First Son[1]

Farewell, thou child of my right hand,[2] and joy;
    My sin was too much hope of thee, loved boy.
Seven years thou wert lent to me, and I thee pay,
    Exacted by thy fate, on the just day.
5 O, could I lose all father, now![3] For why
    Will man lament the state he should envy?
To have so soon 'scaped world's and flesh's rage,
    And, if no other misery, yet age?
Rest in soft peace, and, asked, say, "Here doth lie
10   Ben Jonson his best piece of poetry."
For whose sake, henceforth, all his vows be such,
    As what he loves may never like too much.[4]

Song to Celia

Drink to me only with thine eyes,
    And I will pledge with mine;
Or leave a kiss but in the cup,
    And I'll not look for wine.
5 The thirst that from the soul doth rise
    Doth ask a drink divine;
But might I of Jove's nectar sup,
    I would not change for thine.
I sent thee late a rosy wreath,
10   Not so much honoring thee
As giving it a hope that there
    It could not withered be.

---

1. Benjamin, who died of the plague on his birthday in 1603.
2. In Hebrew, Benjamin means "son of the right hand; dexterous, fortunate."
3. Let go of fatherly feeling.
4. "If you wish . . . to beware of sorrows that gnaw the heart, to no man make yourself too much a comrade" (Martial 12.34, lines 8–11).

But thou thereon didst only breathe,
   And sent'st it back on me;
15 Since when it grows, and smells, I swear,
   Not of itself, but thee.

John Donne
1572–1631

The Good Morrow[1]

I wonder by my troth, what thou, and I
Did, till we loved? Were we not weaned till then?
But sucked on country pleasures, childishly?
Or snorted we in the seven sleepers' den?[2]
5 'Twas so; but this, all pleasures fancies be.
If ever any beauty I did see,
Which I desired, and got, 'twas but a dream of thee.

And now good morrow to our waking souls,
Which watch not one another out of fear;
10 For love, all love of other sights controls,
And makes one little room, an everywhere.
Let sea-discoverers to new worlds have gone,
Let maps to others, worlds on worlds have shown,
Let us possess one world, each hath one, and is one.

15 My face in thine eye, thine in mine appears,
And true plain hearts do in the faces rest.
Where can we find two better hemispheres
Without sharp north, without declining west?
What ever dies was not mixed equally;[3]
20 If our two loves be one, or, thou and I
Love so alike, that none do slacken, none can die.

A Valediction: Forbidding Mourning[1]

As virtuous men pass mildly away,
   And whisper to their souls, to go,
Whilst some of their sad friends do say,
   The breath goes now, and some say, no:

1. Donne's love poems, written over a period of 20 years, cannot be dated with any certainty. They were first printed in 1633, scattered throughout the entire collection of poems. Then, in the 1635 edition, the love poems were printed as a group under the title *Songs and Sonnets*. There is no certainty that the titles were chosen by Donne.
2. Legendary cave where seven Ephesian youths were put to sleep by God to escape the persecution of Christians by the Emperor Decius (249).
3. According to ancient medicine, death was caused by an imbalance of elements in the body.

1. In his *Life of Dr. John Donne* (1640), Walton describes the occasion as Donne's farewell to his wife before his journey to France in 1611.

5   So let us melt, and make no noise,
       No tear-floods, nor sigh-tempests move,
     'Twere profanation° of our joys   *desecration*
       To tell the laity[2] of our love.

     Moving of th'earth brings harms and fears,
10   Men reckon what it did and meant,
     But trepidation of the spheres,[3]
       Though greater far, is innocent.

     Dull sublunary[4] lovers' love
       (Whose soul is sense) cannot admit
15   Absence, because it doth remove
       Those things which elemented° it.   *composed*

     But we by a love, so much refined,
       That our selves know not what it is,
     Inter-assurèd of the mind,
20   Care less, eyes, lips, and hands to miss.

     Our two souls therefore, which are one,
       Though I must go, endure not yet
     A breach, but an expansion,
       Like gold to airy thinness beat.[5]

25   If they be two, they are two so
       As stiff twin compasses[6] are two,
     Thy soul the fixed foot, makes no show
       To move, but doth, if th' other do.

     And though it in the center sit,
30   Yet when the other far doth roam,
     It leans, and hearkens after it,
       And grows erect, as that comes home.

     Such wilt thou be to me, who must
       Like th' other foot, obliquely run;
35   Thy firmness makes my circle just,°   *complete*
       And makes me end, where I begun.

from Holy Sonnets

Divine Meditations

6

Death be not proud, though some have called thee
Mighty and dreadful, for thou are not so.
For, those, whom thou think'st thou dost overthrow,

---

2. The uninitiated.
3. Though the movement of the spheres is greater than an earthquake, we feel its effects less.
4. Under the sphere of the moon, hence sensual.

5. Gold was beaten to produce gold leaf. "Airy" suggests their love will become so fine that it will be spiritual.
6. A common emblem of constancy amidst change.

Die not, poor death, nor yet canst thou kill me;
5   From rest and sleep, which but thy pictures be,
Much pleasure, then from thee, much more must flow,
And soonest our best men with thee do go,
Rest of their bones, and soul's delivery.
Thou art slave to fate, chance, kings, and desperate men,
10   And dost with poison, war, and sickness dwell,
And poppy,° or charms can make us sleep as well,   *a narcotic*
And better than thy stroke; why swell'st° thou then?   *grow in pride*
One short sleep past, we wake eternally,
And death shall be no more. Death thou shalt die.[1]

Lady Mary Wroth
1586?–1652?

from A Crown of Sonnets Dedicated to Love[1]
77

In this strange labyrinth how shall I turn?
    Ways° are on all sides while the way I miss: *paths*
    If to the right hand, there, in love I burn;
    Let me go forward, therein danger is;
5   If to the left, suspicion hinders bliss,
    Let me turn back, shame cries I ought return,
    Nor faint° though crosses with my fortunes kiss;[2]   *lose heart*
    Stand still is harder, although sure to mourn.[3]
Thus let me take the right, or left-hand way,
10   Go forward, or stand still, or back retire;
    I must these doubts endure without allay°   *relief*
    Or help, but travail[4] find for my best hire.
Yet that which most my troubled sense doth move
Is to leave all, and take the thread of love.[5]

1. "The last enemy that shall be destroyed is death" (1 Corinthians 15.26).
1. The crown (Italian *corona*) is a form in which the last line of each poem is repeated as the first line of the next. The last poem of the sequence ends with the first line of the first poem.
2. Though troubles embrace my luck, or fate.
3. It is more difficult to do nothing, although this is sure to make me mourn.
4. Hard work, with word play on "Travel," which occurs in the 1621 text.
5. An allusion to the myth of Ariadne, beloved of Theseus, to whom she gave a thread to unwind behind him on his path through the labyrinth so that, after slaying the Minotaur, he could retrace his steps on his way out.

Robert Herrick
1591–1674

from HESPERIDES
The Argument of His Book[1]

I sing of brooks, of blossoms, birds, and bowers,
Of April, May, of June, and July flowers.
I sing of Maypoles, hock carts, wassails, wakes,[2]
Of bridegrooms, brides, and of their bridal cakes.
5   I write of youth, of love, and have access
By these, to sing of cleanly wantonness.°   *carefree abandon*
I sing of dews, of rains, and piece by piece,
Of balm, of oil, of spice, and ambergris.[3]
I sing of times trans-shifting;[4] and I write
10   How roses first came red, and lilies white.
I write of groves, of twilights, and I sing
The court of Mab,[5] and of the fairy king.
I write of hell; I sing (and ever shall)
Of Heaven, and hope to have it after all.

Delight in Disorder

A sweet disorder in the dress
Kindles in clothes a wantonness:
A lawn° about the shoulders thrown   *scarf*
Into a fine distraction;
5   An erring° lace, which here and there   *wandering*
Enthralls the crimson stomacher:[1]
A cuff neglectful, and thereby
Ribbons to flow confusedly:
A winning wave, deserving note,
10   In the tempestuous petticoat;
A carelesse shoestring, in whose tie
I see a wild civility:
Do more bewitch me, than when art
Is too precise[2] in every part.

To the Virgins, to Make Much of Time

Gather ye rosebuds while ye may,
    Old time is still a-flying;[1]
And this same flower that smiles today,
    Tomorrow will be dying.

---

1. All of Herrick's poems were published in 1648. The "Argument" introduces the book's themes.
2. Hock carts: harvest wagons; wassails: drinking toasts; wakes: celebrations in honor of the dedication of a parish church.
3. Secretion from the intestines of sperm whales, used to make perfume.

4. Times changing and passing; the cycle of the seasons.
5. Queen of the fairies.
1. Ornamental covering for the chest worn under the lacing of the bodice.
2. "Precise" was often used to describe the strictness of the Puritans.
1. The Latin tag *tempus fugit* ("time flies").

5 The glorious lamp of heaven, the sun,
  The higher he's a-getting;
 The sooner will his race be run,[2]
  And nearer he's to setting.

 That age is best, which is the first,
10 When youth and blood are warmer;
 But being spent, the worse, and worst
  Times still succeed the former.

 Then be not coy, but use your time,
  And while ye may, go marry;
15 For having lost but once your prime,
  You may for ever tarry.

Andrew Marvell
1621–1678

To His Coy Mistress[1]

Had we but world enough, and time,
This coyness, Lady, were no crime.
We would sit down, and think which way
To walk, and pass our long love's day.
5 Thou by the Indian Ganges' side
Shouldst rubies find: I by the tide
Of Humber would complain.[2] I would
Love you ten years before the flood:
And you should if you please refuse
10 Till the conversion of the Jews.[3]
My vegetable love should grow
Vaster than empires, and more slow.[4]
An hundred years should go to praise
Thine eyes, and on thy forehead gaze.
15 Two hundred to adore each breast:
But thirty thousand to the rest.
An age at least to every part,
And the last age should show your heart.
For Lady you deserve this state;
20 Nor would I love at lower rate.
 But at my back I always hear
Times wingèd chariot hurrying near:
And yonder all before us lie
Deserts of vast eternity.

2. In Greek mythology, the sun was seen as the chariot of Apollo drawn across the sky each day as in a race.
1. A poem on the theme of *carpe diem* ("seize the day") that includes a blazon, or description of the lady from head to toe, and a logical argument: "If . . . But . . . Therefore."
2. Marvell grew up in Hull on the Humber River.

3. The end of time: the Flood occurred in the distant past, and Christians prophesied that Jews would convert to Christianity at the end of the world.
4. The "vegetable" was characterized only by growth, in contrast to the sensitive, which felt, and the rational, which could reason.

25 Thy beauty shall no more be found;
    Nor, in thy marble vault, shall sound
    My echoing song: then worms shall try
    That long preserved virginity:
    And your quaint honor turn to dust;[5]
30 And into ashes all my lust.
    The grave's a fine and private place,
    But none, I think, do there embrace.
        Now, therefore, while the youthful hue
    Sits on thy skin like morning dew,[6]
35 And while thy willing soul transpires
    At every pore with instant fires,
    Now let us sport us while we may;
    And now, like amorous birds of prey,
    Rather at once our time devour,
40 Than languish in his slow-chapped° power.   *slowly biting*
    Let us roll all our strength, and all
    Our sweetness, up into one ball:
    And tear our pleasures with rough strife,
    Thorough the iron gates of life.[7]
45 Thus, though we cannot make our sun
    Stand still, yet we will make him run.[8]

John Milton

1608–1674

How Soon Hath Time

    How soon hath time the subtle thief of youth,
        Stol'n on his wing my three and twentieth year![1]
        My hasting days fly on with full career,°   *speed*
        But my late spring no bud or blossom shew'th.
5   Perhaps my semblance° might deceive the truth,   *appearance*
        That I to manhood am arrived so near,
        And inward ripeness doth much less appear,
        That some more timely-happy spirits[2] endu'th.°   *gives, endows*
    Yet be it less or more, or soon or slow,
10   It shall be still° in strictest measure even,°   *always / level with*
        To that same lot, however mean or high,
    Toward which Time leads me, and the will of Heaven;
        All is, if I have grace to use it so,
        As ever in my great task Master's° eye.   *God's*

---

5. "Quaint honor," proud chastity.
6. In the 1681 Folio, "dew" reads "glue," and in two manuscripts the rhymes in lines 33 and 34 are "glue" and "dew."
7. One manuscript reads "grates" for "gates."
8. Joshua made the sun stand still in the war against Gibeon (see Joshua 10.12).

1. Written when Milton was 23, this sonnet was published in 1645.
2. Those individuals of Milton's age who have already achieved success.

When I Consider How My Light Is Spent[1]

When I consider how my light is spent,
　Ere half my days, in this dark world and wide,
　And that one talent which is death to hide,[2]
　Lodged with me useless, though my soul more bent
5　To serve therewith my Maker, and present
　My true account, lest he returning chide,
　Doth God exact day-labor, light denied,
　I fondly° ask; but Patience to prevent   *foolishly*
　That murmur, soon replies, "God doth not need
10　Either man's work or his own gifts,[3] who best
　Bear his mild yoke,[4] they serve him best, his state
　Is kingly. Thousands at his bidding speed
　And post o'er land and ocean without rest:
　They also serve who only stand and wait."

from **Paradise Lost**[1]

from **Book 1**

　Of Man's First Disobedience, and the Fruit
　Of that Forbidden Tree, whose mortal[2] taste
　Brought Death into the World, and all our woe,[3]
　With loss of *Eden*, till one greater Man[4]
5　Restore us, and regain the blissful Seat,
　Sing Heav'nly Muse,[5] that on the secret top
　Of *Oreb*, or of *Sinai*, didst inspire
　That Shepherd, who first taught the chosen Seed,[6]
　In the Beginning how the Heav'ns and Earth
10　Rose out of *Chaos*: Or if *Sion* Hill[7]
　Delight thee more, and *Siloa's* Brook[8] that flow'd
　Fast° by the Oracle of God; I thence   *close*
　Invoke thy aid to my advent'rous Song,
　That with no middle flight intends to soar

1. Probably written around 1652, as Milton's blindness became complete.
2. In the parable of the talents, Jesus tells of a servant who is given a talent (a large sum of money) to keep for his master. He buries the money; his master condemns him for not having invested it wisely. Matthew 25.14–30.
3. See Job 22.2.
4. See Matthew 11.30: "My yoke is easy."
1. Our text is taken from Merritt Y. Hughes, ed., *John Milton Complete Poems and Major Prose*, and the notes are adapted from John Carey and Alastair Fowler, eds., *The Poems of John Milton*.
2. "Death-bringing" (Latin *mortalis*) but also "to mortals."
3. This definition of the first sin follows Calvin's Catechism.
4. Christ, in Pauline theology the second Adam (see Romans 5.19). The people and events referred to in these lines have a typological connection, i.e., the Christian interpretation of the Old Testament as a prefiguration of the New.

5. Rhetorically, lines 1–49 are the *invocatio*, consisting of an address to the Muse, and the *principium* that states the whole scope of the poem's action. The "Heavenly Muse," later addressed as the muse of astronomy Urania (7.1), is here identified with the Holy Spirit of the Bible, which inspires Moses.
6. The "Shepherd" is Moses, who was granted the vision of the burning bush on Mount Oreb (Exodus 3) and received the Law, either on Mount Oreb (Deuteronomy 4.10) or on its lower part, Mount Sinai (Exodus 19.20). Moses, the first Jewish writer, taught "the chosen seed," the children of Israel, about the beginning of the world in Genesis.
7. The sanctuary, a place of ceremonial song but also (Isaiah 2.3) of oracular pronouncements.
8. A spring immediately west of Mount Zion and beside Calvary, often used as a symbol of the operation of the Holy Ghost.

15	Above th' *Aonian* Mount,[9] while it pursues
	Things unattempted yet in Prose or Rhyme.[10]
	And chiefly Thou O Spirit, that dost prefer
	Before all Temples th' upright heart and pure,[11]
	Instruct me, for Thou know'st; Thou from the first
20	Wast present, and with mighty wings outspread
	Dove-like satst brooding on the vast Abyss
	And mad'st it pregnant:[12] What in me is dark
	Illumine, what is low raise and support;
	That to the highth of this great Argument°
25	I may assert Eternal Providence,
	And justify[13] the ways of God to men.
	Say first, for Heav'n hides nothing from thy view
	Nor the deep Tract of Hell, say first what cause
	Mov'd our Grand[14] Parents in that happy State,
30	Favor'd of Heav'n so highly, to fall off
	From thir Creator, and transgress his Will
	For° one restraint, Lords of the World besides?°
	Who first seduc'd them to that foul revolt?
	Th' infernal Serpent;[15] hee it was, whose guile
35	Stirr'd up with Envy and Revenge, deceiv'd
	The Mother of Mankind; what time his Pride
	Had cast him out from Heav'n, with all his Host
	Of Rebel Angels, by whose aid aspiring
	To set himself in Glory above his Peers,
40	He trusted to have equall'd the most High,[16]
	If he oppos'd; and with ambitious aim
	Against the Throne and Monarchy of God
	Rais'd impious War in Heav'n and Battle proud
	With vain attempt. Him the Almighty Power
45	Hurl'd headlong flaming from th' Ethereal Sky[17]
	With hideous ruin and combustion down
	To bottomless perdition, there to dwell
	In Adamantine Chains[18] and penal Fire,
	Who durst defy th' Omnipotent to Arms.
50	Nine times the Space that measures Day and Night[19]
	To mortal men, hee with his horrid crew

theme (gloss for line 24, "Argument")

because of / otherwise (gloss for line 32, "For" / "besides")

9. Helicon, sacred to the Muses.
10. Ironically translating Ariosto's boast in the invocation to *Orlando Furioso*.
11. The Spirit is the voice of God, which inspired the Hebrew prophets.
12. Identifying the Spirit present at the creation (Genesis 1.2) with the Spirit in the form of a dove that descended on Jesus at the beginning of his ministry (John 1.32). Vast: large; deserted (Latin *vastus*).
13. Does not mean merely "demonstrate logically" but has its biblical meaning and implies spiritual rather than rational understanding.
14. Implies not only greatness, but also inclusiveness of generality or parentage.
15. "That old serpent, called the Devil, and Satan" (Revelation 12.9) both because Satan entered the body of a serpent to tempt Eve and because his nature is guileful and dangerous to humans.
16. Satan's crime was not his aspiring "above his peers" but aspiring "To set himself in [divine] Glory." Numerous verbal echoes relate lines 40–48 to the biblical accounts of the fall and binding of Lucifer, in 2 Peter 2.4, Revelation 20.1–2, and Isaiah 14.12–15: "Thou hast said . . . I will exalt my throne above the stars of God . . . I will be like the most High. Yet thou shalt be brought down to hell."
17. Mingling an allusion to Luke 10.18, "I beheld Satan as lightning fall from heaven," with one to Homer, *Iliad* 1.591, Hephaistos "hurled from the ethereal threshold."
18. 2 Peter 2.4; "God spared not the angels that sinned, but . . . delivered them into chains of darkness."
19. The devils fall for the same number of days that the Titans fall from heaven when overthrown by the Olympian gods (see Hesiod, *Theogony* 664–735).

Lay vanquisht, rolling in the fiery Gulf
Confounded though immortal: But his doom
Reserv'd him to more wrath; for now the thought
55 Both of lost happiness and lasting pain
Torments him; round he throws his baleful° eyes   *evil, suffering*
That witness'd huge affliction and dismay
Mixt with obdúrate° pride and steadfast hate: *unyielding*
At once as far as Angels' ken° he views   *power of vision*
60 The dismal° Situation waste and wild,   *dreadful, sinister*
A Dungeon horrible, on all sides round
As one great Furnace flam'd, yet from those flames
No light, but rather darkness visible
Serv'd only to discover sights of woe,[20]
65 Regions of sorrow, doleful shades, where peace
And rest can never dwell, hope never comes
That comes to all;[21] but torture without end
Still urges,° and a fiery Deluge, fed   *presses*
With ever-burning Sulphur unconsum'd:
70 Such place Eternal Justice had prepar'd
For those rebellious, here thir Prison ordained
In utter° darkness, and thir portion set   *complete, outer*
As far remov'd from God and light of Heav'n
As from the Center thrice to th' utmost Pole.[22]
75 O how unlike the place from whence they fell!
There the companions of his fall, o'erwhelm'd
With Floods and Whirlwinds of tempestuous fire,
He soon discerns, and welt'ring by his side
One next himself in power, and next in crime,
80 Long after known in *Palestine,* and nam'd
Beëlzebub.[23] To whom th' Arch-Enemy,
And thence in Heav'n call'd Satan,[24] with bold words
Breaking the horrid silence thus began.[25]
        If thou beest hee; But O how fall'n! how chang'd
85 From him, who in the happy Realms of Light
Cloth'd with transcendent brightness didst outshine
Myriads though bright:[26] If he whom mutual league,
United thoughts and counsels, equal hope,
And hazard in the Glorious Enterprise,
90 Join'd with me once, now misery hath join'd
In equal ruin: into what Pit thou seest
From what highth fall'n, so much the stronger prov'd

20. See the account of the land of the dead in Job 10.22: "the light is as darkness."
21. The phrase echoes Dante's *Inferno:* III.9 "All hope abandon, ye who enter here."
22. Milton refers to the Ptolemaic universe in which the earth is at the center of ten concentric spheres. Milton draws attention to the numerical proportion, heaven-earth:earth-hell—i.e., earth divides the interval between heaven and hell in the proportion that Neoplatonists believed should be maintained between reason and con-cupiscence.
23. Hebrew, "Lord of the flies"; Matthew 12.24, "the prince of the devils."
24. Hebrew, "enemy." After his rebellion, Satan's "former name" (Lucifer) was no longer used (5.658).
25. Rhetorically, the opening of the action proper. The 41-line speech beginning here, the first speech in the book, exactly balances the last, which also is spoken by Satan and also consists of 41 lines (1.622–62).
26. The break in grammatical concord (between "him" and "didst") reflects Satan's doubt whether Beelzebub is present and so whether second-person forms are appropriate.

He with his Thunder: and till then who knew
The force of those dire Arms? yet not for those,
95   Nor what the Potent Victor in his rage
Can else inflict, do I repent or change,
Though chang'd in outward luster; that fixt mind
And high disdain, from sense of injur'd merit,
That with the mightiest rais'd me to contend,
100   And to the fierce contention brought along
Innumerable force of Spirits arm'd
That durst dislike his reign, and mee preferring,
His utmost power with adverse power oppos'd
In dubious Battle on the Plains of Heav'n,
105   And shook his throne.[27] What though the field be lost?
All is not lost; the unconquerable Will,
And study° of revenge, immortal hate,   *pursuit*
And courage never to submit or yield:
And what is else not to be overcome?
110   That Glory[28] never shall his wrath or might
Extort from me. To bow and sue for grace
With suppliant knee, and deify his power
Who from the terror of this Arm so late
Doubted° his Empire, that were low indeed,   *feared for*
115   That were an ignominy and shame beneath
This downfall; since by Fate the strength of Gods
And this Empyreal substance cannot fail,[29]
Since through experience of this great event
In Arms not worse, in foresight much advanc't,
120   We may with more successful hope resolve
To wage by force or guile eternal War
Irreconcilable to our grand Foe,
Who now triúmphs, and in th' excess of joy
Sole reigning holds the Tyranny of Heav'n.[30]
125   So spake th' Apostate Angel, though in pain,
Vaunting aloud, but rackt with deep despair:
And him thus answer'd soon his bold Compeer.°   *comrade*
    O Prince, O Chief of many Throned Powers,
That led th' imbattl'd Seraphim[31] to War
130   Under thy conduct, and in dreadful deeds
Fearless, endanger'd Heav'n's perpetual King;
And put to proof his high Supremacy,
Whether upheld by strength, or Chance, or Fate;[32]
Too well I see and rue the dire event,
135   That with sad overthrow and foul defeat
Hath lost us Heav'n, and all this mighty Host

27. The Son's chariot, not Satan's armies, shakes heaven to its foundations, as we learn in Book 6. Throughout the present passage, Satan sees himself as the hero of a pagan epic.
28. Either "the glory of overcoming me" or "my glory of will."
29. Implying not only that as angels they are immortal, but also that the continuance of their strength is assured by fate.

30. An obvious instance of the devil's bias.
31. The traditional nine orders of angels are seraphim, cherubim, thrones, dominions, virtues, powers, principalities, archangels, and angels, but Milton does not use these terms systematically.
32. The main powers recognized in the devils' ideology. God's power rests on a quality that does not occur to Beelzebub: goodness.

In horrible destruction laid thus low,
As far as Gods and Heav'nly Essences
Can perish: for the mind and spirit remains
140   Invincible, and vigor soon returns,
Though all our Glory extinct, and happy state
Here swallow'd up in endless misery.
But what if he our Conqueror (whom I now
Of force° believe Almighty, since no less   *necessarily*
145   Than such could have o'erpow'rd such force as ours)
Have left us this our spirit and strength entire
Strongly to suffer and support our pains,
That we may so suffice° his vengeful ire,   *satisfy*
Or do him mightier service as his thralls
150   By right of War, whate'er his business be
Here in the heart of Hell to work in Fire,
Or do his Errands in the gloomy Deep;
What can it then avail though yet we feel
Strength undiminisht, or eternal being
155   To undergo eternal punishment?[33]
Whereto with speedy words th' Arch-fiend repli'd.
    Fall'n Cherub, to be weak is miserable
Doing or Suffering: but of this be sure,
To do aught good never will be our task,
160   But ever to do ill our sole delight,
As being the contrary to his high will
Whom we resist.[34] If then his Providence
Out of our evil seek to bring forth good,
Our labor must be to pervert that end,
165   And out of good still to find means of evil;
Which oft-times may succeed, so as perhaps
Shall grieve him, if I fail not, and disturb
His inmost counsels from thir destin'd aim.
But see the angry Victor hath recall'd
170   His Ministers of vengeance and pursuit
Back to the Gates of Heav'n: the Sulphurous Hail
Shot after us in storm, o'erblown hath laid°   *subdued*
The fiery Surge, that from the Precipice
Of Heav'n receiv'd us falling, and the Thunder,
175   Wing'd with red Lightning and impetuous rage,
Perhaps hath spent his shafts, and ceases now
To bellow through the vast and boundless Deep.
Let us not slip° th' occasion, whether scorn,   *lose*
Or satiate fury yield it from our Foe.
180   Seest thou yon dreary Plain, forlorn and wild,
The seat of desolation, void of light,
Save what the glimmering of these livid flames
Casts pale and dreadful? Thither let us tend

33. Existing eternally, merely so that our punishment may also be eternal.
34. This fundamental disobedience and disorientation make Satan's heroic virtue into the corresponding excess of vice. Lines 163–65 look forward to 12.470–78 and Adam's wonder at the astonishing reversal whereby God will turn the Fall into an occasion for good.

From off the tossing of these fiery waves,
185   There rest, if any rest can harbor there,
And reassembling our afflicted° Powers,   *downcast*
Consult how we may henceforth most offend°   *harm*
Our Enemy, our own loss how repair,
How overcome this dire Calamity,
190   What reinforcement we may gain from Hope,
If not what resolution from despair.
       Thus Satan talking to his nearest Mate
With Head up-lift above the wave, and Eyes
That sparkling blaz'd, his other Parts besides
195   Prone on the Flood, extended long and large
Lay floating many a rood,° in bulk as huge   *six to eight yards*
As whom the Fables name of monstrous size,
Titanian, or *Earth-born*, that warr'd on *Jove*,
Briareos or *Typhon*,[35] whom the Den
200   By ancient *Tarsus*[36] held, or that Sea-beast
Leviathan,[37] which God of all his works
Created hugest that swim th' Ocean stream:
Him haply slumb'ring on the *Norway* foam
The Pilot of some small night-founder'd° Skiff,   *sunk in night*
205   Deeming some Island, oft, as Seamen tell,
With fixed Anchor in his scaly rind
Moors by his side under the Lee, while Night
Invests° the Sea, and wished Morn delays: *wraps*
So stretcht out huge in length the Arch-fiend lay
210   Chain'd on the burning Lake, nor ever thence
Had ris'n or heav'd his head, but that the will
And high permission of all-ruling Heaven
Left him at large to his own dark designs,
That with reiterated crimes he might
215   Heap on himself damnation, while he sought
Evil to others, and enrag'd might see
How all his malice serv'd but to bring forth
Infinite goodness, grace and mercy shown
On Man by him seduc't, but on himself
220   Treble confusion, wrath and vengeance pour'd.
Forthwith upright he rears from off the Pool
His mighty Stature; on each hand the flames
Driv'n backward slope thir pointing spires, and roll'd
In billows, leave i' th' midst a horrid° Vale.   *bristling*
225   Then with expanded wings he steers his flight
Aloft, incumbent[38] on the dusky Air
That felt unusual weight, till on dry Land

35. The serpent-legged *Briareos* was a Titan, the serpent-headed *Typhon* (Typhoeus) a Giant. Each was a son of Earth; each fought against Jupiter; and each was eventually confined beneath Aetna (see lines 232–37). Typhon was so powerful that when he first made war on the Olympians, they had to resort to metamorphoses to escape (Ovid, *Metamorphoses* 5.325–31 and 346–58).

36. The biblical Tarsus was the capital of Cilicia, and both Pindar and Aeschylus describe Typhon's habitat as a Cilician cave or "den."
37. The monster of Job 41, identified in Isaiah's prophecy of judgement as "the crooked serpent" (Isaiah 27.1) but also sometimes thought of as a whale.
38. Pressing with his weight.

He lights, if it were Land that ever burn'd
With solid, as the Lake with liquid fire
230 And such appear'd in hue;[39] as when the force
Of subterranean wind transports a Hill
Torn from *Pelorus*,[40] or the shatter'd side
Of thund'ring *AEtna*, whose combustible
And fuell'd entrails thence conceiving Fire,
235 Sublim'd[41] with Mineral fury,[42] aid the Winds,
And leave a singed bottom all involv'd°   *wreathed*
With stench and smoke: Such resting found the sole
Of unblest feet. Him follow'd his next Mate,
Both glorying to have scap't the *Stygian*[43] flood
240 As Gods, and by thir own recover'd strength,
Not by the sufferance of supernal Power.
    Is this the Region, this the Soil, the Clime,
Said then the lost Arch-Angel, this the seat
That we must change° for Heav'n, this mournful gloom   *exchange*
245 For that celestial light? Be it so, since he
Who now is Sovran can dispose and bid
What shall be right: fardest° from him is best   *farthest*
Whom reason hath equall'd, force hath made supreme
Above his equals. Farewell happy Fields
250 Where Joy for ever dwells: Hail horrors, hail
Infernal world, and thou profoundest Hell
Receive thy new Possessor: One who brings
A mind not to be chang'd by Place or Time.
The mind is its own place, and in itself
255 Can make a Heav'n of Hell, a Hell of Heav'n.[44]
What matter where, if I be still the same,
And what I should be, all but less than hee
Whom Thunder hath made greater? Here at least
We shall be free; th' Almighty hath not built
260 Here for his envy, will not drive us hence:
Here we may reign secure, and in my choice
To reign is worth ambition[45] though in Hell:
Better to reign in Hell, than serve in Heav'n.
But wherefore let we then our faithful friends,
265 Th' associates and copartners of our loss
Lie thus astonisht on th' oblivious Pool,[46]
And call them not to share with us their part
In this unhappy Mansion: or once more
With rallied Arms to try what may be yet
270 Regain'd in Heav'n, or what more lost in Hell? * * *

---

39. In the 17th century, "hue" referred to surface appearance and texture as well as color.
40. Pelorus and Aetna are volcanic mountains in Sicily.
41. Converted directly from solid to vapor by volcanic heat in such a way as to resolidify on cooling.
42. Disorder of minerals, or subterranean disorder.
43. Of the River Styx—i.e., hellish.

44. The view that heaven and hell are states of mind was held by Amaury de Bene, a medieval heretic often cited in 17th-century accounts of atheism.
45. Worth striving for (Latin *ambitio*). Satan refers not merely to a mental state but also to an active effort that is the price of power.
46. The pool attended by forgetfulness.

from **Book 9**

But neither here seek I, no nor in Heav'n
125   To dwell, unless by maistring Heav'n's Supreme;
Nor hope to be myself less miserable
By what I seek, but others to make such
As I, though thereby worse to me redound:
For only in destroying I find ease
130   To my relentless thoughts; and him destroy'd,
Or won to what may work his utter loss,
For whom all this was made, all this will soon
Follow, as to him linkt in weal or woe,
In woe then: that destruction wide may range:[1]
135   To mee shall be the glory sole among
Th'infernal Powers, in one day to have marr'd
What he *Almight* styl'd, six Nights and Days
Continu'd making, and who knows how long
Before had been contriving, though perhaps
140   Not longer than since I in one Night freed
From servitude inglorious well nigh half
Th' Angelic Name, and thinner left the throng
Of his adorers: hee to be aveng'd,
And to repair his numbers thus impair'd,
145   Whether such virtue° spent of old now fail'd   power
More Angels to Create, if they at least
Are his Created, or to spite us more,
Determin'd to advance into our room
A Creature form'd of Earth, and him endow,
150   Exalted from so base original,
With Heav'nly spoils, our spoils; What he decreed
He effected; Man he made, and for him built
Magnificent this World, and Earth his seat,
Him Lord pronounc'd, and, O indignity!
155   Subjected to his service Angel wings,
And flaming Ministers to watch and tend
Thir earthy Charge: Of these the vigilance
I dread, and to elude, thus wrapt in mist
Of midnight vapor glide obscure, and pry
160   In every Bush and Brake, where hap may find
The Serpent sleeping, in whose mazy folds
To hide me, and the dark intent I bring.
O foul descent! that I who erst contended
With Gods to sit the highest, am now constrain'd
165   Into a Beast, and mixt with bestial slime,
This essence to incarnate and imbrute,
That to the highth of Deity aspir'd;
But what will not Ambition and Revenge
Descend to? who aspires must down as low

1. The created cosmos will follow humans to destruction.

170 As high he soar'd, obnoxious° first or last   *exposed*
    To basest things. Revenge, at first though sweet,
    Bitter ere long back on itself recoils;
    Let it, I reck not, so it light well aim'd,
    Since higher I fall short, on him who next
175 Provokes my envy, this new Favorite
    Of Heav'n, this Man of Clay, Son of despite,
    Whom us the more to spite his Maker rais'd
    From dust: spite then with spite is best repaid.
        So saying, through each Thicket Dank or Dry,
180 Like a black mist low creeping, he held on
    His midnight search, where soonest he might find
    The Serpent: him fast sleeping soon he found
    In Labyrinth of many a round self-roll'd,
    His head the midst, well stor'd with subtle wiles:
185 Not yet in horrid Shade or dismal Den,
    Nor nocent° yet, but on the grassy Herb   *harmful, guilty*
    Fearless unfear'd he slept: in at his Mouth
    The Devil enter'd, and his brutal sense,
    In heart or head, possessing soon inspir'd
190 With act intelligential; but his sleep
    Disturb'd not, waiting close° th' approach of Morn.   *concealed*
    Now whenas sacred Light began to dawn
    In *Eden* on the humid Flow'rs, that breath'd
    Thir morning incense, when all things that breathe,
195 From th' Earth's great Altar send up silent praise
    To the Creator, and his Nostrils fill
    With grateful Smell, forth came the human pair
    And join'd thir vocal Worship to the Choir
    Of Creatures wanting voice; that done, partake
200 The season, prime for sweetest Scents and Airs:
    Then cómmune how that day they best may ply
    Thir growing work: for much thir work outgrew
    The hands' dispatch of two Gard'ning so wide.

Samuel Pepys
1633–1703

from **The Diary**
[THE FIRE OF LONDON]

[2 September 1666] Lord's Day. Some of our maids sitting up late last night to get things ready against our feast today, Jane called us up,[1] about 3 in the morning, to tell us of a great fire they saw in the City. So I rose, and slipped on my nightgown and went to her window, and thought it to be on the back side of Mark Lane at the furthest; but being unused to such fires as followed, I thought it far enough off, and so went to bed again and to sleep. About 7 rose again to dress myself, and there looked out at the window and saw the fire not so much as it was, and further off. So to my closet[2] to set things to rights after yesterday's cleaning. By and by Jane comes and tells me that she hears that above 300 houses have been burned down tonight by the fire we saw, and that it was now burning down all Fish Street by London Bridge. So I made myself ready presently, and walked to the Tower and there got up upon one of the high places, Sir J. Robinson's little son going up with me; and there I did see the houses at that end of the bridge all on fire, and an infinite great fire on this and the other side the end of the bridge—which, among other people, did trouble me for poor little Mitchell and our Sarah on the bridge.[3] So down, with my heart full of trouble, to the Lieutenant of the Tower, who tells me that it begun this morning in the King's baker's house in Pudding Lane, and that it hath burned down St. Magnus's Church and most part of Fish Street already. So I down to the water-side and there got a boat and through bridge,[4] and there saw a lamentable fire. Poor Mitchell's house, as far as the Old Swan, already burned that way and the fire running further, that in a very little time it got as far as the Steelyard while I was there. Everybody endeavoring to remove their goods, and flinging into the river or bringing them into lighters[5] that lay off. Poor people staying in their houses as long as till the very fire touched them, and then running into boats or clambering from one pair of stair by the water-side to another. And among other things, the poor pigeons I perceive were loath to leave their houses, but hovered about the windows and balconies till they were some of them burned, their wings, and fell down.

Having stayed, and in an hour's time seen the fire rage every way, and nobody to my sight endeavoring to quench it, but to remove their goods and leave all to the fire; and having seen it get as far as the Steelyard, and the wind mighty high and driving it into the City, and everything, after so long a drought, proving combustible, even the very stones of churches, and among other things, the poor steeple by which pretty Mrs. Horsley lives, and whereof my old school-fellow Elborough is parson, taken fire in the very top and there burned till it fall down—I to Whitehall with a gentleman with me who desired to go off from the Tower to see the fire in my boat—to Whitehall, and there up to the King's closet in the chapel, where people came about me and I did give them an account dismayed them all; and word was carried in to the King, so I was called for and did tell the King and Duke of York what I saw, and that unless his Majesty did command hous-

---

1. Called, woke
2. Private room, study.
3. London Bridge was lined with shops and houses, including the liquor shop of Pepys's friend Michael

Mitchell and the residence of his former servant Sarah.
4. Under the bridge.
5. Barges.

es to be pulled down, nothing could stop the fire. They seemed much troubled, and the King commanded me to go to my Lord Mayor from him and command him to spare no houses but to pull down before the fire every way. The Duke of York bid me tell him that if he would have any more soldiers, he shall; and so did my Lord Arlington afterward, as a great secret. Here meeting with Captain Cocke, I in his coach, which he lent me, and Creed with me, to Paul's; and there walked along Watling Street as well as I could, every creature coming away loaden with goods to save—and here and there sick people carried away in beds. Extraordinary good goods carried in carts and on backs. At last met my Lord Mayor in Canning Street, like a man spent, with a hankercher about his neck. To the King's message, he cried like a fainting woman, "Lord, what can I do? I am spent! People will not obey me. I have been pulling down houses. But the fire overtakes us faster than we can do it." That he needed no more soldiers; and that for himself, he must go and refresh himself, having been up all night. So he left me, and I him, and walked home—seeing people all almost distracted and no manner of means used to quench the fire. The houses too, so very thick thereabouts, and full of matter for burning, as pitch and tar, in Thames Street—and warehouses of oil and wines and brandy and other things. Here I saw Mr. Isaac Houblon, that handsome man—prettily dressed and dirty at his door at Dowgate, receiving some of his brothers' things whose houses were on fire; and as he says, have been removed twice already, and he doubts (as it soon proved) that they must be in a little time removed from his house also—which was a sad consideration. And to see the churches all filling with goods, by people who themselves should have been quietly there at this time.

By this time it was about 12 a-clock, and so home and there find my guests, which was Mr. Wood and his wife, Barbary Shelden, and also Mr. Moone—she mighty fine, and her husband, for aught I see, a likely man. But Mr. Moone's design and mine, which was to look over my closet and please him with the sight thereof, which he hath long desired, was wholly disappointed, for we were in great trouble and disturbance at this fire, not knowing what to think of it. However, we had an extraordinary good dinner, and as merry as at this time we could be.

While at dinner, Mrs. Batelier came to inquire after Mr. Woolfe and Stanes (who it seems are related to them), whose houses in Fish Street are all burned, and they in a sad condition. She would not stay in the fright.

As soon as dined, I and Moone away and walked through the City, the streets full of nothing but people and horses and carts loaden with goods, ready to run over one another, and removing goods from one burned house to another—they now removing out of Canning Street (which received goods in the morning) into Lombard Street and further; and among others, I now saw my little goldsmith Stokes receiving some friend's goods, whose house itself was burned the day after. We parted at Paul's, he home and I to Paul's Wharf, where I had appointed a boat to attend me; and took in Mr. Carkesse and his brother, whom I met in the street, and carried them below and above bridge, to and again, to see the fire, which was now got further, both below and above, and no likelihood of stopping it. Met with the King and Duke of York in their barge, and with them to Queenhithe and there called Sir Richard Browne to them. Their order was only to pull down houses apace, and so below bridge at the water-side; but little was or could be done, the fire coming upon them so fast. Good hopes there was of stopping it at the Three Cranes above, and at Buttolph's Wharf below bridge, if care be used; but the wind carries it into the City, so as we know not by the water-side what it doth there.

River full of lighters and boats taking in goods, and good goods swimming in the water; and only, I observed that hardly one lighter or boat in three that had the goods of a house in, but there was a pair of virginals[6] in it. Having seen as much as I could now, I away to Whitehall by appointment, and there walked to St. James's Park, and there met my wife and Creed and Wood and his wife and walked to my boat, and there upon the water again, and to the fire up and down, it still increasing and the wind great. So near the fire as we could for smoke; and all over the Thames, with one's face in the wind you were almost burned with a shower of fire-drops—this is very true—so as houses were burned by these drops and flakes of fire, three or four, nay five or six houses, one from another. When we could endure no more upon the water, we to a little alehouse on the Bankside over against the Three Cranes, and there stayed till it was dark almost and saw the fire grow; and as it grow darker, appeared more and more, and in corners and upon steeples and between churches and houses, as far as we could see up the hill of the City, in a most horrid malicious bloody flame, not like the fine flame of an ordinary fire. Barbary and her husband away before us. We stayed till, it being darkish, we saw the fire as only one entire arch of fire from this to the other side the bridge, and in a bow up the hill, for an arch of above a mile long. It made me weep to see it. The churches, houses, and all on fire and flaming at once, and a horrid noise the flames made, and the cracking of houses at their ruin. So home with a sad heart, and there find everybody discoursing and lamenting the fire; and poor Tom Hayter[7] came with some few of his goods saved out of his house, which is burned upon Fish Street Hill. I invited him to lie at my house, and did receive his goods: but was deceived in his lying there, the noise coming every moment of the growth of the fire, so as we were forced to begin to pack up our own goods and prepare for their removal. And did by moonshine (it being brave,[8] dry, and moonshine and warm weather) carry much of my goods into the garden, and Mr. Hayter and I did remove my money and iron-chests into my cellar—as thinking that the safest place. And got my bags of gold into my office ready to carry away, and my chief papers of accounts also there, and my tallies into a box by themselves. So great was our fear, as Sir W. Batten had carts come out of the country to fetch away his goods this night. We did put Mr. Hayter, poor man, to bed a little; but he got but very little rest, so much noise being in my house, taking down of goods.

[3 September 1666] About 4 a-clock in the morning, my Lady Batten sent me a cart to carry away all my money and plate and best things to Sir W. Rider's at Bethnell Green; which I did, riding myself in my nightgown in the cart; and Lord, to see how the streets and the highways are crowded with people, running and riding and getting of carts at any rate to fetch away things. I find Sir W. Rider tired with being called up[9] all night and receiving things from several friends. His house full of goods—and much of Sir W. Batten and Sir W. Penn's.[10] I am eased at my heart to have my treasure so well secured. Then home with much ado to find a way. Nor any sleep all this night to me nor my poor wife. But then, and all this day, she and I and all my people laboring to get away the rest of our things, and did get Mr. Tooker to get me a lighter to take them in, and we did carry them (myself some) over Tower Hill, which was by this time full of people's goods, bringing their goods thither. And down to the lighter, which lay at the

6. A small harpsichord.
7. One of Pepys's clerks in the Navy Office.
8. Pleasant.

9. Called on, woken.
10. William Penn, Pepys's colleague on the Navy Board (and father of the founder of Pennsylvania).

next quay above the Tower Dock. And here was my neighbor's wife, Mrs. Buckworth, with her pretty child and some few of her things, which I did willingly give way to be saved with mine. But there was no passing with anything through the postern,[11] the crowd was so great.

The Duke of York came this day by the office and spoke to us, and did ride with his guard up and down the City to keep all quiet (he being now general, and having the care of all).

This day, Mercer being not at home, but against her mistress's order gone to her mother's, and my wife going thither to speak with W. Hewer, met her there and was angry; and her mother saying that she was not a prentice girl, to ask leave every time she goes abroad, my wife with good reason was angry, and when she came home, bid her be gone again. And so she went away, which troubled me; but yet less than it would, because of the condition we are in fear of coming into in a little time, of being less able to keep one in her quality. At night, lay down a little upon a quilt of W. Hewer in the office (all my own things being packed up or gone); and after me, my poor wife did the like—we having fed upon the remains of yesterday's dinner, having no fire nor dishes, nor any opportunity of dressing anything.

[4 September 1666] Up by break of day to get away the remainder of my things, which I did by a lighter at the Iron Gate; and my hands so few, that it was the afternoon before we could get them all away.

Sir W. Penn and I to Tower Street, and there met the fire burning three or four doors beyond Mr. Howell's; whose goods, poor man (his trays and dishes, shovels, etc., were flung all along Tower Street in the kennels, and people working therewith from one end to the other), the fire coming on in that narrow street, on both sides, with infinite fury. Sir W. Batten, not knowing how to remove his wine, did dig a pit in the garden and laid it in there; and I took the opportunity of laying all the papers of my office that I could not otherwise dispose of. And in the evening Sir W. Penn and I did dig another and put our wine in it, and I my parmesan cheese as well as my wine and some other things.

The Duke of York was at the office this day at Sir W. Penn's, but I happened not to be within. This afternoon, sitting melancholy with Sir W. Penn in our garden and thinking of the certain burning of this office without extraordinary means, I did propose for the sending up of all our workmen from Woolwich and Deptford yards (none whereof yet appeared), and to write to Sir W. Coventry to have the Duke of York's permission to pull down houses rather then lose this office, which would much hinder the King's business. So Sir W. Penn he went down this night, in order to the sending them up tomorrow morning; and I wrote to Sir W. Coventry about the business, but received no answer.

This night Mrs. Turner (who, poor woman, was removing her goods all this day—good goods, into the garden, and knew not how to dispose of them)—and her husband supped with my wife and I at night in the office, upon a shoulder of mutton from the cook's, without any napkin or anything, in a sad manner but were merry. Only, now and then walking into the garden and saw how horridly the sky looks, all on a fire in the night, was enough to put us out of our wits; and indeed it was extremely dreadful—for it looks just as if it was at us, and the whole heaven on fire. I after supper walked in the dark down to Tower Street, and there saw it all on fire at the Trinity House on that side

11. Back or side gate.

and the Dolphin Tavern on this side, which was very near us—and the fire with extra-ordinary vehemence. Now begins the practice of blowing up of houses in Tower Street, those next the Tower, which at first did frighten people more than anything; but it stopped the fire where it was done—it bringing down the houses to the ground in the same places they stood, and then it was easy to quench what little fire was in it, though it kindled nothing almost. W. Hewer this day went to see how his mother did, and comes late home, but telling us how he hath been forced to remove her to Islington, her house in Pye Corner being burned. So that it is got so far that way and all the Old Bailey, and was running down to Fleet Street. And Paul's is burned, and all Cheap-side. I wrote to my father this night; but the post-house being burned, the letter could not go.

Mary, Lady Chudleigh
1656–1710

To the Ladies

	Wife and servant are the same,	
	But only differ in the name:	
	For when that fatal knot is tied,	
	Which nothing, nothing can divide:	
5	When she the word *obey* has said,	
	And man by law supreme has made,	
	Then all that's kind is laid aside,	
	And nothing left but state° and pride:	*dignity*
	Fierce as an Eastern Prince he grows,	
10	And all his innate rigor shows:	
	Then but to look, to laugh, or speak,	
	Will the nuptial contract break.	
	Like mutes she signs alone must make,	
	And never any freedom take:	
15	But still be governed by a nod,	
	And fear her husband as her God:	
	Him still must serve, him still obey,	
	And nothing act, and nothing say,	
	But what her haughty lord thinks fit,	
20	Who with the power, has all the wit.°	*intelligence*
	Then shun, oh! shun that wretched state,	
	And all the fawning flatterers hate:	
	Value your selves, and men despise,	
	You must be proud, if you'll be wise.	

1703

Jonathan Swift
1667–1745

Introduction to Gulliver's Travel's

GULLIVER'S TRAVELS   Travels into Several Remote Nations of the World. In Four Parts. By Lemuel Gulliver—better known as Gulliver's Travels—was first published in late October 1726 and enjoyed instant success. One contemporary observer noted that "several thousands sold in a week," and Swift's London friends wrote to him in Dublin to say that everyone was reading and talking about Gulliver. Readers continue to be fascinated by Swift's masterpiece: since 1945, more than 500 books and scholarly articles have been devoted to Gulliver's Travels. Variously classified as an early novel, an imaginary voyage, a moral and political allegory, and even a children's story, Lemuel Gulliver's four journeys, representing the four directions of the globe, comprise a survey of the human condition: a comic, ironic, and sometimes harrowing answer to the question, "What does it mean to be a human being?"

In the first voyage, the diminutive citizens of Lilliput represent human small-mindedness and petty ambitions. Filled with self-importance, the Lilliputians are cruel, treacherous, malicious, and destructive. The perspective is reversed in the second voyage to Brobdingnag, land of giants, where Gulliver has the stature of a Lilliputian. He is humbled by his own helplessness and, finding the huge bodies of the Brobdingnagians grotesque, he realizes how repulsive the Lilliputians must have found him. When Gulliver gives the wise king an account of the political affairs of England—which manifest hypocrisy, avarice, and hatred—the enlightened monarch concludes that most of the country's inhabitants must be "the most pernicious race of little odious vermin that Nature ever suffered to crawl upon the surface of the earth." In the third voyage (which was written last), Gulliver visits the flying island of Laputa and the metropolis of Lagado, on an adjacent continent, where he encounters the misuse of human reason. In Laputa, those who are supposedly "wise" lack all common sense and practical ability; at Lagado, the Academy of Projectors is staffed by professors who waste both money and intelligence on absurd endeavors. Swift aims his satire at so-called intellectuals—especially the "virtuosi," or amateur scientists of the Royal Society—who live in the world of their own speculations and so fail to use their gifts for the common good. Throughout Gulliver's Travels that which is admirable is held up to expose corruption in the reader's world, and that which is deplorable is identified with the institutions and practices associated with contemporary Europe, particularly Britain.

Gulliver's fourth voyage finds him on the island of the Houyhnhnms, horses endowed with reason, whose highly rational and well-ordered (though emotionally sterile) society is contrasted with the violence, selfishness, and brutality of the Yahoos, irrational beasts who bear a disconcerting resemblance to humans. In his foolish pride, Gulliver believes that he can escape the human condition and live as a stoical Houyhnhnm, even when he returns to his family in England. Of course, Gulliver is neither Houyhnhnm nor Yahoo, but a man. His time in Houyhnhnm-land does not teach him to be more rational or compassionate, but makes him more foolish, derelict in his duties as husband, father, and citizen. Instead of seeking to become a better man, Gulliver strives to become what he is not—with results that are both tragic and farcical. Although the poet Edward Young charged Swift with having "blasphemed a nature little lower than that of the angels" in satirizing the follies of humankind, Gulliver's Travels reveals the Dean of Saint Patrick's to be more a humanist than a misanthrope. With brilliantly modulated ironic self-awareness, Swift's painful comedy of exposure to the truth of human frailty demonstrates that there is no room for the distortions of human pride in a world where our practices are so evidently at variance with our principles. Swift advances no program of social reform, but provokes a new recognition—literally, a rethinking—of our own humanity.

from Gulliver's Travels

from Part 4. A Voyage to the Country of the Houyhnhnms[1]

CHAPTER 1

The author sets out as Captain of a ship. His men conspire against him, confine him a long time to his cabin, set him on shore in an unknown land. He travels up into the country. The Yahoos,[2] a strange sort of animal, described. The author meets two Houyhnhnms.

I continued at home with my wife and children about five months in a very happy condition, if I could have learned the lesson of knowing when I was well. I left my poor wife big with child, and accepted an advantageous offer made me to be Captain of the *Adventure*,[3] a stout merchantman of 350 tons: for I understood navigation well, and being grown weary of a surgeon's employment at sea, which however I could exercise upon occasion, I took a skillful young man of that calling, one Robert Purefoy,[4] into my ship. We set sail from Portsmouth upon the seventh day of September, 1710; on the fourteenth, we met with Captain Pocock[5] of Bristol, at Teneriffe,[6] who was going to the bay of Campeche, to cut logwood. On the sixteenth, he was parted from us by a storm; I heard since my return, that his ship foundered, and none escaped, but one cabin boy. He was an honest man, and a good sailor, but a little too positive in his own opinions, which was the cause of his destruction, as it hath been of several others. For if he had followed my advice, he might at this time have been safe at home with his family as well as myself.

I had several men died in my ship of calentures,[7] so that I was forced to get recruits out of Barbados, and the Leeward Islands, where I touched by[8] the direction of the merchants who employed me, which I had soon too much cause to repent; for I found afterwards that most of them had been buccaneers. I had fifty hands on board, and my orders were, that I should trade with the Indians in the South Sea, and make what discoveries I could. These rogues whom I had picked up debauched my other men, and they all formed a conspiracy to seize the ship and secure me; which they did one morning, rushing into my cabin, and binding me hand and foot, threatening to throw me overboard, if I offered to stir. I told them, I was their prisoner, and would submit. This they made me swear to do, and then unbound me, only fastening one of my legs with a chain near my bed, and placed a sentry at my door with his piece charged,[9] who was commanded to shoot me dead, if I attempted my liberty. They sent me down victuals and drink, and took the government of the ship to themselves. Their design was to turn pirates, and plunder the Spaniards, which they could not do

---

1. Pronounced "whinnims," to mimic the sound of a horse's whinny, though some scholars have offered more complex interpretations of this name. With characteristic irony, Swift probably chose horses to represent rational creatures because the philosopher John Locke (1632–1704) and Bishop Edward Stillingfleet (1635–1699) had argued extensively about how one might distinguish man as a rational animal from an evidently irrational animal, such as a horse.

2. The name may be derived from similarly titled African or Guianan tribes. The animals represent sinful, fallen humanity, and their juxtaposition with the Houyhnhnms is designed to question belief in the innate rationality of humankind and the superiority of humans over other creatures.

3. The name of two ships of the notorious pirate Captain William Kidd (d. 1701). Kidd, originally commissioned to capture pirates, was also subject to a mutiny.

4. "Pure faith," associating Gulliver with the overzealous Puritans.

5. Probably modeled on the dogmatic Captain Dampier (1652–1715), who had spent three years logcutting around the Campeche Bay, on the Yucatan Peninsula, in the Gulf of Mexico. His violent disagreements with his lieutenant led to a court martial.

6. One of the Canary Islands, off the northwestern coast of Africa.

7. Tropical fevers.

8. Landed according to.

9. Gun loaded.

till they got more men. But first they resolved to sell the goods in the ship, and then go to Madagascar[10] for recruits, several among them having died since my confinement. They sailed many weeks, and traded with the Indians, but I knew not what course they took, being kept close prisoner in my cabin, and expecting nothing less than to be murdered, as they often threatened me.

Upon the ninth day of May, 1711, one James Welch came down to my cabin; and said he had orders from the Captain to set me ashore. I expostulated with him, but in vain; neither would he so much as tell me who their new captain was. They forced me into the longboat, letting me put on my best suit of clothes, which were good as new, and a small bundle of linen, but no arms except my hanger;[11] and they were so civil as not to search my pockets, into which I conveyed what money I had, with some other little necessaries. They rowed about a league; and then set me down on a strand.[12] I desired them to tell me what country it was. They all swore, they knew no more than myself, but said, that the Captain (as they called him) was resolved, after they had sold the lading,[13] to get rid of me in the first place where they discovered land. They pushed off immediately, advising me to make haste, for fear of being overtaken by the tide, and bade me farewell.

In this desolate condition I advanced forward, and soon got upon firm ground, where I sat down on a bank to rest myself, and consider what I had best to do. When I was a little refreshed, I went up into the country, resolving to deliver myself to the first savages I should meet, and purchase my life from them by some bracelets, glass rings, and other toys,[14] which sailors usually provide themselves with in those voyages, and whereof I had some about me: the land was divided by long rows of trees, not regularly planted, but naturally growing; there was great plenty of grass, and several fields of oats. I walked very circumspectly for fear of being surprised, or suddenly shot with an arrow from behind or on either side. I fell into a beaten road, where I saw many tracks of human feet, and some of cows, but most of horses. At last I beheld several animals in a field, and one or two of the same kind sitting in trees. Their shape was very singular, and deformed, which a little discomposed me, so that I lay down behind a thicket to observe them better. Some of them coming forward near the place where I lay, gave me an opportunity of distinctly marking[15] their form. Their heads and breasts were covered with a thick hair, some frizzled and others lank; they had beards like goats, and a long ridge of hair down their backs, and the foreparts of their legs and feet, but the rest of their bodies were bare, so that I might see their skins, which were of a brown buff color. They had no tails, nor any hair at all on their buttocks, except about the anus; which, I presume, Nature had placed there to defend them as they sat on the ground; for this posture they used, as well as lying down, and often stood on their hind feet. They climbed high trees, as nimbly as a squirrel, for they had strong extended claws before and behind, terminating in sharp points, and hooked. They would often spring, and bound, and leap with prodigious agility. The females were not so large as the males; they had long lank hair on their heads, and only a sort of down on the rest of their bodies. * * * Their dugs[16] hung between their forefeet, and often reached almost to the ground as they walked. The hair of both sexes was of several colors, brown, red, black, and yellow. Upon the whole, I never beheld in all my travels so disagreeable an animal, nor one against

10. A popular meeting place for pirates.
11. A short sword, typically hung from the belt.
12. The shore; in this context, apparently a spit extending into the sea.

13. Cargo.
14. Trinkets.
15. Observing.
16. Breasts.

which I naturally conceived so strong an antipathy. So that thinking I had seen enough, full of contempt and aversion, I got up and pursued the beaten road, hoping it might direct me to the cabin of some Indian. I had not gone far when I met one of these creatures full in my way, and coming up directly to me. The ugly monster, when he saw me, distorted several ways every feature of his visage, and stared as at an object he had never seen before; then approaching nearer, lifted up his forepaw, whether out of curiosity or mischief, I could not tell. But I drew my hanger, and gave him a good blow with the flat side of it; for I durst not strike him with the edge, fearing the inhabitants might be provoked against me, if they should come to know, that I had killed or maimed any of their cattle. When the beast felt the smart, he drew back, and roared so loud, that a herd of at least forty came flocking about me from the next field, howling and making odious faces; but I ran to the body of a tree, and leaning my back against it, kept them off, by waving my hanger. Several of this cursed brood getting hold of the branches behind leaped up into the tree, from whence they began to discharge their excrements on my head: however, I escaped pretty well, by sticking close to the stem of the tree, but was almost stifled with the filth, which fell about me on every side.

In the midst of this distress, I observed them all to run away on a sudden as fast as they could, at which I ventured to leave the tree, and pursue the road, wondering what it was that could put them into this flight. But looking on my left hand, I saw a horse walking softly in the field, which my persecutors having sooner discovered, was the cause of their flight. The horse started a little when he came near me, but soon recovering himself, looked full in my face with manifest tokens of wonder: he viewed my hands and feet, walking round me several times. I would have pursued my journey, but he placed himself directly in the way, yet looking with a very mild aspect, never offering the least violence. We stood gazing at each other for some time; at last I took the boldness to reach my hand towards his neck, with a design to stroke it, using the common style and whistle of jockeys when they are going to handle a strange horse. But this animal, seeming to receive my civilities with disdain, shook his head, and bent his brows, softly raising up his left forefoot to remove my hand. Then he neighed three or four times, but in so different a cadence, that I almost began to think he was speaking to himself in some language of his own.

While he and I were thus employed, another horse came up; who applying[17] himself to the first in a very formal manner, they gently struck each other's right hoof before, neighing several times by turns, and varying the sound, which seemed to be almost articulate. They went some paces off, as if it were to confer together, walking side by side, backward and forward, like persons deliberating upon some affair of weight, but often turning their eyes towards me, as it were to watch that I might not escape. I was amazed to see such actions and behavior in brute beasts, and concluded with myself, that if the inhabitants of this country were endued with a proportionable degree of reason, they must needs be the wisest people upon earth. This thought gave me so much comfort, that I resolved to go forward until I could discover some house or village, or meet with any of the natives, leaving the two horses to discourse together as they pleased. But the first, who was a dapple-grey, observing me to steal off, neighed after me in so expressive a tone, that I fancied myself to understand what he meant; whereupon I turned back, and came near him, to expect[18] his farther commands. But concealing my

---

17. Addressing.   18. Await.

fear as much as I could, for I began to be in some pain,[19] how this adventure might terminate; and the reader will easily believe I did not much like my present situation.

The two horses came up close to me, looking with great earnestness upon my face and hands. The grey steed rubbed my hat all round with his right forehoof, and discomposed it so much, that I was forced to adjust it better, by taking it off, and settling it again; whereat both he and his companion (who was a brown bay) appeared to be much surprised; the latter felt the lappet[20] of my coat, and finding it to hang loose about me, they both looked with new signs of wonder. He stroked my right hand, seeming to admire the softness, and color; but he squeezed it so hard between his hoof and his pastern,[21] that I was forced to roar; after which they both touched me with all possible tenderness. They were under great perplexity about my shoes and stockings, which they felt very often, neighing to each other, and using various gestures, not unlike those of a philosopher,[22] when he would attempt to solve some new and difficult phenomenon.

Upon the whole, the behavior of these animals was so orderly and rational, so acute and judicious, that I at last concluded, they must needs be magicians, who had thus metamorphosed themselves upon some design, and seeing a stranger in the way, were resolved to divert themselves with him; or perhaps were really amazed at the sight of a man so very different in habit, feature, and complexion from those who might probably live in so remote a climate.[23] Upon the strength of this reasoning, I ventured to address them in the following manner: Gentlemen, if you be conjurers, as I have good cause to believe, you can understand any language; therefore I make bold to let your Worships know, that I am a poor distressed Englishman, driven by his misfortunes upon your coast, and I entreat one of you, to let me ride upon his back, as if he were a real horse, to some house or village, where I can be relieved. In return of which favor, I will make you a present of this knife and bracelet (taking them out of my pocket). The two creatures stood silent while I spoke, seeming to listen with great attention; and when I had ended, they neighed frequently towards each other, as if they were engaged in serious conversation. I plainly observed that their language expressed the passions[24] very well, and the words might with little pains be resolved into an alphabet more easily than the Chinese.

I could frequently distinguish the word *Yahoo*, which was repeated by each of them several times; and although it were impossible for me to conjecture what it meant, yet while the two horses were busy in conversation, I endeavored to practice this word upon my tongue; and as soon as they were silent, I boldly pronounced *Yahoo* in a loud voice, imitating, at the same time, as near as I could, the neighing of a horse; at which they were both visibly surprised, and the grey repeated the same word twice, as if he meant to teach me the right accent, wherein I spoke after him as well as I could, and found myself perceivably to improve every time, although very far from any degree of perfection. Then the bay tried me with a second word, much harder to be pronounced; but reducing it to the English *orthography*,[25] may be spelled thus, *Houyhnhnm*. I did not succeed in this so well as the former, but after two or three farther trials, I had better fortune; and they both appeared amazed at my capacity.

After some farther discourse, which I then conjectured might relate to me, the two friends took their leaves, with the same compliment of striking each other's hoof;

19. Began to be worried.
20. Lapel.
21. Part of a horse's foot between the fetlock (a projection of the lower leg) and the hoof.

22. Scientist.
23. Region.
24. Emotions.
25. Spelling.

and the grey made me signs that I should walk before him; wherein I thought it prudent to comply, till I could find a better director. When I offered to slacken my pace, he would cry *Hhuun, Hhuun*; I guessed his meaning, and gave him to understand, as well as I could, that I was weary, and not able to walk faster; upon which, he would stand a while to let me rest.

CHAPTER 2

The author conducted by a Houyhnhnm to his house. The house described. The author's reception. The food of the Houyhnhnms. The author in distress for want of meat, is at last relieved. His manner of feeding in that country.

Having traveled about three miles, we came to a long kind of building, made of timber stuck in the ground, and wattled across;[1] the roof was low, and covered with straw. I now began to be a little comforted, and took out some toys, which travelers usually carry for presents to the savage Indians of America and other parts, in hopes the people of the house would be thereby encouraged to receive me kindly. The horse made me a sign to go in first; it was a large room with a smooth, clay floor, and a rack[2] and manger extending the whole length on one side. There were three nags,[3] and two mares, not eating, but some of them sitting down upon their hams,[4] which I very much wondered at; but wondered more to see the rest employed in domestic business. The last seemed but ordinary cattle; however, this confirmed my first opinion, that a people who could so far civilize brute animals, must needs excel in wisdom all the nations of the world. The grey came in just after, and thereby prevented any ill treatment, which the others might have given me. He neighed to them several times in a style of authority, and received answers.

Beyond this room there were three others, reaching the length of the house, to which you passed through three doors, opposite to each other, in the manner of a vista;[5] we went through the second room towards the third; here the grey walked in first, beckoning me to attend:[6] I waited in the second room, and got ready my presents, for the master and mistress of the house: they were two knives, three bracelets of false pearl, a small looking glass, and a bead necklace. The horse neighed three or four times, and I waited to hear some answers in a human voice, but I heard no other returns than in the same dialect, only one or two a little shriller than his. I began to think that this house must belong to some person of great note among them, because there appeared so much ceremony before I could gain admittance. But, that a man of quality should be served all by horses, was beyond my comprehension. I feared my brain was disturbed by my sufferings and misfortunes: I roused myself, and looked about me in the room where I was left alone; this was furnished as the first, only after a more elegant manner. I rubbed mine eyes often, but the same objects still occurred. I pinched my arms and sides, to awake myself, hoping I might be in a dream. I then absolutely concluded, that all these appearances could be nothing else but necromancy[7] and magic. But I had no time to pursue these reflections; for the grey horse came to the door, and made me a sign to follow him into the third room, where I saw a very comely mare,

1. Filled in with twigs and branches.
2. Hayrack for the feed.
3. Ponies.
4. Buttocks.

5. Long, narrow view (usually between rows of trees).
6. Wait.
7. Sorcery.

together with a colt and foal, sitting on their haunches, upon mats of straw, not unartfully made, and perfectly neat and clean.

The mare, soon after my entrance, rose from her mat, and coming up close, after having nicely[8] observed my hands and face, gave me a most contemptuous look; then turning to the horse, I heard the word *Yahoo* often repeated betwixt them; the meaning of which word I could not then comprehend, although it were the first I had learned to pronounce; but I was soon better informed, to my everlasting mortification: for the horse beckoning to me with his head, and repeating the word *Hhuun, Hhuun,* as he did upon the road, which I understood was to attend him, led me out into a kind of court, where was another building at some distance from the house. Here we entered, and I saw three of those detestable creatures, which I first met after my landing, feeding upon roots, and the flesh of some animals, which I afterwards found to be that of asses and dogs, and now and then a cow dead by accident or disease.[9] They were all tied by the neck with strong withes,[10] fastened to a beam; they held their food between the claws of their forefeet, and tore it with their teeth.

The master horse ordered a sorrel nag, one of his servants, to untie the largest of these animals, and take him into the yard. The beast and I were brought close together, and our countenances diligently compared, both by master and servant, who thereupon repeated several times the word *Yahoo.* My horror and astonishment are not to be described, when I observed, in this abominable animal, a perfect human figure; the face of it indeed was flat and broad, the nose depressed, the lips large, and the mouth wide. But these differences are common to all savage nations, where the lineaments of the countenance are distorted by the natives suffering[11] their infants to lie groveling on the earth, or by carrying them on their backs, nuzzling with their face against the mother's shoulders. The forefeet of the Yahoo differed from my hands in nothing else but the length of the nails, the coarseness and brownness of the palms, and the hairiness on the backs. There was the same resemblance between our feet, with the same differences, which I knew very well, though the horses did not, because of my shoes and stockings; the same in every part of our bodies, except as to hairiness and color, which I have already described.

The great difficulty that seemed to stick with the two horses, was, to see the rest of my body so very different from that of a Yahoo, for which I was obliged to my clothes, whereof they had no conception: the sorrel nag offered me a root, which he held (after their manner, as we shall describe in its proper place) between his hoof and pastern; I took it in my hand, and having smelt it, returned it to him as civilly as I could. He brought out of the Yahoo's kennel a piece of ass's flesh, but it smelt so offensively that I turned from it with loathing; he then threw it to the Yahoo, by whom it was greedily devoured. He afterwards showed me a wisp of hay, and a fetlock full of oats; but I shook my head, to signify, that neither of these were food for me. And indeed, I now apprehended, that I must absolutely starve, if I did not get to some of my own species: for as to those filthy Yahoos, although there were few greater lovers of mankind, at that time, than myself; yet I confess I never saw any sensitive[12] being so detestable on all accounts; and the more I came near them, the more hateful they grew, while I stayed in that country. This the master horse

8. Closely.
9. The Yahoos eat food listed in Leviticus (11.3, 27, 39–40) as unclean, suggesting that they exemplify the human condition distorted and debased by sin.
10. Leashes.
11. Allowing.
12. "Having sense or perception, but not reason" (Johnson's *Dictionary*).

observed by my behavior, and therefore sent the Yahoo back to his kennel. He then put his forehoof to his mouth, at which I was much surprised, although he did it with ease, and with a motion that appeared perfectly natural, and made other signs to know what I would eat; but I could not return him such an answer as he was able to apprehend; and if he had understood me, I did not see how it was possible to contrive any way for finding myself nourishment. While we were thus engaged, I observed a cow passing by, whereupon I pointed to her, and expressed a desire to let me go and milk her. This had its effect; for he led me back into the house, and ordered a mare-servant to open a room, where a good store of milk lay in earthen and wooden vessels, after a very orderly and cleanly manner. She gave me a large bowl full, of which I drank very heartily, and found myself well refreshed.

About noon I saw coming towards the house a kind of vehicle drawn like a sledge by four Yahoos. There was in it an old steed, who seemed to be of quality; he alighted with his hind feet forward, having by accident got a hurt in his left forefoot. He came to dine with our horse, who received him with great civility. They dined in the best room, and had oats boiled in milk for the second course, which the old horse ate warm, but the rest cold. Their mangers were placed circular in the middle of the room, and divided into several partitions, round which they sat on their haunches upon bosses[13] of straw. In the middle was a large rack with angles answering to every partition of the manger. So that each horse and mare ate their own hay, and their own mash of oats and milk, with much decency and regularity. The behavior of the young colt and foal appeared very modest, and that of the master and mistress extremely cheerful and complaisant[14] to their guest. The grey ordered me to stand by him, and much discourse passed between him and his friend concerning me, as I found by the stranger's often looking on me, and the frequent repetition of the word Yahoo.

I happened to wear my gloves, which the master grey observing, seemed perplexed, discovering signs of wonder what I had done to my forefeet; he put his hoof three or four times to them, as if he would signify, that I should reduce them to their former shape, which I presently did, pulling off both my gloves, and putting them into my pocket. This occasioned farther talk, and I saw the company was pleased with my behavior, whereof I soon found the good effects. I was ordered to speak the few words I understood, and while they were at dinner, the master taught me the names for oats, milk, fire, water, and some others; which I could readily pronounce after him, having from my youth a great facility in learning languages.

When dinner was done, the master horse took me aside, and by signs and words made me understand the concern he was in, that I had nothing to eat. Oats in their tongue are called *hlunnh*. This word I pronounced two or three times; for although I had refused them at first, yet upon second thoughts, I considered that I could contrive to make of them a kind of bread, which might be sufficient with milk to keep me alive, till I could make my escape to some other country, and to creatures of my own species. The horse immediately ordered a white mare-servant of his family to bring me a good quantity of oats in a sort of wooden tray. These I heated before the fire as well as I could, and rubbed them till the husks came off, which I made a shift[15]to winnow from the grain; I ground and beat them between two stones, then took water, and made them into a paste or cake, which I toasted at the fire, and ate warm with milk. It was at first a very insipid diet, although common enough in many parts of Europe, but grew

13. Piles or seats.
14. Courteous.

15. Attempted.

tolerable by time; and having been often reduced to hard fare in my life, this was not the first experiment I had made how easily nature is satisfied.[16] And I cannot but observe, that I never had one hour's sickness, while I stayed in this island. 'Tis true, I sometimes made a shift to catch a rabbit, or bird, by springes[17] made of Yahoos' hairs, and I often gathered wholesome herbs, which I boiled, or ate as salads with my bread, and now and then, for a rarity, I made a little butter, and drank the whey. I was at first at a great loss for salt; but custom soon reconciled the want of it; and I am confident that the frequent use of salt among us is an effect of luxury, and was first introduced only as a provocative to drink; except where it is necessary for preserving of flesh in long voyages, or in places remote from great markets. For we observe no animal to be fond of it but man:[18] and as to myself, when I left this country, it was a great while before I could endure the taste of it in anything that I ate.

This is enough to say upon the subject of my diet, wherewith other travelers fill their books, as if the readers were personally concerned whether we fared[19] well or ill. However, it was necessary to mention this matter, lest the world should think it impossible that I could find sustenance for three years in such a country, and among such inhabitants.

When it grew towards evening, the master horse ordered a place for me to lodge in; it was but six yards from the house, and separated from the stable of the Yahoos. Here I got some straw, and covering myself with my own clothes, slept very sound. But I was in a short time better accommodated, as the reader shall know hereafter, when I come to treat more particularly about my way of living.

CHAPTER 3

The author studious to learn the language, the Houyhnhnm his master assists in teaching him. The language described. Several Houyhnhnms of quality come out of curiosity to see the author. He gives his master a short account of his voyage.

My principal endeavor was to learn the language, which my master (for so I shall henceforth call him) and his children, and every servant of his house were desirous to teach me. For they looked upon it as a prodigy that a brute animal should discover[1] such marks of a rational creature. I pointed to everything, and inquired the name of it, which I wrote down in my journal book when I was alone, and corrected my bad accent, by desiring those of the family to pronounce it often. In this employment, a sorrel nag, one of the under servants, was very ready to assist me.

In speaking, they pronounce through the nose and throat, and their language approaches nearest to the High Dutch or German, of any I know in Europe; but is much more graceful and significant.[2] The Emperor Charles V made almost the same observation, when he said, that if he were to speak to his horse, it should be in High Dutch.[3]

The curiosity and impatience of my master were so great, that he spent many hours of his leisure to instruct me. He was convinced (as he afterwards told me) that I must be a Yahoo, but my teachableness, civility, and cleanliness astonished him;

16. A commonplace idea in ancient satire; Swift may here be mocking it.
17. Snares.
18. This is, of course, untrue, but Gulliver's subsequent dislike of salt indicates his dislike of human society in general.

19. A pun on "fare," meaning both food and "to get along."
1. Display.
2. Expressive.
3. I.e., German; Charles V of Spain (1500–1551) was believed to have said that he would address his God in Spanish, his mistress in Italian, and his horse in German.

which were qualities altogether so opposite to those animals. He was most perplexed about my clothes, reasoning sometimes with himself, whether they were a part of my body; for I never pulled them off till the family were asleep, and got them on before they waked in the morning. My master was eager to learn from whence I came, how I acquired those appearances of reason, which I discovered in all my actions, and to know my story from my own mouth, which he hoped he should soon do by the great proficiency I made in learning and pronouncing their words and sentences. To help my memory, I formed all I learned into the English alphabet, and writ the words down with the translations. This last, after some time, I ventured to do in my master's presence. It cost me much trouble to explain to him what I was doing; for the inhabitants have not the least idea of books or literature.

In about ten weeks' time I was able to understand most of his questions, and in three months could give him some tolerable answers. He was extremely curious to know from what part of the country I came, and how I was taught to imitate a rational creature, because the Yahoos (whom he saw I exactly resembled in my head, hands, and face, that were only visible), with some appearance of cunning, and the strongest disposition to mischief, were observed to be the most unteachable of all brutes. I answered, that I came over the sea, from a far place, with many others of my own kind, in a great hollow vessel made of the bodies of trees. That my companions forced me to land on this coast, and then left me to shift for myself. It was with some difficulty, and by the help of many signs, that I brought him to understand me. He replied, that I must needs be mistaken, or that I *said the thing which was not*. (For they have no word in their language to express lying or falsehood.) He knew it was impossible[4] that there could be a country beyond the sea, or that a parcel of brutes could move a wooden vessel whither they pleased upon water. He was sure no Houyhnhnm alive could make such a vessel, or would trust Yahoos to manage it.

The word *Houyhnhnm*, in their tongue, signifies a *horse*, and in its etymology, the *Perfection of Nature*. I told my master, that I was at a loss for expression, but would improve as fast as I could; and hoped in a short time I should be able to tell him wonders: he was pleased to direct his own mare, his colt and foal, and the servants of the family to take all opportunities of instructing me, and every day for two or three hours, he was at the same pains himself: several horses and mares of quality in the neighborhood came often to our house upon the report spread of a wonderful Yahoo, that could speak like a Houyhnhnm, and seemed in his words and actions to discover some glimmerings of reason. These delighted to converse with me; they put many questions, and received such answers as I was able to return. By all which advantages, I made so great a progress, that in five months from my arrival, I understood whatever was spoke, and could express myself tolerably well.

The Houyhnhnms who came to visit my master, out of a design of seeing and talking with me, could hardly believe me to be a right[5] Yahoo, because my body had a different covering from others of my kind. They were astonished to observe me without the usual hair or skin, except on my head, face, and hands; but I discovered that secret to my master, upon an accident, which happened about a fortnight before.

I have already told the reader, that every night when the family were gone to bed, it was my custom to strip and cover myself with my clothes: it happened one morning early, that my master sent for me, by the sorrel nag, who was his valet; when

4. The Houyhnhnm thus shows himself to be so dependent on reason that he is dogmatic in his ignorance, unable (like rationalists in religion) to accept what he does not know by his own reasoning.
5. True.

he came, I was fast asleep, my clothes fallen off on one side, and my shirt above my waist. I awaked at the noise he made, and observed him to deliver his message in some disorder; after which he went to my master, and in a great fright gave him a very confused account of what he had seen: this I presently discovered; for going as soon as I was dressed, to pay my attendance upon his Honor, he asked me the meaning of what his servant had reported, that I was not the same thing when I slept as I appeared to be at other times; that his valet assured him, some part of me was white, some yellow, at least not so white, and some brown.

I had hitherto concealed the secret of my dress, in order to distinguish myself as much as possible, from that cursed race of Yahoos; but now I found it in vain to do so any longer. Besides, I considered that my clothes and shoes would soon wear out, which already were in a declining condition, and must be supplied by some contrivance from the hides of Yahoos or other brutes; whereby the whole secret would be known: I therefore told my master, that in the country from whence I came, those of my kind always covered their bodies with the hairs of certain animals prepared by art, as well for decency, as to avoid inclemencies of air both hot and cold; of which, as to my own person, I would give him immediate conviction, if he pleased to command me; only desiring his excuse, if I did not expose those parts that Nature taught us to conceal. He said my discourse was all very strange, but especially the last part; for he could not understand why Nature should teach us to conceal what Nature had given. That neither himself nor family were ashamed of any parts of their bodies; but however I might do as I pleased. Whereupon, I first unbuttoned my coat, and pulled it off. I did the same with my waistcoat;[6] I drew off my shoes, stockings, and breeches. I let my shirt down to my waist, and drew up the bottom, fastening it like a girdle about my middle to hide my nakedness.

My master observed the whole performance with great signs of curiosity and admiration. He took up all my clothes in his pastern, one piece after another, and examined them diligently; he then stroked my body very gently, and looked round me several times, after which he said, it was plain I must be a perfect Yahoo; but that I differed very much from the rest of my species, in the softness, and whiteness, and smoothness of my skin, my want of hair in several parts of my body, the shape and shortness of my claws behind and before, and my affectation of walking continually on my two hinder feet. He desired to see no more, and gave me leave to put on my clothes again, for I was shuddering with cold.

I expressed my uneasiness at his giving me so often the appellation of *Yahoo*, an odious animal, for which I had so utter an hatred and contempt; I begged he would forbear applying that word to me, and take the same order in his family, and among his friends whom he suffered to see me. I requested likewise, that the secret of my having a false covering to my body might be known to none but himself, at least as long as my present clothing should last; for, as to what the sorrel nag his valet had observed, his Honor might command him to conceal it.

All this my master very graciously consented to,[7] and thus the secret was kept till my clothes began to wear out, which I was forced to supply by several contrivances, that shall hereafter be mentioned. In the meantime, he desired I would go on with my utmost diligence to learn their language, because he was more astonished at my capacity for speech and reason, than at the figure of my body, whether it were

6. Vest.

7. The Houyhnhnms may have no word for "lying," but they can hide the truth.

covered or no; adding, that he waited with some impatience to hear the wonders which I promised to tell him.

From thenceforward he doubled the pains he had been at to instruct me; he brought me into all company, and made them treat me with civility, because, as he told them privately, this would put me into good humor, and make me more diverting.

Every day when I waited on him, beside the trouble he was at in teaching, he would ask me several questions concerning myself, which I answered as well as I could; and by those means he had already received some general ideas, though very imperfect. It would be tedious to relate the several steps, by which I advanced to a more regular conversation: but the first account I gave of myself in any order and length, was to this purpose:

That, I came from a very far country, as I already had attempted to tell him, with about fifty more of my own species; that we traveled upon the seas, in a great hollow vessel made of wood, and larger than his Honor's house. I described the ship to him in the best terms I could, and explained by the help of my handkerchief displayed, how it was driven forward by the wind. That upon a quarrel among us, I was set on shore on this coast, where I walked forward without knowing whither, till he delivered me from the persecution of those execrable Yahoos. He asked me, who made the ship, and how it was possible that the Houyhnhnms of my country would leave it to the management of brutes? My answer was, that I durst proceed no farther in my relation, unless he would give me his word and honor that he would not be offended, and then I would tell him the wonders I had so often promised. He agreed; and I went on by assuring him, that the ship was made by creatures like myself, who in all the countries I had traveled, as well as in my own, were the only governing, rational animals; and that upon my arrival hither, I was as much astonished to see the Houyhnhnms act like rational beings, as he or his friends could be in finding some marks of reason in a creature he was pleased to call a Yahoo, to which I owned my resemblance in every part, but could not account for their degenerate and brutal nature. I said farther, that if good fortune ever restored me to my native country, to relate my travels hither, as I resolved to do, everybody would believe that I *said the thing which was not;* that I invented the story out of my own head; and with all possible respect to himself, his family, and friends, and under his promise of not being offended, our countrymen would hardly think it probable, that a Houyhnhnm should be the presiding creature of a nation, and a Yahoo the brute.

Chapter 4

The Houyhnhnms' notion of truth and falsehood. The author's discourse disapproved by his master. The author gives a more particular account of himself, and the accidents of his voyage.

My master heard me with great appearances of uneasiness in his countenance, because *doubting* or *not believing,* are so little known in this country, that the inhabitants cannot tell how to behave themselves under such circumstances. And I remember in frequent discourses with my master concerning the nature of manhood,[1] in other parts of the world, having occasion to talk of *lying,* and *false representation,* it was with much difficulty that he comprehended what I meant, although he had otherwise a most acute judgment. For he argued thus: that the use of speech was

1. Human nature.

to make us understand one another, and to receive information of facts; now if any one *said the thing which was not,* these ends were defeated; because I cannot properly be said to understand him, and I am so far from receiving information, that he leaves me worse than in ignorance, for I am led to believe a thing *black* when it is *white,* and *short* when it is *long.* And these were all the notions he had concerning that faculty of *lying,* so perfectly well understood, and so universally practiced among human creatures.

To return from this digression; when I asserted that the Yahoos were the only governing animal in my country, which my master said was altogether past his conception, he desired to know, whether we had Houyhnhnms among us, and what was their employment: I told him, we had great numbers, that in summer they grazed in the fields, and in winter were kept in houses, with hay and oats, where Yahoo servants were employed to rub their skins smooth, comb their manes, pick their feet, serve them with food, and make their beds. I understand you well, said my master; it is now very plain, from all you have spoken, that whatever share of reason the Yahoos pretend to, the Houyhnhnms are your masters;[2] I heartily wish our Yahoos would be so tractable. I begged his Honor would please to excuse me from proceeding any farther, because I was very certain that the account he expected from me would be highly displeasing. But he insisted in commanding me to let him know the best and the worst: I told him, he should be obeyed. I owned, that the Houyhnhnms among us, whom we called *horses,* were the most generous and comely animal we had, that they excelled in strength and swiftness; and when they belonged to persons of quality, employed in traveling, racing, or drawing chariots, they were treated with much kindness and care, till they fell into diseases, or became foundered in the feet;[3] but then they were sold, and used to all kind of drudgery till they died; after which their skins were stripped and sold for what they were worth, and their bodies left to be devoured by dogs and birds of prey.[4] But the common race of horses had not so good fortune, being kept by farmers and carriers and other mean people, who put them to greater labor, and fed them worse. I described as well as I could, our way of riding, the shape and use of a bridle, a saddle, a spur, and a whip, of harness and wheels. I added, that we fastened plates of a certain hard substance called *iron* at the bottom of their feet, to preserve their hoofs from being broken by the stony ways on which we often traveled.

My master, after some expressions of great indignation, wondered how we dared to venture upon a Houyhnhnm's back, for he was sure that the weakest servant in his house would be able to shake off the strongest Yahoo, or by lying down, and rolling upon his back, squeeze the brute to death. I answered, that our horses were trained up from three or four years old to the several uses we intended them for; that if any of them proved intolerably vicious, they were employed for carriages; that they were severely beaten while they were young, for any mischievous tricks; that the males, designed for the common use of riding or draft, were generally *castrated* about two years after their birth, to take down their spirits, and make them more tame and gentle; that they were indeed sensible of rewards and punishments; but his Honor would please to consider, that they had not the least tincture of reason any more than the Yahoos in this country.

2. Possibly a satire on the English love of horses.
3. Until their feet give in from overwork.
4. Swift mockingly paraphrases the *Iliad* 1.4–6: "The souls of mighty Chiefs untimely slain; / Whose limbs unburied on the naked shore, / Devouring dogs and hungry vultures tore" (Pope's translation).

It put me to the pains of many circumlocutions to give my master a right idea of what I spoke; for their language doth not abound in variety of words, because their wants and passions are fewer than among us. But it is impossible to express his noble resentment at our savage treatment of the Houyhnhnm race, particularly after I had explained the manner and use of *castrating* horses among us, to hinder them from propagating their kind, and to render them more servile. He said, if it were possible there could be any country where Yahoos alone were endued with reason, they certainly must be the governing animal, because reason will in time always prevail against brutal strength. But, considering the frame of our bodies, and especially of mine, he thought no creature of equal bulk was so ill-contrived for employing that reason in the common offices of life; whereupon he desired to know whether those among whom I lived, resembled me or the Yahoos of his country. I assured him, that I was as well shaped as most of my age, but the younger and the females were much more soft and tender, and the skins of the latter generally as white as milk. He said, I differed indeed from other Yahoos, being much more cleanly, and not altogether so deformed, but in point of real advantage, he thought I differed for the worse. That my nails were of no use either to my fore or hinder feet; as to my forefeet, he could not properly call them by that name, for he never observed me to walk upon them; that they were too soft to bear the ground; that I generally went with them uncovered, neither was the covering I sometimes wore on them of the same shape, or so strong as that on my feet behind. That I could not walk with any security, for if either of my hinder feet slipped, I must inevitably fall. He then began to find fault with other parts of my body, the flatness of my face, the prominence of my nose, mine eyes placed directly in front, so that I could not look on either side without turning my head, that I was not able to feed myself, without lifting one of my forefeet to my mouth, and therefore Nature had placed those joints to answer that necessity. He knew not what could be the use of those several clefts and divisions in my feet behind; that these were too soft to bear the hardness and sharpness of stones without a covering made from the skin of some other brute; that my whole body wanted a fence against heat and cold, which I was forced to put on and off every day with tediousness and trouble. And lastly, that he observed every animal in this country naturally to abhor the Yahoos, whom the weaker avoided, and the stronger drove from them. So that supposing us to have the gift of reason, he could not see how it were possible to cure that natural antipathy which every creature discovered[5] against us; nor consequently, how we could tame and render them serviceable. However, he would (as he said) debate that matter no farther, because he was more desirous to know my own story, the country where I was born, and the several actions and events of my life before I came hither.

I assured him, how extremely desirous I was that he should be satisfied in every point; but I doubted much, whether it would be possible for me to explain myself on several subjects whereof his Honor could have no conception, because I saw nothing in his country to which I could resemble[6] them. That, however, I would do my best, and strive to express myself by similitudes, humbly desiring his assistance when I wanted proper words; which he was pleased to promise me.

I said, my birth was of honest parents, in an island called England, which was remote from this country, as many days' journey as the strongest of his Honor's servants could travel in the annual course of the sun. That I was bred a surgeon, whose

5. Displayed.   6. Compare.

trade it is to cure wounds and hurts in the body, got by accident or violence; that my country was governed by a female man, whom we called a *Queen*. That I left it to get riches,[7] whereby I might maintain myself and family when I should return. That in my last voyage, I was commander of the ship, and had about fifty Yahoos under me, many of which died at sea, and I was forced to supply[8] them by others picked out from several nations. That our ship was twice in danger of being sunk; the first time by a great storm, and the second, by striking against a rock. Here my master interposed, by asking me, how I could persuade strangers out of different countries to venture with me, after the losses I had sustained, and the hazards I had run. I said, they were fellows of desperate fortunes, forced to fly from the places of their birth, on account of their poverty or their crimes. Some were undone by lawsuits; others spent all they had in drinking, whoring, and gaming; others fled for treason; many for murder, theft, poisoning, robbery, perjury, forgery, coining false money, for committing rapes or sodomy, for flying from their colors,[9] or deserting to the enemy, and most of them had broken prison; none of these durst return to their native countries for fear of being hanged, or of starving in a jail; and therefore were under a necessity of seeking a livelihood in other places.

During this discourse, my master was pleased often to interrupt me. I had made use of many circumlocutions in describing to him the nature of the several crimes, for which most of our crew had been forced to fly their country. This labor took up several days' conversation before he was able to comprehend me. He was wholly at a loss to know what could be the use or necessity of practicing those vices. To clear up which I endeavored to give him some ideas of the desire of power and riches, of the terrible effects of lust, intemperance, malice, and envy. All this I was forced to define and describe by putting of cases, and making suppositions. After which, like one whose imagination was struck with something never seen or heard of before, he would lift up his eyes with amazement and indignation. Power, government, war, law, punishment, and a thousand other things had no terms, wherein that language could express them, which made the difficulty almost insuperable to give my master any conception of what I meant. But being of an excellent understanding, much improved by contemplation and converse, he at last arrived at a competent knowledge of what human nature in our parts of the world is capable to perform, and desired I would give him some particular account of that land, which we call Europe, but especially, of my own country.

from CHAPTER 9

A grand debate at the general Assembly of the Houyhnhnms, and how it was determined. The learning of the Houyhnhnms. Their buildings. Their manner of burials. The defectiveness of their language.

One of these grand Assemblies was held in my time, about three months before my departure, whither my master went as the Representative of our district. In this Council was resumed their old debate, and indeed, the only debate that ever happened in their country; whereof my master after his return gave me a very particular account.

The question to be debated, was, whether the Yahoos should be exterminated from the face of the earth. One of the *members* for the affirmative offered several

---

7. Gulliver originally stated that he undertook his second and third voyages out of a desire to travel: he now reads all human motivation in the worst possible light.

8. Replace.

9. Deserting their regiment in the army.

arguments of great strength and weight, alleging, that as the Yahoos were the most filthy, noisome, and deformed animal which Nature ever produced, so they were the most restive and indocible,[1] mischievous, and malicious: they would privately suck the teats of the Houyhnhnms' cows, kill and devour their cats, trample down their oats and grass, if they were not continually watched, and commit a thousand other extravagancies. He took notice of a general tradition, that Yahoos had not been always in their country, but, that many ages ago, two of these brutes appeared together upon a mountain,[2] whether produced by the heat of the sun upon corrupted mud and slime, or from the ooze and froth of the sea, was never known.[3] That these Yahoos engendered, and their brood in a short time grew so numerous as to overrun and infest the whole nation. That the Houyhnhnms, to get rid of this evil, made a general hunting, and at last enclosed the whole herd; and destroying the elder, every Houyhnhnm kept two young ones in a kennel, and brought them to such a degree of tameness, as an animal so savage by nature can be capable of acquiring; using them for draft and carriage. That there seemed to be much truth in this tradition, and that those creatures could not be *ylnhniamshy* (or *aborigines* of the land) because of the violent hatred the Houyhnhnms, as well as all other animals, bore them; which although their evil disposition sufficiently deserved, could never have arrived at so high a degree, if they had been *aborigines,* or else they would have long since been rooted out. That the inhabitants taking a fancy to use the service of the Yahoos, had very imprudently neglected to cultivate the breed of *asses,* which were a comely animal, easily kept, more tame and orderly, without any offensive smell, strong enough for labor, although they yield to the other in agility of body; and if their braying be no agreeable sound, it is far preferable to the horrible howlings of the Yahoos.[4]

Several others declared their sentiments to the same purpose, when my master proposed an expedient to the assembly, whereof he had indeed borrowed the hint from me. He approved of the tradition, mentioned by the Honorable Member who spoke before, and affirmed, that the two Yahoos said to be first seen among them had been driven thither over the sea; that coming to land, and being forsaken by their companions, they retired to the mountains, and degenerating by degrees, became in process of time, much more savage than those of their own species in the country from whence these two originals came. The reason of his assertion was, that he had now in his possession a certain wonderful[5] Yahoo (meaning myself), which most of them had heard of, and many of them had seen. He then related to them, how he first found me: that my body was all covered with an artificial composure of the skins and hairs of other animals; that I spoke in a language of my own, and had thoroughly learned theirs; that I had related to him the accidents which brought me thither; that when he saw me without my covering, I was an exact Yahoo in every part, only of a whiter color, less hairy, and with shorter claws. He added, how I had endeavored to persuade him, that in my own and other countries the Yahoos acted as the governing, rational animal, and held the Houyhnhnms in servitude; that he observed in me all the qualities of a Yahoo, only a little more civilized by some tinc-

1. Unteachable.
2. Probably Milton's "steep savage Hill," the garden of Eden (*Paradise Lost,* 4.172).
3. Humans are supposed to be of divine origin, but the Yahoos represent such a degraded form of humanity that they (like, it was believed, insects on the Nile's banks) were formed from the action of the sun on mud.

4. The commonplace comparison of humans to asses was one Swift had previously used in *A Tale of a Tub* (1704) and *The Battle of the Books* (1704).
5. Amazing, unusual.

ture of reason, which however was in a degree as far inferior to the Houyhnhnm race, as the Yahoos of their country were to me;[6] that, among other things, I mentioned a custom we had of *castrating* Houyhnhnms when they were young, in order to render them tame; that the operation was easy and safe; that it was no shame to learn wisdom from brutes, as industry is taught by the ant, and building by the swallow. (For so I translate the word *lyhannh*, although it be a much larger fowl.) That this invention might be practiced upon the younger Yahoos here, which, besides rendering them tractable and fitter for use, would in an age put an end to the whole species without destroying life. That, in the meantime the Houyhnhnms should be exhorted to cultivate the breed of asses, which, as they are in all respects more valuable brutes, so they have this advantage, to be fit for service at five years old, which the others are not till twelve.

This was all my master thought fit to tell me at that time, of what passed in the grand Council. But he was pleased to conceal[7] one particular, which related personally to myself, whereof I soon felt the unhappy effect, as the reader will know in its proper place, and from whence I date all the succeeding misfortunes of my life. ✳ ✳ ✳

CHAPTER 10

The author's economy[1] and happy life among the Houyhnhnms. His great improvement in virtue, by conversing with them. Their conversations. The author hath notice given him by his master that he must depart from the country. He falls into a swoon for grief, but submits. He contrives and finishes a canoe, by the help of a fellow servant, and puts to sea at a venture.[2]

I had settled my little economy to my own heart's content. My master had ordered a room to be made for me after their manner, about six yards from the house, the sides and floors of which I plastered with clay, and covered with rush mats of my own contriving; I had beaten hemp, which there grows wild, and made of it a sort of ticking;[3] this I filled with the feathers of several birds I had taken with springes made of Yahoos' hairs, and were excellent food. I had worked[4] two chairs with my knife, the sorrel nag helping me in the grosser[5] and more laborious part. When my clothes were worn to rags, I made myself others with the skins of rabbits, and of a certain beautiful animal about the same size, called *nnuhnoh*, the skin of which is covered with a fine down. Of these I likewise made very tolerable stockings. I soled my shoes with wood which I cut from a tree, and fitted to the upper leather, and when this was worn out, I supplied it with the skins of Yahoos dried in the sun. I often got honey out of hollow trees, which I mingled with water,[6] or ate it with my bread. No man could more verify the truth of these two maxims, *That nature is very easily satisfied*; and, *That necessity is the mother of invention*. I enjoyed perfect health of body and tranquillity of mind; I did not feel the treachery or inconstancy of a friend, nor the injuries of a secret or open enemy. I had no occasion of bribing, flattering, or pimping, to procure the favor of any great man or of his minion. I wanted no fence[7]

---

6. Gulliver falls between the Houyhnhnms and the Yahoos in reason, as he did between the Lilliputians and the Brobdingnagians in size.
7. Another indication that the Houyhnhnms are not completely honest or candid.
1. Method of living.

2. Without further planning.
3. Sturdy material used for making mattress covering.
4. Made.
5. Heavier, larger.
6. Honey-sweetened water was a Utopian drink.
7. Defense.

against fraud or oppression; here was neither physician to destroy my body, nor lawyer to ruin my fortune; no informer to watch my words and actions, or forge accusations against me for hire; here were no jibers, censurers, backbiters, pickpockets, highwaymen, housebreakers, attorneys, bawds, buffoons, gamesters, politicians, wits, splenetics, tedious talkers, controvertists, ravishers, murderers, robbers, virtuosos;[8] no leaders or followers of party and faction; no encouragers to vice, by seducement or examples; no dungeon, axes, gibbets, whipping posts, or pillories; no cheating shopkeepers or mechanics;[9] no pride, vanity, or affectation; no fops, bullies, drunkards, strolling whores, or poxes;[10] no ranting, lewd, expensive wives; no stupid, proud pendants; no importunate, overbearing, quarrelsome, noisy, roaring, empty, conceited, swearing companions; no scoundrels, raised from the dust upon the merit of their vices, or nobility thrown into it on account of their virtues; no lords, fiddlers, judges, or dancing masters.[11]

I had the favor of being admitted to[12] several Houyhnhnms, who came to visit or dine with my master; where his Honor graciously suffered me to wait in the room, and listen to their discourse. Both he and his company would often descend to ask me questions, and receive my answers. I had also sometimes the honor of attending my master in his visits to others. I never presumed to speak, except in answer to a question, and then I did it with inward regret, because it was a loss of so much time for improving myself; but I was infinitely delighted with the station of a humble auditor in such conversations, where nothing passed but what was useful, expressed in the fewest and most significant words; where (as I have already said) the greatest *decency* was observed, without the least degree of ceremony; where no person spoke without being pleased himself, and pleasing his companions; where there was no interruption, tediousness, heat,[13] or difference of sentiments. They have a notion, that when people are met together, a short silence doth much improve conversation: this I found to be true, for during those little intermissions of talk, new ideas would arise in their minds, which very much enlivened the discourse. Their subjects are generally on friendship and benevolence, or order and economy, sometimes upon the visible operations of Nature, or ancient traditions, upon the bounds and limits of virtue, upon the unerring rules of reason, or upon some determinations to be taken at the next great Assembly, and often upon the various excellencies of *poetry*. I may add without vanity, that my presence often gave them sufficient matter for discourse, because it afforded my master an occasion of letting his friends into the history of me and my country, upon which they were all pleased to descant in a manner not very advantageous to humankind; and for that reason I shall not repeat what they said: only I may be allowed to observe, that his Honor, to my great admiration, appeared to understand the nature of Yahoos much better than myself. He went through all our vices and follies, and discovered many which I had never mentioned to him, by only supposing what qualities a Yahoo of their country, with a small proportion of reason, might be capable of exerting; and concluded, with too much probability, how vile as well as miserable such a creature must be.

I freely confess, that all the little knowledge I have of any value, was acquired by the lectures I received from my master, and from hearing the discourses of him

8. One knowledgeable or interested in apparently trivial "scientific" pursuits.
9. Laborers.
10. Venereal diseases.

11. That necessary tutor for the socially aspiring, the dancing master (usually French), was a particular figure of fun; he usually accompanied himself on the fiddle.
12. Allowed to meet.
13. Heat of argument.

and his friends; to which I should be prouder to listen, than to dictate to the greatest and wisest assembly in Europe. I admired the strength, comeliness, and speed of the inhabitants; and such a constellation of virtues in such amiable persons produced in me the highest veneration. At first, indeed, I did not feel that natural awe which the Yahoos and all other animals bear towards them, but it grew upon me by degrees, much sooner than I imagined, and was mingled with a respectful love and gratitude, that they would condescend to distinguish me from the rest of my species.

When I thought of my family, my friends, my countrymen, or human race in general, I considered them as they really were, Yahoos in shape and disposition, perhaps a little more civilized, and qualified with the gift of speech, but making no other use of reason, than to improve and multiply those vices, whereof their brethren in this country had only the share that Nature allotted them. When I happened to behold the reflection of my own form in a lake or a fountain, I turned away my face in horror and detestation of myself,[14] and could better endure the sight of a common Yahoo, than of my own person. By conversing with the Houyhnhnms, and looking upon them with delight, I fell to imitate their gait and gesture, which is now grown into a habit, and my friends often tell me in a blunt way, that I *trot like a horse*; which, however, I take for a great compliment; neither shall I disown, that in speaking I am apt to fall into the voice and manner of the Houyhnhnms, and hear myself ridiculed on that account without the least mortification.

In the midst of all this happiness, when I looked upon myself to be fully settled for life, my master sent for me one morning a little earlier than his usual hour. I observed by his countenance that he was in some perplexity, and at a loss how to begin what he had to speak. After a short silence, he told me, he did not know how I would take what he was going to say; that in the last general Assembly, when the affair of the Yahoos was entered upon, the representatives had taken offense at his keeping a Yahoo (meaning myself) in his family more like a Houyhnhnm, than a brute animal. That he was known frequently to converse with me, as if he could receive some advantage or pleasure in my company; that such a practice was not agreeable to reason or Nature, or a thing ever heard of before among them. The Assembly did therefore *exhort* him, either to employ me like the rest of my species, or command me to swim back to the place from whence I came. That the first of these expedients was utterly rejected by all the Houyhnhnms who had ever seen me at his house or their own, for they alleged, that because I had some rudiments of reason, added to the natural pravity[15] of those animals, it was to be feared, I might be able to seduce them into the woody and mountainous parts of the country, and bring them in troops by night to destroy the Houyhnhnms' cattle, as being naturally of the ravenous[16] kind, and averse from labor.

My master added, that he was daily pressed by the Houyhnhnms of the neighborhood to have the Assembly's *exhortation* executed, which he could not put off much longer. He doubted[17] it would be impossible for me to swim to another country, and therefore wished I would contrive some sort of vehicle resembling those I had described to him, that might carry me on the sea, in which work I should have the assistance of his own servants, as well as those of his neighbors. He concluded, that

---

14. A mocking reversal both of a common pattern in pastoral love poetry and of the Greek myth of Narcissus.
15. Depravity.

16. Rapacious, predatory, or greedy.
17. Feared.

for his own part he could have been content to keep me in his service as long as I lived, because he found I had cured myself of some bad habits and dispositions, by endeavoring, as far as my inferior nature was capable, to imitate the Houyhnhnms.

I should here observe to the reader, that a decree of the general Assembly in this country is expressed by the word *hnhloayn*, which signifies an *exhortation*, as near as I can render it, for they have no conception how a rational creature can be *compelled*, but only advised, or *exhorted*, because no person can disobey reason, without giving up his claim to be a rational creature.

I was struck with the utmost grief and despair at my master's discourse, and being unable to support the agonies I was under, I fell into a swoon at his feet; when I came to myself, he told me, that he concluded I had been dead. (For these people are subject to no such imbecilities of nature.) I answered, in a faint voice, that death would have been too great an happiness; that although I could not blame the Assembly's *exhortation*, or the urgency[18] of his friends, yet in my weak and corrupt judgment, I thought it might consist[19] with reason to have been less rigorous. That I could not swim a league, and probably the nearest land to theirs might be distant above a hundred; that many materials, necessary for making a small vessel to carry me off, were wholly wanting in this country, which, however, I would attempt in obedience and gratitude to his Honor, although I concluded the thing to be impossible, and therefore looked on myself as already devoted to destruction. That the certain prospect of an unnatural death was the least of my evils: for, supposing I should escape with life by some strange adventure, how could I think with temper[20] of passing my days among Yahoos, and relapsing into my old corruptions, for want of examples to lead and keep me within the paths of virtue? That I knew too well upon what solid reasons all the determinations of the wise Houyhnhnms were founded, not to be shaken by arguments of mine, a miserable Yahoo; and therefore after presenting him with my humble thanks for the offer of his servants' assistance in making a vessel, and desiring a reasonable time for so difficult a work, I told him I would endeavor to preserve a wretched being; and, if ever I returned to England, was not without hopes of being useful to my own species, by celebrating the praises of the renowned Houyhnhnms, and proposing their virtues to the imitation of mankind.

My master in a few words made me a very gracious reply, allowed me the space of two *months* to finish my boat; and ordered the sorrel nag, my fellow servant (for so at this distance I may presume to call him) to follow my instructions, because I told my master, that his help would be sufficient, and I knew he had a tenderness for me.

In his company my first business was to go to that part of the coast, where my rebellious crew had ordered me to be set on shore. I got upon a height, and looking on every side into the sea, fancied I saw a small island, towards the northeast: I took out my pocket glass, and could then clearly distinguish it about five leagues off, as I computed; but it appeared to the sorrel nag to be only a blue cloud: for, as he had no conception of any country beside his own, so he could not be as expert in distinguishing remote objects at sea, as we who so much converse[21] in that element.

After I had discovered this island, I considered no farther; but resolved it should, if possible, be the first place of my banishment, leaving the consequence to Fortune.

I returned home, and consulting with the sorrel nag, we went into a copse at some distance, where I with my knife, and he with a sharp flint fastened very artifi-

---

18. Urging.
19. Be consistent.

20. Calmness.
21. Are familiar with.

cially, after their manner, to a wooden handle, cut down several oak wattles about the thickness of a walking staff, and some larger pieces. But I shall not trouble the reader with a particular description of my own mechanics; let it suffice to say, that in six weeks' time, with the help of the sorrel nag, who performed the parts that required most labor, I finished a sort of Indian canoe, but much larger, covering it with the skins of Yahoos well stitched together, with hempen threads of my own making. My sail was likewise composed of the skins of the same animal; but I made use of the youngest I could get, the older being too tough and thick, and I likewise provided myself with four paddles. I laid in a stock of boiled flesh, of rabbits and fowls, and took with me two vessels, one filled with milk, and the other with water.

I tried my canoe in a large pond near my master's house, and then corrected in it what was amiss; stopping all the chinks with Yahoos' tallow, till I found it staunch,[22] and able to bear me and my freight. And when it was as complete as I could possibly make it, I had it drawn on a carriage very gently by Yahoos, to the seaside, under the conduct of the sorrel nag, and another servant.

When all was ready, and the day came for my departure, I took leave of my master and lady, and the whole family, mine eyes flowing with tears, and my heart quite sunk with grief. But his Honor, out of curiosity, and perhaps (if I may speak it without vanity) partly out of kindness, was determined to see me in my canoe, and got several of his neighboring friends to accompany him. I was forced to wait above an hour for the tide, and then observing the wind very fortunately bearing towards the island, to which I intended to steer my course, I took a second leave of my master, but as I was going to prostrate myself to kiss his hoof, he did me the honor to raise it gently to my mouth. I am not ignorant how much I have been censured for mentioning this last particular. For my detractors are pleased to think it improbable, that so illustrious a person should descend to give so great a mark of distinction to a creature so inferior as I. Neither have I forgot, how apt some travelers are to boast of extraordinary favors they have received.[23] But if these censurers were better acquainted with the noble and courteous disposition of the Houyhnhnms, they would soon change their opinion.

I paid my respects to the rest of the Houyhnhnms in his Honor's company; then getting into my canoe, I pushed off from shore.

22. Watertight.
23. Swift heightens the absurdity of Gulliver's action, and draws attention to his later misanthropy.

Alexander Pope
1688–1744

from An Essay on Criticism

Of all the causes which conspire to blind
Man's erring judgment, and misguide the mind,
What the weak head with strongest bias[1] rules,
Is pride, the never-failing vice of fools.
205 Whatever Nature has in worth denied,
She gives in large recruits° of needful° pride;   *supplies / needed*
For as in bodies, thus in souls, we find
What wants° in blood and spirits, swelled with wind;   *is lacking*
Pride, where wit fails, steps in to our defense,
210 And fills up all the mighty void of sense!
If once right reason drives that cloud away,
Truth breaks upon us with resistless day;
Trust not yourself; but your defects to know,
Make use of every friend—and every foe.
215   A little learning is a dang'rous thing;
Drink deep, or taste not the Pierian spring:[2]
There shallow draughts[3] intoxicate the brain,
And drinking largely sobers us again.
Fired at first sight with what the Muse imparts,
220 In fearless youth we tempt° the heights of Arts,   *attempt*
While from the bounded° level of our mind,   *limited*
Short views we take, nor see the lengths behind,
But more advanced, behold with strange surprise
New, distant scenes of endless science[4] rise!
225 So pleased at first, the towering Alps we try,
Mount o'er the vales, and seem to tread the sky;
Th' eternal snows appear already past,
And the first clouds and mountains seem the last:
But those attained, we tremble to survey
230 The growing labors of the lengthened way,
Th' increasing prospect tires our wandering eyes,
Hills peep o'er hills, and Alps on Alps arise! * * *
285   Thus critics, of less judgment than caprice,
Curious,° not knowing, not exact, but nice,°   *picky / fussy*
Form short ideas; and offend in arts
(As most in manners) by a love to parts.[5]
Some to conceit[6] alone their taste confine,
290 And glitt'ring thoughts struck out at every line;
Pleased with a work where nothing's just or fit;
One glaring chaos and wild heap of wit:
Poets like painters, thus, unskilled to trace
The naked Nature and the living grace,

1. Not only prejudice but a kind of bowling ball. (In bowls, the bias ball is one weighted to roll obliquely.)
2. Hippocrene, the stream associated with the Muses.
3. I.e., drinking small amounts.
4. Knowledge, subjects requiring study.
5. Individual talents.
6. Extravagant use of metaphor.

295	With gold and jewels cover every part,	
	And hide with ornaments their want° of art.	*lack*
	True wit is Nature to advantage dressed,	
	What oft was thought, but ne'er so well expressed,	
	Something, whose truth convinced at sight we find,	
300	That gives us back the image of our mind:	
	As shades° more sweetly recommend the light,	*shadows*
	So modest plainness sets off sprightly wit:	
	For works may have more wit than does 'em good,	
	As bodies perish through excess of blood.[7]	

Introduction to The Rape of the Lock

"New things are made familiar, and familiar things are made new," wrote Samuel Johnson about the most accomplished poem of Pope's younger years. "The whole detail of a female day is brought before us invested with so much art of decoration that, though nothing is disguised, everything is striking."

Only a poet with formidable imaginative powers could have made a great mock-heroic poem out of such unpromising materials. When Robert, Lord Petre, cut a love-lock from the head of Arabella Fermor without her permission, the two young people, both in their early twenties, quarreled bitterly. Their families, leading members of the Roman Catholic gentry once on the friendliest terms, became seriously estranged. Pope's friend John Caryll, who saw himself as a mediator among the group, asked him "to write a poem to make a jest of it, and laugh them together."

Pope's first effort was a poem in two cantos, *The Rape of the Locke*, printed in 1712 with some of his other pieces and the work of other poets. Two years later, Pope separately published *The Rape of the Lock*, enlarged to five cantos by the addition of the "machinery" of the sylphs and gnomes, and by the game of Ombre. The poem reached its final form in 1717 when Pope added the moralizing declamation of Clarissa (5.7–35), a parody of the speech of Sarpedon to Glaucus in the *Iliad*. The mock-epic tenor of the five-canto poem was clearly influenced by Pope's translation of the *Iliad*, his main project while most of *The Rape of the Lock* was being composed. Other influences were Homer's *Odyssey*, Virgil's *Aeneid*, Milton's *Paradise Lost*, and Boileau's *Le Lutrin* (1674, 1683), a mock-heroic satire on clerical infighting over the placement of a lectern. Yoking together the mundanely trivial and the mythically heroic as he follows the course of Belinda's day, Pope produced a vivid, yet affectionate, mockery of the fashions and sexual mores common in his own social circle.

The arming of the champion for war became the application of Belinda's (i.e., Arabella's) make-up for the battle of the sexes; the larger-than-life gods of classical mythology became miniature cartoon-like sylphs; Aeneas' voyage up the Tiber became Belinda's progress up the Thames; the depiction of Achilles' shield became the description of Belinda's petticoat; the test of single combat became the game of cards; the hero's journey to the underworld became the gnome's adventure in the Cave of Spleen; and the rape of Helen that started the Trojan War became the "rape" (stealing) of Belinda's hair that began an unpleasant social squabble. All the trappings of classical epic are here: the divine messenger appearing to the hero in a dream, the sacrifice to the gods, the inspirational speech to the troops before battle, the epic feast, the violent melee, and the final triumphant apotheosis. Throughout the poem, the enormous distance between the trivial *matter* and the heroic *manner* produces brilliantly comic results.

7. Apoplexy, it was thought, was caused by such an excess.

from The Rape of the Lock

from CANTO 1

What dire offense from am'rous causes springs,
What mighty contests rise from trivial things,
I sing[1]—This verse to Caryll, Muse! is due;
This, ev'n Belinda may vouchsafe to view:

5   Slight is the subject, but not so the praise,
If she inspire, and he approve my lays.°   *verses*
   Say what strange motive, Goddess!° could compel   *his Muse*
A well-bred lord t' assault a gentle belle?
Oh say what stranger cause, yet unexplored,

10 Could make a gentle belle reject a lord?
In tasks so bold, can little men engage,
And in soft bosoms dwells such mighty rage?
   Sol through white curtains shot a tim'rous ray,
And op'd those eyes that must eclipse the day;

15 Now lapdogs[2] give themselves the rousing shake,
And sleepless lovers, just at twelve, awake:
Thrice rung the bell, the slipper knocked the ground,[3]
And the pressed watch returned a silver sound.[4]
Belinda still her downy pillow pressed,

20 Her guardian Sylph prolonged the balmy rest. * * *

from CANTO 3

125   But when to mischief mortals bend their will,
How soon they find fit instruments of ill!
Just then, Clarissa drew with tempting grace
A two-edged weapon from her shining case;
So ladies in romance assist their knight,

130 Present the spear, and arm him for the fight.
He takes the gift with rev'rence, and extends
The little engine° on his fingers' ends,   *instrument*
This just behind Belinda's neck he spread,
As o'er the fragrant steams she bends her head:

135 Swift to the lock a thousand sprites repair,
A thousand wings, by turns, blow back the hair,
And thrice they twitched the diamond in her ear,
Thrice she looked back, and thrice the foe drew near. * * *

   The peer now spreads the glitt'ring forfex° wide,   *scissors*
T' enclose the lock; now joins it, to divide.
Ev'n then, before the fatal engine closed,

150 A wretched Sylph too fondly interposed;
Fate urged the shears, and cut the Sylph in twain

---

1. Pope begins with the ancient epic formula of "proposition" of the work as a whole, and "invocation" of the gods' assistance, continuing with the traditional epic questions.
2. Small dogs imported from Asia were highly fashionable ladies' pets at this time.

3. Belinda rings the bell and then finally bangs her slipper on the floor to call her maid.
4. The popular "pressed watch" chimed the hour and quarter hours when its stem was pressed, saving its owner from striking a match to see the time.

(But airy substance soon unites again)[1]
The meeting points the sacred hair dissever
From the fair head, forever and forever!
155   Then flashed the living lightning from her eyes,
And screams of horror rend th' affrighted skies.
Not louder shrieks to pitying Heav'n are cast,
When husbands or when lapdogs breathe their last,
Or when rich china vessels, fall'n from high,
160   In glitt'ring dust and painted fragments lie!
    Let wreaths of triumph now my temples twine,
(The victor cried) the glorious prize is mine!
While fish in streams, or birds delight in air,
Or in a coach and six[2] the British fair,
165   As long as *Atalantis*[3] shall be read,
Or the small pillow grace a lady's bed,[4]
While visits shall be paid on solemn days,
When numerous wax lights[5] in bright order blaze,
While nymphs take treats, or assignations give,
170   So long my honor, name, and praise shall live!
    What time would spare, from steel receives its date,°   *end*
And monuments, like men, submit to fate!
Steel could the labor of the gods destroy,
And strike to dust th' imperial tow'rs of Troy;[6]
175   Steel could the works of mortal pride confound,
And hew triumphal arches to the ground.
What wonder then, fair nymph! thy hairs should feel
The conqu'ring force of unresisted steel?

from CANTO 4

But anxious cares the pensive nymph oppressed,
And secret passions labored in her breast.
Not youthful kings in battle seized alive,
Not scornful virgins who their charms survive,
5   Not ardent lovers robbed of all their bliss,
Not ancient ladies when refused a kiss,
Not tyrants fierce that unrepenting die,
Not Cynthia when her manteau's° pinned awry,   *gown's*
E'er felt such rage, resentment, and despair,
10   As thou, sad virgin! for thy ravished hair. * * *

1. *Milton* lib. 6 [Pope's note], citing *Paradise Lost* 6.329–31, "The girding sword with discontinuous wound / Passed through him, but the ethereal substance closed / Not long divisible. . . ."
2. A carriage drawn by six horses; a symbol of wealth and prestige.
3. The scandalous *Atalantis: Secret Memoirs and Manners of Several Persons of Quality* (1709), by Mary Delarivière Manley.
4. Said to be a place where ladies hid romance novels and other contraband.
5. Candles made of wax, rather than the cheaper tallow. Evening social visits were an essential part of the fashionable woman's routine.
6. Even Troy, fabled to have been built by Apollo and Poseidon, was destroyed by arms.

from CANTO 5

    Then cease, bright nymph! to mourn thy ravished hair
Which adds new glory to the shining sphere!
Not all the tresses that fair head can boast
Shall draw such envy as the lock you lost.
145   For, after all the murders of your eye,
When, after millions slain, yourself shall die;
When those fair suns[1] shall set, as set they must,
And all those tresses shall be laid in dust;
This lock, the Muse shall consecrate to fame,
150   And mid'st the stars inscribe Belinda's name!

Thomas Gray
1716–1771

Elegy Written in a Country Churchyard

The curfew tolls the knell of parting day,
The lowing herd wind slowly o'er the lea,
The plowman homeward plods his weary way,
And leaves the world to darkness and to me.

5   Now fades the glimmering landscape on the sight,
And all the air a solemn stillness holds,
Save where the beetle wheels his droning flight,
And drowsy tinklings lull the distant folds;

Save that from yonder ivy-mantled tower
10   The moping owl does to the moon complain
Of such as, wand'ring near her secret bower,
Molest her ancient solitary reign.

Beneath those rugged elms, that yew-tree's shade,
Where heaves the turf in many a mouldering heap,
15   Each in his narrow cell for ever laid,
The rude forefathers of the hamlet sleep.

The breezy call of incense-breathing morn,
The swallow twitt'ring from the straw-built shed,
The cock's shrill clarion, or the echoing horn,
20   No more shall rouse them from their lowly bed.

For them no more the blazing hearth shall burn,
Or busy housewife ply her evening care:
No children run to lisp their sire's return,
Or climb his knees the envied kiss to share.

25   Oft did the harvest to their sickle yield,
Their furrow oft the stubborn glebe° has broke;   *clod of earth*
How jocund did they drive their team afield!

---

1. I.e., her eyes.

How bowed the woods beneath their sturdy stroke!

Let not Ambition mock their useful toil,
30   Their homely joys, and destiny obscure;
Nor Grandeur hear, with a disdainful smile,
The short and simple annals of the poor.

The boast of heraldry, the pomp of power,
And all that beauty, all that wealth e'er gave,
35   Awaits alike th' inevitable hour.
The paths of glory lead but to the grave.

Nor you, ye Proud, impute to these the fault,
If Mem'ry o'er their tomb no trophies raise,
Where through the long-drawn aisle and fretted vault
40   The pealing anthem swells the note of praise.

Can storied urn or animated bust
Back to its mansion call the fleeting breath?
Can Honor's voice provoke the silent dust,
Or Flatt'ry soothe the dull cold ear of Death?

45   Perhaps in this neglected spot is laid
Some heart once pregnant with celestial fire;
Hands that the rod of empire might have swayed,
Or waked to ecstasy the living lyre.

But Knowledge to their eyes her ample page
50   Rich with the spoils of time did ne'er unroll;
Chill Penury repressed their noble rage,
And froze the genial current of the soul.

Full many a gem of purest ray serene,
The dark unfathomed caves of ocean bear:
55   Full many a flower is born to blush unseen,
And waste its sweetness on the desert air.

Some village-Hampden[1] that with dauntless breast
The little tyrant of his fields withstood;
Some mute inglorious Milton here may rest,
60   Some Cromwell guiltless of his country's blood.

Th' applause of listening senates to command,
The threats of pain and ruin to despise,
To scatter plenty o'er a smiling land,
And read their history in a nation's eyes,

65   Their lot forbade: nor circumscribed alone
Their growing virtues, but their crimes confined;
Forbade to wade through slaughter to a throne,
And shut the gates of mercy on mankind,

1. John Hampden (1594–1643), Parliamentary statesman and general in the Civil Wars, famed for his firm defiance of Charles I.

The struggling pangs of conscious truth to hide,
70   To quench the blushes of ingenuous shame,
Or heap the shrine of Luxury and Pride
With incense kindled at the Muse's flame.[2]

Far from the madding crowd's ignoble strife,
Their sober wishes never learned to stray;
75   Along the cool sequestered vale of life
They kept the noiseless tenor of their way.

Yet ev'n these bones from insult to protect
Some frail memorial still erected nigh,
With uncouth rhymes and shapeless sculpture decked,
80   Implores the passing tribute of a sigh.

Their name, their years, spelt by th' unlettered muse,
The place of fame and elegy supply:
And many a holy text around she strews,
That teach the rustic moralist to die.

85   For who to dumb Forgetfulness a prey,
This pleasing anxious being e'er resigned,
Left the warm precincts of the cheerful day,
Nor cast one longing ling'ring look behind?

On some fond breast the parting soul relies,
90   Some pious drops the closing eye requires;
Ev'n from the tomb the voice of nature cries,
Ev'n in our ashes live their wonted fires.

For thee, who mindful of th' unhonored dead
Dost in these lines their artless tale relate;
95   If chance, by lonely Contemplation led,
Some kindred spirit shall inquire thy fate,

Haply some hoary-headed swain may say,
"Oft have we seen him at the peep of dawn
Brushing with hasty steps the dews away
100   To meet the sun upon the upland lawn.

"There at the foot of yonder nodding beech
That wreathes its old fantastic roots so high,
His listless length at noontide would he stretch,
And pore upon the brook that babbles by.

2. According to Gray's friend William Mason, the poem originally concluded at this juncture with the following four stanzas, preserved in a manuscript at Eton College:

The thoughtless world to majesty may bow
Exalt the brave, and idolize success,
But more to innocence their safety owe
Than power and genius e'er conspired to bless.

And thou, who mindful of the unhonored dead
Dost in these notes their artless tale relate

By night and lonely contemplation led
To linger in the gloomy walks of fate,

Hark how the sacred calm, that broods around
Bids ev'ry fierce tumultuous passion cease
In still small accents whisp'ring from the ground
A grateful earnest of eternal peace.

No more with reason and thyself at strife;
Give anxious cares and endless wishes room
But through the cool sequestered vale of life
Pursue the silent tenor of thy doom.

105   "Hard by yon wood, now smiling as in scorn,
          Mutt'ring his wayward fancies he would rove,
          Now drooping, woeful wan, like one forlorn,
          Or crazed with care, or crossed in hopeless love.

          "One morn I missed him on the 'customed hill,
110   Along the heath and near his favorite tree;
          Another came; nor yet beside the rill,
          Nor up the lawn, nor at the wood was he;

          "The next with dirges due in sad array
          Slow through the church-way path we saw him borne.
115   Approach and read (for thou can'st read) the lay,
          Graved on the stone beneath yon aged thorn."

The Epitaph

Here rests his head upon the lap of earth
A youth to fortune and to fame unknown.
Fair Science frowned not on his humble birth,
120   *And Melancholy marked him for her own.*

Large was his bounty, and his soul sincere,
Heaven did a recompense as largely send:
He gave to Mis'ry all he had, a tear,
He gained from Heav'n ('twas all he wished) a friend.

125   *No farther seek his merits to disclose,*
Or draw his frailties from their dread abode,
(There they alike in trembling hope repose)
The bosom of his Father and his God.

1746–1750   1751

Samuel Johnson
1709–1784

from A Dictionary of the English Language

FUNK. n.s. A stink. A low word.

IMAGINÁTION. n.s. [*imaginatio*, Lat. *imagination*, Fr. from *imagine*.]

1. Fancy; the power of forming ideal pictures; the power of representing things absent to one's self or others.

> *Imagination* I understand to be the representation of an individual thought. *Imagination* is of three kinds: joined with belief of that which is to come; joined with memory of that which is past; and of things present, or as if they were present: for I comprehend in this imagination feigned and at pleasure, as if one should imagine such a man to be in the vestments of a pope, or to have wings.
>
> —Bacon

> Our simple apprehension of corporal objects, if present, is sense; if absent, *imagination:* when we would perceive a material object, our fancies present us with its idea.
>
> —Glanville

> O whither shall I run, or which way fly
> The sight of this so horrid spectacle,
> Which erst my eyes beheld, and yet behold!
> For dire *imagination* still pursues me.
>
> —Milton

> Where beams of warm *imagination* play,
> The memory's soft figures melt away.
>
> —Pope

2. Conception; image in the mind; idea.

> Sometimes despair darkens all her *imaginations*; sometimes the active passion of love cheers and clears her invention.
>
> —Sidney

> Princes have but their titles for their glories,
> An outward honor for an inward toil;
> And, for unfelt *imaginations*,
> They often feel a world of restless cares.
>
> —Shakespeare, *Richard III*

> Better I were distract,
> So should my thoughts be severed from my griefs;
> And woes, by wrong *imaginations*, lose

---

1. All entries are from the fourth edition of Johnson's *Dictionary* (1773), the last that Johnson prepared. Each entry is presented complete, with etymology, definitions, illustrations.

The knowledge of themselves.

—Shakespeare, *King Lear*

His *imaginations* were often as just as they were bold and strong.

—Dennis

3. Contrivance; scheme.

Thou hast seen all their vengeance, and all their *imaginations* against me.

—Bible (Lamentations 3.60)

4. An unsolid or fanciful opinion.

We are apt to think that space, in itself, is actually boundless; to which *imagination*, the idea of space, of itself leads us.

—Locke

JÚDGMENT. n.s. [*jugement*, Fr.]

1. The power of discerning the relations between one term or one proposition and another.

O *judgment!* thou art fled to brutish beasts,
And men have lost their reason.

—Shakespeare, *Julius Caesar*

The faculty, which God has given man to supply the want of certain knowledge, is *judgment*, whereby the mind takes any proposition to be true or false, without perceiving a demonstrative evidence in the proofs.

—Locke

Judgment is that whereby we join ideas together by affirmation or negation; so, this tree is high.

—Watts

2. Doom; the right or power of passing judgment.

If my suspect be false, forgive me, God;
For *judgment* only doth belong to thee.

—Shakespeare, *Henry VI*

3. The act of exercising judicature; judicatory.

They gave *judgment* upon him.

—Bible (2 Kings)

When thou, O Lord, shalt stand disclosed
In majesty severe,
And sit in *judgment* on my soul,
O how shall I appear?

—Addison's *Spectator*

4. Determination; decision.

Where distinctions or identities are purely material, the *judgment* is made by the imagination, otherwise by the understanding.

—Glanville's *Scepsis*

We shall make a certain *judgment* what kind of dissolution that earth was capable of.

—Burnet's *Theory*

Reason ought to accompany the exercise of our senses, whenever we would form a just *judgment* of things proposed to our inquiry.

—Watts

5. The quality of distinguishing propriety and impropriety; criticism.

Judgment, a cool and slow faculty, attends not a man in the rapture of poetical composition.

—Dennis

'Tis with our *judgments* as our watches, none
Go just alike; yet each believes his own.

—Pope

6. Opinion; notion.

I see men's *judgments* are
A parcel of their fortunes, and things outward
Draw the inward quality after them,
To suffer all alike.

—Shakespeare, *Antony and Cleopatra*

When she did think my master loved her well,
She, in my *judgment*, was as fair as you.

—Shakespeare

7. Sentence against a criminal.

When he was brought again to th' bar, to hear
His knell rung out, his *judgment*, he was stirred
With agony.

—Shakespeare, *Henry VIII*

The chief priests informed me, desiring to have *judgment* against him.

—Bible (Acts 25.15)

On Adam last this *judgment* he pronounced.

—Milton

8. Condemnation. This is a theological use.

The *judgment* was by one to condemnation; but the free gift is of many offenses unto justification.

—Bible (Romans 5.16)

The precepts, promises, and threatenings of the Gospel will rise up in *judgment* against us, and the articles of our faith will be so many articles of accusation.

—Tillotson

9. Punishment inflicted by Providence, with reference to some particular crime.

This *judgment* of the heavens that makes us tremble,
Touches us not with pity.

—Shakespeare, *King Lear*

We cannot be guilty of greater uncharitableness, than to interpret afflictions as punishments and *judgments*: it aggravates the evil to him who suffers, when he looks upon himself as the mark of divine vengeance.

—Addison's *Spectator*

10. Distribution of justice.

> The Jews made insurrection against Paul, and brought him to the *judgment* seat.
>
> —Bible (Acts 18.12)

> Your dishonor
> Mangles true *judgment*, and bereaves the state
> Of that integrity which should become it.
>
> —Shakespeare, *Coriolanus*

> In *judgments* between rich and poor, consider not what the poor man needs, but what is his own.
>
> —Taylor

> A bold and wise petitioner goes strait to the throne and *judgment* seat of the monarch.
>
> —Arbuthnot and Pope

11. Judiciary law; statute.

> If ye hearken to these *judgments*, and keep and do them, the Lord thy God shall keep unto thee the covenant.
>
> —Bible (Deuteronomy)

12. The last doom.

> The dreadful *judgment* day
> So dreadful will not be as was his sight.
>
> —Shakespeare, *Henry VI*

LEXICÓGRAPHER. n.s. [λεξικον and γραφειν; *lexicographe*, Fr.] A writer of dictionaries; a harmless drudge, that busies himself in tracing the original, and detailing the signification of words.

> Commentators and *lexicographers* acquainted with the Syriac language, have given these hints in their writings on scripture.
>
> —Watt's *Improvement of the Mind*

VACÚITY. n.s. [*vacuitas*; from *vacuus*, Lat. *vacuité*, Fr.]

1. Emptiness; state of being unfilled.

> Hunger is such a state of *vacuity*, as to require a fresh supply of aliment.
>
> —Arbuthnot

2. Space unfilled; space unoccupied.

> In filling up *vacuities*, turning out shadows and ceremonies, by explicit prescription of substantial duties, which those shadows did obscurely represent.
>
> —Hammond's *Fund*

> He, that seat soon failing, meets
> A vast *vacuity*.
>
> —Milton

> Body and space are quite different things, and a *vacuity* is interspersed among the particles of matter.
>
> —Bentley

God, who alone can answer all our longings, and fill every *vacuity* of our soul, should entirely possess our heart.

—Rogers

Redeeming still at night these *vacuities* of the day.

—Fell

3. Inanity; want of reality.

The soul is seen, like other things, in the mirror of its effects: but if they'll run behind the glass to catch at it, their expectations will meet with *vacuity* and emptiness.

—Glanville

James Boswell
1740–1795

from The Life of Samuel Johnson, LL.D.
[INTRODUCTION; BOSWELL'S METHOD]

To write the Life of him who excelled all mankind in writing the lives of others, and who, whether we consider his extraordinary endowments or his various works, has been equaled by few in any age, is an arduous, and may be reckoned in me a presumptuous task.

Had Dr. Johnson written his own life, in conformity with the opinion which he has given, that every man's life may be best written by himself;[1] had he employed in the preservation of his own history, that clearness of narration and elegance of language in which he has embalmed so many eminent persons, the world would probably have had the most perfect example of biography that was ever exhibited. But although he at different times, in a desultory manner, committed to writing many particulars of the progress of his mind and fortunes, he never had preserving diligence enough to form them into a regular composition. Of these memorials a few have been preserved; but the greater part was consigned by him to the flames, a few days before his death.

As I had the honor and happiness of enjoying his friendship for upwards of twenty years; as I had the scheme of writing his life constantly in view; as he was well apprised of this circumstance, and from time to time obligingly satisfied my inquiries, by communicating to me the incidents of his early years; as I acquired a facility in recollecting, and was very assiduous in recording, his conversation, of which the extraordinary vigor and vivacity constituted one of the first features of his character; and as I have spared no pains in obtaining materials concerning him, from every quarter where I could discover that they were to be found, and have been favored with the most liberal communications by his friends; I flatter myself that few biographers have entered upon such a work as this with more advantages; independent of literary abilities, in which I am not vain enough to compare myself with some great names who have gone before me in this kind of writing. * * *

Instead of melting down my materials into one mass, and constantly speaking in my own person, by which I might have appeared to have more merit in the exe-

1. In *Idler* No. 84.

cution of the work, I have resolved to adopt and enlarge upon the excellent plan of Mr. Mason, in his *Memoirs* of Gray.[2] Wherever narrative is necessary to explain, connect, and supply, I furnish it to the best of my abilities; but in the chronological series of Johnson's life, which I trace as distinctly as I can, year by year, I produce, wherever it is in my power, his own minutes,[3] letters, or conversation, being convinced that this mode is more lively, and will make my readers better acquainted with him, than even most of those were who actually knew him, but could know him only partially; whereas there is here an accumulation of intelligence from various points, by which his character is more fully understood and illustrated.

Indeed I cannot conceive a more perfect mode of writing any man's life than not only relating all the most important events of it in their order, but interweaving what he privately wrote, and said, and thought; by which mankind are enabled as it were to see him live, and to "live o'er each scene"[4] with him, as he actually advanced through the several stages of his life. Had his other friends been as diligent and ardent as I was, he might have been almost entirely preserved. As it is, I will venture to say that he will be seen in this work more completely than any man who has ever yet lived.

And he will be seen as he really was; for I profess to write, not his panegyric, which must be all praise, but his Life; which, great and good as he was, must not be supposed to be entirely perfect. To be as he was, is indeed subject of panegyric enough to any man in this state of being; but in every picture there should be shade as well as light, and when I delineate him without reserve, I do what he himself recommended, both by his precept[5] and his example. * * *

What I consider as the peculiar value of the following work is the quantity that it contains of Johnson's conversation; which is universally acknowledged to have been eminently instructive and entertaining; and of which the specimens that I have given upon a former occasion have been received with so much approbation that I have good grounds for supposing that the world will not be indifferent to more ample communications of a similar nature. * * *

I am fully aware of the objections which may be made to the minuteness on some occasions of my detail of Johnson's conversation, and how happily it is adapted for the petty exercise of ridicule, by men of superficial understanding and ludicrous fancy;[6] but I remain firm and confident in my opinion, that minute particulars are frequently characteristic,[7] and always amusing, when they relate to a distinguished man. I am therefore exceedingly unwilling that anything, however slight, which my illustrious friend thought it worth his while to express, with any degree of point,[8] should perish. * * *

Of one thing I am certain, that considering how highly the small portion which we have of the table talk and other anecdotes of our celebrated writers[9] is valued, and how earnestly it is regretted that we have not more, I am justified in preserving rather too many of Johnson's sayings than too few; especially as from the diversity of

---

2. William Mason constructed his *Memoirs* of Thomas Gray (1775) around a selection of the poet's letters.
3. Memoranda.
4. "To wake the soul by tender strokes of art, / To raise the genius, and to mend the heart, / To make mankind in conscious virtue bold, / Live o'er each scene, and be what they behold" (lines 1–4 of Pope's prologue to Addison's *Cato*).
5. Boswell proceeds to quote from Rambler No. 60 in which Johnson articulates his biographical principles.

6. Boswell's Hebridean journal had already been parodied in print for its "minuteness" and "detail."
7. Revealing of character.
8. "Remarkable turn of words or thought" (Johnson's *Dictionary*).
9. E.g., Joseph Spence's *Anecdotes, Observations and Characters of Books and Men, Collected from the Conversation of Mr. Pope*, which (though unpublished until 1820) Johnson drew on for his *Life of Pope*.

dispositions it cannot be known with certainty beforehand, whether what may seem trifling to some, and perhaps to the collector himself, may not be most agreeable to many; and the greater number that an author can please in any degree, the more pleasure does there arise to a benevolent mind.

To those who are weak enough to think this a degrading task, and the time and labor which have been devoted to it misemployed, I shall content myself with opposing the authority of the greatest man of any age, Julius Caesar, of whom Bacon observes, that "in his book of Apothegms which he collected, we see that he esteemed it more honor to make himself but a pair of tables, to take the wise and pithy words of others, than to have every word of his own to be made an apothegm or an oracle."

Having said thus much by way of introduction, I commit the following pages to the candor of the Public.

Anna Letitia Barbauld
1743–1825

The Mouse's Petition to Dr. Priestley[1]

O hear a pensive prisoner's prayer,
    For liberty that sighs;
And never let thine heart be shut
    Against the wretch's cries!

5   For here forlorn and sad I sit,
    Within the wiry grate;
And tremble at the approaching morn,
    Which brings impending fate.

If e'er thy breast with freedom glowed,
10   And spurned a tyrant's chain,
Let not thy strong oppressive force
    A free-born mouse detain!

O do not stain with guiltless blood
    Thy hospitable hearth;
15   Nor triumph that thy wiles betrayed
    A prize so little worth.

The scattered gleanings of a feast
    My frugal meals supply;
But if thine unrelenting heart
20   That slender boon deny,—

The cheerful light, the vital air,
    Are blessings widely given;
Let nature's commoners enjoy
    The common gifts of heaven.

1. The title in early editions is *The Mouse's Petition, Found in the trap where he had been confined all night,* accompanied by a motto from Virgil's *Aeneid* (6.853): "Parcere subjectis & debellare superbos" [To spare the conquered, and subdue the proud]. Joseph Priestley (1733–1804), political radical and eminent chemist who discovered oxygen, had been testing the properties of gases on captured household mice. Tradition has it that Barbauld's petition succeeded, and this mouse was released.

25 The well-taught philosophic mind
        To all compassion gives:
    Casts round the world an equal eye,
        And feels for all that lives.

    If mind,—as ancient sages taught,—
30   A never-dying flame,
    Still shifts through matter's varying forms,
        In every form the same;

    Beware, lest in the worm you crush
        A brother's soul you find;
35 And tremble lest thy luckless hand
        Dislodge a kindred mind.

    Or, if this transient gleam of day
        Be *all* of life we share,
    Let pity plead within thy breast
40   That little *all* to spare.

    So may thy hospitable board
        With wealth and peace be crowned;
    And every charm of heartfelt ease
        Beneath thy roof be found.

45 So when destruction lurks unseen,
        Which men, like mice, may share,
    May some kind angel clear thy path,
        And break the hidden snare.

1771   1773

William Blake

1757–1827

Introduction to Songs of Innocence and of Experience

Blake's most popular work appeared in two phases. In 1789 he published *Songs of Innocence;* five years later he bound these poems with a set of new poems in a volume titled *Songs of Innocence and of Experience Shewing the two contrary States of the Human Soul.* "Innocence" and "Experience" are definitions of consciousness that rethink Milton's existential-mythic states of "Paradise" and the "Fall." Blake's categories are modes of perception that tend to coordinate with a chronological story that would become standard in Romanticism: childhood is a time and a state of protected "innocence," but it is a qualified innocence, not immune to the fallen world and its institutions. This world sometimes impinges on childhood itself, and in any event becomes known through "experience," a state of being marked by the loss of childhood vitality, by fear and inhibition, by social and political corruption, and by the manifold oppression of Church, State, and the ruling classes. The volume's "Contrary States" are sometimes signaled by patently repeated or contrasted titles: in *Innocence, Infant Joy,* in *Experience, Infant Sorrow;* in *Innocence, The Lamb,* in *Experience, The Fly* and *The Tyger.*

    These contraries are not constructed as simple oppositions, however. Unlike Milton's narrative of the Fall from Paradise, Blake shows either state of soul possible at any moment. Some children, even infants, have already lost their innocence through a soiling contact with the world;

some adults, particularly joyously visionary poets, seem able to retain a kind of innocent vitality even as they enter the world of experience. Moreover, the values of "Innocence" and "Experience" are themselves complex. At times, the innocent state of soul reflects a primary, untainted vitality of imagination; but at other times, Blake, like Mary Wollstonecraft, implicates innocence with dangerous ignorance and vulnerability to oppression. Thus, in their rhetorical structure, the poems may present an innocent speaker against dark ironies that a more experienced reader, alert to social and political evil, will grasp. But just as trickily, experience can also define an imagination self-darkened by its own "mind-forg'd manacles." Blake's point is not that children are pure and adults fallen, or that children are naive and adults perspicacious. The contrary possibilities coexist, with different plays and shades of emphasis in different poems. And these values are often further complicated by the ambiguous significance of the illustrations that accompany and often frame the poems' texts. Sometimes these illustrations sustain the speaker's tone and point of view (e.g., *The Lamb*), and sometimes (e.g., *The Little Black Boy*) they offer an ironic counter-commentary.

from SONGS OF INNOCENCE AND OF EXPERIENCE

SHEWING THE TWO CONTRARY STATES OF THE HUMAN SOUL

from *Songs of Innocence*

The Lamb

Little Lamb who made thee
Dost thou know who made thee
Gave thee life & bid thee feed,
By the stream & o'er the mead;
5   Gave thee clothing of delight,
Softest clothing wooly bright;
Gave thee such a tender voice,
Making all the vales rejoice:
    Little Lamb who made thee
10   Dost thou know who made thee

Little Lamb, I'll tell thee.
Little Lamb, I'll tell thee;
He is called by thy name
For he calls himself a Lamb:
15   He is meek & he is mild,
He became a little child:
I a child & thou a lamb,
We are called by his name.
    Little Lamb God bless thee
20   Little Lamb God bless thee

The Chimney Sweeper[1]

When my mother died I was very young
And my father sold me while yet my tongue
Could scarcely cry weep weep weep weep.[2]
So your chimneys I sweep & in soot I sleep.

5   Theres little Tom Dacre, who cried when his head
That curl'd like a lambs back, was shav'd, so I said:
Hush Tom never mind it, for when your head's bare
You know that the soot cannot spoil your white hair

And so he was quiet, & that very night,
10   As Tom was a sleeping he had such a sight,
That thousands of sweepers Dick, Joe, Ned & Jack
Were all of them lock'd up in coffins of black,

And by came an Angel who had a bright key,
And he open'd the coffins & set them all free.
15   Then down a green plain leaping laughing they run
And wash in a river and shine in the Sun.

Then naked & white, all their bags left behind,
They rise upon clouds, and sport in the wind
And the Angel told Tom if he'd be a good boy,
20   He'd have God for his father & never want joy

And so Tom awoke and we rose in the dark
And got with our bags & our brushes to work.
Tho' the morning was cold, Tom was happy & warm
So if all do their duty they need not fear harm.[3]

1. Chimney-sweeps were mostly young boys, whose impoverished parents sold them into the business, or who were orphans, outcasts, or illegitimate children with no other means of living. It was filthy, health-ruining labor, aggravated by overwork and inadequate clothing, food, and shelter. Among the hazards were burns, permanently blackened skin, deformed legs, black lung disease, and cancer of the scrotum. Protective legislation passed in 1788 was never enforced. Blake's outrage at this exploitation also sounds in "London." Admiring the poem, Charles Lamb sent it to James Montgomery (a topical poet and radical-press editor) for inclusion in *The Chimney-Sweeper's Friend, and Climbing Boy's Album* (1824), which he was assembling for the Society for Ameliorating the Condition of Infant Chimney-Sweepers.
2. With a relevant pun, the child's lisping street cry advertising his trade, "sweep! sweep!"
3. A typical conduct homily.

from Songs of Experience

The Fly

Little Fly
Thy summer's play,
My thoughtless hand
Has brush'd away.[1]

Am not I
A fly like thee?
Or art not thou
A man like me?

For I dance
And drink & sing:
Till some blind hand
Shall brush my wing.

If thought is life
And strength & breath:[2]
And the want
Of thought is death;

Then am I
A happy fly,
If I live,
Or if I die.

William Blake, *The Fly,* from *Songs of Experience.* The activities depicted seem "innocent": a girl bats a shuttlecock; a nurse guides a boy's early steps. But the poem-text provokes a view of the girl as a potential fly-swatter, and, in another frame of reference, of both little ones as analogues to the "little fly." Blake's plate makes the order of the stanzas ambiguous: should we read down or across? Courtesy of Bridgeman Art Library. © Fitzwilliam Museum, University of Cambridge, UK.

1. Cf. the blinded Gloucester's bitterly rueful comment in *King Lear:* "As flies to wanton boys, are we to th' gods, / They kill us for their sport" (4.1.36–37).

2. Cf. Descartes' famous statement: "I think, therefore I am."

The Tyger[1]

Tyger Tyger, burning bright,
In the forests of the night;[2]
What immortal hand or eye,
Could frame thy fearful symmetry?

5   In what distant deeps or skies,
Burnt the fire of thine eyes?
On what wings dare he aspire?[3]
What the hand dare sieze the fire?

And what shoulder & what art,
10   Could twist the sinews of thy heart?
And when thy heart began to beat,
What dread hand? & what dread feet?[4]

What the hammer? what the chain,
In what furnace was thy brain?
15   What the anvil? what dread grasp,
Dare its deadly terrors clasp!

When the stars threw down their spears
And water'd heaven with their tears:[5]
Did he smile his work to see?[6]
20   Did he who made the Lamb make thee?[7]

Tyger Tyger burning bright,
In the forests of the night:
What immortal hand or eye,
Dare frame thy fearful symmetry?

1. See Color Plate 18.
2. Not just a time of day but a metaphysical location, characterized by forest mazes—the terrain that conducts to Hell in Dante's *Inferno*.
3. Icarus, with his father Dedalus, fashioned wings of feathers and wax to escape from prison. Icarus became enchanted with flight and, ignoring his father's cautions, soared too close to the sun; the wax melted and he fell to his death in the sea.
4. One engraving has, "What dread hand Formd thy dread feet?"

5. In the war in Heaven, *Paradise Lost* (bk. 6), Satan, rebelling against God's authority, is defeated by the Son and driven down to Hell. Blake's verb leaves it undecidable whether the stars "threw down their spears" in desperate surrender or in defiance.
6. In a notebook draft, Blake wrote "did he laugh his work to see."
7. An allusion to Jesus, "The Lamb of God" (John 1.29 and 1.36) and, indirectly, to the poem in *Songs of Innocence*, with Blake as the maker.

A POISON TREE

I was angry with my friend:
I told my wrath, my wrath did end.
I was angry with my foe:
I told it not, my wrath did grow.

5   And I waterd it in fears,
Night & morning with my tears:
And I sunned it with smiles.
And with soft deceitful wiles.

And it grew both day and night.
10   Till it bore an apple bright.
And my foe beheld it shine.
And he knew that it was mine.

And into my garden stole.
When the night had veild the pole.
15   In the morning glad I see.
My foe outstretchd beneath the tree.

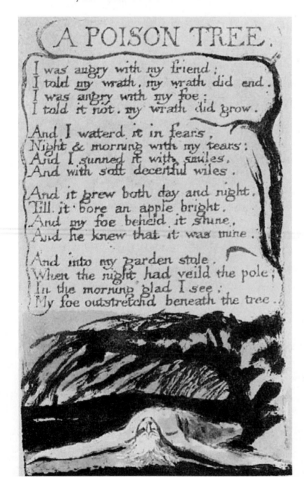

William Blake. *A Poison Tree,*
from *Songs of Experience.* The
poem was originally titled "Christian Forbearance." The tail of the
"y" in "My" at the beginning of
the last line becomes a clockwise
frame of the whole, as a branch
of the poison tree. The outstretched body is in the posture
of a crucifixion. Courtesy of
Bridgeman Art Library.
© Fitzwilliam Museum, University
of Cambridge, UK.

Olaudah Equiano
c. 1745–1797

from **The Interesting Narrative of the Life of Olaudah Equiano**
or *Gustavus Vassa, the African*
[THE SLAVE SHIP AND ITS CARGO]

The first object that saluted my eyes when I arrived on the coast was the sea, and a slave ship, which was then riding at anchor, and waiting for its cargo.[1] These filled me with astonishment, that was soon converted into terror, which I am yet at a loss to describe, and much more the then feelings of my mind when I was carried on board. I was immediately handled and tossed up to see if I was sound, by some of the crew; and I was now persuaded that I had got into a world of bad spirits, and that they were going to kill me. Their complexions too, differing so much from ours, their long hair, and the language they spoke, which was very different from any I had ever heard, united to confirm me in this belief. Indeed such were the horrors of my views and fears at the moment, that if ten thousand worlds had been my own, I would have freely parted with them all to have exchanged my condition with the meanest slave in my own country. When I looked round the ship too, and saw a large furnace or copper boiling and a multitude of black people, of every description, chained together, every one of their countenances expressing dejection and sorrow, I no longer doubted of my fate; and, quite overpowered with horror and anguish, I fell motionless on the deck, and fainted. When I recovered a little, I found some black people about me, who I believed were some of those who brought me on board, and had been receiving their pay: they talked to me in order to cheer me, but all in vain. I asked them if we were not to be eaten by those white men with horrible looks, red faces, and long hair. They told me I was not: and one of the crew brought me a small portion of spirituous liquor in a wine glass; but, being afraid of him, I would not take it out of his hand. One of the blacks therefore took it from him and gave it to me, and I took a little down my palate, which, instead of reviving me, as they thought it would, threw me into the greatest consternation at the strange feeling it produced, having never tasted any such liquor before.

Soon after this the blacks who brought me on board went off, and left me abandoned to despair. I now saw myself deprived of all chance of returning to my native country, or even the least glimpse of gaining the shore, which I now considered as friendly; and I even wished for my former slavery, in preference to my present situation, which was filled with horrors of every kind, still heightened by my ignorance of what I was to undergo. I was not long suffered to indulge my grief. I was soon put down under the decks, and there I received such a salutation in my nostrils as I had never experienced in my life: so that, with the loathsomeness of the stench, and with my crying together, I became so sick and low that I was not able to eat, nor had I the least desire to taste any thing. I now wished for the last friend, death, to relieve me; but soon, to my grief, two of the white men offered me eatables; and, on my refusing to eat, one of them held me fast by the hands, and laid me across, I think, the windlass, and tied my feet, while the other flogged me severely. I had never experienced any thing of this kind before, and although, not being used to the water, I naturally

---

1. Captured by slavers along with his sister, Equiano was soon separated from her and sold to different masters over a period of several months before reaching the African coast for shipment to Barbados.

feared that element the first time I saw it, yet nevertheless, could I have got over the nettings, I would have jumped over the side, but I could not; and besides the crew used to watch us very closely, who were not chained down to the decks, lest we should leap into the water. I have seen some of these poor African prisoners most severely cut for attempting to do so, and hourly whipped for not eating. This indeed was often the case with myself. In a little time after, amongst the poor chained men, I found some of my own nation, which in a small degree gave ease to my mind. I inquired of these what was to be done with us. They gave me to understand we were to be carried to these white people's country to work for them. I was then a little revived, and thought if it were no worse than working, my situation was not so desperate. But still I feared I should be put to death, the white people looked and acted, as I thought, in so savage a manner; for I had never seen among any people such instances of brutal cruelty: and this is not only shewn towards us blacks, but also to some of the whites themselves. One white man in particular I saw, when we were permitted to be on deck, flogged so unmercifully with a large rope near the foremast, that he died in consequence of it; and they tossed him over the side as they would have done a brute. This made me fear these people the more; and I expected nothing less than to be treated in the same manner. I could not help expressing my fearful apprehensions to some of my countrymen; I asked them if these people had no country, but lived in this hollow place, the ship. They told me they did not, but came from a distant one. "Then," said I, "how comes it, that in all our country we never heard of them?" They told me, because they lived so very far off. I then asked, where their women were: had they any like themselves. I was told they had. "And why," said I, "do we not see them?" They answered, because they were left behind. I asked how the vessel could go. They told me they could not tell; but that there was cloth put upon the masts by the help of the ropes I saw, and then the vessel went on; and the white men had some spell or magic they put in the water, when they liked, in order to stop the vessel. I was exceedingly amazed at this account, and really thought they were spirits. I therefore wished much to be from amongst them, for I expected they would sacrifice me; but my wishes were in vain, for we were so quartered that it was impossible for any of us to make our escape.

Mary Wollstonecraft
1759–1797

from A Vindication of the Rights of Woman

After considering the historic page, and viewing the living world with anxious solicitude, the most melancholy emotions of sorrowful indignation have depressed my spirits, and I have sighed when obliged to confess, that either nature has made a great difference between man and man, or that the civilization which has hitherto taken place in the world has been very partial. I have turned over various books written on the subject of education, and patiently observed the conduct of parents and the management of schools; but what has been the result?—a profound conviction that the neglected education of my fellow-creatures is the grand source of the misery I deplore; and that women, in particular, are rendered weak and wretched by a variety of concurring causes, originating from one hasty conclusion. The conduct and manners of women, in fact, evidently prove that their minds are not in a healthy state; for, like the flowers which are planted in too rich a soil, strength and usefulness are sacrificed to beauty; and the flaunting leaves, after having pleased a fastidious eye, fade, disregarded on the stalk, long before the season when they ought to have arrived at maturity.—One cause of this barren blooming I attribute to a false system of education, gathered from the books written on this subject by men who, considering females rather as women than human creatures, have been more anxious to make them alluring mistresses than affectionate wives and rational mothers; and the understanding of the sex has been so bubbled[1] by this specious homage, that the civilized women of the present century, with a few exceptions, are only anxious to inspire love, when they ought to cherish a nobler ambition, and by their abilities and virtues exact respect.

In a treatise, therefore, on female rights and manners, the works which have been particularly written for their improvement must not be overlooked; especially when it is asserted, in direct terms, that the minds of women are enfeebled by false refinement; that the books of instruction, written by men of genius, have had the same tendency as more frivolous productions; and that, in the true style of Mahometanism, they are treated as a kind of subordinate beings, and not as a part of the human species,[2] when improveable reason is allowed to be the dignified distinction which raises men above the brute creation, and puts a natural sceptre in a feeble hand.

Yet, because I am a woman, I would not lead my readers to suppose that I mean violently to agitate the contested question respecting the equality or inferiority of the sex; but as the subject lies in my way, and I cannot pass it over without subjecting the main tendency of my reasoning to misconstruction, I shall stop a moment to deliver, in a few words, my opinion.—In the government of the physical world it is observable that the female in point of strength is, in general, inferior to the male. This is the law of nature; and it does not appear to be suspended or abrogated in favour of woman. A degree of physical superiority cannot, therefore, be denied—and it is a noble prerogative! But not content with this natural pre-eminence, men endeavour to sink us still lower, merely to render us alluring objects for a moment; and women, intoxicated by the adoration which men, under the influence of their senses, pay them, do not seek to obtain a durable interest in their hearts, or to become the friends of the fellow creatures who find amusement in their society.

1. Gas-filled; deluded.
2. A European misconception that the sacred texts of Islam stated that women lack souls and therefore have no afterlife in Heaven.

I am aware of an obvious inference:—from every quarter have I heard exclamations against masculine women; but where are they to be found? If by this appellation men mean to inveigh against their ardour in hunting, shooting, and gaming, I shall most cordially join in the cry; but if it be against the imitation of manly virtues, or, more properly speaking, the attainment of those talents and virtues, the exercise of which ennobles the human character, and which raise females in the scale of animal being, when they are comprehensively termed mankind;—all those who view them with a philosophic eye must, I should think, wish with me, that they may every day grow more and more masculine.

Robert Burns

1759–1796

To a Mouse

On Turning Her Up in Her Nest with the Plough, November, 1785

Wee, sleekit,° cowrin, tim'rous beastie, *sleek*
O, what a panic's in thy breastie!
Thou need na start awa sae° hasty *so*
Wi' bickering brattle!° *scurry*
I wad be laith° to rin an' chase thee, *loath*
Wi' murdering pattle!° *plough-scraper*

I'm truly sorry man's dominion
Has broken Nature's social union,
An' justifies that ill opinion
Which makes thee startle
At me, thy poor, earth-born companion
An' fellow mortal!

I doubt na, whyles,° but thou may thieve; *sometimes*
What then? poor beastie, thou maun° live! *must*
A daimen icker in a thrave° *odd ear in 24 sheaves*
'S a sma' request;
I'll get a blessin wi' the lave,° *rest*
An' never miss 't!

Thy wee-bit housie, too, in ruin!
Its silly wa's° the win's are strewin! *feeble walls*
An' naething, now, to big° a new ane, *build*
O' foggage° green! *coarse grass*
An' bleak December's win's ensuin,
Baith snell° an' keen! *bitter*

Thou saw the fields laid bare an' waste,
An' weary winter comin fast,
An' cozie here, beneath the blast,
Thou thought to dwell,
Till crash! the cruel coulter° past *plow-blade*
Out thro' thy cell.

That wee bit heap o' leaves an' stibble,°   *stubble*
Has cost thee monie a weary nibble!
Now thou's turned out, for a' thy trouble,
    But° house or hald,°   *without / goods*
35 To thole° the winter's sleety dribble,   *endure*
    An' cranreuch° cauld!   *hoarfrost*

But Mousie, thou art no thy lane,°   *not alone*
In proving foresight may be vain:
The best-laid schemes o' mice an' men
40   Gang aft agley,°   *go oft awry*
An' lea'e us nought but grief an' pain,
    For promis'd joy!

Still thou art blest, compared wi' me!
The present only toucheth thee:
45 But och! I backward cast my e'e,
    On prospects drear!
An' forward, tho' I canna see,
    I guess an' fear!
1785   1786

A Red, Red Rose[1]

O, my luve is like a red, red rose,
    That's newly sprung in June.
O, my luve is like the melodie,
    That's sweetly play'd in tune.

5 As fair art thou, my bonie lass,
    So deep in luve am I,
And I will luve thee still, my dear,
    Till a' the seas gang° dry.   *go*

Till a' the seas gang dry, my dear,
10   And the rocks melt wi' the sun!
And I will luve thee still, my dear,
    While the sands o' life shall run.

And fare thee weel, my only luve,
    And fare thee weel a while!
15 And I will come again, my luve,
    Tho' it were ten thousand mile!
1794   1796

1. This poem incorporates elements of several old ballads and folk songs, a common practice of amalgamation at which Burns had great success.

William Wordsworth
1770–1850

Lines Written in Early Spring

I heard a thousand blended notes,
While in a grove I sate reclined,
In that sweet mood when pleasant thoughts
Bring sad thoughts to the mind.

5   To her fair works did nature link
The human soul that through me ran;
And much it griev'd my heart to think
What man has made of man.

Through primrose-tufts, in that sweet bower,
10   The periwinkle trail'd its wreathes;
And 'tis my faith that every flower
Enjoys the air it breathes.

The birds around me hopp'd and play'd:
Their thoughts I cannot measure,°   *assess, put in meters*
15   But the least motion which they made,
It seem'd a thrill of pleasure.

The budding twigs spread out their fan,
To catch the breezy air;
And I must think, do all I can,
20   That there was pleasure there.

If I these thoughts may not prevent,
If such be of my creed the plan,
Have I not reason to lament
What man has made of man?

1798   1798

Lines Written a Few Miles above Tintern Abbey
On Revisiting the Banks of the Wye during a Tour, July 13, 1798

Five years have passed; five summers, with the length
Of five long winters! and again I hear
These waters, rolling from their mountain-springs
With a sweet inland murmur.[1]—Once again
5   Do I behold these steep and lofty cliffs,
Which on a wild secluded scene impress
Thoughts of more deep seclusion; and connect
The landscape with the quiet of the sky.
The day is come when I again repose
10   Here, under this dark sycamore, and view
These plots of cottage-ground, these orchard-tufts,
Which, at this season, with their unripe fruits,
Among the woods and copses lose themselves,
Nor, with their green and simple hue, disturb

1. The river is not affected by the tides a few miles above Tintern [Wordsworth's note, 1798].

15 The wild green landscape. Once again I see
These hedge-rows, hardly hedge-rows, little lines
Of sportive wood run wild; these pastoral farms
Green to the very door; and wreathes of smoke
Sent up, in silence, from among the trees,
20 With some uncertain notice, as might seem,
Of vagrant dwellers in the houseless woods,
Or of some hermit's cave, where by his fire
The hermit° sits alone.   *religious recluse*

       Though absent long,
These forms of beauty have not been to me,
25 As is a landscape to a blind man's eye:
But oft, in lonely rooms, and mid the din
Of towns and cities, I have owed to them,
In hours of weariness, sensations sweet,
Felt in the blood, and felt along the heart,
30 And passing even into my purer mind
With tranquil restoration:—feelings too
Of unremembered pleasure; such, perhaps,
As may have had no trivial influence
On that best portion of a good man's life;
35 His little, nameless, unremembered acts
Of kindness and of love. Nor less, I trust,
To them I may have owed another gift,
Of aspect more sublime; that blessed mood,
In which the burthen° of the mystery,[2]   *burden*
40 In which the heavy and the weary weight
Of all this unintelligible world
Is lighten'd:—that serene and blessed mood,
In which the affections gently lead us on,
Until, the breath of this corporeal frame,
45 And even the motion of our human blood
Almost suspended, we are laid asleep
In body, and become a living soul:
While with an eye made quiet by the power
Of harmony, and the deep power of joy,
50 We see into the life of things.

          If this
Be but a vain belief, yet, oh! how oft,
In darkness, and amid the many shapes
Of joyless day-light; when the fretful stir
Unprofitable, and the fever of the world,
55 Have hung upon the beatings of my heart,[3]
How oft, in spirit, have I turned to thee
O sylvan Wye! Thou wanderer through the wood
How often has my spirit turned to thee!

And now, with gleams of half-extinguish'd thought,
60 With many recognitions dim and faint,

2. Keats thought this phrase the core of Wordsworth's "genius."
3. Echoing Macbeth's sense of life's fitful fever (3.2.23)

and Hamlet's view of life as "weary, stale, flat, and unprofitable" (1.2.133).

And somewhat of a sad perplexity,
The picture of the mind revives again:
While here I stand, not only with the sense
Of present pleasure, but with pleasing thoughts
65   That in this moment there is life and food
For future years. And so I dare to hope
Though changed, no doubt, from what I was, when first
I came among these hills; when like a roe
I bounded o'er the mountains, by the sides
70   Of the deep rivers, and the lonely streams,
Wherever nature led; more like a man
Flying from something that he dreads, than one
Who sought the thing he loved. For nature then
(The coarser pleasures of my boyish days,
75   And their glad animal movements all gone by,)
To me was all in all.—I cannot paint
What then I was. The sounding cataract
Haunted me like a passion: the tall rock,
The mountain, and the deep and gloomy wood,
80   Their colours and their forms, were then to me
An appetite: a feeling and a love,
That had no need of a remoter charm,
By thought supplied, or any interest
Unborrowed from the eye.—That time is past,
85   And all its aching joys are now no more,
And all its dizzy raptures. Not for this
Faint° I, nor mourn nor murmur: other gifts   *lose heart*
Have followed, for such loss, I would believe,
Abundant recompence. For I have learned
90   To look on nature, not as in the hour
Of thoughtless youth, but hearing oftentimes
The still, sad music of humanity,
Not harsh nor grating, though of ample power
To chasten and subdue. And I have felt
95   A presence that disturbs me with the joy
Of elevated thoughts; a sense sublime
Of something far more deeply interfused,
Whose dwelling is the light of setting suns,
And the round ocean, and the living air,
100   And the blue sky, and in the mind of man,
A motion and a spirit, that impels
All thinking things, all objects of all thought,
And rolls through all things. Therefore am I still
A lover of the meadows and the woods,
105   And mountains; and of all that we behold
From this green earth; of all the mighty world
Of eye and ear, both what they half-create,[4]
And what perceive; well pleased to recognize
In nature and the language of the sense,

4. This line has a close resemblance to an admirable line of Young, the exact expression of which I cannot recollect [Wordsworth's note]. He is thinking of Edward Young's "half create the wondrous world they see" (*The Complaint or Night Thoughts* [1744], 6.427).

110 The anchor of my purest thoughts, the nurse,
The guide, the guardian of my heart, and soul
Of all my moral being.

                Nor, perchance,
If I were not thus taught, should I the more
Suffer my genial° spirits to decay: *creative*
115 For thou art with me, here, upon the banks
Of this fair river; thou, my dearest Friend,[5]
My dear, dear Friend, and in thy voice I catch°   *sense, arrest*
The language of my former heart, and read
My former pleasures in the shooting lights
120 Of thy wild eyes. Oh! yet a little while
May I behold in thee what I was once,
My dear, dear Sister! And this prayer I make,
Knowing that Nature never did betray
The heart that loved her; 'tis her privilege,
125 Through all the years of this our life, to lead
From joy to joy: for she can so inform
The mind that is within us, so impress
With quietness and beauty, and so feed
With lofty thoughts, that neither evil tongues,[6]
130 Rash judgments, nor the sneers of selfish men,
Nor greetings where no kindness is, nor all
The dreary intercourse of daily life,
Shall e'er prevail against us, or disturb
Our chearful faith that all which we behold
135 Is full of blessings. Therefore let the moon
Shine on thee in thy solitary walk;
And let the misty mountain winds be free
To blow against thee: and in after years,
When these wild ecstasies shall be matured
140 Into a sober pleasure, when thy mind
Shall be a mansion for all lovely forms,
Thy memory be as a dwelling-place
For all sweet sounds and harmonies; Oh! then,
If solitude, or fear, or pain, or grief,
145 Should be thy portion,° with what healing thoughts   *dowry, bequest*
Of tender joy wilt thou remember me,
And these my exhortations! Nor, perchance,
If I should be, where I no more can hear
Thy voice, nor catch from thy wild eyes these gleams
150 Of past existence, wilt thou then forget
That on the banks of this delightful stream
We stood together; and that I, so long
A worshipper of Nature, hither came,
Unwearied in that service: rather say
155 With warmer love, oh! with far deeper zeal

5. His sister Dorothy. The language echoes Psalm 23: "Yea, through I walk through the valley of the shadow of death, I will fear no evil: for thou art with me."

6. An echo of Milton's claim to "Sing with mortal voice, unchang'd / To hoarse or mute, though fall'n on evil days, / . . . and evil tongues" (*Paradise Lost* 7.24–26).

Of holier love. Nor wilt thou then forget,
That after many wanderings, many years
Of absence, these steep woods and lofty cliffs,
And this green pastoral landscape, were to me
160   More dear, both for themselves, and for thy sake.
1798   1798

Song ("She dwelt among th' untrodden ways")

She dwelt among th' untrodden ways
    Beside the springs of Dove,[1]
A Maid whom there were none to praise
    And very few to love:

5   A Violet by a mossy stone
    Half-hidden from the Eye![2]
—Fair, as a star when only one
    Is shining in the sky!

She *liv'd* unknown, and few could know
10   When Lucy ceas'd to be;
But she is in her Grave, and Oh!
    The difference to me!

1798   1800

The world is too much with us

The world is too much with us; late and soon,
Getting and spending, we lay waste our powers:
Little we see in nature that is ours;
We have given our hearts away, a sordid boon!
5   The Sea that bares her bosom to the moon;
The Winds that will be howling at all hours
And are up-gathered now like sleeping flowers;
For this, for everything, we are out of tune;
It moves us not. Great God! I'd rather be
10   A Pagan° suckled in a creed outworn;   *pre-Christian*
So might I, standing on this pleasant lea,
Have glimpses that would make me less forlorn;
Have sight of Proteus rising from the sea;
Or hear old Triton blow his wreathed horn.[1]

1. A river in England.
2. See Gray's *Elegy Written in a Country Churchyard:* "Full
many a flower is born to blush unseen" (55).

1. Proteus is the shape-changing herdsman of the sea;
Triton, usually depicted blowing a conch shell, is a sea
deity. Cf. the personified "Sea" in line 5.

Composed upon Westminster Bridge, Sept. 3, 1802[1]

Earth has not anything to shew more fair:
Dull would he be of soul who could pass by
A sight so touching in its majesty:
This City now doth like a garment wear
5   The beauty of the morning; silent, bare,
Ships, towers, domes, theatres, and temples lie
Open unto the fields, and to the sky;
All bright and glittering in the smokeless air.
Never did sun more beautifully steep
10   In his first splendour, valley, rock, or hill;
Ne'er saw I, never felt, a calm so deep!
The river glideth at his own sweet will:
Dear God! the very houses seem asleep;
And all that mighty heart is lying still!

It is a beauteous Evening[1]

It is a beauteous Evening, calm and free;
The holy time is quiet as a Nun
Breathless with adoration; the broad sun
Is sinking down in its tranquillity;
5   The gentleness of heaven is on the Sea:[2]
Listen! the mighty Being is awake
And doth with his eternal motion make
A sound like thunder—everlastingly.
Dear Child! dear Girl! that walkest with me here,[3]
10   If thou appear'st untouch'd by solemn thought,
Thy nature is not therefore less divine:
Thou liest in Abraham's bosom[4] all the year;
And worshipp'st at the Temple's inner shrine,
God being with thee when we know it not.

I wandered lonely as a cloud[1]

I wandered lonely as a cloud
That floats on high o'er vales and hills,
When all at once I saw a crowd,
A host, of golden daffodils;
5   Beside the lake, beneath the trees,
Fluttering and dancing in the breeze.

1. "Composed on the roof of a coach, on my way to France" [I.F., 1843]. For a description of the circumstances, see Dorothy Wordsworth's *Grasmere Journals*, July 1802, page 197. Wordsworth misremembered the date as September (the time of his return, not his departure), and gave the year as 1803 (corrected to 1802 in the edition of 1838). His confusion about the date may have had to do with his anxiety about his reunion with—and final departure from—Annette Vallon and their daughter Caroline.

1. This was composed on the beach near Calais, in the autumn of 1802 [Wordsworth's note, 1843].
2. In 1836 Wordsworth changed "is on" to "broods o'er."
3. Wordsworth's daughter Caroline.
4. Christ's description of the resting place for heaven-bound souls (Luke 16.22).
1. Compare Dorothy Wordsworth's *Grasmere Journal*, 15 April 1802, page 197.

Continuous as the stars that shine
And twinkle on the milky way,
They stretched in never-ending line
10   Along the margin of a bay:
Ten thousand saw I at a glance,
Tossing their heads in sprightly dance.

The waves beside them danced; but they
Outdid the sparkling waves in glee:—
15   A Poet could not but be gay,
In such a jocund company:
I gazed—and gazed—but little thought
What wealth the show to me had brought:

For oft when on my couch I lie
20   In vacant or in pensive mood,
They flash upon that inward eye
Which is the bliss of solitude;[2]
And then my heart with pleasure fills,
And dances with the daffodils.

1804/1815   1807/1815

My heart leaps up

My heart leaps up when I behold
    A Rainbow in the sky:
So was it when my life began;
So is it now I am a Man;
5   So be it when I shall grow old,
    Or let me die!
The Child is Father of the Man;
And I could wish my days to be
Bound each to each by natural piety.

1802   1807

Dorothy Wordsworth
1771–1855

from The Grasmere Journals
[A VISION OF THE MOON]

[*18 March 1802*] * * * As we came along Ambleside vale in the twilight—it was a grave evening—there was something in the air that compelled me to serious thought—the hills were large, closed in by the sky. It was nearly dark * * * night was come on & the moon was overcast. But as I climbed Moss the moon came out from behind a Moun-

---

2. Lines 21–22 were composed by Wordsworth's wife. He thought them the "two best lines," though Coleridge called them "mental bombast" (*Biographia Literaria*, ch. 22).

tain Mass of Black clouds—O the unutterable darkness of the sky & the Earth below the Moon! & the glorious brightness of the moon itself! There was a vivid sparkling streak of light at this end of Rydale water but the rest was very dark & Loughrigg fell and Silver How were white & bright as if they were covered with hoar frost.[1] The moon retired again & appeared & disappeared several times before I reached home. Once there was no moonlight to be seen but upon the Island house & the promontory of the Island where it stands, "That needs must be a holy place" &c—&c.[2] I had many many exquisite feelings and when I saw this lowly Building in the waters among the dark & lofty hills, with that bright soft light upon it—it made me more than half a poet. I was tired when I reached home. I could not sit down to reading & tried to write verses but alas! I gave up expecting William & went soon to bed. Fletcher's carts came home late.[3]

[A FIELD OF DAFFODILS]

Thursday 15th. [*April 1802*] * * * When we were in the woods beyond Gowbarrow[1] park we saw a few daffodils close to the water side, we fancied that the lake had floated the seeds ashore & that the little colony had so sprung up—But as we went along there were more & yet more & at last under the boughs of the trees, we saw that there was a long belt of them along the shore, about the breadth of a country turnpike road.[2] I never saw daffodils so beautiful they grew among the mossy stones about & about them, some rested their heads upon these stones as on a pillow for weariness & the rest tossed & reeled & danced & seemed as if they verily laughed with the wind that blew upon them over the Lake, they looked so gay ever glancing ever changing. This wind blew directly over the lake to them. There was here & there a little knot & a few stragglers a few yards higher up but they were so few as not to disturb the simplicity & unity & life of that one busy highway. We rested again & again. The Bays were stormy, & we heard the waves at different distances and in the middle of the water like the Sea.

[THE CIRCUMSTANCES OF "COMPOSED UPON WESTMINISTER BRIDGE"[1]]

[*27 July 1802*] * * * After various troubles & disasters we left London on Saturday morning at 1/2 past 5 or 6. * * * we mounted the Dover Coach at Charing Cross. It was a beautiful morning. The City, St Pauls, with the River & a multitude of little Boats, made a most beautiful sight as we crossed Westminster Bridge. The houses were not overhung by their cloud of smoke & they were spread out endlessly, yet the sun shone so brightly with such a pure light that there was even something like the purity of one of nature's own grand Spectacles.

1. The places mentioned are White Moss Common, Rydale water (a lake nearby Grasmere Lake and the Common), and two peaks to the south of these lakes, Loughrigg and Silver How.
2. Perhaps recalling an early draft of Coleridge's *Kubla Khan*, line 14, or William's feeling in *Home at Grasmere* that "dwellers in this holy place / Must need themselves be hallow'd" (366–67).
3. William's ride, via the mail carrier.
1. Several miles away in another part of the Lake district, near Patterdale on Ullswater.

2. Dorothy erased the next words, "the end we did not see." Cf. W. Wordsworth's poem, *I wandered lonely as a cloud*: "They stretched in never-ending line."
1. See page 195; William and Dorothy are on their way to Calais, France, sailing from Dover, to settle affairs with Annette Vallon and her daughter by William, Caroline, prior to William's marriage to Mary Hutchinson in October. The City is Westminster, a district of London where Parliament, Westminster Abbey, and Buckingham Palace are located; St. Paul's is the chief Anglican church. Westminster Bridge crosses the Thames river.

Samuel Taylor Coleridge
1772–1834

from The Rime of the Ancient Mariner

An ancient Mariner
meeteth three Gallants
bidden to a wedding-
feast, and detaineth
one.

IT is an ancient Mariner,
And he stoppeth one of three.
"By thy long gray beard and glittering eye,
Now wherefore stopp'st thou me?

"The Bridegroom's doors are opened wide,   5
And I am next of kin;
The guests are met, the feast is set:
May'st hear the merry din."

He holds him with his skinny hand,
"There was a ship," quoth he.   10
"Hold off! unhand me, grey-beard loon!"
Eftsoons° his hand dropt he.   *immediately*

The wedding-guest is
spellbound by the eye
of the old sea-faring
man, and constrained
to hear his tale.

He holds him with his glittering eye—
The wedding-guest stood still,
And listens like a three years' child: 15
The Mariner hath his will.

The wedding-guest sat on a stone:
He can not choose but hear;
And thus spake on that ancient man,
The bright-eyed Mariner.   20

The ship was cheer'd, the harbour clear'd,
Merrily did we drop
Below the kirk,° below the hill.   *church*
Below the light-house top.

The Mariner tells how
the ship sailed
southward with a good
wind and fair weather,
till it reached the line.

The Sun came up upon the left,   25
Out of the sea came he;
And he shone bright, and on the right
Went down into the sea.

Higher and higher every day,
Till over the mast at noon—   30
The Wedding-Guest here beat his breast,
For he heard the loud bassoon.

The wedding-guest
heareth the bridal
music; but the Mariner
continueth his tale.

The bride hath paced into the hall,
Red as a rose is she;
Nodding their heads before her goes   35
The merry minstrelsy.

The Wedding-Guest he beat his breast,
Yet he can not choose but hear;

And thus spake on that ancient man,
The bright-eyed Mariner.   40

And now the STORM-BLAST came, and he
Was tyrannous and strong:
He struck with his o'ertaking wings,
And chased us south along.

With sloping masts and dipping prow,   45
As who pursued with yell and blow
Still treads the shadow of his foe
And forward bends his head,
The ship drove fast, loud roared the blast,
And southward aye° we fled.   *continuously*

And now there came both mist and snow,
And it grew wondrous cold:
And ice, mast-high, came floating by,
As green as emerald.

And through the drifts the snowy clifts   55
Did send a dismal sheen:
Nor shapes of men nor beast we ken°—   *knew*
The ice was all between.

The ice was here, the ice was there,
The ice was all around: 60
It cracked and growled, and roared and howled,
Like noises in a swound!

At length did cross an Albatross,
Thorough the fog it came;
As if it had been a Christian soul,   65
We hailed it in God's name.

It ate the food it ne'er had eat,
And round and round it flew.
The ice did split with a thunder-fit;
The helmsman steered us through!   70

And a good south wind sprung up behind;
The Albatross did follow,
And every day, for food or play,
Came to the mariner's hollo!

In mist or cloud, on mast or shroud,   75
It perched for vespers nine;
Whiles all the night, through fog-smoke white,
Glimmered the white moon-shine.

"God save thee, ancient Mariner!
From the fiends, that plague thee thus!—   80
Why look'st thou so?"—With my cross-bow
I shot the ALBATROSS. * * *

Part the Sixth

FIRST VOICE.

"But tell me, tell me! speak again,   410
Thy soft response renewing—
What makes that ship drive on so fast?
What is the OCEAN doing?"

SECOND VOICE.

"Still as a slave before his lord,
The OCEAN hath no blast;   415
His great bright eye most silently
Up to the Moon is cast—

If he may know which way to go;
For she guides him smooth or grim.
See, brother, see! how graciously   420
She looketh down on him."

FIRST VOICE.

The Mariner hath been cast into a trance; for the angelic power causeth the vessel to drive northward, faster than human life could endure.

"But why drives on that ship so fast,
Without or wave or wind?"

SECOND VOICE.

"The air is cut away before,
And closes from behind.   425

Fly, brother, fly! more high, more high!
Or we shall be belated:
For slow and slow that ship will go,
When the Mariner's trance is abated."

The supernatural motion is retarded; the Mariner awakes, and his penance begins anew.

I woke, and we were sailing on   430
As in a gentle weather:
'Twas night, calm night, the moon was high;
The dead men stood together.

All stood together on the deck,
For a charnel-dungeon fitter: 435
All fixed on me their stony eyes,
That in the Moon did glitter.

The pang, the curse, with which they died,
Had never passed away:
I could not draw my eyes from theirs,   440
Nor turn them up to pray.

The curse is finally expiated.

And now this spell was snapt: once more
I viewed the ocean green,
And looked far forth, yet little saw
Of what had else been seen—   445

Like one, that on a lonesome road
Doth walk in fear and dread,
And having once turn'd round, walks on,
And turns no more his head;

Because he knows, a frightful fiend   450
Doth close behind him tread.

But soon there breathed a wind on me,
Nor sound nor motion made:
Its path was not upon the sea,
In ripple or in shade.   455

It raised my hair, it fanned my cheek
Like a meadow-gale of spring—
It mingled strangely with my fears,
Yet it felt like a welcoming.

Swiftly, swiftly flew the ship,   460
Yet she sailed softly too:
Sweetly, sweetly blew the breeze—
On me alone it blew.

And the ancient
Mariner beholdeth his
native country.

Oh! dream of joy! is this indeed
The light-house top I see?   465
Is this the hill? is this the kirk?
Is this mine own countree?

We drifted o'er the harbour-bar,
And I with sobs did pray—
O let me be awake, my God!   470
Or let me sleep alway.

The harbour-bay was clear as glass,
So smoothly it was strewn!
And on the bay the moonlight lay,
And the shadow of the moon.   475

The rock shone bright, the kirk no less,
That stands above the rock:
The moonlight steeped in silentness
The steady weathercock.

And the bay was white with silent light,   480
Till rising from the same,

The angelic spirits
leave the dead bodies,

Full many shapes, that shadows were,
In crimson colours came.

And appear in their
own forms of light.

A little distance from the prow
Those crimson shadows were: 485
I turned my eyes upon the deck—
Oh, Christ! what saw I there!

Each corse lay flat, lifeless and flat,
And, by the holy rood!°   *cross*
A man all light, a seraph-man,   490
On every corse there stood.

This seraph-band, each waved his hand:
It was a heavenly sight!

They stood as signals to the land,
Each one a lovely light;   495

This seraph-band, each waved his hand,
No voice did they impart—
No voice; but oh! the silence sank
Like music on my heart.

But soon I heard the dash of oars,   500
I heard the Pilot's cheer;
My head was turned perforce away
And I saw a boat appear.

The Pilot, and the Pilot's boy,
I heard them coming fast: 505
Dear Lord in Heaven! it was a joy
The dead men could not blast.

I saw a third—I heard his voice:
It is the Hermit good!
He singeth loud his godly hymns   510
That he makes in the wood.
He'll shrieve° my soul, he'll wash away   *absolve*
The Albatross's blood.

Part the Seventh

The Hermit of the Wood,

This Hermit good lives in that wood
Which slopes down to the sea.   515
How loudly his sweet voice he rears!
He loves to talk with marineres
That come from a far countree.

He kneels at morn, and noon, and eve—
He hath a cushion plump: 520
It is the moss that wholly hides
The rotted old oak-stump.

The Skiff-boat neared: I heard them talk,
"Why, this is strange, I trow!
Where are those lights so many and fair,   525
That signal made but now?"

Approacheth the ship with wonder.

"Strange, by my faith!" the Hermit said—
"And they answered not our cheer!
The planks looked warped! and see those sails,
How thin they are and sere!   530
I never saw aught like to them,
Unless perchance it were

"Brown skeletons of leaves that lag
My forest-brook along;
When the ivy-tod° is heavy with snow,   *clump*   535

And the owlet whoops to the wolf below,
That eats the she-wolf's young."

"Dear Lord! it hath a fiendish look—
(The Pilot made reply)
I am a-feared"—"Push on, push on!"   540
Said the Hermit cheerily.

The boat came closer to the ship,
But I nor spake nor stirred;
The boat came close beneath the ship,
And straight a sound was heard.   545

The ship suddenly
sinketh.

Under the water it rumbled on,
Still louder and more dread:
It reachd the ship, it split the bay;
The ship went down like lead.

The ancient Mariner is
saved in the Pilot's
boat.

Stunned by that loud and dreadful sound,   550
Which sky and ocean smote,
Like one that hath been seven days drowned,
My body lay afloat;
But swift as dreams, myself I found
Within the Pilot's boat.   555

Upon the whirl, where sank the ship,
The boat spun round and round;
And all was still, save that the hill
Was telling of the sound.

I moved my lips—the Pilot shrieked   560
And fell down in a fit;
The holy Hermit raised his eyes,
And prayed where he did sit.

I took the oars: the Pilot's boy,
Who now doth crazy go,   565
Laughed loud and long, and all the while
His eyes went to and fro.
"Ha! ha!" quoth he, "full plain I see,
The Devil knows how to row."

And now, all in my own countree,   570
I stood on the firm land!
The Hermit stepped forth from the boat,
And scarcely he could stand.

The ancient Mariner
earnestly entreateth
the Hermit to shrieve
him; and the penance
of life falls on him.

"O shrieve me, shrieve me, holy man!"
The Hermit crossed his brow.   575
"Say quick," quoth he, "I bid thee say—
What manner of man art thou?"

Forthwith this frame of mine was wrenched
With a woeful agony,

Which forced me to begin my tale;   580
And then it left me free.

And ever and anon
throughout his future
life an agony
constraineth him to
travel from land to
land,
Since then, at an uncertain hour,
That agony returns:
And till my ghastly tale is told,
This heart within me burns.   585

I pass, like night, from land to land;
I have strange power of speech;
That moment that his face I see,
I know the man that must hear me:
To him my tale I teach.   590

What loud uproar bursts from that door!
The wedding-guests are there:
But in the garden-bower the bride
And bride-maids singing are;
And hark the little vesper bell,   595
Which biddeth me to prayer!

O Wedding-Guest! this soul hath been
Alone on a wide wide sea:
So lonely 'twas, that God himself
Scarce seemed there to be.   600

O sweeter than the marriage-feast,
'Tis sweeter far to me,
To walk together to the kirk
With a goodly company!—

To walk together to the kirk,   605
And all together pray,
While each to his great Father bends,
Old men, and babes, and loving friends,
And youths and maidens gay!

And to teach by his
own example, love and
reverence to all things
that God made and
loveth.
Farewell, farewell! but this I tell   610
To thee, thou Wedding-Guest!
He prayeth well, who loveth well
Both man and bird and beast.

He prayeth best, who loveth best
All things both great and small;   615
For the dear God who loveth us,
He made and loveth all."

The Mariner, whose eye is bright,
Whose beard with age is hoar,
Is gone: and now the Wedding-Guest   620
Turned from the bridegroom's door.

He went like one that hath been stunned,
And is of sense forlorn:
A sadder and a wiser man,
He rose the morrow morn.   625

1817–1834   1817

Kubla Khan[1]

In Xanadu did KUBLA KHAN
A stately pleasure-dome decree:
Where ALPH, the sacred river, ran
Through caverns measureless to man
5   Down to a sunless sea.
So twice five miles of fertile ground
With walls and towers were girdled round;
And here were gardens bright with sinuous rills,
Where blossom'd many an incense-bearing tree;
10   And here were forests ancient as the hills,
And folding sunny spots of greenery.

But oh that deep romantic chasm which slanted
Down the green hill athwart a cedarn cover!
A savage place! as holy and inchanted
15   As e'er beneath a waning moon was haunted
By woman wailing for her demon-lover!
And from this chasm, with ceaseless turmoil seething,
As if this earth in fast thick pants were breathing,
A mighty fountain momently was forced:
20   Amid whose swift half-intermitted Burst
Huge fragments vaulted like rebounding hail,
Or chaffy grain beneath the thresher's flail:
And mid these dancing rocks at once and ever
It flung up momently the sacred river.
25   Five miles meandering with a mazy motion
Through wood and dale the sacred river ran,
Then reached the caverns measureless to man,
And sank in tumult to a lifeless ocean:
And 'mid this tumult Kubla heard from far
30   Ancestral voices prophesying war!
            The shadow of the dome of pleasure
            Floated midway on the waves;
            Where was heard the mingled measure
            From the fountain and the caves.
35   It was a miracle of rare device,
A sunny pleasure-dome with caves of ice!

            A damsel with a dulcimer
            In a vision once I saw:

1. Kubla Khan was the grandson of Genghis Khan and Emperor of China in the 13th century.

It was an Abyssinian maid
40   And on her dulcimer she play'd,
Singing of Mount Abora.
Could I revive within me
Her symphony and song,
To such a deep delight 'twould win me,
45   That with music loud and long,
I would build that dome in air,
That sunny dome! those caves of ice!
And all who heard should see them there,
And all should cry, Beware! Beware!
50   His flashing eyes, his floating hair!
Weave a circle round him thrice,
And close your eyes with holy dread:
For he on honey-dew hath fed,
And drank[2] the milk of Paradise.

1797–1798   1816

George Gordon, Lord Byron
1788–1824

She walks in beauty[1]

1

She walks in beauty, like the night
    Of cloudless climes and starry skies;
And all that's best of dark and bright
    Meet in her aspect and her eyes:
5   Thus mellow'd to that tender light
    Which heaven to gaudy day denies.

2

One shade the more, one ray the less,
    Had half impair'd the nameless grace
Which waves in every raven tress,
10   Or softly lightens o'er her face;
Where thoughts serenely sweet express
    How pure, how dear their dwelling-place.

3

And on that cheek, and o'er that brow,
    So soft, so calm, yet eloquent,
15   The smiles that win, the tints that glow,
    But tell of days in goodness spent,
A mind at peace with all below,
    A heart whose love is innocent!

1814   1815

---

2. Changed to "drunk" in 1832.
1. The first poem in *Hebrew Melodies*, a collection initiated by Jewish composer Isaac Nathan, and published with
his music. The subject is Anne Wilmot, the wife of
Byron's cousin, whom he had seen at a party wearing
"mourning, with dark spangles on her dress."

from CHILDE HAROLD'S PILGRIMAGE, CANTO THE THIRD[1]

[BYRON'S STRAINED IDEALISM. APOSTROPHE TO HIS DAUGHTER]

111

Thus far have I proceeded in a theme
Renew'd with no kind auspices°:—to feel   *hopeful signs*
We are not what we have been, and to deem
We are not what we should be,—and to steel
1035 The heart against itself; and to conceal,
With a proud caution, love, or hate, or aught,—
Passion or feeling, purpose, grief, or zeal,—
Which is the tyrant spirit of our thought,
Is a stern task of soul:—No matter,—it is taught.

112

1040 And for these words, thus woven into song,
It may be that they are a harmless wile,—
The colouring of the scenes which fleet along,
Which I would seize, in passing, to beguile
My breast, or that of others, for a while.
1045 Fame is the thirst of youth,—but I am not
So young as to regard men's frown or smile,
As loss or guerdon° of a glorious lot;   *prize*
I stood and stand alone,—remember'd or forgot.

113

I have not loved the world, nor the world me;
1050 I have not flatter'd its rank breath,[2] nor bow'd
To its idolatries a patient knee,—
Nor coin'd my cheek to smiles,—nor cried aloud
In worship of an echo; in the crowd
They could not deem me one of such; I stood
1055 Among them, but not of them; in a shroud
Of thoughts which were not their thoughts, and still could,
Had I not filed[3] my mind, which thus itself subdued.

114

I have not loved the world, not the world me,—
But let us part fair foes; I do believe,
1060 Though I have found them not, that there may be
Words which are things,—hopes which will not deceive,

1. The first two cantos of *Childe Harold's Pilgrimage* appeared in 1812. As their subtitle "A Romaunt" indicated, Byron had adopted the form of romance for his unnervingly contemporary poem. The Spenserian stanzas and mock-archaisms—a "childe" is a youth of noble birth—played discordantly against the account of his travels in 1809–1811 through Spain (and his acerbic commentary on the Peninsular War) and then on into parts of Greece unfrequented by Westerners. The overwhelming success of the poem ensured that Byron would be identified with Childe Harold. Byron protested, but the connection is reinforced by the manuscripts themselves, which disclose that Childe Harold was once

Childe Burun, an ancient form of his family name. Canto 3, published in 1816, is independent, though the continuity reflects the degree to which protagonist and poet had come to figure each other. Byron left England on 25 April 1816, and wrote the opening stanzas while crossing the Channel.
2. See Shakespeare, *Coriolanus*, 3.1.66–67. Byron frequently voices himself through allusions to Shakespeare's willful Roman general, who retorts to the plebeians who banish him: "I banish you" (3.3.124).
3. Defiled. Byron adds a note citing Shakespeare's *Macbeth*, 3.1.65

And virtues which are merciful, nor weave
Snares for the failing: I would also deem
O'er others' griefs that some sincerely grieve;
1065   That two, or one, are almost what they seem,—
That goodness is no name, and happiness no dream.

115

My daughter! with thy name this song begun—
My daughter! with thy name thus much shall end—
I see thee not,—I hear thee not,—but none
1070   Can be so wrapt in thee; thou art the friend
To whom the shadows of far years extend:
Albeit my brow thou never should'st behold,
My voice shall with thy future visions blend
And reach into thy heart,—when mine is cold,—
1075   A token and a tone, even from thy father's mould.

116

To aid thy mind's developement,—to watch
Thy dawn of little joys,—to sit and see
Almost thy very growth,—to view thee catch
Knowledge of objects,—wonders yet to thee!
1080   To hold thee lightly on a gentle knee,
And print on thy soft cheek a parent's kiss,—
This, it should seem, was not reserved for me;
Yet this was in my nature:—as it is,
I know not what is there, yet something like to this.

117

1085   Yet, though dull Hate as duty should be taught,
I know that thou wilt love me; though my name
Should be shut from thee, as a spell still fraught
With desolation,—and a broken claim:
Though the grave closed between us,—'twere the same,
1090   I know that thou wilt love me; though to drain
My blood from out thy being were an aim,
And an attainment,—all would be in vain,—
Still thou would'st love me, still that more than life retain.

118

The child of love,—though born in bitterness
1095   And nurtured in convulsion. Of thy sire
These were the elements,—and thine no less.
As yet such are around thee,—but thy fire
Shall be more temper'd, and thy hope far higher.
Sweet be thy cradled slumbers! O'er the sea,
1100   And from the mountains where I now respire,
Fain would I waft such blessing upon thee,
As, with a sigh, I deem thou might'st have been to me!

from DON JUAN

from **Canto 1**

1

I want a hero: an uncommon want,
  When every year and month sends forth a new one,
Till, after cloying the gazettes with cant,
  The age discovers he is not the true one;
5 Of such as these I should not care to vaunt,
  I'll therefore take our ancient friend Don Juan—
We all have seen him, in the pantomime,
Sent to the devil somewhat ere his time.[1] * * *

6

Most epic poets plunge "in medias res"
  (Horace makes this the heroic turnpike road),[2]
And then your hero tells, whene'er you please,
  What went before—by way of episode,
45 While seated after dinner at his ease,
  Beside his mistress in some soft abode,
Palace, or garden, paradise, or cavern,
Which serves the happy couple for a tavern.

7

That is the usual method, but not mine—
50   —My way is to begin with the beginning;
The regularity of my design
  Forbids all wandering as the worst of sinning,[3]
And therefore I shall open with a line
  (Although it cost me half an hour in spinning)
55 Narrating somewhat of Don Juan's father,
And also of his mother, if you'd rather.

8

In Seville was he born, a pleasant city,
  Famous for oranges and women—he
Who has not seen it will be much to pity,
60   So says the proverb—and I quite agree;
Of all the Spanish towns is none more pretty,
  Cadiz perhaps—but that you soon may see:—
Don Juan's parents lived beside the river,
A noble stream, and call'd the Guadalquivir. * * *

1. Popular melodrama portrayed Don Juan as a seducer who ends in hell; Byron plays against his own reputation as notorious lover by presenting Juan as an innocent boy overwhelmed by women. His attention may have been drawn to the figure by Coleridge's discussion in *Biographia Literaria* (ch. 23). "Juan" is Anglicized into two syllables, as the rhymes with "true one" and "new one" indicate. "Inez" rhymes with "fine as" and "Jóse" with "nosey."

2. In *Ars Poetica* Horace recommends that the epic poet begin dramatically, like Homer, by taking the audience directly "into the midst of things."
3. That is, digression, literally "off the path." The Latin word for "wandering," *erratus*, also means "sinning."

10

His mother was a learned lady, famed
      For every branch of every science known—
75 In every Christian language ever named,
      With virtues equall'd by her wit alone,
She made the cleverest people quite ashamed,
      And even the good with inward envy groan,
Finding themselves so very much exceeded
80 In their own way by all the things that she did. * * *

13

She knew the Latin—that is, "the Lord's prayer,"
      And Greek—the alphabet—I'm nearly sure;
She read some French romances here and there,
100   Although her mode of speaking was not pure;
For native Spanish she had no great care,
      At least her conversation was obscure;
Her thoughts were theorems, her words a problem,
As if she deem'd that mystery would ennoble 'em. * * *

16

In short, she was a walking calculation,
      Miss Edgeworth's novels stepping from their covers,
Or Mrs. Trimmer's books on education,
      Or "Cœlebs' Wife" set out in quest of lovers,[4]
125 Morality's prim personification,
      In which not Envy's self a flaw discovers;
To others' share let "female errors fall,"[5]
For she had not even one—the worst of all. * * *

20

Now Donna Inez had, with all her merit,
      A great opinion of her own good qualities;
155 Neglect, indeed, requires a saint to bear it,
      And such, indeed, she was in her moralities;
But then she had a devil of a spirit,
      And sometimes mix'd up fancies with realities,
And let few opportunities escape
160 Of getting her liege lord into a scrape. * * *

23

Don Jóse and his lady quarrell'd—*why*,
      Not any of the many could divine,
Though several thousand people chose to try,
180   'Twas surely no concern of theirs nor mine;
I loathe that low vice—curiosity;
      But if there's any thing in which I shine,
'Tis in arranging all my friends' affairs,
Not having, of my own, domestic cares.

---

4. Maria Edgeworth was a popular Irish novelist and educational writer; Sarah Trimmer (1741–1810) was a popular writer on education and of children's books. *Cœlebs in Search of a Wife* (1809)—its title deliberately misquoted by Byron—was the only, but quite successful, novel of Hannah More.
5. Alexander Pope, *The Rape of the Lock* (1714), 2.17.

24

185 And so I interfered, and with the best
        Intentions, but their treatment was not kind;
    I think the foolish people were possess'd,
        For neither of them could I ever find,
    Although their porter afterwards confess'd—
190   But that's no matter, and the worst's behind,
    For little Juan o'er me threw, down stairs,
    A pail of housemaid's water unawares.

25

    A little curly-headed, good-for-nothing,
        And mischief-making monkey from his birth;
195 His parents ne'er agreed except in doting
        Upon the most unquiet imp on earth;
    Instead of quarrelling, had they been but both in
        Their senses, they'd have sent young master forth
    To school, or had him soundly whipp'd at home,
200 To teach him manners for the time to come.

26

    Don Jóse and the Donna Inez led
        For some time an unhappy sort of life,
    Wishing each other, not divorced, but dead;
        They lived respectably as man and wife,
205 Their conduct was exceedingly well-bred,
        And gave no outward signs of inward strife,
    Until at length the smother'd fire broke out,
    And put the business past all kind of doubt.

27

    For Inez call'd some druggists, and physicians,
210   And tried to prove her loving lord was *mad*,[6]
    But as he had some lucid intermissions,
        She next decided he was only *bad*;
    Yet when they ask'd her for her depositions,
        No sort of explanation could be had,
215 Save that her duty both to man and God
    Required this conduct—which seem'd very odd.

28

    She kept a journal, where his faults were noted,
        And open'd certain trunks of books and letters,
    All which might, if occasion served, be quoted;
220   And then she had all Seville for abettors,
    Besides her good old grandmother (who doted);
        The hearers of her case became repeaters,
    Then advocates, inquisitors, and judges,
    Some for amusement, others for old grudges. * * *

6. As Byron believed Lady Byron had tried to do; stanzas 27 and 28 replay details of their separation.

32

Their friends had tried at reconciliation,
250   Then their relations, who made matters worse.
('Twere hard to tell upon a like occasion
    To whom it may be best to have recourse—
I can't say much for friend or yet relation):
    The lawyers did their utmost for divorce,
255   But scarce a fee was paid on either side
Before, unluckily, Don Jóse died. * * *

37

Dying intestate,° Juan was sole heir   *without a will*
290   To a chancery suit, and messuages,° and lands,   *houses*
Which, with a long minority and care,
    Promised to turn out well in proper hands:
Inez became sole guardian, which was fair,
    And answer'd but to nature's just demands;
295   An only son left with an only mother
Is brought up much more wisely than another.

38

Sagest of women, even of widows, she
    Resolved that Juan should be quite a paragon,
And worthy of the noblest pedigree:
300   (His sire was of Castile, his dam from Aragon.)
Then for accomplishments of chivalry,
    In case our lord the king should go to war again,
He learn'd the arts of riding, fencing, gunnery,
And how to scale a fortress—or a nunnery. * * *

Percy Bysshe Shelley
1792–1822

Ozymandias[1]

I met a traveller from an antique land
Who said: "Two vast and trunkless° legs of stone   *lacking a torso*
Stand in the desert. . . . Near them on the sand,
Half sunk, a shattered visage° lies, whose frown,   *face*
5   And wrinkled lip, and sneer of cold command,
Tell that its sculptor well those passions read
Which yet survive, stamped on these lifeless things,
The hand that mocked them, and the heart that fed.[2]
And on the pedestal, these words appear:

1. Ozymandias (the Greek name for Ramses II) reigned 1292–1225 B.C.; he is thought to be the pharaoh of Exodus whom Moses challenged. The story of the statue and its inscription is taken from the Greek historian Diodorus Siculus, 1st century B.C.
2. The sculptor read well those passions that survive his hand (that mocked them) and the tyrant's heart (that fed them); "mocked": "imitated," with a sense of caricature or derision. The passions survive both on the images of the stone fragments and in the hearts of modern tyrants; Shelley published this sonnet in 1818 in Leigh Hunt's radical paper, *The Examiner*.

10   "My name is Ozymandias, King of Kings:
      Look on my works, ye Mighty, and despair!"[3]
      Nothing beside remains. Round the decay
      Of that colossal[4] Wreck, boundless and bare,
      The lone and level sands stretch far away."

1817   1818

Ode to the West Wind[1]

1

O wild West Wind, thou breath of Autumn's being,
Thou from whose unseen presence the leaves dead
Are driven like ghosts from an enchanter fleeing,

Yellow, and black, and pale, and hectic° red,   *feverish*
5   Pestilence-stricken multitudes![2] O Thou
      Who chariotest to their dark wintry bed

The winged seeds, where they lie cold and low,
Each like a corpse within its grave, until
Thine azure sister of the Spring° shall blow   *spring wind*

10   Her clarion° o'er the dreaming earth, and fill   *shrill trumpet*
      (Driving sweet buds like flocks to feed in air)
      With living hues and odours plain and hill:

Wild Spirit, which art moving everywhere;
Destroyer and Preserver;[3] hear, O hear!

2

15   Thou on whose stream, mid the steep sky's commotion,
      Loose clouds like earth's decaying leaves are shed,
      Shook from the tangled boughs of heaven and ocean,

Angels° of rain and lightning! there are spread   *messengers*
On the blue surface of thine airy surge,
20   Like the bright hair uplifted from the head

Of some fierce Maenad, even from the dim verge
Of the horizon to the zenith's height,
The locks of the approaching storm.[4] Thou dirge°   *funeral chant*

---

3. According to Diodorus, this is the actual boast; by Shelley's time, its language echoes ironically against the subsequent application of this title to Christ.
4. An adjective derived from "colossus," the term in antiquity for any large statue; there were several such of 50–60 feet in height in ancient Egypt. Shelley is also recalling the depiction of Julius Caesar by one of the conspirators in his assassination: "he doth bestride the narrow world / Like a Colossus" (*Julius Caesar* 1.2.135–36).
1. There is a long tradition, as old as the Bible, of wind as metaphor of life and inspiration—particularly the West Wind, as bearer of new weather, the harbinger of future seasons, events, and transformations, not only in the natural weather, but by symbolic extension, in emotional, spiritual, and political life. The Latin word for "wind," *spiritus*, also means "breath" (1) and soul or spirit (13, 61–62), as well as being the root-word for "inspiration" (a taking-in of energy).

2. An allusion to a traditional epic simile (Milton, Dante, Virgil) comparing the dead to wind-driven fallen leaves.
3. Titles for major Hindu gods, Siva the Destroyer and Vishnu the Preserver.
4. The Greek god of wine Bacchus was attended by Maenads, female votaries who danced in wild worship. Viewing a sculpture of them in Florence, Shelley commented: "The tremendous spirit of superstition aided by drunkenness . . . seems to have caught them in its whirlwinds, and to bear them over the earth as the rapid volutions of a tempest have the ever-changing trunk of a water-spout. . . . Their hair, loose and floating, seems caught in tempest of their own tumultuous motion." Associated in general with vegetation, Bacchus was fabled to die in the autumn and be reborn in the spring.

Of the dying year, to which this closing night
25   Will be the dome of a vast sepulchre,
Vaulted with all thy congregated might

Of vapours, from whose solid atmosphere
Black rain, and fire, and hail, will burst: Oh hear!

3

Thou who didst waken from his summer dreams
30   The blue Mediterranean, where he lay,
Lulled by the coil of his crystalline streams,

Beside a pumice° isle in Baiae's bay,   *volcanic*
And saw in sleep old palaces and towers
Quivering within the wave's intenser day,

35   All overgrown with azure moss, and flowers
So sweet, the sense faints picturing them!⁵ Thou
For whose path the Atlantic's level powers

Cleave themselves into chasms, while far below
The sea-blooms and the oozy woods which wear
40   The sapless foliage of the ocean, know

Thy voice, and suddenly grow grey with fear,
And tremble and despoil themselves:⁶ O hear!

4

If I were a dead leaf thou mightest bear;
If I were a swift cloud to fly with thee;
45   A wave to pant beneath thy power, and share

The impulse of thy strength, only less free
Than thou, O uncontrollable! if even
I were as in my boyhood, and could be

The comrade of thy wanderings over heaven,
50   As then, when to outstrip thy skiey speed
Scarce seemed a vision,—I would ne'er have striven

As thus with thee in prayer in my sore need.
Oh lift me as a wave, a leaf, a cloud!
I fall upon the thorns of life!⁷ I bleed!

55   A heavy weight of hours has chained and bowed
One too like thee—tameless, and swift, and proud.

5

Make me thy lyre,⁸ even as the forest is:
What if my leaves are falling like its own?
The tumult of thy mighty harmonies

60   Will take from both a deep autumnal tone,
Sweet though in sadness. Be thou, Spirit fierce,
My spirit! Be thou me, impetuous one!⁹

5. Ruins of imperial Roman villas in the Bay of Baiae, west of Naples.
6. In a note, Shelley says he is alluding to the seasonal change (despoiling) of seaweed, a process he imagines as instigated by the autumn wind.
7. A risky self-comparison to Jesus' torture by a crown of thorns.
8. A wind-harp, an image used in Coleridge's *The Eolian Harp*.
9. Shelley hazards the ungrammatical objective case ("me" instead of "I") not only to chime with "Be" but also to represent himself as an object.

Drive my dead thoughts over the universe,
Like withered leaves, to quicken a new birth;
65   And, by the incantation of this verse,

Scatter, as from an unextinguished hearth
Ashes and sparks, my words among mankind!
Be through my lips to unawakened earth

The trumpet of a prophecy! O Wind,
70   If Winter comes, can Spring be far behind?

1819   1820

To a Sky-Lark

Hail to thee, blithe Spirit!
    Bird thou never wert—
That from Heaven or near it
    Pourest thy full heart
5   In profuse strains of unpremeditated art.[1]

Higher still and higher
    From the earth thou springest,
Like a cloud of fire;
    The blue deep thou wingest,
10   And singing still dost soar, and soaring ever singest.

In the golden lightning
    Of the sunken sun,
O'er which clouds are bright'ning,
    Thou dost float and run,
15   Like an unbodied joy whose race is just begun.

The pale purple even°   *evening*
    Melts around thy flight;
Like a star of Heaven,
    In the broad daylight
20   Thou art unseen, but yet I hear thy shrill delight—

Keen as are the arrows
    Of that silver sphere°   *morning star*
Whose intense lamp narrows
    In the white dawn clear
25   Until we hardly see—we feel, that it is there.

All the earth and air
    With thy voice is loud,
As, when night is bare,
    From one lonely cloud
30   The moon rains out her beams, and Heaven is overflowed.

---

1. The skylark sings only in flight; Shelley evokes Milton's thanks to his "Celestial patroness," who "inspires / Easy [his] unpremeditated Verse" (*Paradise Lost* 9.21–24).

What thou art we know not;
　　What is most like thee?
From rainbow clouds there flow not
　　Drops so bright to see
35 As from thy presence showers a rain of melody:—

Like a Poet hidden
　　In the light of thought,
Singing hymns unbidden,
　　Till the world is wrought
40 To sympathy with hopes and fears it heeded not:

Like a high-born maiden
　　In a palace tower,
Soothing her love-laden
　　Soul in secret hour
45 With music sweet as love which overflows her bower:

Like a glow-worm golden
　　In a dell of dew,
Scattering unbeholden
　　Its aerial hue
50 Among the flowers and grass which screen it from the view:

Like a rose embowered
　　In its own green leaves,
By warm winds deflowered,
　　Till the scent it gives
55 Makes faint with too much sweet these heavy-winged thieves:

Sound of vernal° showers   *springtime*
　　On the twinkling grass,
Rain-awakened flowers,
　　All that ever was,
60 Joyous and clear and fresh,—thy music doth surpass.

Teach us, Sprite° or Bird,   *spirit, fairy*
　　What sweet thoughts are thine:
I have never heard
　　Praise of love or wine
65 That panted forth a flood of rapture so divine.

Chorus Hymeneal°   *wedding song*
　　Or triumphal° chaunt,   *military*
Matched with thine, would be all
　　But an empty vaunt—
70 A thing wherein we feel there is some hidden want.

What objects are the fountains
　　Of thy happy strain?
What fields, or waves, or mountains?
　　What shapes of sky or plain?
75 What love of thine own kind? what ignorance of pain?

With thy clear keen joyance
    Languor cannot be:
Shadow of annoyance
    Never came near thee:
80 Thou lovest—but ne'er knew love's sad satiety.°   (over)fullness

Waking or asleep,
    Thou of death must deem
Things more true and deep
    Than we mortals dream,
85 Or how could thy notes flow in such a crystal stream?

We look before and after,[2]
    And pine for what is not:
Our sincerest laughter
    With some pain is fraught;
90 Our sweetest songs are those that tell of saddest thought.

Yet if we could scorn
    Hate and pride and fear,
If we were things born
    Not to shed a tear,
95 I know not how thy joy we ever should come near.

Better than all measures
    Of delightful sound,
Better than all treasures
    That in books are found,
100 Thy skill to poet were, thou scorner of the ground!

Teach me half the gladness
    That thy brain must know,
Such harmonious madness[3]
    From my lips would flow
105 The world should listen then—as I am listening now.

1820   1820

---

2. Echoing Hamlet's comment on the human capability of "looking before and after" (4.4.36), as well as alluding to Wordsworth's use of this phrase in Preface to Lyrical Ballads.

3. Echoing Wordsworth's rhyme in Resolution and Independence: "We Poets in our youth begin in gladness; / But thereof come in the end despondency and madness" (48–49).

John Keats
1795–1821

On First Looking into Chapman's Homer[1]

Much have I travell'd in the realms of gold,
   And many goodly states and kingdoms seen;
   Round many western islands have I been
Which bards in fealty to Apollo° hold.   *god of poetry*
5   Oft of one wide expanse had I been told
     That deep-brow'd Homer ruled as his demesne;°   *realm*
     Yet did I never breathe its pure serene°   *clear sky*
Till I heard Chapman speak out loud and bold:
Then felt I like some watcher of the skies
10   When a new planet swims into his ken;[2]
Or like stout Cortez when with eagle eyes
    He star'd at the Pacific—and all his men
Look'd at each other with a wild surmise—
    Silent, upon a peak in Darien.[3]

1816   1816, 1817

Sonnet: When I have fears

When I have fears that I may cease to be[1]
   Before my pen has glean'd my teeming brain,
Before high piled books in charact'ry°   *written symbols*
   Hold like rich garners the full-ripened grain;
5   When I behold upon the night's starred face,
   Huge cloudy symbols of a high romance,
And think that I may never live to trace
   Their shadows with the magic hand of chance;
And when I feel, fair creature of an hour,
10   That I shall never look upon thee more,
Never have relish in the fairy power
   Of unreflecting love—then on the shore
Of the wide world I stand alone and think,
Till love and fame to nothingness do sink.

January 1818   1848

1. Written the morning after Keats had stayed up all night with Clarke reading George Chapman's vibrant, early 17th-century translation of Homer at a time when Pope's rendering in polished heroic couplets was the standard. Keats describes his reading as a Homeric voyage through the Greek isles where classical literature had its golden age. In *A Defence of Poesie* (1595), Sidney wrote that poets "deliver a golden" world from the "brazen" world of nature. Keats extends the language of traveling in "realms of gold" to Renaissance-era voyages of discovery to the New World in quest of gold by adventurers such as the conquistador of Mexico, Cortez.

2. Uranus was discovered in 1781; ken: range of apprehension.
3. Mountain range in eastern Panama.
1. Keats's sonnet plays several allusive echoes: Shakespeare's "When I do count the clock that tells the time"; Wordsworth's "few could know / When Lucy ceased to be" (*She dwelt among th'untrodden ways*; see page 194); Shelley's lament that by 1816 the radical Wordsworth should "cease to be" (*To Wordsworth*); Milton's sonnet, "When I consider how my light is spent / Ere half my days, in this dark world and wide . . ."

Ode to a Nightingale[1]

1

My heart aches, and a drowsy numbness pains
  My sense, as though of hemlock I had drunk,
Or emptied some dull opiate to the drains
  One minute past, and Lethe-wards had sunk:[2]
5 'Tis not through envy of thy happy lot,
  But being too happy in thine happiness,—
    That thou, light-winged Dryad° of the trees,   *wood-nymph*
      In some melodious plot
Of beechen green, and shadows numberless,
10   Singest of summer in full-throated ease.

2

O, for a draught of vintage!° that hath been   *wine*
  Cool'd a long age in the deep-delved earth,
Tasting of Flora and the country green,
  Dance, and Provençal song, and sunburnt mirth![3]
15 O for a beaker full of the warm South,
  Full of the true, the blushful Hippocrene,[4]
    With beaded bubbles winking at the brim,
      And purple-stained mouth;
That I might drink, and leave the world unseen,[5]
20   And with thee fade away into the forest dim:

3

Fade far away, dissolve, and quite forget
  What thou among the leaves hast never known,
The weariness, the fever, and the fret
  Here, where men sit and hear each other groan;
25 Where palsy shakes a few, sad, last gray hairs,
  Where youth grows pale, and spectre-thin, and dies;[6]
    Where but to think is to be full of sorrow
      And leaden-eyed despairs,
Where Beauty cannot keep her lustrous eyes,
30   Or new Love pine at them beyond to-morrow.

4

Away! away! for I will fly to thee,
  Not charioted by Bacchus and his pards,[7]
But on the viewless wings of Poesy,
  Though the dull brain perplexes and retards:
35   Already with thee! tender is the night,

1. First published in *Annals of the Fine Arts*, 1819. Keats's stanza incorporates sonnet elements: a Shakespearean quatrain (*abab*) followed by a Petrarchan sestet (*cdecde*), also the form of the ode on "Melancholy." The nightingale in literary tradition (including Milton, Wordsworth, Coleridge) often evokes Ovid's story of Philomela. Keats was also inspired by an actual nightingale's song at the house where he was living.
2. In small doses hemlock is a sedative; in large doses, such as Socrates', it is fatal; an opiate is any sense-duller, particularly opium, widely used as a painkiller; Lethe is the mythic river of the underworld whose waters produce forgetfulness of previous life.
3. Magician Merlin dwells "in a deep delve, farre from the view of day, / That of no living wight he mote be found" (*Faerie Queene* 3.3.7). Flora: Roman goddess of flowers.

Provence: region in southern France famed for troubadours.
4. The fountain of the muses on Mount Helicon.
5. "Unseen" can modify both "I" and "world."
6. An echo of Wordsworth's memory in *Tintern Abbey* of himself in "darkness, and amid the many shapes / Of joyless day-light; when the fretful stir / Unprofitable, and the fever of the world, / Have hung upon the beatings of my heart" (52–55). Both Wordsworth and Keats recall Macbeth's envy of Duncan "in his grave; / After life's fitful fever he sleeps well" (*Macbeth* 3.322–323). Also echoed is Wordsworth's image of an ideal life "from diminution safe and weakening age; / While man grows old, and dwindles, and decays" (*Excursion* 4.759–60).
7. Bacchus, god of wine and revelry, whose chariot is drawn by leopards.

And haply° the Queen-Moon is on her throne,   *happily, perhaps*
    Cluster'd around by all her starry Fays;°   *fairies*
        But here there is no light,
    Save what from heaven is with the breezes blown
40   Through verdurous glooms and winding mossy ways.

5

I cannot see what flowers are at my feet,
    Nor what soft incense hangs upon the boughs,
But, in embalmed darkness, guess each sweet
    Wherewith the seasonable month endows
45 The grass, the thicket, and the fruit-tree wild;
    White hawthorn, and the pastoral eglantine;
        Fast fading violets cover'd up in leaves;
        And mid-May's eldest child,
    The coming musk-rose, full of dewy wine,
50   The murmurous haunt of flies on summer eves.[8]

6

Darkling° I listen; and, for many a time   *in the dark*
    I have been half in love with easeful Death,
Call'd him soft names in many a mused rhyme,
    To take into the air my quiet breath;
55 Now more than ever seems it rich to die,
    To cease upon the midnight with no pain,
        While thou art pouring forth thy soul abroad
        In such an ecstasy!
    Still wouldst thou sing, and I have ears in vain—
60   To thy high requiem° become a sod.   *funeral mass*

7

Thou wast not born for death, immortal Bird!
    No hungry generations tread thee down;
The voice I hear this passing night was heard
    In ancient days by emperor and clown:°   *rustic, peasant*
65 Perhaps the self-same song that found a path
    Through the sad heart of Ruth, when, sick for home,
    She stood in tears amid the alien corn;[9]
        The same that oft-times hath
    Charm'd magic casements, opening on the foam
70   Of perilous seas, in faery lands forlorn.

8

Forlorn! the very word is like a bell
    To toll me back from thee to my sole self!
Adieu! the fancy cannot cheat so well[10]
    As she is fam'd to do, deceiving elf.

---

8. This guessing of flowers echoes Oberon's description in *A Midsummer Night's Dream* of a verdant bank where one may find a snake-skin whose juices make a sleeper fall in love with whatever is first seen on waking (2.1.249–58).
9. See Ruth 1–2: compelled by famine to leave her home, Ruth eked out a living as a gleaner in faraway fields.
10. The adieu echoes the opening line of Charlotte Smith's *On the Departure of the Nightingale* (1784), "Sweet poet of the woods!—a long adieu!" The closing question bears several echoes: *Psyche* 5–6; the opening of Spenser's *Amoretti* 77: "Was it a dreame, or did I see it playne?";

Hazlitt's remark that "Spenser was the poet of our waking dreams," his "music . . . lulling the senses into a deep oblivion of the jarring noises of the world from which we have no wish ever to be recalled" (*On Chaucer and Spenser*, 1818); a spellbound lover's confusion in *Midsummer Night's Dream:* "Are you sure / That we are awake? It seesm to me / That yet we sleep, we dream" (4.1.194–96); Wordsworth's lament in the "Intimations" *Ode*, "Whither is fled the visionary gleam? / Where is it now, the glory and the dream?" (56–57), and his phrase "waking dream" in *Yarrow Visited* (pub. 1815).

75   Adieu! adieu! thy plaintive anthem fades
              Past the near meadows, over the still stream,
              Up the hill-side; and now 'tis buried deep
                    In the next valley-glades:
              Was it a vision, or a waking dream?
              Fled is that music:—Do I wake or sleep?

Charles Dickens
1812–1870

from Dombey and Son
[THE COMING OF THE RAILWAY]

The first shock of a great earthquake had, just at that period, rent the whole neighbourhood to its centre.[1] Traces of its course were visible on every side. Houses were
knocked down; streets broken through and stopped; deep pits and trenches dug in
the ground; enormous heaps of earth and clay thrown up; buildings that were
undermined and shaking, propped by great beams of wood. Here, a chaos of carts,
overthrown and jumbled together, lay topsy-turvy at the bottom of a steep unnatural hill; there, confused treasures of iron soaked and rusted in something that had
accidentally become a pond. Everywhere were bridges that led nowhere; thorough-
fares that were wholly impassable; Babel towers[2] of chimneys, wanting half their
height; temporary wooden houses and enclosures, in the most unlikely situations;
carcases of ragged tenements, and fragments of unfinished walls and arches, and
piles of scaffolding, and wildernesses of bricks, and giant forms of cranes, and
tripods straddling above nothing. There were a hundred thousand shapes and substances of incompleteness, wildly mingled out of their places, upside down, burrow-
ing in the earth, aspiring in the air, mouldering in the water, and unintelligible as
any dream. Hot springs and fiery eruptions, the usual attendants upon earthquakes,
lent their contributions of confusion to the scene. Boiling water hissed and heaved
within dilapidated walls; whence, also, the glare and roar of flames came issuing
forth; and mounds of ashes blocked up rights of way, and wholly changed the law
and custom of the neighbourhood.

In short, the yet unfinished and unopened Railroad was in progress; and, from
the very core of all this dire disorder, trailed smoothly away, upon its mighty course of
civilisation and improvement.

But as yet, the neighbourhood was shy to own the Railroad. One or two bold
speculators had projected streets; and one had built a little, but had stopped among
the mud and ashes to consider farther of it. A bran-new Tavern, redolent of fresh
mortar and size, and fronting nothing at all, had taken for its sign The Railway Arms;
but that might be rash enterprise—and then it hoped to sell drink to the workmen.
So, the Excavators' House of Call had sprung up from a beer-shop; and the old-
established Ham and Beef Shop had become the Railway Eating House, with a roast
leg of pork daily, through interested motives of a similar immediate and popular

---

1. Dickens is describing the construction of the London-
Birmingham railway, which demolished many buildings
in Camden Town, an area in London he knew as a boy.
The line opened in 1838.

2. The tower of Babel was supposed to have been built
high enough to reach heaven (Genesis 11).

description. Lodging-house keepers were favourable in like manner; and for the like reasons were not to be trusted. The general belief was very slow. There were frowzy fields, and cow-houses, and dunghills, and dustheaps, and ditches, and gardens, and summer-houses, and carpet-beating grounds, at the very door of the Railway. Little tumuli[3] of oyster shells in the oyster season, and of lobster shells in the lobster season, and of broken crockery and faded cabbage leaves in all seasons, encroached upon its high places. Posts, and rails, and old cautions to trespassers, and backs of mean houses, and patches of wretched vegetation, stared it out of countenance. Nothing was the better for it, or thought of being so. If the miserable waste ground lying near it could have laughed, it would have laughed it to scorn, like many of the miserable neighbours.

1846

from Hard Times
[COKETOWN]

Coketown, to which Messrs Bounderby and Gradgrind[1] now walked, was a triumph of fact; it had no greater taint of fancy in it than Mrs Gradgrind herself. Let us strike the key-note, Coketown, before pursuing our tune.

It was a town of red brick, or of brick that would have been red if the smoke and ashes had allowed it; but, as matters stood it was a town of unnatural red and black like the painted face of a savage. It was a town of machinery and tall chimneys, out of which interminable serpents of smoke trailed themselves for ever and ever, and never got uncoiled. It had a black canal in it, and a river that ran purple with ill-smelling dye, and vast piles of building full of windows where there was a rattling and a trembling all day long, and where the piston of the steam-engine worked monotonously up and down, like the head of an elephant in a state of melancholy madness. It contained several large streets all very like one another, and many small streets still more like one another, inhabited by people equally like one another, who all went in and out at the same hours, with the same sound upon the same pavements, to do the same work, and to whom every day was the same as yesterday and tomorrow, and every year the counterpart of the last and the next.

These attributes of Coketown were in the main inseparable from the work by which it was sustained; against them were to be set off, comforts of life which found their way all over the world, and elegancies of life which made, we will not ask how much of the fine lady, who could scarcely bear to hear the place mentioned. The rest of its features were voluntary, and they were these.

You saw nothing in Coketown but what was severely workful. If the members of a religious persuasion built a chapel there—as the members of eighteen religious persuasions had done—they made it a pious warehouse of red brick, with sometimes (but this only in highly ornamented examples) a bell in a bird-cage on the top of it. The solitary exception was the New Church; a stuccoed edifice with a square steeple over the door, terminating in four short pinnacles like florid wooden legs. All the public inscriptions in the town were painted alike, in severe characters of black and white. The jail might have been the infirmary, the infirmary might have been the jail, the town-hall might have been either, or both, or any-

3. Artificial mounds. Oysters, a luxury today, were popular with poor people in Dickens's day; in *Pickwick Papers* Sam Weller says: "Poverty and oysters always seem to go together."

1. Bounderby is a mill owner; Gradgrind runs a school on Utilitarian principles.

thing else, for anything that appeared to the contrary in the graces of their con-struction. Fact, fact, fact, everywhere in the material aspect of the town; fact, fact, fact, everywhere in the immaterial. The M'Choakumchild school was all fact, and the school of design was all fact, and the relations between master and man were all fact, and everything was fact between the lying-in hospital and the cemetery, and what you couldn't state in figures, or show to be purchaseable in the cheapest market and saleable in the dearest, was not, and never should be, world without end, Amen.[2]

A town so sacred to fact, and so triumphant in its assertion, of course got on well? Why no, not quite well. No? Dear me!

No. Coketown did not come out of its own furnaces, in all respects like gold that had stood the fire. First, the perplexing mystery of the place was, Who belonged to the eighteen denominations? Because, whoever did, the labouring peo-ple did not. It was very strange to walk through the streets on a Sunday morning, and note how few of *them* the barbarous jangling of bells that was driving the sick and nervous mad, called away from their own quarter, from their own close rooms, from the corners of their own streets, where they lounged listlessly, gazing at all the church and chapel going, as at a thing with which they had no manner of concern. Nor was it merely the stranger who noticed this, because there was a native organi-zation in Coketown itself, whose members were to be heard of in the House of Commons every session, indignantly petitioning for acts of parliament that should make these people religious by main force. Then, came the Teetotal Society, who complained that these same people *would* get drunk, and showed in tabular state-ments that they did get drunk, and proved at tea parties that no inducement, human or Divine (except a medal), would induce them to forego their custom of getting drunk. Then, came the chemist and druggist, with other tabular statements, showing that when they didn't get drunk, they took opium. Then, came the experi-enced chaplain of the jail, with more tabular statements, outdoing all the previous tabular statements, and showing that the same people *would* resort to low haunts, hidden from the public eye, where they heard low singing and saw low dancing, and mayhap joined in it; and where A. B., aged twenty-four next birthday, and committed for eighteen months' solitary, had himself said (not that he had ever shown himself particularly worthy of belief) his ruin began, as he was perfectly sure and confident that otherwise he would have been a tip-top moral specimen. Then, came Mr Gradgrind and Mr Bounderby, the two gentlemen at this present moment walking through Coketown, and both eminently practical, who could, on occasion, furnish more tabular statements derived from their own personal experience, and illustrated by cases they had known and seen, from which it clearly appeared—in short it was the only clear thing in the case—that these same people were a bad lot altogether, gentlemen; that do what you would for them they were never thankful for it, gentlemen; that they were restless, gentlemen; that they never knew what they wanted; that they lived upon the best, and bought fresh butter, and insisted on Mocha coffee, and rejected all but prime parts of meat, and yet were eternally dissatisfied and unmanageable.

1854

---

2. The conclusion of the Anglican form of the Lord's Prayer.

Elizabeth Barrett Browning
1806–1861

from Sonnets from the Portuguese[1]

38

First time he kissed me, he but only kissed
The fingers of this hand wherewith I write;
And ever since, it grew more clean and white,
Slow to world-greetings, quick with its "Oh, list,"°   listen
5   When the angels speak. A ring of amethyst
I could not wear here, plainer to my sight,
Than that first kiss. The second passed in height
The first, and sought the forehead, and half missed,
Half falling on the hair. O beyond meed!°   deserving
10 That was the chrism[2] of love, which love's own crown,
With sanctifying sweetness, did precede.
The third upon my lips was folded down
In perfect, purple state; since when, indeed,
I have been proud and said, "My love, my own."

43

How do I love thee? Let me count the ways.
I love thee to the depth and breadth and height
My soul can reach, when feeling out of sight
For the ends of Being and ideal Grace.
5   I love thee to the level of everyday's
Most quiet need, by sun and candle-light.
I love thee freely, as men strive for Right;
I love thee purely, as they turn from Praise.
I love thee with the passion put to use
10 In my old griefs, and with my childhood's faith.
I love thee with a love I seemed to lose
With my lost saints,—I love with the breath,
Smiles, tears, of all my life!—and, if God choose,
I shall but love thee better after death.

1845–1847   1850

---

1. These very personal poems chronicle Elizabeth Barrett's courtship with Robert Browning. She did not show them to him until after they were married, when he pronounced them "the finest sonnets written in any language since Shakespeare's." He overcame her reluctance to publish them by proposing the somewhat cryptic title implying that they are merely translations.
2. Consecrated oil used to anoint during a coronation.

from Aurora Leigh[1]
from Book 5
[EPIC ART AND MODERN LIFE]

The critics say that epics have died out
140 With Agamemnon and the goat-nursed gods;[2]
I'll not believe it. I could never deem,
As Payne Knight[3] did (the mythic mountaineer
Who travelled higher than he was born to live,
And showed sometimes the goitre in his throat[4]
145 Discoursing of an image seen through fog),
That Homer's heroes measured twelve feet high.
They were but men:—his Helen's hair turned grey
Like any plain Miss Smith's who wears a front;[5]
And Hector's infant whimpered at a plume[6]
150 As yours last Friday at a turkey-cock.
All actual heroes are essential men,
And all men possible heroes: every age,
Heroic in proportions, double-faced,
Looks backward and before, expects a morn
155 And claims an epos.°   *epic poem*

       Ay, but every age
Appears to souls who live in't (ask Carlyle[7])
Most unheroic. Ours, for instance, ours:
The thinkers scout it, and the poets abound
Who scorn to touch it with a finger-tip:
160 A pewter age,[8]—mixed metal, silver-washed;
An age of scum, spooned off the richer past,
An age of patches for old gaberdines,°   *overcoats*
An age of mere transition,[9] meaning nought
Except that what succeeds must shame it quite
165 If God please. That's wrong thinking, to my mind,
And wrong thoughts make poor poems.

         Every age,
Through being beheld too close, is ill-discerned
By those who have not lived past it. We'll suppose
Mount Athos carved, as Alexander schemed,
170 To some colossal statue of a man.[10]

1. Barrett Browning called *Aurora Leigh*, a poem in nine books, a "verse novel." It portrays the struggles of a young poet to find her artistic voice and pursue her vocation despite the obstacles confronting a woman writer.
2. Agamemnon led the Greeks in the Trojan War, as chronicled in Homer's epic, the *Iliad*; Zeus was nursed by a goat.
3. Richard Payne Knight (1750–1824), a classical scholar who speculated about Homer and the Elgin marbles.
4. A swelling of the throat (caused by lack of iodine in the water at high altitudes), symbolizing the foolishness of Payne Knight's utterances.
5. Hairpiece worn over the forehead; artificial bangs.
6. When the Trojan warrior Hector tried to embrace his infant son before going into battle, the baby was terrified of his father's plumed helmet.
7. In *On Heroes and Hero Worship* (1841) Thomas Carlyle urges a renewal of the idea of the heroic.
8. Inferior to the Golden, the Silver, or even the Bronze Age; Hesiod proposed that history is a constant process of decline.
9. In *The Spirit of the Age* (1831) John Stuart Mill says the present era is "an age of transition."
10. Alexander the Great thought of having Mount Athos carved in the form of a gigantic statue of a conqueror, with a basin in one hand to collect water for the pastures below.

The peasants, gathering brushwood in his ear,
Had guessed as little as the browsing goats
Of form or feature of humanity
Up there,—in fact, had travelled five miles off
175 Or ere the giant image broke on them,
Full human profile, nose and chin distinct,
Mouth, muttering rhythms of silence up the sky
And fed at evening with the blood of suns;
Grand torso,—hand, that flung perpetually
180 The largesse of a silver river down
To all the country pastures. 'Tis even thus
With times we live in,—evermore too great
To be apprehended near.

                          But poets should
Exert a double vision; should have eyes
185 To see near things as comprehensively
As if afar they took their point of sight,
And distant things as intimately deep
As if they touched them. Let us strive for this.
I do distrust the poet who discerns
190 No character or glory in his times,
And trundles back his soul five hundred years,
Past moat and drawbridge, into a castle-court,
To sing—oh, not of lizard or of toad
Alive i' the ditch there,—'twere excusable,
195 But of some black chief, half knight, half sheep-lifter,
Some beauteous dame, half chattel and half queen,
As dead as must be, for the greater part,
The poems made on their chivalric bones;
And that's no wonder: death inherits death.

200 Nay, if there's room for poets in this world
A little overgrown (I think there is),
Their sole work is to represent the age,
Their age, not Charlemagne's,[11]—this live, throbbing age,
That brawls, cheats, maddens, calculates, aspires,
205 And spends more passion, more heroic heat,
Betwixt the mirrors of its drawing-rooms,
Than Roland with his knights at Roncesvalles.[12]
To flinch from modern varnish, coat or flounce,
Cry out for togas and the picturesque,
210 Is fatal,—foolish too. King Arthur's self
Was commonplace to Lady Guenever;
And Camelot to minstrels seemed as flat
As Fleet Street to our poets.[13]

11. Charlemagne was king of the Franks (768–814) and emperor of the West, laying the foundation for the Holy Roman Empire.
12. Legendary hero whose defeat at Roncesvalles (in the Spanish Pyrenees) was disastrous for Charlemagne's forces; his exploits are the subject of a medieval epic poem, Le Chanson de Roland.
13. I.e., to his wife Guinevere, even the glorious King Arthur was ordinary, and his kingdom was no more a subject for the poets of his own time than Fleet Street—location of London publishers and newspaper offices—is for the poets of the 19th century.

Never flinch,

But still, unscrupulously epic, catch
215   Upon the burning lava of a song
The full-veined, heaving, double-breasted Age:
That, when the next shall come, the men of that
May touch the impress with reverent hand, and say
"Behold,—behold the paps we all have sucked!
220   This bosom seems to beat still, or at least
It sets ours beating: this is living art,
Which thus presents and thus records true life."

1853–1856   1856

Alfred, Lord Tennyson
1809–1892

The Lady of Shalott[1]
Part 1

On either side the river lie
Long fields of barley and of rye,

William Holman Hunt, *The Lady of Shalott*, from the Moxon edition of Tennyson's poems, 1857. This edition was a high point in Victorian book illustration, including drawings by Rossetti and Millais as well as Hunt. Tennyson, however, complained about this illustration because it depicts the lady entangled in the threads of her tapestry, making her unable to leave the loom, as she does in his poem. Hunt responded: "I had only half a page on which to convey the impression of weird fate, whereas you use about fifteen pages to give expression to the complete idea."

1. The Lady of Shalott is evidently the Elaine of the *Morte d'Arthur*, but I do not think that I had ever heard of the latter when I wrote the former [Tennyson's note]. In Malory, Elaine dies of grief for love of Lancelot, but the curse, the weaving, and the mirror are all Tennyson's inventions.

That clothe the wold° and meet the sky;   *rolling uplands*
And thro' the field the road runs by
5   To many-tower'd Camelot;
And up and down the people go,
Gazing where the lilies blow°   *bloom*
Round an island there below,
          The island of Shalott.

10   Willows whiten, aspens quiver,
Little breezes dusk and shiver
Thro' the wave that runs for ever
By the island in the river
          Flowing down to Camelot.
15   Four gray walls, and four gray towers,
Overlook a space of flowers,
And the silent isle imbowers
          The Lady of Shalott.

By the margin, willow-veil'd,
20   Slide the heavy barges trail'd
By slow horses; and unhail'd
The shallop° flitteth silken-sail'd   *small boat*
          Skimming down to Camelot:
But who hath seen her wave her hand?
25   Or at the casement seen her stand?
Or is she known in all the land,
          The Lady of Shalott?

Only reapers, reaping early
In among the bearded barley,
30   Hear a song that echoes cheerly
From the river winding clearly,
          Down to tower'd Camelot:
And by the moon the reaper weary,
Piling sheaves in uplands airy,
35   Listening, whispers "'Tis the fairy
          Lady of Shalott.'"

Part 2

There she weaves by night and day
A magic web with colours gay.
She has heard a whisper say,
40   A curse is on her if she stay
          To look down to Camelot.
She knows not what the curse may be,
And so she weaveth steadily,
And little other care hath she,
45   The Lady of Shalott.

And moving thro' a mirror clear[2]
That hangs before her all the year,
Shadows of the world appear.
There she sees the highway near
50   Winding down to Camelot:
There the river eddy whirls,
And there the surly village-churls,°   *peasants*
And the red cloaks of market girls,
        Pass onward from Shalott.

55 Sometimes a troop of damsels glad,
An abbot on an ambling pad,°   *horse*
Sometimes a curly shepherd-lad,
Or long-hair'd page in crimson clad,
        Goes by to tower'd Camelot;
60 And sometimes thro' the mirror blue
The knights come riding two and two:
She hath no loyal knight and true,
        The Lady of Shalott.

But in her web she still delights
65 To weave the mirror's magic sights,
For often thro' the silent nights
A funeral, with plumes and lights
        And music, went to Camelot:
Or when the moon was overhead,
70 Came two young lovers lately wed;
"I am half sick of shadows," said
        The Lady of Shalott.

Part 3

A bow-shot from her bower-eaves,
He rode between the barley-sheaves,
75 The sun came dazzling thro' the leaves,
And flamed upon the brazen greaves°   *leg armor*
        Of bold Sir Lancelot.[3]
A red-cross knight for ever kneel'd
To a lady in his shield,[4]
80 That sparkled on the yellow field,
        Beside remote Shalott.

The gemmy bridle glitter'd free,
Like to some branch of stars we see
Hung in the golden Galaxy.
85 The bridle bells rang merrily
        As he rode down to Camelot:

2. Working from the back of their tapestries, weavers placed mirrors on the other side to see the effect of their work.
3. The greatest of King Arthur's knights, Lancelot was in love with Queen Guinevere.

4. Lancelot's shield depicts the Redcrosse Knight—a character in Spenser's *Faerie Queene* who champions holiness—kneeling in homage to his lady.

And from his blazon'd baldric° slung   *ornamented belt*
A mighty silver bugle hung,
And as he rode his armour rung,
90   Beside remote Shalott.

All in the blue unclouded weather
Thick-jewell'd shone the saddle-leather,
The helmet and the helmet-feather
Burn'd like one burning flame together,
95   As he rode down to Camelot.
As often thro' the purple night,
Below the starry clusters bright,
Some bearded meteor, trailing light,
          Moves over still Shalott.

100 His broad clear brow in sunlight glow'd;
On burnish'd hooves his war-horse trode;
From underneath his helmet flow'd
His coal-black curls as on he rode,
          As he rode down to Camelot.
105 From the bank and from the river
He flash'd into the crystal mirror,
"Tirra lirra," by the river
          Sang Sir Lancelot.

She left the web, she left the loom,
110 She made three paces thro' the room,
She saw the water-lily bloom,
She saw the helmet and the plume,
          She look'd down to Camelot.
Out flew the web and floated wide;
115 The mirror crack'd from side to side;
"The curse is come upon me," cried
          The Lady of Shalott.

Part 4

In the stormy east-wind straining,
The pale yellow woods were waning,
120 The broad stream in his banks complaining,
Heavily the low sky raining
          Over tower'd Camelot;
Down she came and found a boat
Beneath a willow left afloat,
125 And round about the prow she wrote
          The Lady of Shalott.

And down the river's dim expanse
Like some bold seër in a trance,
Seeing all his own mischance—
130 With a glassy countenance

       Did she look to Camelot.
And at the closing of the day
She loosed the chain, and down she lay;
The broad stream bore her far away,
135   The Lady of Shalott.

Lying, robed in snowy white
That loosely flew to left and right—
The leaves upon her falling light—
Thro' the noises of the night
140   She floated down to Camelot:
And as the boat-head wound along
The willowy hills and fields among,
They heard her singing her last song,
       The Lady of Shalott.

145   Heard a carol, mournful, holy,
Chanted loudly, chanted lowly,
Till her blood was frozen slowly,
And her eyes were darken'd wholly,
        Turn'd to tower'd Camelot.
150   For ere she reach'd upon the tide
The first house by the water-side,
Singing in her song she died,
       The Lady of Shalott.

Under tower and balcony,
155   By garden-wall and gallery,
A gleaming shape she floated by,
Dead-pale between the houses high,
        Silent into Camelot.
Out upon the wharfs they came;
160   Knight and burgher, lord and dame,
And round the prow they read her name,
       The Lady of Shalott.

Who is this? and what is here?
And in the lighted palace near
165   Died the sound of royal cheer;
And they cross'd themselves for fear,
        All the knights at Camelot:
But Lancelot mused a little space;
He said, "She has a lovely face;
170   God in his mercy lend her grace,
       The Lady of Shalott."

                             1832, 1842

from In Memoriam A. H. H.
Obiit MDCCCXXXIII[1]

54

Oh yet we trust that somehow good
  Will be the final goal of ill,
  To pangs of nature, sins of will,
Defects of doubt, and taints of blood;

5   That nothing walks with aimless feet;
  That not one life shall be destroy'd,
  Or cast as rubbish to the void,
When God hath made the pile complete;

That not a worm is cloven in vain;
10   That not a moth with vain desire
  Is shrivell'd in a fruitless fire,
Or but subserves another's gain.

Behold, we know not anything;
  I can but trust that good shall fall
15   At last—far off—at last, to all,
And every winter change to spring.

So runs my dream: but what am I?
  An infant crying in the night:
  An infant crying for the light:
20 And with no language but a cry.

55

The wish, that of the living whole
  No life may fail beyond the grave,
  Derives it not from what we have
The likest God within the soul?[2]

5   Are God and Nature then at strife,
  That Nature lends such evil dreams?
  So careful of the type[3] she seems,
So careless of the single life;

That I, considering everywhere
10   Her secret meaning in her deeds,
  And finding that of fifty seeds
She often brings but one to bear,

I falter where I firmly trod,
  And falling with my weight of cares
15   Upon the great world's altar-stairs
That slope thro' darkness up to God,

---

1. Died 1833
2. The inner consciousness—the divine in man [Tennyson's note].

3. Species; i.e., Nature ensures the preservation of the species but is indifferent to the fate of the individual.

I stretch lame hands of faith, and grope,
   And gather dust and chaff, and call
   To what I feel is Lord of all,
20   And faintly trust the larger hope.[4]

The Charge of the Light Brigade[1]

1

Half a league, half a league,
Half a league onward,
All in the valley of Death
   Rode the six hundred.
5   "Forward, the Light Brigade!
Charge for the guns!" he said:
Into the valley of Death
   Rode the six hundred.[2]

2

"Forward, the Light Brigade!"
10   Was there a man dismay'd?
Not tho' the soldier knew
   Some one had blunder'd:
Their's not to make reply,
Their's not to reason why,
15   Their's but to do and die:
Into the valley of Death
   Rode the six hundred.

3

Cannon to right of them,
Cannon to left of them,
20   Cannon in front of them
   Volley'd and thunder'd;
Storm'd at with shot and shell,
Boldly they rode and well,
Into the jaws of Death,
25   Into the mouth of Hell
   Rode the six hundred.

4

Flash'd all their sabres bare,
Flash'd as they turn'd in air
Sabring the gunners there,
30   Charging an army, while
   All the world wonder'd:

4. Hallam Tennyson notes: "My father means by 'the larger hope' that the whole human race would through, perhaps, ages of suffering, be at length purified and saved."
1. In 1854, during the Crimean War, a misunderstood order
caused a brigade of 600 British cavalry to make a foolhardy
charge upon the batteries of Russian artillery at Balaclava,
near Sebastopol. More than 400 soldiers were killed.
2. In his Lincolnshire accent, Tennyson apparently pronounced "hundred" as "hunderd"—thus making it an
exact rhyme with "blundered" and "thundered."

Plunged in the battery-smoke
Right thro' the line they broke;
Cossack and Russian
35 Reel'd from the sabre-stroke
　　Shatter'd and sunder'd.
Then they rode back, but not
　　Not the six hundred.

5

Cannon to right of them,
40 Cannon to left of them,
Cannon behind them
　　Volley'd and thunder'd;
Storm'd at with shot and shell,
While horse and hero fell,
45 They that had fought so well
Came thro' the jaws of Death,
Back from the mouth of Hell,
All that was left of them,
　　Left of six hundred.

6

50 When can their glory fade?
O the wild charge they made!
　　All the world wonder'd.
Honour the charge they made!
Honour the Light Brigade,
55 　　Noble six hundred!
1854

1854

Robert Browning
1812–1889

My Last Duchess[1]
Ferrara

That's my last Duchess painted on the wall,
Looking as if she were alive. I call
That piece a wonder, now: Frà Pandolf's[2] hands
Worked busily a day, and there she stands.
5   Will't please you sit and look at her? I said
"Frà Pandolf" by design, for never read
Strangers like you that pictured countenance,
The depth and passion of its earnest glance,
But to myself they turned (since none puts by
10   The curtain I have drawn for you, but I)
And seemed as they would ask me, if they durst,
How such a glance came there; so, not the first
Are you to turn and ask thus. Sir, 'twas not
Her husband's presence only, called that spot
15   Of joy into the Duchess' cheek: perhaps
Frà Pandolf chanced to say "Her mantle laps
Over my lady's wrist too much," or "Paint
Must never hope to reproduce the faint
Half-flush that dies along her throat:" such stuff
20   Was courtesy, she thought, and cause enough
For calling up that spot of joy. She had
A heart—how shall I say?—too soon made glad,
Too easily impressed; she liked whate'er
She looked on, and her looks went everywhere.
25   Sir, 'twas all one! My favour at her breast,
The dropping of the daylight in the West,
The bough of cherries some officious fool
Broke in the orchard for her, the white mule
She rode with round the terrace—all and each
30   Would draw from her alike the approving speech,
Or blush, at least. She thanked men,—good! but thanked
Somehow—I know not how—as if she ranked
My gift of a nine-hundred-years-old name
With anybody's gift. Who'd stoop to blame
35   This sort of trifling? Even had you skill
In speech—(which I have not)—to make your will
Quite clear to such an one, and say, "Just this
Or that in you disgusts me; here you miss,
Or there exceed the mark"—and if she let

1. The speaker is modeled on Alfonso II, Duke of Ferrara, who married the 14-year-old Lucrezia de Medici in 1558. When she died three years later, poisoning was suspected. In 1565 the Duke married the daughter of Ferdinand I, Count of Tyrol.

2. Brother Pandolf, the imaginary painter of the duchess's portrait.

40   Herself be lessoned so, nor plainly set
        Her wits to yours, forsooth, and made excuse,
        —E'en then would be some stooping; and I choose
        Never to stoop. Oh sir, she smiled, no doubt,
        Whene'er I passed her, but who passed without
45   Much the same smile? This grew; I gave commands;
        Then all smiles stopped together. There she stands
        As if alive. Will't please you rise? We'll meet
        The company below, then. I repeat,
        The Count your master's known munificence
50   Is ample warrant that no just pretence
        Of mine for dowry will be disallowed;
        Though his fair daughter's self, as I avowed
        At starting, is my object.[3] Nay, we'll go
        Together down, sir. Notice Neptune, though,
55   Taming a sea-horse, thought a rarity,
        Which Claus of Innsbruck cast in bronze for me!

1842   1842

Love Among the Ruins[1]

1

        Where the quiet-coloured end of evening smiles,
                Miles and miles
        On the solitary pastures where our sheep
                Half-asleep
5   Tinkle homeward thro' the twilight, stray or stop
                As they crop—
        Was the site once of a city great and gay,
                (So they say)
        Of our country's very capital, its prince
10   Ages since
        Held his court in, gathered councils, wielding far
                Peace or war.

2

        Now,—the country does not even boast a tree
                As you see,
15   To distinguish slopes of verdure, certain rills
                From the hills
        Intersect and give a name to, (else they run
                Into one)
        Where the domed and daring palace shot its spires
20   Up like fires
        O'er the hundred-gated circuit of a wall
                Bounding all,
        Made of marble, men might march on nor be pressed
                Twelve abreast.

3. Only now does the reader learn that the duke is con-
ducting negotiations for his second marriage and has
been addressing the envoy of his bride-to-be's father.

1. The poem's scenery suggests the Roman Campagna but
may also allude to archaeological excavations at Babylon,
Nineveh, and Egyptian Thebes. Browning invented this
stanza form.

3

25   And such plenty and perfection, see, of grass
              Never was!
      Such a carpet as, this summer-time, o'erspreads
              And embeds
      Every vestige of the city, guessed alone,
30   Stock or stone—
      Where a multitude of men breathed joy and woe
              Long ago;
      Lust of glory pricked their hearts up, dread of shame
              Struck them tame;
35   And that glory and that shame alike, the gold
              Bought and sold.

4

      Now,—the single little turret that remains
              On the plains,
      By the caper° overrooted, by the gourd   *shrub*
40   Overscored,
      While the patching houseleek's head of blossom winks
              Through the chinks—
      Marks the basement whence a tower in ancient time
              Sprang sublime,
45   And a burning ring, all round, the chariots traced
              As they raced,
      And the monarch and his minions and his dames
              Viewed the games.

5

      And I know, while thus the quiet-coloured eve
50   Smiles to leave
      To their folding, all our many-tinkling fleece
              In such peace,
      And the slopes and rills in undistinguished grey
              Melt away—
55   That a girl with eager eyes and yellow hair
              Waits me there
      In the turret whence the charioteers caught soul
              For the goal,
      When the king looked, where she looks now, breathless, dumb
60   Till I come.

6

      But he looked upon the city, every side,
              Far and wide,
      All the mountains topped with temples, all the glades'
              Colonnades,
65   All the causeys,° bridges, aqueducts,—and then,   *causeways*
              All the men!
      When I do come, she will speak not, she will stand,
              Either hand
      On my shoulder, give her eyes the first embrace
70   Of my face,
      Ere we rush, ere we extinguish sight and speech
              Each on each.

7

In one year they sent a million fighters forth
            South and North,
75   And they built their gods a brazen pillar high
            As the sky,
      Yet reserved a thousand chariots in full force—
            Gold, of course.
      Oh heart! oh blood that freezes, blood that burns!
80   Earth's returns
      For whole centuries of folly, noise and sin!
            Shut them in,
      With their triumphs and their glories and the rest!
            Love is best.

c. 1852   1855

from "Childe Roland to the Dark Tower Came"[1]
(See Edgar's Song in "Lear")[2]

1

My first thought was, he lied in every word,
    That hoary cripple, with malicious eye
    Askance to watch the working of his lie
On mine, and mouth scarce able to afford
5   Suppression of the glee, that pursed and scored
    Its edge, at one more victim gained thereby.

2

What else should he be set for, with his staff?
    What, save to waylay with his lies, ensnare
    All travellers who might find him posted there,
10 And ask the road? I guessed what skull-like laugh
    Would break, what crutch 'gin write my epitaph
    For pastime in the dusty thoroughfare,

3

If at his counsel I should turn aside
    Into that ominous tract which, all agree,
15   Hides the Dark Tower. Yet acquiescingly
I did turn as he pointed: neither pride
Nor hope rekindling at the end descried,
    So much as gladness that some end might be.

4

For, what with my whole world-wide wandering,
20   What with my search drawn out thro' years, my hope
    Dwindled into a ghost not fit to cope

1. Roland was a hero of Charlemagne legends, and a "childe" was a young candidate for knighthood. Although critics have proposed many different interpretations of Roland's strange, nightmarish quest, Browning himself said only that the poem "came upon me as a kind of dream. I had to write it, then and there, and I finished it the same day, I believe. But it was simply that I had to do it. I did not know then what I meant beyond that, and I'm sure I don't know now. But I am very fond of it." 2. In Shakespeare's *King Lear*, Edgar, disguised as the mad beggar Poor Tom, sings: "Child Rowland to the dark tower came; / His word was still, 'Fie, foh and fum, / I smell the blood of a British man'" (3.4.181–83).

With that obstreperous joy success would bring,—
   I hardly tried now to rebuke the spring
      My heart made, finding failure in its scope. * * *

7

Thus, I had so long suffered in this quest,
   Heard failure prophesied so oft, been writ
      So many times among "The Band"—to wit,
40   The knights who to the Dark Tower's search addressed
Their steps—that just to fail as they, seemed best,
      And all the doubt was now—should I be fit?

8

So, quiet as despair, I turned from him,
   That hateful cripple, out of his highway
45   Into the path he pointed. All the day
Had been a dreary one at best, and dim
Was settling to its close, yet shot one grim
   Red leer to see the plain catch its estray.°   *stray animal*

9

For mark! no sooner was I fairly found
50   Pledged to the plain, after a pace or two,
      Than, pausing to throw backward a last view
O'er the safe road, 'twas gone; grey plain all round:
Nothing but plain to the horizon's bound.
      I might go on; nought else remained to do. * * *

19

A sudden little river crossed my path
110   As unexpected as a serpent comes.
      No sluggish tide congenial to the glooms;
This, as it frothed by, might have been a bath
For the friend's glowing hoof—to see the wrarh
      Of its black eddy bespate with flakes and spumes. * * *

21

Which, while I forded,—good saints, how I feared
   To set my foot upon a dead man's cheek,
      Each step, or feel the spear I thrust to seek
For hollows, tangled in his hair or beard!
125   —It may have been a water-rat I speared,
      But, ugh! it sounded like a baby's shriek. * * *

25

145   Then came a bit of stubbed ground, once a wood,
      Next a marsh, it would seem, and now mere earth
      Desperate and done with; (so a fool finds mirth,
Makes a thing and then mars it, till his mood
Changes and off he goes!) within a rood°—   *quarter of an acre*
150   Bog, clay and rubble, sand and stark black dearth.

26

Now blotches rankling, coloured gay and grim,
　　Now patches where some leanness of the soil's
　　Broke into moss or substances like boils;
Then came some palsied oak, a cleft in him
155 Like a distorted mouth that splits its rim
　　Gaping at death, and dies while it recoils.

27

And just as far as ever from the end!
　　Nought in the distance but the evening, nought
　　To point my footstep further! At the thought,
160 A great black bird, Apollyon's[3] bosom-friend,
Sailed past, nor beat his wide wing dragon-penned°   *pinioned*
　　That brushed my cap—perchance the guide I sought.

28

For, looking up, aware I somehow grew,
　　'Spite of the dusk, the plain had given place
165 　　All round to mountains—with such name to grace
Mere ugly heights and heaps now stolen in view.
How thus they had surprised me,—solve it, you!
　　How to get from them was no clearer case.

29

Yet half I seemed to recognize some trick
170 　　Of mischief happened to me, God knows when—
　　In a bad dream perhaps. Here ended, then,
Progress this way. When, in the very nick
Of giving up, one time more, came a click
　　As when a trap shuts—you're inside the den!

30

175 Burningly it came on me all at once,
　　This was the place! those two hills on the right,
　　Crouched like two bulls locked horn in horn in fight;
While to the left, a tall scalped mountain . . . Dunce,
Dotard, a-dozing at the very nonce,°   *moment*
180 　　After a life spent training for the sight!

31

What in the midst lay but the Tower itself?
　　The round squat turret, blind as the fool's heart,[4]
　　Built of brown stone, without a counterpart
In the whole world. The tempest's mocking elf
185 Points to the shipman thus the unseen shelf
　　He strikes on, only when the timbers start.

3. Devil mentioned in Revelation 9.11 and in Bunyan's *Pilgrim's Progress*.   4. "The fool hath said in his heart, There is no God" (Psalm 14.1).

32

Not see? because of night perhaps?—why, day
  Came back again for that! before it left,
  The dying sunset kindled through a cleft:
190 The hills, like giants at a hunting, lay,
Chin upon hand, to see the game at bay,—
  "Now stab and end the creature—to the heft!"°   *hilt*

33

Not hear? when noise was everywhere! it tolled
  Increasing like a bell. Names in my ears
195   Of all the lost adventurers my peers,—
How such a one was strong, and such was bold,
And such was fortunate, yet each of old
  Lost, lost! one moment knelled the woe of years.

34

There they stood, ranged along the hill-sides, met
200   To view the last of me, a living frame
  For one more picture! in a sheet of flame
I saw them and I knew them all. And yet
Dauntless the slug-horn⁵ to my lips I set,
  And blew. "*Childe Roland to the Dark Tower came.*"

c. 1852   1855

5. Scottish word for slogan, or battle cry, though Browning seems to mean "trumpet."

Elizabeth Gaskell
1810–1865

Our Society at Cranford[1]

In the first place, Cranford is in possession of the Amazons;[2] all the holders of houses above a certain rent are women. If a married couple come to settle in the town, somehow the gentleman disappears; he is either fairly frightened to death by being the only man in the Cranford evening parties, or he is accounted for by being with his regiment, his ship, or closely engaged in business all the week in the great neighbouring commercial town of Drumble,[3] distant only twenty miles on a railroad. In short, whatever does become of the gentlemen, they are not at Cranford. What could they do if they were there? The surgeon has his round of thirty miles, and sleeps at Cranford; but every man cannot be a surgeon. For keeping the trim gardens full of choice flowers without a weed to speck them; for frightening away little boys who look wistfully at the said flowers through the railings; for rushing out at the geese that occasionally venture into the gardens if the gates are left open; for deciding all questions of literature and politics without troubling themselves with unnecessary reasons or arguments; for obtaining clear and correct knowledge of everybody's affairs in the parish; for keeping their neat maid-servants in admirable order; for kindness (somewhat dictatorial) to the poor, and real tender good offices to each other whenever they are in distress, the ladies of Cranford are quite sufficient. "A man," as one of them observed to me once, "is *so* in the way in the house!" Although the ladies of Cranford know all each other's proceedings, they are exceedingly indifferent to each other's opinions. Indeed, as each has her own individuality, not to say eccentricity, pretty strongly developed, nothing is so easy as verbal retaliation; but, somehow, good-will reigns among them to a considerable degree.

The Cranford ladies have only an occasional little quarrel, spirited out in a few peppery words and angry jerks of the head; just enough to prevent the even tenor of their lives from becoming too flat. Their dress is very independent of fashion; as they observe, "What does it signify how we dress here at Cranford, where everybody knows us?" And if they go from home, their reason is equally cogent, "What does it signify how we dress here, where nobody knows us?" The materials of their clothes are, in general, good and plain, and most of them are nearly as scrupulous as Miss Tyler, of cleanly memory;[4] but I will answer for it, the last gigot, the last tight and scanty petticoat in wear in England, was seen in Cranford—and seen without a smile.[5]

I can testify to a magnificent family red silk umbrella, under which a gentle little spinster, left alone of many brothers and sisters, used to patter to church on rainy

1. First published as a self-contained story in December 1851 in *Household Words*, a periodical edited by Charles Dickens. Although Gaskell later said that "I never meant to write more," Dickens persuaded her to continue the story in subsequent issues. In 1853 the collected sketches appeared in book form as *Cranford*.
2. In Greek legend, the Amazons were fierce warriors who formed an all-female state.
3. Manchester.
4. The aunt of Robert Southey (1774–1843)—Poet Laureate at the time when *Cranford* takes place—was famous for her passion for cleanliness.
5. By the mid-1830s, the old-fashioned leg-of-mutton sleeve and straight skirt had given way to the hooped skirt.

days. Have you any red silk umbrellas in London? We had a tradition of the first that had ever been seen in Cranford; and the little boys mobbed it, and called it "a stick in petticoats." It might have been the very red silk one I have described, held by a strong father over a troop of little ones; the poor little lady—the survivor of all—could scarcely carry it.

Then there were rules and regulations for visiting and calls; and they were announced to any young people who might be staying in the town, with all the solemnity with which the old Manx laws were read once a year on the Tinwald Mount.[6]

"Our friends have sent to inquire how you are after your journey to-night, my dear" (fifteen miles in a gentleman's carriage); "they will give you some rest to-morrow, but the next day, I have no doubt, they will call; so be at liberty after twelve—from twelve to three are our calling hours."

Then, after they had called—

"It is the third day; I dare say your mamma has told you, my dear, never to let more than three days elapse between receiving a call and returning it; and also, that you are never to stay longer than a quarter of an hour."

"But am I to look at my watch? How am I to find out when a quarter of an hour has passed?"

"You must keep thinking about the time, my dear, and not allow yourself to forget it in conversation."

As everybody had this rule in their minds, whether they received or paid a call, of course no absorbing subject was ever spoken about. We kept ourselves to short sentences of small talk, and were punctual to our time.

I imagine that a few of the gentlefolks of Cranford were poor, and had some difficulty in making both ends meet; but they were like the Spartans,[7] and concealed their smart under a smiling face. We none of us spoke of money, because that subject savoured of commerce and trade, and though some might be poor, we were all aristocratic. The Cranfordians had that kindly *esprit de corps* which made them overlook all deficiencies in success when some among them tried to conceal their poverty. When Mrs Forrester, for instance, gave a party in her baby-house of a dwelling, and the little maiden disturbed the ladies on the sofa by a request that she might get the tea-tray out from underneath, every one took this novel proceeding as the most natural thing in the world, and talked on about household forms and ceremonies as if we all believed that our hostess had a regular servants' hall, second table, with housekeeper and steward, instead of the one little charity-school maiden,[8] whose short ruddy arms could never have been strong enough to carry the tray upstairs, if she had not been assisted in private by her mistress, who now sat in state, pretending not to know what cakes were sent up, though she knew, and we knew, and she knew that we knew, and we knew that she knew that we knew, she had been busy all the morning making tea-bread and sponge-cakes.

There were one or two consequences arising from this general but unacknowledged poverty, and this very much acknowledged gentility, which were not amiss, and which might be introduced into many circles of society to their great improvement. For instance, the inhabitants of Cranford kept early hours, and clattered

6. The population of the Isle of Man customarily assembled once a year on Tynwald Hill to hear the new laws read aloud.
7. The Spartans of ancient Greece were known for their courage and self-control in the face of hardship.
8. Charity schools trained poor children for domestic work; that one such pupil formed Mrs. Forrester's entire domestic staff indicates her meager standard of living.

home in their pattens,[9] under the guidance of a lantern-bearer, about nine o'clock at night; and the whole town was abed and asleep by half-past ten. Moreover, it was considered "vulgar" (a tremendous word in Cranford) to give anything expensive, in the way of eatable or drinkable, at the evening entertainments. Wafer bread-and-butter and sponge-biscuits were all that the Honourable Mrs Jamieson gave; and she was sister-in-law to the late Earl of Glenmire, although she did practise such "elegant economy."

"Elegant economy!" How naturally one falls back into the phraseology of Cranford! There, economy was always "elegant," and money-spending always "vulgar and ostentatious;" a sort of sour-grapeism which made us very peaceful and satisfied. I never shall forget the dismay felt when a certain Captain Brown came to live at Cranford, and openly spoke about his being poor—not in a whisper to an intimate friend, the doors and windows being previously closed, but in the public street! in a loud military voice! alleging his poverty as a reason for not taking a particular house. The ladies of Cranford were already rather moaning over the invasion of their territories by a man and a gentleman. He was a half-pay captain,[10] and had obtained some situation on a neighbouring railroad, which had been vehemently petitioned against by the little town;[11] and if, in addition to his masculine gender, and his connection with the obnoxious railroad, he was so brazen as to talk of being poor—why, then, indeed, he must be sent to Coventry.[12] Death was as true and as common as poverty; yet people never spoke about that, loud out in the streets. It was a word not to be mentioned to ears polite. We had tacitly agreed to ignore that any with whom we associated on terms of visiting equality could ever be prevented by poverty from doing anything that they wished. If we walked to or from a party, it was because the night was so fine, or the air so refreshing, not because sedan-chairs were expensive.[13] If we wore prints, instead of summer silks, it was because we preferred a washing material; and so on, till we blinded ourselves to the vulgar fact that we were, all of us, people of very moderate means. Of course, then, we did not know what to make of a man who could speak of poverty as if it was not a disgrace. Yet, somehow, Captain Brown made himself respected in Cranford, and was called upon, in spite of all resolutions to the contrary. I was surprised to hear his opinions quoted as authority at a visit which I paid to Cranford about a year after he had settled in the town. My own friends had been among the bitterest opponents of any proposal to visit the Captain and his daughters, only twelve months before; and now he was even admitted in the tabooed hours before twelve. True, it was to discover the cause of a smoking chimney, before the fire was lighted; but still Captain Brown walked upstairs, nothing daunted, spoke in a voice too large for the room, and joked quite in the way of a tame man about the house. He had been blind to all the small slights, and omissions of trivial ceremonies, with which he had been received. He had been friendly, though the Cranford ladies had been cool; he had answered small sarcastic compliments in good faith; and with his manly frankness had overpowered all the shrinking which met him as a man who was not ashamed to be poor. And, at last, his excellent masculine common sense, and his facility in devising expedients to overcome domestic dilemmas, had gained him an extraordinary place as authority among the Cranford ladies. He himself went on in

9. Wooden platform shoes to protect one's shoes from mud.
10. A retired officer who stayed on reserve at half pay.
11. The railroads were new, and still looked on with suspicion by many country-dwellers.

12. Ostracized.
13. Enclosed chairs carried by servants; more common in the 18th century.

his course, as unaware of his popularity as he had been of the reverse; and I am sure he was startled one day when he found his advice so highly esteemed as to make some counsel which he had given in jest to be taken in sober, serious earnest.

It was on this subject: An old lady had an Alderney cow, which she looked upon as a daughter. You could not pay the short quarter of an hour call without being told of the wonderful milk or wonderful intelligence of this animal. The whole town knew and kindly regarded Miss Betsy Barker's Alderney; therefore great was the sympathy and regret when, in an unguarded moment, the poor cow tumbled into a lime-pit.[14] She moaned so loudly that she was soon heard and rescued; but meanwhile the poor beast had lost most of her hair, and came out looking naked, cold, and miserable, in a bare skin. Everybody pitied the animal, though a few could not restrain their smiles at her droll appearance. Miss Betsy Barker absolutely cried with sorrow and dismay; and it was said she thought of trying a bath of oil. This remedy, perhaps, was recommended by some one of the number whose advice she asked; but the proposal, if ever it was made, was knocked on the head by Captain Brown's decided "Get her a flannel waistcoat and flannel drawers, ma'am, if you wish to keep her alive. But my advice is, kill the poor creature at once."

Miss Betsy Barker dried her eyes, and thanked the Captain heartily; she set to work, and by-and-by all the town turned out to see the Alderney meekly going to her pasture, clad in dark grey flannel. I have watched her myself many a time. Do you ever see cows dressed in grey flannel in London?

Captain Brown had taken a small house on the outskirts of the town, where he lived with his two daughters. He must have been upwards of sixty at the time of the first visit I paid to Cranford after I had left it as a residence. But he had a wiry, well-trained, elastic figure, a stiff military throw-back of his head, and a springing step, which made him appear much younger than he was. His eldest daughter looked almost as old as himself, and betrayed the fact that his real was more than his apparent age. Miss Brown must have been forty; she had a sickly, pained, careworn expression on her face, and looked as if the gaiety of youth had long faded out of sight. Even when young she must have been plain and hard featured. Miss Jessie Brown was ten years younger than her sister, and twenty shades prettier. Her face was round and dimpled. Miss Jenkyns once said, in a passion against Captain Brown (the cause of which I will tell you presently), "that she thought it was time for Miss Jessie to leave off her dimples, and not always to be trying to look like a child." It was true there was something childlike in her face; and there will be, I think, till she dies, though she should live to a hundred. Her eyes were large blue wondering eyes, looking straight at you; her nose was unformed and snub, and her lips were red and dewy; she wore her hair, too, in little rows of curls, which heightened this appearance. I do not know whether she was pretty or not; but I liked her face, and so did everybody, and I do not think she could help her dimples. She had something of her father's jauntiness of gait and manner; and any female observer might detect a slight difference in the attire of the two sisters—that of Miss Jessie being about two pounds per annum more expensive than Miss Brown's. Two pounds was a large sum in Captain Brown's annual disbursements.

Such was the impression made upon me by the Brown family when I first saw them all together in Cranford Church. The Captain I had met before—on the occasion of the smoky chimney, which he had cured by some simple alteration in the

14. A pit in which tanners dress skins with lime to remove the hair.

flue. In church, he held his double eye-glass to his eyes during the Morning Hymn, and then lifted up his head erect and sang out loud and joyfully. He made the responses louder than the clerk—an old man with a piping feeble voice, who, I think, felt aggrieved at the Captain's sonorous bass, and quavered higher and higher in consequence.

On coming out of church, the brisk Captain paid the most gallant attention to his two daughters. He nodded and smiled to his acquaintances; but he shook hands with none until he had helped Miss Brown to unfurl her umbrella, had relieved her of her prayer-book, and had waited patiently till she, with trembling nervous hands, had taken up her gown to walk through the wet roads.

I wondered what the Cranford ladies did with Captain Brown at their parties. We had often rejoiced, in former days, that there was no gentleman to be attended to, and to find conversation for, at the card-parties. We had congratulated ourselves upon the snugness of the evenings; and, in our love for gentility, and distaste of mankind, we had almost persuaded ourselves that to be a man was to be "vulgar"; so that when I found my friend and hostess, Miss Jenkyns, was going to have a party in my honour, and that Captain and the Miss Browns were invited, I wondered much what would be the course of the evening. Card-tables, with green baize tops, were set out by daylight, just as usual; it was the third week in November, so the evenings closed in about four. Candles, and clean packs of cards were arranged on each table. The fire was made up; the neat maid-servant had received her last directions; and there we stood, dressed in our best, each with a candle-lighter in our hands, ready to dart at the candles as soon as the first knock came. Parties in Cranford were solemn festivities, making the ladies feel gravely elated as they sat together in their best dresses. As soon as three had arrived, we sat down to "Preference," I being the unlucky fourth.[15] The next four comers were put down immediately to another table; and presently the tea-trays, which I had seen set out in the store-room as I passed in the morning, were placed each on the middle of a card-table. The china was delicate egg-shell; the old-fashioned silver glittered with polishing; but the eatables were of the slightest description. While the trays were yet on the tables, Captain and the Miss Browns came in; and I could see that, somehow or other, the Captain was a favourite with all the ladies present. Ruffled brows were smoothed, sharp voices lowered at his approach. Miss Brown looked ill, and depressed almost to gloom. Miss Jessie smiled as usual, and seemed nearly as popular as her father. He immediately and quietly assumed the man's place in the room; attended to every one's wants, lessened the pretty maid-servant's labour by waiting on empty cups and bread-and-butterless ladies; and yet did it all in so easy and dignified a manner, and so much as if it were a matter of course for the strong to attend to the weak, that he was a true man throughout. He played for threepenny points with as grave an interest as if they had been pounds; and yet, in all his attention to strangers, he had an eye on his suffering daughter—for suffering I was sure she was, though to many eyes she might only appear to be irritable. Miss Jessie could not play cards: but she talked to the sitters-out, who, before her coming, had been rather inclined to be cross. She sang, too, to an old cracked piano, which I think had been a spinet[16] in its youth. Miss Jessie sang "Jock of Hazeldean"[17] a little out of tune; but we were none of us musical, though Miss Jenkyns beat time, out of time, by way of appearing to be so.

15. "Unlucky" because only three people can play this card game at once; the dealer has to sit out.

16. An earlier keyboard instrument, popular before the invention of the piano.
17. A ballad written in 1816 by Sir Walter Scott.

It was very good of Miss Jenkyns to do this; for I had seen that, a little before, she had been a good deal annoyed by Miss Jessie Brown's unguarded admission (à propos of Shetland wool) that she had an uncle, her mother's brother, who was a shopkeeper in Edinburgh. Miss Jenkyns tried to drown this confession by a terrible cough—for the Honourable Mrs Jamieson was sitting at the card-table nearest Miss Jessie, and what would she say or think if she found out she was in the same room with a shopkeeper's niece! But Miss Jessie Brown (who had no tact, as we all agreed the next morning) would repeat the information, and assure Miss Pole she could easily get her the identical Shetland wool required, "through my uncle, who has the best assortment of Shetland goods of any one in Edinbro'." It was to take the taste of this out of our mouths, and the sound of this out of our ears, that Miss Jenkyns proposed music; so I say again, it was very good of her to beat time to the song.

When the trays re-appeared with biscuits and wine, punctually at a quarter to nine, there was conversation, comparing of cards, and talking over tricks; but by-and-by Captain Brown sported a bit of literature.

"Have you seen any numbers of 'The Pickwick Papers'?" said he. (They were then publishing in parts.)[18] "Capital thing!"

Now Miss Jenkyns was daughter of a deceased rector of Cranford; and, on the strength of a number of manuscript sermons, and a pretty good library of divinity, considered herself literary, and looked upon any conversation about books as a challenge to her. So she answered and said, "Yes, she had seen them; indeed, she might say she had read them."

"And what do you think of them?" exclaimed Captain Brown. "Aren't they famously good?"

So urged, Miss Jenkyns could not but speak.

"I must say, I don't think they are by any means equal to Dr Johnson.[19] Still, perhaps, the author is young. Let him persevere, and who knows what he may become if he will take the great Doctor for his model?" This was evidently too much for Captain Brown to take placidly; and I saw the words on the tip of his tongue before Miss Jenkyns had finished her sentence.

"It is quite a different sort of thing, my dear madam," he began.

"I am quite aware of that," returned she. "And I make allowances, Captain Brown."

"Just allow me to read you a scene out of this month's number," pleaded he. "I had it only this morning, and I don't think the company can have read it yet."

"As you please," said she, settling herself with an air of resignation. He read the account of the "swarry" which Sam Weller gave at Bath.[20] Some of us laughed heartily. I did not dare, because I was staying in the house. Miss Jenkyns sat in patient gravity. When it was ended, she turned to me, and said with mild dignity—

"Fetch me 'Rasselas,'[21] my dear, out of the bookroom."

When I brought it to her, she turned to Captain Brown—

"Now allow me to read you a scene, and then the present company can judge between your favourite, Mr Boz, and Dr Johnson."

18. Dickens published The Pickwick Papers serially in 1836 and 1837 under the pseudonym "Boz." Although this form of publication was considered "vulgar," the humorous escapades of Mr. Pickwick were phenomenally successful. When Cranford first appeared in Dickens's Household Words, he substituted Thomas Hood for himself, to Gaskell's annoyance.
19. Samuel Johnson (1708–1784) wrote more than a hundred years before Dickens; he was noted for his stately, balanced prose.
20. A reference to an episode in Pickwick Papers where Mr. Pickwick's servant Sam Weller attends a "soirée" for the footmen at Bath. The quick-witted Sam mocks the pompous servants, but they don't realize it.
21. Rasselas is a series of dialogues on moral themes between the prince of Abyssinia and his spiritual mentor, Imlac. Unlike the lively Pickwick, it is a serious and slow-paced philosophical work.

She read one of the conversations between Rasselas and Imlac, in a high-pitched majestic voice: and when she had ended, she said, "I imagine I am now justified in my preference of Dr Johnson as a writer of fiction." The Captain screwed his lips up, and drummed on the table, but he did not speak. She thought she would give a finishing blow or two.

"I consider it vulgar, and below the dignity of literature, to publish in numbers."

"How was the *Rambler*[22] published, ma'am?" asked Captain Brown in a low voice, which I think Miss Jenkyns could not have heard.

"Dr Johnson's style is a model for young beginners. My father recommended it to me when I began to write letters—I have formed my own style upon it; I recommend it to your favourite."

"I should be very sorry for him to exchange his style for any such pompous writing," said Captain Brown.

Miss Jenkyns felt this as a personal affront, in a way of which the Captain had not dreamed. Epistolary writing she and her friends considered as her *forte*. Many a copy of many a letter have I seen written and corrected on the slate, before she "seized the half-hour just previous to post-time to assure" her friends of this or of that; and Dr Johnson was, as she said, her model in these compositions. She drew herself up with dignity, and only replied to Captain Brown's last remark by saying, with marked emphasis on every syllable, "I prefer Dr Johnson to Mr Boz."

It is said—I won't vouch for the fact—that Captain Brown was heard to say, *sotto voce*, "D—n Dr Johnson!" If he did, he was penitent afterwards, as he showed by going to stand near Miss Jenkyns's arm-chair, and endeavouring to beguile her into conversation on some more pleasing subject. But she was inexorable. The next day she made the remark I have mentioned about Miss Jessie's dimples.

2

It was impossible to live a month at Cranford and not know the daily habits of each resident; and long before my visit was ended I knew much concerning the whole Brown trio. There was nothing new to be discovered respecting their poverty; for they had spoken simply and openly about that from the very first. They made no mystery of the necessity for their being economical. All that remained to be discovered was the Captain's infinite kindness of heart, and the various modes in which, unconsciously to himself, he manifested it. Some little anecdotes were talked about for some time after they occurred. As we did not read much, and as all the ladies were pretty well suited with servants, there was a dearth of subjects for conversation. We therefore discussed the circumstance of the Captain taking a poor old woman's dinner out of her hands one very slippery Sunday. He had met her returning from the bakehouse as he came from church, and noticed her precarious footing; and, with the grave dignity with which he did everything, he relieved her of her burden, and steered along the street by her side, carrying her baked mutton and potatoes safely home.[23] This was thought very eccentric; and it was rather expected that he would pay a round of calls, on the Monday morning, to explain and apologise to the Cranford sense of propriety: but he did no such thing: and then it was decided that he was ashamed, and was keeping out of sight. In a kindly pity for him, we began to say,

22. A periodical started in 1750 by Dr. Johnson and written almost entirely by himself.

23. Poor people often brought their meals to cook in the ovens of baker's shops on Sundays and holidays.

"After all, the Sunday morning's occurrence showed great goodness of heart," and it was resolved that he should be comforted on his next appearance amongst us; but, lo! he came down upon us, untouched by any sense of shame, speaking loud and bass as ever, his head thrown back, his wig as jaunty and well-curled as usual, and we were obliged to conclude he had forgotten all about Sunday.

Miss Pole and Miss Jessie Brown had set up a kind of intimacy on the strength of the Shetland wool and the new knitting stitches; so it happened that when I went to visit Miss Pole I saw more of the Browns than I had done while staying with Miss Jenkyns, who had never got over what she called Captain Brown's disparaging remarks upon Dr Johnson as a writer of light and agreeable fiction. I found that Miss Brown was seriously ill of some lingering, incurable complaint, the pain occasioned by which gave the uneasy expression to her face that I had taken for unmitigated crossness. Cross, too, she was at times, when the nervous irritability occasioned by her disease became past endurance. Miss Jessie bore with her at these times, even more patiently than she did with the bitter self-upbraidings by which they were invariably succeeded. Miss Brown used to accuse herself, not merely of hasty and irritable temper, but also of being the cause why her father and sister were obliged to pinch, in order to allow her the small luxuries which were necessaries in her condition. She would so fain have made sacrifices for them, and have lightened their cares, that the original generosity of her disposition added acerbity to her temper. All this was borne by Miss Jessie and her father with more than placidity—with absolute tenderness. I forgave Miss Jessie her singing out of tune, and her juvenility of dress, when I saw her at home. I came to perceive that Captain Brown's dark Brutus wig and padded coat[24] (alas! too often threadbare) were remnants of the military smartness of his youth, which he now wore unconsciously. He was a man of infinite resources, gained in his barrack experience. As he confessed, no one could black his boots to please him except himself; but, indeed, he was not above saving the little maid-servant's labours in every way—knowing, most likely, that his daughter's illness made the place a hard one.

He endeavoured to make peace with Miss Jenkyns soon after the memorable dispute I have named, by a present of a wooden fire-shovel (his own making), having heard her say how much the grating of an iron one annoyed her. She received the present with cool gratitude, and thanked him formally. When he was gone, she bade me put it away in the lumber-room; feeling, probably, that no present from a man who preferred Mr Boz to Dr Johnson could be less jarring than an iron fire-shovel.

Such was the state of things when I left Cranford and went to Drumble. I had, however, several correspondents, who kept me *au fait* as to the proceedings of the dear little town. There was Miss Pole, who was becoming as much absorbed in crochet as she had been once in knitting, and the burden of whose letter was something like, "But don't you forget the white worsted at Flint's" of the old song; for at the end of every sentence of news came a fresh direction as to some crochet commission which I was to execute for her. Miss Matilda Jenkyns (who did not mind being called Miss Matty, when Miss Jenkyns was not by) wrote nice, kind, rambling letters, now and then venturing into an opinion of her own; but suddenly pulling herself up, and either begging me not to name what she had said, as Deborah thought differently, and *she* knew, or else putting in a postscript to the effect that, since writing the

24. A short, curly hairstyle popular during the French Revolution; padded coats were fashionable in the early 19th century.

above, she had been talking over the subject with Deborah, and was quite convinced that, &c.—(here probably followed a recantation of every opinion she had given in the letter). Then came Miss Jenkyns—Debōrah, as she liked Miss Matty to call her, her father having once said that the Hebrew name ought to be so pronounced. I secretly think she took the Hebrew prophetess for a model in character; and, indeed, she was not unlike the stern prophetess[25] in some ways, making allowance, of course, for modern customs and difference in dress. Miss Jenkyns wore a cravat, and a little bonnet like a jockey-cap, and altogether had the appearance of a strong-minded woman; although she would have despised the modern idea of women being equal to men. Equal, indeed! she knew they were superior. But to return to her letters. Everything in them was stately and grand like herself. I have been looking them over (dear Miss Jenkyns, how I honoured her!), and I will give an extract, more especially because it relates to our friend Captain Brown:—

"The Honourable Mrs Jamieson has only just quitted me; and, in the course of conversation, she communicated to me the intelligence that she had yesterday received a call from her revered husband's quondam[26] friend, Lord Mauleverer. You will not easily conjecture what brought his lordship within the precincts of our little town. It was to see Captain Brown, with whom, it appears, his lordship was acquainted in the 'plumed wars,' and who had the privilege of averting destruction from his lordship's head when some great peril was impending over it, off the misnomered Cape of Good Hope. You know our friend the Honourable Mrs Jamieson's deficiency in the spirit of innocent curiosity; and you will therefore not be so much surprised when I tell you she was quite unable to disclose to me the exact nature of the peril in question. I was anxious, I confess, to ascertain in what manner Captain Brown, with his limited establishment, could receive so distinguished a guest; and I discovered that his lordship retired to rest, and, let us hope, to refreshing slumbers, at the Angel Hotel; but shared the Brunonian[27] meals during the two days that he honoured Cranford with his august presence. Mrs Johnson, our civil butcher's wife, informs me that Miss Jessie purchased a leg of lamb; but, besides this, I can hear of no preparation whatever to give a suitable reception to so distinguished a visitor. Perhaps they entertained him with 'the feast of reason and the flow of soul;'[28] and to us, who are acquainted with Captain Brown's sad want of relish for 'the pure wells of English undefiled,'[29] it may be matter for congratulation that he has had the opportunity of improving his taste by holding converse with an elegant and refined member of the British aristocracy. But from some mundane failings who is altogether free?"

Miss Pole and Miss Matty wrote to me by the same post. Such a piece of news as Lord Mauleverer's visit was not to be lost on the Cranford letter-writers: they made the most of it. Miss Matty humbly apologised for writing at the same time as her sister, who was so much more capable than she to describe the honour done to Cranford; but in spite of a little bad spelling, Miss Matty's account gave me the best idea of the commotion occasioned by his lordship's visit, after it had occurred; for, except the people at the Angel, the Browns, Mrs Jamieson, and a little lad his lordship had sworn at for driving a dirty hoop against the aristocratic legs, I could not hear of any one with whom his lordship had held conversation.

---

25. Deborah was one of the leaders of Israel (Judges 4–5).
26. Former.
27. A pretentious, Latinized version of Brown, part of Miss Jenkyns's unintentionally comic imitation of the style of Dr. Johnson.

28. Alexander Pope, *Imitations of Horace*, Satire 1, Book 2.128 (1733).
29. Edmund Spenser, *The Faerie Queene*, 4.2.32 (1596); the reference is to Chaucer.

My next visit to Cranford was in the summer. There had been neither births, deaths, nor marriages since I was there last. Everybody lived in the same house, and wore pretty nearly the same well-preserved, old-fashioned clothes. The greatest event was, that Miss Jenkynses had purchased a new carpet for the drawing-room. Oh, the busy work Miss Matty and I had in chasing the sunbeams, as they fell in an afternoon right down on this carpet through the blindless window! We spread newspapers over the places, and sat down to our book or our work; and, lo! in a quarter of an hour the sun had moved, and was blazing away on a fresh spot; and down again we went on our knees to alter the position of the newspapers. We were very busy, too, one whole morning, before Miss Jenkyns gave her party, in following her directions, and in cutting out and stitching together pieces of newspaper so as to form little paths to every chair set for the expected visitors, lest their shoes might dirty or defile the purity of the carpet. Do you make paper paths for every guest to walk upon in London?

Captain Brown and Miss Jenkyns were not very cordial to each other. The literary dispute, of which I had seen the beginning, was a "raw," the slightest touch on which made them wince. It was the only difference of opinion they had ever had; but that difference was enough. Miss Jenkyns could not refrain from talking *at* Captain Brown; and, though he did not reply, he drummed with his fingers, which action she felt and resented as very disparaging to Dr Johnson. He was rather ostentatious in his preference of the writings of Mr Boz; would walk through the streets so absorbed in them that he all but ran against Miss Jenkyns; and though his apologies were earnest and sincere, and though he did not, in fact, do more than startle her and himself, she owned to me she had rather he had knocked her down, if he had only been reading a higher style of literature. The poor, brave Captain! he looked older, and more worn, and his clothes were very threadbare. But he seemed as bright and cheerful as ever, unless he was asked about his daughter's health.

"She suffers a great deal, and she must suffer more: we do what we can to alleviate her pain;—God's will be done!" He took off his hat at these last words. I found, from Miss Matty, that everything had been done, in fact. A medical man, of high repute in that country neighbourhood, had been sent for, and every injunction he had given was attended to, regardless of expense. Miss Matty was sure they denied themselves many things in order to make the invalid comfortable; but they never spoke about it; and as for Miss Jessie!—"I really think she's an angel," said poor Miss Matty, quite overcome. "To see her way of bearing with Miss Brown's crossness, and the bright face she puts on after she's been sitting up a whole night and scolded above half of it, is quite beautiful. Yet she looks as neat and as ready to welcome the Captain at breakfast-time as if she had been asleep in the Queen's bed all night. My dear! you could never laugh at her prim little curls or her pink bows again if you saw her as I have done." I could only feel very penitent, and greet Miss Jessie with double respect when I met her next. She looked faded and pinched; and her lips began to quiver, as if she was very weak, when she spoke of her sister. But she brightened, and sent back the tears that were glittering in her pretty eyes, as she said—

"But, to be sure, what a town Cranford is for kindness! I don't suppose any one has a better dinner than usual cooked but the best part of all comes in a little covered basin for my sister. The poor people will leave their earliest vegetables at our door for her. They speak short and gruff, as if they were ashamed of it; but I am sure it often goes to my heart to see their thoughtfulness." The tears now came back and overflowed; but after a minute or two she began to scold herself, and ended by going away the same cheerful Miss Jessie as ever.

"But why does not this Lord Mauleverer do something for the man who saved his life?" said I.

"Why, you see, unless Captain Brown has some reason for it, he never speaks about being poor; and he walked along by his lordship looking as happy and cheerful as a prince; and as they never called attention to their dinner by apologies, and as Miss Brown was better that day, and all seemed bright, I dare say his lordship never knew how much care there was in the background. He did send game in the winter pretty often, but now he is gone abroad."

I had often occasion to notice the use that was made of fragments and small opportunities in Cranford; the rose-leaves that were gathered ere they fell to make into a potpourri for some one who had no garden; the little bundles of lavender flowers sent to strew the drawers of some town-dweller, or to burn in the chamber of some invalid. Things that many would despise, and actions which it seemed scarcely worth while to perform, were all attended to in Cranford. Miss Jenkyns stuck an apple full of cloves, to be heated and smell pleasantly in Miss Brown's room; and as she put in each clove she uttered a Johnsonian sentence. Indeed, she never could think of the Browns without talking Johnson; and, as they were seldom absent from her thoughts just then, I heard many a rolling, three-piled sentence.

Captain Brown called one day to thank Miss Jenkyns for many little kindnesses, which I did not know until then that she had rendered. He had suddenly become like an old man; his deep bass voice had a quavering in it, his eyes looked dim, and the lines on his face were deep. He did not—could not—speak cheerfully of his daughter's state, but he talked with manly, pious resignation, and not much. Twice over he said, "What Jessie has been to us, God only knows!" and after the second time, he got up hastily, shook hands all round without speaking, and left the room.

That afternoon we perceived little groups in the street, all listening with faces aghast to some tale or other. Miss Jenkyns wondered what could be the matter for some time before she took the undignified step of sending Jenny out to inquire.

Jenny came back with a white face of terror. "Oh, ma'am! oh, Miss Jenkyns, ma'am! Captain Brown is killed by them nasty cruel railroads!" and she burst into tears. She, along with many others, had experienced the poor Captain's kindness.

"How?—where—where? Good God! Jenny, don't waste time in crying, but tell us something." Miss Matty rushed out into the street at once, and collared the man who was telling the tale.

"Come in—come to my sister at once, Miss Jenkyns, the rector's daughter. Oh, man, man! say it is not true," she cried, as she brought the affrighted carter, sleeking down his hair, into the drawing-room, where he stood with his wet boots on the new carpet, and no one regarded it.

"Please, mum, it is true. I seed it myself," and he shuddered at the recollection. "The Captain was a-reading some new book as he was deep in, a-waiting for the down train; and there was a little lass as wanted to come to its mammy, and gave its sister the slip, and came toddling across the line. And he looked up sudden, at the sound of the train coming, and seed the child, and he darted on the line and cotched it up, and his foot slipped, and the train came over him in no time. O Lord, Lord! Mum, it's quite true—and they've come over to tell his daughters. The child's safe, though, with only a bang on its shoulder as he threw it to its mammy. Poor Captain would be glad of that, mum, wouldn't he? God bless him!" The great rough carter puckered up his manly face, and turned away to hide his tears. I turned to Miss Jenkyns. She looked very ill, as if she were going to faint, and signed to me to open the window.

"Matilda, bring me my bonnet. I must go to those girls. God pardon me, if ever I have spoken contemptuously to the Captain!"

Miss Jenkyns arrayed herself to go out, telling Miss Matilda to give the man a glass of wine. While she was away, Miss Matty and I huddled over the fire, talking in a low and awestruck voice. I know we cried quietly all the time.

Miss Jenkyns came home in a silent mood, and we durst not ask her many questions. She told us that Miss Jessie had fainted, and that she and Miss Pole had had some difficulty in bringing her round; but that, as soon as she recovered, she begged one of them to go and sit with her sister.

"Mr Hoggins says she cannot live many days, and she shall be spared this shock," said Miss Jessie, shivering with feelings to which she dared not give way.

"But how can you manage, my dear?" asked Miss Jenkyns; "you cannot bear up, she must see your tears."

"God will help me—I will not give way—she was asleep when the news came; she may be asleep yet. She would be so utterly miserable, not merely at my father's death, but to think of what would become of me; she is so good to me." She looked up earnestly in their faces with her soft true eyes, and Miss Pole told Miss Jenkyns afterwards she could hardly bear it, knowing, as she did, how Miss Brown treated her sister.

However, it was settled according to Miss Jessie's wish. Miss Brown was to be told her father had been summoned to take a short journey on railway business. They had managed it in some way—Miss Jenkyns could not exactly say how. Miss Pole was to stop with Miss Jessie. Mrs Jamieson had sent to inquire. And this was all we heard that night; and a sorrowful night it was. The next day a full account of the fatal accident was in the county paper which Miss Jenkyns took in. Her eyes were very weak, she said, and she asked me to read it. When I came to the "gallant gentleman was deeply engaged in the perusal of a number of 'Pickwick,' which he had just received," Miss Jenkyns shook her head long and solemnly, and then sighed out, "Poor, dear, infatuated man!"

The corpse was to be taken from the station to the parish church, there to be interred. Miss Jessie had set her heart on following it to the grave; and no dissuasives could alter her resolve. Her restraint upon herself made her almost obstinate; she resisted all Miss Pole's entreaties and Miss Jenkyns's advice. At last Miss Jenkyns gave up the point; and after a silence, which I feared portended some deep displeasure against Miss Jessie, Miss Jenkyns said she should accompany the latter to the funeral.

"It is not fit for you to go alone. It would be against both propriety and humanity were I to allow it."

Miss Jessie seemed as if she did not half like this arrangement; but her obstinacy, if she had any, had been exhausted in her determination to go to the interment. She longed, poor thing, I have no doubt, to cry alone over the grave of the dear father to whom she had been all in all, and to give way, for one little half-hour, uninterrupted by sympathy and unobserved by friendship. But it was not to be. That afternoon Miss Jenkyns sent out for a yard of black crape, and employed herself busily in trimming the little black silk bonnet I have spoken about. When it was finished she put it on, and looked at us for approbation—admiration she despised. I was full of sorrow, but, by one of those whimsical thoughts which come unbidden into our heads, in times of deepest grief, I no sooner saw the bonnet than I was reminded of a helmet; and in that hybrid bonnet, half helmet, half jockey-cap, did Miss Jenkyns attend Captain Brown's funeral, and, I believe, supported Miss Jessie with a tender, indulgent firmness which was invaluable, allowing her to weep her passionate fill before they left.

Miss Pole, Miss Matty, and I, meanwhile attended to Miss Brown: and hard work we found it to relieve her querulous and never-ending complaints. But if we were so weary and dispirited, what must Miss Jessie have been! Yet she came back almost calm, as if she had gained a new strength. She put off her mourning dress, and came in, looking pale and gentle, thanking us each with a soft long pressure of the hand. She could even smile—a faint, sweet, wintry smile—as if to reassure us of her power to endure; but her look made our eyes fill suddenly with tears, more than if she had cried outright.

It was settled that Miss Pole was to remain with her all the watching livelong night; and that Miss Matty and I were to return in the morning to relieve them, and give Miss Jessie the opportunity for a few hours of sleep. But when the morning came, Miss Jenkyns appeared at the breakfast-table, equipped in her helmet-bonnet, and ordered Miss Matty to stay at home, as she meant to go and help to nurse. She was evidently in a state of great friendly excitement, which she showed by eating her breakfast standing, and scolding the household all round.

No nursing—no energetic strong-minded woman could help Miss Brown now. There was that in the room as we entered which was stronger than us all, and made us shrink into solemn awestruck helplessness. Miss Brown was dying. We hardly knew her voice, it was so devoid of the complaining tone we had always associated with it. Miss Jessie told me afterwards that it, and her face too, were just what they had been formerly, when her mother's death left her the young anxious head of the family, of whom only Miss Jessie survived.

She was conscious of her sister's presence, though not, I think, of ours. We stood a little behind the curtain: Miss Jessie knelt with her face near her sister's, in order to catch the last soft awful whispers.

"Oh, Jessie! Jessie! How selfish I have been! God forgive me for letting you sacrifice yourself for me as you did! I have so loved you—and yet I have thought only of myself. God forgive me!"

"Hush, love! hush!" said Miss Jessie, sobbing.

"And my father! my dear, dear father! I will not complain now, if God will give me strength to be patient. But, oh, Jessie! tell my father how I longed and yearned to see him at last, and to ask his forgiveness. He can never know now how I loved him—oh! if I might but tell him, before I die! What a life of sorrow his has been, and I have done so little to cheer him!"

A light came into Miss Jessie's face. "Would it comfort you, dearest, to think that he does know?—would it comfort you, love, to know that his cares, his sorrows"—Her voice quivered, but she steadied it into calmness—"Mary! he has gone before you to the place where the weary are at rest.[30] He knows now how you loved him."

A strange look, which was not distress, came over Miss Brown's face. She did not speak for some time, but then we saw her lips form the words, rather than heard the sound—"Father, mother, Harry, Archy;"—then, as if it were a new idea throwing a filmy shadow over her darkened mind—"But you will be alone, Jessie!"

Miss Jessie had been feeling this all during the silence, I think; for the tears rolled down her cheeks like rain, at these words, and she could not answer at first. Then she put her hands together tight, and lifted them up, and said—but not to us—

"Though He slay me, yet will I trust in Him."[31]

---

30. Job 3.17.   31. Job 13.15.

In a few moments more Miss Brown lay calm and still—never to sorrow or murmur more.

After this second funeral, Miss Jenkyns insisted that Miss Jessie should come to stay with her rather than go back to the desolate house, which, in fact, we learned from Miss Jessie, must now be given up, as she had not wherewithal to maintain it. She had something above twenty pounds a year, besides the interest of the money for which the furniture would sell; but she could not live upon that: and so we talked over her qualifications for earning money.

"I can sew neatly," said she, "and I like nursing. I think, too, I could manage a house, if any one would try me as housekeeper; or I would go into a shop, as saleswoman, if they would have patience with me at first."

Miss Jenkyns declared, in an angry voice, that she should do no such thing; and talked to herself about "some people having no idea of their rank as a captain's daughter," nearly an hour afterwards, when she brought Miss Jessie up a basin of delicately-made arrowroot, and stood over her like a dragoon until the last spoonful was finished; then she disappeared. Miss Jessie began to tell me some more of the plans which had suggested themselves to her, and insensibly fell into talking of the days that were past and gone, and interested me so much I neither knew nor heeded how time passed. We were both startled when Miss Jenkyns reappeared, and caught us crying. I was afraid lest she would be displeased, as she often said that crying hindered digestion, and I knew she wanted Miss Jessie to get strong; but, instead, she looked queer and excited, and fidgeted round us without saying anything. At last she spoke.

"I have been so much startled—no, I've not been at all startled—don't mind me, my dear Miss Jessie—I've been very much surprised—in fact, I've had a caller, whom you knew once, my dear Miss Jessie"—

Miss Jessie went very white, then flushed scarlet, and looked eagerly at Miss Jenkyns.

"A gentleman, my dear, who wants to know if you would see him."

"Is it?—it is not"—stammered out Miss Jessie—and got no farther.

"This is his card," said Miss Jenkyns, giving it to Miss Jessie; and while her head was bent over it, Miss Jenkyns went through a series of winks and odd faces to me, and formed her lips into a long sentence, of which, of course, I could not understand a word.

"May he come up?" asked Miss Jenkyns, at last.

"Oh, yes! certainly!" said Miss Jessie, as much as to say, this is your house, you may show any visitor where you like. She took up some knitting of Miss Matty's and began to be very busy, though I could see how she trembled all over.

Miss Jenkyns rang the bell, and told the servant who answered it to show Major Gordon upstairs; and, presently, in walked a tall, fine, frank-looking man of forty or upwards. He shook hands with Miss Jessie; but he could not see her eyes, she kept them so fixed on the ground. Miss Jenkyns asked me if I would come and help her to tie up the preserves in the store-room; and, though Miss Jessie plucked at my gown, and even looked up at me with begging eye, I durst not refuse to go where Miss Jenkyns asked. Instead of tying up preserves in the store-room, however, we went to talk in the dining-room; and there Miss Jenkyns told me what Major Gordon had told her; how he had served in the same regiment with Captain Brown, and had become acquainted with Miss Jessie, then a sweet-looking, blooming girl of eighteen; how the acquaintance had grown into love on his part, though it had been some years before he had spoken; how, on becoming possessed, through the will of an uncle, of a good estate in Scotland, he had offered and been refused, though with so much agitation and evident distress that he was sure she was not indifferent to him; and how he had discovered that the obstacle was the fell disease which was, even then, too surely threatening her sister. She had mentioned that the surgeons foretold intense suffering; and there was no one but herself to nurse her poor Mary, or cheer and comfort her father during the time of illness. They had had long discussions; and on her refusal to pledge herself to him as his wife when all should be over, he had grown angry, and broken off entirely, and gone abroad, believing that she was a cold-hearted person whom he would do well to forget. He had been travelling in the East, and was on his return home when, at Rome, he saw the account of Captain Brown's death in *Galignani*.[32]

Just then Miss Matty, who had been out all the morning, and had only lately returned to the house, burst in with a face of dismay and outraged propriety.

"Oh, goodness me!" she said. "Deborah, there's a gentleman sitting in the drawing-room with his arm round Miss Jessie's waist!" Miss Matty's eyes looked large with terror.

Miss Jenkyns snubbed her down in an instant.

"The most proper place in the world for his arm to be in. Go away, Matilda, and mind your own business." This from her sister, who had hitherto been a model of feminine decorum, was a blow for poor Miss Matty, and with a double shock she left the room.

The last time I ever saw poor Miss Jenkyns was many years after this. Mrs Gordon had kept up a warm and affectionate intercourse with all at Cranford. Miss Jenkyns, Miss Matty, and Miss Pole had all been to visit her, and returned with wonderful accounts of her house, her husband, her dress, and her looks. For, with happiness, something of her early bloom returned; she had been a year or two younger than we had taken her for. Her eyes were always lovely, and, as Mrs Gordon, her dimples were not out of place. At the time to which I have referred, when I last saw Miss Jenkyns, that lady was old and feeble, and had lost something of her strong mind. Little Flora Gordon was staying with the Misses Jenkyns, and when I came in she was reading aloud to Miss Jenkyns, who lay feeble and changed on the sofa. Flora put down the *Rambler* when I came in.

"Ah!" said Miss Jenkyns, "you find me changed, my dear. I can't see as I used to do. If Flora were not here to read to me, I hardly know how I should get through the day. Did you ever read the *Rambler*? It's a wonderful book—wonderful! and the most improving reading for Flora" (which I dare say it would have been, if she could have read half the words without spelling, and could have understood the meaning of a third), "better than that strange old book, with the queer name, poor Captain Brown was killed for reading—that book by Mr Boz, you know—'Old Poz'; when I was a girl—but that's a long time ago—I acted Lucy in 'Old Poz.' "[33] She babbled on long enough for Flora to get a good long spell at the "Christmas Carol,"[34] which Miss Matty had left on the table.

1851, 1853

32. An English newspaper published in Paris and read by tourists and expatriates.
33. A children's play by Maria Edgeworth (1795); Lucy is the young heroine.
34. Published by Dickens in 1843. The topicality of Dickens's works helps date the events of *Cranford*.

Sir Arthur Conan Doyle
1859–1930

A Scandal in Bohemia[1]

To Sherlock Holmes she is always *the* woman. I have seldom heard him mention her under any other name. In his eyes she eclipses and predominates the whole of her sex. It was not that he felt any emotion akin to love for Irene Adler. All emotions, and that one particularly, were abhorrent to his cold, precise, but admirably balanced mind. He was, I take it, the most perfect reasoning and observing machine that the world has seen; but, as a lover, he would have placed himself in a false position. He never spoke of the softer passions, save with a gibe and a sneer. They were admirable things for the observer—excellent for drawing the veil from men's motives and actions. But for the trained reasoner to admit such intrusions into his own delicate and finely adjusted temperament was to introduce a distracting factor which might throw a doubt upon all his mental results. Grit in a sensitive instrument, or a crack in one of his own high-power lenses, would not be more disturbing than a strong emotion in a nature such as his. And yet there was but one woman to him, and that woman was the late Irene Adler, of dubious and questionable memory.

I had seen little of Holmes lately. My marriage had drifted us away from each other. My own complete happiness, and the home-centred interests which rise up around the man who first finds himself master of his own establishment, were sufficient to absorb all my attention; while Holmes, who loathed every form of society with his whole Bohemian soul,[2] remained in our lodgings in Baker-street, buried among his old books, and alternating from week to week between cocaine and ambition, the drowsiness of the drug, and the fierce energy of his own keen nature. He was still, as ever, deeply attracted by the study of crime, and occupied his immense faculties and extraordinary powers of observation in following out those clues, and clearing up those mysteries, which had been abandoned as hopeless by the official police. From time to time I heard some vague account of his doings: of his summons to Odessa in the case of the Trepoff murder, of his clearing up of the singular tragedy of the Atkinson brothers at Trincomalee, and finally of the mission which he had accomplished so delicately and successfully for the reigning family of Holland. Beyond these signs of his activity, however, which I merely shared with all the readers of the daily press, I knew little of my former friend and companion.

One night—it was on the 20th of March, 1888—I was returning from a journey to a patient (for I had now returned to civil practice),[3] when my way led me through Baker-street. As I passed the well-remembered door, which must always be associated in my mind with my wooing, and with the dark incidents of the Study in Scarlet,[4] I was seized with a keen desire to see Holmes again, and to know how he was employing his extraordinary powers. His rooms were brilliantly lit, and, even as I looked up,

1. First published in *The Strand Magazine* in July 1891.
2. Like the artists in Henri Murger's *Scènes de la vie de Bohème* (1848), Holmes's tastes are aesthetic and eccentric. His bohemianism contrasts with the conventional soul of the King of Bohemia later in the story.
3. Watson, who had been invalided out of the Army medical corps, had resumed private practice upon his marriage.
4. Doyle's first Sherlock Holmes novel (1887).

I saw his tall spare figure pass twice in a dark silhouette against the blind. He was pacing the room swiftly, eagerly, with his head sunk upon his chest, and his hands clasped behind him. To me, who knew his every mood and habit, his attitude and manner told their own story. He was at work again. He had arisen out of his drug-created dreams, and was hot upon the scent of some new problem. I rang the bell, and was shown up to the chamber which had formerly been in part my own.

His manner was not effusive. It seldom was; but he was glad, I think, to see me. With hardly a word spoken, but with a kindly eye, he waved me to an armchair, threw across his case of cigars, and indicated a spirit case and a gasogene in the corner.[5] Then he stood before the fire, and looked me over in his singular introspective fashion.

"Wedlock suits you," he remarked. "I think, Watson, that you have put on seven and a half pounds since I saw you."

"Seven," I answered.

"Indeed, I should have thought a little more. Just a trifle more, I fancy, Watson. And in practice again, I observe. You did not tell me that you intended to go into harness."

"Then, how do you know?"

"I see it, I deduce it. How do I know that you have been getting yourself very wet lately, and that you have a most clumsy and careless servant girl?"

"My dear Holmes," said I, "this is too much. You would certainly have been burned, had you lived a few centuries ago.[6] It is true that I had a country walk on Thursday and came home in a dreadful mess; but, as I have changed my clothes, I can't imagine how you deduce it. As to Mary Jane, she is incorrigible, and my wife has given her notice; but there again I fail to see how you work it out."

He chuckled to himself and rubbed his long nervous hands together.

"It is simplicity itself," said he; "my eyes tell me that on the inside of your left shoe, just where the fire-light strikes it, the leather is scored by six almost parallel cuts. Obviously they have been caused by someone who has very carelessly scraped round the edges of the sole in order to remove crusted mud from it. Hence, you see, my double deduction that you had been out in vile weather, and that you had a particularly malignant boot-slitting specimen of the London slavey.[7] As to your practice, if a gentleman walks into my rooms smelling of iodoform, with a black mark of nitrate of silver upon his right fore-finger, and a bulge on the side of his top-hat to show where he has secreted his stethoscope, I must be dull indeed, if I do not pronounce him to be an active member of the medical profession."

I could not help laughing at the ease with which he explained his process of deduction. "When I hear you give your reasons," I remarked, "the thing always appears to me to be so ridiculously simple that I could easily do it myself, though at each successive instance of your reasoning I am baffled, until you explain your process. And yet I believe that my eyes are as good as yours."

"Quite so," he answered, lighting a cigarette, and throwing himself down into an armchair. "You see, but you do not observe. The distinction is clear. For example, you have frequently seen the steps which lead up from the hall to this room."

"Frequently."

"How often?"

"Well, some hundreds of times."

---

5. I.e., he invited Watson to make himself a drink (a gasogene makes carbonated water).

6. I.e., his uncanny powers would have led to his being burned at the stake as a warlock.

7. Maidservant.

"Then how many are there?"

"How many! I don't know."

"Quite so! You have not observed. And yet you have seen. That is just my point. Now, I know that there are seventeen steps, because I have both seen and observed. By the way, since you are interested in these little problems, and since you are good enough to chronicle one or two of my trifling experiences, you may be interested in this." He threw over a sheet of thick pink-tinted notepaper which had been lying open upon the table. "It came by the last post," said he. "Read it aloud."

The note was undated, and without either signature or address.

"There will call upon you to-night, at a quarter to eight o'clock," it said, "a gentleman who desires to consult you upon a matter of the very deepest moment. Your recent services to one of the Royal Houses of Europe have shown that you are one who may safely be trusted with matters which are of an importance which can hardly be exaggerated. This account of you we have from all quarters received. Be in your chamber then at that hour, and do not take it amiss if your visitor wear a mask."

"This is indeed a mystery," I remarked. "What do you imagine that it means?"

"I have no data yet. It is a capital mistake to theorise before one has data. Insensibly one begins to twist facts to suit theories, instead of theories to suit facts. But the note itself. What do you deduce from it?"

I carefully examined the writing, and the paper upon which it was written.

"The man who wrote it was presumably well to do," I remarked, endeavouring to imitate my companion's processes. "Such paper could not be bought under half a crown a packet. It is peculiarly strong and stiff."

"Peculiar—that is the very word," said Holmes. "It is not an English paper at all. Hold it up to the light."

I did so, and saw a large E with a small g, a P, and a large G with a small t woven into the texture of the paper.

"What do you make of that?" asked Holmes.

"The name of the maker, no doubt; or his monogram, rather."

"Not at all. The G with the small t stands for 'Gesellschaft,' which is the German for 'Company.' It is a customary contraction like our 'Co.' P, of course, stands for 'Papier.' Now for the Eg. Let us glance at our Continental Gazetteer." He took down a heavy brown volume from his shelves. "Eglow, Eglonitz—here we are, Egria. It is in a German-speaking country—in Bohemia,[8] not far from Carlsbad. 'Remarkable as being the scene of the death of Wallenstein, and for its numerous glass factories and paper mills.' Ha, ha, my boy, what do you make of that?" His eyes sparkled, and he sent up a great blue triumphant cloud from his cigarette.

"The paper was made in Bohemia," I said.

"Precisely. And the man who wrote the note is a German. Do you note the peculiar construction of the sentence—'This account of you we have from all quarters received.' A Frenchman or Russian could not have written that. It is the German who is so uncourteous to his verbs. It only remains, therefore, to discover what is wanted by this German who writes upon Bohemian paper, and prefers wearing a mask to showing his face. And here he comes, if I am not mistaken, to resolve all our doubts."

As he spoke there was the sharp sound of horses' hoofs and grating wheels against the curb, followed by a sharp pull at the bell. Holmes whistled.

8. Country in Eastern Central Europe, then part of the Austrian Empire, now part of the Czech Republic. Prague was the capital.

"A pair, by the sound," said he. "Yes," he continued, glancing out of the window. "A nice little brougham and a pair of beauties.[9] A hundred and fifty guineas apiece. There's money in this case, Watson, if there is nothing else."

"I think that I had better go, Holmes."

"Not a bit, Doctor. Stay where you are. I am lost without my Boswell.[10] And this promises to be interesting. It would be a pity to miss it."

"But your client—"

"Never mind him. I may want your help, and so may he. Here he comes. Sit down in that armchair, Doctor, and give us your best attention."

A slow and heavy step, which had been heard upon the stairs and in the passage, paused immediately outside the door. Then there was a loud and authoritative tap.

"Come in!" said Holmes.

A man entered who could hardly have been less than six feet six inches in height, with the chest and limbs of a Hercules. His dress was rich with a richness which would, in England, be looked upon as akin to bad taste. Heavy bands of Astrakhan[11] were slashed across the sleeves and fronts of his double-breasted coat, while the deep blue cloak which was thrown over his shoulders was lined with flame-coloured silk, and secured at the neck with a brooch which consisted of a single flaming beryl. Boots which extended half way up his calves, and which were trimmed at the tops with rich brown fur, completed the impression of barbaric opulence which was suggested by his whole appearance. He carried a broad-brimmed hat in his hand, while he wore across the upper part of his face, extending down past the cheekbones, a black vizard mask,[12] which he had apparently adjusted that very moment, for his hand was still raised to it as he entered. From the lower part of the face he appeared to be a man of strong character, with a thick, hanging lip, and a long straight chin, suggestive of resolution pushed to the length of obstinacy.

"You had my note?" he asked, with a deep harsh voice and a strongly marked German accent. "I told you that I would call." He looked from one to the other of us, as if uncertain which to address.

"Pray take a seat," said Holmes. "This is my friend and colleague, Dr Watson, who is occasionally good enough to help me in my cases. Whom have I the honour to address?"

"You may address me as the Count Von Kramm, a Bohemian nobleman. I understand that this gentleman, your friend, is a man of honour and discretion, whom I may trust with a matter of the most extreme importance. If not, I should much prefer to communicate with you alone."

I rose to go, but Holmes caught me by the wrist and pushed me back into my chair. "It is both, or none," said he. "You may say before this gentleman anything which you may say to me."

The Count shrugged his broad shoulders. "Then I must begin," said he, "by binding you both to absolute secrecy for two years, at the end of that time the matter will be of no importance. At present it is not too much to say that it is of such weight that it may have an influence upon European history."

"I promise," said Holmes.

"And I."

9. A closed four-wheeled carriage drawn by two horses.
10. James Boswell (1740–1795), biographer of Samuel Johnson.

11. A luxurious wool, made from lambs who are killed in their mother's womb.
12. A mask that conceals the eyes.

"You will excuse this mask," continued our strange visitor. "The august person who employs me wishes his agent to be unknown to you, and I may confess at once that the title by which I have just called myself is not exactly my own."

"I was aware of it," said Holmes dryly.

"The circumstances are of great delicacy, and every precaution has to be taken to quench what might grow to be an immense scandal and seriously compromise one of the reigning families of Europe. To speak plainly, the matter implicates the great House of Ormstein, hereditary kings of Bohemia."

"I was also aware of that," murmured Holmes, settling himself down in his arm-chair, and closing his eyes.

Our visitor glanced with some apparent surprise at the languid, lounging figure of the man who had been no doubt depicted to him as the most incisive reasoner, and most energetic agent in Europe. Holmes slowly reopened his eyes, and looked impatiently at his gigantic client.

"If your Majesty would condescend to state your case," he remarked, "I should be better able to advise you."

The man sprang from his chair, and paced up and down the room in uncontrollable agitation. Then, with a gesture of desperation, he tore the mask from his face and hurled it upon the ground. "You are right," he cried, "I am the King. Why should I attempt to conceal it?"

"Why, indeed?" murmured Holmes. "Your Majesty had not spoken before I was aware that I was addressing Wilhelm Gottsreich Sigismond von Ormstein, Grand Duke of Cassel-Felstein, and hereditary King of Bohemia."

"But you can understand," said our strange visitor, sitting down once more and passing his hand over his high, white forehead, "you can understand that I am not accustomed to doing such business in my own person. Yet the matter was so delicate that I could not confide it to an agent without putting myself in his power. I have come *incognito* from Prague for the purpose of consulting you."

"Then, pray consult," said Holmes, shutting his eyes once more.

"The facts are briefly these: Some five years ago, during a lengthy visit to Warsaw, I made the acquaintance of the well-known adventuress Irene Adler. The name is no doubt familiar to you."

"Kindly look her up in my index, Doctor," murmured Holmes, without opening his eyes. For many years he had adopted a system of docketing all paragraphs concerning men and things, so that it was difficult to name a subject or a person on which he could not at once furnish information. In this case I found her biography sandwiched in between that of a Hebrew Rabbi and that of a staff-commander who had written a monograph upon the deep sea fishes.

"Let me see," said Holmes. "Hum! Born in New Jersey in the year 1858. Contralto—hum! La Scala,[13] hum! Prima donna Imperial Opera of Warsaw—Yes! Retired from operatic stage—ha! Living in London—quite so! Your Majesty, as I understand, became entangled with this young person, wrote her some compromising letters, and is now desirous of getting those letters back."

"Precisely so. But how—"

"Was there a secret marriage?"

"None."

"No legal papers or certificates?"

"None."

13. A famous opera house in Milan.

"Then I fail to follow your Majesty. If this young person should produce her letters for blackmailing or other purposes, how is she to prove their authenticity?"

"There is the writing."

"Pooh, pooh! Forgery."

"My private notepaper."

"Stolen."

"My own seal."

"Imitated."

"My photograph."

"Bought."

"We were both in the photograph."

"Oh dear! That is very bad! Your Majesty has indeed committed an indiscretion."

"I was mad—insane."

"You have compromised yourself seriously."

"I was only Crown Prince then. I was young. I am but thirty now."

"It must be recovered."

"We have tried and failed."

"Your Majesty must pay. It must be bought."

"She will not sell."

"Stolen, then."

"Five attempts have been made. Twice burglars in my pay ransacked her house. Once we diverted her luggage when she travelled. Twice she has been waylaid. There has been no result."

"No sign of it?"

"Absolutely none."

Holmes laughed. "It is quite a pretty little problem," said he.

"But a very serious one to me," returned the King, reproachfully.

"Very, indeed. And what does she propose to do with the photograph?"

"To ruin me."

"But how?"

"I am about to be married."

"So I have heard."

"To Clotilde Lothman von Saxe-Meningen, second daughter of the King of Scandinavia. You may know the strict principles of her family. She is herself the very soul of delicacy. A shadow of a doubt as to my conduct would bring the matter to an end."

"And Irene Adler?"

"Threatens to send them the photograph. And she will do it. I know that she will do it. You do not know her, but she has a soul of steel. She has the face of the most beautiful of women, and the mind of the most resolute of men. Rather than I should marry another woman, there are no lengths to which she would not go—none."

"You are sure that she has not sent it yet?"

"I am sure."

"And why?"

"Because she has said that she would send it on the day when the betrothal was publicly proclaimed. That will be next Monday."

"Oh, then, we have three days yet," said Holmes, with a yawn. "That is very fortunate, as I have one or two matters of importance to look into just at present. Your Majesty will, of course, stay in London for the present?"

"Certainly. You will find me at the Langham, under the name of the Count Von Kramm."

"Then I shall drop you a line to let you know how we progress."

"Pray do so. I shall be all anxiety."

"Then, as to money?"

"You have *carte blanche*."[14]

"Absolutely?"

"I tell you that I would give one of the provinces of my kingdom to have that photograph."

"And for present expenses?"

The king took a heavy chamois leather bag from under his cloak, and laid it on the table.

"There are three hundred pounds in gold, and seven hundred in notes," he said.

Holmes scribbled a receipt upon a sheet of his note-book, and handed it to him.

"And mademoiselle's address?" he asked.

"Is Briony Lodge, Serpentine-avenue, St. John's Wood."[15]

Holmes took a note of it. "One other question," said he. "Was the photograph a cabinet?"[16]

"It was."

"Then, good night, your Majesty, and I trust that we shall soon have some good news for you. And good night, Watson," he added, as the wheels of the Royal brougham rolled down the street. "If you will be good enough to call tomorrow afternoon, at three o'clock, I should like to chat this little matter over with you."

2

At three o'clock precisely I was at Baker-street, but Holmes had not yet returned. The landlady informed me that he had left the house shortly after eight o'clock in the morning. I sat down beside the fire, however, with the intention of awaiting him, however long he might be. I was already deeply interested in his inquiry, for, though it was surrounded by none of the grim and strange features which were associated with the two crimes which I have already recorded,[17] still, the nature of the case and the exalted station of his client gave it a character of its own. Indeed, apart from the nature of the investigation which my friend had on hand, there was something in his masterly grasp of a situation, and his keen, incisive reasoning, which made it a pleasure to me to study his system of work, and to follow the quick, subtle methods by which he disentangled the most inextricable mysteries. So accustomed was I to his invariable success that the very possibility of his failing had ceased to enter into my head.

It was close upon four before the door opened, and a drunken-looking groom, ill-kempt and side-whiskered, with an inflamed face and disreputable clothes, walked into the room. Accustomed as I was to my friend's amazing powers in the use of disguises, I had to look three times before I was certain that it was indeed he. With a nod he vanished into the bedroom, whence he emerged in five minutes tweed-suited and respectable, as of old. Putting his hands into his pockets, he stretched out his legs in front of the fire, and laughed heartily for some minutes.

"Well, really!" he cried, and then he choked; and laughed again until he was obliged to lie back, limp and helpless, in the chair.

---

14. I.e., complete freedom of action and unlimited funds.
15. A London area favored by authors, artists, and well-known courtesans.
16. A cabinet photo was 5 ½ by 4 inches.
17. In *A Study in Scarlet* (1887) and *The Sign of the Four* (1890).

"What is it?"

"It's quite too funny. I am sure you could never guess how I employed my morning, or what I ended by doing."

"I can't imagine. I suppose that you have been watching the habits, and perhaps the house, of Miss Irene Adler."

"Quite so, but the sequel was rather unusual. I will tell you, however. I left the house a little after eight o'clock this morning, in the character of a groom out of work. There is a wonderful sympathy and freemasonry among horsey men. Be one of them, and you will know all that there is to know. I soon found Briony Lodge. It is a *bijou* villa,[18] with a garden at the back, but built out in front right up to the road, two stories. Chubb lock to the door. Large sitting-room on the right side, well furnished, with long windows almost to the floor, and those preposterous English window fasteners which a child could open. Behind there was nothing remarkable, save that the passage window could be reached from the top of the coach-house. I walked round it and examined it closely from every point of view, but without noting anything else of interest.

"I then lounged down the street, and found, as I expected, that there was a mews[19] in a lane which runs down by one wall of the garden. I lent the ostlers a hand in rubbing down their horses, and I received in exchange twopence, a glass of half-and-half, two fills of shag tobacco, and as much information as I could desire about Miss Adler, to say nothing of half a dozen other people in the neighbourhood in whom I was not in the least interested, but whose biographies I was compelled to listen to."

"And what of Irene Adler?" I asked.

"Oh, she has turned all the men's heads down in that part. She is the daintiest thing under a bonnet on this planet. So say the Serpentine-mews, to a man. She lives quietly, sings at concerts, drives out at five every day, and returns at seven sharp for dinner. Seldom goes out at other times, except when she sings. Has only one male visitor, but a good deal of him. He is dark, handsome, and dashing; never calls less than once a day, and often twice. He is a Mr Godfrey Norton, of the Inner Temple.[20] See the advantages of a cabman as a confidant. They had driven him home a dozen times from Serpentine-mews, and knew all about him. When I had listened to all that they had to tell, I began to walk up and down near Briony Lodge once more, and to think over my plan of campaign.

"This Godfrey Norton was evidently an important factor in the matter. He was a lawyer. That sounded ominous. What was the relation between them, and what the object of his repeated visits? Was she his client, his friend, or his mistress? If the former, she had probably transferred the photograph to his keeping. If the latter, it was less likely. On the issue of this question depended whether I should continue my work at Briony Lodge, or turn my attention to the gentleman's chambers in the Temple. It was a delicate point, and it widened the field of my inquiry. I fear that I bore you with these details, but I have to let you see my little difficulties, if you are to understand the situation."

"I am following you closely," I answered.

"I was still balancing the matter in my mind, when a hansom cab drove up to Briony Lodge, and a gentleman sprang out. He was a remarkably handsome man, dark, aquiline, and moustached—evidently the man of whom I had heard. He appeared to be in a great hurry, shouted to the cabman to wait, and brushed past the maid who opened the door with the air of a man who was thoroughly at home.

18. A small, charming house.
19. A back lane, used for stables and deliveries.

20. One of the four Inns of Court, where the offices and residences of barristers are located.

"He was in the house about half an hour, and I could catch glimpses of him, in the windows of the sitting-room, pacing up and down, talking excitedly and waving his arms. Of her I could see nothing. Presently he emerged, looking even more flurried than before. As he stepped up to the cab, he pulled a gold watch from his pocket and looked at it earnestly. 'Drive like the devil,' he shouted, 'first to Gross & Hankey's in Regent-street, and then to the church of St. Monica in the Edgware-road. Half a guinea if you do it in twenty minutes!'

"Away they went, and I was just wondering whether I should not do well to follow them, when up the lane came a neat little landau, the coachman with his coat only half buttoned, and his tie under his ear, while all the tags of his harness were sticking out of the buckles. It hadn't pulled up before she shot out of the hall door and into it. I only caught a glimpse of her at the moment, but she was a lovely woman, with a face that a man might die for.

" 'The Church of St. Monica, John,' she cried, 'and half a sovereign if you reach it in twenty minutes.'

"This was quite too good to lose, Watson. I was just balancing whether I should run for it, or whether I should perch behind her landau, when a cab came through the street. The driver looked twice at such a shabby fare; but I jumped in before he could object. 'The Church of St. Monica,' said I, 'and half a sovereign if you reach it in twenty minutes.' It was twenty-five minutes to twelve, and of course it was clear enough what was in the wind.[21]

"My cabby drove fast. I don't think I ever drove faster, but the others were there before us. The cab and the landau with their steaming horses were in front of the door when I arrived. I paid the man, and hurried into the church. There was not a soul there save the two whom I had followed and a surpliced clergyman, who seemed to be expostulating with them. They were all three standing in a knot in front of the altar. I lounged up the side aisle like any other idler who has dropped into a church. Suddenly, to my surprise, the three at the altar faced round to me, and Godfrey Norton came running as hard as he could towards me.

" 'Thank God!' he cried. 'You'll do. Come! Come!'

" 'What then?' I asked.

" 'Come man, come, only three minutes, or it won't be legal.'

"I was half dragged up to the altar, and, before I knew where I was, I found myself mumbling responses which were whispered in my ear, and vouching for things of which I knew nothing, and generally assisting in the secure tying up of Irene Adler, spinster, to Godfrey Norton, bachelor. It was all done in an instant, and there was the gentleman thanking me on the one side and the lady on the other, while the clergyman beamed on me in front. It was the most preposterous position in which I ever found myself in my life, and it was the thought of it that started me laughing just now. It seems that there had been some informality about their licence, that the clergyman absolutely refused to marry them without a witness of some sort, and that my lucky appearance saved the bridegroom from having to sally out into the streets in search of a best man. The bride gave me a sovereign, and I mean to wear it on my watch chain in memory of the occasion."

"This is a very unexpected turn of affairs," said I; "and what then?"

"Well, I found my plans very seriously menaced. It looked as if the pair might take an immediate departure, and so necessitate very prompt and energetic measures on my part. At the church door, however, they separated, he driving back to the

21. Until 1886, marriages could only be legally performed before noon.

Temple, and she to her own house. 'I shall drive out in the Park at five as usual,' she said as she left him. I heard no more. They drove away in different directions, and I went off to make my own arrangements."

"Which are?"

"Some cold beef and a glass of beer," he answered, ringing the bell. "I have been too busy to think of food, and I am likely to be busier still this evening. By the way, Doctor, I shall want your co-operation."

"I shall be delighted."

"You don't mind breaking the law?"

"Not in the least."

"Nor running a chance of arrest?"

"Not in a good cause."

"Oh, the cause is excellent!"

"Then I am your man."

"I was sure that I might rely on you."

"But what is it you wish?"

"When Mrs Turner has brought in the tray I will make it clear to you. Now," he said, as he turned hungrily on the simple fare that our landlady had provided, "I must discuss it while I eat, for I have not much time. It is nearly five now. In two hours we must be on the scene of action. Miss Irene, or Madame, rather, returns from her drive at seven. We must be at Briony Lodge to meet her."

"And what then?"

"You must leave that to me. I have already arranged what is to occur. There is only one point on which I must insist. You must not interfere, come what may. You understand?"

"I am to be neutral?"

"To do nothing whatever. There will probably be some small unpleasantness. Do not join in it. It will end in my being conveyed into the house. Four or five minutes afterwards the sitting-room window will open. You are to station yourself close to that open window."

"Yes."

"You are to watch me, for I will be visible to you."

"Yes."

"And when I raise my hand—so—you will throw into the room what I give you to throw, and will, at the same time, raise the cry of fire. You quite follow me?"

"Entirely."

"It is nothing very formidable," he said, taking a long cigar-shaped roll from his pocket. "It is an ordinary plumber's smoke rocket,[22] fitted with a cap at either end to make it self-lighting. Your task is confined to that. When you raise your cry of fire, it will be taken up by quite a number of people. You may then walk to the end of the street, and I will rejoin you in ten minutes. I hope that I have made myself clear?"

"I am to remain neutral, to get near the window, to watch you, and, at the signal, to throw in this object, then to raise the cry of fire, and to await you at the corner of the street."

"Precisely."

"Then you may entirely rely on me."

"That is excellent. I think perhaps it is almost time that I prepared for the new *rôle* I have to play."

22. A device to test pipes for leaks.

He disappeared into his bedroom, and returned in a few minutes in the character of an amiable and simple-minded Nonconformist clergyman. His broad black hat, his baggy trousers, his white tie, his sympathetic smile, and general look of peering and benevolent curiosity were such as Mr John Hare[23] alone could have equalled. It was not merely that Holmes changed his costume. His expression, his manner, his very soul seemed to vary with every fresh part that he assumed. The stage lost a fine actor, even as science lost an acute reasoner, when he became a specialist in crime.

It was a quarter past six when we left Baker-street, and it still wanted ten minutes to the hour when we found ourselves in Serpentine-avenue. It was already dusk, and the lamps were just being lighted as we paced up and down in front of Briony Lodge, waiting for the coming of its occupant. The house was just such as I had pictured it from Sherlock Holmes's succinct description, but the locality appeared to be less private than I expected. On the contrary, for a small street in a quiet neighbourhood, it was remarkably animated. There was a group of shabbily-dressed men smoking and laughing in a corner, a scissors grinder with his wheel,[24] two guardsmen who were flirting with a nurse-girl, and several well-dressed young men who were lounging up and down with cigars in their mouths.

"You see," remarked Holmes, as we paced to and fro in front of the house, "this marriage rather simplifies matters. The photograph becomes a double-edged weapon now. The chances are that she would be as averse to its being seen by Mr Godfrey Norton, as our client is to its coming to the eyes of his Princess. Now the question is—Where are we to find the photograph?"

"Where, indeed?"

"It is most unlikely that she carries it about with her. It is cabinet size. Too large for easy concealment about a woman's dress. She knows that the King is capable of having her waylaid and searched. Two attempts of the sort have already been made. We may take it then that she does not carry it about with her."

"Where, then?"

"Her banker or her lawyer. There is that double possibility. But I am inclined to think neither. Women are naturally secretive, and they like to do their own secreting. Why should she hand it over to anyone else? She could trust her own guardianship, but she could not tell what indirect or political influence might be brought to bear upon a business man. Besides, remember that she had resolved to use it within a few days. It must be where she can lay her hands upon it. It must be in her own house."

"But it has twice been burgled."

"Pshaw! They did not know how to look."

"But how will you look?"

"I will not look."

"What then?"

"I will get her to show me."

"But she will refuse."

"She will not be able to. But I hear the rumble of wheels. It is her carriage. Now carry out my orders to the letter."

As he spoke the gleam of the sidelights of a carriage came round the curve of the avenue. It was a smart little landau which rattled up to the door of Briony Lodge. As it pulled up one of the loafing men at the corner dashed forward to open the door in the hope of earning a copper, but was elbowed away by another loafer who had rushed up with the same intention. A fierce quarrel broke out, which was increased by the two

23. A popular character actor of the era.   24. A door-to-door knife sharpener.

guardsmen, who took sides with one of the loungers, and by the scissors grinder, who was equally hot upon the other side. A blow was struck, and in an instant the lady, who had stepped from her carriage, was the centre of a little knot of flushed and struggling men who struck savagely at each other with their fists and sticks. Holmes dashed into the crowd to protect the lady; but, just as he reached her, he gave a cry and dropped to the ground, with the blood running freely down his face. At his fall the guardsmen took to their heels in one direction and the loungers in the other, while a number of better dressed people who had watched the scuffle without taking part in it, crowded in to help the lady and to attend to the injured man. Irene Adler, as I will still call her, had hurried up the steps; but she stood at the top with her superb figure outlined against the lights of the hall, looking back into the street.

"Is the poor gentleman much hurt?" she asked.

"He is dead," cried several voices.

"No, no, there's life in him," shouted another. "But he'll be gone before you can get him to hospital."

"He's a brave fellow," said a woman. "They would have had the lady's purse and watch if it hadn't been for him. They were a gang, and a rough one too. Ah, he's breathing now."

"He can't lie in the street. May we bring him in, marm?"

"Surely. Bring him into the sitting-room. There is a comfortable sofa. This way, please!"

Slowly and solemnly he was borne into Briony Lodge, and laid out in the principal room, while I still observed the proceedings from my post by the window. The lamps had been lit, but the blinds had not been drawn, so that I could see Holmes as he lay upon the couch. I do not know whether he was seized with compunction at that moment for the part he was playing, but I know that I never felt more heartily ashamed of myself in my life than when I saw the beautiful creature against whom I was conspiring, or the grace and kindliness with which she waited upon the injured man. And yet it would be the blackest treachery to Holmes to draw back now from the part which he had entrusted to me. I hardened my heart, and took the smoke-rocket from under my ulster.[25] After all, I thought, we are not injuring her. We are but preventing her from injuring another.

Holmes had sat up upon the couch, and I saw him motion like a man who is in need of air. A maid rushed across and threw open the window. At the same instant I saw him raise his hand, and at the signal I tossed my rocket into the room with a cry of "Fire." The word was no sooner out of my mouth than the whole crowd of spectators, well dressed and ill—gentlemen, ostlers, and servant maids—joined in a general shriek of "Fire." Thick clouds of smoke curled through the room, and out at the open window. I caught a glimpse of rushing figures, and a moment later the voice of Holmes from within, assuring them that it was a false alarm. Slipping through the shouting crowd I made my way to the corner of the street, and in ten minutes was rejoiced to find my friend's arm in mine, and to get away from the scene of uproar. He walked swiftly and in silence for some few minutes, until we had turned down one of the quiet streets which lead towards the Edgware-road.

"You did it very nicely, Doctor," he remarked. "Nothing could have been better. It is all right."

"You have the photograph!"

25. A long, loose overcoat.

"I know where it is."

"And how did you find out?"

"She showed me, as I told you that she would."

"I am still in the dark."

"I do not wish to make a mystery," said he laughing. "The matter was perfectly simple. You, of course, saw that everyone in the street was an accomplice. They were all engaged for the evening."

"I guessed as much."

"Then, when the row broke out, I had a little moist red paint in the palm of my hand. I rushed forward, fell down, clapped my hand to my face, and became a piteous spectacle. It is an old trick."

"That also I could fathom."

"Then they carried me in. She was bound to have me in. What else could she do? And into her sitting-room, which was the very room which I suspected. It lay between that and her bedroom, and I was determined to see which. They laid me on a couch, I motioned for air, they were compelled to open the window, and you had your chance."

"How did that help you?"

"It was all-important. When a woman thinks that her house is on fire, her instinct is at once to rush to the thing which she values most. It is a perfectly overpowering impulse, and I have more than once taken advantage of it. In the case of the Darlington Substitution Scandal it was of use to me, and also in the Arnsworth Castle business. A married woman grabs at her baby—an unmarried one reaches for her jewel box. Now it was clear to me that our lady of to-day had nothing in the house more precious to her than what we are in quest of. She would rush to secure it. The alarm of fire was admirably done. The smoke and shouting were enough to shake nerves of steel. She responded beautifully. The photograph is in a recess behind a sliding panel just above the right bell pull. She was there in an instant, and I caught a glimpse of it as she half drew it out. When I cried out that it was a false alarm, she replaced it, glanced at the rocket, rushed from the room, and I have not seen her since. I rose, and, making my excuses, escaped from the house. I hesitated whether to attempt to secure the photograph at once; but the coachman had come in, and, as he was watching me narrowly, it seemed safer to wait. A little over-precipitance may ruin all."

"And now?" I asked.

"Our quest is practically finished. I shall call with the King to-morrow, and with you, if you care to come with us. We will be shown into the sitting-room to wait for the lady, but it is probable that when she comes she may find neither us nor the photograph. It might be a satisfaction to His Majesty to regain it with his own hands."

"And when will you call?"

"At eight in the morning. She will not be up, so that we shall have a clear field. Besides, we must be prompt, for this marriage may mean a complete change in her life and habits. I must wire to the King without delay."

We had reached Baker-street, and had stopped at the door. He was searching his pockets for the key, when someone passing said:—

"Good-night, Mister Sherlock Holmes."

There were several people on the pavement at the time, but the greeting appeared to come from a slim youth in an ulster who had hurried by.

"I've heard that voice before," said Holmes, staring down the dimly lit street. "Now, I wonder who the deuce that could have been."

3

I slept at Baker-street that night, and we were engaged upon our toast and coffee in the morning when the King of Bohemia rushed into the room.

"You have really got it!" he cried, grasping Sherlock Holmes by either shoulder, and looking eagerly into his face.

"Not yet."

"But you have hopes?"

"I have hopes."

"Then, come. I am all impatience to be gone."

"We must have a cab."

"No, my brougham is waiting."

"Then that will simplify matters." We descended, and started off once more for Briony Lodge.

"Irene Adler is married," remarked Holmes.

"Married! When?"

"Yesterday."

"But to whom?"

"To an English lawyer named Norton."

"But she could not love him?"

"I am in hopes that she does."

"And why in hopes?"

"Because it would spare your Majesty all fear of future annoyance. If the lady loves her husband, she does not love your Majesty. If she does not love your Majesty, there is no reason why she should interfere with your Majesty's plan."

"It is true. And yet—! Well! I wish she had been of my own station! What a queen she would have made!" He relapsed into a moody silence which was not broken, until we drew up in Serpentine-avenue.

The door of Briony Lodge was open, and an elderly woman stood upon the steps. She watched us with a sardonic eye as we stepped from the brougham.

"Mr Sherlock Holmes, I believe?" said she.

"I am Mr Holmes," answered my companion, looking at her with a questioning and rather startled gaze.

"Indeed! My mistress told me that you were likely to call. She left this morning with her husband, by the 5.15 train from Charing-cross, for the Continent."

"What!" Sherlock Holmes staggered back, white with chagrin and surprise. "Do you mean that she has left England?"

"Never to return."

"And the papers?" asked the King, hoarsely. "All is lost."

"We shall see." He pushed past the servant, and rushed into the drawing-room, followed by the King and myself. The furniture was scattered about in every direction, with dismantled shelves, and open drawers, as if the lady had hurriedly ransacked them before her flight. Holmes rushed at the bell-pull, tore back a small sliding shutter, and, plunging in his hand, pulled out a photograph and a letter. The photograph was of Irene Adler herself in evening dress, the letter was superscribed to "Sherlock Holmes, Esq. To be left till called for." My friend tore it open, and we all three read it together. It was dated at midnight of the preceding night, and ran in this way:—

"MY DEAR MR SHERLOCK HOLMES,—You really did it very well. You took me in completely. Until after the alarm of fire, I had not a suspicion. But then, when I found how I had betrayed myself, I began to think. I had been warned against you months ago. I had been told that, if the King employed an agent, it would certainly be you. And your address had been given me. Yet, with all this, you made me reveal what you wanted to know. Even after I became suspicious, I found it hard to think evil of such a dear, kind old clergyman. But, you know, I have been trained as an actress myself. Male costume is nothing new to me. I often take advantage of the freedom which it gives. I sent John, the coachman, to watch you, ran upstairs, got into my walking clothes, as I call them, and came down just as you departed.

"Well, I followed you to your door, and so made sure that I was really an object of interest to the celebrated Mr Sherlock Holmes. Then I, rather imprudently, wished you good night, and started for the Temple to see my husband.

"We both thought the best resource was flight, when pursued by so formidable an antagonist; so you will find the nest empty when you call to-morrow. As to the photograph, your client may rest in peace. I love and am loved by a better man than he. The King may do what he will without hindrance from one whom he has cruelly wronged. I keep it only to safeguard myself, and to preserve a weapon which will always secure me from any steps which he might take in the future. I leave a photograph which he might care to possess; and I remain, dear Mr Sherlock Holmes, very truly yours,

"IRENE NORTON, *née* ADLER."

"What a woman—oh, what a woman!" cried the King of Bohemia, when we had all three read this epistle. "Did I not tell you how quick and resolute she was? Would she not have made an admirable queen? Is it not a pity that she was not on my level?"

"From what I have seen of the lady, she seems, indeed, to be on a very different level to your Majesty," said Holmes, coldly. "I am sorry that I have not been able to bring your Majesty's business to a more successful conclusion."

"On the contrary, my dear sir," cried the King. "Nothing could be more successful. I know that her word is inviolate. The photograph is now as safe as if it were in the fire."

"I am glad to hear your Majesty say so."

"I am immensely indebted to you. Pray tell me in what way I can reward you. This ring—." He slipped an emerald snake ring from his finger, and held it out upon the palm of his hand.

"Your Majesty has something which I should value even more highly," said Holmes.

"You have but to name it."

"This photograph!"

The King stared at him in amazement.

"Irene's photograph!" he cried. "Certainly, if you wish it."

"I thank your Majesty. Then there is no more to be done in the matter. I have the honour to wish you a very good morning." He bowed, and, turning away without observing the hand which the King had stretched out to him, he set off in my company for his chambers.

And that was how a great scandal threatened to affect the kingdom of Bohemia, and how the best plans of Mr Sherlock Holmes were beaten by a woman's wit. He used to make merry over the cleverness of women, but I have not heard him do it of late. And when he speaks of Irene Adler, or when he refers to her photograph, it is always under the honourable title of *the* woman.

1891

Matthew Arnold
1822–1888

Dover Beach

The sea is calm to-night.
The tide is full, the moon lies fair
Upon the straits; on the French coast the light
Gleams and is gone; the cliffs of England stand,
5   Glimmering and vast, out in the tranquil bay.
Come to the window, sweet is the night-air!
Only, from the long line of spray
Where the sea meets the moon-blanched land,
Listen! you hear the grating roar
10   Of pebbles which the waves draw back, and fling,
At their return, up the high strand,
Begin, and cease, and then again begin,
With tremulous cadence slow, and bring
The eternal note of sadness in.

15   Sophocles long ago
Heard it on the Aegean,[1] and it brought
Into his mind the turbid ebb and flow
Of human misery; we
Find also in the sound a thought,
20   Hearing it by this distant northern sea.

The Sea of Faith
Was once, too, at the full, and round earth's shore
Lay like the folds of a bright girdle° furled.   *sash*
But now I only hear
25   Its melancholy, long, withdrawing roar,
Retreating, to the breath
Of the night-wind, down the vast edges drear
And naked shingles° of the world.   *pebble beaches*

Ah, love, let us be true
30   To one another! for the world, which seems
To lie before us like a land of dreams,
So various, so beautiful, so new,
Hath really neither joy, nor love, nor light,
Nor certitude, nor peace, nor help for pain;
35   And we are here as on a darkling plain
Swept with confused alarms of struggle and flight,
Where ignorant armies clash by night.

c. 1851   1867

---

1. Sophocles was a 5th century B.C. Greek dramatist; the Aegean Sea lies between Greece and Turkey.

Christina Rossetti
1830–1894

Song

When I am dead, my dearest,
    Sing no sad songs for me;
Plant thou no roses at my head,
    Nor shady cypress tree:
5   Be the green grass above me
    With showers and dewdrops wet;
And if thou wilt, remember,
    And if thou wilt, forget.

I shall not see the shadows,
10   I shall not feel the rain;
I shall not hear the nightingale
    Sing on, as if in pain:
And dreaming through the twilight
    That doth not rise nor set,
15   Haply° I may remember,   *perhaps*
    And haply may forget.

1848   1862

"No, Thank You, John"

I never said I loved you, John:
    Why will you teaze me day by day,
And wax a weariness to think upon
    With always "do" and "pray"?

5   You know I never loved you, John;
    No fault of mine made me your toast:
Why will you haunt me with a face as wan
    As shows an hour-old ghost?

I dare say Meg or Moll would take
10   Pity upon you, if you'd ask:
And pray don't remain single for my sake
    Who can't perform that task.

I have no heart?—Perhaps I have not;
    But then you're mad to take offence
15   That I don't give you what I have not got:
    Use your own common sense.

Let bygones be bygones:
    Don't call me false, who owed not to be true:
I'd rather answer "No" to fifty Johns
20   Than answer "Yes" to you.

Let's mar our pleasant days no more,
   Song-birds of passage, days of youth:
Catch at today, forget the days before:
   I'll wink at your untruth.

25   Let us strike hands as hearty friends;
   No more, no less; and friendship's good:
Only don't keep in view ulterior ends,
   And points not understood

In open treaty. Rise above
30   Quibbles and shuffling off and on:
Here's friendship for you if you like; but love,—
   No, thank you, John.

1860   1862

Promises Like Pie-Crust[1]

Promise me no promises,
   So will I not promise you;
Keep we both our liberties,
   Never false and never true:
5   Let us hold the die uncast,
   Free to come as free to go;
For I cannot know your past,
   And of mine what can you know?

You, so warm, may once have been
10   Warmer towards another one;
I, so cold, may once have seen
   Sunlight, once have felt the sun:
Who shall show us if it was
   Thus indeed in time of old?
15   Fades the image from the glass
   And the fortune is not told.

If you promised, you might grieve
   For lost liberty again;
If I promised, I believe
20   I should fret to break the chain:
Let us be the friends we were,
   Nothing more but nothing less;
Many thrive on frugal fare
   Who would perish of excess.

1861   1896

---

1. English proverb: "Promises are like pie-crust, made to be broken."

Gerard Manley Hopkins
1844–1889

God's Grandeur

The world is charged with the grandeur of God.
   It will flame out, like shining from shook foil;[1]
   It gathers to a greatness, like the ooze of oil
Crushed.[2] Why do men then now not reck° his rod?   *heed*
5 Generations have trod, have trod, have trod;
   And all is seared with trade; bleared, smeared with toil;
   And wears man's smudge and shares man's smell: the soil
Is bare now, nor can foot feel, being shod.

And for° all this, nature is never spent;   *despite*
10   There lives the dearest freshness deep down things;
And though the last lights off the black West went
   Oh, morning, at the brown brink eastward, springs—
Because the Holy Ghost over the bent
   World broods with warm breast and with ah! bright wings.

1877   1895

The Windhover:[1]

To Christ Our Lord

I caught this morning morning's minion,[2] king-
   dom of daylight's dauphin,[3] dapple-dawn-drawn Falcon, in his riding
   Of the rolling level underneath him steady air, and striding
High there, how he rung upon the rein[4] of a wimpling wing
5 In his ecstasy! then off, off forth on swing,
   As a skate's heel sweeps smooth on a bow-bend: the hurl and gliding
   Rebuffed the big wind. My heart in hiding
Stirred for a bird,—the achieve of, the mastery of the thing!

Brute beauty and valour and act, oh, air, pride, plume, here
10   Buckle! AND the fire that breaks from thee then, a billion
Times told lovelier, more dangerous, O my chevalier!

   No wonder of it: shéer plód makes plough down sillion[5]
Shine, and blue-bleak embers, ah my dear,
   Fall, gall[6] themselves, and gash gold-vermilion.

1877   1918

---

1. I mean foil in its sense of leaf or tinsel. . . . Shaken goldfoil gives off broad glares like sheet lightning and also, and this is true of nothing else, owing to its zigzag dints and creasings and network of small many cornered facets, a sort of fork lightning too [Hopkins's note].
2. Oil made by crushing seeds or olives.
1. Kestrel falcon—a small hawk—that appears to hover in the air.

2. Darling, from the French *mignon*.
3. The dauphin was the heir to the French throne.
4. In falconry, a bird rings when it rises in spirals (like a horse circling at the end of a tether or rein). Wimpling means rippling.
5. The furrows of a plowed field.
6. Break their surfaces.

Pied[1] Beauty

Glory be to God for dappled things—
   For skies of couple-colour as a brinded[2] cow;
     For rose-moles all in stipple[3] upon trout that swim;
Fresh-firecoal chestnut-falls;[4] finches' wings;
5   Landscape plotted and pieced—fold, fallow, and plough;[5]
     And áll trádes, their gear and tackle and trim.°   *equipment*

All things counter,[6] original, spare, strange;
   Whatever is fickle, freckled (who knows how?)
     With swift, slow; sweet, sour; adazzle, dim;
10 He fathers-forth whose beauty is past change:
         Praise him.

1877   1918

Lewis Carroll
1832–1898

from Through the Looking-Glass

Jabberwocky[1]

'Twas brillig, and the slithy toves
   Did gyre and gimble in the wabe:
All mimsy were the borogoves,
   And the mome raths outgrabe.

5 "Beware the Jabberwock, my son!
   The jaws that bite, the claws that catch!
Beware the Jubjub bird, and shun
   The frumious Bandersnatch!"

He took his vorpal sword in hand:
10   Long time the manxome foe he sought—
So rested he by the Tumtum tree,
   And stood awhile in thought.

And, as in uffish thought he stood,
   The Jabberwock, with eyes of flame,
15 Came whiffling through the tulgey wood,
   And burbled as it came!

One, two! One, two! And through and through
   The vorpal blade went snicker-snack!
He left it dead, and with its head
20   He went galumphing back.

1. Blotched with different colors.
2. Brindled, having dark patches on a tawny ground.
3. Stippled, painted or drawn with dots instead of lines.
4. Chestnuts as bright as coals [Hopkins's journal].
5. Landscape of differently colored fields, some used as pasture ("fold"), some lying fallow, some plowed.
6. Contrary; "spare" means rare.

1. From *Through the Looking-Glass* (ch. 1). Alice finds a book in which all the words are printed backwards; when she realizes it's a Looking-glass book, she holds it up to the mirror and reads this poem. Afterwards she remarks that "it's *rather* hard to understand!" Later in *Through the Looking-Glass* Humpty Dumpty explicates the poem (see below).

"And, hast thou slain the Jabberwock?
        Come to my arms, my beamish boy!
    O frabjous day! Callooh! Callay!"
        He chortled in his joy.

25   'Twas brillig, and the slithy toves
            Did gyre and gimble in the wabe:
        All mimsy were the borogoves,
            And the mome raths outgrabe.

[HUMPTY DUMPTY ON JABBERWOCKY][1]

"You seem very clever at explaining words, Sir," said Alice. "Would you kindly tell me the meaning of the poem called 'Jabberwocky'?"

"Let's hear it," said Humpty Dumpty. "I can explain all the poems that ever were invented—and a good many that haven't been invented just yet."

This sounded very hopeful, so Alice repeated the first verse:—

> "'Twas brillig, and the slithy toves
>   Did gyre and gimble in the wabe:
> All mimsy were the borogoves,
>   And the mome raths outgrabe."

"That's enough to begin with," Humpty Dumpty interrupted: "there are plenty of hard words there. 'Brillig' means four o'clock in the afternoon—the time when you begin broiling things for dinner."

"That'll do very well," said Alice: "and 'slithy'?"

"Well, 'slithy' means 'lithe and slimy.' 'Lithe' is the same as 'active.' You see it's like a pormanteau[2]—there are two meanings packed up into one word."

"I see it now," Alice remarked thoughtfully: "and what are 'toves'?"

"Well 'toves' are something like badgers—they're something like lizards—and they're something like corkscrews."

"They must be very curious-looking creatures."

"They are that," said Humpty Dumpty; "also they make their nests under sun-dials—also they live on cheese."

"And what's to 'gyre' and to 'gimble'?"

"To 'gyre' is to go round and round like a gyroscope. To 'gimble' is to make holes like a gimlet."

"And 'the wabe' is the grass-plot round a sun-dial, I suppose?" said Alice, surprised at her own ingenuity.

"Of course it is. It's called 'wabe' you know, because it goes a long way before it, and a long way behind it—"

"And a long way beyond it on each side," Alice added.

---

1. From *Through the Looking-Glass* (ch. 6).
2. A word formed by combining two other words (e.g., *brunch*, *motel*). In the preface to *The Hunting of the Snark* (1876), Carroll wrote about the "hard words" in *Jabberwocky*: "Humpty Dumpty's theory, of two meanings packed into one word like a portmanteau, seems to me the right explanation for all. For instance, take the two words 'fuming' and 'furious.' Make up your mind that you will say both words, but leave it unsettled which you will say first. Now open your mouth and speak. If your thoughts incline ever so little towards 'fuming,' you will say 'fuming-furious,' if they turn, by even a hair's breadth, towards 'furious,' you will say 'furious-fuming,' but if you have the rarest of gifts, a perfectly balanced mind, you will say 'frumious.'"

"Exactly so. Well then, *'mimsy'* is 'flimsy and miserable' (there's another portmanteau for you). And a *'borogove'* is a thin shabby-looking bird with its feathers sticking out all round—something like a live mop."

"And then *'mome raths'*?" said Alice. "I'm afraid I'm giving you a great deal of trouble."

"Well, a *'rath'* is a sort of green pig: but *'mome'* I'm not certain about. I think it's short for 'from home'—meaning that they'd lost their way, you know."

"And what does *'outgrabe'* mean?"

"Well, *'outgribing'* is something between bellowing and whistling, with a kind of sneeze in the middle: however, you'll hear it done, maybe—down in the wood yonder—and, when you've once heard it, you'll be *quite* content. Who's been repeating all that hard stuff to you?"

"I read it in a book," said Alice.

Oscar Wilde
1854–1900

The Importance of Being Earnest
A Trivial Comedy for Serious People

FIRST ACT

SCENE: *Morning-room in Algernon's flat in Half Moon Street.*[1] *The room is luxuriously and artistically furnished. The sound of a piano is heard in the adjoining room.*

[*Lane is arranging afternoon tea on the table, and after the music has ceased, Algernon enters.*]

ALGERNON: Did you hear what I was playing, Lane?

LANE: I didn't think it polite to listen, sir.

ALGERNON: I'm sorry for that, for your sake. I don't play accurately—anyone can play accurately—but I play with wonderful expression. As far as the piano is concerned, sentiment is my forte. I keep science for Life.

LANE: Yes, sir.

ALGERNON: And, speaking of the science of Life, have you got the cucumber sandwiches cut for Lady Bracknell?

LANE: Yes, sir. [*Hands them on a salver.*]

ALGERNON [*inspects them, takes two, and sits down on the sofa*]: Oh! . . . by the way, Lane, I see from your book that on Thursday night, when Lord Shoreham and Mr Worthing were dining with me, eight bottles of champagne are entered as having been consumed.

LANE: Yes, sir; eight bottles and a pint.

ALGERNON: Why is it that at a bachelor's establishment the servants invariably drink the champagne? I ask merely for information.

1. A fashionable address in the West End of London.

LANE: I attribute it to the superior quality of the wine, sir. I have often observed that in married households the champagne is rarely of a first-rate brand.

ALGERNON: Good Heavens! Is marriage so demoralizing as that?

LANE: I believe it *is* a very pleasant state, sir. I have had very little experience of it myself up to the present. I have only been married once. That was in consequence of a misunderstanding between myself and a young person.

ALGERNON [*languidly*]: I don't know that I am much interested in your family life, Lane.

LANE: No, sir; it is not a very interesting subject. I never think of it myself.

ALGERNON: Very natural, I am sure. That will do, Lane, thank you.

LANE: Thank you, sir. [*Lane goes out.*]

ALGERNON: Lane's views on marriage seem somewhat lax. Really, if the lower orders don't set us a good example, what on earth is the use of them? They seem, as a class, to have absolutely no sense of moral responsibility.
  [*Enter Lane.*]

LANE: Mr Ernest Worthing.
  [*Enter Jack. Lane goes out.*]

ALGERNON: How are you, my dear Ernest? What brings you up to town?

JACK: Oh, pleasure, pleasure! What else should bring one anywhere? Eating as usual, I see, Algy!

ALGERNON [*stiffly*]: I believe it is customary in good society to take some slight refreshment at five o'clock. Where have you been since last Thursday?

JACK [*sitting down on the sofa*]: In the country.

ALGERNON: What on earth do you do there?

JACK [*pulling off his gloves*]: When one is in town one amuses oneself. When one is in the country one amuses other people. It is excessively boring.

ALGERNON: And who are the people you amuse?

JACK [*airily*]: Oh, neighbours, neighbours.

ALGERNON: Got nice neighbours in your part of Shropshire?[2]

JACK: Perfectly horrid! Never speak to one of them.

ALGERNON: How immensely you must amuse them! [*Goes over and takes sandwich.*] By the way, Shropshire is your county, is it not?

JACK: Eh? Shropshire? Yes, of course. Hallo! Why all these cups? Why cucumber sandwiches? Why such reckless extravagance in one so young? Who is coming to tea?

ALGERNON: Oh! merely Aunt Augusta and Gwendolen.

JACK: How perfectly delightful!

ALGERNON: Yes, that is all very well; but I am afraid Aunt Augusta won't quite approve of your being here.

JACK: May I ask why?

ALGERNON: My dear fellow, the way you flirt with Gwendolen is perfectly disgraceful. It is almost as bad as the way Gwendolen flirts with you.

JACK: I am in love with Gwendolen. I have come up to town expressly to propose to her.

ALGERNON: I thought you had come up for pleasure? . . . I call that business.

JACK: How utterly unromantic you are!

ALGERNON: I really don't see anything romantic in proposing. It is very romantic to be in love. But there is nothing romantic about a definite proposal. Why, one may be accepted. One usually is, I believe. Then the excitement is all over. The

---

2. Worthing's estate is actually in Hertfordshire, which is a long way from Shropshire.

very essence of romance is uncertainty. If I ever get married, I'll certainly try to forget the fact.

JACK: I have no doubt about that, dear Algy. The Divorce Court was specially invented for people whose memories are so curiously constituted.

ALGERNON: Oh! there is no use speculating on that subject. Divorces are made in Heaven—[*Jack puts out his hand to take a sandwich. Algernon at once interferes.*] Please don't touch the cucumber sandwiches. They are ordered specially for Aunt Augusta. [*Takes one and eats it.*]

JACK: Well, you have been eating them all the time.

ALGERNON: That is quite a different matter. She is my aunt. [*Takes plate from below.*] Have some bread and butter. The bread and butter is for Gwendolen. Gwendolen is devoted to bread and butter.

JACK [*advancing to table and helping himself*]: And very good bread and butter it is too.

ALGERNON: Well, my dear fellow, you need not eat as if you were going to eat it all. You behave as if you were married to her already. You are not married to her already, and I don't think you ever will be.

JACK: Why on earth do you say that?

ALGERNON: Well, in the first place girls never marry the men they flirt with. Girls don't think it right.

JACK: Oh, that is nonsense!

ALGERNON: It isn't. It is a great truth. It accounts for the extraordinary number of bachelors that one sees all over the place. In the second place, I don't give my consent.

JACK: Your consent!

ALGERNON: My dear fellow, Gwendolen is my first cousin. And before I allow you to marry her, you will have to clear up the whole question of Cecily. [*Rings bell.*]

JACK: Cecily! What on earth do you mean? What do you mean, Algy, by Cecily? I don't know anyone of the name of Cecily.

[*Enter Lane.*]

ALGERNON: Bring me that cigarette case Mr Worthing left in the smoking-room the last time he dined here.

LANE: Yes, sir. [*Lane goes out.*]

JACK: Do you mean to say you have had my cigarette case all this time? I wish to goodness you had let me know. I have been writing frantic letters to Scotland Yard[3] about it. I was very nearly offering a large reward.

ALGERNON: Well, I wish you would offer one. I happen to be more than usually hard up.

JACK: There is no good offering a large reward now that the thing is found.

[*Enter Lane with the cigarette case on a salver. Algernon takes it at once. Lane goes out.*]

ALGERNON: I think that is rather mean of you, Ernest, I must say. [*Opens case and examines it.*] However, it makes no matter, for, now that I look at the inscription inside, I find that the thing isn't yours after all.

JACK: Of course it's mine. [*Moving to him.*] You have seen me with it a hundred times, and you have no right whatsoever to read what is written inside. It is a very ungentlemanly thing to read a private cigarette case.

ALGERNON: Oh! it is absurd to have a hard-and-fast rule about what one should read and what one shouldn't. More than half of modern culture depends on what one shouldn't read.

3. London police headquarters.

JACK: I am quite aware of the fact, and I don't propose to discuss modern culture. It isn't the sort of thing one should talk of in private. I simply want my cigarette case back.

ALGERNON: Yes; but this isn't your cigarette case. This cigarette case is a present from someone of the name of Cecily, and you said you didn't know anyone of that name.

JACK: Well, if you want to know, Cecily happens to be my aunt.

ALGERNON: Your aunt!

JACK: Yes. Charming old lady she is, too. Lives at Tunbridge Wells.⁴ Just give it back to me, Algy.

ALGERNON [retreating to back of sofa]: But why does she call herself little Cecily if she is your aunt and lives at Tunbridge Wells? [Reading.] "From little Cecily with her fondest love."

JACK [moving to sofa and kneeling upon it]: My dear fellow, what on earth is there in that? Some aunts are tall, some aunts are not tall. That is a matter that surely an aunt may be allowed to decide for herself. You seem to think that every aunt should be exactly like your aunt! That is absurd! For Heaven's sake give me back my cigarette case. [Follows Algernon round the room.]

ALGERNON: Yes. But why does your aunt call you her uncle? "From little Cecily, with her fondest love to her dear Uncle Jack." There is no objection, I admit, to an aunt being a small aunt, but why an aunt, no matter what her size may be, should call her own nephew her uncle, I can't quite make out. Besides, your name isn't Jack at all; it is Ernest.

JACK: It isn't Ernest; it's Jack.

ALGERNON: You have always told me it was Ernest. I have introduced you to everyone as Ernest. You answer to the name of Ernest. You look as if your name was Ernest. You are the most earnest looking person I ever saw in my life. It is perfectly absurd your saying that your name isn't Ernest. It's on your cards. Here is one of them. [Taking it from case.] "Mr Ernest Worthing, B. 4, The Albany." I'll keep this as a proof that your name is Ernest if ever you attempt to deny it to me, or to Gwendolen, or to anyone else. [Puts the card in his pocket.]

JACK: Well, my name is Ernest in town and Jack in the country, and the cigarette case was given to me in the country.

ALGERNON: Yes, but that does not account for the fact that your small Aunt Cecily, who lives at Tunbridge Wells, calls you her dear uncle. Come, old boy, you had much better have the thing out at once.

JACK: My dear Algy, you talk exactly as if you were a dentist. It is very vulgar to talk like a dentist when one isn't a dentist. It produces a false impression.

ALGERNON: Well, that is exactly what dentists always do. Now, go on! Tell me the whole thing. I may mention that I have always suspected you of being a confirmed and secret Bunburyist, and I am quite sure of it now.

JACK: Bunburyist? What on earth do you mean by a Bunburyist?

ALGERNON: I'll reveal to you the meaning of that incomparable expression as soon as you are kind enough to inform me why you are Ernest in town and Jack in the country.

JACK: Well, produce my cigarette case first.

ALGERNON: Here it is. [Hands cigarette case.] Now produce your explanation, and pray make it improbable. [Sits on sofa.]

4. A fashionable resort.

JACK: My dear fellow, there is nothing improbable about my explanation at all. In fact it's perfectly ordinary. Old Mr Thomas Cardew, who adopted me when I was a little boy, made me in his will guardian to his granddaughter, Miss Cecily Cardew. Cecily who addresses me as her uncle from motives of respect that you could not possibly appreciate, lives at my place in the country under the charge of her admirable governess, Miss Prism.

ALGERNON: Where is that place in the country, by the way?

JACK: That is nothing to you, dear boy. You are not going to be invited. . . . I may tell you candidly that the place is not in Shropshire. ·

ALGERNON: I suspected that, my dear fellow! I have Bunburyed all over Shropshire on two separate occasions. Now, go on. Why are you Ernest in town and Jack in the country?

JACK: My dear Algy, I don't know whether you will be able to understand my real motives. You are hardly serious enough. When one is placed in the position of guardian, one has to adopt a very high moral tone on all subjects. It's one's duty to do so. And as a high moral tone can hardly be said to conduce very much to either one's health or one's happiness, in order to get up to town I have always pretended to have a younger brother of the name of Ernest, who lives in the Albany, and gets into the most dreadful scrapes. That, my dear Algy, is the whole truth pure and simple.

ALGERNON: The truth is rarely pure and never simple. Modern life would be very tedious if it were either, and modern literature a complete impossibility!

JACK: That wouldn't be at all a bad thing.

ALGERNON: Literary criticism is not your forte, my dear fellow. Don't try it. You should leave that to people who haven't been at a University. They do it so well in the daily papers. What you really are is a Bunburyist. I was quite right in saying you were a Bunburyist. You are one of the most advanced Bunburyists I know.

JACK: What on earth do you mean?

ALGERNON: You have invented a very useful younger brother called Ernest, in order that you may be able to come up to town as often as you like. I have invented an invaluable permanent invalid called Bunbury, in order that I may be able to go down into the country whenever I choose. Bunbury is perfectly invaluable. If it wasn't for Bunbury's extraordinary bad health, for instance, I wouldn't be able to dine with you at Willis's[5] tonight, for I have been really engaged[6] to Aunt Augusta for more than a week.

JACK: I haven't asked you to dine with me anywhere tonight.

ALGERNON: I know. You are absurdly careless about sending out invitations. It is very foolish of you. Nothing annoys people so much as not receiving invitations.

JACK: You had much better dine with your Aunt Augusta.

ALGERNON: I haven't the smallest intention of doing anything of the kind. To begin with, I dined there on Monday, and once a week is quite enough to dine with one's own relations. In the second place, whenever I do dine there I am always treated as a member of the family, and sent down[7] with either no woman at all, or two. In the third place, I know perfectly well whom she will place me next to, tonight. She will place me next Mary Farquhar, who always flirts with her own husband across the dinner-table. That is not very pleasant. Indeed, it is not even decent . . . and that sort of thing is enormously on the increase. The amount of women in London who

---

5. An expensive London restaurant.
6. I.e., pledged to attend her dinner party.

7. Sent in to the dining room as someone's escort.

flirt with their own husbands is perfectly scandalous. It looks so bad. It is simply washing one's clean linen in public. Besides, now that I know you to be a confirmed Bunburyist I naturally want to talk to you about Bunburying. I want to tell you the rules.

JACK: I'm not a Bunburyist at all. If Gwendolen accepts me, I am going to kill my brother, indeed I think I'll kill him in any case. Cecily is a little too much interested in
him. It is rather a bore. So I am going to get rid of Ernest. And I strongly advise you
to do the same with Mr . . . with your invalid friend who has the absurd name.

ALGERNON: Nothing will induce me to part with Bunbury, and if you ever get
married, which seems to me extremely problematic, you will be very glad to
know Bunbury. A man who marries without knowing Bunbury has a very
tedious time of it.

JACK: That is nonsense. If I marry a charming girl like Gwendolen, and she is the
only girl I ever saw in my life that I would marry, I certainly won't want to
know Bunbury.

ALGERNON: Then your wife will. You don't seem to realize, that in married life
three is company and two is none.

JACK [*sententiously*]: That, my dear young friend, is the theory that the corrupt
French Drama[8] has been propounding for the last fifty years.

ALGERNON: Yes; and that the happy English home has proved in half the time.

JACK: For heaven's sake, don't try to be cynical. It's perfectly easy to be cynical.

ALGERNON: My dear fellow, it isn't easy to be anything nowadays. There's such a
lot of beastly competition about. [*The sound of an electric bell is heard.*] Ah! that
must be Aunt Augusta. Only relatives, or creditors, ever ring in that Wagnerian
manner.[9] Now, if I get her out of the way for ten minutes, so that you can have an
opportunity for proposing to Gwendolen, may I dine with you tonight at Willis's?

JACK: I suppose so, if you want to.

ALGERNON: Yes, but you must be serious about it. I hate people who are not serious about meals. It is so shallow of them.

[*Enter Lane.*]

LANE: Lady Bracknell and Miss Fairfax.

[*Algernon goes forward to meet them. Enter Lady Bracknell and Gwendolen.*]

LADY BRACKNELL: Good afternoon, dear Algernon, I hope you are behaving
very well.

ALGERNON: I'm feeling very well, Aunt Augusta.

LADY BRACKNELL: That's not quite the same thing. In fact the two things rarely
go together. [*Sees Jack and bows to him with icy coldness.*]

ALGERNON [*to Gwendolen*]: Dear me, you are smart![10]

GWENDOLEN: I am always smart! Aren't I, Mr Worthing?

JACK: You're quite perfect, Miss Fairfax.

GWENDOLEN: Oh! I hope I am not that. It would leave no room for developments,
and I intend to develop in many directions. [*Gwendolen and Jack sit down together
in the corner.*]

LADY BRACKNELL: I'm sorry if we are a little late, Algernon, but I was obliged to
call on dear Lady Harbury. I hadn't been there since her poor husband's death. I
never saw a woman so altered; she looks quite twenty years younger. And now I'll
have a cup of tea, and one of those nice cucumber sandwiches you promised me.

8. Late 19th-century French plays frequently focused on
marital infidelity.
9. I.e., loud and dramatic, like the grand operas of

Richard Wagner (1813–1883).
10. Chic.

ALGERNON: Certainly, Aunt Augusta. [*Goes over to tea-table.*]

LADY BRACKNELL: Won't you come and sit here, Gwendolen?

GWENDOLEN: Thanks, mamma, I'm quite comfortable where I am.

ALGERNON [*picking up empty plate in horror*]: Good heavens! Lane! Why are there no cucumber sandwiches? I ordered them specially.

LANE [*gravely*]: There were no cucumbers in the market this morning, sir. I went down twice.

ALGERNON: No cucumbers!

LANE: No, sir. Not even for ready money.

ALGERNON: That will do, Lane, thank you.

LANE: Thank you, sir. [*Goes out.*]

ALGERNON: I am greatly distressed, Aunt Augusta, about there being no cucumbers, not even for ready money.

LADY BRACKNELL: It really makes no matter, Algernon. I had some crumpets with Lady Harbury, who seems to me to be living entirely for pleasure now.

ALGERNON: I hear her hair has turned quite gold from grief.

LADY BRACKNELL: It certainly has changed its colour. From what cause I, of course, cannot say. [*Algernon crosses and hands tea.*] Thank you. I've quite a treat for you tonight, Algernon. I am going to send you down with Mary Farquhar. She is such a nice woman, and so attentive to her husband. It's delightful to watch them.

ALGERNON: I am afraid, Aunt Augusta, I shall have to give up the pleasure of dining with you tonight after all.

LADY BRACKNELL [*frowning*]: I hope not, Algernon. It would put my table completely out. Your uncle would have to dine upstairs. Fortunately he is accustomed to that.

ALGERNON: It is a great bore, and, I need hardly say, a terrible disappointment to me, but the fact is I have just had a telegram to say that my poor friend Bunbury is very ill again. [*Exchanges glances with Jack.*] They seem to think I should be with him.

LADY BRACKNELL: It is very strange. This Mr Bunbury seems to suffer from curiously bad health.

ALGERNON: Yes; poor Bunbury is a dreadful invalid.

LADY BRACKNELL: Well, I must say, Algernon, that I think it is high time that Mr Bunbury made up his mind whether he was going to live or to die. This shilly-shallying with the question is absurd. Nor do I in any way approve of the modern sympathy with invalids. I consider it morbid. Illness of any kind is hardly a thing to be encouraged in others. Health is the primary duty of life. I am always telling that to your poor uncle, but he never seems to take much notice . . . as far as any improvement in his ailments goes. I should be much obliged if you would ask Mr Bunbury, from me, to be kind enough not to have a relapse on Saturday, for I rely on you to arrange my music for me. It is my last reception, and one wants something that will encourage conversation, particularly at the end of the season[11] when everyone has practically said whatever they had to say, which, in most cases, was probably not much.

ALGERNON: I'll speak to Bunbury, Aunt Augusta, if he is still conscious, and I think I can promise you he'll be all right by Saturday. Of course the music is a great difficulty. You see, if one plays good music, people don't listen, and if one plays bad music people don't talk. But I'll run over the programme I've drawn out, if you will kindly come into the next room for a moment.

---

11. Fashionable people left their country estates to spend the social season in London; it began in late spring and lasted through July.

LADY BRACKNELL: Thank you, Algernon. It is very thoughtful of you. [*Rising, and following Algernon.*] I'm sure the programme will be delightful, after a few expurgations. French songs I cannot possibly allow. People always seem to think that they are improper, and either look shocked, which is vulgar, or laugh, which is worse. But German sounds a thoroughly respectable language, and indeed, I believe is so. Gwendolen, you will accompany me.

GWENDOLEN: Certainly, mamma.

[*Lady Bracknell and Algernon go into the music-room, Gwendolen remains behind.*]

JACK: Charming day it has been, Miss Fairfax.

GWENDOLEN: Pray don't talk to me about the weather, Mr Worthing. Whenever people talk to me about the weather, I always feel quite certain that they mean something else. And that makes me so nervous.

JACK: I do mean something else.

GWENDOLEN: I thought so. In fact, I am never wrong.

JACK: And I would like to be allowed to take advantage of Lady Bracknell's temporary absence . . .

GWENDOLEN: I would certainly advise you to do so. Mamma has a way of coming back suddenly into a room that I have often had to speak to her about.

JACK [*nervously*]: Miss Fairfax, ever since I met you I have admired you more than any girl . . . I have ever met since . . . I met you.

GWENDOLEN: Yes, I am quite aware of the fact. And I often wish that in public, at any rate, you had been more demonstrative. For me you have always had an irresistible fascination. Even before I met you I was far from indifferent to you. [*Jack looks at her in amazement.*] We live, as I hope you know, Mr Worthing, in an age of ideals. The fact is constantly mentioned in the more expensive monthly magazines, and has reached the provincial pulpits I am told: and my ideal has always been to love some one of the name of Ernest. There is something in that name that inspires absolute confidence. The moment Algernon first mentioned to me that he had a friend called Ernest, I knew I was destined to love you.

JACK: You really love me, Gwendolen?

GWENDOLEN: Passionately!

JACK: Darling! You don't know how happy you've made me.

GWENDOLEN: My own Ernest!

JACK: But you don't really mean to say that you couldn't love me if my name wasn't Ernest?

GWENDOLEN: But your name is Ernest.

JACK: Yes, I know it is. But supposing it was something else? Do you mean to say you couldn't love me then?

GWENDOLEN [*glibly*]: Ah! that is clearly a metaphysical speculation, and like most metaphysical speculations has very little reference at all to the actual facts of real life, as we know them.

JACK: Personally, darling, to speak quite candidly, I don't much care about the name of Ernest . . . I don't think the name suits me at all.

GWENDOLEN: It suits you perfectly. It is a divine name. It has a music of its own. It produces vibrations.

JACK: Well, really, Gwendolen, I must say that I think there are lots of other much nicer names. I think Jack, for instance, a charming name.

GWENDOLEN: Jack? . . . No, there is very little music in the name Jack, if any at all, indeed. It does not thrill. It produces absolutely no vibrations . . . I have known several Jacks, and they all, without exception, were more than usually plain. Besides, Jack is a notorious domesticity for John! And I pity any woman who is married to a man called John. She would probably never be allowed to know the entrancing pleasure of a single moment's solitude. The only really safe name is Ernest.

JACK: Gwendolen, I must get christened at once—I mean we must get married at once. There is no time to be lost.

GWENDOLEN: Married, Mr Worthing?[12]

JACK [astounded]: Well . . . surely. You know that I love you, and you led me to believe, Miss Fairfax, that you were not absolutely indifferent to me.

GWENDOLEN: I adore you. But you haven't proposed to me yet. Nothing has been said at all about marriage. The subject has not even been touched on.

JACK: Well . . . may I propose to you now?

GWENDOLEN: I think it would be an admirable opportunity. And to spare you any possible disappointment, Mr Worthing, I think it only fair to tell you quite frankly beforehand that I am fully determined to accept you.

JACK: Gwendolen!

GWENDOLEN: Yes, Mr Worthing, what have you got to say to me?

JACK: You know what I have got to say to you.

GWENDOLEN: Yes, but you don't say it.

JACK: Gwendolen, will you marry me? [Goes on his knees.]

GWENDOLEN: Of course I will, darling. How long you have been about it! I am afraid you have had very little experience in how to propose.

JACK: My own one, I have never loved anyone in the world but you.

GWENDOLEN: Yes, but men often propose for practice. I know my brother Gerald does. All my girl-friends tell me so. What wonderfully blue eyes you have, Ernest! They are quite, quite, blue. I hope you will always look at me just like that, especially when there are other people present.

[Enter Lady Bracknell.]

LADY BRACKNELL: Mr Worthing! Rise, sir, from this semi-recumbent posture. It is most indecorous.

GWENDOLEN: Mamma! [He tries to rise; she restrains him.] I must beg you to retire. This is no place for you. Besides, Mr Worthing has not quite finished yet.

LADY BRACKNELL: Finished what, may I ask?

GWENDOLEN: I am engaged to Mr Worthing, mamma. [They rise together.]

LADY BRACKNELL: Pardon me, you are not engaged to anyone. When you do become engaged to some one, I, or your father, should his health permit him, will inform you of the fact. An engagement should come on a young girl as a surprise, pleasant or unpleasant, as the case may be. It is hardly a matter that she could be allowed to arrange for herself. . . . And now I have a few questions to put to you, Mr Worthing. While I am making these inquiries, you, Gwendolen, will wait for me below in the carriage.

GWENDOLEN [reproachfully]: Mamma!

LADY BRACKNELL: In the carriage, Gwendolen! [Gwendolen goes to the door. She and Jack blow kisses to each other behind Lady Bracknell's back. Lady Bracknell looks vaguely about as if she could not understand what the noise was. Finally turns round.] Gwendolen, the carriage!

GWENDOLEN: Yes, mamma. [Goes out, looking back at Jack.]

12. Gwendolen reverts to using Jack's last name when she is reminded that he has not yet formally proposed.

LADY BRACKNELL [*sitting down*]: You can take a seat, Mr Worthing.
  [*Looking in her pocket for note-book and pencil.*]
JACK: Thank you, Lady Bracknell, I prefer standing.
LADY BRACKNELL [*pencil and note-book in hand*]: I feel bound to tell you that you
  are not down on my list of eligible young men, although I have the same list as the
  dear Duchess of Bolton has. We work together, in fact. However, I am quite ready
  to enter your name, should your answers be what a really affectionate mother
  requires. Do you smoke?
JACK: Well, yes, I must admit I smoke.
LADY BRACKNELL: I am glad to hear it. A man should always have an occupation
  of some kind. There are far too many idle men in London as it is. How old are you?
JACK: Twenty-nine.
LADY BRACKNELL: A very good age to be married at. I have always been of opinion
  that a man who desires to get married should know either everything or nothing.
  Which do you know?
JACK [*after some hesitation*]: I know nothing, Lady Bracknell.
LADY BRACKNELL: I am pleased to hear it. I do not approve of anything that
  tampers with natural ignorance. Ignorance is like a delicate exotic fruit; touch it
  and the bloom is gone. The whole theory of modern education is radically
  unsound. Fortunately in England, at any rate, education produces no effect whatsoever. If it did, it would prove a serious danger to the upper classes, and probably
  lead to acts of violence in Grosvenor Square.[13] What is your income?
JACK: Between seven and eight thousand a year.
LADY BRACKNELL [*makes a note in her book*]: In land, or in investments?
JACK: In investments, chiefly.
LADY BRACKNELL: That is satisfactory. What between the duties expected of
  one during one's lifetime, and the duties exacted from one after one's death,[14]
  land has ceased to be either a profit or a pleasure. It gives one position, and prevents one from keeping it up. That's all that can be said about land.
JACK: I have a country house with some land, of course, attached to it, about fifteen hundred acres, I believe; but I don't depend on that for my real income. In
  fact, as far as I can make out, the poachers are the only people who make anything out of it.
LADY BRACKNELL: A country house! How many bedrooms? Well, that point can
  be cleared up afterwards. You have a town house, I hope? A girl with a simple,
  unspoiled nature, like Gwendolen, could hardly be expected to reside in the country.
JACK: Well, I own a house in Belgrave Square,[15] but it is let by the year to Lady
  Bloxham. Of course, I can get it back whenever I like, at six months' notice.
LADY BRACKNELL: Lady Bloxham? I don't know her.
JACK: Oh, she goes about very little. She is a lady considerably advanced in years.
LADY BRACKNELL: Ah, nowadays that is no guarantee of respectability of char-
  acter. What number in Belgrave Square?
JACK: 149.
LADY BRACKNELL [*shaking her head*]: The unfashionable side. I thought there
  was something. However, that could easily be altered.
JACK: Do you mean the fashion, or the side?

13. A fashionable area in the West End of London.   15. A fashionable West End address in Belgravia.
14. "Death duties" are inheritance taxes.

LADY BRACKNELL [*sternly*]: Both, if necessary, I presume. What are your politics?

JACK: Well, I am afraid I really have none. I am a Liberal Unionist.[16]

LADY BRACKNELL: Oh, they count as Tories. They dine with us. Or come in the evening, at any rate. Now to minor matters. Are your parents living?

JACK: I have lost both my parents.

LADY BRACKNELL: Both? To lose one parent may be regarded as a misfortune— to lose *both* seems like carelessness. Who was your father? He was evidently a man of some wealth. Was he born in what the Radical papers call the purple of commerce, or did he rise from the ranks of the aristocracy?

JACK: I am afraid I really don't know. The fact is, Lady Bracknell, I said I had lost my parents. It would be nearer the truth to say that my parents seem to have lost me . . . I don't actually know who I am by birth. I was . . . well, I was found.

LADY BRACKNELL: Found!

JACK: The late Mr Thomas Cardew, an old gentleman of a very charitable and kindly disposition, found me, and gave me the name of Worthing, because he happened to have a first-class ticket for Worthing in his pocket at the time. Worthing is a place in Sussex. It is a seaside resort.

LADY BRACKNELL: Where did the charitable gentleman who had a first-class ticket for this seaside resort find you?

JACK [*gravely*]: In a hand-bag.

LADY BRACKNELL: A hand-bag?

JACK [*very seriously*]: Yes, Lady Bracknell. I was in a hand-bag—a somewhat large, black leather hand-bag, with handles to it—an ordinary hand-bag in fact.

LADY BRACKNELL: In what locality did this Mr James, or Thomas, Cardew come across this ordinary hand-bag?

JACK: In the cloak-room at Victoria Station. It was given to him in mistake for his own.

LADY BRACKNELL: The cloak-room at Victoria Station?

JACK: Yes. The Brighton line.

LADY BRACKNELL: The line is immaterial. Mr Worthing, I confess I feel somewhat bewildered by what you have just told me. To be born, or at any rate bred, in a hand-bag, whether it had handles or not, seems to me to display a contempt for the ordinary decencies of family life that reminds one of the worst excesses of the French Revolution. And I presume you know what that unfortunate movement led to? As for the particular locality in which the hand-bag was found, a cloakroom at a railway station might serve to conceal a social indiscretion—has probably, indeed, been used for that purpose before now—but it could hardly be regarded as an assured basis for a recognized position in good society.

JACK: May I ask you then what you would advise me to do? I need hardly say I would do anything in the world to ensure Gwendolen's happiness.

LADY BRACKNELL: I would strongly advise you, Mr Worthing, to try and acquire some relations as soon as possible, and to make a definite effort to produce at any rate one parent, of either sex, before the season is quite over.

JACK: Well, I don't see how I could possibly manage to do that. I can produce the hand-bag at any moment. It is in my dressing-room at home. I really think that should satisfy you, Lady Bracknell.

LADY BRACKNELL: Me, sir! What has it to do with me? You can hardly imagine that I and Lord Bracknell would dream of allowing our only daughter—a girl

---

16. In 1886 Liberal Unionists joined the Conservatives (the "Tories") in voting against the Liberal Prime Minister Gladstone's bill supporting Home Rule for Ireland.

brought up with the utmost care—to marry into a cloak-room, and form an alliance with a parcel? Good morning, Mr Worthing!

[*Lady Bracknell sweeps out in majestic indignation.*]

JACK: Good morning! [*Algernon, from the other room, strikes up the Wedding March. Jack looks perfectly furious, and goes to the door.*] For goodness' sake don't play that ghastly tune, Algy! How idiotic you are!

[*The music stops, and Algernon enters cheerily.*]

ALGERNON: Didn't it go off all right, old boy? You don't mean to say Gwendolen refused you? I know it is a way she has. She is always refusing people. I think it is most ill-natured of her.

JACK: Oh, Gwendolen is as right as a trivet.[17] As far as she is concerned, we are engaged. Her mother is perfectly unbearable. Never met such a Gorgon[18] . . . I don't really know what a Gorgon is like, but I am quite sure Lady Bracknell is one. In any case, she is a monster, without being a myth, which is rather unfair . . . I beg your pardon, Algy, I suppose I shouldn't talk about your own aunt in that way before you.

ALGERNON: My dear boy, I love hearing my relations abused. It is the only thing that makes me put up with them at all. Relations are simply a tedious pack of people, who haven't got the remotest knowledge of how to live, nor the smallest instinct about when to die.

JACK: Oh, that is nonsense!

ALGERNON: It isn't!

JACK: Well, I won't argue about the matter. You always want to argue about things.

ALGERNON: That is exactly what things were originally made for.

JACK: Upon my word, if I thought that, I'd shoot myself . . . [*A pause.*] You don't think there is any chance of Gwendolen becoming like her mother in about a hundred and fifty years, do you Algy?

ALGERNON: All women become like their mothers. That is their tragedy. No man does. That's his.

JACK: Is that clever?

ALGERNON: It is perfectly phrased! and quite as true as any observation in civilized life should be.

JACK: I am sick to death of cleverness. Everybody is clever nowadays. You can't go anywhere without meeting clever people. The thing has become an absolute public nuisance. I wish to goodness we had a few fools left.

ALGERNON: We have.

JACK: I should extremely like to meet them. What do they talk about?

ALGERNON: The fools? Oh! about the clever people, of course.

JACK: What fools!

ALGERNON: By the way, did you tell Gwendolen the truth about your being Ernest in town, and Jack in the country?

JACK [*in a very patronizing manner*]: My dear fellow, the truth isn't quite the sort of thing one tells to a nice sweet refined girl. What extraordinary ideas you have about the way to behave to a woman!

ALGERNON: The only way to behave to a woman is to make love to her,[19] if she is pretty, and to someone else if she is plain.

JACK: Oh, that is nonsense.

---

17. Reliable and steady, like a stand used to hold a pot over the fire.

18. A mythical female monster with snakes for hair.

19. I.e., to flirt with or court her.

ALGERNON: What about your brother? What about the profligate Ernest?

JACK: Oh, before the end of the week I shall have got rid of him. I'll say he died in Paris of apoplexy. Lots of people die of apoplexy, quite suddenly, don't they?

ALGERNON: Yes, but it's hereditary, my dear fellow. It's a sort of thing that runs in families. You had much better say a severe chill.

JACK: You are sure a severe chill isn't hereditary, or anything of that kind?

ALGERNON: Of course it isn't!

JACK: Very well, then. My poor brother Ernest is carried off suddenly in Paris, by a severe chill. That gets rid of him.

ALGERNON: But I thought you said that . . . Miss Cardew was a little too much interested in your poor brother Ernest? Won't she feel his loss a good deal?

JACK: Oh, that is all right. Cecily is not a silly romantic girl, I am glad to say. She has got a capital appetite, goes long walks, and pays no attention at all to her lessons.

ALGERNON: I would rather like to see Cecily.

JACK: I will take very good care you never do. She is excessively pretty, and she is only just eighteen.

ALGERNON: Have you told Gwendolen yet that you have an excessively pretty ward who is only just eighteen?

JACK: Oh! one doesn't blurt these things out to people. Cecily and Gwendolen are perfectly certain to be extremely great friends. I'll bet you anything you like that half an hour after they have met, they will be calling each other sister.

ALGERNON: Women only do that when they have called each other a lot of other things first. Now, my dear boy, if we want to get a good table at Willis's, we really must go and dress. Do you know it is nearly seven?

JACK [*irritably*]: Oh! it always is nearly seven.

ALGERNON: Well, I'm hungry.

JACK: I never knew you when you weren't. . . .

ALGERNON: What shall we do after dinner? Go to a theatre?

JACK: Oh no! I loathe listening.

ALGERNON: Well, let us go to the Club?

JACK: Oh, no! I hate talking.

ALGERNON: Well, we might trot round to the Empire[20] at ten?

JACK: Oh, no! I can't bear looking at things. It is so silly.

ALGERNON: Well, what shall we do?

JACK: Nothing!

ALGERNON: It is awfully hard work doing nothing. However, I don't mind hard work where there is no definite object of any kind.

[*Enter Lane.*]

LANE: Miss Fairfax.

[*Enter Gwendolen. Lane goes out.*]

ALGERNON: Gwendolen, upon my word!

GWENDOLEN: Algy, kindly turn your back. I have something very particular to say to Mr Worthing.

ALGERNON: Really, Gwendolen, I don't think I can allow this at all.

GWENDOLEN: Algy, you always adopt a strictly immoral attitude towards life. You are not quite old enough to do that.

[*Algernon retires to the fireplace.*]

20. A popular music hall.

JACK: My own darling!

GWENDOLEN: Ernest, we may never be married. From the expression on mamma's face I fear we never shall. Few parents nowadays pay any regard to what their children say to them. The old-fashioned respect for the young is fast dying out. Whatever influence I ever had over mamma, I lost at the age of three. But although she may prevent us from becoming man and wife, and I may marry someone else, and marry often, nothing that she can possibly do can alter my eternal devotion to you.

JACK: Dear Gwendolen!

GWENDOLEN: The story of your romantic origin, as related to me by mamma, with unpleasing comments, has naturally stirred the deeper fibres of my nature. Your Christian name has an irresistible fascination. The simplicity of your character makes you exquisitely incomprehensible to me. Your town address at the Albany I have. What is your address in the country?

JACK: The Manor House, Woolton, Hertfordshire.

[*Algernon, who has been carefully listening, smiles to himself, and writes the address on his shirt-cuff. Then picks up the Railway Guide.*]

GWENDOLEN: There is a good postal service, I suppose? It may be necessary to do something desperate. That of course will require serious consideration. I will communicate with you daily.

JACK: My own one!

GWENDOLEN: How long do you remain in town?

JACK: Till Monday.

GWENDOLEN: Good! Algy, you may turn round now.

ALGERNON: Thanks, I've turned round already.

GWENDOLEN: You may also ring the bell.

JACK: You will let me see you to your carriage, my own darling?

GWENDOLEN: Certainly.

JACK [*to Lane, who now enters*]: I will see Miss Fairfax out.

LANE: Yes, sir. [*Jack and Gwendolen go off.*]

[*Lane presents several letters on a salver to Algernon. It is to be surmised that they are bills, as Algernon, after looking at the envelopes, tears them up.*]

ALGERNON: A glass of sherry, Lane.

LANE: Yes, sir.

ALGERNON: Tomorrow, Lane, I'm going Bunburying.

LANE: Yes, sir.

ALGERNON: I shall probably not be back till Monday. You can put up my dress clothes, my smoking jacket, and all the Bunbury suits . . .

LANE: Yes, sir. [*Handing sherry.*]

ALGERNON: I hope tomorrow will be a fine day, Lane.

LANE: It never is, sir.

ALGERNON: Lane, you're a perfect pessimist.

LANE: I do my best to give satisfaction, sir.

[*Enter Jack. Lane goes off.*]

JACK: There's a sensible, intellectual girl! the only girl I ever cared for in my life. [*Algernon is laughing immoderately.*] What on earth are you so amused at?

ALGERNON: Oh, I'm a little anxious about poor Bunbury, that is all.

JACK: If you don't take care, your friend Bunbury will get you into a serious scrape some day.

ALGERNON: I love scrapes. They are the only things that are never serious.

JACK: Oh, that's nonsense, Algy. You never talk anything but nonsense.

ALGERNON: Nobody ever does.

[*Jack looks indignantly at him, and leaves the room. Algernon lights a cigarette, reads his shirt-cuff, and smiles.*]   ACT DROP

SECOND ACT

SCENE: *Garden at the Manor House. A flight of gray stone steps leads up to the house. The garden, an old-fashioned one, full of roses. Time of year, July. Basket chairs, and a table covered with books, are set under a large yew tree.*

[*Miss Prism discovered seated at the table. Cecily is at the back watering flowers.*]

MISS PRISM [*calling*]: Cecily, Cecily! Surely such a utilitarian occupation as the watering of flowers is rather Moulton's duty than yours? Especially at a moment when intellectual pleasures await you. Your German grammar is on the table. Pray open it at page fifteen. We will repeat yesterday's lesson.

CECILY [*coming over very slowly*]: But I don't like German. It isn't at all a becoming language. I know perfectly well that I look quite plain after my German lesson.

MISS PRISM: Child, you know how anxious your guardian is that you should improve yourself in every way. He laid particular stress on your German, as he was leaving for town yesterday. Indeed, he always lays stress on your German when he is leaving for town.

CECILY: Dear Uncle Jack is so very serious! Sometimes he is so serious that I think he cannot be quite well.

MISS PRISM [*drawing herself up*]: Your guardian enjoys the best of health, and his gravity of demeanour is especially to be commended in one so comparatively young as he is. I know no one who has a higher sense of duty and responsibility.

CECILY: I suppose that is why he often looks a little bored when we three are together.

MISS PRISM: Cecily! I am surprised at you. Mr Worthing has many troubles in his life. Idle merriment and triviality would be out of place in his conversation. You must remember his constant anxiety about that unfortunate young man his brother.

CECILY: I wish Uncle Jack would allow that unfortunate young man, his brother, to come down here sometimes. We might have a good influence over him, Miss Prism. I am sure you certainly would. You know German, and geology, and things of that kind influence a man very much. [*Cecily begins to write in her diary.*]

MISS PRISM [*shaking her head*]: I do not think that even I could produce any effect on a character that according to his own brother's admission is irretrievably weak and vacillating. Indeed I am not sure that I would desire to reclaim him. I am not in favour of this modern mania for turning bad people into good people at a moment's notice. As a man sows so let him reap.[1] You must put away your diary, Cecily. I really don't see why you should keep a diary at all.

CECILY: I keep a diary in order to enter the wonderful secrets of my life. If I didn't write them down I should probably forget all about them.

MISS PRISM: Memory, my dear Cecily, is the diary that we all carry about with us.

CECILY: Yes, but it usually chronicles the things that have never happened, and couldn't possibly have happened. I believe that Memory is responsible for nearly all the three-volume novels that Mudie sends us.[2]

1. "Be not deceived; God is not mocked: for whatsoever a man soweth, that shall he also reap" (Galatians 6.7).
2. Mudie's Select Library lent novels to subscribers for a fee; at the time of this play, both Mudie's and the three-volume novel were becoming outmoded.

MISS PRISM: Do not speak slightly of the three-volume novel, Cecily. I wrote one myself in earlier days.

CECILY: Did you really, Miss Prism? How wonderfully clever you are! I hope it did not end happily? I don't like novels that end happily. They depress me so much.

MISS PRISM: The good ended happily, and the bad unhappily. That is what Fiction means.

CECILY: I suppose so. But it seems very unfair. And was your novel ever published?

MISS PRISM: Alas! no. The manuscript unfortunately was abandoned. I use the word in the sense of lost or mislaid. To your work, child, these speculations are profitless.

CECILY [smiling]: But I see dear Dr Chasuble coming up through the garden.

MISS PRISM [rising and advancing]: Dr Chasuble! This is indeed a pleasure.
      [Enter Canon Chasuble.][3]

CHASUBLE: And how are we this morning? Miss Prism, you are, I trust, well?

CECILY: Miss Prism has just been complaining of a slight headache. I think it would do her so much good to have a short stroll with you in the Park, Dr Chasuble.

MISS PRISM: Cecily, I have not mentioned anything about a headache.

CECILY: No, dear Miss Prism, I know that, but I felt instinctively that you had a headache. Indeed I was thinking about that, and not about my German lesson, when the Rector came in.

CHASUBLE: I hope Cecily, you are not inattentive.

CECILY: Oh, I am afraid I am.

CHASUBLE: That is strange. Were I fortunate enough to be Miss Prism's pupil, I would hang upon her lips. [Miss Prism glares.] I spoke metaphorically.—My metaphor was drawn from bees. Ahem! Mr Worthing I suppose, has not returned from town yet?

MISS PRISM: We do not expect him till Monday afternoon.

CHASUBLE: Ah yes, he usually likes to spend his Sunday in London. He is not one of those whose sole aim is enjoyment, as, by all accounts, that unfortunate young man his brother seems to be. But I must not disturb Egeria[4] and her pupil any longer.

MISS PRISM: Egeria? My name is Laetitia, Doctor.

CHASUBLE [bowing]: A classical allusion merely, drawn from the Pagan authors. I shall see you both no doubt at Evensong?[5]

MISS PRISM: I think, dear Doctor, I will have a stroll with you. I find I have a headache after all, and a walk might do it good.

CHASUBLE: With pleasure, Miss Prism, with pleasure. We might go as far as the schools and back.

MISS PRISM: That would be delightful. Cecily, you will read your Political Economy in my absence. The chapter on the Fall of the Rupee you may omit.[6] It is somewhat too sensational. Even these metallic problems have their melodramatic side. [Goes down the garden with Dr Chasuble.]

CECILY [picks up books and throws them back on table]: Horrid Political Economy! Horrid Geography! Horrid, horrid German!
      [Enter Merriman with a card on a salver.]

MERRIMAN: Mr Ernest Worthing has just driven over from the station. He has brought his luggage with him.

CECILY [takes the card and reads it]: "Mr Ernest Worthing, B.4 The Albany, W." Uncle Jack's brother! Did you tell him Mr Worthing was in town?

3. A canon is a cathedral clergyman; a chasuble is a vestment.
4. Roman goddess of fountains; her name was used for a woman who instructed other women.
5. Evening church services.
6. The declining value of the Indian rupee would hurt British civil servants in India, who were paid in rupees.

MERRIMAN: Yes, Miss. He seemed very much disappointed. I mentioned that you and Miss Prism were in the garden. He said he was anxious to speak to you privately for a moment.

CECILY: Ask Mr Ernest Worthing to come here. I suppose you had better talk to the housekeeper about a room for him.

MERRIMAN: Yes, Miss. [*Merriman goes off.*]

CECILY: I have never met any really wicked person before. I feel rather frightened. I am so afraid he will look just like everyone else.

[*Enter Algernon, very gay and debonair.*]

He does!

ALGERNON [*raising his hat*]: You are my little cousin Cecily, I'm sure.

CECILY: You are under some strange mistake. I am not little. In fact, I believe I am more than usually tall for my age. [*Algernon is rather taken aback.*] But I am your cousin Cecily. You, I see from your card, are Uncle Jack's brother, my cousin Ernest, my wicked cousin Ernest.

ALGERNON: Oh! I am not really wicked at all, cousin Cecily. You mustn't think that I am wicked.

CECILY: If you are not, then you have certainly been deceiving us all in a very inexcusable manner. I hope you have not been leading a double life, pretending to be wicked and being really good all the time. That would be hypocrisy.

ALGERNON [*looks at her in amazement*]: Oh! Of course I have been rather reckless.

CECILY: I am glad to hear it.

ALGERNON: In fact, now you mention the subject, I have been very bad in my own small way.

CECILY: I don't think you should be so proud of that, although I am sure it must have been very pleasant.

ALGERNON: It is much pleasanter being here with you.

CECILY: I can't understand how you are here at all. Uncle Jack won't be back till Monday afternoon.

ALGERNON: That is a great disappointment. I am obliged to go up by the first train on Monday morning. I have a business appointment that I am anxious . . . to miss.

CECILY: Couldn't you miss it anywhere but in London?

ALGERNON: No: the appointment is in London.

CECILY: Well, I know, of course, how important it is not to keep a business engagement, if one wants to retain any sense of the beauty of life, but still I think you had better wait till Uncle Jack arrives. I know he wants to speak to you about your emigrating.

ALGERNON: About my what?

CECILY: Your emigrating. He has gone up to buy your outfit.

ALGERNON: I certainly wouldn't let Jack buy my outfit. He has no taste in neckties at all.

CECILY: I don't think you will require neckties. Uncle Jack is sending you to Australia.[7]

ALGERNON: Australia! I'd sooner die.

CECILY: Well, he said at dinner on Wednesday night, that you would have to choose between this world, the next world, and Australia.

ALGERNON: Oh, well! The accounts I have received of Australia and the next world are not particularly encouraging. This world is good enough for me, cousin Cecily.

CECILY: Yes, but are you good enough for it?

---

7. Australia was no longer a penal colony, but it was still a place where families sent their ne'er-do-well sons.

ALGERNON: I'm afraid I'm not that. That is why I want you to reform me. You might make that your mission, if you don't mind, cousin Cecily.

CECILY: I'm afraid I've no time, this afternoon.

ALGERNON: Well, would you mind my reforming myself this afternoon?

CECILY: It is rather Quixotic[8] of you. But I think you should try.

ALGERNON: I will. I feel better already.

CECILY: You are looking a little worse.

ALGERNON: That is because I am hungry.

CECILY: How thoughtless of me. I should have remembered that when one is going to lead an entirely new life, one requires regular and wholesome meals. Won't you come in?

ALGERNON: Thank you. Might I have a buttonhole[9] first? I never have any appetite unless I have a buttonhole first.

CECILY: A Maréchal Niel?[10] [*Picks up scissors.*]

ALGERNON: No, I'd sooner have a pink rose.

CECILY: Why? [*Cuts a flower.*]

ALGERNON: Because you are like a pink rose, Cousin Cecily.

CECILY: I don't think it can be right for you to talk to me like that. Miss Prism never says such things to me.

ALGERNON: Then Miss Prism is a short-sighted old lady. [*Cecily puts the rose in his buttonhole.*] You are the prettiest girl I ever saw.

CECILY: Miss Prism says that all good looks are a snare.

ALGERNON: They are a snare that every sensible man would like to be caught in.

CECILY: Oh! I don't think I would care to catch a sensible man. I shouldn't know what to talk to him about.

   [*They pass into the house. Miss Prism and Dr Chasuble return.*]

MISS PRISM: You are too much alone, dear Dr Chasuble. You should get married. A misanthrope I can understand—a womanthrope, never!

CHASUBLE [*with a scholar's shudder*][11]: Believe me, I do not deserve so neologistic a phrase. The precept as well as the practice of the Primitive Church was distinctly against matrimony.[12]

MISS PRISM [*sententiously*]: That is obviously the reason why the Primitive Church has not lasted up to the present day. And you do not seem to realize, dear Doctor, that by persistently remaining single, a man converts himself into a permanent public temptation. Men should be more careful; this very celibacy leads weaker vessels astray.

CHASUBLE: But is a man not equally attractive when married?

MISS PRISM: No married man is ever attractive except to his wife.

CHASUBLE: And often, I've been told, not even to her.

MISS PRISM: That depends on the intellectual sympathies of the woman. Maturity can always be depended on. Ripeness can be trusted. Young women are green. [*Dr Chasuble starts.*] I spoke horticulturally. My metaphor was drawn from fruits. But where is Cecily?

---

8. Hopelessly idealistic, like Don Quixote.
9. A flower to wear in his lapel.
10. A yellow rose.
11. He shudders because Miss Prism has mangled the language by coining a word, "womanthrope," to describe someone who dislikes women, instead of using the cor-

rect term, "misogynist." A neologism is a newly invented word.
12. Protestant clergy are allowed to marry, but as a High Church Anglican, Chasuble is interested in preserving the rituals and practices of the early Catholic church.

CHASUBLE: Perhaps she followed us to the schools.

[*Enter Jack slowly from the back of the garden. He is dressed in the deepest mourning, with crape hat-band and black gloves.*]

MISS PRISM: Mr Worthing!

CHASUBLE: Mr Worthing?

MISS PRISM: This is indeed a surprise. We did not look for you till Monday afternoon.

JACK [*shakes Miss Prism's hand in a tragic manner*]: I have returned sooner than I expected. Dr Chasuble, I hope you are well?

CHASUBLE: Dear Mr Worthing, I trust this garb of woe does not betoken some terrible calamity?

JACK: My brother.

MISS PRISM: More shameful debts and extravagance?

CHASUBLE: Still leading his life of pleasure?

JACK [*shaking his head*]: Dead!

CHASUBLE: Your brother Ernest dead?

JACK: Quite dead.

MISS PRISM: What a lesson for him! I trust he will profit by it.

CHASUBLE: Mr Worthing, I offer you my sincere condolence. You have at least the consolation of knowing that you were always the most generous and forgiving of brothers.

JACK: Poor Ernest! He had many faults, but it is a sad, sad blow.

CHASUBLE: Very sad indeed. Were you with him at the end?

JACK: No. He died abroad; in Paris, in fact. I had a telegram last night from the manager of the Grand Hotel.

CHASUBLE: Was the cause of death mentioned?

JACK: A severe chill, it seems.

MISS PRISM: As a man sows, so shall he reap.

CHASUBLE [*raising his hand*]: Charity, dear Miss Prism, charity! None of us are perfect. I myself am peculiarly susceptible to draughts. Will the interment take place here?

JACK: No. He seemed to have expressed a desire to be buried in Paris.

CHASUBLE: In Paris! [*Shakes his head.*] I fear that hardly points to any very serious state of mind at the last. You would no doubt wish me to make some slight allusion to this tragic domestic affliction next Sunday. [*Jack presses his hand convulsively.*] My sermon on the meaning of the manna in the wilderness[13] can be adapted to almost any occasion, joyful, or, as in the present case, distressing. [*All sigh.*] I have preached it at harvest celebrations, christenings, confirmations, on days of humiliation and festal days. The last time I delivered it was in the Cathedral, as a charity sermon on behalf of the Society for the Prevention of Discontent among the Upper Orders. The Bishop, who was present, was much struck by some of the analogies I drew.

JACK: Ah! that reminds me, you mentioned christenings I think, Dr Chasuble? I suppose you know how to christen all right? [*Dr Chasuble looks astounded.*] I mean, of course, you are continually christening, aren't you?

MISS PRISM: It is, I regret to say, one of the Rector's most constant duties in this parish. I have often spoken to the poorer classes on the subject. But they don't seem to know what thrift is.

CHASUBLE: But is there any particular infant in whom you are interested, Mr Worthing? Your brother was, I believe, unmarried, was he not?

---

13. An episode in Exodus 16.

JACK: Oh, yes.

MISS PRISM [*bitterly*]: People who live entirely for pleasure usually are.

JACK: But it is not for any child, dear Doctor. I am very fond of children. No! the fact is, I would like to be christened myself, this afternoon, if you have nothing better to do.

CHASUBLE: But surely, Mr Worthing, you have been christened already?

JACK: I don't remember anything about it.

CHASUBLE: But have you any grave doubts on the subject?

JACK: I certainly intend to have. Of course I don't know if the thing would bother you in any way, or if you think I am a little too old now.

CHASUBLE: Not at all. The sprinkling, and, indeed, the immersion of adults is a perfectly canonical practice.

JACK: Immersion!

CHASUBLE: You need have no apprehensions. Sprinkling is all that is necessary, or indeed I think advisable. Our weather is so changeable. At what hour would you wish the ceremony performed?

JACK: Oh, I might trot round about five if that would suit you.

CHASUBLE: Perfectly, perfectly! In fact I have two similar ceremonies to perform at that time. A case of twins that occurred recently in one of the outlying cottages on your own estate. Poor Jenkins the carter, a most hard-working man.

JACK: Oh! I don't see much fun in being christened along with other babies. It would be childish. Would half-past five do?

CHASUBLE: Admirably! Admirably! [*Takes out watch.*] And now, dear Mr Worthing, I will not intrude any longer into a house of sorrow. I would merely beg you not to be too much bowed down by grief. What seem to us bitter trials are often blessings in disguise.

MISS PRISM: This seems to me a blessing of an extremely obvious kind.

[*Enter Cecily from the house.*]

CECILY: Uncle Jack! Oh, I am pleased to see you back. But what horrid clothes you have got on! Do go and change them.

MISS PRISM: Cecily!

CHASUBLE: My child! my child!

[*Cecily goes towards Jack; he kisses her brow in a melancholy manner.*]

CECILY: What is the matter, Uncle Jack? Do look happy! You look as if you had toothache, and I have got such a surprise for you. Who do you think is in the dining-room? Your brother!

JACK: Who?

CECILY: Your brother Ernest. He arrived about half an hour ago.

JACK: What nonsense! I haven't got a brother.

CECILY: Oh, don't say that. However badly he may have behaved to you in the past he is still your brother. You couldn't be so heartless as to disown him. I'll tell him to come out. And you will shake hands with him, won't you, Uncle Jack? [*Runs back into the house.*]

CHASUBLE: These are very joyful tidings.

MISS PRISM: After we had all been resigned to his loss, his sudden return seems to me peculiarly distressing.

JACK: My brother is in the dining-room? I don't know what it all means. I think it is perfectly absurd.

[*Enter Algernon and Cecily hand in hand. They come slowly up to Jack.*]

JACK: Good heavens! [*Motions Algernon away.*]

ALGERNON: Brother John, I have come down from town to tell you that I am very sorry for all the trouble I have given you, and that I intend to lead a better life in the future.

[*Jack glares at him and does not take his hand.*]

CECILY: Uncle Jack, you are not going to refuse your own brother's hand?

JACK: Nothing will induce me to take his hand. I think his coming down here disgraceful. He knows perfectly well why.

CECILY: Uncle Jack, do be nice. There is some good in everyone. Ernest has just been telling me about his poor invalid friend Mr Bunbury whom he goes to visit so often. And surely there must be much good in one who is kind to an invalid, and leaves the pleasures of London to sit by a bed of pain.

JACK: Oh! he has been talking about Bunbury has he?

CECILY: Yes, he has told me all about poor Mr Bunbury, and his terrible state of health.

JACK: Bunbury! Well, I won't have him talk to you about Bunbury or about anything else. It is enough to drive one perfectly frantic.

ALGERNON: Of course I admit that the faults were all on my side. But I must say that I think that Brother John's coldness to me is peculiarly painful. I expected a more enthusiastic welcome, especially considering it is the first time I have come here.

CECILY: Uncle Jack, if you don't shake hands with Ernest I will never forgive you.

JACK: Never forgive me?

CECILY: Never, never, never!

JACK: Well, this is the last time I shall ever do it. [*Shakes hands with Algernon and glares.*]

CHASUBLE: It's pleasant, is it not, to see so perfect a reconciliation? I think we might leave the two brothers together.

MISS PRISM: Cecily, you will come with us.

CECILY: Certainly, Miss Prism. My little task of reconciliation is over.

CHASUBLE: You have done a beautiful action today, dear child.

MISS PRISM: We must not be premature in our judgements.

CECILY: I feel very happy. [*They all go off.*]

JACK: You young scoundrel, Algy, you must get out of this place as soon as possible. I don't allow any Bunburying here.

[*Enter Merriman.*]

MERRIMAN: I have put Mr Ernest's things in the room next to yours, sir. I suppose that is all right?

JACK: What?

MERRIMAN: Mr Ernest's luggage, sir. I have unpacked it and put it in the room next to your own.

JACK: His luggage?

MERRIMAN: Yes, sir. Three portmanteaus, a dressing-case, two hat-boxes, and a large luncheon-basket.

ALGERNON: I am afraid I can't stay more than a week this time.

JACK: Merriman, order the dog-cart[14] at once. Mr Ernest has been suddenly called back to town.

MERRIMAN: Yes, sir. [*Goes back into the house.*]

ALGERNON: What a fearful liar you are, Jack. I have not been called back to town at all.

14. A horse-drawn cart with seats, and a box for hunting dogs.

JACK: Yes, you have.

ALGERNON: I haven't heard anyone call me.

JACK: Your duty as a gentleman calls you back.

ALGERNON: My duty as a gentleman has never interfered with my pleasures in the smallest degree.

JACK: I can quite understand that.

ALGERNON: Well, Cecily is a darling.

JACK: You are not to talk of Miss Cardew like that. I don't like it.

ALGERNON: Well, I don't like your clothes. You look perfectly ridiculous in them. Why on earth don't you go up and change? It is perfectly childish to be in deep mourning for a man who is actually staying for a whole week with you in your house as a guest. I call it grotesque.

JACK: You are certainly not staying with me for a whole week as a guest or anything else. You have got to leave . . . by the four-five train.

ALGERNON: I certainly won't leave you so long as you are in mourning. It would be most unfriendly. If I were in mourning you would stay with me, I suppose. I should think it very unkind if you didn't.

JACK: Well, will you go if I change my clothes?

ALGERNON: Yes, if you are not too long. I never saw anybody take so long to dress, and with such little result.

JACK: Well, at any rate, that is better than being always over-dressed as you are.

ALGERNON: If I am occasionally a little over-dressed, I make up for it by being always immensely over-educated.

JACK: Your vanity is ridiculous, your conduct an outrage, and your presence in my garden utterly absurd. However, you have got to catch the four-five, and I hope you will have a pleasant journey back to town. This Bunburying, as you call it, has not been a great success for you. [*Goes into the house.*]

ALGERNON: I think it has been a great success. I'm in love with Cecily, and that is everything.

[*Enter Cecily at the back of the garden. She picks up the can and begins to water the flowers.*]

But I must see her before I go, and make arrangements for another Bunbury. Ah, there she is.

CECILY: Oh, I merely came back to water the roses. I thought you were with Uncle Jack.

ALGERNON: He's gone to order the dog-cart for me.

CECILY: Oh, is he going to take you for a nice drive?

ALGERNON: He's going to send me away.

CECILY: Then have we got to part?

ALGERNON: I am afraid so. It's a painful parting.

CECILY: It is always painful to part from people whom one has known for a very brief space of time. The absence of old friends one can endure with equanimity. But even a momentary separation from anyone to whom one has just been introduced is almost unbearable.

ALGERNON: Thank you.

[*Enter Merriman.*]

MERRIMAN: The dog-cart is at the door, sir.

[*Algernon looks appealingly at Cecily.*]

CECILY: It can wait, Merriman . . . for . . . five minutes.

MERRIMAN: Yes, Miss. [*Exit Merriman.*]

ALGERNON: I hope, Cecily, I shall not offend you if I state quite frankly and openly that you seem to me to be in every way the visible personification of absolute perfection.

CECILY: I think your frankness does you great credit, Ernest. If you will allow me I will copy your remarks into my diary. [*Goes over to table and begins writing in diary.*]

ALGERNON: Do you really keep a diary? I'd give anything to look at it. May I?

CECILY: Oh no. [*Puts her hand over it.*] You see, it is simply a very young girl's record of her own thoughts and impressions, and consequently meant for publication. When it appears in volume form I hope you will order a copy. But pray, Ernest, don't stop. I delight in taking down from dictation. I have reached "absolute perfection." You can go on. I am quite ready for more.

ALGERNON [*somewhat taken aback*]: Ahem! Ahem!

CECILY: Oh, don't cough, Ernest. When one is dictating one should speak fluently and not cough. Besides, I don't know how to spell a cough. [*Writes as Algernon speaks.*]

ALGERNON [*speaking very rapidly*]: Cecily, ever since I first looked upon your wonderful and incomparable beauty, I have dared to love you wildly, passionately, devotedly, hopelessly.

CECILY: I don't think that you should tell me that you love me wildly, passionately, devotedly, hopelessly. Hopelessly doesn't seem to make much sense, does it?

ALGERNON: Cecily!

[*Enter Merriman.*]

MERRIMAN: The dog-cart is waiting, sir.

ALGERNON: Tell it to come round next week, at the same hour.

MERRIMAN [*looks at Cecily, who makes no sign*]: Yes, sir. [*Merriman retires.*]

CECILY: Uncle Jack would be very much annoyed if he knew you were staying on till next week, at the same hour.

ALGERNON: Oh, I don't care about Jack. I don't care for anybody in the whole world but you. I love you, Cecily. You will marry me, won't you?

CECILY: You silly boy! Of course. Why, we have been engaged for the last three months.

ALGERNON: For the last three months?

CECILY: Yes, it will be exactly three months on Thursday.

ALGERNON: But how did we become engaged?

CECILY: Well, ever since dear Uncle Jack first confessed to us that he had a younger brother who was very wicked and bad, you of course have formed the chief topic of conversation between myself and Miss Prism. And of course a man who is much talked about is always very attractive. One feels there must be something in him after all. I daresay it was foolish of me, but I fell in love with you, Ernest.

ALGERNON: Darling! And when was the engagement actually settled?

CECILY: On the 14th of February last. Worn out by your entire ignorance of my existence, I determined to end the matter one way or the other, and after a long struggle with myself I accepted you under this dear old tree here. The next day I bought this little ring in your name, and this is the little bangle with the true lovers' knot I promised you always to wear.

ALGERNON: Did I give you this? It's very pretty, isn't it?

CECILY: Yes, you've wonderfully good taste, Ernest. It's the excuse I've always given for your leading such a bad life. And this is the box in which I keep all your dear letters. [*Kneels at table, opens box, and produces letters tied up with blue ribbon.*]

ALGERNON: My letters! But my own sweet Cecily, I have never written you any letters.

CECILY: You need hardly remind me of that, Ernest. I remember only too well that I was forced to write your letters for you. I wrote always three times a week, and sometimes oftener.

ALGERNON: Oh, do let me read them, Cecily?

CECILY: Oh, I couldn't possibly. They would make you far too conceited. [*Replaces box.*] The three you wrote me after I had broken off the engagement are so beautiful, and so badly spelled, that even now I can hardly read them without crying a little.

ALGERNON: But was our engagement ever broken off?

CECILY: Of course it was. On the 22nd of last March. You can see the entry if you like. [*Shows diary.*] "Today I broke off my engagement with Ernest. I feel it is better to do so. The weather still continues charming."

ALGERNON: But why on earth did you break it off? What had I done? I had done nothing at all. Cecily, I am very much hurt indeed to hear you broke it off. Particularly when the weather was so charming.

CECILY: It would hardly have been a really serious engagement if it hadn't been broken off at least once. But I forgave you before the week was out.

ALGERNON [*crossing to her, and kneeling*]: What a perfect angel you are, Cecily.

CECILY: You dear romantic boy. [*He kisses her, she puts her fingers through his hair.*] I hope your hair curls naturally, does it?

ALGERNON: Yes, darling, with a little help from others.

CECILY: I am so glad.

ALGERNON: You'll never break off our engagement again, Cecily?

CECILY: I don't think I could break it off now that I have actually met you. Besides, of course, there is the question of your name.

ALGERNON: Yes, of course. [*Nervously.*]

CECILY: You must not laugh at me, darling, but it had always been a girlish dream of mine to love some one whose name was Ernest. [*Algernon rises, Cecily also.*] There is something in that name that seems to inspire absolute confidence. I pity any poor married woman whose husband is not called Ernest.

ALGERNON: But, my dear child, do you mean to say you could not love me if I had some other name?

CECILY: But what name?

ALGERNON: Oh, any name you like—Algernon—for instance . . .

CECILY: But I don't like the name of Algernon.

ALGERNON: Well, my own dear, sweet, loving little darling, I really can't see why you should object to the name of Algernon. It is not at all a bad name. In fact, it is rather an aristocratic name. Half of the chaps who get into the Bankruptcy Court are called Algernon. But seriously, Cecily . . . [*moving to her*] . . . if my name was Algy, couldn't you love me?

CECILY [*rising*]: I might respect you, Ernest, I might admire your character, but I fear that I should not be able to give you my undivided attention.

ALGERNON: Ahem! Cecily! [*Picking up hat.*] Your Rector here is, I suppose, thoroughly experienced in the practice of all the rites and ceremonials of the Church?

CECILY: Oh yes. Dr Chasuble is a most learned man. He has never written a single book, so you can imagine how much he knows.

ALGERNON: I must see him at once on a most important christening—I mean on most important business.

CECILY: Oh!

ALGERNON: I shan't be away more than half an hour.

CECILY: Considering that we have been engaged since February the 14th, and that I only met you today for the first time, I think it is rather hard that you should leave me for so long a period as half an hour. Couldn't you make it twenty minutes?

ALGERNON: I'll be back in no time. [*Kisses her and rushes down the garden.*]

CECILY: What an impetuous boy he is! I like his hair so much. I must enter his proposal in my diary.

[*Enter Merriman.*]

MERRIMAN: A Miss Fairfax has just called to see Mr Worthing. On very important business Miss Fairfax states.

CECILY: Isn't Mr Worthing in his library?

MERRIMAN: Mr Worthing went over in the direction of the Rectory some time ago.

CECILY: Pray ask the lady to come out here; Mr Worthing is sure to be back soon. And you can bring tea.

MERRIMAN: Yes, Miss. [*Goes out.*]

CECILY: Miss Fairfax! I suppose one of the many good elderly women who are associated with Uncle Jack in some of his philanthropic work in London. I don't quite like women who are interested in philanthropic work. I think it is so forward of them.

[*Enter Merriman.*]

MERRIMAN: Miss Fairfax.

[*Enter Gwendolen. Exit Merriman.*]

CECILY [*advancing to meet her*]: Pray let me introduce myself to you. My name is Cecily Cardew.

GWENDOLEN: Cecily Cardew? [*Moving to her and shaking hands.*] What a very sweet name! Something tells me that we are going to be great friends. I like you already more than I can say. My first impressions of people are never wrong.

CECILY: How nice of you to like me so much after we have known each other such a comparatively short time. Pray sit down.

GWENDOLEN [*still standing up*]: I may call you Cecily, may I not?

CECILY: With pleasure!

GWENDOLEN: And you will always call me Gwendolen, won't you.

CECILY: If you wish.

GWENDOLEN: Then that is all quite settled, is it not?

CECILY: I hope so.

[*A pause. They both sit down together.*]

GWENDOLEN: Perhaps this might be a favourable opportunity for my mentioning who I am. My father is Lord Bracknell. You have never heard of papa, I suppose?

CECILY: I don't think so.

GWENDOLEN: Outside the family circle, papa, I am glad to say, is entirely unknown. I think that is quite as it should be. The home seems to me to be the proper sphere for the man. And certainly once a man begins to neglect his domestic duties he becomes painfully effeminate, does he not? And I don't like that. It makes men so very attractive. Cecily, mamma, whose views on education are remarkably strict, has brought me up to be extremely short-sighted; it is part of her system; so do you mind my looking at you through my glasses?

CECILY: Oh! not at all, Gwendolen. I am very fond of being looked at.

GWENDOLEN [*after examining Cecily carefully through a lorgnette*]: You are here on a short visit I suppose.

CECILY: Oh no! I live here.

GWENDOLEN [*severely*]: Really? Your mother, no doubt, or some female relative of advanced years, resides here also?

CECILY: Oh no! I have no mother, nor, in fact, any relations.

GWENDOLEN: Indeed?

CECILY: My dear guardian, with the assistance of Miss Prism, has the arduous task of looking after me.

GWENDOLEN: Your guardian?

CECILY: Yes, I am Mr Worthing's ward.

GWENDOLEN: Oh! It is strange he never mentioned to me that he had a ward. How secretive of him! He grows more interesting hourly. I am not sure, however, that the news inspires me with feelings of unmixed delight. [*Rising and going to her.*] I am very fond of you, Cecily; I have liked you ever since I met you! But I am bound to state that now that I know that you are Mr Worthing's ward, I cannot help expressing a wish you were—well just a little older than you seem to be— and not quite so very alluring in appearance. In fact, if I may speak candidly—

CECILY: Pray do! I think that whenever one has anything unpleasant to say, one should always be quite candid.

GWENDOLEN: Well, to speak with perfect candour, Cecily, I wish that you were fully forty-two, and more than usually plain for your age. Ernest has a strong upright nature. He is the very soul of truth and honour. Disloyalty would be as impossible to him as deception. But even men of the noblest possible moral character are extremely susceptible to the influence of the physical charms of others. Modern, no less than Ancient History, supplies us with many most painful examples of what I refer to. If it were not so, indeed, History would be quite unreadable.

CECILY: I beg your pardon, Gwendolen, did you say Ernest?

GWENDOLEN: Yes.

CECILY: Oh, but it is not Mr Ernest Worthing who is my guardian. It is his brother— his elder brother.

GWENDOLEN [*sitting down again*]: Ernest never mentioned to me that he had a brother.

CECILY: I am sorry to say they have not been on good terms for a long time.

GWENDOLEN: Ah! that accounts for it. And now that I think of it I have never heard any man mention his brother. The subject seems distasteful to most men. Cecily, you have lifted a load from my mind. I was growing almost anxious. It would have been terrible if any cloud had come across a friendship like ours, would it not? Of course you are quite, quite sure that it is not Mr Ernest Worthing who is your guardian?

CECILY: Quite sure. [*A pause.*] In fact, I am going to be his.

GWENDOLEN [*enquiringly*]: I beg your pardon?

CECILY [*rather shy and confidingly*]: Dearest Gwendolen, there is no reason why I should make a secret of it to you. Our little county newspaper is sure to chronicle the fact next week. Mr Ernest Worthing and I are engaged to be married.

GWENDOLEN [*quite politely, rising*]: My darling Cecily, I think there must be some slight error. Mr Ernest Worthing is engaged to me. The announcement will appear in the "Morning Post" on Saturday at the latest.

CECILY [*very politely, rising*]: I am afraid you must be under some misconception. Ernest proposed to me exactly ten minutes ago. [*Shows diary.*]

GWENDOLEN [*examines diary through her lorgnette carefully*]: It is certainly very curious, for he asked me to be his wife yesterday afternoon at 5.30. If you would care to verify the incident, pray do so. [*Produces diary of her own.*] I never travel without my diary.

One should always have something sensational to read in the train. I am so sorry, dear Cecily, if it is any disappointment to you, but I am afraid I have the prior claim.

CECILY: It would distress me more than I can tell you, dear Gwendolen, if it caused you any mental or physical anguish, but I feel bound to point out that since Ernest proposed to you he clearly has changed his mind.

GWENDOLEN [*meditatively*]: If the poor fellow has been entrapped into any foolish promise I shall consider it my duty to rescue him at once, and with a firm hand.

CECILY [*thoughtfully and sadly*]: Whatever unfortunate entanglement my dear boy may have got into, I will never reproach him with it after we are married.

GWENDOLEN: Do you allude to me, Miss Cardew, as an entanglement? You are presumptuous. On an occasion of this kind it becomes more than a moral duty to speak one's mind. It becomes a pleasure.

CECILY: Do you suggest, Miss Fairfax, that I entrapped Ernest into an engagement? How dare you? This is no time for wearing the shallow mask of manners. When I see a spade I call it a spade.

GWENDOLEN [*satirically*]: I am glad to say that I have never seen a spade. It is obvious that our social spheres have been widely different.

[*Enter Merriman, followed by the footman. He carries a salver, table cloth, and plate stand. Cecily is about to retort. The presence of the servants exercises a restraining influence, under which both girls chafe.*]

MERRIMAN: Shall I lay tea here as usual, Miss?

CECILY [*sternly, in a calm voice*]: Yes, as usual.

[*Merriman begins to clear table and lay cloth. A long pause. Cecily and Gwendolen glare at each other.*]

GWENDOLEN: Are there many interesting walks in the vicinity, Miss Cardew?

CECILY: Oh! yes! a great many. From the top of one of the hills quite close one can see five counties.

GWENDOLEN: Five counties! I don't think I should like that. I hate crowds.

CECILY [*sweetly*]: I suppose that is why you live in town?

[*Gwendolen bites her lip, and beats her foot nervously with her parasol.*]

GWENDOLEN [*looking round*]: Quite a well-kept garden this is, Miss Cardew.

CECILY: So glad you like it, Miss Fairfax.

GWENDOLEN: I had no idea there were any flowers in the country.

CECILY: Oh, flowers are as common here, Miss Fairfax, as people are in London.

GWENDOLEN: Personally, I cannot understand how anybody manages to exist in the country, if anybody who is anybody does. The country always bores me to death.

CECILY: Ah! This is what the newspapers call agricultural depression,[15] is it not? I believe the aristocracy are suffering very much from it just at present. It is almost an epidemic amongst them, I have been told. May I offer you some tea, Miss Fairfax?

GWENDOLEN [*with elaborate politeness*]: Thank you. [*Aside.*] Detestable girl! But I require tea!

CECILY [*sweetly*]: Sugar?

GWENDOLEN [*superciliously*]: No, thank you. Sugar is not fashionable any more.

[*Cecily looks angrily at her, takes up the tongs and puts four lumps of sugar into the cup.*]

CECILY [*severely*]: Cake or bread and butter?

GWENDOLEN [*in a bored manner*]: Bread and butter, please. Cake is rarely seen at the best houses nowadays.

15. A pun on the word "depression"; beginning in the 1870s, British agriculture had been in a slump, causing losses and hardship among landowners.

CECILY [*cuts a very large slice of cake, and puts it on the tray*]: Hand that to Miss Fairfax.

[*Merriman does so, and goes out with footman. Gwendolen drinks the tea and makes a grimace. Puts down cup at once, reaches out her hand to the bread and butter, looks at it, and finds it is cake. Rises in indignation.*]

GWENDOLEN: You have filled my tea with lumps of sugar, and though I asked most distinctly for bread and butter, you have given me cake. I am known for the gentleness of my disposition, and the extraordinary sweetness of my nature, but I warn you, Miss Cardew, you may go too far.

CECILY [*rising*]: To save my poor, innocent, trusting boy from the machinations of any other girl there are no lengths to which I would not go.

GWENDOLEN: From the moment I saw you I distrusted you. I felt that you were false and deceitful. I am never deceived in such matters. My first impressions of people are invariably right.

CECILY: It seems to me, Miss Fairfax, that I am trespassing on your valuable time. No doubt you have many other calls of a similar character to make in the neighbourhood.

[*Enter Jack.*]

GWENDOLEN [*catching sight of him*]: Ernest! My own Ernest!

JACK: Gwendolen! Darling! [*Offers to kiss her.*]

GWENDOLEN [*drawing back*]: A moment! May I ask if you are engaged to be married to this young lady? [*Points to Cecily.*]

JACK [*laughing*]: To dear little Cecily! Of course not! What could have put such an idea into your pretty little head?

GWENDOLEN: Thank you. You may! [*Offers her cheek.*]

CECILY [*very sweetly*]: I knew there must be some misunderstanding, Miss Fairfax. The gentleman whose arm is at present round your waist is my dear guardian, Mr John Worthing.

GWENDOLEN: I beg your pardon?

CECILY: This is Uncle Jack.

GWENDOLEN [*receding*]: Jack! Oh!

[*Enter Algernon.*]

CECILY: Here is Ernest.

ALGERNON [*goes straight over to Cecily without noticing anyone else*]: My own love! [*Offers to kiss her.*]

CECILY [*drawing back*]: A moment, Ernest! May I ask you—are you engaged to be married to this young lady?

ALGERNON [*looking round*]: To what young lady? Good heavens! Gwendolen!

CECILY: Yes, to good heavens, Gwendolen, I mean to Gwendolen.

ALGERNON [*laughing*]: Of course not! What could have put such an idea into your pretty little head?

CECILY: Thank you. [*Presenting her cheek to be kissed.*] You may.

[*Algernon kisses her.*]

GWENDOLEN: I felt there was some slight error, Miss Cardew. The gentleman who is now embracing you is my cousin, Mr Algernon Moncrieff.

CECILY [*breaking away from Algernon*]: Algernon Moncrieff! Oh!

[*The two girls move towards each other and put their arms round each other's waists as if for protection.*]

CECILY: Are you called Algernon?

ALGERNON: I cannot deny it.

CECILY: Oh!

GWENDOLEN: Is your name really John?

JACK [standing rather proudly]: I could deny it if I liked. I could deny anything if I liked. But my name certainly is John. It has been John for years.

CECILY [to Gwendolen]: A gross deception has been practised on both of us.

GWENDOLEN: My poor wounded Cecily!

CECILY: My sweet wronged Gwendolen!

GWENDOLEN [slowly and seriously]: You will call me sister, will you not?
   [They embrace. Jack and Algernon groan and walk up and down.]

CECILY [rather brightly]: There is just one question I would like to be allowed to ask my guardian.

GWENDOLEN: An admirable idea! Mr Worthing, there is just one question I would like to be permitted to put to you. Where is your brother Ernest? We are both engaged to be married to your brother Ernest, so it is a matter of some importance to us to know where your brother Ernest is at present.

JACK [slowly and hesitatingly]: Gwendolen—Cecily—It is very painful for me to be forced to speak the truth. It is the first time in my life that I have ever been reduced to such a painful position, and I am really quite inexperienced in doing anything of the kind. However I will tell you quite frankly that I have no brother Ernest. I have no brother at all. I never had a brother in my life, and I certainly have not the smallest intention of ever having one in the future.

CECILY [surprised]: No brother at all?

JACK [cheerily]: None!

GWENDOLEN [severely]: Had you never a brother of any kind?

JACK [pleasantly]: Never. Not even of any kind.

GWENDOLEN: I am afraid it is quite clear, Cecily, that neither of us is engaged to be married to anyone.

CECILY: It is not a very pleasant position for a young girl suddenly to find herself in. Is it?

GWENDOLEN: Let us go into the house. They will hardly venture to come after us there.

CECILY: No, men are so cowardly, aren't they?
   [They retire into the house with scornful looks.]

JACK: This ghastly state of things is what you call Bunburying, I suppose?

ALGERNON: Yes, and a perfectly wonderful Bunbury it is. The most wonderful Bunbury I have ever had in my life.

JACK: Well, you've no right whatsoever to Bunbury here.

ALGERNON: That is absurd. One has a right to Bunbury anywhere one chooses. Every serious Bunburyist knows that.

JACK: Serious Bunburyist! Good heavens!

ALGERNON: Well, one must be serious about something, if one wants to have any amusement in life. I happen to be serious about Bunburying. What on earth you are serious about I haven't got the remotest idea. About everything, I should fancy. You have such an absolutely trivial nature.

JACK: Well, the only small satisfaction I have in the whole of this wretched business is that your friend Bunbury is quite exploded. You won't be able to run down to the country quite so often as you used to do, dear Algy. And a very good thing too.

ALGERNON: Your brother is a little off colour, isn't he, dear Jack? You won't be able to disappear to London quite so frequently as your wicked custom was. And not a bad thing either.

JACK: As for your conduct towards Miss Cardew, I must say that your taking in a sweet, simple, innocent girl like that is quite inexcusable. To say nothing of the fact that she is my ward.

ALGERNON: I can see no possible defence at all for your deceiving a brilliant, clever, thoroughly experienced young lady like Miss Fairfax. To say nothing of the fact that she is my cousin.

JACK: I wanted to be engaged to Gwendolen, that is all. I love her.

ALGERNON: Well, I simply wanted to be engaged to Cecily. I adore her.

JACK: There is certainly no chance of your marrying Miss Cardew.

ALGERNON: I don't think there is much likelihood, Jack, of you and Miss Fairfax being united.

JACK: Well, that is no business of yours.

ALGERNON: If it was my business, I wouldn't talk about it. [*Begins to eat muffins.*] It is very vulgar to talk about one's business. Only people like stockbrokers do that, and then merely at dinner parties.

JACK: How you can sit there, calmly eating muffins when we are in this horrible trouble, I can't make out. You seem to me to be perfectly heartless.

ALGERNON: Well, I can't eat muffins in an agitated manner. The butter would probably get on my cuffs. One should always eat muffins quite calmly. It is the only way to eat them.

JACK: I say it's perfectly heartless your eating muffins at all, under the circumstances.

ALGERNON: When I am in trouble, eating is the only thing that consoles me. Indeed, when I am in really great trouble, as anyone who knows me intimately will tell you, I refuse everything except food and drink. At the present moment I am eating muffins because I am unhappy. Besides, I am particularly fond of muffins. [*Rising.*]

JACK [*rising*]: Well, that is no reason why you should eat them all in that greedy way.

[*Takes muffins from Algernon.*]

ALGERNON [*offering tea-cake*]: I wish you would have tea-cake instead. I don't like tea-cake.

JACK: Good heavens! I suppose a man may eat his own muffins in his own garden.

ALGERNON: But you have just said it was perfectly heartless to eat muffins.

JACK: I said it was perfectly heartless of you, under the circumstances. That is a very different thing.

ALGERNON: That may be. But the muffins are the same. [*He seizes the muffin-dish from Jack.*]

JACK: Algy, I wish to goodness you would go.

ALGERNON: You can't possibly ask me to go without having some dinner. It's absurd. I never go without my dinner. No one ever does, except vegetarians and people like that. Besides I have just made arrangements with Dr Chasuble to be christened at a quarter to six under the name of Ernest.

JACK: My dear fellow, the sooner you give up that nonsense the better. I made arrangements this morning with Dr Chasuble to be christened myself at 5.30, and I naturally will take the name of Ernest. Gwendolen would wish it. We can't both be christened Ernest. It's absurd. Besides, I have a perfect right to be christened if I like. There is no evidence at all that I ever have been christened by anybody. I should think it extremely probable I never was, and so does Dr Chasuble. It is entirely different in your case. You have been christened already.

ALGERNON: Yes, but I have not been christened for years.

JACK: Yes, but you have been christened. That is the important thing.

ALGERNON: Quite so. So I know my constitution can stand it. If you are not quite sure about your ever having been christened, I must say I think it rather dangerous your venturing on it now. It might make you very unwell. You can hardly have forgotten that someone very closely connected with you was very nearly carried off this week in Paris by a severe chill.

JACK: Yes, but you said yourself that a severe chill was not hereditary.

ALGERNON: It usen't to be, I know—but I daresay it is now. Science is always making wonderful improvements in things.

JACK [picking up the muffin-dish]: Oh, that is nonsense; you are always talking nonsense.

ALGERNON: Jack, you are at the muffins again! I wish you wouldn't. There are only two left. [Takes them.] I told you I was particularly fond of muffins.

JACK: But I hate tea-cake.

ALGERNON: Why on earth then do you allow tea-cake to be served up for your guests? What ideas you have of hospitality!

JACK: Algernon! I have already told you to go. I don't want you here. Why don't you go!

ALGERNON: I haven't quite finished my tea yet! and there is still one muffin left.
    [Jack groans, and sinks into a chair. Algernon still continues eating.]   ACT DROP

THIRD ACT

SCENE: Morning-room[1] at the Manor House.

[Gwendolen and Cecily are at the window, looking out into the garden.]

GWENDOLEN: The fact that they did not follow us at once into the house, as anyone else would have done, seems to me to show that they have some sense of shame left.

CECILY: They have been eating muffins. That looks like repentance.

GWENDOLEN [after a pause]: They don't seem to notice us at all. Couldn't you cough?

CECILY: But I haven't got a cough.

GWENDOLEN: They're looking at us. What effrontery!

CECILY: They're approaching. That's very forward of them.

GWENDOLEN: Let us preserve a dignified silence.

CECILY: Certainly. It's the only thing to do now.
    [Enter Jack followed by Algernon. They whistle some dreadful popular air from a British Opera.][2]

GWENDOLEN: This dignified silence seems to produce an unpleasant effect.

CECILY: A most distasteful one.

GWENDOLEN: But we will not be the first to speak.

CECILY: Certainly not.

GWENDOLEN: Mr Worthing, I have something very particular to ask you. Much depends on your reply.

1. An informal room for receiving morning calls from friends (afternoon visitors were received in the formal drawing room).

2. Probably a reference to Gilbert and Sullivan, who had made fun of Wilde and the Aesthetic movement in Patience (1881).

CECILY: Gwendolen, your common sense is invaluable. Mr Moncrieff, kindly answer me the following question. Why did you pretend to be my guardian's brother?

ALGERNON: In order that I might have an opportunity of meeting you.

CECILY [to Gwendolen]: That certainly seems a satisfactory explanation, does it not?

GWENDOLEN: Yes, dear, if you can believe him.

CECILY: I don't. But that does not affect the wonderful beauty of his answer.

GWENDOLEN: True. In matters of grave importance, style, not sincerity is the vital thing. Mr Worthing, what explanation can you offer to me for pretending to have a brother? Was it in order that you might have an opportunity of coming up to town to see me as often as possible?

JACK: Can you doubt it, Miss Fairfax?

GWENDOLEN: I have the gravest doubts upon the subject. But I intend to crush them. This is not the moment for German scepticism.[3] [Moving to Cecily.] Their explanations appear to be quite satisfactory, especially Mr Worthing's. That seems to me to have the stamp of truth upon it.

CECILY: I am more than content with what Mr Moncrieff said. His voice alone inspires one with absolute credulity.

GWENDOLEN: Then you think we should forgive them?

CECILY: Yes. I mean no.

GWENDOLEN: True! I had forgotten. There are principles at stake that one cannot surrender. Which of us should tell them? The task is not a pleasant one.

CECILY: Could we not both speak at the same time?

GWENDOLEN: An excellent idea! I nearly always speak at the same time as other people. Will you take the time from me?

CECILY: Certainly.

[Gwendolen beats time with uplifted finger.]

GWENDOLEN AND CECILY [speaking together]: Your Christian names are still an insuperable barrier. That is all!

JACK AND ALGERNON [speaking together]: Our Christian names! Is that all? But we are going to be christened this afternoon.

GWENDOLEN [to Jack]: For my sake you are prepared to do this terrible thing?

JACK: I am.

CECILY [to Algernon]: To please me you are ready to face this fearful ordeal?

ALGERNON: I am!

GWENDOLEN: How absurd to talk of the equality of the sexes! Where questions of self-sacrifice are concerned, men are infinitely beyond us.

JACK: We are. [Clasps hands with Algernon.]

CECILY: They have moments of physical courage of which we women know absolutely nothing.

GWENDOLEN [to Jack]: Darling!

ALGERNON [to Cecily]: Darling! [They fall into each other's arms.]

[Enter Merriman. When he enters he coughs loudly, seeing the situation.]

MERRIMAN: Ahem! Ahem! Lady Bracknell!

JACK: Good heavens!

[Enter Lady Bracknell. The couples separate in alarm.] [Exit Merriman.]

LADY BRACKNELL: Gwendolen! What does this mean?

GWENDOLEN: Merely that I am engaged to be married to Mr Worthing, mamma.

3. Many 19th-century German scholars were skeptical in their treatment of religious texts.

LADY BRACKNELL: Come here. Sit down. Sit down immediately. Hesitation of any kind is a sign of mental decay in the young, of physical weakness in the old. [*Turns to Jack.*] Apprised, sir, of my daughter's sudden flight by her trusty maid, whose confidence I purchased by means of a small coin, I followed her at once by a luggage train. Her unhappy father is, I am glad to say, under the impression that she is attending a more than usually lengthy lecture by the University Extension Scheme on the Influence of a permanent income on Thought. I do not propose to undeceive him. Indeed I have never undeceived him on any question. I would consider it wrong. But of course, you will clearly understand that all communication between yourself and my daughter must cease immediately from this moment. On this point, as indeed on all points, I am firm.

JACK: I am engaged to be married to Gwendolen, Lady Bracknell!

LADY BRACKNELL: You are nothing of the kind, sir. And now, as regards Algernon! . . . Algernon!

ALGERNON: Yes, Aunt Augusta.

LADY BRACKNELL: May I ask if it is in this house that your invalid friend Mr Bunbury resides?

ALGERNON [*stammering*]: Oh! No! Bunbury doesn't live here. Bunbury is somewhere else at present. In fact, Bunbury is dead.

LADY BRACKNELL: Dead! When did Mr Bunbury die? His death must have been extremely sudden.

ALGERNON [*airily*]: Oh! I killed Bunbury this afternoon. I mean poor Bunbury died this afternoon.

LADY BRACKNELL: What did he die of?

ALGERNON: Bunbury? Oh, he was quite exploded.

LADY BRACKNELL: Exploded! Was he the victim of a revolutionary outrage?[4] I was not aware that Mr Bunbury was interested in social legislation. If so, he is well punished for his morbidity.

ALGERNON: My dear Aunt Augusta, I mean he was found out! The doctors found out that Bunbury could not live, that is what I mean—so Bunbury died.

LADY BRACKNELL: He seems to have had great confidence in the opinion of his physicians. I am glad, however, that he made up his mind at the last to some definite course of action, and acted under proper medical advice. And now that we have finally got rid of this Mr Bunbury, may I ask, Mr Worthing, who is that young person whose hand my nephew Algernon is now holding in what seems to me a peculiarly unnecessary manner?

JACK: That lady is Miss Cecily Cardew, my ward.

[*Lady Bracknell bows coldly to Cecily.*]

ALGERNON: I am engaged to be married to Cecily, Aunt Augusta.

LADY BRACKNELL: I beg your pardon?

CECILY: Mr Moncrieff and I are engaged to be married, Lady Bracknell.

LADY BRACKNELL [*with a shiver, crossing to the sofa and sitting down*]: I do not know whether there is anything peculiarly exciting in the air of this particular part of Hertfordshire, but the number of engagements that go on seems to me considerably above the proper average that statistics have laid down for our guidance. I think some preliminary enquiry on my part would not be out of place. Mr Worthing, is Miss Cardew at all connected with any of the larger railway stations in

4. Anarchy and political assassination were much in the news; Wilde's earliest drama, *Vera, or the Nihilists* (1881), dealt with the subject.

London? I merely desire information. Until yesterday I had no idea that there were any families or persons whose origins was a Terminus.[5]

[*Jack looks perfectly furious, but restrains himself.*]

JACK [*in a clear, cold voice*]: Miss Cardew is the granddaughter of the late Mr Thomas Cardew of 149, Belgrave Square, S.W.; Gervase Park, Dorking, Surrey; and the Sporran, Fifeshire, N.B.[6]

LADY BRACKNELL: That sounds not unsatisfactory. Three addresses always inspire confidence, even in tradesmen. But what proof have I of their authenticity?

JACK: I have carefully preserved the Court Guides[7] of the period. They are open to your inspection, Lady Bracknell.

LADY BRACKNELL [*grimly*]: I have known strange errors in that publication.

JACK: Miss Cardew's family solicitors are Messrs Markby, Markby, and Markby.

LADY BRACKNELL: Markby, Markby, and Markby? A firm of the very highest position in their profession. Indeed I am told that one of the Mr Markbys is occasionally to be seen at dinner parties. So far I am satisfied.

JACK [*very irritably*]: How extremely kind of you, Lady Bracknell! I have also in my possession, you will be pleased to hear, certificates of Miss Cardew's birth, baptism, whooping cough, registration, vaccination, confirmation, and the measles; both the German and the English variety.

LADY BRACKNELL: Ah! A life crowded with incident, I see; though perhaps somewhat too exciting for a young girl. I am not myself in favour of premature experiences. [*Rises, looks at her watch.*] Gwendolen! the time approaches for our departure. We have not a moment to lose. As a matter of form, Mr Worthing, I had better ask you if Miss Cardew has any little fortune?

JACK: Oh! about a hundred and thirty thousand pounds in the Funds.[8] That is all. Goodbye, Lady Bracknell. So pleased to have seen you.

LADY BRACKNELL [*sitting down again*]: A moment, Mr Worthing. A hundred and thirty thousand pounds! And in the Funds! Miss Cardew seems to me a most attractive young lady, now that I look at her. Few girls of the present day have any really solid qualities, any of the qualities that last, and improve with time. We live, I regret to say, in an age of surfaces. [*To Cecily.*] Come over here, dear. [*Cecily goes across.*] Pretty child! your dress is sadly simple, and your hair seems almost as Nature might have left it. But we can soon alter all that. A thoroughly experienced French maid produces a really marvellous result in a very brief space of time. I remember recommending one to young Lady Lancing, and after three months her own husband did not know her.

JACK [*aside*]: And after six months nobody knew her.

LADY BRACKNELL [*glares at Jack for a few moments. Then bends, with a practised smile, to Cecily.*]: Kindly turn round, sweet child. [*Cecily turns completely round.*] No, the side view is what I want. [*Cecily presents her profile.*] Yes, quite as I expected. There are distinct social possibilities in your profile. The two weak points in our age are its want of principle and its want of profile. The chin a little higher, dear. Style largely depends on the way the chin is worn. They are worn very high, just at present. Algernon!

ALGERNON: Yes, Aunt Augusta!

---

5. A railway station at the end of the line.
6. North Britain, i.e., Scotland.
7. Annual publications listing the names and London addresses of the upper classes.
8. The Consolidated Funds, reliable interest-bearing government bonds.

LADY BRACKNELL: There are distinct social possibilities in Miss Cardew's profile.

ALGERNON: Cecily is the sweetest, dearest, prettiest girl in the whole world. And I don't care twopence about social possibilities.

LADY BRACKNELL: Never speak disrespectfully of Society, Algernon. Only people who can't get into it do that. [*To Cecily.*] Dear child, of course you know that Algernon has nothing but his debts to depend upon. But I do not approve of mercenary marriages. When I married Lord Bracknell I had no fortune of any kind. But I never dreamed for a moment of allowing that to stand in my way. Well, I suppose I must give my consent.

ALGERNON: Thank you, Aunt Augusta.

LADY BRACKNELL: Cecily, you may kiss me!

CECILY [*kisses her*]: Thank you, Lady Bracknell.

LADY BRACKNELL: You may also address me as Aunt Augusta for the future.

CECILY: Thank you, Aunt Augusta.

LADY BRACKNELL: The marriage, I think, had better take place quite soon.

ALGERNON: Thank you, Aunt Augusta.

CECILY: Thank you, Aunt Augusta.

LADY BRACKNELL: To speak frankly, I am not in favour of long engagements. They give people the opportunity of finding out each other's character before marriage, which I think is never advisable.

JACK: I beg your pardon for interrupting you, Lady Bracknell, but this engagement is quite out of the question. I am Miss Cardew's guardian, and she cannot marry without my consent until she comes of age. That consent I absolutely decline to give.

LADY BRACKNELL: Upon what grounds may I ask? Algernon is an extremely, I may almost say an ostentatiously, eligible young man. He has nothing, but he looks everything. What more can one desire?

JACK: It pains me very much to have to speak frankly to you, Lady Bracknell, about your nephew, but the fact is that I do not approve at all of his moral character. I suspect him of being untruthful.

[*Algernon and Cecily look at him in indignant amazement.*]

LADY BRACKNELL: Untruthful! My nephew Algernon? Impossible! He is an Oxonian.[9]

JACK: I fear there can be no possible doubt about the matter. This afternoon, during my temporary absence in London on an important question of romance, he obtained admission to my house by means of the false pretence of being my brother. Under an assumed name he drank, I've just been informed by my butler, an entire pint bottle of my Perrier-Jouet, Brut, '89; a wine I was specially reserving for myself. Continuing his disgraceful deception, he succeeded in the course of the afternoon in alienating the affections of my only ward. He subsequently stayed to tea, and devoured every single muffin. And what makes his conduct all the more heartless is, that he was perfectly well aware from the first that I have no brother, that I never had a brother, and that I don't intend to have a brother, not even of any kind. I distinctly told him so myself yesterday afternoon.

LADY BRACKNELL: Ahem! Mr Worthing, after careful consideration I have decided entirely to overlook my nephew's conduct to you.

---

9. I.e., he attended Oxford University.

JACK: That is very generous of you, Lady Bracknell. My own decision, however, is unalterable. I decline to give my consent.

LADY BRACKNELL [to Cecily]: Come here, sweet child. [Cecily goes over.] How old are you, dear?

CECILY: Well, I am really only eighteen, but I always admit to twenty when I go to evening parties.

LADY BRACKNELL: You are perfectly right in making some slight alteration. Indeed, no woman should ever be quite accurate about her age. It looks so calculating. . . . [In a meditative manner.] Eighteen, but admitting to twenty at evening parties. Well, it will not be very long before you are of age and free from the restraints of tutelage. So I don't think your guardian's consent is, after all, a matter of any importance.

JACK: Pray excuse me, Lady Bracknell, for interrupting you again, but it is only fair to tell you that according to the terms of her grandfather's will Miss Cardew does not come legally of age till she is thirty-five.

LADY BRACKNELL: That does not seem to me to be a grave objection. Thirty-five is a very attractive age. London society is full of women of the very highest birth who have, of their own free choice, remained thirty-five for years. Lady Dumbleton is an instance in point. To my own knowledge she has been thirty-five ever since she arrived at the age of forty, which was many years ago now. I see no reason why our dear Cecily should not be even still more attractive at the age you mention than she is at present. There will be a large accumulation of property.

CECILY: Algy, could you wait for me till I was thirty-five?

ALGERNON: Of course I could, Cecily. You know I could.

CECILY: Yes, I felt it instinctively, but I couldn't wait all that time. I hate waiting even five minutes for anybody. It always makes me rather cross. I am not punctual myself, I know, but I do like punctuality in others, and waiting, even to be married, is quite out of the question.

ALGERNON: Then what is to be done, Cecily?

CECILY: I don't know, Mr Moncrieff.

LADY BRACKNELL: My dear Mr Worthing, as Miss Cardew states positively that she cannot wait till she is thirty-five—a remark which I am bound to say seems to me to show a somewhat impatient nature—I would beg of you to reconsider your decision.

JACK: But my dear Lady Bracknell, the matter is entirely in your own hands. The moment you consent to my marriage with Gwendolen, I will most gladly allow your nephew to form an alliance with my ward.

LADY BRACKNELL [rising and drawing herself up]: You must be quite aware that what you propose is out of the question.

JACK: Then a passionate celibacy is all that any of us can look forward to.

LADY BRACKNELL: That is not the destiny I propose for Gwendolen. Algernon, of course, can choose for himself. [Pulls out her watch.] Come, dear; [Gwendolen rises.] we have already missed five, if not six, trains. To miss any more might expose us to comment on the platform.

[Enter Dr Chasuble.]

CHASUBLE: Everything is quite ready for the christenings.

LADY BRACKNELL: The christenings, sir! Is not that somewhat premature?

CHASUBLE [looking rather puzzled, and pointing to Jack and Algernon]: Both these gentlemen have expressed a desire for immediate baptism.

LADY BRACKNELL: At their age? The idea is grotesque and irreligious! Algernon, I forbid you to be baptized. I will not hear of such excesses. Lord Bracknell would be highly displeased if he learned that that was the way in which you wasted your time and money.

CHASUBLE: Am I to understand then that there are to be no christenings at all this afternoon?

JACK: I don't think that, as things are now, it would be of much practical value to either of us, Dr Chasuble.

CHASUBLE: I am grieved to hear such sentiments from you, Mr Worthing. They savour of the heretical views of the Anabaptists,[10] views that I have completely refuted in four of my unpublished sermons. However, as your present mood seems to be one peculiarly secular, I will return to the church at once. Indeed, I have just been informed by the pew-opener[11] that for the last hour and a half Miss Prism has been waiting for me in the vestry.

LADY BRACKNELL [*starting*]: Miss Prism! Did I hear you mention a Miss Prism?

CHASUBLE: Yes, Lady Bracknell. I am on my way to join her.

LADY BRACKNELL: Pray allow me to detain you for a moment. This matter may prove to be one of vital importance to Lord Bracknell and myself. Is this Miss Prism a female of repellent aspect, remotely connected with education?

CHASUBLE [*somewhat indignantly*]: She is the most cultivated of ladies, and the very picture of respectability.

LADY BRACKNELL: It is obviously the same person. May I ask what position she holds in your household?

CHASUBLE [*severely*]: I am a celibate, madam.

JACK [*interposing*]: Miss Prism, Lady Bracknell, has been for the last three years Miss Cardew's esteemed governess and valued companion.

LADY BRACKNELL: In spite of what I hear of her, I must see her at once. Let her be sent for.

CHASUBLE [*looking off*]: She approaches; she is nigh.

[*Enter Miss Prism hurriedly.*]

MISS PRISM: I was told you expected me in the vestry, dear Canon. I have been waiting for you there for an hour and three quarters. [*Catches sight of Lady Bracknell who has fixed her with a stony glare. Miss Prism grows pale and quails. She looks anxiously round as if desirous to escape.*]

LADY BRACKNELL [*in a severe, judicial voice*]: Prism! [*Miss Prism bows her head in shame.*] Come here, Prism! [*Miss Prism approaches in a humble manner.*] Prism! Where is that baby? [*General consternation. The Canon starts back in horror. Algernon and Jack pretend to be anxious to shield Cecily and Gwendolen from hearing the details of a terrible public scandal.*] Twenty-eight years ago, Prism, you left Lord Bracknell's house, Number 104, Upper Grosvenor Street, in charge of a perambulator that contained a baby, of the male sex. You never returned. A few weeks later, through the elaborate investigations of the Metropolitan police, the perambulator was discovered at midnight, standing by itself in a remote corner of Bayswater.[12] It contained the manuscript of a three-volume novel of more than usually revolting sentimentality. [*Miss Prism starts in involuntary indignation.*] But the baby was not there! [*Everyone looks at Miss Prism.*] Prism! Where is that baby? [*A pause.*]

MISS PRISM: Lady Bracknell, I admit with shame that I do not know. I only wish I did. The plain facts of the case are these. On the morning of the day you mention,

10. A 16th-century Protestant sect that believed in adult baptism.
11. Usher.

12. An area in the West End of London, near Kensington Gardens.

a day that is for ever branded on my memory, I prepared as usual to take the baby out in its perambulator. I had also with me a somewhat old, but capacious hand-bag in which I had intended to place the manuscript of a work of fiction that I had written during my few unoccupied hours. In a moment of mental abstraction, for which I never can forgive myself, I deposited the manuscript in the bassinette, and placed the baby in the hand-bag.

JACK [*who has been listening attentively*]: But where did you deposit the hand-bag?

MISS PRISM: Do not ask me, Mr Worthing.

JACK: Miss Prism, this is a matter of no small importance to me. I insist on knowing where you deposited the hand-bag that contained that infant.

MISS PRISM: I left it in the cloak-room of one of the larger railway stations in London.

JACK: What railway station?

MISS PRISM [*quite crushed*]: Victoria. The Brighton line. [*Sinks into a chair.*]

JACK: I must retire to my room for a moment. Gwendolen, wait here for me.

GWENDOLEN: If you are not too long, I will wait here for you all my life.

[*Exit Jack in great excitement.*]

CHASUBLE: What do you think this means, Lady Bracknell?

LADY BRACKNELL: I dare not even suspect, Dr Chasuble. I need hardly tell you that in families of high position strange coincidences are not supposed to occur. They are hardly considered the thing.

[*Noises heard overhead as if someone was throwing trunks about. Everyone looks up.*]

CECILY: Uncle Jack seems strangely agitated.

CHASUBLE: Your guardian has a very emotional nature.

LADY BRACKNELL: This noise is extremely unpleasant. It sounds as if he was having an argument. I dislike arguments of any kind. They are always vulgar, and often convincing.

CHASUBLE [*looking up*]: It has stopped now. [*The noise is redoubled.*]

LADY BRACKNELL: I wish he would arrive at some conclusion.

GWENDOLEN: This suspense is terrible. I hope it will last.

[*Enter Jack with a hand-bag of black leather in his hand.*]

JACK [*rushing over to Miss Prism*]: Is this the hand-bag, Miss Prism? Examine it carefully before you speak. The happiness of more than one life depends on your answer.

MISS PRISM [*calmly*]: It seems to be mine. Yes, here is the injury it received through the upsetting of a Gower Street omnibus in younger and happier days. Here is the stain on the lining caused by the explosion of a temperance beverage, an incident that occurred at Leamington. And here, on the lock, are my initials. I had forgotten that in an extravagant mood I had had them placed there. The bag is undoubtedly mine. I am delighted to have it so unexpectedly restored to me. It has been a great inconvenience being without it all these years.

JACK [*in a pathetic voice*]: Miss Prism, more is restored to you than this hand-bag. I was the baby you placed in it.

MISS PRISM [*amazed*]: You?

JACK [*embracing her*]: Yes . . . mother!

MISS PRISM [*recoiling in indignant astonishment*]: Mr Worthing! I am unmarried!

JACK: Unmarried! I do not deny that is a serious blow. But after all, who has the right to cast a stone against one who has suffered?[13] Cannot repentance wipe out an act

---

13. Jesus saves a woman who is about to be stoned for committing adultery, saying, "He that is without sin among you, let him first cast a stone at her" (John 8.7).

of folly? Why should there be one law for men, and another for women? Mother, I forgive you. [*Tries to embrace her again.*]

MISS PRISM [*still more indignant*]: Mr Worthing, there is some error. [*Pointing to Lady Bracknell.*] There is the lady who can tell you who you really are.

JACK [*after a pause*]: Lady Bracknell, I hate to seem inquisitive, but would you kindly inform me who I am?

LADY BRACKNELL: I am afraid that the news I have to give you will not altogether please you. You are the son of my poor sister, Mrs Moncrieff, and consequently Algernon's elder brother.

JACK: Algy's elder brother! Then I have a brother after all. I knew I had a brother! I always said I had a brother! Cecily—how could you have ever doubted that I had a brother. [*Seizes hold of Algernon.*] Dr Chasuble, my unfortunate brother. Miss Prism, my unfortunate brother. Gwendolen, my unfortunate brother. Algy, you young scoundrel, you will have to treat me with more respect in the future. You have never behaved to me like a brother in all your life.

ALGERNON: Well, not till today, old boy, I admit. I did my best, however, though I was out of practice. [*Shakes hands.*]

GWENDOLEN [*to Jack*]: My own! But what own are you? What is your Christian name, now that you have become someone else?

JACK: Good heavens! . . . I had quite forgotten that point. Your decision on the subject of my name is irrevocable, I suppose?

GWENDOLEN: I never change, except in my affections.

CECILY: What a noble nature you have, Gwendolen!

JACK: Then the question had better be cleared up at once. Aunt Augusta, a moment. At the time when Miss Prism left me in the hand-bag, had I been christened already?

LADY BRACKNELL: Every luxury that money could buy, including christening, had been lavished on you by your fond and doting parents.

JACK: Then I was christened! That is settled. Now, what name was I given? Let me know the worst.

LADY BRACKNELL: Being the eldest son you were naturally christened after your father.

JACK [*irritably*]: Yes, but what was my father's Christian name?

LADY BRACKNELL [*meditatively*]: I cannot at the present moment recall what the General's Christian name was. But I have no doubt he had one. He was eccentric, I admit. But only in later years. And that was the result of the Indian climate, and marriage, and indigestion, and other things of that kind.

JACK: Algy! Can't you recollect what our father's Christian name was?

ALGERNON: My dear boy, we were never even on speaking terms. He died before I was a year old.

JACK: His name would appear in the Army Lists of the period, I suppose, Aunt Augusta?

LADY BRACKNELL: The General was essentially a man of peace, except in his domestic life. But I have no doubt his name would appear in any military directory.

JACK: The Army Lists of the last forty years are here. These delightful records should have been my constant study. [*Rushes to bookcase and tears the books out.*] M. Generals . . . Mallam, Maxbohm,[14] Magley, what ghastly names they have— Markby, Migsby, Mobbs, Moncrieff! Lieutenant 1840, Captain, Lieutenant-Colonel, Colonel, General 1869, Christian names, Ernest John. [*Puts book very qui-*

---

14. A pun on the name of Wilde's friend Max Beerbohm.

etly down and speaks quite calmly.] I always told you, Gwendolen, my name was Ernest, didn't I? Well, it is Ernest after all. I mean it naturally is Ernest.

LADY BRACKNELL: Yes, I remember now that the General was called Ernest. I knew I had some particular reason for disliking the name.

GWENDOLEN: Ernest! My own Ernest! I felt from the first that you could have no other name!

JACK: Gwendolen, it is a terrible thing for a man to find out suddenly that all his life he has been speaking nothing but the truth. Can you forgive me?

GWENDOLEN: I can. For I feel that you are sure to change.

JACK: My own one!

CHASUBLE [*to Miss Prism*]: Laetitia! [*Embraces her.*]

MISS PRISM [*enthusiastically*]: Frederick! At last!

ALGERNON: Cecily! [*Embraces her.*] At last!

JACK: Gwendolen! [*Embraces her.*] At last!

LADY BRACKNELL: My nephew, you seem to be displaying signs of triviality.

JACK: On the contrary, Aunt Augusta, I've now realized for the first time in my life the vital Importance of Being Earnest.

TABLEAU   CURTAIN

1894, performed 1895   1899

Joseph Conrad
1857–1924

from Heart of Darkness

"It was upward of thirty days before I saw the mouth of the big river. We anchored off the seat of the government. But my work would not begin till some two hundred miles farther on. So as soon as I could I made a start for a place thirty miles higher up.

"I had my passage on a little sea-going steamer. Her captain was a Swede, and knowing me for a seaman, invited me on the bridge. He was a young man, lean, fair, and morose, with lanky hair and a shuffling gait. As we left the miserable little wharf, he tossed his head contemptuously at the shore. 'Been living there?' he asked. I said, 'Yes.' 'Fine lot these government chaps—are they not?' he went on, speaking English with great precision and considerable bitterness. 'It is funny what some people will do for a few francs a month. I wonder what becomes of that kind when it goes up country?' I said to him I expected to see that soon. 'So-o-o!' he exclaimed. He shuffled athwart, keeping one eye ahead vigilantly. 'Don't be too sure,' he continued. 'The other day I took up a man who hanged himself on the road. He was a Swede, too.' 'Hanged himself! Why, in God's name?' I cried. He kept on looking out watchfully. 'Who knows? The sun too much for him, or the country perhaps.'

"At last we opened a reach. A rocky cliff appeared, mounds of turned-up earth by the shore, houses on a hill, others, with iron roofs, amongst a waste of excavations, or hanging to the declivity. A continuous noise of the rapids above hovered over this scene of inhabited devastation. A lot of people, mostly black and naked, moved about like ants. A jetty projected into the river. A blinding sunlight drowned all this at times in a sudden recrudescence of glare. 'There's your Company's station,' said the Swede, pointing to three wooden barrack-like structures on the rocky slope. 'I will send your things up. Four boxes did you say? So. Farewell.'

"I came upon a boiler wallowing in the grass, then found a path leading up the hill. It turned aside for the boulders, and also for an undersized railway-truck lying there on its back with its wheels in the air. One was off. The thing looked as dead as the carcass of some animal. I came upon more pieces of decaying machinery, a stack of rusty rails. To the left a clump of trees made a shady spot, where dark things seemed to stir feebly. I blinked, the path was steep. A horn tooted to the right, and I saw the black people run. A heavy and dull detonation shook the ground, a puff of smoke came out of the cliff, and that was all. No change appeared on the face of the rock. They were building a railway. The cliff was not in the way or anything; but this objectless blasting was all the work going on.

"A slight clinking behind me made me turn my head. Six black men advanced in a file, toiling up the path. They walked erect and slow, balancing small baskets full of earth on their heads, and the clink kept time with their footsteps. Black rags were wound round their loins, and the short ends behind wagged to and fro like tails. I could see every rib, the joints of their limbs were like knots in a rope; each had an iron collar on his neck, and all were connected together with a chain whose bights swung between them, rhythmically clinking. Another report from the cliff made me think suddenly of that ship of war I had seen firing into a continent. It was the same kind of ominous voice; but these men could by no stretch of imagination be called enemies. They were called criminals, and the outraged law, like the bursting shells, had come to them, an insoluble mystery from over the sea. All their meagre breasts panted together, the violently dilated nostrils quivered, the eyes stared stonily up-hill. They passed me within six inches, without a glance, with that complete, deathlike indifference of unhappy savages. Behind this raw matter one of the reclaimed, the product of the new forces at work, strolled despondently, carrying a rifle by its middle. He had a uniform jacket with one button off, and seeing a white man on the path, hoisted his weapon to his shoulder with alacrity. This was simple prudence, white men being so much alike at a distance that he could not tell who I might be. He was speedily reassured, and with a large, white, rascally grin, and a glance at his charge, seemed to take me into partnership in his exalted trust. After all, I also was a part of the great cause of these high and just proceedings.

"Instead of going up, I turned and descended to the left. My idea was to let that chain-gang get out of sight before I climbed the hill. You know I am not particularly tender; I've had to strike and to fend off. I've had to resist and to attack sometimes—that's only one way of resisting—without counting the exact cost, according to the demands of such sort of life as I had blundered into. I've seen the devil of violence, and the devil of greed, and the devil of hot desire; but, by all the stars! these were strong, lusty, red-eyed devils, that swayed and drove men—men, I tell you. But as I stood on this hillside, I foresaw that in the blinding sunshine of that land I would become acquainted with a flabby, pretending, weak-eyed devil of a rapacious and pitiless folly. How insidious he could be, too, I was only to find out several months later and a thousand miles farther. For a moment I stood appalled, as though by a warning. Finally I descended the hill, obliquely, towards the trees I had seen.

"I avoided a vast artificial hole somebody had been digging on the slope, the purpose of which I found it impossible to divine. It wasn't a quarry or a sandpit, anyhow. It was just a hole. It might have been connected with the philanthropic desire of giving the criminals something to do. I don't know. Then I nearly fell into a very narrow ravine, almost no more than a scar in the hillside. I discovered that a lot of imported drainage-pipes for the settlement had been tumbled in there. There wasn't one that was not broken. It was a wanton smash-up. At last I got under the trees. My purpose was to stroll into the shade for a moment; but no sooner within than it seemed to me I had stepped into the gloomy circle of some Inferno. The rapids were near, and an uninterrupted, uniform, headlong, rushing noise filled the mournful stillness of the grove, where not a breath stirred, not a leaf moved, with a mysterious sound—as though the tearing pace of the launched earth had suddenly become audible.

"Black shapes crouched, lay, sat between the trees, leaning against the trunks, clinging to the earth, half coming out, half effaced within the dim light, in all the attitudes of pain, abandonment, and despair. Another mine on the cliff went off, followed by a slight shudder of the soil under my feet. The work was going on. The work! And this was the place where some of the helpers had withdrawn to die.

"They were dying slowly—it was very clear. They were not enemies, they were not criminals, they were nothing earthly now,—nothing but black shadows of disease and starvation, lying confusedly in the greenish gloom. Brought from all the recesses of the coast in all the legality of time contracts, lost in uncongenial surroundings, fed on unfamiliar food, they sickened, became inefficient, and were then allowed to crawl away and rest. These moribund shapes were free as air—and nearly as thin. I began to distinguish the gleam of eyes under the trees. Then, glancing down, I saw a face near my hand. The black bones reclined at full length with one shoulder against the tree, and slowly the eyelids rose and the sunken eyes looked up at me, enormous and vacant, a kind of blind, white flicker in the depths of the orbs, which died out slowly. The man seemed young—almost a boy—but you know with them it's hard to tell. I found nothing else to do but to offer him one of my good Swede's ship's biscuits I had in my pocket. The fingers closed slowly on it and held—there was no other movement and no other glance. He had tied a bit of white worsted round his neck— Why? Where did he get it? Was it a badge—an ornament—a charm—a propitiatory act? Was there any idea at all connected with it? It looked startling round his black neck, this bit of white thread from beyond the seas.

"Near the same tree two more bundles of acute angles sat with their legs drawn up. One, with his chin propped on his knees, stared at nothing, in an intolerable and appalling manner: his brother phantom rested its forehead, as if overcome with a great weariness; and all about others were scattered in every pose of contorted collapse, as in some picture of a massacre or a pestilence. While I stood horror-struck, one of these creatures rose to his hands and knees, and went off on all-fours towards the river to drink. He lapped out of his hand, then sat up in the sunlight, crossing his shins in front of him, and after a time let his woolly head fall on his breastbone.

"I didn't want any more loitering in the shade, and I made haste towards the station. When near the buildings I met a white man, in such an unexpected elegance of get-up that in the first moment I took him for a sort of vision. I saw a high starched collar, white cuffs, a light alpaca jacket, snowy trousers, a clear silk necktie, and varnished boots. No hat. Hair parted, brushed, oiled, under a green-lined parasol held in a big white hand. He was amazing, and had a penholder behind his ear.

"I shook hands with this miracle, and I learned he was the Company's chief accountant, and that all the book-keeping was done at this station. He had come out for a moment, he said, 'to get a breath of fresh air.' The expression sounded wonderfully odd, with its suggestion of sedentary desk-life. I wouldn't have mentioned the fellow to you at all, only it was from his lips that I first heard the name of the man who is so indissolubly connected with the memories of that time. Moreover, I respected the fellow. Yes; I respected his collars, his vast cuffs, his brushed hair. His appearance was certainly that of a hairdresser's dummy; but in the great demoralisation of the land he kept up his appearance. That's backbone. His starched collars and got-up shirt-fronts were achievements of character. He had been out nearly three years; and, later on, I could not help asking him how he managed to sport such linen. He had just the faintest blush, and said modestly, 'I've been teaching one of the native women about the station. It was difficult. She had a distaste for the work.' Thus this man had verily accomplished something. And he was devoted to his books, which were in apple-pie order.

Bernard Shaw
1856–1950

Pygmalion

Preface: A Professor of Phonetics

As will be seen later on, Pygmalion needs, not a preface, but a sequel, which I have supplied in its due place.

The English have no respect for their language, and will not teach their children to speak it. They cannot spell it because they have nothing to spell it with but an old foreign alphabet of which only the consonants—and not all of them—have any agreed speech value. Consequently no man can teach himself what it should sound like from reading it; and it is impossible for an Englishman to open his mouth without making some other Englishman despise him. Most European languages are now accessible in black and white to foreigners: English and French are not thus accessible even to Englishmen and Frenchmen. The reformer we need most today is an energetic phonetic enthusiast: that is why I have made such a one the hero of a popular play.

There have been heroes of that kind crying in the wilderness for many years past. When I became interested in the subject towards the end of the eighteen-seventies, the illustrious Alexander Melville Bell, the inventor of Visible Speech, had emigrated to Canada, where his son invented the telephone; but Alexander J. Ellis was still a London patriarch, with an impressive head always covered by a velvet skull cap, for which he would apologize to public meetings in a very courtly manner. He and Tito Pagliardini, another phonetic veteran, were men whom it was impossible to dislike. Henry Sweet, then a young man, lacked their sweetness of character: he was about as conciliatory to conventional mortals as Ibsen[1] or Samuel Butler.[2] His great ability as a phonetician (he was, I think, the best of them all at his job) would have entitled him to high official recognition, and perhaps enabled him to popularize his subject, but for his Satanic contempt for all academic dignitaries and persons in general who thought more of Greek than of phonetics. Once, in the days when the Imperial Institute rose in South Kensington, and Joseph Chamberlain[3] was booming the Empire, I induced the editor of a leading monthly review to commission an article from Sweet on the imperial importance of his subject. When it arrived, it contained nothing but a savagely derisive attack on a professor of language and literature whose chair Sweet regarded as proper to a phonetic expert only. The article, being libellous, had to be returned as impossible; and I had to renounce my dream of dragging its author into the limelight. When I met him afterwards, for the first time for many years, I found to my astonishment that he, who had been a quite tolerably presentable young man, had actually managed by sheer scorn to alter his personal appearance until he had become a sort of walking repudiation of Oxford and all its traditions. It must have been largely in his own despite that he was squeezed into something called a Readership of phonetics there. The future of phonetics rests probably with his pupils, who all swore by him; but nothing could bring the man himself into any sort of compliance with the university to which he nevertheless clung by divine right in an intensely

---

1. Henrik Ibsen (1828–1906), Norwegian playwright whose realist plays dealing with contemporary social problems were a large influence on Shaw.

2. Samuel Butler (1835–1902), whose satirical novels were admired by Shaw.

3. Joseph Chamberlain (1836–1914), British statesman.

Oxonian way. I daresay his papers, if he has left any, include some satires that may be published without too destructive results fifty years hence. He was, I believe, not in the least an ill-natured man: very much the opposite, I should say; but he would not suffer fools gladly; and to him all scholars who were not rabid phoneticians were fools.

Those who knew him will recognize in my third act the allusion to the Current Shorthand in which he used to write postcards. It may be acquired from a four and sixpenny manual published by the Clarendon Press. The postcards which Mrs Higgins describes are such as I have received from Sweet. I would decipher a sound which a cockney would represent by *zerr*, and a Frenchman by *seu*, and then write demanding with some heat what on earth it meant. Sweet, with boundless contempt for my stupidity, would reply that it not only meant but obviously was the word Result, as no other word containing that sound, and capable of making sense with the context, existed in any language spoken on earth. That less expert mortals should require fuller indications was beyond Sweet's patience. Therefore, though the whole point of his Current Shorthand is that it can express every sound in the language perfectly, vowels as well as consonants, and that your hand has to make no stroke except the easy and current ones with which you write m, n, and u, l, p, and q, scribbling them at whatever angle comes easiest to you, his unfortunate determination to make this remarkable and quite legible script serve also as a shorthand reduced it in his own practice to the most inscrutable of cryptograms. His true objective was the provision of a full, accurate, legible script for our language; but he was led past that by his contempt for the popular Pitman system of shorthand, which he called the Pitfall system. The triumph of Pitman was a triumph of business organization: there was a weekly paper to persuade you to learn Pitman: there were cheap textbooks and exercise books and transcripts of speeches for you to copy, and schools where experienced teachers coached you up to the necessary proficiency. Sweet could not organize his market in that fashion. He might as well have been the Sybil who tore up the leaves of prophecy that nobody would attend to. The four and sixpenny manual, mostly in his lithographed hand-writing, that was never vulgarly advertized, may perhaps some day be taken up by a syndicate and pushed upon the public as The Times pushed the Encyclopaedia Britannica; but until then it will certainly not prevail against Pitman. I have bought three copies of it during my lifetime; and I am informed by the publishers that its cloistered existence is still a steady and healthy one. I actually learned the system two several[4] times; and yet the shorthand in which I am writing these lines is Pitman's. And the reason is, that my secretary cannot transcribe Sweet, having been perforce taught in the schools of Pitman. In America I could use the commercially organized Gregg shorthand, which has taken a hint from Sweet by making its letters writable (current, Sweet would have called them) instead of having to be geometrically drawn like Pitman's; but all these systems, including Sweet's, are spoilt by making them available for verbatim reporting, in which complete and exact spelling and word division are impossible. A complete and exact phonetic script is neither practicable nor necessary for ordinary use; but if we enlarge our alphabet to the Russian size, and make our spelling as phonetic as Spanish, the advance will be prodigious.

Pygmalion[5] Higgins is not a portrait of Sweet, to whom the adventure of Eliza Doolittle would have been impossible; still, as will be seen, there are touches of Sweet in the play. With Higgins's physique and temperament Sweet might have set the Thames on fire. As it was, he impressed himself professionally on Europe to an

4. Different.
5. In Greek myth, Pygmalion was king of Cyprus and a sculptor; he fell in love with his own creation, and Aphrodite brought the statue, Galatea, to life.

extent that made his comparative personal obscurity, and the failure of Oxford to do justice to his eminence, a puzzle to foreign specialists in his subject. I do not blame Oxford, because I think Oxford is quite right in demanding a certain social amenity from its nurslings (heaven knows it is not exorbitant in its requirements!); for although I well know how hard it is for a man of genius with a seriously underrated subject to maintain serene and kindly relations with the men who underrate it, and who keep all the best places for less important subjects which they profess without originality and sometimes without much capacity for them, still, if he overwhelms them with wrath and disdain, he cannot expect them to heap honors on him.

Of the later generations of phoneticians I know little. Among them towered Robert Bridges, to whom perhaps Higgins may owe his Miltonic sympathies, though here again I must disclaim all portraiture. But if the play makes the public aware that there are such people as phoneticians, and that they are among the most important people in England at present, it will serve its turn.

I wish to boast that Pygmalion has been an extremely successful play, both on stage and screen, all over Europe and North America as well as at home. It is so intensely and deliberately didactic, and its subject is esteemed so dry, that I delight in throwing it at the heads of the wiseacres who repeat the parrot cry that art should never be didactic. It goes to prove my contention that great art can never be anything else.

Finally, and for the encouragement of people troubled with accents that cut them off from all high employment, I may add that the change wrought by Professor Higgins in the flower-girl is neither impossible nor uncommon. The modern concierge's daughter who fulfils her ambition by playing the Queen of Spain in Ruy Blas at the Théâtre Français is only one of many thousands of men and women who have sloughed off their native dialects and acquired a new tongue. Our West End shop assistants and domestic servants are bi-lingual. But the thing has to be done scientifically, or the last state of the aspirant may be worse than the first. An honest slum dialect is more tolerable than the attempts of phonetically untaught persons to imitate the plutocracy. Ambitious flower-girls who read this play must not imagine that they can pass themselves off as fine ladies by untutored imitation. They must learn their alphabet over again, and different, from a phonetic expert. Imitation will only make them ridiculous.

NOTE FOR TECHNICIANS. A complete representation of the play as printed for the first time in this edition is technically possible only on the cinema screen or on stages furnished with exceptionally elaborate machinery. For ordinary theatrical use the scenes separated by rows of asterisks are to be omitted.

In the dialogue an e upside down indicates the indefinite vowel, sometimes called obscure or neutral, for which, though it is one of the commonest sounds in English speech, our wretched alphabet has no letter.

ACT 1

London at 11.15 p.m. Torrents of heavy summer rain. Cab whistles blowing frantically in all directions. Pedestrians running for shelter into the portico of St Paul's church (not Wren's[1] cathedral but Inigo Jones's[2] church in Covent Garden vegetable market), among them a lady and her daughter in evening dress. All are peering out gloomily at the rain, except one man with his back turned to the rest, wholly preoccupied with a notebook in which he is writing.

The church clock strikes the first quarter.

---

1. Sir Christopher Wren (1632–1723), English architect.   2. Inigo Jones (1573–1652), English architect.

THE DAUGHTER [*in the space between the central pillars, close to the one on her left*]: I'm getting chilled to the bone. What can Freddy be doing all this time? He's been gone twenty minutes.

THE MOTHER [*on her daughter's right*]: Not so long. But he ought to have got us a cab by this.

A BYSTANDER [*on the lady's right*]: He wont get no cab not until half-past eleven, missus, when they come back after dropping their theatre fares.

THE MOTHER: But we must have a cab. We cant stand here until half-past eleven. It's too bad.

THE BYSTANDER: Well it aint my fault, missus.

THE DAUGHTER: If Freddy had a bit of gumption, he would have got one at the theatre door.

THE MOTHER: What could he have done, poor boy?

THE DAUGHTER: Other people get cabs. Why couldnt he?

[*Freddy rushes in out of the rain from the Southampton Street side, and comes between them closing a dripping umbrella. He is a young man of twenty, in evening dress, very wet round the ankles.*]

THE DAUGHTER: Well, havnt you got a cab?

FREDDY: Theres not one to be had for love or money.

THE MOTHER: Oh, Freddy, there must be one. You cant have tried.

THE DAUGHTER: It's too tiresome. Do you expect us to go and get one ourselves?

FREDDY: I tell you theyre all engaged. The rain was so sudden: nobody was prepared; and everybody had to take a cab. Ive been to Charing Cross one way and nearly to Ludgate Circus the other; and they were all engaged.

THE MOTHER: Did you try Trafalgar Square?

FREDDY: There wasnt one at Trafalgar Square.

THE DAUGHTER: Did you try?

FREDDY: I tried as far as Charing Cross Station. Did you expect me to walk to Hammersmith?

THE DAUGHTER: You havnt tried at all.

THE MOTHER: You really are very helpless, Freddy. Go again; and dont come back until you have found a cab.

FREDDY: I shall simply get soaked for nothing.

THE DAUGHTER: And what about us? Are we to stay here all night in this draught, with next to nothing on? You selfish pig—

FREDDY: Oh, very well: I'll go. I'll go. [*He opens his umbrella and dashes off Strandwards, but comes into collision with a flower girl who is hurrying in for shelter, knocking her basket out of her hands. A blinding flash of lightning, followed instantly by a rattling peal of thunder, orchestrates the incident.*]

THE FLOWER GIRL: Nah then, Freddy: look wh'y' gowin, deah.

FREDDY: Sorry. [*He rushes off.*]

THE FLOWER GIRL [*picking up her scattered flowers and replacing them in the basket*]: Theres menners f'yer! Tǝ -oo banches o voylets trod into the mad.

[*She sits down on the plinth of the column, sorting her flowers, on the lady's right. She is not at all a romantic figure. She is perhaps eighteen, perhaps twenty, hardly older. She wears a little sailor hat of black straw that has long been exposed to the dust and soot of London and has seldom if ever been brushed. Her hair needs washing rather badly: its mousy color can hardly be natural. She wears a shoddy black coat that reaches*] *nearly to her knees and is shaped to her waist. She has a brown skirt with a coarse apron. Her boots are much the worse for wear. She is no doubt as clean as she can afford to be; but compared to the ladies she is very dirty. Her features are no worse than theirs; but their condition leaves something to be desired; and she needs the services of a dentist.*]

THE MOTHER: How do you know that my son's name is Freddy, pray?

THE FLOWER GIRL: Ow, eez, yə -ooa san, is e? Wal, fewd dan y' d-ooty bawmz a mather should, eed now bettern to spawl a pore gel's flahrzn than ran away athaht pyin. Will ye-oo py me f'them? [*Here, with apologies, this desperate attempt to represent her dialect without a phonetic alphabet must be abandoned as unintelligible outside London.*]

THE DAUGHTER: Do nothing of the sort, mother. The idea!

THE MOTHER: Please allow me, Clara. Have you any pennies?

THE DAUGHTER: No. Ive nothing smaller than sixpence.

THE FLOWER GIRL [*hopefully*]: I can give you change for a tanner, kind lady.

THE MOTHER [*to Clara*]: Give it to me. [*Clara parts reluctantly.*] Now [*to the girl*] This is for your flowers.

THE FLOWER GIRL: Thank you kindly, lady.

THE DAUGHTER: Make her give you the change. These things are only a penny a bunch.

THE MOTHER: Do hold your tongue, Clara. [*To the girl*] You can keep the change.

THE FLOWER GIRL: Oh, thank you, lady.

THE MOTHER: Now tell me how you know that young gentleman's name.

THE FLOWER GIRL: I didnt.

THE MOTHER: I heard you call him by it. Dont try to deceive me.

THE FLOWER GIRL [*protesting*]: Who's trying to deceive you? I called him Freddy or Charlie same as you might yourself if you was talking to a stranger and wished to be pleasant.

THE DAUGHTER: Sixpence thrown away! Really, mamma, you might have spared Freddy that. [*She retreats in disgust behind the pillar.*]

[*An elderly gentleman of the amiable military type rushes into the shelter, and closes a dripping umbrella. He is in the same plight as Freddy, very wet about the ankles. He is in evening dress, with a light overcoat. He takes the place left vacant by the daughter.*]

THE GENTLEMAN: Phew!

THE MOTHER [*to the gentleman*]: Oh, sir, is there any sign of its stopping?

THE GENTLEMAN: I'm afraid not. It started worse than ever about two minutes ago. [*He goes to the plinth beside the flower girl; puts up his foot on it; and stoops to turn down his trouser ends.*]

THE MOTHER: Oh dear! [*She retires sadly and joins her daughter.*]

THE FLOWER GIRL [*taking advantage of the military gentleman's proximity to establish friendly relations with him*]: If it's worse, it's a sign it's nearly over. So cheer up, Captain; and buy a flower off a poor girl.

THE GENTLEMAN: I'm sorry. I havnt any change.

THE FLOWER GIRL: I can give you change, Captain.

THE GENTLEMAN: For a sovereign? Ive nothing less.

THE FLOWER GIRL: Garn! Oh do buy a flower off me, Captain. I can change half-a-crown. Take this for tuppence.

THE GENTLEMAN: Now dont be troublesome: theres a good girl. [*Trying his pockets.*] I really havnt any change—Stop: heres three hapence, if thats any use to you [*he retreats to the other pillar*].

THE FLOWER GIRL [*disappointed, but thinking three halfpence better than nothing*]: Thank you, sir.

THE BYSTANDER [*to the girl*]: You be careful: give him a flower for it. Theres a bloke here behind taking down every blessed word youre saying. [*All turn to the man who is taking notes.*]

THE FLOWER GIRL [*springing up terrified*]: I aint done nothing wrong by speaking to the gentleman. Ive a right to sell flowers if I keep off the kerb. [*Hysterically.*] I'm a respectable girl: so help me. I never spoke to him except to ask him to buy a flower off me.

[*General hubbub, mostly sympathetic to the flower girl, but deprecating her excessive sensibility. Cries of Dont start hollerin. Who's hurting you? Nobody's going to touch you. Whats the good of fussing? Steady on. Easy easy, etc., come from the elderly staid spectators, who pat her comfortingly. Less patient ones bid her shut her head, or ask her roughly what is wrong with her. A remoter group, not knowing what the matter is, crowd in and increase the noise with question and answer: Whats the row? What-she-do? Where is he? A tec³ taking her down. What! him? Yes: him over there: Took money off the gentleman, etc.*]

THE FLOWER GIRL [*breaking through them to the gentleman, crying wildly*]: Oh, sir, dont let him charge me. You dunno what it means to me. Theyll take away my character and drive me on the streets for speaking to gentlemen. They—

THE NOTE TAKER [*coming forward on her right, the rest crowding after him*]: There! there! there! there! Who's hurting you, you silly girl? What do you take me for?

THE BYSTANDER: It's aw rawt: e's a genleman: look at his bə -oots. [*Explaining to the note taker.*] She thought you was a copper's nark, sir.

THE NOTE TAKER [*with quick interest*]: Whats a copper's nark?

THE BYSTANDER [*inapt at definition*]: It's a—well, it's a copper's nark, as you might say. What else would you call it? A sort of informer.

THE FLOWER GIRL [*still hysterical*]: I take my Bible oath I never said a word—

THE NOTE TAKER [*overbearing but good-humored*]: Oh, shut up, shut up. Do I look like a policeman?

THE FLOWER GIRL [*far from reassured*]: Then what did you take down my words for? How do I know whether you took me down right? You just shew⁴ me what youve wrote about me. [*The note taker opens his book and holds it steadily under her nose, though the pressure of the mob trying to read it over his shoulders would upset a weaker man.*] Whats that? That aint proper writing. I cant read that.

THE NOTE TAKER: I can. [*Reads, reproducing her pronunciation exactly.*] "Cheer ap, Keptin; n' baw ya flahr orf a pore gel."

THE FLOWER GIRL [*much distressed*]: It's because I called him Captain. I meant no harm. [*To the gentleman.*] Oh, sir, dont let him lay a charge agen me for a word like that. You—

THE GENTLEMAN: Charge! I make no charge. [*To the note taker.*] Really, sir, if you are a detective, you need not begin protecting me against molestation by young women until I ask you. Anybody could see that the girl meant no harm.

---

3. Detective.   4. Show.

THE BYSTANDERS GENERALLY [*demonstrating against police espionage*]: Course they could. What business is it of yours? You mind your own affairs. He wants promotion, he does. Taking down people's words! Girl never said a word to him. What harm if she did? Nice thing a girl cant shelter from the rain without being insulted, etc., etc., etc. [*She is conducted by the more sympathetic demonstrators back to her plinth, where she resumes her seat and struggles with her emotion.*]

THE BYSTANDER: He aint a tec. He's a blooming busy-body: thats what he is. I tell you, look at his bə -oots.

THE NOTE TAKER [*turning on him genially*]: And how are all your people down at Selsey?

THE BYSTANDER [*suspiciously*]: Who told you my people come from Selsey?

THE NOTE TAKER: Never you mind. They did. [*To the girl.*] How do you come to be up so far east? You were born in Lisson Grove.

THE FLOWER GIRL [*appalled*]: Oh, what harm is there in my leaving Lisson Grove? It wasnt fit for a pig to live in; and I had to pay four-and-six a week. [*In tears.*] Oh, boo—hoo—oo—

THE NOTE TAKER: Live where you like; but stop that noise.

THE GENTLEMAN [*to the girl*]: Come, come! he cant touch you: you have a right to live where you please.

A SARCASTIC BYSTANDER [*thrusting himself between the note taker and the gentleman*]: Park Lane, for instance. I'd like to go into the Housing Question with you, I would.

THE FLOWER GIRL [*subsiding into a brooding melancholy over her basket, and talking very low-spiritedly to herself*]: I'm a good girl, I am.

THE SARCASTIC BYSTANDER [*not attending to her*]: Do you know where I come from?

THE NOTE TAKER [*promptly*]: Hoxton.

[*Titterings. Popular interest in the note taker's performance increases.*]

THE SARCASTIC ONE [*amazed*]: Well, who said I didnt? Bly me! you know everything, you do.

THE FLOWER GIRL [*still nursing her sense of injury*]: Aint no call to meddle with me, he aint.

THE BYSTANDER [*to her*]: Of course he aint. Dont you stand it from him. [*To the note taker.*] See here: what call have you to know about people what never offered to meddle with you?

THE FLOWER GIRL: Let him say what he likes. I dont want to have no truck with him.

THE BYSTANDER: You take us for dirt under your feet, dont you? Catch you taking liberties with a gentleman!

THE SARCASTIC BYSTANDER: Yes: tell him where he come from if you want to go fortune-telling.

THE NOTE TAKER: Cheltenham, Harrow, Cambridge, and India.

THE GENTLEMAN: Quite right.

[*Great laughter. Reaction in the note taker's favor. Exclamations of* He knows all about it. Told him proper. Hear him tell the toff where he come from? etc.]

THE GENTLEMAN: May I ask, sir, do you do this for your living at a music hall?

THE NOTE TAKER: I've thought of that. Perhaps I shall some day.

[*The rain has stopped; and the persons on the outside of the crowd begin to drop off.*]

THE FLOWER GIRL [*resenting the reaction*]: He's no gentleman, he aint, to interfere with a poor girl.

THE DAUGHTER [*out of patience, pushing her way rudely to the front and displacing the
gentleman, who politely retires to the other side of the pillar*]: What on earth is Freddy
doing? I shall get pneumownia if I stay in this draught any longer.

THE NOTE TAKER [*to himself, hastily making a note of her pronunciation of "monia"*]:
Earlscourt.

THE DAUGHTER [*violently*]: Will you please keep your impertinent remarks to
yourself.

THE NOTE TAKER: Did I say that out loud? I didnt mean to. I beg your pardon.
Your mother's Epsom, unmistakeably.

THE MOTHER [*advancing between the daughter and the note taker*]: How very curious! I was brought up in Largelady Park, near Epsom.

THE NOTE TAKER [*uproariously amused*]: Ha! ha! what a devil of a name! Excuse
me. [*To the daughter.*] You want a cab, do you?

THE DAUGHTER: Dont dare speak to me.

THE MOTHER: Oh, please, please, Clara. [*Her daughter repudiates her with an angry
shrug and retires haughtily.*] We should be so grateful to you, sir, if you found us a
cab. [*The note taker produces a whistle.*] Oh, thank you. [*She joins her daughter. The
note taker blows a piercing blast.*]

THE SARCASTIC BYSTANDER: There! I knowed he was a plain-clothes copper.

THE BYSTANDER: That aint a police whistle: thats a sporting whistle.

THE FLOWER GIRL [*still preoccupied with her wounded feelings*]: He's no right to
take away my character. My character is the same to me as any lady's.

THE NOTE TAKER: I dont know whether youve noticed it; but the rain stopped
about two minutes ago.

THE BYSTANDER: So it has. Why didnt you say so before? And us losing our time
listening to your silliness! [*He walks off towards the Strand.*]

THE SARCASTIC BYSTANDER: I can tell where you come from. You come from
Anwell. Go back there.

THE NOTE TAKER [*helpfully*]: Hanwell.

THE SARCASTIC BYSTANDER [*affecting great distinction of speech*]: Thenk you,
teacher. Haw haw! So long. [*He touches his hat with mock respect and strolls off.*]

THE FLOWER GIRL: Frightening people like that! How would he like it himself?

THE MOTHER: It's quite fine now, Clara. We can walk to a motor bus. Come. [*She
gathers her skirts above her ankles and hurries off towards the Strand.*]

THE DAUGHTER: But the cab—[*her mother is out of hearing*]. Oh, how tiresome!
[*She follows angrily.*]

[*All the rest have gone except the note taker, the gentleman, and the flower girl, who
sits arranging her basket, and still pitying herself in murmurs.*]

THE FLOWER GIRL: Poor girl! Hard enough for her to live without being worried
and chivied.

THE GENTLEMAN [*returning to his former place on the note taker's left*]: How do you
do it, if I may ask?

THE NOTE TAKER: Simply phonetics. The science of speech. Thats my profession: also my hobby. Happy is the man who can make a living by his hobby! You
can spot an Irishman or a Yorkshireman by his brogue. *I* can place any man within six miles. I can place him within two miles in London. Sometimes within two
streets.

THE FLOWER GIRL: Ought to be ashamed of himself, unmanly coward!

THE GENTLEMAN: But is there a living in that?

THE NOTE TAKER: Oh, yes. Quite a fat one. This is an age of upstarts. Men begin in Kentish Town with £80 a year, and end in Park Lane with a hundred thousand. They want to drop Kentish Town; but they give themselves away every time they open their mouths. Now I can teach them—

THE FLOWER GIRL: Let him mind his own business and leave a poor girl—

THE NOTE TAKER [*explosively*]: Woman: cease this detestable boohooing instantly: or else seek the shelter of some other place of worship.

THE FLOWER GIRL [*with feeble defiance*]: Ive a right to be here if I like, same as you.

THE NOTE TAKER: A woman who utters such depressing and disgusting sounds has no right to be anywhere—no right to live. Remember that you are a human being with a soul and the divine gift of articulate speech: that your native language is the language of Shakespear and Milton and The Bible; and dont sit there crooning like a bilious pigeon.

THE FLOWER GIRL [*quite overwhelmed, looking up at him in mingled wonder and deprecation without daring to raise her head*]: Ah-ah-ah-ow-ow-ow-oo!

THE NOTE TAKER [*whipping out his book*]: Heavens! what a sound! [*He writes; then holds out the book and reads, reproducing her vowels exactly.*] Ah-ah-ah-ow-ow-ow-oo!

THE FLOWER GIRL [*tickled by the performance, and laughing in spite of herself*]: Garn!

THE NOTE TAKER: You see this creature with her kerbstone English: the English that will keep her in the gutter to the end of her days. Well, sir, in three months I could pass that girl off as a duchess at an ambassador's garden party. I could even get her a place as lady's maid or shop assistant, which requires better English.

THE FLOWER GIRL: What's that you say?

THE NOTE TAKER: Yes, you squashed cabbage leaf, you disgrace to the noble architecture of these columns, you incarnate insult to the English language: I could pass you off as the Queen of Sheba. [*To the Gentleman.*] Can you believe that?

THE GENTLEMAN: Of course I can. I am myself a student of Indian dialects; and—

THE NOTE TAKER [*eagerly*]: Are you? Do you know Colonel Pickering, the author of Spoken Sanscrit?

THE GENTLEMAN: I am Colonel Pickering. Who are you?

THE NOTE TAKER: Henry Higgins, author of Higgins's Universal Alphabet.

PICKERING [*with enthusiasm*]: I came from India to meet you.

HIGGINS: I was going to India to meet you.

PICKERING: Where do you live?

HIGGINS: 27A Wimpole Street. Come and see me tomorrow.

PICKERING: I'm at the Carlton. Come with me now and lets have a jaw over some supper.

HIGGINS: Right you are.

THE FLOWER GIRL [*to Pickering, as he passes her*]: Buy a flower, kind gentleman. I'm short for my lodging.

PICKERING: I really havnt any change. I'm sorry. [*He goes away.*]

HIGGINS [*shocked at the girl's mendacity*]: Liar. You said you could change half-a-crown.

THE FLOWER GIRL [*rising in desperation*]: You ought to be stuffed with nails, you ought. [*Flinging the basket at his feet.*] Take the whole blooming basket for sixpence. [*The church clock strikes the second quarter.*]

HIGGINS [*hearing in it the voice of God, rebuking him for his Pharisaic want of charity to the poor girl*]: A reminder. [*He raises his hat solemnly; then throws a handful of money into the basket and follows Pickering.*]

THE FLOWER GIRL [*picking up a half-crown*]: Ah-ow-ooh! [*picking up a couple of florins*] Aaah-ow-ooh! [*picking up several coins*] Aaaaaah-ow-ooh! [*picking up a half-sovereign*] Aaaaaaaaaaaah-ow-ooh!!!

FREDDY [*springing out of a taxicab*]: Got one at last. Hallo! [*To the girl.*] Where are the two ladies that were here?

THE FLOWER GIRL: They walked to the bus when the rain stopped.

FREDDY: And left me with a cab on my hands! Damnation!

THE FLOWER GIRL [*with grandeur*]: Never mind, young man. I'm going home in a taxi. [*She sails off to the cab. The driver puts his hand behind him and holds the door firmly shut against her. Quite understanding his mistrust, she shews him her handful of money.*] A taxi fare aint no object to me, Charlie. [*He grins and opens the door.*] Here. What about the basket?

THE TAXIMAN: Give it here. Tuppence extra.

LIZA: No: I dont want nobody to see it. [*She crushes it into the cab and gets in, continuing the conversation through the window.*] Goodbye, Freddy.

FREDDY [*dazedly raising his hat*]: Goodbye.

TAXIMAN: Where to?

LIZA: Bucknam Pellis [Buckingham Palace].

TAXIMAN: What d'ye mean—Bucknam Pellis?

LIZA: Dont you know where it is? In the Green Park, where the King lives. Goodbye, Freddy. Dont let me keep you standing there. Goodbye.

FREDDY: Goodbye. [*He goes.*]

TAXIMAN: Here? Whats this about Bucknam Pellis? What business have you at Bucknam Pellis?

LIZA: Of course I havnt none. But I wasnt going to let him know that. You drive me home.

TAXIMAN: And wheres home?

LIZA: Angel Court, Drury Lane, next Meiklejohn's oil shop.

TAXIMAN: That sounds more like it, Judy. [*He drives off.*]

*   *   *

Let us follow the taxi to the entrance to Angel Court, a narrow little archway between two shops, one of them Meiklejohn's oil shop. When it stops there, Eliza gets out, dragging her basket with her.

LIZA: How much?

TAXIMAN [*indicating the taximeter*]: Cant you read? A shilling.

LIZA: A shilling for two minutes!!

TAXIMAN: Two minutes or ten: it's all the same.

LIZA: Well. I dont call it right.

TAXIMAN: Ever been in a taxi before?

LIZA [*with dignity*]: Hundreds and thousands of times, young man.

TAXIMAN [*laughing at her*]: Good for you. Judy, Keep the shilling, darling, with best love from all at home. Good luck! [*He drives off.*]

LIZA [*humiliated*]: Impidence!

[*She picks up the basket and trudges up the alley with it to her lodging: a small room with very old wall paper hanging loose in the damp places. A broken pane in the window is mended with paper. A portrait of a popular actor and a fashion plate of ladies' dresses, all wildly beyond poor Eliza's means, both torn from newspapers, are pinned up on the wall. A birdcage hangs in the window; but its tenant died long ago: it remains as a memorial only.*

These are the only visible luxuries: the rest is the irreducible minimum of poverty's needs: a wretched bed heaped with all sorts of coverings that have any warmth in them, a draped packing case with a basin and jug on it and a little looking glass over it, a chair and table, the refuse of some suburban kitchen, and an American alarum clock on the shelf above the unused fireplace: the whole lighted with a gas lamp with a penny in the slot meter. Rent: four shillings a week.

Here Eliza, chronically weary, but too excited to go to bed, sits, counting her new riches and dreaming and planning what to do with them, until the gas goes out, when she enjoys for the first time the sensation of being able to put in another penny without grudging it. This prodigal mood does not extinguish her gnawing sense of the need for economy sufficiently to prevent her from calculating that she can dream and plan in bed more cheaply and warmly than sitting up without a fire. So she takes off her shawl and skirt and adds them to the miscellaneous bedclothes. Then she kicks off her shoes and gets into bed without any further change.]

ACT 2

Next day at 11 a.m. Higgins's laboratory in Wimpole Street. It is a room on the first floor, looking on the street, and was meant for the drawing room. The double doors are in the middle of the back wall; and persons entering find in the corner to their right two tall file cabinets at right angles to one another against the wall. In this corner stands a flat writing-table, on which are a phonograph, a laryngoscope, a row of tiny organ pipes with a bellows, a set of lamp chimneys for singing flames with burners attached to a gas plug in the wall by an indiarubber tube, several tuning-forks of different sizes, a life-size image of half a human head, shewing in section the vocal organs, and a box containing a supply of wax cylinders for the phonograph.

Further down the room, on the same side, is a fireplace, with a comfortable leather-covered easy-chair at the side of the hearth nearest the door, and a coal-scuttle. There is a clock on the mantel-piece. Between the fireplace and the phonograph table is a stand for newspapers.

On the other side of the central door, to the left of the visitor, is a cabinet of shallow drawers. On it is a telephone and the telephone directory. The corner beyond, and most of the side wall, is occupied by a grand piano, with the keyboard at the end furthest from the door, and a bench for the player extending the full length of the keyboard. On the piano is a dessert dish heaped with fruit and sweets, mostly chocolates.

The middle of the room is clear. Besides the easy-chair, the piano bench, and two chairs at the phonograph table, there is one stray chair. It stands near the fireplace. On the walls, engravings: mostly Piranesis[1] and mezzotint[2] portraits. No paintings.

Pickering is seated at the table, putting down some cards and a tuning-fork which he has been using. Higgins is standing up near him, closing two or three file drawers which are hanging out. He appears in the morning light as a robust, vital, appetizing sort of man of forty or thereabouts, dressed in a professional-looking black frock-coat with a white linen collar and black silk tie. He is of the energetic scientific type, heartily, even violently interested in everything that can be studied as a scientific subject, and careless about himself and other people, including their feelings. He is,

---

1. Giovanni Piranesi (1720–1778), Italian architect and engraver.   2. Prints produced with copper or steel engraved plates.

in fact, but for his years and size, rather like a very impetuous baby 'taking notice' eagerly and loudly, and requiring almost as much watching to keep him out of unintended mischief. His manner varies from genial bullying when he is in a good humor to stormy petulance when anything goes wrong: but he is so entirely frank and void of malice that he remains likeable even in his least reasonable moments.

HIGGINS [*as he shuts the last drawer*]: Well, I think thats the whole show.

PICKERING: It's really amazing. I havnt taken half of it in, you know.

HIGGINS: Would you like to go over any of it again?

PICKERING [*rising and coming to the fireplace, where he plants himself with his back to the fire*]: No, thank you: not now. I'm quite done up for this morning.

HIGGINS [*following him, and standing beside him on his left*]: Tired of listening to sounds?

PICKERING: Yes. It's a fearful strain. I rather fancied myself because I can pronounce twenty-four distinct vowel sounds; but your hundred and thirty beat me. I cant hear a bit of difference between most of them.

HIGGINS [*chuckling, and going over to the piano to eat sweets*]: Oh, that comes with practice. You hear no difference at first; but you keep on listening, and presently you find theyre all as different as A from B. [*Mrs Pearce looks in: she is Higgins's housekeeper.*] Whats the matter?

MRS PEARCE [*hesitating, evidently perplexed*]: A young woman asks to see you, sir.

HIGGINS: A young woman! What does she want?

MRS PEARCE: Well, sir, she says youll be glad to see her when you know what she's come about. She's quite a common girl, sir. Very common indeed. I should have sent her away, only I thought perhaps you wanted her to talk into your machines. I hope Ive not done wrong; but really you see such queer people sometimes—youll excuse me, I'm sure, sir—

HIGGINS: Oh, thats all right, Mrs Pearce. Has she an interesting accent?

MRS PEARCE: Oh, something dreadful, sir, really. I dont know how you can take an interest in it.

HIGGINS [*to Pickering*]: Lets have her up. Shew her up, Mrs Pearce. [*He rushes across to his working table and picks out a cylinder to use on the phonograph.*]

MRS PEARCE [*only half resigned to it*]: Very well, sir. It's for you to say. [*She goes downstairs.*]

HIGGINS: This is rather a bit of luck. I'll shew you how I make records. We'll set her talking; and I'll take it down first in Bell's Visible Speech; then in broad Romic; and then we'll get her on the phonograph so that you can turn her on as often as you like with the written transcript before you.

MRS PEARCE [*returning*]: This is the young woman, sir.

[*The flower girl enters in state. She has a hat with three ostrich feathers, orange, sky-blue, and red. She has a nearly clean apron and the shoddy coat has been tidied a little. The pathos of this deplorable figure, with its innocent vanity and consequential air, touches Pickering, who has already straightened himself in the presence of Mrs Pearce. But as to Higgins, the only distinction he makes between men and women is that when he is neither bullying nor exclaiming to the heavens against some featherweight cross, he coaxes women as a child coaxes its nurse when it wants to get anything out of her.*]

HIGGINS [*brusquely, recognizing her with unconcealed disappointment, and at once, baby-like, making an intolerable grievance of it*]: Why, this is the girl I jotted down last night. She's no use: Ive got all the records I want of the Lisson Grove lingo; and I'm not going to waste another cylinder on it. [*To the girl.*] Be off with you: I dont want you.

THE FLOWER GIRL: Dont you be so saucy. You aint heard what I come for yet. [*To Mrs Pearce, who is waiting at the door for further instructions.*] Did you tell him I come in a taxi?

MRS PEARCE: Nonsense, girl! what do you think a gentleman like Mr Higgins cares what you came in?

THE FLOWER GIRL: Oh, we are proud! He aint above giving lessons, not him: I heard him say so. Well, I aint come here to ask for any compliment; and if my money's not good enough I can go elsewhere.

HIGGINS: Good enough for what?

THE FLOWER GIRL: Good enough for yə -oo. Now you know, dont you? I'm coming to have lessons, I am. And to pay for em tə -oo: make no mistake.

HIGGINS [*stupent*][3]: Well!!! [*Recovering his breath with a gasp.*] What do you expect me to say to you?

THE FLOWER GIRL: Well, if you was a gentleman, you might ask me to sit down, I think. Dont I tell you I'm bringing you business?

HIGGINS: Pickering: shall we ask this baggage to sit down, or shall we throw her out of the window?

THE FLOWER GIRL [*running away in terror to the piano, where she turns at bay*]: Ah-ah-oh-ow-ow-ow-oo! [*Wounded and whimpering.*] I wont be called a baggage when Ive offered to pay like any lady.

[*Motionless, the two men stare at her from the other side of the room, amazed.*]

PICKERING [*gently*]: But what is it you want?

THE FLOWER GIRL: I want to be a lady in a flower shop stead of sellin at the corner of Tottenham Court Road. But they wont take me unless I can talk more genteel. He said he could teach me. Well, here I am ready to pay him—not asking any favor—and he treats me zif I was dirt.

MRS PEARCE: How can you be such a foolish ignorant girl as to think you could afford to pay Mr Higgins?

THE FLOWER GIRL: Why shouldnt I? I know what lessons cost as well as you do; and I'm ready to pay.

HIGGINS: How much?

THE FLOWER GIRL [*coming back to him triumphant*]: Now youre talking! I thought youd come off it when you saw a chance of getting back a bit of what you chucked at me last night. [*Confidentially.*] Youd had a drop in, hadnt you?

HIGGINS [*peremptorily*]: Sit down.

THE FLOWER GIRL: Oh, if youre going to make a compliment of it—

HIGGINS [*thundering at her*]: Sit down.

MRS PEARCE [*severely*]: Sit down, girl. Do as youre told.

THE FLOWER GIRL: Ah-ah-ah-ow-ow-oo! [*She stands, half rebellious, half-bewildered.*]

PICKERING [*very courteous*]: Wont you sit down? [*He places the stray chair near the hearthrug between himself and Higgins.*]

LIZA [*coyly*]: Dont mind if I do. [*She sits down. Pickering returns to the hearthrug.*]

HIGGINS: Whats your name?

THE FLOWER GIRL: Liza Doolittle.

HIGGINS [*declaiming gravely*]: Eliza, Elizabeth, Betsy and Bess,
    They went to the woods to get a bird's nes':

3. Astonished.

PICKERING: They found a nest with four eggs in it:

HIGGINS: They took one apiece, and left three in it.

[*They laugh heartily at their own fun.*]

LIZA: Oh, dont be silly.

MRS PEARCE [*placing herself behind Eliza's chair*]: You mustnt speak to the gentleman like that.

LIZA: Well, why wont he speak sensible to me?

HIGGINS: Come back to business. How much do you propose to pay me for the lessons?

LIZA: Oh, I know whats right. A lady friend of mine gets French lessons for eighteenpence an hour from a real French gentleman. Well, you wouldnt have the face to ask me the same for teaching me my own language as you would for French; so I wont give more than a shilling. Take it or leave it.

HIGGINS [*walking up and down the room, ratting his keys and his cash in his pockets*]: You know, Pickering, if you consider a shilling, not as a simple shilling, but as a percentage of this girl's income, it works out as fully equivalent to sixty or seventy guineas from a millionaire.

PICKERING: How so?

HIGGINS: Figure it out. A millionaire has about £150 a day. She earns about half-a-crown.

LIZA [*haughtily*]: Who told you I only—

HIGGINS [*continuing*]: She offers me two-fifths of her day's income for a lesson. Two-fifths of a millionaire's income for a day would be somewhere about £60. It's handsome. By George, it's enormous! it's the biggest offer I ever had.

LIZA [*rising, terrified*]: Sixty pounds! What are you talking about? I never offered you sixty pounds. Where would I get—

HIGGINS: Hold your tongue.

LIZA [*weeping*]: But I aint got sixty pounds. Oh—

MRS PEARCE: Dont cry, you silly girl. Sit down. Nobody is going to touch your money.

HIGGINS: Somebody is going to touch you, with a broom-stick, if you dont stop snivelling. Sit down.

LIZA [*obeying slowly*]: Ah-ah-ah-ow-oo-o! One would think you was my father.

HIGGINS: If I decide to teach you, I'll be worse than two fathers to you. Here [*he offers her his silk handkerchief*]!

LIZA: Whats this for?

HIGGINS: To wipe your eyes. To wipe any part of your face that feels moist. Remember: thats your handkerchief; and thats your sleeve. Dont mistake the one for the other if you wish to become a lady in a shop.

[*Liza, utterly bewildered, stares helplessly at him.*]

MRS PEARCE: It's no use talking to her like that, Mr Higgins: she doesnt understand you. Besides, youre quite wrong: she doesnt do it that way at all. [*She takes the handkerchief.*]

LIZA [*snatching it*]: Here! You give me that handkerchief. He gev it to me, not to you.

PICKERING [*laughing*]: He did. I think it must be regarded as her property, Mrs Pearce.

MRS PEARCE [*resigning herself*]: Serve you right, Mr Higgins.

PICKERING: Higgins: I'm interested. What about the ambassador's garden party? I'll say youre the greatest teacher alive if you make that good. I'll bet you all the expenses of the experiment you cant do it. And I'll pay for the lessons.

LIZA: Oh, you are real good. Thank you, Captain.

HIGGINS [*tempted, looking at her*]: It's almost irresistible. She's so deliciously low— so horribly dirty—

LIZA [*protesting extremely*]: Ah-ah-ah-ah-ow-oo-oo!!! I aint dirty: I washed my face and hands afore I come, I did.

PICKERING: Youre certainly not going to turn her head with flattery, Higgins.

MRS PEARCE [*uneasy*]: Oh, dont say that, sir: theres more ways than one of turn-ing a girl's head; and nobody can do it better than Mr Higgins, though he may not always mean it. I do hope, sir, you wont encourage him to do anything foolish.

HIGGINS [*becoming excited as the idea grows on him*]: What is life but a series of inspired follies? The difficulty is to find them to do. Never lose a chance: it doesnt come every day. I shall make a duchess of this draggletailed guttersnipe.

LIZA [*strongly deprecating this view of her*]: Ah-ah-ah-ow-ow-oo!

HIGGINS: [*carried away*]: Yes: in six months—in three if she has a good ear and a quick tongue—I'll take her anywhere and pass her off as anything. We'll start today: now! this moment! Take her away and clean her, Mrs Pearce. Monkey Brand,[4] if it wont come off any other way. Is there a good fire in the kitchen?

MRS PEARCE [*protesting*]: Yes; but—

HIGGINS [*storming on*]: Take all her clothes off and burn them. Ring up Whiteley or somebody for new ones. Wrap her up in brown paper til they come.

LIZA: Youre no gentleman, youre not, to talk of such things. I'm a good girl, I am; and I know what the like of you are, I do.

HIGGINS: We want none of your Lisson Grove prudery here, young woman. Youve got to learn to behave like a duchess. Take her away, Mrs Pearce. If she gives you any trouble, wallop her.

LIZA [*springing up and running between Pickering and Mrs Pearce for protection*]: No! I'll call the police, I will.

MRS PEARCE: But Ive no place to put her.

HIGGINS: Put her in the dustbin.

LIZA: Ah-ah-ah-ow-ow-oo!

PICKERING: Oh come, Higgins! Be reasonable.

MRS PEARCE [*resolutely*]: You must be reasonable, Mr Higgins: really you must. You cant walk over everybody like this.

[*Higgins, thus scolded, subsides. The hurricane is succeeded by a zephyr of amiable surprise.*]

HIGGINS [*with professional exquisiteness of modulation*]: I walk over everybody! My dear Mrs Pearce, my dear Pickering, I never had the slightest intention of walking over anyone. All I propose is that we should be kind to this poor girl. We must help her to prepare and fit herself for her new station in life. If I did not express myself clearly it was because I did not wish to hurt her delicacy, or yours.

[*Liza, reassured, steals back to her chair.*]

MRS PEARCE [*to Pickering*]: Well, did you ever hear anything like that, sir?

PICKERING [*laughing heartily*]: Never, Mrs Pearce: never.

---

4. Widely advertised brand of household cleanser—"won't wash clothes!"

HIGGINS [*patiently*]: Whats the matter?

MRS PEARCE: Well, the matter is, sir, that you cant take a girl up like that as if you were picking up a pebble on the beach.

HIGGINS: Why not?

MRS PEARCE: Why not! But you dont know anything about her. What about her parents? She may be married.

LIZA: Garn!

HIGGINS: There! As the girl very properly says, Garn! Married indeed! Dont you know that a woman of that class looks a worn out drudge of fifty a year after she's married?

LIZA: Whood marry me?

HIGGINS [*suddenly resorting to the most thrillingly beautiful low tones in his best elocutionary style*]: By George, Eliza, the streets will be strewn with the bodies of men shooting themselves for your sake before Ive done with you.

MRS PEARCE: Nonsense, sir. You mustnt talk like that to her.

LIZA [*rising and squaring herself determinedly*]: I'm going away. He's off his chump, he is. I dont want no balmies teaching me.

HIGGINS [*wounded in his tenderest point by her insensibility to his elocution*]: Oh, indeed! I'm mad, am I? Very well, Mrs Pearce: you neednt order the new clothes for her. Throw her out.

LIZA [*whimpering*]: Nah-ow. You got no right to touch me.

MRS PEARCE: You see now what comes of being saucy. [*Indicating the door.*] This way, please.

LIZA [*almost in tears*]: I didnt want no clothes. I wouldnt have taken them. [*She throws away the handkerchief.*] I can buy my own clothes.

HIGGINS [*deftly retrieving the handkerchief and intercepting her on her reluctant way to the door*]: Youre an ungrateful wicked girl. This is my return for offering to take you out of the gutter and dress you beautifully and make a lady of you.

MRS PEARCE: Stop, Mr Higgins. I wont allow it. It's you that are wicked. Go home to your parents, girl; and tell them to take better care of you.

LIZA: I aint got no parents. They told me I was big enough to earn my own living and turned me out.

MRS PEARCE: Wheres your mother?

LIZA: I aint got no mother. Her that turned me out was my sixth stepmother. But I done without them. And I'm a good girl, I am.

HIGGINS: Very well, then, what on earth is all this fuss about? The girl doesnt belong to anybody—is no use to anybody but me. [*He goes to Mrs Pearce and begins coaxing.*] You can adopt her, Mrs Pearce: I'm sure a daughter would be a great amusement to you. Now dont make any more fuss. Take her downstairs; and—

MRS PEARCE: But whats to become of her? Is she to be paid anything? Do be sensible, sir.

HIGGINS: Oh, pay her whatever is necessary: put it down in the housekeeping book. [*Impatiently.*] What on earth will she want with money? She'll have her food and her clothes. She'll only drink if you give her money.

LIZA [*turning on him*]: Oh you are a brute. It's a lie: nobody ever saw the sign of liquor on me. [*To Pickering.*] Oh, sir: youre a gentleman: dont let him speak to me like that.

PICKERING [*in good-humored remonstrance*]: Does it occur to you, Higgins, that the girl has some feelings?

HIGGINS [*looking critically at her*]: Oh no, I dont think so. Not any feelings that we need bother about. [*Cheerily.*] Have you, Eliza?

LIZA: I got my feelings same as anyone else.

HIGGINS [*to Pickering, reflectively*]: You see the difficulty?

PICKERING: Eh? What difficulty?

HIGGINS: To get her to talk grammar. The mere pronunciation is easy enough.

LIZA: I dont want to talk grammar. I want to talk like a lady in a flower-shop.

MRS PEARCE: Will you please keep to the point, Mr Higgins. I want to know on what terms the girl is to be here. Is she to have any wages? And what is to become of her when youve finished your teaching? You must look ahead a little.

HIGGINS [*impatiently*]: Whats to become of her if I leave her in the gutter? Tell me that, Mrs Pearce.

MRS PEARCE: Thats her own business, not yours. Mr Higgins.

HIGGINS: Well, when Ive done with her, we can throw her back into the gutter; and then it will be her own business again; so thats all right.

LIZA: Oh, youve no feeling heart in you: you dont care for nothing but yourself. [*She rises and takes the floor resolutely.*] Here! Ive had enough of this. I'm going [*making for the door*]. You ought to be ashamed of yourself, you ought.

HIGGINS [*snatching a chocolate cream from the piano, his eyes suddenly beginning to twinkle with mischief*]: Have some chocolates, Eliza.

LIZA [*halting, tempted*]: How do I know what might be in them? Ive heard of girls being drugged by the like of you.

[*Higgins whips out his penknife; cuts a chocolate in two; puts one half into his mouth and bolts it; and offers her the other half.*]

HIGGINS: Pledge of good faith. Eliza. I eat one half: you eat the other. [*Liza opens her mouth to retort: he pops the half chocolate into it.*] You shall have boxes of them, barrels of them, every day. You shall live on them. Eh?

LIZA [*who has disposed of the chocolate after being nearly choked by it*]: I wouldnt have ate it, only I'm too ladylike to take it out of my mouth.

HIGGINS: Listen, Eliza. I think you said you came in a taxi.

LIZA: Well, what if I did? Ive as good a right to take a taxi as anyone else.

HIGGINS: You have, Eliza; and in future you shall have as many taxis as you want. You shall go up and down and round the town in a taxi every day. Think of that, Eliza.

MRS PEARCE: Mr Higgins: youre tempting the girl. It's not right. She should think of the future.

HIGGINS: At her age! Nonsense! Time enough to think of the future when you havnt any future to think of. No, Eliza: do as this lady does: think of other people's futures; but never think of your own. Think of chocolates, and taxis, and gold, and diamonds.

LIZA: No: I dont want no gold and no diamonds. I'm a good girl, I am. [*She sits down again, with an attempt at dignity.*]

HIGGINS: You shall remain so, Eliza, under the care of Mrs Pearce. And you shall marry an officer in the Guards, with a beautiful moustache: the son of a marquis, who will disinherit him for marrying you, but will relent when he sees your beauty and goodness—

PICKERING: Excuse me, Higgins: but I really must interfere. Mrs Pearce is quite right. If this girl is to put herself in your hands for six months for an experiment in teaching, she must understand thoroughly what she's doing.

HIGGINS: How can she? She's incapable of understanding anything. Besides, do any of us understand what we are doing? If we did, would we ever do it?

PICKERING: Very clever, Higgins; but not to the present point. [*To Eliza.*] Miss Doolittle—

LIZA [*overwhelmed*]: Ah-ah-ow-oo!

HIGGINS: There! Thats all youll get out of Eliza. Ah-ah-ow-oo! No use explaining. As a military man you ought to know that. Give her her orders: thats enough for her. Eliza: you are to live here for the next six months, learning how to speak beautifully, like a lady in a florist's shop. If youre good and do whatever youre told, you shall sleep in a proper bedroom, and have lots to eat, and money to buy chocolates and take rides in taxis. If youre naughty and idle you will sleep in the back kitchen among the black beetles, and be walloped by Mrs Pearce with a broomstick. At the end of six months you shall go to Buckingham Palace in a carriage, beautifully dressed. If the King finds out youre not a lady, you will be taken by the police to the Tower of London, where your head will be cut off as a warning to other presumptuous flower girls. If you are not found out, you shall have a present of seven-and-sixpence to start life with as a lady in a shop. If you refuse this offer you will be a most ungrateful wicked girl; and the angels will weep for you. [*To Pickering.*] Now are you satisfied, Pickering? [*To Mrs Pearce.*] Can I put it more plainly and fairly, Mrs Pearce?

MRS PEARCE [*patiently*]: I think youd better let me speak to the girl properly in private. I dont know that I can take charge of her or consent to the arrangement at all. Of course I know you dont mean her any harm; but when you get what you call interested in people's accents, you never think or care what may happen to them or you. Come with me, Eliza.

HIGGINS: Thats all right. Thank you, Mrs Pearce. Bundle her off to the bathroom.

LIZA [*rising reluctantly and suspiciously*]: Youre a great bully, you are. I wont stay here if I dont like. I wont let nobody wallop me. I never asked to go to Bucknam Palace, I didnt. I was never in trouble with the police, not me. I'm a good girl—

MRS PEARCE: Dont answer back, girl. You dont understand the gentleman. Come with me. [*She leads the way to the door, and holds it open for Eliza.*]

LIZA [*as she goes out*]: Well, what I say is right. I wont go near the King, not if I'm going to have my head cut off. If I'd known what I was letting myself in for, I wouldnt have come here. I always been a good girl; and I never offered to say a word to him; and I dont owe him nothing; and I dont care; and I wont be put upon; and I have my feelings the same as anyone else—

[*Mrs Pearce shuts the door; and Eliza's plaints are no longer audible.*]

*   *   *

Eliza is taken upstairs to the third floor greatly to her surprise; for she expected to be taken down to the scullery. There Mrs Pearce opens a door and takes her into a spare bedroom.

MRS PEARCE: I will have to put you here. This will be your bedroom.

LIZA: O-h, I couldnt sleep here, missus. It's too good for the likes of me. I should be afraid to touch anything. I aint a duchess yet, you know.

MRS PEARCE: You have got to make yourself as clean as the room: then you wont be afraid of it. And you must call me Mrs Pearce, not missus. [*She throws open the door of the dressing-room, now modernized as a bathroom.*]

LIZA: Gawd! whats this? Is this where you wash clothes? Funny sort of copper[5] I call it.

---

5. Kettle to boil laundry.

MRS PEARCE: It is not a copper. This is where we wash ourselves, Eliza, and where I am going to wash you.

LIZA: You expect me to get into that and wet myself all over! Not me. I should catch my death. I knew a woman did it every Saturday night; and she died of it.

MRS PEARCE: Mr Higgins has the gentlemen's bathroom down-stairs; and he has a bath every morning, in cold water.

LIZA: Ugh! He's made of iron, that man.

MRS PEARCE: If you are to sit with him and the Colonel and be taught you will have to do the same. They wont like the smell of you if you dont. But you can have the water as hot as you like. There are two taps: hot and cold.

LIZA [weeping]: I couldnt. I dursnt. Its not natural: It would kill me. Ive never had a bath in my life: not what youd call a proper one.

MRS PEARCE: Well, dont you want to be clean and sweet and decent, like a lady? You know you cant be a nice girl inside if youre a dirty slut outside.

LIZA: Boohoo!!!!

MRS PEARCE: Now stop crying and go back into your room and take off all your clothes. Then wrap yourself in this [taking down a gown from its peg and handing it to her] and come back to me. I will get the bath ready.

LIZA [all tears]: I cant. I wont. I'm not used to it. Ive never took off all my clothes before. It's not right: it's not decent.

MRS PEARCE: Nonsense, child. Dont you take off all your clothes every night when you go to bed?

LIZA [amazed]: No. Why should I? I should catch my death. Of course I take off my skirt.

MRS PEARCE: Do you mean that you sleep in the underclothes you wear in the daytime?

LIZA: What else have I to sleep in?

MRS PEARCE: You will never do that again as long as you live here. I will get you a proper nightdress.

LIZA: Do you mean change into cold things and lie awake shivering half the night? You want to kill me, you do.

MRS PEARCE: I want to change you from a frowzy[6] slut to a clean respectable girl fit to sit with the gentlemen in the study. Are you going to trust me and do what I tell you or be thrown out and sent back to your flower basket?

LIZA: But you dont know what the cold is to me. You dont know how I dread it.

MRS PEARCE: Your bed wont be cold here: I will put a hot water bottle in it. [Pushing her into the bedroom.] Off with you and undress.

LIZA: Oh, if only I'd a known what a dreadful thing it is to be clean I'd never have come. I didnt know when I was well off. I—[Mrs Pearce pushes her through the door, but leaves it partly open lest her prisoner should take to flight.]

[Mrs Pearce puts on a pair of white rubber sleeves, and fills the bath, mixing hot and cold, and testing the result with the bath thermometer. She perfumes it with a handful of bath salts and adds a palmful of mustard. She then takes a formidable looking long handled scrubbing brush and soaps it profusely with a ball of scented soap.

Eliza comes back with nothing on but the bath gown huddled tightly round her, a piteous spectacle of abject terror.]

MRS PEARCE: Now come along. Take that thing off.

LIZA: Oh I couldnt, Mrs Pearce: I reely couldnt. I never done such a thing.

6. Dirty, untidy.

MRS PEARCE: Nonsense. Here: step in and tell me whether it's hot enough for you.

LIZA: Ah-oo! Ah-oo! It's too hot.

MRS PEARCE [*deftly snatching the gown away and throwing Eliza down on her back*]: It wont hurt you. [*She sets to work with the scrubbing brush.*]

[*Eliza's screams are heartrending.*]

*   *   *

Meanwhile the Colonel has been having it out with Higgins about Eliza. Pickering has come from the hearth to the chair and seated himself astride of it with his arms on the back to cross-examine him.

PICKERING: Excuse the straight question, Higgins. Are you a man of good character where women are concerned?

HIGGINS [*moodily*]: Have you ever met a man of good character where women are concerned?

PICKERING: Yes: very frequently.

HIGGINS [*dogmatically, lifting himself on his hands to the level of the piano, and sitting on it with a bounce*]: Well, I havnt. I find that the moment I let a woman make friends with me, she becomes jealous, exacting, suspicious, and a damned nuisance. I find that the moment I let myself make friends with a woman, I become selfish and tyrannical. Women upset everything. When you let them into your life, you find that the woman is driving at one thing and youre driving at another.

PICKERING: At what, for example?

HIGGINS [*coming off the piano restlessly*]: Oh, Lord knows! I suppose the woman wants to live her own life; and the man wants to live his; and each tries to drag the other on to the wrong track. One wants to go north and the other south; and the result is that both have to go east, though they both hate the east wind. [*He sits down on the bench at the keyboard.*] So here I am, a confirmed old bachelor, and likely to remain so.

PICKERING [*rising and standing over him gravely*]: Come, Higgins! You know what I mean. If I'm to be in this business I shall feel responsible for that girl. I hope it's understood that no advantage is to be taken of her position.

HIGGINS: What! That thing! Sacred. I assure you. [*Rising to explain.*] You see, she'll be a pupil; and teaching would be impossible unless pupils were sacred. Ive taught scores of American millionairesses how to speak English: the best looking women in the world. I'm seasoned. They might as well be blocks of wood. I might as well be a block of wood. It's—

[*Mrs Pearce opens the door. She has Eliza's hat in her hand. Pickering retires to the easy-chair at the hearth and sits down.*]

HIGGINS [*eagerly*]: Well, Mrs Pearce: is it all right?

MRS PEARCE [*at the door*]: I just wish to trouble you with a word, if I may, Mr Higgins.

HIGGINS: Yes, certainly. Come in. [*She comes forward.*] Dont burn that, Mrs Pearce. I'll keep it as a curiosity. [*He takes the hat.*]

MRS PEARCE: Handle it carefully, sir, please. I had to promise her not to burn it; but I had better put it in the oven for a while.

HIGGINS [*putting it down hastily on the piano*]: Oh! thank you. Well, what have you to say to me?

PICKERING: Am I in the way?

MRS PEARCE: Not at all, sir. Mr Higgins: will you please be very particular what you say before the girl?

HIGGINS [*sternly*]: Of course. I'm always particular about what I say. Why do you say this to me?

MRS PEARCE [*unmoved*]: No sir: youre not at all particular when youve mislaid anything or when you get a little impatient. Now it doesnt matter before me: I'm used to it. But you really must not swear before the girl.

HIGGINS [*indignantly*]: I swear! [*Most emphatically.*] I never swear. I detest the habit. What the devil do you mean?

MRS PEARCE [*stolidly*]: Thats what I mean, sir. You swear a great deal too much. I dont mind your damning and blasting, and what the devil and where the devil and who the devil—

HIGGINS: Mrs Pearce: this language from your lips! Really!

MRS PEARCE [*not to be put off*]: —but there is a certain word I must ask you not to use. The girl used it herself when she began to enjoy the bath. It begins with the same letter as bath.[7] She knows no better: she learnt it at her mother's knee. But she must not hear it from your lips.

HIGGINS [*loftily*]: I cannot charge myself with having ever uttered it, Mrs Pearce. [*She looks at him steadfastly. He adds, hiding an uneasy conscience with a judicial air.*] Except perhaps in a moment of extreme and justifiable excitement.

MRS PEARCE: Only this morning, sir, you applied it to your boots, to the butter, and to the brown bread.

HIGGINS: Oh, that! Mere alliteration, Mrs Pearce, natural to a poet.

MRS PEARCE: Well, sir, whatever you choose to call it. I beg you not to let the girl hear you repeat it.

HIGGINS: Oh, very well, very well. Is that all?

MRS PEARCE: No, sir. We shall have to be very particular with this girl as to personal cleanliness.

HIGGINS: Certainly. Quite right. Most important.

MRS PEARCE: I mean not to be slovenly about her dress or untidy in leaving things about.

HIGGINS [*going to her solemnly*]: Just so. I intended to call your attention to that. [*He passes on to Pickering, who is enjoying the conversation immensely.*] It is these little things that matter, Pickering. Take care of the pence and the pounds will take care of themselves is as true of personal habits as of money. [*He comes to anchor on the hearthrug, with the air of a man in an unassailable position.*]

MRS PEARCE: Yes, sir. Then might I ask you not to come down to breakfast in your dressing-gown, or at any rate not to use it as a napkin to the extent you do, sir. And if you would be so good as not to eat everything off the same plate, and to remember not to put the porridge saucepan out of your hand on the clean tablecloth, it would be a better example to the girl. You know you nearly choked yourself with a fishbone in the jam only last week.

HIGGINS [*routed from the hearthrug and drifting back to the piano*]: I may do these things sometimes in absence of mind; but surely I dont do them habitually. [*Angrily.*] By the way: my dressing-gown smells most damnably of benzine.

MRS PEARCE: No doubt it does, Mr Higgins. But if you will wipe your fingers—

HIGGINS [*yelling*]: Oh very well, very well: I'll wipe them in my hair in future.

MRS PEARCE: I hope youre not offended, Mr Higgins.

---

7. The word in question is "bloody" which, at the time the play was written and produced, was a vulgar term not used in polite society.

HIGGINS [*shocked at finding himself thought capable of an unamiable sentiment*]: Not at all, not at all. Youre quite right, Mrs Pearce: I shall be particularly careful before the girl. Is that all?

MRS PEARCE: No, sir. Might she use some of those Japanese dresses you brought from abroad? I really cant put her back into her old things.

HIGGINS: Certainly. Anything you like. Is that all?

MRS PEARCE: Thank you, sir. Thats all. [*She goes out.*]

HIGGINS: You know, Pickering, that woman has the most extraordinary ideas about me. Here I am, a shy, diffident sort of man. Ive never been able to feel really grown-up and tremendous, like other chaps. And yet she's firmly persuaded that I'm an arbitrary overbearing bossing kind of person. I cant account for it.

[*Mrs Pearce returns.*]

MRS PEARCE: If you please, sir, the trouble's beginning already. Theres a dustman downstairs, Alfred Doolittle, wants to see you. He says you have his daughter here.

PICKERING [*rising*]: Phew! I say!

HIGGINS [*promptly*]: Send the blackguard[8] up.

MRS PEARCE: Oh, very well, sir. [*She goes out.*]

PICKERING: He may not be a blackguard, Higgins.

HIGGINS: Nonsense. Of course he's a blackguard.

PICKERING: Whether he is or not, I'm afraid we shall have some trouble with him.

HIGGINS [*confidently*]: Oh no: I think not. If theres any trouble he shall have it with me, not I with him. And we are sure to get something interesting out of him.

PICKERING: About the girl?

HIGGINS: No, I mean his dialect.

PICKERING: Oh!

MRS PEARCE [*at the door*]: Doolittle, sir. [*She admits Doolittle and retires.*]

[*Alfred Doolittle is an elderly but vigorous dustman, clad in the costume of his profession, including a hat with a back brim covering his neck and shoulders. He has well marked and rather interesting features, and seems equally free from fear and conscience. He has a remarkably expressive voice, the result of a habit of giving vent to his feelings without reserve. His present pose is that of wounded honor and stern resolution.*]

DOOLITTLE [*at the door, uncertain which of the two gentlemen is his man*]: Professor Iggins?

HIGGINS: Here, Good morning. Sit down.

DOOLITTLE: Morning, Governor. [*He sits down magisterially.*] I come about a very serious matter, Governor.

HIGGINS [*to Pickering*]: Brought up in Hounslow. Mother Welsh, I should think. [*Doolittle opens his mouth, amazed. Higgins continues.*] What do you want, Doolittle?

DOOLITTLE [*menacingly*]: I want my daughter: thats what I want. See?

HIGGINS: Of course you do. Youre her father, arnt you? You dont suppose anyone else wants her, do you? I'm glad to see you have some spark of family feeling left. She's upstairs. Take her away at once.

DOOLITTLE [*rising, fearfully taken aback*]: What!

HIGGINS: Take her away. Do you suppose I'm going to keep your daughter for you?

DOOLITTLE [*remonstrating*]: Now, now, look here, Governor. Is this reasonable? Is it fairity[9] to take advantage of a man like this? The girl belongs to me. You got her. Where do I come in? [*He sits down again.*]

8. Scoundrel.   9. Fair play.

HIGGINS: Your daughter had the audacity to come to my house and ask me to teach her how to speak properly so that she could get a place in a flower-shop. This gentleman and my housekeeper have been here all the time. [*Bullying him.*] How dare you come here and attempt to blackmail me? You sent her here on purpose.

DOOLITTLE [*protesting*]: No, Governor.

HIGGINS: You must have. How else could you possibly know that she is here?

DOOLITTLE: Dont take a man up like that, Governor.

HIGGINS: The police shall take you up. This is a plant—a plot to extort money by threats. I shall telephone for the police. [*He goes resolutely to the telephone and opens the directory.*]

DOOLITTLE: Have I asked you for a brass farthing? I leave it to the gentleman here: have I said a word about money?

HIGGINS [*throwing the book aside and marching down on Doolittle with a poser[10]*]: What else did you come for?

DOOLITTLE [*sweetly*]: Well, what would a man come for? Be human, Governor.

HIGGINS [*disarmed*]: Alfred: did you put her up to it?

DOOLITTLE: So help me, Governor, I never did. I take my Bible oath I aint seen the girl these two months past.

HIGGINS: Then how did you know she was here?

DOOLITTLE [*"most musical, most melancholy"*]: I'll tell you, Governor, if youll only let me get a word in. I'm willing to tell you. I'm wanting to tell you. I'm waiting to tell you.

HIGGINS: Pickering: this chap has a certain natural gift of rhetoric. Observe the rhythm of his native woodnotes wild. "I'm willing to tell you: I'm wanting to tell you: I'm waiting to tell you." Sentimental rhetoric! Thats the Welsh strain in him. It also accounts for his mendacity[11] and dishonesty.

PICKERING: Oh, please, Higgins: I'm west country[12] myself. [*To Doolittle.*] How did you know the girl was here if you didnt send her?

DOOLITTLE: It was like this, Governor. The girl took a boy in the taxi to give him a jaunt. Son of her landlady, he is. He hung about on the chance of her giving him another ride home. Well, she sent him back for her luggage when she heard you was willing for her to stop here. I met the boy at the corner of Long Acre and Endell Street.

HIGGINS: Public house. Yes?

DOOLITTLE: The poor man's club, Governor: why shouldnt I?

PICKERING: Do let him tell his story, Higgins.

DOOLITTLE: He told me what was up. And I ask you, what was my feelings and my duty as a father? I says to the boy, "You bring me the luggage," I says—

PICKERING: Why didnt you go for it yourself?

DOOLITTLE: Landlady wouldnt have trusted me with it, Governor. She's that kind of woman: you know. I had to give the boy a penny afore he trusted me with it, the little swine. I brought it to her just to oblige you like, and make myself agreeable. Thats all.

HIGGINS: How much luggage?

DOOLITTLE: Musical instrument, Governor. A few pictures, a trifle of jewlery, and a bird-cage. She said she didn't want no clothes. What was I to think from that, Governor? I ask you as a parent what was I to think?

---

10. Puzzle
11. Tendency to lie.

12. From the west of England—perhaps even Wales.

HIGGINS: So you came to rescue her from worse than death eh?

DOOLITTLE [*appreciatively: relieved at being so well understood*]: Just so, Governor. Thats right.

PICKERING: But why did you bring her luggage if you intended to take her away?

DOOLITTLE: Have I said a word about taking her away? Have I now?

HIGGINS [*determinedly*]: Youre going to take her away, double quick. [*He crosses to the hearth and rings the bell.*]

DOOLITTLE [*rising*]: No, Governor. Dont say that. I'm not the man to stand in my girl's light. Heres a career opening for her as you might say; and—

[*Mrs Pearce opens the door and awaits orders.*]

HIGGINS: Mrs Pearce: this is Eliza's father. He has come to take her away. Give her to him. [*He goes back to the piano, with an air of washing his hands of the whole affair.*]

DOOLITTLE: No. This is a misunderstanding. Listen here—

MRS PEARCE: He cant take her away, Mr Higgins: how can he? You told me to burn her clothes.

DOOLITTLE: Thats right. I cant carry the girl through the streets like a blooming monkey, can I? I put it to you.

HIGGINS: You have put it to me that you want your daughter. Take your daughter. If she has no clothes go out and buy her some.

DOOLITTLE [*desperate*]: Wheres the clothes she come in? Did I burn them or did your missus here?

MRS PEARCE: I am the housekeeper, if you please. I have sent for some clothes for the girl. When they come you can take her away. You can wait in the kitchen. This way, please.

[*Doolittle, much troubled, accompanies her to the door; then hesitates: finally turns confidentially to Higgins.*]

DOOLITTLE: Listen here, Governor. You and me is men of the world, aint we?

HIGGINS: Oh! Men of the world, are we? Youd better go, Mrs Pearce.

MRS PEARCE: I think so, indeed, sir. [*She goes, with dignity.*]

PICKERING: The floor is yours, Mr Doolittle.

DOOLITTLE [*to Pickering*]: I thank you, Governor. [*To Higgins, who takes refuge on the piano bench, a little overwhelmed by the proximity of his visitor; for Doolittle has a professional flavor of dust about him.*] Well, the truth is, Ive taken a sort of fancy to you, Governor; and if you want the girl, I'm not so set on having her back home again but what I might be open to an arrangement. Regarded in the light of a young woman, she's a fine handsome girl. As a daughter she's not worth her keep; and so I tell you straight. All I ask is my rights as a father; and youre the last man alive to expect me to let her go for nothing; for I can see youre one of the straight sort, Governor. Well, whats a five-pound note to you? and whats Eliza to me? [*He turns to his chair and sits down judicially.*]

PICKERING: I think you ought to know, Doolittle, that Mr Higgins's intentions are entirely honorable.

DOOLITTLE: Course they are, Governor. If I thought they wasn't, I'd ask fifty.

HIGGINS [*revolted*]: Do you mean to say that you would sell your daughter for £50?

DOOLITTLE: Not in a general way I wouldnt; but to oblige a gentleman like you I'd do a good deal, I do assure you.

PICKERING: Have you no morals, man?

DOOLITTLE [*unabashed*]: Cant afford them, Governor. Neither could you if you was as poor as me. Not that I mean any harm, you know. But if Liza is going to have a bit out of this, why not me too?

HIGGINS [*troubled*]: I dont know what to do, Pickering. There can be no question that as a matter of morals it's a positive crime to give this chap a farthing. And yet I feel a sort of rough justice in his claim.

DOOLITTLE: Thats it, Governor. Thats all I say. A father's heart, as it were.

PICKERING: Well, I know the feeling; but really it seems hardly right—

DOOLITTLE: Dont say that, Governor. Dont look at it that way. What am I, Governors both? I ask you, what am I? I'm one of the undeserving poor: thats what I am. Think of what that means to a man. It means that he's up agen middle class morality all the time. If theres anything going, and I put in for a bit of it, it's always the same story: "Youre undeserving: so you cant have it." But my needs is as great as the most deserving widow's that ever got money out of six different charities in one week for the death of the same husband. I dont need less than a deserving man: I need more. I dont eat less hearty than him; and I drink a lot more. I want a bit of amusement, cause I'm a thinking man. I want cheerfulness and a song and a band when I feel low. Well, they charge me just the same for everything as they charge the deserving. What is middle class morality? Just an excuse for never giving me anything. Therefore, I ask you, as two gentlemen, not to play that game on me. I'm playing straight with you. I aint pretending to be deserving. I'm undeserving; and I mean to go on being undeserving. I like it; and thats the truth. Will you take advantage of a man's nature to do him out of the price of his own daughter what he's brought up and fed and clothed by the sweat of his brow until she's growed big enough to be interesting to you two gentlemen? Is five pounds unreasonable? I put it to you: and I leave it to you.

HIGGINS [*rising, and going over to Pickering*]: Pickering: if we were to take this man in hand for three months, he could choose between a seat in the Cabinet and a popular pulpit in Wales.

PICKERING: What do you say to that, Doolittle?

DOOLITTLE: Not me, Governor, thank you kindly. Ive heard all the preachers and all the prime ministers—for I'm a thinking man and game for politics or religion or social reform same as all the other amusements—and I tell you it's a dog's life any way you look at it. Undeserving poverty is my line. Taking one station in society with another, it's—it's—well, it's the only one that has any ginger in it, to my taste.

HIGGINS: I suppose we must give him a fiver.

PICKERING: He'll make a bad use of it, I'm afraid.

DOOLITTLE: Not me, Governor, so help me I wont. Dont you be afraid that I'll save it and spare it and live idle on it. There wont be a penny of it left by Monday: I'll have to go to work same as if I'd never had it. It wont pauperize me, you bet. Just one good spree for myself and the missus, giving pleasure to ourselves and employment to others, and satisfaction to you to think it's not been throwed away. You couldnt spend it better.

HIGGINS: [*taking out his pocket book and coming between Doolittle and the piano*]: This is irresistible. Lets give him ten. [*He offers two notes to the dustman.*]

DOOLITTLE: No, Governor. She wouldnt have the heart to spend ten; and perhaps I shouldnt neither. Ten pounds is a lot of money: it makes a man feel prudent like; and then good-bye to happiness. You give me what I ask you, Governor: not a penny more, and not a penny less.

PICKERING: Why dont you marry that missus of yours? I rather draw the line at encouraging that sort of immorality.

DOOLITTLE: Tell her so. Governor: tell her so. I'm willing. It's me that suffers by it. Ive no hold on her. I got to be agreeable to her. I got to give her presents. I got to buy her clothes something sinful. I'm a slave to that woman, Governor, just because I'm not her lawful husband. And she knows it too. Catch her marrying me! Take my advice, Governor—marry Eliza while she's young and dont know no better. If you dont youll be sorry for it after. If you do, she'll be sorry for it after; but better her than you, because youre a man, and she's only a woman and dont know how to be happy anyhow.

HIGGINS: Pickering: If we listen to this man another minute, we shall have no convictions left. [To Doolittle.] Five pounds I think you said.

DOOLITTLE: Thank you kindly, Governor.

HIGGINS: Youre sure you wont take ten?

DOOLITTLE: Not now. Another time, Governor.

HIGGINS [handing him a five-pound note]: Here you are.

DOOLITTLE: Thank you, Governor. Good morning. [He hurries to the door, anxious to get away with his booty. When he opens it he is confronted with a dainty and exquisitely clean young Japanese lady in a simple blue cotton kimono printed cunningly with small white jasmine blossoms. Mrs Pearce is with her. He gets out of her way deferentially and apologizes.] Beg pardon, miss.

THE JAPANESE LADY: Garn! Dont you know you own daughter?

DOOLITTLE: [exclaiming] Bly me! It's Eliza!
HIGGINS: {simul- } Whats that? This!
PICKERING: [taneously] By Jove!

LIZA: Dont I look silly?

HIGGINS: Silly?

MRS PEARCE [at the door]: Now, Mr Higgins, please dont say anything to make the girl conceited about herself.

HIGGINS [conscientiously]: Oh! Quite right, Mrs Pearce. [To Eliza.] Yes: damned silly.

MRS PEARCE: Please, sir.

HIGGINS [correcting himself]: I mean extremely silly.

LIZA: I should look all right with my hat on. [She takes up her hat; puts it on; and walks across the room to the fireplace with a fashionable air.]

HIGGINS: A new fashion, by George! And it ought to look horrible!

DOOLITTLE: [with fatherly pride]: Well, I never thought she'd clean up as good looking as that, Governor. She's a credit to me, aint she?

LIZA: I tell you, it's easy to clean up here. Hot and cold water on tap, just as much as you like, there is. Woolly towels, there is; and a towel horse[13] so hot, it burns your fingers. Soft brushes to scrub yourself, and a wooden bowl of soap smelling like primroses. Now I know why ladies is so clean. Washing's a treat for them. Wish they could see what it is for the like of me!

HIGGINS: I'm glad the bathroom met with your approval.

LIZA: It didnt: not all of it; and I dont care who hears me say it. Mrs Pearce knows.

HIGGINS: What was wrong, Mrs Pearce?

MRS PEARCE [blandly]: Oh, nothing, sir. It doesnt matter.

LIZA: I had a good mind to break it. I didn't know which way to look. But I hung a towel over it, I did.

HIGGINS: Over what?

---

13. Towel rack.

MRS PEARCE: Over the looking-glass sir.

HIGGINS: Doolittle: you have brought your daughter up too strictly.

DOOLITTLE: Me! I never brought her up at all, except to give her a lick of a strap now and again. Dont put it on me, Governor. She aint accustomed to it, you see: thats all. But she'll soon pick up your free-and-easy ways.

LIZA: I'm a good girl, I am; and I wont pick up no free-and-easy ways.

HIGGINS: Eliza: if you say again that youre a good girl, your father shall take you home.

LIZA: Not him. You dont know my father. All he come here for was to touch you for some money to get drunk on.

DOOLITTLE: Well, what else would I want money for? To put into the plate in church, I suppose. [*She puts out her tongue at him. He is so incensed by this that Pickering presently finds it necessary to step between them.*] Dont you give me none of your lip; and dont let me hear you giving this gentleman any of it neither, or youll hear from me about it. See?

HIGGINS: Have you any further advice to give her before you go, Doolittle? Your blessing, for instance.

DOOLITTLE: No, Governor: I aint such a mug as to put up my children to all I know myself. Hard enough to hold them in without that. If you want Eliza's mind improved, Governor, you do it yourself with a strap. So long, gentlemen. [*He turns to go.*]

HIGGINS [*impressively*]: Stop. Youll come regularly to see your daughter. It's your duty, you know. My brother is a clergyman; and he could help you in your talks with her.

DOOLITTLE [*evasively*]: Certainly. I'll come, Governor. Not just this week, because I have a job at a distance. But later on you may depend on me. Afternoon, gentlemen. Afternoon, maam. [*He touches his hat to Mrs Pearce, who disdains the salutation and goes out. He winks at Higgins, thinking him probably a fellow-sufferer from Mrs Pearce's difficult disposition, and follows her.*]

LIZA: Dont you believe the old liar. He'd as soon you set a bull-dog on him as a clergyman. You wont see him again in a hurry.

HIGGINS: I dont want to, Eliza. Do you?

LIZA: Not me. I dont want never to see him again. I dont. He's a disgrace to me, he is, collecting dust, instead of working at his trade.

PICKERING: What is his trade, Eliza?

LIZA: Talking money out of other people's pockets into his own. His proper trade's a navvy[14]; and he works at it sometimes too—for exercise—and earns good money at it. Aint you going to call me Miss Doolittle any more?

PICKERING: I beg your pardon, Miss Doolittle. It was a slip of the tongue.

LIZA: Oh, I dont mind; only it sounded so genteel. I should just like to take a taxi to the corner of Tottenham Court Road and get out there and tell it to wait for me, just to put the girls in their place a bit. I wouldnt speak to them, you know.

PICKERING: Better wait til we get you something really fashionable.

HIGGINS: Besides, you shouldnt cut your old friends now that you have risen in the world. Thats what we call snobbery.

LIZA: You dont call the like of them my friends now, I should hope. Theyve took it out of me often enough with their ridicule when they had the chance; and now I mean to get a bit of my own back. But if I'm to have fashionable clothes, I'll wait.

14. Manual laborer.

I should like to have some. Mrs Pearce says youre going to give me some to wear in bed at night different to what I wear in the daytime; but it do seem a waste of money when you could get something to shew. Besides, I never could fancy changing into cold things on a winter night.

MRS PEARCE [*coming back*]: Now, Eliza. The new things have come for you to try on.

LIZA: Ah-ow-oo-ooh! [*She rushes out.*]

MRS PEARCE [*following her*]: Oh, dont rush about like that, girl. [*She shuts the door behind her.*]

HIGGINS: Pickering: we have taken on a stiff job.

PICKERING [*with conviction*]: Higgins: we have.

*   *   *

There seems to be some curiosity as to what Higgins's lessons to Eliza were like. Well, here is a sample: the first one.

Picture Eliza, in her new clothes, and feeling her inside put out of step by a lunch, dinner, and breakfast of a kind to which it is unaccustomed, seated with Higgins and the Colonel in the study, feeling like a hospital out-patient at a first encounter with the doctors.

Higgins, constitutionally unable to sit still, discomposes her still more by striding restlessly about. But for the reassuring presence and quietude of her friend the Colonel she would run for her life, even back to Drury Lane.

HIGGINS: Say your alphabet.

LIZA: I know my alphabet. Do you think I know nothing? I dont need to be taught like a child.

HIGGINS [*thundering*]: Say your alphabet.

PICKERING: Say it, Miss Doolittle. You will understand presently. Do what he tells you; and let him teach you in his own way.

LIZA: Oh well, if you put it like that—Ahyee, bə yee, cə yee, də yee—

HIGGINS [*with the roar of a wounded lion*]: Stop. Listen to this, Pickering. This is what we pay for as elementary education. This unfortunate animal has been locked up for nine years in school at our expense to teach her to speak and read the language of Shakespear and Milton. And the result is Ahyee, Bə -yee, Cə -yee, Də -yee. [*To Eliza.*] Say A, B, C, D.

LIZA [*almost in tears*]: But I'm saying it. Ahyee, Bə yee, Cə -yee—

HIGGINS: Stop. Say a cup of tea.

LIZA: A cappə tə -ee.

HIGGINS: Put your tongue forward until it squeezes against the top of your lower teeth. Now say cup.

LIZA: C-c-c—I cant. C-Cup.

PICKERING: Good. Splendid, Miss Doolittle.

HIGGINS: By Jupiter, she's done it at the first shot. Pickering: we shall make a duchess of her. [*To Eliza.*] Now do you think you could possibly say tea? Not tə -yee, mind: if you ever say bə -yee cə -yee də -yee again you shall be dragged round the room three times by the hair of your head. [*Fortissimo.*] T, T, T, T.

LIZA [*weeping*]: I cant hear no difference cep that it sounds more genteel-like when you say it.

HIGGINS: Well, if you can hear that difference, what the devil are you crying for? Pickering: give her a chocolate.

PICKERING: No, no. Never mind crying a little, Miss Doolittle: you are doing very well; and the lessons wont hurt. I promise you I wont let him drag you round the room by your hair.

HIGGINS: Be off with you to Mrs Pearce and tell her about it. Think about it. Try to do it by yourself: and keep your tongue well forward in your mouth instead of trying to roll it up and swallow it. Another lesson at half-past four this afternoon. Away with you.

[*Eliza, still sobbing, rushes from the room.*]

And that is the sort of ordeal poor Eliza has to go through for months before we meet her again on her first appearance in London society of the professional class.

ACT 3

It is Mrs Higgins's at-home day.[1] Nobody has yet arrived. Her drawing room, in a flat on Chelsea Embankment, has three windows looking on the river; and the ceiling is not so lofty as it would be in an older house of the same pretension. The windows are open, giving access to a balcony with flowers in pots. If you stand with your face to the windows, you have the fireplace on your left and the door in the right-hand wall close to the corner nearest the windows.

Mrs Higgins was brought up on Morris[2] and Burne Jones[3]; and her room, which is very unlike her son's room in Wimpole Street, is not crowded with furniture and little tables and nicknacks. In the middle of the room there is a big ottoman; and this, with the carpet, the Morris wallpapers, and the Morris chintz window curtains and brocade covers of the ottoman and its cushions, supply all the ornament, and are much too handsome to be hidden by odds and ends of useless things. A few good oil-paintings from the exhibitions in the Grosvenor Gallery thirty years ago (the Burne Jones, not the Whistler[4] side of them) are on the walls. The only landscape is a Cecil Lawson[5] on the scale of a Rubens[6]. There is a portrait of Mrs Higgins as she was when she defied the fashion in her youth in one of the beautiful Rossettian[7] costumes which, when caricatured by people who did not understand, led to the absurdities of popular estheticism in the eighteen-seventies.

In the corner diagonally opposite the door Mrs Higgins, now over sixty and long past taking the trouble to dress out of the fashion, sits writing at an elegantly simple writing-table with a bell button within reach of her hand. There is a Chippendale chair further back in the room between her and the window nearest her side. At the other side of the room, further forward, is an Elizabethan chair roughly carved in the taste of Inigo Jones. On the same side a piano in a decorated case. The corner between the fireplace and the window is occupied by a divan cushioned in Morris chintz.

It is between four and five in the afternoon.

The door is opened violently; and Higgins enters with his hat on.

MRS HIGGINS [*dismayed*]: Henry! [*Scolding him.*] What are you doing here today? It is my at-home day: you promised not to come. [*As he bends to kiss her, she takes his hat off, and presents it to him.*]

HIGGINS: Oh bother! [*He throws the hat down on the table.*]

MRS HIGGINS: Go home at once.

HIGGINS [*kissing her*]: I know, mother. I came on purpose.

MRS HIGGINS: But you mustnt. I'm serious, Henry. You offend all my friends: they stop coming whenever they meet you.

HIGGINS: Nonsense! I know I have no small talk; but people dont mind. [*He sits on the settee.*]

1. Reception of visitors in one's home in genteel society.
2. William Morris (1834–1896), English graphic artist, poet, and social reformer.
3. Sir Edward Coley Burne-Jones (1833–1898), English painter and designer.
4. James Abbott McNeill Whistler (1834–1903), American avant-garde painter who did much of his work living in London.
5. Cecil Gordon Lawson (1851–1882), English landscape painter.
6. Peter Paul Rubens (1577–1640), Flemish painter.
7. Dante Gabriel Rossetti (1828–1882), painter and poet, founder of the Pre-Raphaelite Brotherhood.

MRS HIGGINS: Oh! dont they? Small talk indeed! What about your large talk? Really, dear, you mustnt stay.

HIGGINS: I must. Ive a job for you. A phonetic job.

MRS HIGGINS: No use, dear. I'm sorry; but I cant get round your vowels; and though I like to get pretty postcards in your patent shorthand, I always have to read the copies in ordinary writing you so thoughtfully send me.

HIGGINS: Well, this isnt a phonetic job.

MRS HIGGINS: You said it was.

HIGGINS: Not your part of it. Ive picked up a girl.

MRS HIGGINS: Does that mean that some girl has picked you up?

HIGGINS: Not at all. I dont mean a love affair.

MRS HIGGINS: What a pity!

HIGGINS: Why?

MRS HIGGINS: Well, you never fall in love with anyone under forty-five. When will you discover that there are some rather nice-looking young women about?

HIGGINS: Oh, I cant be bothered with young women. My idea of a lovable woman is somebody as like you as possible. I shall never get into the way of seriously liking young women: some habits lie too deep to be changed. [*Rising abruptly and walking about, jingling his money and his keys in his trouser pockets.*] Besides, theyre all idiots.

MRS HIGGINS: Do you know what you would do if you really loved me, Henry?

HIGGINS: Oh bother! What? Marry, I suppose.

MRS HIGGINS: No. Stop fidgeting and take your hands out of your pockets. [*With a gesture of despair, he obeys and sits down again.*] Thats a good boy. Now tell me about the girl.

HIGGINS: She's coming to see you.

MRS HIGGINS: I dont remember asking her.

HIGGINS: You didnt. *I* asked her. If youd known her you wouldnt have asked her.

MRS HIGGINS: Indeed! Why?

HIGGINS: Well, It's like this. She's a common flower-girl. I picked her off the kerbstone.

MRS HIGGINS: And invited her to my at-home!

HIGGINS [*rising and coming to her to coax her*]: Oh, thatll be all right. Ive taught her to speak properly; and she has strict orders as to her behavior. She's to keep to two subjects: the weather and everybody's health—Fine day and How do you do, you know—and not to let herself go on things in general. That will be safe.

MRS HIGGINS: Safe! To talk about our health! About our insides! Perhaps about our outsides! How could you be so silly, Henry?

HIGGINS [*impatiently*]: Well, she must talk about something. [*He controls himself and sits down again.*] Oh, she'll be all right; dont you fuss. Pickering is in it with me. Ive a sort of bet on that I'll pass her off as a duchess in six months. I started on her some months ago; and she's getting on like a house on fire. I shall win my bet. She has a quick ear; and she's been easier to teach than my middle-class pupils because she's had to learn a complete new language. She talks English almost as you talk French.

MRS HIGGINS: Thats satisfactory, at all events.

HIGGINS: Well, it is and it isnt.

MRS HIGGINS: What does that mean?

HIGGINS: You see, Ive got her pronunciation all right; but you have to consider not only how a girl pronounces, but what she pronounces; and thats where—
[*They are interrupted by the parlormaid, announcing guests.*]

THE PARLORMAID: Mrs and Miss Eynsford Hill. [*She withdraws.*]

HIGGINS: Oh Lord! [*He rises: snatches his hat from the table; and makes for the door; but before he reaches it his mother introduces him.*]
[*Mrs and Miss Eynsford Hill are the mother and daughter who sheltered from the rain in Covent Garden. The mother is well bred, quiet, and has the habitual anxiety of straitened means. The daughter has acquired a gay air of being very much at home in society; the bravado of genteel poverty.*]

MRS EYNSFORD HILL [*to Mrs Higgins*]: How do you do? [*They shake hands.*]

MISS EYNSFORD HILL: How d'you do? [*She shakes.*]

MRS HIGGINS [*introducing*]: My son Henry.

MRS EYNSFORD HILL: Your celebrated son! I have so longed to meet you, Professor Higgins.

HIGGINS [*glumly, making no movement in her direction*]: Delighted. [*He backs against the piano and bows brusquely.*]

MISS EYNSFORD HILL [*going to him with confident familiarity*]: How do you do?

HIGGINS [*staring at her*]: Ive seen you before somewhere. I havnt the ghost of a notion where; but Ive heard your voice. [*Drearily*] It doesnt matter. Youd better sit down.

MRS HIGGINS: I'm sorry to say that my celebrated son has no manners. You mustnt mind him.

MISS EYNSFORD HILL [*gaily*]: I dont. [*She sits in the Elizabethan chair.*]

MRS EYNSFORD HILL [*a little bewildered*]: Not at all. [*She sits on the ottoman between her daughter and Mrs Higgins, who has turned her chair away from the writing-table.*]

HIGGINS: Oh, have I been rude? I didnt mean to be.
[*He goes to the central window, through which, with his back to the company, he contemplates the river and the flowers in Battersea Park on the opposite bank as if they were a frozen desert.*
The parlormaid returns, ushering in Pickering.]

THE PARLORMAID: Colonel Pickering. [*She withdraws.*]

PICKERING: How do you do, Mrs Higgins?

MRS HIGGINS: So glad youve come. Do you know Mrs Eynsford Hill—Miss Eynsford Hill? [*Exchange of bows. The Colonel brings the Chippendale chair a little forward between Mrs Hill and Mrs Higgins, and sits down.*]

PICKERING: Has Henry told you what weve come for?

HIGGINS [*over his shoulder*]: We were interrupted: damn it!

MRS HIGGINS: Oh Henry, Henry, really!

MRS EYNSFORD HILL [*half rising*]: Are we in the way?

MRS HIGGINS [*rising and making her sit down again*]: No, no. You couldnt have come more fortunately; we want you to meet a friend of ours.

HIGGINS [*turning hopefully*]: Yes, by George! We want two or three people. Youll do as well as anybody else.
[*The parlormaid returns, ushering Freddy.*]

THE PARLORMAID: Mr Eynsford Hill.

HIGGINS [*almost audibly, past endurance*]: God of Heaven! Another of them.

FREDDY [*shaking hands with Mrs Higgins*]: Ahdedo?

MRS HIGGINS: Very good of you to come. [*Introducing.*] Colonel Pickering.

FREDDY [*bowing*]: Ahdedo?

MRS HIGGINS: I dont think you know my son, Professor Higgins.

FREDDY [*going to Higgins*]: Ahdedo?

HIGGINS [*looking at him much as if he were a pickpocket*]: I'll take my oath Ive met you before somewhere. Where was it?

FREDDY: I dont think so.

HIGGINS [*resignedly*]: It dont matter, anyhow. Sit down.

> [*He shakes Freddy's hand and almost slings him on to the ottoman with his face to the window; then comes round to the other side of it.*]

HIGGINS: Well, here we are, anyhow! [*He sits down on the ottoman next Mrs Eynsford Hill, on her left.*] And now, what the devil are we going to talk about until Eliza comes?

MRS HIGGINS: Henry: you are the life and soul of the Royal Society's soirées; but really youre rather trying on more commonplace occasions.

HIGGINS: Am I? Very sorry. [*Beaming suddenly.*] I suppose I am, you know. [*Uproariously.*] Ha, ha!

MISS EYNSFORD HILL [*who considers Higgins quite eligible matrimonially*]: I sympathize. *I* havnt any small talk. If people would only be frank and say what they really think!

HIGGINS [*relapsing into gloom*]: Lord forbid!

MRS EYNSFORD HILL [*taking up her daughter's cue*]: But why?

HIGGINS: What they think they ought to think is bad enough, Lord knows; but what they really think would break up the whole show. Do you suppose it would be really agreeable if I were to come out now with what I really think?

MISS EYNSFORD HILL [*gaily*]: Is it so very cynical?

HIGGINS: Cynical! Who the dickens said it was cynical? I mean it wouldnt be decent.

MRS EYNSFORD HILL [*seriously*]: Oh! I'm sure you dont mean that, Mr Higgins.

HIGGINS: You see, we're all savages, more or less. We're supposed to be civilized and cultured—to know all about poetry and philosophy and art and science, and so on; but how many of us know even the meanings of these names? [*To Miss Hill.*] What do you know of poetry? [*To Mrs Hill.*] What do you know of science? [*Indicating Freddy.*] What does he know of art or science or anything else? What the devil do you imagine I know of philosophy?

MRS HIGGINS [*warningly*]: Or of manners, Henry?

THE PARLORMAID [*opening the door*]: Miss Doolittle. [*She withdraws.*]

HIGGINS [*rising hastily and running to Mrs Higgins*]: Here she is, mother. [*He stands on tiptoe and makes signs over his mother's head to Eliza to indicate to her which lady is her hostess.*]

> [*Eliza, who is exquisitely dressed, produces an impression of such remarkable distinction and beauty as she enters that they all rise, quite fluttered. Guided by Higgins's signals, she comes to Mrs Higgins with studied grace.*]

LIZA [*speaking with pedantic correctness of pronunciation and great beauty of tone*]: How do you do, Mrs Higgins? [*She gasps slightly in making sure of the H in Higgins, but is quite successful.*] Mr Higgins told me I might come.

MRS HIGGINS [*cordially*]: Quite right: I'm very glad indeed to see you.

PICKERING: How do you do, Miss Doolittle?

LIZA [*shaking hands with him*]: Colonel Pickering, is it not?

MRS EYNSFORD HILL: I feel sure we have met before, Miss Doolittle. I remember your eyes.

LIZA: How do you do? [*She sits down on the ottoman gracefully in the place just left vacant by Higgins.*]

MRS EYNSFORD HILL [*introducing*]: My daughter Clara.

LIZA: How do you do?

CLARA [*impulsively*]: How do you do? [*She sits down on the ottoman beside Eliza, devouring her with her eyes.*]

FREDDY [*coming to their side of the ottoman*]: Ive certainly had the pleasure.

MRS EYNSFORD HILL [*introducing*]: My son Freddy.

LIZA: How do you do?

[*Freddy bows and sits down in the Elizabethan chair, infatuated.*]

HIGGINS [*suddenly*]: By George, yes: It all comes back to me! [*They stare at him.*] Covent Garden! [*Lamentably.*] What a damned thing!

MRS HIGGINS: Henry, please! [*He is about to sit on the edge of the table.*] Dont sit on my writing-table: youll break it.

HIGGINS [*sulkily*]: Sorry.

[*He goes to the divan, stumbling into the fender and over the fire-irons on his way; extricating himself with muttered imprecations; and finishing his disastrous journey by throwing himself so impatiently on the divan that he almost breaks it. Mrs Higgins looks at him, but controls herself and says nothing.*

A long and painful pause ensues.]

MRS HIGGINS [*at last, conversationally*]: Will it rain, do you think?

LIZA: The shallow depression in the west of these islands is likely to move slowly in an easterly direction. There are no indications of any great change in the barometrical situation.

FREDDY: Ha! ha! how awfully funny!

LIZA: What is wrong with that, young man? I bet I got it right.

FREDDY: Killing!

MRS EYNSFORD HILL: I'm sure I hope it wont turn cold. Theres so much influenza about. It runs right through our whole family regularly every spring.

LIZA [*darkly*]: My aunt died of influenza: so they said.

MRS EYNSFORD HILL [*clicks her tongue sympathetically*]: !!!

LIZA [*in the same tragic tone*]: But it's my belief they done the old woman in.

MRS HIGGINS [*puzzled*]: Done her in?

LIZA: Y-e-e-e-es, Lord love you! Why should she die of influenza? She come through diphtheria right enough the year before. I saw her with my own eyes. Fairly blue with it, she was. They all thought she was dead; but my father he kept ladling gin down her throat til she came to so sudden that she bit the bowl off the spoon.

MRS EYNSFORD HILL [*startled*]: Dear me!

LIZA [*piling up the indictment*]: What call would a woman with that strength in her have to die of influenza? What become of her new straw hat that should have come to me? Somebody pinched it; and what I say is, them as pinched it done her in.

MRS EYNSFORD HILL: What does doing her in mean?

HIGGINS [*hastily*]: Oh, thats the new small talk. To do a person in means to kill them.

MRS EYNSFORD HILL [to Eliza, horrified]: You surely dont believe that your aunt was killed?

LIZA: Do I not! Them she lived with would have killed her for a hat-pin, let alone a hat.

MRS EYNSFORD HILL: But it cant have been right for your father to pour spirits down her throat like that. It might have killed her.

LIZA: Not her. Gin was mother's milk to her. Besides, he'd poured so much down his own throat that he knew the good of it.

MRS EYNSFORD HILL: Do you mean that he drank?

LIZA: Drank! My word! Something chronic.

MRS EYNSFORD HILL: How dreadful for you!

LIZA: Not a bit. It never did him no harm what I could see. But then he did not keep it up regular. [Cheerfully.] On the burst, as you might say, from time to time. And always more agreeable when he had a drop in. When he was out of work, my mother used to give him fourpence and tell him to go out and not come back until he'd drunk himself cheerful and loving-like. Theres lots of women has to make their husbands drunk to make them fit to live with. [Now quite at her ease.] You see, it's like this. If a man has a bit of a conscience, it always takes him when he's sober; and then it makes him low-spirited. A drop of booze just takes that off and makes him happy. [To Freddy, who is in convulsions of suppressed laughter.] Here! What are you sniggering at?

FREDDY: The new small talk. You do it so awfully well.

LIZA: If I was doing it proper, what was you laughing at? [To Higgins.] Have I said anything I oughtnt?

MRS HIGGINS [interposing]: Not at all, Miss Doolittle.

LIZA: Well, thats a mercy, anyhow. [Expansively.] What I always say is—

HIGGINS [rising and looking at his watch]: Ahem!

LIZA [looking round at him; taking the hint; and rising]: Well: I must go. [They all rise. Freddy goes to the door.] So pleased to have met you. Goodbye. [She shakes hands with Mrs Higgins.]

MRS HIGGINS: Goodbye.

LIZA: Goodbye, Colonel Pickering.

PICKERING: Goodbye, Miss Doolittle. [They shake hands].

LIZA [nodding to the others]: Goodbye, all.

FREDDY [opening the door for her]: Are you walking across the Park, Miss Doolittle? If so—

LIZA [perfectly elegant diction]: Walk! Not bloody likely. [Sensation.] I am going in a taxi. [She goes out.]

[Pickering gasps and sits down. Freddy goes out on the balcony to catch another glimpse of Eliza.]

MRS EYNSFORD HILL [suffering from shock]: Well, I really cant get used to the new ways.

CLARA [throwing herself discontentedly into the Elizabethan chair]: Oh, it's all right, mamma, quite right. People will think we never go anywhere or see anybody if you are so old-fashioned.

MRS EYNSFORD HILL: I daresay I am very old-fashioned; but I do hope you wont begin using that expression, Clara. I have got accustomed to hear you talking about men as rotters, and calling everything filthy and beastly; though I do think it horrible and unladylike. But this last is really too much. Dont you think so, Colonel Pickering?

PICKERING: Dont ask me, Ive been away in India for several years; and manners have changed so much that I sometimes dont know whether I'm at a respectable dinner-table or in a ship's forecastle.

CLARA: It's all a matter of habit. Theres no right or wrong in it. Nobody means anything by it. And it's so quaint, and gives such a smart emphasis to things that are not in themselves very witty. I find the new small talk delightful and quite innocent.

MRS EYNSFORD HILL [rising]: Well, after that, I think it's time for us to go.
    [Pickering and Higgins rise.]

CLARA [rising]: Oh yes: we have three at-homes to go to still. Goodbye, Mrs Higgins. Goodbye, Colonel Pickering. Goodbye, Professor Higgins.

HIGGINS [coming grimly at her from the divan, and accompanying her to the door]: Goodbye. Be sure you try on that small talk at the three at-homes. Dont be nervous about it. Pitch it in strong.

CLARA [all smiles]: I will. Goodbye. Such nonsense, all this early Victorian prudery!

HIGGINS [tempting her]: Such damned nonsense!

CLARA: Such bloody nonsense!

MRS EYNSFORD HILL [convulsively]: Clara!

CLARA: Ha! ha! [She goes out radiant, conscious of being thoroughly up to date, and is heard descending the stairs in a stream of silvery laughter.]

FREDDY [to the heavens at large]: Well, I ask you—[He gives it up, and comes to Mrs Higgins.] Goodbye.

MRS HIGGINS [shaking hands]: Goodbye. Would you like to meet Miss Doolittle again?

FREDDY [eagerly]: Yes, I should, most awfully.

MRS HIGGINS: Well, you know my days.

FREDDY: Yes. Thanks awfully. Goodbye. [He goes out.]

MRS EYNSFORD HILL: Goodbye, Mr Higgins.

HIGGINS: Goodbye. Goodbye.

MRS EYNSFORD HILL [to Pickering]: It's no use. I shall never be able to bring myself to use that word.

PICKERING: Dont. It's not compulsory, you know. Youll get on quite well without it.

MRS EYNSFORD HILL: Only, Clara is so down on me if I am not positively reeking with the latest slang. Goodbye.

PICKERING: Goodbye. [They shake hands.]

MRS EYNSFORD HILL [to Mrs Higgins]: You mustnt mind Clara. [Pickering, catching from her lowered tone that this is not meant for him to hear, discreetly joins Higgins at the window.] We're so poor! and she gets so few parties, poor child! She doesnt quite know. [Mrs Higgins, seeing that her eyes are moist, takes her hand sympathetically and goes with her to the door.] But the boy is nice. Dont you think so?

MRS HIGGINS: Oh, quite nice. I shall always be delighted to see him.

MRS EYNSFORD HILL: Thank you, dear. Goodbye. [She goes out.]

HIGGINS [eagerly]: Well? Is Eliza presentable? [He swoops on his mother and drags her to the ottoman, where she sits down in Eliza's place with her son on her left.]
    [Pickering returns to his chair on her right.]

MRS HIGGINS: You silly boy, of course she's not presentable. She's a triumph of your art and of her dressmaker's; but if you suppose for a moment that she doesnt give herself away in every sentence she utters, you must be perfectly cracked about her.

PICKERING: But dont you think something might be done? I mean something to eliminate the sanguinary element from her conversation.

MRS HIGGINS: Not as long as she is in Henry's hands.

HIGGINS [*aggrieved*]: Do you mean that my language is improper?

MRS HIGGINS: No, dearest: it would be quite proper—say on a canal barge; but it would not be proper for her at a garden party.

HIGGINS [*deeply injured*]: Well I must say—

PICKERING [*interrupting him*]: Come, Higgins: you must learn to know yourself. I havnt heard such language as yours since we used to review the volunteers in Hyde Park twenty years ago.

HIGGINS [*sulkily*]: Oh, well, if you say so, I suppose I dont always talk like a bishop.

MRS HIGGINS [*quieting Henry with a touch*]: Colonel Pickering: will you tell me what is the exact state of things in Wimpole Street?

PICKERING [*cheerfully: as if this completely changed the subject*]: Well, I have come to live there with Henry. We work together at my Indian Dialects; and we think it more convenient—

MRS HIGGINS: Quite so. I know all about that: it's an excellent arrangement. But where does this girl live?

HIGGINS: With us, of course. Where should she live?

MRS HIGGINS: But on what terms? Is she a servant? If not, what is she?

PICKERING [*slowly*]: I think I know what you mean, Mrs Higgins.

HIGGINS: Well, dash me if I do! Ive had to work at the girl every day for months to get her to her present pitch. Besides, she's useful. She knows where my things are, and remembers my appointments and so forth.

MRS HIGGINS: How does your housekeeper get on with her?

HIGGINS: Mrs Pearce? Oh, she's jolly glad to get so much taken off her hands; for before Eliza came, she used to have to find things and remind me of my appointments. But she's got some silly bee in her bonnet about Eliza. She keeps saying "You dont think, sir": doesnt she, Pick?

PICKERING: Yes: thats the formula. "You dont think, sir." Thats the end of every conversation about Eliza.

HIGGINS: As if I ever stop thinking about the girl and her confounded vowels and consonants. I'm worn out, thinking about her, and watching her lips and her teeth and her tongue, not to mention her soul, which is the quaintest of the lot.

MRS HIGGINS: You certainly are a pretty pair of babies, playing with your live doll.

HIGGINS: Playing! The hardest job I ever tackled: make no mistake about that, mother. But you have no idea how frightfully interesting it is to take a human being and change her into a quite different human being by creating a new speech for her. It's filling up the deepest gulf that separates class from class and soul from soul.

PICKERING [*drawing his chair closer to Mrs Higgins and bending over to her eagerly*]: Yes: it's enormously interesting. I assure you. Mrs Higgins, we take Eliza very seriously. Every week—every day almost—there is some new change. [*Closer again.*] We keep records of every stage—dozens of gramophone disks and photographs—

HIGGINS [*assailing her at the other ear*]: Yes, by George: it's the most absorbing experiment I ever tackled. She regularly fills our lives up: doesnt she, Pick?

PICKERING: We're always talking Eliza.

HIGGINS: Teaching Eliza.

PICKERING: Dressing Eliza.

MRS HIGGINS: What!

HIGGINS: Inventing new Elizas.

HIGGINS: ⎫		You know, she has the most extraordinary quickness of ear;
PICKERING: ⎭		I assure you, my dear Mrs Higgins, that girl
HIGGINS: ⎫		just like a parrot. Ive tried her with every
PICKERING: ⎭		is a genius. She can play the piano quite beautifully.
HIGGINS: ⎫		possible sort of sound that a human being can make—
PICKERING: ⎭		We have taken her to classical concerts and to music
HIGGINS: ⎫	*[speaking*	Continental dialects, African dialects, Hottentot
PICKERING: ⎭	*together]*	halls; and it's all the same to her: she plays everything
HIGGINS: ⎫		clicks, things it took me years to get hold of; and
PICKERING: ⎭		she hears right off when she comes home, whether it's
HIGGINS: ⎫		she picks them up like a shot, right away, as if she had
PICKERING: ⎭		Beethoven and Brahms or Lehar and Lionel Monckton;
HIGGINS: ⎫		been at it all her life.
PICKERING: ⎭		though six months ago, she'd never as much as touched a piano—

MRS HIGGINS [*putting her fingers in her ears, as they are by this time shouting one another down with an intolerable noise*]: Sh-sh-sh—sh!
[*They stop.*]

PICKERING: I beg your pardon. [*He draws his chair back apologetically.*]

HIGGINS: Sorry. When Pickering starts shouting nobody can get a word in edgeways.

MRS HIGGINS: Be quiet, Henry, Colonel Pickering: dont you realize that when Eliza walked into Wimpole Street, something walked in with her?

PICKERING: Her father did. But Henry soon got rid of him.

MRS HIGGINS: It would have been more to the point if her mother had. But as her mother didnt something else did.

PICKERING: But what?

MRS HIGGINS [*unconsciously dating herself by the word*]: A problem.

PICKERING: Oh I see. The problem of how to pass her off as a lady.

HIGGINS: I'll solve that problem. Ive half solved it already.

MRS HIGGINS: No, you two infinitely stupid male creatures: the problem of what is to be done with her afterwards.

HIGGINS: I dont see anything in that. She can go her own way, with all the advantages I have given her.

MRS HIGGINS: The advantages of that poor woman who was here just now! The manners and habits that disqualify a fine lady from earning her own living without giving her a fine lady's income! Is that what you mean?

PICKERING [*indulgently, being rather bored*]: Oh, that will be all right, Mrs Higgins. [*He rises to go.*]

HIGGINS [*rising also*]: We'll find her some light employment.

PICKERING: She's happy enough. Dont you worry about her. Goodbye. [*He shakes hands as if he were consoling a frightened child, and makes for the door.*]

HIGGINS: Anyhow, theres no good bothering now. The thing's done. Goodbye, mother. [*He kisses her, and follows Pickering.*]

PICKERING [*turning for a final consolation*]: There are plenty of openings. We'll do whats right. Goodbye.

HIGGINS [*to Pickering as they go out together*]: Lets take her to the Shakespear exhibition at Earls Court.

PICKERING: Yes: lets. Her remarks will be delicious.

HIGGINS: She'll mimic all the people for us when we get home.

PICKERING: Ripping. [*Both are heard laughing as they go down-stairs.*]

MRS HIGGINS [*rises with an impatient bounce, and returns to her work at the writing-table. She sweeps a litter of disarranged papers out of the way; snatches a sheet of paper from her stationery case; and tries resolutely to write. At the third time she gives it up; flings down her pen; grips the table angrily and exclaims*]: Oh, men! men!! men!!!

*   *   *

Clearly Eliza will not pass as a duchess yet; and Higgins's bet remains unwon. But the six months are not yet exhausted; and just in time Eliza does actually pass as a princess. For a glimpse of how she did it imagine an Embassy in London one summer evening after dark. The hall door has an awning and a carpet across the sidewalk to the kerb, because a grand reception is in progress. A small crowd is lined up to see the guests arrive.

A Rolls-Royce car drives up. Pickering in evening dress, with medals and orders, alights, and hands out Eliza, in opera cloak, evening dress, diamonds, fan, flowers and all accessories. Higgins follows. The car drives off; and the three go up the steps and into the house, the door opening for them as they approach.

Inside the house they find themselves in a spacious hall from which the grand staircase rises. On the left are the arrangements for the gentlemen's cloaks. The male guests are depositing their hats and wraps there.

On the right is a door leading to the ladies' cloakroom. Ladies are going in cloaked and coming out in splendor. Pickering whispers to Eliza and points out the ladies' room. She goes into it. Higgins and Pickering take off their overcoats and take tickets for them from the attendant.

One of the guests, occupied in the same way, has his back turned. Having taken his ticket, he turns round and reveals himself as an important looking young man with an astonishingly hairy face. He has an enormous moustache, flowing out into luxuriant whiskers. Waves of hair cluster on his brow. His hair is cropped closely at the back, and glows with oil. Otherwise he is very smart. He wears several worthless orders. He is evidently a foreigner, guessable as a whiskered Pandour[8] from Hungary: but in spite of the ferocity of his moustache he is amiable and genially voluble.

Recognizing Higgins, he flings his arms wide apart and approaches him enthusiastically.

WHISKERS: Maestro, maestro. [*He embraces Higgins and kisses him on both cheeks.*] You remember me?

HIGGINS: No I dont. Who the devil are you?

WHISKERS: I am your pupil: your first pupil, your best and greatest pupil. I am little Nepommuck, the marvellous boy. I have made your name famous throughout Europe. You teach me phonetic. You cannot forget ME.

HIGGINS: Why dont you shave?

NEPOMMUCK: I have not your imposing appearance, your chin, your brow. Nobody notices me when I shave. Now I am famous: they call me Hairy Faced Dick.

HIGGINS: And what are you doing here among all these swells?

NEPOMMUCK: I am interpreter. I speak 32 languages. I am indispensable at these international parties. You are great cockney specialist: you place a man anywhere in London the moment he open his mouth. I place any man in Europe.

[*A footman hurries down the grand staircase and comes to Nepommuck.*]

FOOTMAN: You are wanted upstairs. Her Excellency cannot understand the Greek gentleman.

NEPOMMUCK: Thank you, yes, immediately.

---

8. Member of the legendarily cruel Croatian militia.

[*The footman goes and is lost in the crowd.*]

NEPOMMUCK. [*to Higgins*]: This Greek diplomatist pretends he cannot speak nor understand English. He cannot deceive me. He is the son of a Clerkenwell watchmaker. He speaks English so villainously that he dare not utter a word of it without betraying his origin. I help him to pretend; but I make him pay through the nose. I make them all pay. Ha ha! [*He hurries upstairs.*]

PICKERING: Is this fellow really an expert? Can he find out Eliza and blackmail her?

HIGGINS: We shall see. If he finds her out I lose my bet.

[*Eliza comes from the cloakroom and joins them.*]

PICKERING: Well, Eliza, now for it. Are you ready?

LIZA: Are you nervous, Colonel?

PICKERING: Frightfully. I feel exactly as I felt before my first battle. It's the first time that frightens.

LIZA: It is not the first time for me, Colonel. I have done this fifty times—hundreds of times—in my little piggery in Angel Court in my day-dreams. I am in a dream now. Promise me not to let Professor Higgins wake me; for if he does I shall forget everything and talk as I used to in Drury Lane.

PICKERING: Not a word, Higgins. [*To Eliza.*] Now ready?

LIZA: Ready.

PICKERING: Go.

[*They mount the stairs, Higgins last. Pickering whispers to the footman on the first landing.*]

FIRST LANDING FOOTMAN: Miss Doolittle, Colonel Pickering, Professor Higgins.

SECOND LANDING FOOTMAN: Miss Doolittle, Colonel Pickering, Professor Higgins.

[*At the top of the staircase the Ambassador and his wife, with Nepommuck at her elbow, are receiving.*]

HOSTESS [*taking Eliza's hand*]: How d'ye do?

HOST [*same play*]: How d'ye do? How d'ye do, Pickering?

LIZA [*with a beautiful gravity that awes her hostess*]: How do you do? [*She passes on to the drawing room.*]

HOSTESS: Is that your adopted daughter, Colonel Pickering? She will make a sensation.

PICKERING: Most kind of you to invite her for me. [*He passes on.*]

HOSTESS [*to Nepommuck*]: Find out all about her.

NEPOMMUCK [*bowing*]: Excellency—[*He goes into the crowd.*]

HOST: How d'ye do, Higgins? You have a rival here tonight. He introduced himself as your pupil. Is he any good?

HIGGINS: He can learn a language in a fortnight—knows dozens of them. A sure mark of a fool. As a phonetician, no good whatever.

HOSTESS: How d'ye do, Professor?

HIGGINS: How do you do? Fearful bore for you this sort of thing. Forgive my part in it. [*He passes on.*]

[*In the drawing room and its suite of salons the reception is in full swing. Eliza passes through. She is so intent on her ordeal that she walks like a somnambulist in a desert instead of a débutante in a fashionable crowd. They stop talking to look at her, admiring her dress, her jewels, and her strangely attractive self. Some of the younger ones at the back stand on their chairs to see.*]

*The Host and Hostess come in from the staircase and mingle with their guests.
Higgins, gloomy and contemptuous of the whole business, comes into the group where
they are chatting.*]

HOSTESS: Ah, here is Professor Higgins: he will tell us. Tell us all about the wonderful young lady, Professor.

HIGGINS [*almost morosely*]: What wonderful young lady?

HOSTESS: You know very well. They tell me there has been nothing like her in London since people stood on their chairs to look at Mrs Langtry.[9]

[*Nepommuck joins the group, full of news.*]

HOSTESS: Ah, here you are at last, Nepommuck. Have you found out all about the Doolittle lady?

NEPOMMUCK: I have found out all about her. She is a fraud.

HOSTESS: A fraud! Oh no.

NEPOMMUCK: YES, yes. She cannot deceive me. Her name cannot be Doolittle.

HIGGINS: Why?

NEPOMMUCK: Because Doolittle is an English name. And she is not English.

HOSTESS: Oh, nonsense! She speaks English perfectly.

NEPOMMUCK: Too perfectly. Can you shew me any English woman who speaks English as it should be spoken? Only foreigners who have been taught to speak it speak it well.

HOSTESS: Certainly she terrified me by the way she said How d'ye do. I had a schoolmistress who talked like that; and I was mortally afraid of her. But if she is not English what is she?

NEPOMMUCK: Hungarian.

ALL THE REST: Hungarian!

NEPOMMUCK: Hungarian. And of royal blood. I am Hungarian. My blood is royal.

HIGGINS: Did you speak to her in Hungarian?

NEPOMMUCK: I did. She was very clever. She said "Please speak to me in English: I do not understand French." French! She pretends not to know the difference between Hungarian and French. Impossible: she knows both.

HIGGINS: And the blood royal? How did you find that out?

NEPOMMUCK: Instinct, maestro, instinct. Only the Magyar races can produce that air of the divine right, those resolute eyes. She is a princess.

HOST: What do you say, Professor?

HIGGINS: I say an ordinary London girl out of the gutter and taught to speak by an expert. I place her in Drury Lane.

NEPOMMUCK: Ha ha ha! Oh, maestro, maestro, you are mad on the subject of cockney dialects. The London gutter is the whole world for you.

HIGGINS [*to the Hostess*]: What does your Excellency say?

HOSTESS: Oh, of course I agree with Nepommuck. She must be a princess at least.

HOST: Not necessarily legitimate, of course. Morganatic[10] perhaps. But that is undoubtedly her class.

HIGGINS: I stick to my opinion.

HOSTESS: Oh, you are incorrigible.

---

9. Lillie Langtry (1852–1929), English actress and celebrity spokesperson for Pears' soap.
10. Form of marriage in which partners of unequal social station agree that neither the lower-ranking spouse nor any children will have a claim to the higher-ranking spouse's titles or property.

[*The group breaks up, leaving Higgins isolated. Pickering joins him.*]

PICKERING: Where is Eliza? We must keep an eye on her.

[*Eliza joins them.*]

LIZA: I dont think I can bear much more. The people all stare so at me. An old lady has just told me that I speak exactly like Queen Victoria. I am sorry if I have lost your bet. I have done my best: but nothing can make me the same as these people.

PICKERING: You have not lost it, my dear. You have won it ten times over.

HIGGINS: Let us get out of this. I have had enough of chattering to these fools.

PICKERING: Eliza is tired; and I am hungry. Let us clear out and have supper somewhere.

ACT 4

The Wimpole Street laboratory. Midnight. Nobody in the room. The clock on the mantelpiece strikes twelve. The fire is not alight: it is a summer night.

Presently Higgins and Pickering are heard on the stairs.

HIGGINS [*calling down to Pickering*]: I say, Pick: lock up, will you? I shant be going out again.

PICKERING: Right. Can Mrs Pearce go to bed? We dont want anything more, do we?

HIGGINS: Lord, no!

[*Eliza opens the door and is seen on the lighted landing in all the finery in which she has just won Higgins's bet for him. She comes to the hearth, and switches on the electric lights there. She is tired: her pallor contrasts strongly with her dark eyes and hair; and her expression is almost tragic. She takes off her cloak; puts her fan and gloves on the piano; and sits down on the bench, brooding and silent. Higgins, in evening dress, with overcoat and hat, comes in, carrying a smoking jacket which he has picked up downstairs. He takes off the hat and overcoat; throws them carelessly on the newspaper stand; disposes of his coat in the same way; puts on the smoking jacket; and throws himself wearily into the easy-chair at the hearth. Pickering, similarly attired, comes in. He also takes off his hat and overcoat, and is about to throw them on Higgins's when he hesitates.*]

PICKERING: I say: Mrs Pearce will row if we leave these things lying about in the drawing room.

HIGGINS: Oh, chuck them over the bannisters into the hall. She'll find them there in the morning and put them away all right. She'll think we were drunk.

PICKERING: We are, slightly. Are there any letters?

HIGGINS: I didnt look. [*Pickering takes the overcoats and hats and goes downstairs. Higgins begins half singing half yawning an air from La Fanciulla del Golden West. Suddenly he stops and exclaims.*] I wonder where the devil my slippers are!

[*Eliza looks at him darkly; then rises suddenly and leaves the room.*

Higgins yawns again, and resumes his song.

Pickering returns, with the contents of the letterbox in his hand.]

PICKERING: Only circulars, and this coroneted billet-doux[1] for you. [*He throws the circulars into the fender, and posts himself on the hearthrug, with his back to the grate.*]

HIGGINS [*glancing at the billet-doux*]: Money-lender. [*He throws the letter after the circulars.*]

---

1. Love letter.

[*Eliza returns with a pair of large down-at-heel slippers. She places them on the carpet before Higgins, and sits as before without a word.*]

HIGGINS [*yawning again*]: Oh Lord! What an evening! What a crew! What a silly tomfoolery! [*He raises his shoe to unlace it, and catches sight of the slippers. He stops unlacing and looks at them as if they had appeared there of their own accord.*] Oh! theyre there, are they?

PICKERING [*stretching himself*]: Well, I feel a bit tired. It's been a long day. The garden party, a dinner party, and the reception! Rather too much of a good thing. But youve won your bet, Higgins. Eliza did the trick, and something to spare, eh?

HIGGINS [*fervently*]: Thank God it's over!

[*Eliza flinches violently; but they take no notice of her; and she recovers herself and sits stonily as before.*]

PICKERING: Were you nervous at the garden party? I was. Eliza didnt seem a bit nervous.

HIGGINS: Oh, she wasnt nervous. I knew she'd be all right. No: it's the strain of putting the job through all these months that has told on me. It was interesting enough at first, while we were at the phonetics; but after that I got deadly sick of it. If I hadnt backed myself to do it I should have chucked the whole thing up two months ago. It was a silly notion: the whole thing has been a bore.

PICKERING: Oh come! the garden party was frightfully exciting. My heart began beating like anything.

HIGGINS: Yes, for the first three minutes. But when I saw we were going to win hands down, I felt like a bear in a cage, hanging about doing nothing. The dinner was worse: sitting gorging there for over an hour, with nobody but a damned fool of a fashionable woman to talk to! I tell you, Pickering, never again for me. No more artificial duchesses. The whole thing has been simple purgatory.

PICKERING: Youve never been broken in properly to the social routine. [*Strolling over to the piano.*] I rather enjoy dipping into it occasionally myself: it makes me feel young again. Anyhow, it was a great success: an immense success. I was quite frightened once or twice because Eliza was doing it so well. You see, lots of the real people cant do it at all: theyre such fools that they think style comes by nature to people in their position; and so they never learn. Theres always something professional about doing a thing superlatively well.

HIGGINS: Yes: thats what drives me mad: the silly people dont know their own silly business. [*Rising.*] However, it's over and done with; and now I can go to bed at last without dreading tomorrow.

[*Eliza's beauty becomes murderous.*]

PICKERING: I think I shall turn in too. Still, it's been a great occasion: a triumph for you. Goodnight. [*He goes.*]

HIGGINS [*following him*]: Goodnight. [*Over his shoulder, at the door.*] Put out the lights, Eliza; and tell Mrs Pearce not to make coffee for me in the morning: I'll take tea. [*He goes out.*]

[*Eliza tries to control herself and feel indifferent as she rises and walks across to the hearth to switch off the lights. By the time she gets there she is on the point of screaming. She sits down in Higgins's chair and holds on hard to the arms. Finally she gives way and flings herself furiously on the floor, raging.*]

HIGGINS [*in despairing wrath outside*]: What the devil have I done with my slippers? [*He appears at the door.*]

LIZA [*snatching up the slippers, and hurling them at him one after the other with all her force*]: There are your slippers. And there. Take your slippers; and may you never have a day's luck with them!

HIGGINS [*astounded*]: What on earth—! [*He comes to her.*] Whats the matter? Get up. [*He pulls her up.*] Anything wrong?

LIZA [*breathless*]: Nothing wrong—with you. Ive won your bet for you, havnt I? Thats enough for you. *I* dont matter, I suppose.

HIGGINS: You won my bet! You! Presumptuous insect! *I* won it. What did you throw those slippers at me for?

LIZA: Because I wanted to smash your face. I'd like to kill you, you selfish brute. Why didnt you leave me where you picked me out of—in the gutter? You thank God it's all over, and that now you can throw me back again there, do you? [*She crisps her fingers frantically.*]

HIGGINS [*looking at her in cool wonder*]: The creature is nervous, after all.

LIZA [*gives a suffocated scream of fury, and instinctively darts her nails at his face*]: !!

HIGGINS [*catching her wrists*]: Ah! would you? Claws in, you cat. How dare you shew your temper to me? Sit down and be quiet. [*He throws her roughly into the easy-chair.*]

LIZA [*crushed by superior strength and weight*]: Whats to become of me? Whats to become of me?

HIGGINS: How the devil do I know whats to become of you? What does it matter what becomes of you?

LIZA: You dont care. I know you dont care. You wouldnt care if I was dead. I'm nothing to you—not so much as them slippers.

HIGGINS [*thundering*]: Those slippers.

LIZA [*with bitter submission*]: Those slippers. I didnt think it made any difference now.

[*A pause. Eliza hopeless and crushed. Higgins a little uneasy.*]

HIGGINS [*in his loftiest manner*]: Why have you begun going on like this? May I ask whether you complain of your treatment here?

LIZA: No.

HIGGINS: Has anybody behaved badly to you? Colonel Pickering? Mrs Pearce? Any of the servants?

LIZA: No.

HIGGINS: I presume you dont pretend that *I* have treated you badly?

LIZA: No.

HIGGINS: I am glad to hear it. [*He moderates his tone.*] Perhaps youre tired after the strain of the day. Will you have a glass of champagne? [*He moves towards the door.*]

LIZA: No. [*Recollecting her manners.*] Thank you.

HIGGINS [*good-humored again*]: This has been coming on you for some days. I suppose it was natural for you to be anxious about the garden party. But thats all over now. [*He pats her kindly on the shoulder. She writhes.*] Theres nothing more to worry about.

LIZA: No. Nothing more for you to worry about. [*She suddenly rises and gets away from him by going to the piano bench, where she sits and hides her face.*] Oh God! I wish I was dead.

HIGGINS [*staring after her in sincere surprise*]: Why? In heaven's name, why? [*Reasonably, going to her.*] Listen to me, Eliza. All this irritation is purely subjective.

LIZA: I dont understand. I'm too ignorant.

HIGGINS: It's only imagination. Low spirits and nothing else. Nobody's hurting you. Nothing's wrong. You go to bed like a good girl and sleep it off. Have a little cry and say your prayers: that will make you comfortable.

LIZA: I heard your prayers. "Thank God it's all over!"

HIGGINS [*impatiently*]: Well, dont you thank God it's all over? Now you are free and can do what you like.

LIZA [*pulling herself together in desperation*]: What am I fit for? What have you left me fit for? Where am I to go? What am I to do? Whats to become of me?

HIGGINS [*enlightened, but not at all impressed*]: Oh, thats whats worrying you, is it? [*He thrusts his hands into his pockets, and walks about in his usual manner, rattling the contents of his pockets, as if condescending to a trivial subject out of pure kindness.*] I shouldnt bother about it if I were you. I should imagine you wont have much difficulty in settling yourself somewhere or other, though I hadnt quite realized that you were going away. [*She looks quickly at him: he does not look at her, but examines the dessert stand on the piano and decides that he will eat an apple.*] You might marry, you know. [*He bites a large piece out of the apple and munches it noisily.*] You see, Eliza, all men are not confirmed old bachelors like me and the Colonel. Most men are the marrying sort (poor devils!); and youre not bad-looking: it's quite a pleasure to look at you sometimes—not now, of course, because youre crying and looking as ugly as the very devil; but when youre all right and quite yourself, youre what I should call attractive. That is, to the people in the marrying line, you understand. You go to bed and have a good nice rest; and then get up and look at yourself in the glass; and you wont feel so cheap.

[*Eliza again looks at him, speechless, and does not stir.*
The look is quite lost on him: he eats his apple with a dreamy expression of happiness, as it is quite a good one.]

HIGGINS [*a genial afterthought occurring to him*]: I daresay my mother could find some chap or other who would do very well.

LIZA: We were above that at the corner of Tottenham Court Road.

HIGGINS [*waking up*]: What do you mean?

LIZA: I sold flowers. I didnt sell myself. Now youve made a lady of me I'm not fit to sell anything else. I wish youd left me where you found me.

HIGGINS [*slinging the core of the apple decisively into the grate*]: Tosh, Eliza. Dont you insult human relations by dragging all this cant about buying and selling into it. You neednt marry the fellow if you dont like him.

LIZA: What else am I to do?

HIGGINS: Oh, lots of things. What about your old idea of a florist's shop? Pickering could set you up in one: he has lots of money. [*Chuckling.*] He'll have to pay for all those togs you have been wearing today; and that, with the hire of the jewellery, will make a big hole in two hundred pounds. Why, six months ago you would have thought it the millennium to have a flower shop of your own. Come! youll be all right. I must clear off to bed: I'm devilish sleepy. By the way, I came down for something: I forget what it was.

LIZA: Your slippers.

HIGGINS: Oh yes, of course. You shied them at me. [*He picks them up, and is going out when she rises and speaks to him.*]

LIZA: Before you go, sir—

HIGGINS [*dropping the slippers in his surprise at her calling him Sir*]: Eh?

LIZA: Do my clothes belong to me or to Colonel Pickering?

HIGGINS [*coming back into the room as if her question were the very climax of unreason*]: What the devil use would they be to Pickering?

LIZA: He might want them for the next girl you pick up to experiment on.

HIGGINS [*shocked and hurt*]: Is that the way you feel towards us?

LIZA: I dont want to hear anything more about that. All I want to know is whether anything belongs to me. My own clothes were burnt.

HIGGINS: But what does it matter? Why need you start bothering about that in the middle of the night?

LIZA: I want to know what I may take away with me. I dont want to be accused of stealing.

HIGGINS [*now deeply wounded*]: Stealing! You shouldnt have said that. Eliza. That shews a want of feeling.

LIZA: I'm sorry. I'm only a common ignorant girl; and in my station I have to be careful. There cant be any feelings between the like of you and the like of me. Please will you tell me what belongs to me and what doesnt?

HIGGINS [*very sulky*]: You may take the whole damned houseful if you like. Except the jewels. Theyre hired. Will that satisfy you? [*He turns on his heel and is about to go in extreme dudgeon.[2]*]

LIZA [*drinking in his emotion like nectar, and nagging him to provoke a further supply*]: Stop, please. [*She takes off her jewels.*] Will you take these to your room and keep them safe? I dont want to run the risk of their being missing.

HIGGINS [*furious*]: Hand them over. [*She puts them into his hands.*] If these belonged to me instead of to the jeweller, I'd ram them down your ungrateful throat. [*He perfunctorily thrusts them into his pockets, unconsciously decorating himself with the protruding ends of the chains.*]

LIZA [*taking a ring off*]: This ring isnt the jeweller's: it's the one you bought me in Brighton. I dont want it now. [*Higgins dashes the ring violently into the fireplace, and turns on her so threateningly that she crouches over the piano with her hands over her face, and exclaims.*] Dont you hit me.

HIGGINS: Hit you! You infamous creature, how dare you accuse me of such a thing? It is you who have hit me. You have wounded me to the heart.

LIZA [*thrilling with hidden joy*]: I'm glad. Ive got a little of my own back, anyhow.

HIGGINS [*with dignity, in his finest professional style*]: You have caused me to lose my temper: a thing that has hardly ever happened to me before. I prefer to say noth-ing more tonight. I am going to bed.

LIZA [*pertly*]: Youd better leave a note for Mrs Pearce about the coffee; for she wont be told by me.

HIGGINS [*formally*]: Damn Mrs Pearce; and damn the coffee: and damn you; and [*wildly*] damn my own folly in having lavished my hard-earned knowledge and the treasure of my regard and intimacy on a heartless guttersnipe. [*He goes out with impressive decorum, and spoils it by slamming the door savagely*].

[*Eliza goes down on her knees on the hearthrug to look for the ring. When she finds it she considers for a moment what to do with it. Finally she flings it down on the dessert stand and goes upstairs in a tearing rage.*]

*   *   *

2. Anger, irritation.

The furniture of Eliza's room has been increased by a big wardrobe and a sumptuous dressing-table. She comes in and switches on the electric light. She goes to the wardrobe; opens it; and pulls out a walking dress, a hat, and a pair of shoes, which she throws on the bed. She takes off her evening dress and shoes: then takes a padded hanger from the wardrobe: adjusts it carefully in the evening dress; and hangs it, in the wardrobe, which she shuts with a slam. She puts on her walking shoes, her walking dress, and hat. She takes her wrist watch from the dressing-table and fastens it on. She pulls on her gloves: takes her vanity bag; and looks into it to see that her purse is there before hanging it on her wrist. She makes for the door. Every movement expresses her furious resolution.

She takes a last look at herself in the glass.

She suddenly puts out her tongue at herself; then leaves the room, switching off the electric light at the door.

Meanwhile, in the street outside, Freddy Eynsford Hill, lovelorn, is gazing up at the second floor, in which one of the windows is still lighted.

The light goes out.

FREDDY: Goodnight, darling, darling, darling.

[*Eliza comes out, giving the door a considerable bang behind her.*]

LIZA: Whatever are you doing here?

FREDDY: Nothing. I spend most of my nights here. It's the only place where I'm happy. Dont laugh at me, Miss Doolittle.

LIZA: Dont you call me Miss Doolittle, do you hear? Liza's good enough for me. [*She breaks down and grabs him by the shoulders.*] Freddy: you dont think I'm a heartless guttersnipe, do you?

FREDDY: Oh no, no, darling: how can you imagine such a thing? You are the loveliest, dearest—

[*He loses all self-control and smothers her with kisses. She, hungry for comfort, responds. They stand there in one another's arms.*

An elderly police constable arrives.]

CONSTABLE [*scandalized*]: Now then! Now then!! Now then!!!

[*They release one another hastily.*]

FREDDY: Sorry, constable. Weve only just become engaged.

[*They run away.*

The constable shakes his head, reflecting on his own courtship and on the vanity of human hopes. He moves off in the opposite direction with slow professional steps.

The flight of the lovers takes them to Cavendish Square. There they halt to consider their next move.]

LIZA [*out of breath*]: He didnt half give me a fright, that copper. But you answered him proper.

FREDDY: I hope I havnt taken you out of your way. Where were you going?

LIZA: To the river.

FREDDY: What for?

LIZA: To make a hole in it.

FREDDY [*horrified*]: Eliza, darling. What do you mean? What's the matter?

LIZA: Never mind. It doesnt matter now. Theres nobody in the world now but you and me, is there?

FREDDY: Not a soul.

[*They indulge in another embrace, and are again surprised by a much younger constable.*]

SECOND CONSTABLE: Now then, you two! What's this? Where do you think you are? Move along here, double quick.

FREDDY: As you say, sir, double quick.

[*They run away again, and are in Hanover Square before they stop for another conference.*]

FREDDY: I had no idea the police were so devilishly prudish.

LIZA: It's their business to hunt girls off the streets.

FREDDY: We must go somewhere. We cant wander about the streets all night.

LIZA: Cant we? I think it'd be lovely to wander about for ever.

FREDDY: Oh, darling.

[*They embrace again, oblivious of the arrival of a crawling taxi. It stops.*]

TAXIMAN: Can I drive you and the lady anywhere, sir?

[*They start asunder.*]

LIZA: Oh, Freddy, a taxi. The very thing.

FREDDY: But, damn it, Ive no money.

LIZA: I have plenty. The Colonel thinks you should never go out without ten pounds in your pocket. Listen. We'll drive about all night; and in the morning I'll call on old Mrs Higgins and ask her what I ought to do. I'll tell you all about it in the cab. And the police wont touch us there.

FREDDY: Righto! Ripping. [*To the Taximan.*] Wimbledon Common. [*They drive off.*]

ACT 5

Mrs Higgins's drawing room. She is at her writing-table as before. The parlormaid comes in.

THE PARLORMAID [*at the door*]: Mr Henry, maam, is downstairs with Colonel Pickering.

MRS HIGGINS: Well, shew them up.

THE PARLORMAID: Theyre using the telephone, maam. Telephoning to the police, I think.

MRS HIGGINS: What!

THE PARLORMAID [*coming further in and lowering her voice*]: Mr Henry is in a state, maam. I thought I'd better tell you.

MRS HIGGINS: If you had told me that Mr Henry was not in a state it would have been more surprising. Tell them to come up when theyve finished with the police. I suppose he's lost something.

THE PARLORMAID: Yes, maam [*Going.*]

MRS HIGGINS: Go upstairs and tell Miss Doolittle that Mr Henry and the Colonel are here. Ask her not to come down til I send for her.

THE PARLORMAID: Yes, maam.

[*Higgins bursts in. He is, as the parlormaid has said, in a state.*]

HIGGINS: Look here, mother: heres a confounded thing!

MRS HIGGINS: Yes, dear. Good morning. [*He checks his impatience and kisses her, whilst the parlormaid goes out.*] What is it?

HIGGINS: Eliza's bolted.

MRS HIGGINS [*calmly continuing her writing*]: You must have frightened her.

HIGGINS: Frightened her! nonsense! She was left last night, as usual, to turn out the lights and all that; and instead of going to bed she changed her clothes and went right off: her bed wasnt slept in. She came in a cab for her things before seven this morning; and that fool Mrs Pearce let her have them without telling me a word about it. What am I to do?

MRS HIGGINS: Do without, I'm afraid, Henry. The girl has a perfect right to leave if she chooses.

HIGGINS [*wandering distractedly across the room*]: But I cant find anything. I dont know what appointments Ive got. I'm—[*Pickering comes in. Mrs Higgins puts down her pen and turns away from the writing-table.*]

PICKERING [*shaking hands*]: Good morning. Mrs Higgins. Has Henry told you? [*He sits down on the ottoman.*]

HIGGINS: What does that ass of an inspector say? Have you offered a reward?

MRS HIGGINS [*rising in indignant amazement*]: You dont mean to say you have set the police after Eliza?

HIGGINS: Of course. What are the police for? What else could we do? [*He sits in the Elizabethan chair.*]

PICKERING: The inspector made a lot of difficulties. I really think he suspected us of some improper purpose.

MRS HIGGINS: Well, of course he did. What right have you to go to the police and give the girl's name as if she were a thief, or a lost umbrella, or something? Really! [*She sits down again, deeply vexed.*]

HIGGINS: But we want to find her.

PICKERING: We cant let her go like this, you know, Mrs Higgins. What were we to do?

MRS HIGGINS: You have no more sense, either of you, than two children. Why— [*The parlormaid comes in and breaks off the conversation.*]

THE PARLORMAID: Mr Henry: a gentleman wants to see you very particular. He's been sent on from Wimpole Street.

HIGGINS: Oh, bother! I cant see anyone now. Who is it?

THE PARLORMAID: A Mr Doolittle, sir.

PICKERING: Doolittle! Do you mean the dustman?

THE PARLORMAID: Dustman! Oh no, sir: a gentleman.

HIGGINS [*springing up excitedly*]: By George, Pick, it's some relative of hers that she's gone to. Somebody we know nothing about. [*To the parlormaid.*] Send him up, quick.

THE PARLORMAID: Yes, sir. [*She goes.*]

HIGGINS [*eagerly, going to his mother*]: Genteel relatives! now we shall hear something. [*He sits down in the Chippendale chair.*]

MRS HIGGINS: Do you know any of her people?

PICKERING: Only her father: the fellow we told you about.

THE PARLORMAID [*announcing*]: Mr Doolittle. [*She withdraws*].
    [*Doolittle enters. He is resplendently dressed as for a fashionable wedding, and might, in fact, be the bridegroom. A flower in his buttonhole, a dazzling silk hat, and patent leather shoes complete the effect. He is too concerned with the business he has come on to notice Mrs Higgins. He walks straight to Higgins, and accosts him with vehement reproach.*]

DOOLITTLE [*indicating his own person*]: See here! Do you see this? You done this.

HIGGINS: Done what, man?

DOOLITTLE: This, I tell you. Look at it. Look at this hat. Look at this coat.

PICKERING: Has Eliza been buying you clothes?

DOOLITTLE: Eliza! not she. Why would she buy me clothes?

MRS HIGGINS: Good morning, Mr Doolittle. Wont you sit down?

DOOLITTLE [*taken aback as he becomes conscious that he has forgotten his hostess*]: Asking your pardon, maam. [*He approaches her and shakes her proffered hand.*] Thank you. [*He sits down on the ottoman, on Pickering's right.*] I am that full of what has happened to me that I cant think of anything else.

HIGGINS: What the dickens has happened to you?

DOOLITTLE: I shouldnt mind if it had only happened to me: anything might happen to anybody and nobody to blame but Providence, as you might say. But this is something that you done to me: yes, you, Enry Iggins.

HIGGINS: Have you found Eliza?

DOOLITTLE: Have you lost her?

HIGGINS: Yes.

DOOLITTLE: You have all the luck, you have. I aint found her: but she'll find me quick enough now after what you done to me.

MRS HIGGINS: But what has my son done to you. Mr Doolittle?

DOOLITTLE: Done to me! Ruined me. Destroyed my happiness. Tied me up and delivered me into the hands of middle class morality.

HIGGINS [rising intolerantly and standing over Doolittle]: Youre raving. Youre drunk. Youre mad. I gave you five pounds. After that I had two conversations with you, at half-a-crown an hour. Ive never seen you since.

DOOLITTLE: Oh! Drunk am I? Mad am I? Tell me this. Did you or did you not write a letter to an old blighter in America that was giving five millions to found Moral Reform Societies all over the world, and that wanted you to invent a universal language for him?

HIGGINS: What! Ezra D. Wannafeller! He's dead. [He sits down again carelessly.]

DOOLITTLE: Yes: he's dead; and I'm done for. Now did you or did you not write a letter to him to say that the most original moralist at present in England, to the best of your knowledge, was Alfred Doolittle, a common dustman?

HIGGINS: Oh, after your first visit I remember making some silly joke of the kind.

DOOLITTLE: Ah! You may well call it a silly joke. It put the lid on me right enough. Just give him the chance he wanted to shew that Americans is not like us: that they reckonize and respect merit in every class of life, however humble. Them words is in his blooming will, in which, Henry Higgins, thanks to your silly joking, he leaves me a share in his Pre-digested Cheese Trust worth three thousand a year on condition that I lecture for his Wannafeller Moral Reform World League as often as they ask me up to six times a year.

HIGGINS: The devil he does! Whew! [Brightening suddenly.] What a lark!

PICKERING: A safe thing for you, Doolittle. They wont ask you twice.

DOOLITTLE: It aint the lecturing I mind. I'll lecture them blue in the face, I will, and not turn a hair. It's making a gentleman of me that I object to. Who asked him to make a gentleman of me? I was happy. I was free. I touched pretty nigh everybody for money when I wanted it, same as I touched you, Enry Iggins. Now I am worrited[1]: tied neck and heels: and everybody touches me for money. It's a fine thing for you, says my solicitor. Is it? says I. You mean it's a good thing for you, I says. When I was a poor man and had a solicitor once when they found a pram in the dust cart, he got me off, and got shut of me and got me shut of him as quick as he could. Same with the doctors: used to shove me out of the hospital before I could hardly stand on my legs, and nothing to pay. Now they finds out that I'm not a healthy man and cant live unless they looks after me twice a day. In the house I'm not let do a hand's turn for myself: somebody else must do it and touch me for it. A year ago I hadnt a relative in the world except two or three that wouldnt speak to me. Now Ive fifty, and not a decent week's wages among the lot of them. I have to live for others and not for myself: thats middle class morality. You talk of losing Eliza. Dont you be anxious: I bet she's on my doorstep by this:

---

1. Worried.

she that could support herself easy by selling flowers if I wasnt respectable. And the next one to touch me will be you, Enry Iggins. I'll have to learn to speak middle class language from you, instead of speaking proper English. Thats where youll come in; and I daresay thats what you done it for.

MRS HIGGINS: But, my dear Mr Doolittle, you need not suffer all this if you are really in earnest. Nobody can force you to accept this bequest. You can repudiate it. Isnt that so, Colonel Pickering?

PICKERING: I believe so.

DOOLITTLE [*softening his manner in deference to her sex*]: Thats the tragedy of it, maam. It's easy to say chuck it; but I havnt the nerve. Which of us has? We're all intimidated. Intimidated, maam: thats what we are. What is there for me if I chuck it but the workhouse in my old age? I have to dye my hair already to keep my job as a dustman. If I was one of the deserving poor, and had put by a bit, I could chuck it; but then why should I, acause[2] the deserving poor might as well be millionaires for all the happiness they ever has. They dont know what happiness is. But I, as one of the undeserving poor, have nothing between me and the pauper's uniform but this here blasted three thousand a year that shoves me into the middle class. (Excuse the expression, maam; youd use it yourself if you had my provocation.) Theyve got you every way you turn: it's a choice between the Skilly of the workhouse and the Char Bydis[3] of the middle class; and I havnt the nerve for the workhouse. Intimidated: thats what I am. Broke. Bought up. Happier men than me will call for my dust, and touch me for their tip; and I'll look on helpless, and envy them. And thats what your son has brought me to. [*He is overcome by emotion.*]

MRS HIGGINS: Well, I'm very glad youre not going to do anything foolish, Mr Doolittle. For this solves the problem of Eliza's future. You can provide for her now.

DOOLITTLE [*with melancholy resignation*]: Yes, maam: I'm expected to provide for everyone now, out of three thousand a year.

HIGGINS [*jumping up*]: Nonsense! he cant provide for her. He shant provide for her. She doesnt belong to him. I paid him five pounds for her. Doolittle: either youre an honest man or a rogue.

DOOLITTLE [*tolerantly*]: A little of both, Henry, like the rest of us: a little of both.

HIGGINS: Well, you took that money for the girl; and you have no right to take her as well.

MRS HIGGINS: Henry: dont be absurd. If you want to know where Eliza is, she is upstairs.

HIGGINS [*amazed*]: Upstairs!!! Then I shall jolly soon fetch her downstairs. [*He makes resolutely for the door.*]

MRS HIGGINS [*rising and following him*]: Be quiet, Henry. Sit down.

HIGGINS: I—

MRS HIGGINS: Sit down, dear; and listen to me.

HIGGINS: Oh very well, very well, very well. [*He throws himself ungraciously on the ottoman, with his face towards the windows.*] But I think you might have told us this half an hour ago.

MRS HIGGINS: Eliza came to me this morning. She told me of the brutal way you two treated her.

2. Because.
3. In his odyssey to return home to Ithaca, the Greek hero Odysseus had to sail carefully between the paired hazards of Scylla, a monster who would pluck and eat mariners who passed too close, and Charybdis, an enormous whirlpool.

HIGGINS [*bouncing up again*]: What!

PICKERING [*rising also*]: My dear Mrs Higgins, she's been telling you stories. We didnt treat her brutally. We hardly said a word to her; and we parted on particularly good terms. [*Turning on Higgins.*] Higgins: did you bully her after I went to bed?

HIGGINS: Just the other way about. She threw my slippers in my face. She behaved in the most outrageous way. I never gave her the slightest provocation. The slippers came bang into my face the moment I entered the room—before I had uttered a word. And used perfectly awful language.

PICKERING [*astonished*]: But why? What did we do to her?

MRS HIGGINS: I think I know pretty well what you did. The girl is naturally rather affectionate, I think. Isnt she, Mr Doolittle?

DOOLITTLE: Very tender-hearted, maam. Takes after me.

MRS HIGGINS: Just so. She had become attached to you both. She worked very hard for you, Henry. I dont think you quite realize what anything in the nature of brain work means to a girl of her class. Well, it seems that when the great day of trial came, and she did this wonderful thing for you without making a single mistake, you two sat there and never said a word to her, but talked together of how glad you were that it was all over and how you had been bored with the whole thing. And then you were surprised because she threw your slippers at you! I should have thrown the fire-irons at you.

HIGGINS: We said nothing except that we were tired and wanted to go to bed. Did we, Pick?

PICKERING [*shrugging his shoulders*]: That was all.

MRS HIGGINS [*ironically*]: Quite sure?

PICKERING: Absolutely, Really, that was all.

MRS HIGGINS: You didnt thank her, or pet her, or admire her, or tell her how splendid she'd been.

HIGGINS [*impatiently*]: But she knew all about that. We didnt make speeches to her, if thats what you mean.

PICKERING [*conscience stricken*]: Perhaps we were a little inconsiderate. Is she very angry?

MRS HIGGINS [*returning to her place at the writing-table*]: Well, I'm afraid she wont go back to Wimpole Street, especially now that Mr Doolittle is able to keep up the position you have thrust on her; but she says she is quite willing to meet you on friendly terms and to let bygones be bygones.

HIGGINS [*furious*]: Is she, by George? Ho!

MRS HIGGINS: If you promise to behave yourself, Henry, I'll ask her to come down. If not, go home: for you have taken up quite enough of my time.

HIGGINS: Oh, all right. Very well. Pick: you behave yourself. Let us put on our best Sunday manners for this creature that we picked out of the mud. [*He flings himself sulkily into the Elizabethan chair.*]

DOOLITTLE [*remonstrating*]: Now, now, Enry Iggins! Have some consideration for my feelings as a middle class man.

MRS HIGGINS: Remember your promise, Henry. [*She presses the bell-button on the writing-table.*] Mr Doolittle: will you be so good as to step out on the balcony for a moment. I dont want Eliza to have the shock of your news until she has made it up with these two gentlemen. Would you mind?

DOOLITTLE: As you wish, lady. Anything to help Henry to keep her off my hands. [*He disappears through the window.*]

[*The parlormaid answers the bell. Pickering sits down in Doolittle's place.*]

MRS HIGGINS: Ask Miss Doolittle to come down, please.

THE PARLORMAID: Yes, maam. [*She goes out.*]

MRS HIGGINS: Now, Henry: be good.

HIGGINS: I am behaving myself perfectly.

PICKERING: He is doing his best, Mrs Higgins.

[*A pause. Higgins throws back his head; stretches out his legs; and begins to whistle.*]

MRS HIGGINS: Henry, dearest, you dont look at all nice in that attitude.

HIGGINS [*pulling himself together*]: I was not trying to look nice, mother.

MRS HIGGINS: It doesnt matter, dear. I only wanted to make you speak.

HIGGINS: Why?

MRS HIGGINS: Because you cant speak and whistle at the same time.

[*Higgins groans. Another very trying pause.*]

HIGGINS [*springing up, out of patience*]: Where the devil is that girl? Are we to wait here all day?

[*Eliza enters, sunny, self-possessed, and giving a staggeringly convincing exhibition of ease of manner. She carries a little work-basket, and is very much at home. Pickering is too much taken aback to rise.*]

LIZA: How do you do, Professor Higgins? Are you quite well?

HIGGINS [*choking*]: Am I— [*He can say no more.*]

LIZA: But of course you are: you are never ill. So glad to see you again, Colonel Pickering. [*He rises hastily; and they shake hands.*] Quite chilly this morning, isnt it? [*She sits down on his left. He sits beside her.*]

HIGGINS: Dont you dare try this game on me. I taught it to you; and it doesnt take me in. Get up and come home; and dont be a fool.

[*Eliza takes a piece of needlework from her basket, and begins to stitch at it, without taking the least notice of this outburst.*]

MRS HIGGINS: Very nicely put, indeed, Henry. No woman could resist such an invitation.

HIGGINS: You let her alone, mother. Let her speak for herself. You will jolly soon see whether she has an idea that I havnt put into her head or a word that I havnt put into her mouth. I tell you I have created this thing out of the squashed cabbage leaves of Covent Garden; and now she pretends to play the fine lady with me.

MRS HIGGINS [*placidly*]: Yes, dear; but youll sit down, wont you?

[*Higgins sits down again, savagely.*]

LIZA [*to Pickering, taking no apparent notice of Higgins, and working away deftly*]: Will you drop me altogether now that the experiment is over, Colonel Pickering?

PICKERING: Oh dont. You mustnt think of it as an experiment. It shocks me, somehow.

LIZA: Oh, I'm only a squashed cabbage leaf—

PICKERING [*impulsively*]: No.

LIZA [*continuing quietly*]: —but I owe so much to you that I should be very unhappy if you forgot me.

PICKERING: It's very kind of you to say so, Miss Doolittle.

LIZA: It's not because you paid for my dresses. I know you are generous to everybody with money. But it was from you that I learnt really nice manners; and that is what makes one a lady, isnt it? You see it was so very difficult for me with the example of Professor Higgins always before me. I was brought up to be just like him, unable to control myself, and using bad language on the slightest provocation. And I should never have known that ladies and gentlemen didnt behave like that if you hadnt been there.

HIGGINS: Well!!

PICKERING: Oh, thats only his way, you know. He doesnt mean it.

LIZA: Oh, *I* didnt mean it either, when I was a flower girl. It was only my way. But you see I did it; and thats what makes the difference after all.

PICKERING: No doubt. Still, he taught you to speak; and I couldnt have done that, you know.

LIZA [*trivially*]: Of course: that is his profession.

HIGGINS: Damnation!

LIZA [*continuing*]: It was just like learning to dance in the fashionable way: there was nothing more than that in it. But do you know what began my real education?

PICKERING: What?

LIZA [*stopping her work for a moment*]: Your calling me Miss Doolittle that day when I first came to Wimpole Street. That was the beginning of self-respect for me. [*She resumes her stitching.*] And there were a hundred little things you never noticed, because they came naturally to you. Things about standing up and taking off your hat and opening doors—

PICKERING: Oh, that was nothing.

LIZA: Yes: things that shewed you thought and felt about me as if I were something better than a scullery-maid; though of course I know you would have been just the same to a scullery-maid if she had been let into the drawing room. You never took off your boots in the dining room when I was there.

PICKERING: You mustnt mind that. Higgins takes off his boots all over the place.

LIZA: I know. I am not blaming him. It is his way, isnt it? But it made such a difference to me that you didnt do it. You see, really and truly, apart from the things anyone can pick up (the dressing and the proper way of speaking, and so on), the difference between a lady and a flower girl is not how she behaves, but how she's treated. I shall always be a flower girl to Professor Higgins, because he always treats me as a flower girl, and always will; but I know I can be a lady to you, because you always treat me as a lady, and always will.

MRS HIGGINS: Please dont grind your teeth. Henry.

PICKERING: Well, this is really very nice of you, Miss Doolittle.

LIZA: I should like you to call me Eliza, now, if you would.

PICKERING: Thank you. Eliza, of course.

LIZA: And I should like Professor Higgins to call me Miss Doolittle.

HIGGINS: I'll see you damned first.

MRS HIGGINS: Henry! Henry!

PICKERING [*laughing*]: Why dont you slang back at him? Dont stand it. It would do him a lot of good.

LIZA: I cant. I could have done it once but now I cant go back to it. You told me, you know, that when a child is brought to a foreign country, it picks up the language in a few weeks, and forgets its own. Well, I am a child in your country. I have forgotten my own language, and can speak nothing but yours. Thats the real break-off with the corner of Tottenham Court Road. Leaving Wimpole Street finishes it.

PICKERING [*much alarmed*]: Oh! but youre coming back to Wimpole Street, arnt you? Youll forgive Higgins?

HIGGINS [*rising*]: Forgive! Will she, by George! Let her go. Let her find out how she can get on without us. She will relapse into the gutter in three weeks without me at her elbow.

[*Doolittle appears at the centre window. With a look of dignified reproach at Higgins, he comes slowly and silently to his daughter, who, with her back to the window, is unconscious of his approach.*]

PICKERING: He's incorrigible, Eliza. You wont relapse, will you?

LIZA: No: not now. Never again. I have learnt my lesson. I dont believe I could utter one of the old sounds if I tried. [*Doolittle touches her on her left shoulder. She drops her work, losing her self-possession utterly at the spectacle of her father's splendor.*] A-a-a-a-ah-ow-ooh!

HIGGINS [*with a crow of triumph*]: Aha! Just so. A-a-a-ahowooh! A-a-a-ahowooh! A-a-a-ahowooh! Victory! Victory! [*He throws himself on the divan, folding his arms, and spraddling arrogantly.*]

DOOLITTLE: Can you blame the girl? Dont look at me like that, Eliza. It aint my fault. Ive come into some money.

LIZA: You must have touched a millionaire this time, dad.

DOOLITTLE: I have. But I'm dressed something special today. I'm going to St George's. Hanover Square. Your stepmother is going to marry me.

LIZA [*angrily*]: Youre going to let yourself down to marry that low common woman!

PICKERING [*quietly*]: He ought to, Eliza. [*To Doolittle.*] Why has she changed her mind?

DOOLITTLE [*sadly*]: Intimidated, Governor. Intimidated. Middle class morality claims its victim. Wont you put on your hat, Liza, and come and see me turned off?

LIZA: If the Colonel says I must. I—I'll [*almost sobbing*] I'll demean myself. And get insulted for my pains, like enough.

DOOLITTLE: Dont be afraid: she never comes to words with anyone now, poor woman! respectability has broke all the spirit out of her.

PICKERING [*squeezing Eliza's elbow gently*]: Be kind to them, Eliza. Make the best of it.

LIZA [*forcing a little smile for him through her vexation*]: Oh well, just to shew theres no ill feeling. I'll be back in a moment. [*She goes out.*]

DOOLITTLE [*sitting down beside Pickering*]: I feel uncommon nervous about the ceremony, Colonel. I wish youd come and see me through it.

PICKERING: But youve been through it before, man. You were married to Eliza's mother.

DOOLITTLE: Who told you that, Colonel?

PICKERING: Well, nobody told me. But I concluded—naturally—

DOOLITTLE: No: that aint the natural way, Colonel: It's only the middle class way. My way was always the undeserving way. But dont say nothing to Eliza. She dont know: I always had a delicacy about telling her.

PICKERING: Quite right. We'll leave it so, if you dont mind.

DOOLITTLE: And youll come to the church, Colonel, and put me through straight?

PICKERING: With pleasure. As far as a bachelor can.

MRS HIGGINS: May I come, Mr Doolittle? I should be very sorry to miss your wedding.

DOOLITTLE: I should indeed be honored by your condescension, maam; and my poor old woman would take it as a tremenjous compliment. She's been very low, thinking of the happy days that are no more.

MRS HIGGINS [*rising*]: I'll order the carriage and get ready. [*The men rise, except Higgins.*] I shant be more than fifteen minutes. [*As she goes to the door Eliza comes in, hatted and buttoning her gloves.*] I'm going to the church to see your father married, Eliza. You had better come in the brougham[4] with me. Colonel Pickering can go on with the bridegroom.

[*Mrs Higgins goes out. Eliza comes to the middle of the room between the centre window and the ottoman. Pickering joins her.*]

DOOLITTLE: Bridegroom! What a word! It makes a man realize his position, somehow. [*He takes up his hat and goes towards the door.*]

PICKERING: Before I go, Eliza, do forgive Higgins and come back to us.

LIZA: I dont think dad would allow me. Would you, dad?

DOOLITTLE [*sad but magnanimous*]: They played you off very cunning, Eliza, them two sportsmen. If it had been only one of them, you could have nailed him. But you see, there was two; and one of them chaperoned the other, as you might say. [*To Pickering.*] It was artful of you, Colonel: but I bear no malice: I should have done the same myself. I been the victim of one woman after another all my life, and I dont grudge you two getting the better of Liza. I shant interfere. It's time for us to go, Colonel. So long, Henry. See you in St George's, Eliza. [*He goes out.*]

PICKERING [*coaxing*]: Do stay with us, Eliza. [*He follows Doolittle.*]

[*Eliza goes out on the balcony to avoid being alone with Higgins. He rises and joins her there. She immediately comes back into the room and makes for the door; but he goes along the balcony quickly and gets his back to the door before she reaches it.*]

HIGGINS: Well, Eliza, youve had a bit of your own back, as you call it. Have you had enough? and are you going to be reasonable? Or do you want any more?

LIZA: You want me back only to pick up your slippers and put up with your tempers and fetch and carry for you.

HIGGINS: I havnt said I wanted you back at all.

LIZA: Oh, indeed. Then what are we talking about?

HIGGINS: About you, not about me. If you come back I shall treat you just as I have always treated you. I cant change my nature; and I dont intend to change my manners. My manners are exactly the same as Colonel Pickering's.

LIZA: Thats not true. He treats a flower girl as if she was a duchess.

HIGGINS: And I treat a duchess as if she was a flower girl.

LIZA: I see. [*She turns away composedly, and sits on the ottoman, facing the window.*] The same to everybody.

HIGGINS: Just so.

LIZA: Like father.

HIGGINS [*grinning, a little taken down*]: Without accepting the comparison at all points, Eliza, it's quite true that your father is not a snob, and that he will be quite at home in any station of life to which his eccentric destiny may call him. [*Seriously.*] The great secret, Eliza, is not having bad manners or good manners or any other particular sort of manners, but having the same manner for all human souls: in short, behaving as if you were in Heaven, where there are no third-class carriages, and one soul is as good as another.

LIZA: Amen. You are a born preacher.

HIGGINS [*irritated*]: The question is not whether I treat you rudely, but whether you ever heard me treat anyone else better.

4. Four-wheeled horse carriage.

LIZA [*with sudden sincerity*]: I dont care how you treat me. I dont mind your swearing at me. I shouldnt mind a black eye: Ive had one before this. But [*standing up and facing him*] I wont be passed over.

HIGGINS: Then get out of my way; for I wont stop for you. You talk about me as if I were a motor bus.

LIZA: So you are a motor bus: all bounce and go, and no consideration for anyone. But I can do without you: dont think I cant.

HIGGINS: I know you can. I told you you could.

LIZA [*wounded, getting away from him to the other side of the ottoman with her face to the hearth*]: I know you did, you brute. You wanted to get rid of me.

HIGGINS: Liar.

LIZA: Thank you. [*She sits down with dignity.*]

HIGGINS: You never asked yourself, I suppose, whether I could do without you.

LIZA [*earnestly*]: Dont you try to get round me. Youll have to do without me.

HIGGINS [*arrogant*]: I can do without anybody. I have my own soul: my own spark of divine fire. But [*with sudden humility*] I shall miss you, Eliza. [*He sits down near her on the ottoman.*] I have learnt something from your idiotic notions: I confess that humbly and gratefully. And I have grown accustomed to your voice and appearance. I like them, rather.

LIZA: Well, you have both of them on your gramophone and in your book of photographs. When you feel lonely without me, you can turn the machine on. It's got no feelings to hurt.

HIGGINS: I cant turn your soul on. Leave me those feelings; and you can take away the voice and the face. They are not you.

LIZA: Oh, you are a devil. You can twist the heart in a girl as easy as some could twist her arms to hurt her. Mrs Pearce warned me. Time and again she has wanted to leave you; and you always got round her at the last minute. And you dont care a bit for her. And you dont care a bit for me.

HIGGINS: I care for life, for humanity; and you are a part of it that has come my way and been built into my house. What more can you or anyone ask?

LIZA: I wont care for anybody that doesnt care for me.

HIGGINS: Commercial principles, Eliza. Like [*reproducing her Covent Garden pronunciation with professional exactness*] s'yollin voylets, isnt it?

LIZA: Dont sneer at me. It's mean to sneer at me.

HIGGINS: I have never sneered in my life. Sneering doesnt become either the human face or the human soul. I am expressing my righteous contempt for Commercialism. I dont and wont trade in affection. You call me a brute because you couldnt buy a claim on me by fetching my slippers and finding my spectacles. You were a fool: I think a woman fetching a man's slippers is a disgusting sight: did I ever fetch your slippers? I think a good deal more of you for throwing them in my face. No use slaving for me and then saying you want to be cared for: who cares for a slave? If you come back, come back for the sake of good fellowship; for youll get nothing else. Youve had a thousand times as much out of me as I have out of you; and if you dare to set up your little dog's tricks of fetching and carrying slippers against my creation of a Duchess Eliza. I'll slam the door in your silly face.

LIZA: What did you do it for if you didnt care for me?

HIGGINS [*heartily*]: Why, because it was my job.

LIZA: You never thought of the trouble it would make for me.

HIGGINS: Would the world ever have been made if its maker had been afraid of making trouble? Making life means making trouble. Theres only one way of escaping trouble; and thats killing things. Cowards, you notice, are always shrieking to have troublesome people killed.

LIZA: I'm no preacher: I dont notice things like that. I notice that you dont notice me.

HIGGINS [*jumping up and walking about intolerantly*]: Eliza: youre an idiot. I waste the treasures of my Miltonic mind by spreading them before you. Once for all, understand that I go my way and do my work without caring twopence what happens to either of us. I am not intimidated, like your father and your stepmother. So you can come back or go to the devil: which you please.

LIZA: What am I to come back for?

HIGGINS [*bouncing up on his knees on the ottoman and leaning over it to her*]: For the fun of it. Thats why I took you on.

LIZA [*with averted face*]: And you may throw me out tomorrow if I dont do everything you want me to?

HIGGINS: Yes; and you may walk out tomorrow if I dont do everything you want me to.

LIZA: And live with my stepmother?

HIGGINS: Yes, or sell flowers.

LIZA: Oh! If I only could go back to my flower basket! I should be independent of both you and father and all the world! Why did you take my independence from me? Why did I give it up? I'm a slave now, for all my fine clothes.

HIGGINS: Not a bit. I'll adopt you as my daughter and settle money on you if you like. Or would you rather marry Pickering?

LIZA [*looking fiercely round at him*]: I wouldnt marry you if you asked me; and youre nearer my age than what he is.

HIGGINS [*gently*]: Than he is: not "than what he is."

LIZA [*losing her temper and rising*]: I'll talk as I like. Youre not my teacher now.

HIGGINS [*reflectively*]: I dont suppose Pickering would, though. He's as confirmed an old bachelor as I am.

LIZA: Thats not what I want; and dont you think it. Ive always had chaps enough wanting me that way. Freddy Hill writes to me twice and three times a day, sheets and sheets.

HIGGINS [*disagreeably surprised*]: Damn his impudence! [*He recoils and finds himself sitting on his heels.*]

LIZA: He has a right to if he likes, poor lad. And he does love me.

HIGGINS [*getting off the ottoman*]: You have no right to encourage him.

LIZA: Every girl has a right to be loved.

HIGGINS: What! By fools like that?

LIZA: Freddy's not a fool. And if he's weak and poor and wants me, may be he'd make me happier than my betters that bully me and dont want me.

HIGGINS: Can he make anything of you? Thats the point.

LIZA: Perhaps I could make something of him. But I never thought of us making anything of one another; and you never think of anything else. I only want to be natural.

HIGGINS: In short, you want me to be as infatuated about you as Freddy? Is that it?

LIZA: No I dont. Thats not the sort of feeling I want from you. And dont you be too sure of yourself or of me. I could have been a bad girl if I'd liked. Ive seen

more of some things than you, for all your learning. Girls like me can drag gentlemen down to make love to them easy enough. And they wish each other dead the
next minute.

HIGGINS: Of course they do. Then what in thunder are we quarrelling about?

LIZA [*much troubled*]: I want a little kindness. I know I'm a common ignorant girl, and
you a book-learned gentleman; but I'm not dirt under your feet. What I done [*correct-
ing herself*] what I did was not for the dresses and the taxis: I did it because we were
pleasant together and I come—came—to care for you; not to want you to make love
to me, and not forgetting the difference between us, but more friendly like.

HIGGINS: Well, of course. Thats just how I feel. And how Pickering feels. Eliza:
youre a fool.

LIZA: Thats not a proper answer to give me [*she sinks on the chair at the writing-table
in tears*].

HIGGINS: It's all youll get until you stop being a common idiot. If youre going to be
a lady, youll have to give up feeling neglected if the men you know dont spend
half their time snivelling over you and the other half giving you black eyes. If you
cant stand the coldness of my sort of life, and the strain of it, go back to the gutter.
Work til youre more a brute than a human being: and then cuddle and squabble
and drink til you fall asleep. Oh, it's a fine life, the life of the gutter. It's real: it's
warm: it's violent: you can feel it through the thickest skin: you can taste it and
smell it without any training or any work. Not like Science and Literature and
Classical Music and Philosophy and Art. You find me cold, unfeeling, selfish, dont
you? Very well: be off with you to the sort of people you like. Marry some sentimental hog or other with lots of money, and a thick pair of lips to kiss you with
and a thick pair of boots to kick you with. If you cant appreciate what youve got,
youd better get what you can appreciate.

LIZA [*desperate*]: Oh, you are a cruel tyrant. I cant talk to you: you turn everything
against me: I'm always in the wrong. But you know very well all the time that
youre nothing but a bully. You know I cant go back to the gutter, as you call it,
and that I have no real friends in the world but you and the Colonel. You know
well I couldnt bear to live with a low common man after you two; and it's wicked
and cruel of you to insult me by pretending I could. You think I must go back to
Wimpole Street because I have nowhere else to go but father's. But dont you be
too sure that you have me under your feet to be trampled on and talked down. I'll
marry Freddy, I will, as soon as I'm able to support him.

HIGGINS [*thunderstruck*]: Freddy!!! that young fool! That poor devil who couldnt
get a job as an errand boy even if he had the guts to try for it! Woman: do you not
understand that I have made you a consort for a king?

LIZA: Freddy loves me: that makes him king enough for me. I dont want him to
work: he wasnt brought up to it as I was. I'll go and be a teacher.

HIGGINS: Whatll you teach, in heaven's name?

LIZA: What you taught me. I'll teach phonetics.

HIGGINS: Ha! Ha! ha!

LIZA: I'll offer myself as an assistant to that hairyfaced Hungarian.

HIGGINS [*rising in a fury*]: What! That impostor! That humbug! That toadying
ignoramus! Teach him my methods! my discoveries! You take one step in his
direction and I'll wring your neck. [*He lays hands on her.*] Do you hear?

LIZA [*defiantly non-resistant*]: Wring away. What do I care? I knew youd strike me
some day. [*He lets her go, stamping with rage at having forgotten himself, and recoils so*

hastily that he stumbles back into his seat on the ottoman.] Aha! Now I know how to deal with you. What a fool I was not to think of it before! You cant take away the knowledge you gave me. You said I had a finer ear than you. And I can be civil and kind to people, which is more than you can. Aha! [*Purposely dropping her aitches to annoy him.*] Thats done you, Enry Iggins, it az. Now I dont care that [*snapping her fingers*] for your bullying and your big talk. I'll advertize it in the papers that your duchess is only a flower girl that you taught, and that she'll teach anybody to be a duchess just the same in six months for a thousand guineas. Oh, when I think of myself crawling under your feet and being trampled on and called names, when all the time I had only to lift up my finger to be as good as you, I could just kick myself.

HIGGINS [*wondering at her*]: You damned impudent slut, you! But it's better than snivelling; better than fetching slippers and finding spectacles, isnt it? [*Rising.*] By George, Eliza, I said I'd make a woman of you; and I have. I like you like this.

LIZA: Yes: you can turn round and make up to me now that I'm not afraid of you, and can do without you.

HIGGINS: Of course I do, you little fool. Five minutes ago you were like a millstone round my neck. Now youre a tower of strength: a consort battleship. You and I and Pickering will be three old bachelors instead of only two men and a silly girl.

[*Mrs Higgins returns, dressed for the wedding. Eliza instantly becomes cool and elegant.*]

MRS HIGGINS: The carriage is waiting, Eliza. Are you ready?

LIZA: Quite. Is the Professor coming?

MRS HIGGINS: Certainly not. He cant behave himself in church. He makes remarks out loud all the time on the clergyman's pronunciation.

LIZA: Then I shall not see you again, Professor. Goodbye. [*She goes to the door.*]

MRS HIGGINS [*coming to Higgins*]: Goodbye, dear.

HIGGINS: Goodbye, mother. [*He is about to kiss her, when he recollects something.*] Oh, by the way, Eliza, order a ham and a Stilton cheese, will you? And buy me a pair of reindeer gloves, number eights, and a tie to match that new suit of mine. You can choose the color. [*His cheerful, careless, vigorous voice shews that he is incorrigible.*]

LIZA [*disdainfully*]: Number eights are too small for you if you want them lined with lamb's wool. You have three new ties that you have forgotten in the drawer of your washstand. Colonel Pickering prefers double Gloucester to Stilton; and you dont notice the difference. I telephoned Mrs Pearce this morning not to forget the ham. What you are to do without me I cannot imagine. [*She sweeps out.*]

MRS HIGGINS: I'm afraid youve spoilt that girl, Henry. I should be uneasy about you and her if she were less fond of Colonel Pickering.

HIGGINS: Pickering! Nonsense: she's going to marry Freddy. Ha ha! Freddy! Freddy!! Ha ha ha ha ha!!!!! [*He roars with laughter as the play ends.*]

Sequel

The rest of the story need not be shewn in action, and indeed, would hardly need telling if our imaginations were not so enfeebled by their lazy dependence on the ready-mades and reach-me-downs of the ragshop in which Romance keeps its stock of "happy endings" to misfit all stories. Now, the history of Eliza Doolittle, though called a romance because the transfiguration it records seems exceedingly improbable, is common enough. Such transfigurations have been achieved by hundreds of resolutely ambitious young women since Nell Gwynne[1] set them the example by playing queens and fascinating kings in the theatre in which she began by selling oranges. Nevertheless, people in all directions have assumed, for no other reason than that she became the heroine of a romance, that she must have married the hero of it. This is unbearable, not only because her little drama, if acted on such a thoughtless assumption, must be spoiled, but because the true sequel is patent to anyone with a sense of human nature in general, and of feminine instinct in particular.

Eliza, in telling Higgins she would not marry him if he asked, was not coquetting: she was announcing a well-considered decision. When a bachelor interests, and dominates, and teaches, and becomes important to a spinster, as Higgins with Eliza, she always, if she has character enough to be capable of it, considers very seriously indeed whether she will play for becoming that bachelor's wife, especially if he is so little interested in marriage that a determined and devoted woman might capture him if she set herself resolutely to do it. Her decision will depend a good deal on whether she is really free to choose; and that, again, will depend on her age and income. If she is at the end of her youth, and has no security for her livelihood, she will marry him because she must marry anybody who will provide for her. But at Eliza's age a good-looking girl does not feel that pressure: she feels free to pick and choose. She is therefore guided by her instinct in the matter. Eliza's instinct tells her not to marry Higgins. It does not tell her to give him up. It is not in the slightest doubt as to his remaining one of the strongest personal interests in her life. It would be very sorely strained if there was another woman likely to supplant her with him. But as she feels sure of him on that last point, she has no doubt at all as to her course, and would not have any, even if the difference of twenty years in age, which seems so great to youth, did not exist between them.

As our own instincts are not appealed to by her conclusion, let us see whether we cannot discover some reason in it. When Higgins excused his indifference to young women on the ground that they had an irresistible rival in his mother, he gave the clue to his inveterate old-bachelordom. The case is uncommon only to the extent that remarkable mothers are uncommon. If an imaginative boy has a sufficiently rich mother who has intelligence, personal grace, dignity of character without harshness, and a cultivated sense of the best art of her time to enable her to make her house beautiful, she sets a standard for him against which very few women can struggle, besides effecting for him a disengagement of his affections, his sense of beauty, and his idealism from his specifically sexual impulses. This makes him a standing puzzle to the huge number of uncultivated people who have been brought up in tasteless homes by commonplace or disagreeable parents, and to whom, consequently, literature, painting, sculpture, music, and affectionate personal relations come as modes of sex if they come at all. The word passion means nothing else to them; and that Higgins could have a passion for phonetics and idealize his mother instead of Eliza, would seem to them absurd and unnatural. Nevertheless, when we look round and see that hardly anyone is too ugly or disagreeable to find a wife or a husband if he or she wants one, whilst many old maids and bachelors are above the average in quality and culture, we

---

1. Nell Gwynne (1650–1687), London theatre vendor, actor, and later mistress of Charles II.

cannot help suspecting that the disentanglement of sex from the associations with which it is commonly confused, a disentanglement which persons of genius achieve by sheer intellectual analysis, is sometimes produced or aided by parental fascination.

Now, though Eliza was incapable of thus explaining to herself Higgins's formidable powers of resistance to the charm that prostrated Freddy at the first glance, she was instinctively aware that she could never obtain a complete grip of him, or come between him and his mother (the first necessity of the married woman). To put it shortly, she knew that for some mysterious reason he had not the makings of a married man in him, according to her conception of a husband as one to whom she would be his nearest and fondest and warmest interest. Even had there been no mother-rival, she would still have refused to accept an interest in herself that was secondary to philosophic interests. Had Mrs Higgins died, there would still have been Milton and the Universal Alphabet. Landor's remark that to those who have the greatest power of loving, love is a secondary affair, would not have recommended Landor to Eliza. Put that along with her resentment of Higgins's domineering superiority, and her mistrust of his coaxing cleverness in getting round her and evading her wrath when he had gone too far with his impetuous bullying, and you will see that Eliza's instinct had good grounds for warning her not to marry her Pygmalion.

And now, whom did Eliza marry? For if Higgins was a predestinate old bachelor, she was most certainly not a predestinate old maid. Well, that can be told very shortly to those who have not guessed it from the indications she has herself given them.

Almost immediately after Eliza is stung into proclaiming her considered determination not to marry Higgins, she mentions the fact that young Mr Frederick Eynsford Hill is pouring out his love for her daily through the post. Now Freddy is young, practically twenty years younger than Higgins: he is a gentleman (or, as Eliza would qualify him, a toff[2]), and speaks like one. He is nicely dressed, is treated by the Colonel as an equal, loves her unaffectedly, and is not her master, nor ever likely to dominate her in spite of his advantage of social standing. Eliza has no use for the foolish romantic tradition that all women love to be mastered, if not actually bullied and beaten. "When you go to women" says Nietzsche[3] "take your whip with you." Sensible despots have never confined that precaution to women: they have taken their whips with them when they have dealt with men, and been slavishly idealized by the men over whom they have flourished the whip much more than by women. No doubt there are slavish women as well as slavish men; and women, like men, admire those that are stronger than themselves. But to admire a strong person and to live under that strong person's thumb are two different things. The weak may not be admired and hero-worshipped; but they are by no means disliked or shunned; and they never seem to have the least difficulty in marrying people who are too good for them. They may fail in emergencies: but life is not one long emergency: it is mostly a string of situations for which no exceptional strength is needed, and with which even rather weak people can cope if they have a stronger partner to help them out. Accordingly, it is a truth everywhere in evi-

2. Fashionable gentleman.
3. Friedrich Nietzsche (1844–1900), German philosopher whose rejection of traditional Judeo-Christian ethics and belief in the natural moral superiority of certain individuals fascinated Shaw, finding its most direct expression in his play Man and Superman (1903).

dence that strong people, masculine or feminine, not only do not marry stronger people, but do not shew any preference for them in selecting their friends. When a lion meets another with a louder roar "the first lion thinks the last a bore." The man or woman who feels strong enough for two, seeks for every other quality in a partner than strength.

The converse is also true. Weak people want to marry strong people who do not frighten them too much: and this often leads them to make the mistake we describe metaphorically as "biting off more than they can chew." They want too much for too little; and when the bargain is unreasonable beyond all bearing, the union becomes impossible: it ends in the weaker party being either discarded or borne as a cross, which is worse. People who are not only weak, but silly or obtuse as well, are often in these difficulties.

This being the state of human affairs, what is Eliza fairly sure to do when she is placed between Freddy and Higgins? Will she look forward to a lifetime of fetching Higgins's slippers or to a lifetime of Freddy fetching hers? There can be no doubt about the answer. Unless Freddy is biologically repulsive to her, and Higgins biologically attractive to a degree that overwhelms all her other instincts, she will, if she marries either of them, marry Freddy.

And that is just what Eliza did.

Complications ensued; but they were economic, not romantic. Freddy had no money and no occupation. His mother's jointure,[4] a last relic of the opulence of Largelady Park, had enabled her to struggle along in Earlscourt with an air of gentility, but not to procure any serious secondary education for her children, much less give the boy a profession. A clerkship at thirty shillings a week was beneath Freddy's dignity, and extremely distasteful to him besides. His prospects consisted of a hope that if he kept up appearances somebody would do something for him. The something appeared vaguely to his imagination as a private secretaryship or a sinecure of some sort. To his mother it perhaps appeared as a marriage to some lady of means who could not resist her boy's niceness. Fancy her feelings when he married a flower girl who had become disclassed under extraordinary circumstances which were now notorious!

It is true that Eliza's situation did not seem wholly ineligible. Her father, though formerly a dustman, and now fantastically disclassed, had become extremely popular in the smartest society by a social talent which triumphed over every prejudice and every disadvantage. Rejected by the middle class, which he loathed, he had shot up at once into the highest circles by his wit, his dustmanship (which he carried like a banner), and his Nietzschean transcendence of good and evil. At intimate ducal dinners he sat on the righthand of the Duchess; and in country houses he smoked in the pantry and was made much of by the butler when he was not feeding in the dining room and being consulted by cabinet ministers. But he found it almost as hard to do all this on four thousand a year as Mrs Eynsford Hill to live in Earlscourt on an income so pitiably smaller that I have not the heart to disclose its exact figure. He absolutely refused to add the last straw to his burden by contributing to Eliza's support.

Thus Freddy and Eliza, now Mr and Mrs Eynsford Hill, would have spent a penniless honeymoon but for a wedding present of £500 from the Colonel to Eliza. It

---

4. Estate settled upon a widow by her late husband.

lasted a long time because Freddy did not know how to spend money, never having had any to spend, and Eliza, socially trained by a pair of old bachelors, wore her clothes as long as they held together and looked pretty, without the least regard to their being many months out of fashion. Still, £500 will not last two young people for ever; and they both knew, and Eliza felt as well, that they must shift themselves in the end. She could quarter herself on Wimpole Street because it had come to be her home; but she was quite aware that she ought not to quarter Freddy there, and that it would not be good for his character if she did.

Not that the Wimpole Street bachelors objected. When she consulted them, Higgins declined to be bothered about her housing problem when that solution was so simple. Eliza's desire to have Freddy in the house with her seemed of no more importance than if she had wanted an extra piece of bedroom furniture. Pleas as to Freddy's character, and the moral obligation on him to earn his own living, were lost on Higgins. He denied that Freddy had any character, and declared that if he tried to do any useful work some competent person would have the trouble of undoing it: a procedure involving a net loss to the community, and great unhappiness to Freddy himself, who was obviously intended by Nature for such light work as amusing Eliza, which, Higgins declared, was a much more useful and honorable occupation than working in the city. When Eliza referred again to her project of teaching phonetics, Higgins abated not a jot of his violent opposition to it. He said she was not within ten years of being qualified to meddle with his pet subject: and as it was evident that the Colonel agreed with him, she felt she could not go against them in this grave matter, and that she had no right, without Higgins's consent, to exploit the knowledge he had given her: for his knowledge seemed to her as much his private property as his watch: Eliza was no communist. Besides, she was superstitiously devoted to them both, more entirely and frankly after her marriage than before it.

It was the Colonel who finally solved the problem, which had cost him much perplexed cogitation. He one day asked Eliza, rather shyly, whether she had quite given up her notion of keeping a flower shop. She replied that she had thought of it, but had put it out of her head, because the Colonel had said, that day at Mrs Higgins's, that it would never do. The Colonel confessed that when he said that, he had not quite recovered from the dazzling impression of the day before. They broke the matter to Higgins that evening. The sole comment vouchsafed by him very nearly led to a serious quarrel with Eliza. It was to the effect that she would have in Freddy an ideal errand boy.

Freddy himself was next sounded on the subject. He said he had been thinking of a shop himself; though it had presented itself to his pennilessness as a small place in which Eliza should sell tobacco at one counter whilst he sold newspapers at the opposite one. But he agreed that it would be extraordinarily jolly to go early every morning with Eliza to Covent Garden and buy flowers on the scene of their first meeting: a sentiment which earned him many kisses from his wife. He added that he had always been afraid to propose anything of the sort, because Clara would make an awful row about a step that must damage her matrimonial chances, and his mother could not be expected to like it after clinging for so many years to that step of the social ladder on which retail trade is impossible.

This difficulty was removed by an event highly unexpected by Freddy's mother. Clara, in the course of her incursions into those artistic circles which were the highest within her reach, discovered that her conversational qualifications were expected to include a grounding in the novels of Mr H. G. Wells.[5] She borrowed them in various directions so energetically that she swallowed them all within two months. The result was a conversion of a kind quite common today. A modern Acts of the Apostles would fill fifty whole Bibles if anyone were capable of writing it.

Poor Clara, who appeared to Higgins and his mother as a disagreeable and ridiculous person, and to her own mother as in some inexplicable way a social failure, had never seen herself in either light; for, though to some extent ridiculed and mimicked in West Kensington like everybody else there, she was accepted as a rational and normal—or shall we say inevitable?—sort of human being. At worst they called her The Pusher; but to them no more than to herself had it ever occurred that she was pushing the air, and pushing it in a wrong direction. Still, she was not happy. She was growing desperate. Her one asset, the fact that her mother was what the Epsom greengrocer called a carriage lady, had no exchange value, apparently. It had prevented her from getting educated, because the only education she could have afforded was education with the Earlscourt greengrocer's daughter. It had led her to seek the society of her mother's class; and that class simply would not have her, because she was much poorer than the greengrocer, and, far from being able to afford a maid, could not afford even a house-maid, and had to scrape along at home with an illiberally treated general servant. Under such circumstances nothing could give her an air of being a genuine product of Largelady Park. And yet its tradition made her regard a marriage with anyone within her reach as an unbearable humiliation. Commercial people and professional people in a small way were odious to her. She ran after painters and novelists; but she did not charm them; and her bold attempts to pick up and practise artistic and literary talk irritated them. She was, in short, an utter failure, an ignorant, incompetent, pretentious, unwelcome, penniless, useless little snob; and though she did not admit these disqualifications (for nobody ever faces unpleasant truths of this kind until the possibility of a way out dawns on them) she felt their effects too keenly to be satisfied with her position.

Clara had a startling eyeopener when, on being suddenly wakened to enthusiasm by a girl of her own age who dazzled her and produced in her a gushing desire to take her for a model, and gain her friendship, she discovered that this exquisite apparition had graduated from the gutter in a few months time. It shook her so violently, that when Mr H. G. Wells lifted her on the point of his puissant pen, and placed her at the angle of view from which the life she was leading and the society to which she clung appeared in its true relation to real human needs and worthy social structure, he effected a conversion and a conviction of sin comparable to the most sensational feats of General Booth[6] or Gypsy Smith.[7] Clara's snobbery went bang. Life suddenly began to move with her. Without knowing how or why, she began to make friends and enemies. Some of the acquaintances to whom she had been a tedious or indifferent or ridiculous affliction, dropped her: others became cordial. To her amazement she found that some "quite nice" people were saturated with Wells, and that this accessibility to ideas was the secret of their niceness. People she had thought deeply religious and had tried to conciliate on that tack with disastrous results, suddenly took an interest in her, and

5. H(erbert) G(eorge) Wells (1866–1946), English novelist and writer of science fiction, who shared Shaw's zeal for social reform, while their passion meant they were often at odds.

6. ("General") William Booth (1829–1912), English religious reformer and founder of the Salvation Army.
7. Rodney ("Gypsy") Smith (1860–1947), popular British preacher and evangelist.

revealed a hostility to conventional religion which she had never conceived possible except among the most desperate characters. They made her read Galsworthy; and Galsworthy exposed the vanity of Largelady Park and finished her. It exasperated her to think that the dungeon in which she had languished for so many unhappy years had been unlocked all the time, and that the impulses she had so carefully struggled with and stifled for the sake of keeping well with society, were precisely those by which alone she could have come into any sort of sincere human contact. In the radiance of these discoveries, and the tumult of their reaction, she made a fool of herself as freely and conspicuously as when she so rashly adopted Eliza's expletive in Mrs Higgins's drawing room; for the new-born Wellsian had to find her bearings almost as ridiculously as a baby; but nobody hates a baby for its ineptitudes, or thinks the worse of it for trying to eat the matches; and Clara lost no friends by her follies. They laughed at her to her face this time; and she had to defend herself and fight it out as best she could.

When Freddy paid a visit to Earlscourt (which he never did when he could possibly help it) to make the desolating announcement that he and his Eliza were thinking of blackening the Largelady scutcheon by opening a shop, he found the little household already convulsed by a prior announcement from Clara that she also was going to work in an old furniture shop in Dover Street, which had been started by a fellow Wellsian. This appointment Clara owed, after all, to her old social accomplishment of Push. She had made up her mind that, cost what it might, she would see Mr Wells in the flesh; and she had achieved her end at a garden party. She had better luck than so rash an enterprise deserved, Mr Wells came up to her expectations. Age had not withered him, nor could custom stale his infinite variety in half an hour. His pleasant neatness and compactness, his small hands and feet, his teeming ready brain, his unaffected accessibility, and a certain fine apprehensiveness which stamped him as susceptible from his topmost hair to his tipmost toe, proved irresistible. Clara talked of nothing else for weeks and weeks afterwards. And as she happened to talk to the lady of the furniture shop, and that lady also desired above all things to know Mr Wells and sell pretty things to him, she offered Clara a job on the chance of achieving that end through her.

And so it came about that Eliza's luck held, and the expected opposition to the flower shop melted away. The shop is in the arcade of a railway station not very far from the Victoria and Albert Museum; and if you live in that neighborhood you may go there any day and buy a buttonhole from Eliza.

Now here is a last opportunity for romance. Would you not like to be assured that the shop was an immense success, thanks to Eliza's charms and her early business experience in Covent Garden? Alas! the truth is the truth: the shop did not pay for a long time, simply because Eliza and her Freddy did not know how to keep it. True, Eliza had not to begin at the very beginning: she knew the names and prices of the cheaper flowers; and her elation was unbounded when she found that Freddy, like all youths educated at cheap, pretentious, and thoroughly inefficient schools, knew a little Latin. It was very little, but enough to make him appear to her a Porson or Bentley,[8] and to put him at his ease with botanical nomenclature. Unfortunately he knew nothing else; and Eliza, though she could count money up to eighteen shillings or so, and had acquired a certain familiarity with the language

---

8. Richard Porson (1759–1808), English classical scholar; Richard Bentley (1662–1742), English classical scholar satirized by Jonathan Swift in *The Battle of the Books*.

of Milton from her struggles to qualify herself for winning Higgins's bet, could not write out a bill without utterly disgracing the establishment. Freddy's power of stating in Latin that Balbus built a wall[9] and that Gaul was divided into three parts did not carry with it the slightest knowledge of accounts or business: Colonel Pickering had to explain to him what a cheque book and a bank account meant. And the pair were by no means easily teachable. Freddy backed up Eliza in her obstinate refusal to believe that they could save money by engaging a bookkeeper with some knowledge of the business. How, they argued, could you possibly save money by going to extra expense when you already could not make both ends meet? But the Colonel, after making the ends meet over and over again, at last gently insisted; and Eliza, humbled to the dust by having to beg from him so often, and stung by the uproarious derision of Higgins, to whom the notion of Freddy succeeding at anything was a joke that never palled, grasped the fact that business, like phonetics, has to be learned.

On the piteous spectacle of the pair spending their evenings in shorthand schools and polytechnic classes, learning book-keeping and typewriting with incipient junior clerks, male and female, from the elementary schools, let me not dwell. There were even classes at the London School of Economics, and a humble personal appeal to the director of that institution to recommend a course bearing on the flower business. He, being a humorist, explained to them the method of the celebrated Dickensian essay on Chinese Metaphysics by the gentleman who read an article on China and an article on Metaphysics and combined the information. He suggested that they should combine the London School with Kew Gardens. Eliza, to whom the procedure of the Dickensian gentleman seemed perfectly correct (as in fact it was) and not in the least funny (which was only her ignorance), took the advice with entire gravity. But the effort that cost her the deepest humiliation was a request to Higgins, whose pet artistic fancy, next to Milton's verse, was calligraphy, and who himself wrote a most beautiful Italian hand, that he would teach her to write. He declared that she was congenitally incapable of forming a single letter worthy of the least of Milton's words; but she persisted; and again he suddenly threw himself into the task of teaching her with a combination of stormy intensity, concentrated patience, and occasional bursts of interesting disquisition on the beauty and nobility, the august mission and destiny, of human handwriting. Eliza ended by acquiring an extremely uncommercial script which was a positive extension of her personal beauty, and spending three times as much on stationery as anyone else because certain qualities and shapes of paper became indispensable to her. She could not even address an envelope in the usual way because it made the margins all wrong.

Their commercial schooldays were a period of disgrace and despair for the young couple. They seemed to be learning nothing about flower shops. At last they gave it up as hopeless, and shook the dust of the shorthand schools, and the polytechnics, and the London School of Economics from their feet for ever. Besides, the business was in some mysterious way beginning to take care of itself. They had somehow forgotten their objections to employing other people. They came to the conclusion that their own way was the best, and that they had really a remarkable talent for business. The Colonel, who had been compelled for some years to keep a sufficient sum on current account at

---

9. From Cicero's *Letters to Atticus* 12.2; a common schoolboy's Latin translation exercise.

his bankers to make up their deficits, found that the provision was unnecessary: the young people were prospering. It is true that there was not quite fair play between them and their competitors in trade. Their week-ends in the country cost them nothing, and saved them the price of their Sunday dinners; for the motor car was the Colonel's; and he and Higgins paid the hotel bills. Mr F. Hill, florist and greengrocer (they soon discovered that there was money in asparagus; and asparagus led to other vegetables), had an air which stamped the business as classy; and in private life he was still Frederick Eynsford Hill, Esquire. Not that there was any swank about him; nobody but Eliza knew that he had been christened Frederick Challoner. Eliza herself swanked like anything.

That is all. That is how it has turned out. It is astonishing how much Eliza still manages to meddle in the housekeeping at Wimpole Street in spite of the shop and her own family. And it is notable that though she never nags her husband, and frankly loves the Colonel as if she were his favorite daughter, she has never got out of the habit of nagging Higgins that was established on the fatal night when she won his bet for him. She snaps his head off on the faintest provocation, or on none. He no longer dares to tease her by assuming an abysmal inferiority of Freddy's mind to his own. He storms and bullies and derides; but she stands up to him so ruthlessly that the Colonel has to ask her from time to time to be kinder to Higgins; and it is the only request of his that brings a mulish expression into her face. Nothing but some emergency or calamity great enough to break down all likes and dislikes, and throw them both back on their common humanity—and may they be spared any such trial!—will ever alter this. She knows that Higgins does not need her, just as her father did not need her. The very scrupulousness with which he told her that day that he had become used to having her there, and dependent on her for all sorts of little services, and that he should miss her if she went away (it would never have occurred to Freddy or the Colonel to say anything of the sort) deepens her inner certainty that she is "no more to him than them slippers"; yet she has a sense, too, that his indifference is deeper than the infatuation of commoner souls. She is immensely interested in him. She has even secret mischievous moments in which she wishes she could get him alone, on a desert island, away from all ties and with nobody else in the world to consider, and just drag him off his pedestal and see him making love like any common man. We all have private imaginations of that sort. But when it comes to business, to the life that she really leads as distinguished from the life of dreams and fancies, she likes Freddy and she likes the Colonel; and she does not like Higgins and Mr Doolittle. Galatea never does quite like Pygmalion; his relation to her is too godlike to be altogether agreeable.

Thomas Hardy
1840–1928

On the Departure Platform

We kissed at the barrier; and passing through
She left me, and moment by moment got
Smaller and smaller, until to my view
    She was but a spot;

5   A wee white spot of muslin fluff
That down the diminishing platform bore
Through hustling crowds of gentle and rough
    To the carriage door.

Under the lamplight's fitful glowers,
10   Behind dark groups from far and near,
Whose interests were apart from ours,
    She would disappear,

Then show again, till I ceased to see
That flexible form, that nebulous white;
15   And she who was more than my life to me
    Had vanished quite. . . .

We have penned new plans since that fair fond day,
And in season she will appear again—
Perhaps in the same soft white array—
20   But never as then!

—"And why, young man, must eternally fly
A joy you'll repeat, if you love her well?"
—O friend, nought happens twice thus; why,
    I cannot tell!

1909

The Convergence of the Twain
(Lines on the loss of the "Titanic")[1]

1
In a solitude of the sea
Deep from human vanity,
And the Pride of Life that planned her, stilly couches she.
2
Steel chambers, late the pyres
5   Of her salamandrine° fires,   *white-hot*
Cold currents thrid°, and turn to rhythmic tidal lyres.   *thread*

---

1. The largest ocean-liner of its day, the supposedly unsinkable *Titanic* sank on 15 April 1912 on its maiden voyage after colliding with an iceberg; two thirds of its 2,200 passengers died.

3
Over the mirrors meant
To glass the opulent
The sea-worm crawls—grotesque, slimed, dumb, indifferent.

4
10   Jewels in joy designed
To ravish the sensuous mind
Lie lightless, all their sparkles bleared and black and blind.

5
Dim moon-eyed fishes near
Gaze at the gilded gear
15   And query: "What does this vaingloriousness down here?" . . .

6
Well: while was fashioning
This creature of cleaving wing,
The Immanent Will that stirs and urges everything

7
Prepared a sinister mate
20   For her—so gaily great—
A Shape of Ice, for the time far and dissociate.[2]

8
And as the smart ship grew
In stature, grace, and hue,
In shadowy silent distance grew the Iceberg too.

9
25   Alien they seemed to be:
No mortal eye could see
The intimate welding of their later history,

10
Or sign that they were bent
By paths coincident
30   On being anon twin halves of one august event,

11
Till the Spinner of the Years
Said "Now!" And each one hears,
And consummation comes, and jars two hemispheres.

1912   1912

---

2. According to Hardy, the Immanent Will is that which secretly guides events.

William Butler Yeats
1865–1939

The Lake Isle of Innisfree[1]

I will arise and go now, and go to Innisfree,
And a small cabin build there, of clay and wattles° made: *woven twigs*
Nine bean-rows will I have there, a hive for the honey-bee,
And live alone in the bee-loud glade.

5   And I shall have some peace there, for peace comes dropping slow,
Dropping from the veils of the morning to where the cricket sings;
There midnight's all a glimmer, and noon a purple glow,
And evening full of the linnet's° wings.   *song bird*

I will arise and go now, for always night and day
10   I hear lake water lapping with low sounds by the shore;
While I stand on the roadway, or on the pavements grey,
I hear it in the deep heart's core.

1890   1890

The Wild Swans at Coole[1]

The trees are in their autumn beauty,
The woodland paths are dry,
Under the October twilight the water
Mirrors a still sky;
5   Upon the brimming water among the stones
Are nine-and-fifty swans.

The nineteenth autumn has come upon me
Since I first made my count;
I saw, before I had well finished,
10   All suddenly mount
And scatter wheeling in great broken rings
Upon their clamorous wings.

I have looked upon those brilliant creatures,
And now my heart is sore.
15   All's changed since I, hearing at twilight,
The first time on this shore,
The bell-beat of their wings above my head,
Trod with a lighter tread.

Unwearied still, lover by lover,
20   They paddle in the cold
Companionable streams or climb the air;
Their hearts have not grown old;

---

1. A small island in Lough Gill outside the town of Sligo, near the border with Northern Ireland.

1. Coole Park was the name of the estate of Yeats's patron Lady Gregory in Galway.

Passion or conquest, wander where they will,
Attend upon them still.

25   But now they drift on the still water,
Mysterious, beautiful;
Among what rushes will they build,
By what lake's edge or pool
Delight men's eyes when I awake some day
30   To find they have flown away?

1916   1917

Sailing to Byzantium[1]

1

That is no country for old men. The young
In one another's arms, birds in the trees,
—Those dying generations—at their song,
The salmon-falls, the mackerel-crowded seas,
5   Fish, flesh, or fowl, commend all summer long
Whatever is begotten, born, and dies.
Caught in that sensual music all neglect
Monuments of unageing intellect.

2

An aged man is but a paltry thing,
10   A tattered coat upon a stick, unless
Soul clap its hands and sing, and louder sing
For every tatter in its mortal dress,
Nor is there singing school but studying
Monuments of its own magnificence;
15   And therefore I have sailed the seas and come
To the holy city of Byzantium.

3

O sages standing in God's holy fire
As in the gold mosaic of a wall,
Come from the holy fire, perne° in a gyre,   *spin*
20   And be the singing-masters of my soul.
Consume my heart away; sick with desire
And fastened to a dying animal
It knows not what it is; and gather me
Into the artifice of eternity.

4

25   Once out of nature I shall never take
My bodily form from any natural thing,
But such a form as Grecian goldsmiths make
Of hammered gold and gold enamelling
To keep a drowsy Emperor awake;—
30   Or set upon a golden bough to sing
To lords and ladies of Byzantium
Of what is past, or passing, or to come.

1926   1927

1. Constantinople, now called Istanbul, capital of the Byzantine Empire and the holy city of Eastern Christianity.

James Joyce
1882–1941

The Dead

Lily, the caretaker's daughter, was literally run off her feet. Hardly had she brought one gentleman into the little pantry behind the office on the ground floor and helped him off with his overcoat than the wheezy hall-door bell clanged again and she had to scamper along the bare hallway to let in another guest. It was well for her she had not to attend to the ladies also. But Miss Kate and Miss Julia had thought of that and had converted the bathroom upstairs into a ladies' dressing-room. Miss Kate and Miss Julia were there, gossiping and laughing and fussing, walking after each other to the head of the stairs, peering down over the banisters and calling down to Lily to ask her who had come.

It was always a great affair, the Misses Morkan's annual dance. Everybody who knew them came to it, members of the family, old friends of the family, the members of Julia's choir, any of Kate's pupils that were grown up enough and even some of Mary Jane's pupils too. Never once had it fallen flat. For years and years it had gone off in splendid style as long as anyone could remember; ever since Kate and Julia, after the death of their brother Pat, had left the house in Stoney Batter[1] and taken Mary Jane, their only niece, to live with them in the dark gaunt house on Usher's Island,[2] the upper part of which they had rented from Mr Fulham, the cornfactor on the ground floor. That was a good thirty years ago if it was a day. Mary Jane, who was then a little girl in short clothes, was now the main prop of the household for she had the organ in Haddington Road.[3] She had been through the Academy[4] and gave a pupils' concert every year in the upper room of the Antient Concert Rooms. Many of her pupils belonged to better-class families on the Kingstown and Dalkey line.[5] Old as they were, her aunts also did their share. Julia, though she was quite grey, was still the leading soprano in Adam and Eve's,[6] and Kate, being too feeble to go about much, gave music lessons to beginners on the old square piano in the back room. Lily, the caretaker's daughter, did housemaid's work for them. Though their life was modest they believed in eating well; the best of everything: diamond-bone sirloins, three-shilling tea and the best bottled stout.[7] But Lily seldom made a mistake in the orders so that she got on well with her three mistresses. They were fussy, that was all. But the only thing they would not stand was back answers.

Of course they had good reason to be fussy on such a night. And then it was long after ten o'clock and yet there was no sign of Gabriel and his wife. Besides they were dreadfully afraid that Freddy Malins might turn up screwed.[8] They would not wish for worlds that any of Mary Jane's pupils should see him under the influence; and when he was like that it was sometimes very hard to manage him. Freddy Malins always came late but they wondered what could be keeping Gabriel: and that was what brought them every two minutes to the banisters to ask Lily had Gabriel or Freddy come.

1. A district in northwest Dublin.
2. Two adjoining quays on the south side of the River Liffey.
3. Played the organ in a church on the Haddington Road.
4. Royal Academy of Music.
5. The train line connecting Dublin to the affluent suburbs south of the city.
6. A Dublin church.
7. An extra-strength ale.
8. Drunk.

—O, Mr Conroy, said Lily to Gabriel when she opened the door for him, Miss Kate and Miss Julia thought you were never coming. Good-night, Mrs Conroy.

—I'll engage⁹ they did, said Gabriel, but they forget that my wife here takes three mortal hours to dress herself.

He stood on the mat, scraping the snow from his goloshes, while Lily led his wife to the foot of the stairs and called out:

—Miss Kate, here's Mrs Conroy.

Kate and Julia came toddling down the dark stairs at once. Both of them kissed Gabriel's wife, said she must be perished alive and asked was Gabriel with her.

—Here I am as right as the mail, Aunt Kate! Go on up. I'll follow, called out Gabriel from the dark.

He continued scraping his feet vigorously while the three women went upstairs, laughing, to the ladies' dressing-room. A light fringe of snow lay like a cape on the shoulders of his overcoat and like toecaps on the toes of his goloshes; and, as the buttons of his overcoat slipped with a squeaking noise through the snow-stiffened frieze, a cold fragrant air from out-of-doors escaped from crevices and folds.

—Is it snowing again, Mr Conroy? asked Lily.

She had preceded him into the pantry to help him off with his overcoat. Gabriel smiled at the three syllables she had given his surname and glanced at her. She was a slim, growing girl, pale in complexion and with hay-coloured hair. The gas in the pantry made her look still paler. Gabriel had known her when she was a child and used to sit on the lowest step nursing a rag doll.

—Yes, Lily, he answered, and I think we're in for a night of it.

He looked up at the pantry ceiling, which was shaking with the stamping and shuffling of feet on the floor above, listened for a moment to the piano and then glanced at the girl, who was folding his overcoat carefully at the end of a shelf.

—Tell me, Lily, he said in a friendly tone, do you still go to school?

—O no, sir, she answered. I'm done schooling this year and more.

—O, then, said Gabriel gaily, I suppose we'll be going to your wedding one of these fine days with your young man, eh?

The girl glanced back at him over her shoulder and said with great bitterness:

—The men that is now is only all palaver¹⁰ and what they can get out of you.

Gabriel coloured as if he felt he had made a mistake and, without looking at her, kicked off his goloshes and flicked actively with his muffler at his patent-leather shoes.

He was a stout tallish young man. The high colour of his cheeks pushed upwards even to his forehead where it scattered itself in a few formless patches of pale red; and on his hairless face there scintillated restlessly the polished lenses and the bright gilt rims of the glasses which screened his delicate and restless eyes. His glossy black hair was parted in the middle and brushed in a long curve behind his ears where it curled slightly beneath the groove left by his hat.

When he had flicked lustre into his shoes he stood up and pulled his waistcoat down more tightly on his plump body. Then he took a coin rapidly from his pocket.

—O Lily, he said, thrusting it into her hands, it's Christmas-time, isn't it? Just . . . here's a little. . . .

He walked rapidly towards the door.

—O no, sir! cried the girl, following him. Really, sir, I wouldn't take it.

9. Wager.   10. Empty talk.

—Christmas-time! Christmas-time! said Gabriel, almost trotting to the stairs and waving his hand to her in deprecation.

The girl, seeing that he had gained the stairs, called out after him:

—Well, thank you, sir.

He waited outside the drawing-room door until the waltz should finish, listening to the skirts that swept against it and to the shuffling of feet. He was still discomposed by the girl's bitter and sudden retort. It had cast a gloom over him which he tried to dispel by arranging his cuffs and the bows of his tie. Then he took from his waistcoat pocket a little paper and glanced at the headings he had made for his speech. He was undecided about the lines from Robert Browning for he feared they would be above the heads of his hearers. Some quotation that they could recognise from Shakespeare or from the Melodies[11] would be better. The indelicate clacking of the men's heels and the shuffling of their soles reminded him that their grade of culture differed from his. He would only make himself ridiculous by quoting poetry to them which they could not understand. They would think that he was airing his superior education. He would fail with them just as he had failed with the girl in the pantry. He had taken up a wrong tone. His whole speech was a mistake from first to last, an utter failure.

Just then his aunts and his wife came out of the ladies' dressing-room. His aunts were two small plainly dressed old women. Aunt Julia was an inch or so taller. Her hair, drawn low over the tops of her ears, was grey; and grey also, with darker shadows, was her large flaccid face. Though she was stout in build and stood erect her slow eyes and parted lips gave her the appearance of a woman who did not know where she was or where she was going. Aunt Kate was more vivacious. Her face, healthier than her sister's, was all puckers and creases, like a shrivelled red apple, and her hair, braided in the same old-fashioned way, had not lost its ripe nut colour.

They both kissed Gabriel frankly. He was their favourite nephew, the son of their dead elder sister, Ellen, who had married T.J. Conroy of the Port and Docks.

—Gretta tells me you're not going to take a cab back to Monkstown[12] to-night, Gabriel, said Aunt Kate.

—No, said Gabriel, turning to his wife, we had quite enough of that last year, hadn't we. Don't you remember, Aunt Kate, what a cold Gretta got out of it? Cab windows rattling all the way, and the east wind blowing in after we passed Merrion. Very jolly it was. Gretta caught a dreadful cold.

Aunt Kate frowned severely and nodded her head at every word.

—Quite right, Gabriel, quite right, she said. You can't be too careful.

—But as for Gretta there, said Gabriel, she'd walk home in the snow if she were let.

Mrs Conroy laughed.

—Don't mind him, Aunt Kate, she said. He's really an awful bother, what with green shades for Tom's eyes at night and making him do the dumb-bells, and forcing Eva to eat the stirabout.[13] The poor child! And she simply hates the sight of it! . . . O, but you'll never guess what he makes me wear now!

She broke out into a peal of laughter and glanced at her husband, whose admiring and happy eyes had been wandering from her dress to her face and hair. The two aunts laughed heartily too, for Gabriel's solicitude was a standing joke with them.

11. Thomas Moore's *Irish Melodies*, a perennial favorite volume of poetry.
12. An elegant suburb south of Dublin.
13. Porridge.

—Goloshes! said Mrs Conroy. That's the latest. Whenever it's wet underfoot I must put on my goloshes. Tonight even he wanted me to put them on, but I wouldn't. The next thing he'll buy me will be a diving suit.

Gabriel laughed nervously and patted his tie reassuringly while Aunt Kate nearly doubled herself, so heartily did she enjoy the joke. The smile soon faded from Aunt Julia's face and her mirthless eyes were directed towards her nephew's face. After a pause she asked:

—And what are goloshes, Gabriel?

—Goloshes, Julia! exclaimed her sister. Goodness me, don't you know what goloshes are? You wear them over your . . . over your boots, Gretta, isn't it?

—Yes, said Mrs Conroy. Guttapercha[14] things. We both have a pair now. Gabriel says everyone wears them on the continent.

—O, on the continent, murmured Aunt Julia, nodding her head slowly.

Gabriel knitted his brows and said, as if he were slightly angered:

—It's nothing very wonderful but Gretta thinks it very funny because she says the word reminds her of Christy Minstrels.[15]

—But tell me, Gabriel, said Aunt Kate, with brisk tact. Of course, you've seen about the room. Gretta was saying . . .

—O, the room is all right, replied Gabriel. I've taken one in the Gresham.[16]

—To be sure, said Aunt Kate, by far the best thing to do. And the children, Gretta, you're not anxious about them?

—O, for one night, said Mrs Conroy. Besides, Bessie will look after them.

—To be sure, said Aunt Kate again. What a comfort it is to have a girl like that, one you can depend on! There's that Lily, I'm sure I don't know what has come over her lately. She's not the girl she was at all.

Gabriel was about to ask his aunt some questions on this point but she broke off suddenly to gaze after her sister who had wandered down the stairs and was craning her neck over the banisters.

—Now, I ask you, she said, almost testily, where is Julia going? Julia! Julia! Where are you going?

Julia, who had gone halfway down one flight, came back and announced blandly:

—Here's Freddy.

At the same moment a clapping of hands and a final flourish of the pianist told that the waltz had ended. The drawing-room door was opened from within and some couples came out. Aunt Kate drew Gabriel aside hurriedly and whispered into his ear:

—Slip down, Gabriel, like a good fellow and see if he's all right, and don't let him up if he's screwed. I'm sure he's screwed. I'm sure he is.

Gabriel went to the stairs and listened over the banisters. He could hear two persons talking in the pantry. Then he recognised Freddy Malins' laugh. He went down the stairs noisily.

—It's such a relief, said Aunt Kate to Mrs Conroy, that Gabriel is here. I always feel easier in my mind when he's here. . . . Julia, there's Miss Daly and Miss Power will take some refreshment. Thanks for your beautiful waltz, Miss Daly. It made lovely time.

14. Rubberized fabric.
15. A 19th-century minstrel show.
16. The most elegant hotel in Dublin.

A tall wizen-faced man, with a stiff grizzled moustache and swarthy skin, who was passing out with his partner said:

—And may we have some refreshment, too, Miss Morkan?

—Julia, said Aunt Kate summarily, and here's Mr Browne and Miss Furlong. Take them in, Julia, with Miss Daly and Miss Power.

—I'm the man for the ladies, said Mr Browne, pursing his lips until his moustache bristled and smiling in all his wrinkles. You know, Miss Morkan, the reason they are so fond of me is—

He did not finish his sentence, but, seeing that Aunt Kate was out of earshot, at once led the three young ladies into the back room. The middle of the room was occupied by two square tables placed end to end, and on these Aunt Julia and the caretaker were straightening and smoothing a large cloth. On the sideboard were arrayed dishes and plates, and glasses and bundles of knives and forks and spoons. The top of the closed square piano served also as a sideboard for viands[17] and sweets. At a smaller sideboard in one corner two young men were standing, drinking hop-bitters.[18]

Mr Browne led his charges thither and invited them all, in jest, to some ladies' punch, hot, strong and sweet. As they said they never took anything strong he opened three bottles of lemonade for them. Then he asked one of the young men to move aside, and, taking hold of the decanter, filled out for himself a goodly measure of whisky. The young men eyed him respectfully while he took a trial sip.

—God help me, he said, smiling, it's the doctor's orders.

His wizened face broke into a broader smile, and the three young ladies laughed in musical echo to his pleasantry, swaying their bodies to and fro, with nervous jerks of their shoulders. The boldest said:

—O, now, Mr Browne, I'm sure the doctor never ordered anything of the kind.

Mr Browne took another sip of his whisky and said, with sidling mimicry:

—Well, you see, I'm like the famous Mrs Cassidy, who is reported to have said: *Now, Mary Grimes, if I don't take it, make me take it, for I feel I want it.*

His hot face had leaned forward a little too confidentially and he had assumed a very low Dublin accent so that the young ladies, with one instinct, received his speech in silence. Miss Furlong, who was one of Mary Jane's pupils, asked Miss Daly what was the name of the pretty waltz she had played; and Mr Browne, seeing that he was ignored, turned promptly to the two young men who were more appreciative.

A red-faced young woman, dressed in pansy, came into the room, excitedly clapping her hands and crying:

—Quadrilles![19] Quadrilles!

Close on her heels came Aunt Kate, crying:

—Two gentlemen and three ladies, Mary Jane!

—O, here's Mr Bergin and Mr Kerrigan, said Mary Jane. Mr Kerrigan, will you take Miss Power? Miss Furlong, may I get you a partner, Mr Bergin. O, that'll just do now.

—Three ladies, Mary Jane, said Aunt Kate.

The two young gentlemen asked the ladies if they might have the pleasure, and Mary Jane turned to Miss Daly.

—O, Miss Daly, you're really awfully good, after playing for the last two dances, but really we're so short of ladies to-night.

—I don't mind in the least, Miss Morkan.

17. Meats.
18. Dry ale.

19. A French square dance.

—But I've a nice partner for you, Mr Bartell D'Arcy, the tenor. I'll get him to sing later on. All Dublin is raving about him.

—Lovely voice, lovely voice! said Aunt Kate.

As the piano had twice begun the prelude to the first figure Mary Jane led her recruits quickly from the room. They had hardly gone when Aunt Julia wandered slowly into the room, looking behind her at something.

—What is the matter, Julia? asked Aunt Kate anxiously. Who is it?

Julia, who was carrying in a column of table-napkins, turned to her sister and said, simply, as if the question had surprised her:

—It's only Freddy, Kate, and Gabriel with him.

In fact right behind her Gabriel could be seen piloting Freddy Malins across the landing. The latter, a young man of about forty, was of Gabriel's size and build, with very round shoulders. His face was fleshy and pallid, touched with colour only at the thick hanging lobes of his ears and at the wide wings of his nose. He had coarse features, a blunt nose, a convex and receding brow, tumid and protruded lips. His heavy-lidded eyes and the disorder of his scanty hair made him look sleepy. He was laughing heartily in a high key at a story which he had been telling Gabriel on the stairs and at the same time rubbing the knuckles of his left fist backwards and forwards into his left eye.

—Good-evening, Freddy, said Aunt Julia.

Freddy Malins bade the Misses Morkan good-evening in what seemed an off-hand fashion by reason of the habitual catch in his voice and then, seeing that Mr Browne was grinning at him from the sideboard, crossed the room on rather shaky legs and began to repeat in an undertone the story he had just told to Gabriel.

—He's not so bad, is he? said Aunt Kate to Gabriel.

Gabriel's brows were dark but he raised them quickly and answered:

—O no, hardly noticeable.

—Now, isn't he a terrible fellow! she said. And his poor mother made him take the pledge on New Year's Eve. But come on, Gabriel, into the drawing-room.

Before leaving the room with Gabriel she signalled to Mr Browne by frowning and shaking her forefinger in warning to and fro. Mr Browne nodded in answer and, when she had gone, said to Freddy Malins:

—Now, then, Teddy, I'm going to fill you out a good glass of lemonade just to buck you up.

Freddy Malins, who was nearing the climax of his story, waved the offer aside impatiently but Mr Browne, having first called Freddy Malins' attention to a disarray in his dress, filled out and handed him a full glass of lemonade. Freddy Malins' left hand accepted the glass mechanically, his right hand being engaged in the mechanical readjustment of his dress. Mr Browne, whose face was once more wrinkling with mirth, poured out for himself a glass of whisky while Freddy Malins exploded, before he had well reached the climax of his story, in a kink of high-pitched bronchitic laughter and, setting down his untasted and overflowing glass, began to rub the knuckles of his left fist backwards and forwards into his left eye, repeating words of his last phrase as well as his fit of laughter would allow him.

Gabriel could not listen while Mary Jane was playing her Academy piece, full of runs and difficult passages, to the hushed drawing-room. He liked music but the piece she was playing had no melody for him and he doubted whether it had any melody for the other listeners, though they had begged Mary Jane to play something. Four young men, who had come from the refreshment-room to stand in the door-way at the sound of the piano, had gone away quietly in couples after a few minutes. The only persons who seemed to follow the music were Mary Jane herself, her hands racing along the key-board or lifted from it at the pauses like those of a priestess in momentary imprecation, and Aunt Kate standing at her elbow to turn the page.

Gabriel's eyes, irritated by the floor, which glittered with beeswax under the heavy chandelier, wandered to the wall above the piano. A picture of the balcony scene in *Romeo and Juliet* hung there and beside it was a picture of the two murdered princes[20] in the Tower which Aunt Julia had worked in red, blue and brown wools when she was a girl. Probably in the school they had gone to as girls that kind of work had been taught, for one year his mother had worked for him as a birthday present a waistcoat of purple tabinet,[21] with little foxes' heads upon it, lined with brown satin and having round mulberry buttons. It was strange that his mother had had no musical talent though Aunt Kate used to call her the brains carrier of the Morkan family. Both she and Julia had always seemed a little proud of their serious and matronly sister. Her photograph stood before the pierglass.[22] She held an open book on her knees and was pointing out something in it to Constantine who, dressed in a man-o'-war suit, lay at her feet. It was she who had chosen the names for her sons for she was very sensible of the dignity of family life. Thanks to her, Constantine was now senior curate in Balbriggan[23] and, thanks to her, Gabriel himself had taken his degree in the Royal University.[24] A shadow passed over his face as he remembered her sullen opposition to his marriage. Some slighting phrases she had used still rankled in his memory; she had once spoken of Gretta as being country cute and that was not true of Gretta at all. It was Gretta who had nursed her during all her last long illness in their house at Monkstown.

He knew that Mary Jane must be near the end of her piece for she was playing again the opening melody with runs of scales after every bar and while he waited for the end the resentment died down in his heart. The piece ended with a trill of octaves in the treble and a final deep octave in the bass. Great applause greeted Mary Jane as, blushing and rolling up her music nervously, she escaped from the room. The most vigorous clapping came from the four young men in the doorway who had gone away to the refreshment-room at the beginning of the piece but had come back when the piano had stopped.

Lancers[25] were arranged. Gabriel found himself partnered with Miss Ivors. She was a frank-mannered talkative young lady, with a freckled face and prominent brown eyes. She did not wear a low-cut bodice and the large brooch which was fixed in the front of her collar bore on it an Irish device.

When they had taken their places she said abruptly:

—I have a crow to pluck with you.

—With me? said Gabriel.

She nodded her head gravely.

—What is it? asked Gabriel, smiling at her solemn manner.

—Who is G. C.? answered Miss Ivors, turning her eyes upon him.

Gabriel coloured and was about to knit his brows, as if he did not understand, when she said bluntly:

—O, innocent Amy! I have found out that you write for *The Daily Express*.[26] Now, aren't you ashamed of yourself?

20. The young sons of Edward IV, murdered in the Tower of London by order of their uncle, Edward III.
21. Silk and wool fabric.
22. A large high mirror.
23. Seaport 19 miles southeast of Dublin.

24. The Royal University of Ireland, established in 1882.
25. A type of quadrille for 8 or 16 people.
26. A conservative paper opposed to the struggle for Irish independence.

—Why should I be ashamed of myself? asked Gabriel, blinking his eyes and try-ing to smile.

—Well, I'm ashamed of you, said Miss Ivors frankly. To say you'd write for a rag like that. I didn't think you were a West Briton.[27]

A look of perplexity appeared on Gabriel's face. It was true that he wrote a literary column every Wednesday in *The Daily Express,* for which he was paid fifteen shillings. But that did not make him a West Briton surely. The books he received for review were almost more welcome than the paltry cheque. He loved to feel the covers and turn over the pages of newly printed books. Nearly every day when his teaching in the college was ended he used to wander down the quays to the second-hand booksellers, to Hickey's on Bachelor's Walk, to Webb's or Massey's on Aston's Quay, or to O'Clo-hissey's in the by-street. He did not know how to meet her charge. He wanted to say that literature was above politics. But they were friends of many years' standing and their careers had been parallel, first at the University and then as teachers: he could not risk a grandiose phrase with her. He continued blinking his eyes and trying to smile and murmured lamely that he saw nothing political in writing reviews of books.

When their turn to cross had come he was still perplexed and inattentive. Miss Ivors promptly took his hand in a warm grasp and said in a soft friendly tone:

—Of course, I was only joking. Come, we cross now.

When they were together again she spoke of the University question[28] and Gabriel felt more at ease. A friend of hers had shown her his review of Browning's poems. That was how she had found out the secret: but she liked the review immensely. Then she said suddenly:

—O, Mr Conroy, will you come for an excursion to the Aran Isles[29] this summer? We're going to stay there a whole month. It will be splendid out in the Atlantic. You ought to come. Mr Clancy is coming, and Mr Kilkelly and Kathleen Kearney. It would be splendid for Gretta too if she'd come. She's from Connacht,[30] isn't she?

—Her people are, said Gabriel shortly.

—But you will come, won't you? said Miss Ivors, laying her warm hand eagerly on his arm.

—The fact is, said Gabriel, I have already arranged to go—

—Go where? asked Miss Ivors.

—Well, you know, every year I go for a cycling tour with some fellows and so—

—But where? asked Miss Ivors.

—Well, we usually go to France or Belgium or perhaps Germany, said Gabriel awkwardly.

—And why do you go to France and Belgium, said Miss Ivors, instead of visiting your own land?

—Well, said Gabriel, it's partly to keep in touch with the languages and partly for a change.

—And haven't you your own language to keep in touch with—Irish? asked Miss Ivors.

27. Disparaging term for people wishing to identify Ire-land as British.
28. Ireland's oldest and most prestigious university, Trini-ty College, was open only to Protestants; the "University question" involved, in part, the provision of quality uni-versity education to Catholics.

29. Islands off the west coast of Ireland where the people still retained their traditional culture and spoke Irish.
30. A province on the west coast of Ireland.

—Well, said Gabriel, if it comes to that, you know, Irish is not my language.

Their neighbours had turned to listen to the cross-examination. Gabriel glanced right and left nervously and tried to keep his good humour under the ordeal which was making a blush invade his forehead.

—And haven't you your own land to visit, continued Miss Ivors, that you know nothing of, your own people, and your own country?

—O, to tell you the truth, retorted Gabriel suddenly, I'm sick of my own country, sick of it!

—Why? asked Miss Ivors.

Gabriel did not answer for his retort had heated him.

—Why? repeated Miss Ivors.

They had to go visiting together and, as he had not answered her, Miss Ivors said warmly:

—Of course, you've no answer.

Gabriel tried to cover his agitation by taking part in the dance with great energy. He avoided her eyes for he had seen a sour expression on her face. But when they met in the long chain he was surprised to feel his hand firmly pressed. She looked at him from under her brows for a moment quizzically until he smiled. Then, just as the chain was about to start again, she stood on tiptoe and whispered into his ear:

—West Briton!

When the lancers were over Gabriel went away to a remote corner of the room where Freddy Malins' mother was sitting. She was a stout feeble old woman with white hair. Her voice had a catch in it like her son's and she stuttered slightly. She had been told that Freddy had come and that he was nearly all right. Gabriel asked her whether she had had a good crossing. She lived with her married daughter in Glasgow and came to Dublin on a visit once a year. She answered placidly that she had had a beautiful crossing and that the captain had been most attentive to her. She spoke also of the beautiful house her daughter kept in Glasgow, and of all the nice friends they had there. While her tongue rambled on Gabriel tried to banish from his mind all memory of the unpleasant incident with Miss Ivors. Of course the girl or woman, or whatever she was, was an enthusiast but there was a time for all things. Perhaps he ought not to have answered her like that. But she had no right to call him a West Briton before people, even in joke. She had tried to make him ridiculous before people, heckling him and staring at him with her rabbit's eyes.

He saw his wife making her way towards him through the waltzing couples. When she reached him she said into his ear:

—Gabriel, Aunt Kate wants to know won't you carve the goose as usual. Miss Daly will carve the ham and I'll do the pudding.

—All right, said Gabriel.

—She's sending in the younger ones first as soon as this waltz is over so that we'll have the table to ourselves.

—Were you dancing? asked Gabriel.

—Of course I was. Didn't you see me? What words had you with Molly Ivors?

—No words. Why? Did she say so?

—Something like that. I'm trying to get that Mr D'Arcy to sing. He's full of conceit, I think.

—There were no words, said Gabriel moodily, only she wanted me to go for a trip to the west of Ireland and I said I wouldn't.

His wife clasped her hands excitedly and gave a little jump.

—O, do go, Gabriel, she cried. I'd love to see Galway again.

—You can go if you like, said Gabriel coldly.

She looked at him for a moment, then turned to Mrs Malins and said:

—There's a nice husband for you, Mrs Malins.

While she was threading her way back across the room Mrs Malins, without adverting to the interruption, went on to tell Gabriel what beautiful places there were in Scotland and beautiful scenery. Her son-in-law brought them every year to the lakes and they used to go fishing. Her son-in-law was a splendid fisher. One day he caught a fish, a beautiful big big fish, and the man in the hotel boiled it for their dinner.

Gabriel hardly heard what she said. Now that supper was coming near he began to think again about his speech and about the quotation. When he saw Freddy Malins coming across the room to visit his mother Gabriel left the chair free for him and retired into the embrasure of the window. The room had already cleared and from the back room came the clatter of plates and knives. Those who still remained in the drawing-room seemed tired of dancing and were conversing quietly in little groups. Gabriel's warm trembling fingers tapped the cold pane of the window. How cool it must be outside! How pleasant it would be to walk out alone, first along by the river and then through the park! The snow would be lying on the branches of the trees and forming a bright cap on the top of the Wellington Monument.[31] How much more pleasant it would be there than at the supper-table!

He ran over the headings of his speech: Irish hospitality, sad memories, the Three Graces, Paris, the quotation from Browning. He repeated to himself a phrase he had written in his review: *One feels that one is listening to a thought-tormented music.* Miss Ivors had praised the review. Was she sincere? Had she really any life of her own behind all her propagandism? There had never been any ill-feeling between them until that night. It unnerved him to think that she would be at the supper-table, looking up at him while he spoke with her critical quizzing eyes. Perhaps she would not be sorry to see him fail in his speech. An idea came into his mind and gave him courage. He would say, alluding to Aunt Kate and Aunt Julia: *Ladies and Gentlemen, the generation which is now on the wane among us may have had its faults but for my part I think it had certain qualities of hospitality, of humour, of humanity, which the new and very serious and hypereducated generation that is growing up around us seems to me to lack.* Very good: that was one for Miss Ivors. What did he care that his aunts were only two ignorant old women?

A murmur in the room attracted his attention. Mr Browne was advancing from the door, gallantly escorting Aunt Julia, who leaned upon his arm, smiling and hanging her head. An irregular musketry of applause escorted her also as far as the piano and then, as Mary Jane seated herself on the stool, and Aunt Julia, no longer smiling, half turned so as to pitch her voice fairly into the room, gradually ceased. Gabriel recognised the prelude. It was that of an old song of Aunt Julia's—*Arrayed for the Bridal.*[32] Her voice, strong and clear in tone, attacked with great spirit the runs which embellish the air and though she sang very rapidly she did not miss even the smallest of the grace notes. To follow the voice, without looking at the singer's face, was to feel and share the excitement of swift and secure flight. Gabriel applauded

---

31. A monument to the Duke of Wellington, an Irish-born English military hero, located in Phoenix Park, Dublin's major public park.

32. A popular but challenging song set to music from Bellini's opera *I Puritani* (1835).

loudly with all the others at the close of the song and loud applause was borne in from the invisible supper-table. It sounded so genuine that a little colour struggled into Aunt Julia's face as she bent to replace in the music-stand the old leather-bound song-book that had her initials on the cover. Freddy Malins, who had listened with his head perched sideways to hear her better, was still applauding when every-one else had ceased and talking animatedly to his mother who nodded her head gravely and slowly in acquiescence. At last, when he could clap no more, he stood up suddenly and hurried across the room to Aunt Julia whose hand he seized and held in both his hands, shaking it when words failed him or the catch in his voice proved too much for him.

—I was just telling my mother, he said, I never heard you sing so well, never. No, I never heard your voice so good as it is to-night. Now! Would you believe that now? That's the truth. Upon my word and honour that's the truth. I never heard your voice sound so fresh and so . . . so clear and fresh, never.

Aunt Julia smiled broadly and murmured something about compliments as she released her hand from his grasp. Mr Browne extended his open hand towards her and said to those who were near him in the manner of a showman introducing a prodigy to an audience:

—Miss Julia Morkan, my latest discovery!

He was laughing very heartily at this himself when Freddy Malins turned to him and said:

—Well, Browne, if you're serious you might make a worse discovery. All I can say is I never heard her sing half so well as long as I am coming here. And that's the honest truth.

—Neither did I, said Mr. Browne. I think her voice has greatly improved.

Aunt Julia shrugged her shoulders and said with meek pride:

—Thirty years ago I hadn't a bad voice as voices go.

—I often told Julia, said Aunt Kate emphatically, that she was simply thrown away in that choir. But she never would be said by me.

She turned as if to appeal to the good sense of the others against a refractory child while Aunt Julia gazed in front of her, a vague smile of reminiscence playing on her face.

—No, continued Aunt Kate, she wouldn't be said or led by anyone, slaving there in that choir night and day, night and day. Six o'clock on Christmas morning! And all for what?

—Well, isn't it for the honour of God, Aunt Kate? asked Mary Jane, twisting round on the piano-stool and smiling.

Aunt Kate turned fiercely on her niece and said:

—I know all about the honour of God, Mary Jane, but I think it's not at all hon-ourable for the pope to turn out the women out of the choirs that have slaved there all their lives and put little whipper-snappers of boys over their heads. I suppose it is for the good of the Church if the pope does it. But it's not just, Mary Jane, and it's not right.

She had worked herself into a passion and would have continued in defence of her sister for it was a sore subject with her but Mary Jane, seeing that all the dancers had come back, intervened pacifically:

—Now, Aunt Kate, you're giving scandal to Mr Browne who is of the other persuasion.

Aunt Kate turned to Mr Browne, who was grinning at this allusion to his reli-gion, and said hastily:

—O, I don't question the pope's being right. I'm only a stupid old woman and I wouldn't presume to do such a thing. But there's such a thing as common everyday politeness and gratitude. And if I were in Julia's place I'd tell that Father Healy straight up to his face . . .

—And besides, Aunt Kate, said Mary Jane, we really are all hungry and when we are hungry we are all very quarrelsome.

—And when we are thirsty we are also quarrelsome, added Mr Browne.

—So that we had better go to supper, said Mary Jane, and finish the discussion afterwards.

On the landing outside the drawing-room Gabriel found his wife and Mary Jane trying to persuade Miss Ivors to stay for supper. But Miss Ivors, who had put on her hat and was buttoning her cloak, would not stay. She did not feel in the least hungry and she had already overstayed her time.

—But only for ten minutes, Molly, said Mrs Conroy. That won't delay you.

—To take a pick itself, said Mary Jane, after all your dancing.

—I really couldn't, said Miss Ivors.

—I am afraid you didn't enjoy yourself at all, said Mary Jane hopelessly.

—Ever so much, I assure you, said Miss Ivors, but you really must let me run off now.

—But how can you get home? asked Mrs Conroy.

—O, it's only two steps up the quay.

Gabriel hesitated a moment and said:

—If you will allow me, Miss Ivors, I'll see you home if you really are obliged to go.

But Miss Ivors broke away from them.

—I won't hear of it, she cried. For goodness sake go in to your suppers and don't mind me. I'm quite well able to take care of myself.

—Well, you're the comical girl, Molly, said Mrs Conroy frankly.

—*Beannacht libh*,[33] cried Miss Ivors, with a laugh, as she ran down the staircase.

Mary Jane gazed after her, a moody puzzled expression on her face, while Mrs Conroy leaned over the banisters to listen for the hall-door. Gabriel asked himself was he the cause of her abrupt departure. But she did not seem to be in ill humour: she had gone away laughing. He stared blankly down the staircase.

At that moment Aunt Kate came toddling out of the supper-room, almost wringing her hands in despair.

—Where is Gabriel? she cried. Where on earth is Gabriel? There's everyone waiting in there, stage to let, and nobody to carve the goose!

—Here I am, Aunt Kate! cried Gabriel, with sudden animation, ready to carve a flock of geese, if necessary.

A fat brown goose lay at one end of the table and at the other end, on a bed of creased paper strewn with sprigs of parsley, lay a great ham, stripped of its outer skin and peppered over with crust crumbs, a neat paper frill round its shin and beside this was a round of spiced beef. Between these rival ends ran parallel lines of side-dishes: two little minsters of jelly, red and yellow; a shallow dish full of blocks of blancmange and red jam, a large green leaf-shaped dish with a stalk-shaped handle, on which lay bunches of purple raisins and peeled almonds, a companion dish on which lay a solid rectangle of Smyrna figs, a dish of custard topped with grated nutmeg, a small bowl full of chocolates and sweets wrapped in gold and silver papers and a glass vase in

33. Farewell (Irish).

which stood some tall celery stalks. In the centre of the table there stood, as sentries to a fruit-stand which upheld a pyramid of oranges and American apples, two squat old-fashioned decanters of cut glass, one containing port and the other dark sherry. On the closed square piano a pudding in a huge yellow dish lay in waiting and behind it were three squads of bottles of stout and ale and minerals, drawn up according to the colours of their uniforms, the first two black, with brown and red labels, the third and smallest squad white, with transverse green sashes.

Gabriel took his seat boldly at the head of the table and, having looked to the edge of the carver, plunged his fork firmly into the goose. He felt quite at ease now for he was an expert carver and liked nothing better than to find himself at the head of a well-laden table.

—Miss Furlong, what shall I send you? he asked. A wing or a slice of the breast?

—Just a small slice of the breast.

—Miss Higgins, what for you?

—O, anything at all, Mr Conroy.

While Gabriel and Miss Daly exchanged plates of goose and plates of ham and spiced beef Lily went from guest to guest with a dish of hot floury potatoes wrapped in a white napkin. This was Mary Jane's idea and she had also suggested apple sauce for the goose but Aunt Kate had said that plain roast goose without apple sauce had always been good enough for her and she hoped she might never eat worse. Mary Jane waited on her pupils and saw that they got the best slices and Aunt Kate and Aunt Julia opened and carried across from the piano bottles of stout and ale for the gentlemen and bottles of minerals for the ladies. There was a great deal of confusion and laughter and noise, the noise of orders and counter-orders, of knives and forks, of corks and glass-stoppers. Gabriel began to carve second helpings as soon as he had finished the first round without serving himself. Everyone protested loudly so that he compromised by taking a long draught of stout for he had found the carving hot work. Mary Jane settled down quietly to her supper but Aunt Kate and Aunt Julia were still toddling round the table, walking on each other's heels, getting in each other's way and giving each other unheeded orders. Mr Browne begged of them to sit down and eat their suppers and so did Gabriel but they said there was time enough so that, at last, Freddy Malins stood up and, capturing Aunt Kate, plumped her down on her chair amid general laughter.

When everyone had been well served Gabriel said, smiling:

—Now, if anyone wants a little more of what vulgar people call stuffing let him or her speak.

A chorus of voices invited him to begin his own supper and Lily came forward with three potatoes which she had reserved for him.

—Very well, said Gabriel amiably, as he took another preparatory draught, kindly forget my existence, ladies and gentlemen, for a few minutes.

He set to his supper and took no part in the conversation with which the table covered Lily's removal of the plates. The subject of talk was the opera company which was then at the Theatre Royal. Mr Bartell D'Arcy, the tenor, a dark-complexioned young man with a smart moustache, praised very highly the leading contralto of the company but Miss Furlong thought she had a rather vulgar style of production. Freddy Malins said there was a negro chieftain singing in the second part of the Gaiety pantomime who had one of the finest tenor voices he had ever heard.

—Have you heard him? he asked Mr Bartell D'Arcy across the table.

—No, answered Mr Bartell D'Arcy carelessly.

—Because, Freddy Malins explained, now I'd be curious to hear your opinion of him. I think he has a grand voice.

—It takes Teddy to find out the really good things, said Mr Browne familiarly to the table.

—And why couldn't he have a voice too? asked Freddy Malins sharply. Is it because he's only a black?

Nobody answered this question and Mary Jane led the table back to the legitimate opera. One of her pupils had given her a pass for *Mignon*. Of course it was very fine, she said, but it made her think of poor Georgina Burns. Mr Browne could go back farther still, to the old Italian companies that used to come to Dublin—Tietjens, Ilma de Murzka, Campanini, the great Trebelli, Giuglini, Ravelli, Aramburo.[34] Those were the days, he said, when there was something like singing to be heard in Dublin. He told too of how the top gallery of the old Royal used to be packed night after night, of how one night an Italian tenor had sung five encores to *Let Me Like a Soldier Fall*, introducing a high C every time, and of how the gallery boys would sometimes in their enthusiasm unyoke the horses from the carriage of some great *prima donna* and pull her themselves through the streets to her hotel. Why did they never play the grand old operas now, he asked, *Dinorah*, *Lucrezia Borgia?* Because they could not get the voices to sing them: that was why.

—O, well, said Mr Bartell D'Arcy, I presume there are as good singers to-day as there were then.

—Where are they? asked Mr Browne defiantly.

—In London, Paris, Milan, said Mr Bartell D'Arcy warmly. I suppose Caruso,[35] for example, is quite as good, if not better than any of the men you have mentioned.

—Maybe so, said Mr Browne. But I may tell you I doubt it strongly.

—O, I'd give anything to hear Caruso sing, said Mary Jane.

—For me, said Aunt Kate, who had been picking a bone, there was only one tenor. To please me, I mean. But I suppose none of you ever heard of him.

—Who was he, Miss Morkan? asked Mr Bartell D'Arcy politely.

—His name, said Aunt Kate, was Parkinson. I heard him when he was in his prime and I think he had then the purest tenor voice that was ever put into a man's throat.

—Strange, said Mr Bartell D'Arcy. I never even heard of him.

—Yes, yes, Miss Morkan is right, said Mr Browne. I remember hearing of old Parkinson but he's too far back for me.

—A beautiful pure sweet mellow English tenor, said Aunt Kate with enthusiasm.

Gabriel having finished, the huge pudding was transferred to the table. The clatter of forks and spoons began again. Gabriel's wife served out spoonfuls of the pudding and passed the plates down the table. Midway down they were held up by Mary Jane, who replenished them with raspberry or orange jelly or with blancmange and jam. The pudding was of Aunt Julia's making and she received praises for it from all quarters. She herself said that it was not quite brown enough.

—Well, I hope, Miss Morkan, said Mr Browne, that I'm brown enough for you because, you know, I'm all brown.

All the gentlemen, except Gabriel, ate some of the pudding out of compliment to Aunt Julia. As Gabriel never ate sweets the celery had been left for him. Freddy

34. Famous 19th-century operatic singers.   35. Enrico Caruso (1874–1921), a famous tenor.

Malins also took a stalk of celery and ate it with his pudding. He had been told that celery was a capital thing for the blood and he was just then under doctor's care. Mrs Malins, who had been silent all through the supper, said that her son was going down to Mount Melleray[36] in a week or so. The table then spoke to Mount Melleray, how bracing the air was down there, how hospitable the monks were and how they never asked for a penny-piece from their guests.

—And do you mean to say, asked Mr Browne incredulously, that a chap can go down there and put up there as if it were a hotel and live on the fat of the land and then come away without paying a farthing?

—O, most people give some donation to the monastery when they leave, said Mary Jane.

—I wish we had an institution like that in our Church, said Mr Browne candidly.

He was astonished to hear that the monks never spoke, got up at two in the morning and slept in their coffins. He asked what they did it for.

—That's the rule of the order, said Aunt Kate firmly.

—Yes, but why? asked Mr Browne.

Aunt Kate repeated that it was the rule, that was all. Mr Browne still seemed not to understand. Freddy Malins explained to him, as best he could, that the monks were trying to make up for the sins committed by all the sinners in the outside world. The explanation was not very clear for Mr Browne grinned and said:

—I like that idea very much but wouldn't a comfortable spring bed do them as well as a coffin?

—The coffin, said Mary Jane, is to remind them of their last end.

As the subject had grown lugubrious it was buried in a silence of the table during which Mrs Malins could be heard saying to her neighbour in an indistinct undertone:

—They are very good men, the monks, very pious men.

The raisins and almonds and figs and apples and oranges and chocolates and sweets were now passed about the table and Aunt Julia invited all the guests to have either port or sherry. At first Mr Bartell D'Arcy refused to take either but one of his neighbours nudged him and whispered something to him upon which he allowed his glass to be filled. Gradually as the last glasses were being filled the conversation ceased. A pause followed, broken only by the noise of the wine and by unsettlings of chairs. The Misses Morkan, all three, looked down at the tablecloth. Someone coughed once or twice and then a few gentlemen patted the table gently as a signal for silence. The silence came and Gabriel pushed back his chair and stood up.

The patting at once grew louder in encouragement and then ceased altogether. Gabriel leaned his ten trembling fingers on the tablecloth and smiled nervously at the company. Meeting a row of upturned faces he raised his eyes to the chandelier. The piano was playing a waltz tune and he could hear the skirts sweeping against the drawing-room door. People, perhaps, were standing in the snow on the quay outside, gazing up at the lighted windows and listening to the waltz music. The air was pure there. In the distance lay the park where the trees were weighted with snow. The Wellington Monument wore a gleaming cap of snow that flashed westward over the white field of Fifteen Acres.[37]

He began:

—Ladies and Gentlemen.

---

36. Site of a Trappist monastery in the south of Ireland.   37. A section of Phoenix Park.

—It has fallen to my lot this evening, as in years past, to perform a very pleasing task but a task for which I am afraid my poor powers as a speaker are all too inadequate.

—No, no! said Mr Browne.

—But, however that may be, I can only ask you tonight to take the will for the deed and to lend me your attention for a few moments while I endeavour to express to you in words what my feelings are on this occasion.

—Ladies and Gentlemen. It is not the first time that we have gathered together under this hospitable roof, around this hospitable board. It is not the first time that we have been the recipients—or perhaps, I had better say, the victims—of the hospitality of certain good ladies.

He made a circle in the air with his arm and paused. Everyone laughed or smiled at Aunt Kate and Aunt Julia and Mary Jane who all turned crimson with pleasure. Gabriel went on more boldly:

—I feel more strongly with every recurring year that our country has no tradition which does it so much honour and which it should guard so jealously as that of its hospitality. It is a tradition that is unique as far as my experience goes (and I have visited not a few places abroad) among the modern nations. Some would say, perhaps, that with us it is rather a failing than anything to be boasted of. But granted even that, it is, to my mind, a princely failing, and one that I trust will long be cultivated among us. Of one thing, at least, I am sure. As long as this one roof shelters the good ladies aforesaid—and I wish from my heart it may do so for many and many a long year to come—the tradition of genuine warm-hearted courteous Irish hospitality, which our forefathers have handed down to us and which we in turn must hand down to our descendants, is still alive among us.

A hearty murmur of assent ran round the table. It shot through Gabriel's mind that Miss Ivors was not there and that she had gone away discourteously: and he said with confidence in himself:

—Ladies and Gentlemen.

—A new generation is growing up in our midst, a generation actuated by new ideas and new principles. It is serious and enthusiastic for these new ideas and its enthusiasm, even when it is misdirected, is, I believe, in the main sincere. But we are living in a sceptical and, if I may use the phrase, a thought-tormented age: and sometimes I fear that this new generation, educated or hypereducated as it is, will lack those qualities of humanity, of hospitality, of kindly humour which belonged to an older day. Listening to-night to the names of all those great singers of the past it seemed to me, I must confess, that we were living in a less spacious age. Those days might, without exaggeration, be called spacious days: and if they are gone beyond recall let us hope, at least, that in gatherings such as this we shall still speak of them with pride and affection, still cherish in our hearts the memory of those dead and gone great ones whose fame the world will not willingly let die.

—Hear, hear! said Mr Browne loudly.

—But yet, continued Gabriel, his voice falling into a softer inflection, there are always in gatherings such as this sadder thoughts that will recur to our minds: thoughts of the past, of youth, of changes, of absent faces that we miss here to-night. Our path through life is strewn with many such sad memories: and were we to brood upon them always we could not find the heart to go on bravely with our work among the living. We have all of us living duties and living affections which claim, and rightly claim, our strenuous endeavours.

—Therefore, I will not linger on the past. I will not let any gloomy moralising intrude upon us here to-night. Here we are gathered together for a brief moment from the bustle and rush of our everyday routine. We are met here as friends, in the spirit of good-fellowship, as colleagues, also to a certain extent, in the true spirit of *camaraderie*, and as the guests of—what shall I call them?—the Three Graces[38] of the Dublin musical world.

The table burst into applause and laughter at this sally. Aunt Julia vainly asked each of her neighbors in turn to tell her what Gabriel had said.

—He says we are the Three Graces, Aunt Julia, said Mary Jane.

Aunt Julia did not understand but she looked up, smiling, at Gabriel, who continued in the same vein:

—Ladies and Gentlemen.

—I will not attempt to play to-night the part that Paris[39] played on another occasion. I will not attempt to choose between them. The task would be an invidious one and one beyond my poor powers. For when I view them in turn, whether it be our chief hostess herself, whose good heart, whose too good heart, has become a byword with all who know her, or her sister, who seems to be gifted with perennial youth and whose singing must have been a surprise and a revelation to us all to-night, or, last but not least, when I consider our youngest hostess, talented, cheerful, hard-working and the best of nieces, I confess, Ladies and Gentlemen, that I do not know to which of them I should award the prize.

Gabriel glanced down at his aunts and, seeing the large smile on Aunt Julia's face and the tears which had risen to Aunt Kate's eyes, hastened to his close. He raised his glass of port gallantly, while every member of the company fingered a glass expectantly, and said loudly:

—Let us toast them all three together. Let us drink to their health, wealth, long life, happiness and prosperity and may they long continue to hold the proud and self-won position which they hold in their profession and the position of honour and affection which they hold in our hearts.

All the guests stood up, glass in hand, and, turning towards the three seated ladies, sang in unison, with Mr Browne as leader:

> *For they are jolly gay fellows,*
> *For they are jolly gay fellows,*
> *For they are jolly gay fellows,*
> *Which nobody can deny.*

Aunt Kate was making frank use of her handkerchief and even Aunt Julia seemed moved. Freddy Malins beat time with his pudding-fork and the singers turned towards one another, as if in melodious conference, while they sang, with emphasis:

> *Unless he tells a lie,*
> *Unless he tells a lie.*

Then, turning once more towards their hostesses, they sang:

> *For they are jolly gay fellows,*
> *For they are jolly gay fellows,*
> *For they are jolly gay fellows,*
> *Which nobody can deny.*

38. Companions to the Muses in Greek mythology.
39. Paris was the judge of a divine beauty contest in which Hera, Athena, and Aphrodite competed; his selection of Aphrodite was, indirectly, the cause of the Trojan War.

The acclamation which followed was taken up beyond the door of the supper-room by many of the other guests and renewed time after time, Freddy Malins acting as officer with his fork on high.

The piercing morning air came into the hall where they were standing so that Aunt Kate said:

—Close the door, somebody. Mrs Malins will get her death of cold.

—Browne is out there, Aunt Kate, said Mary Jane.

—Browne is everywhere, said Aunt Kate, lowering her voice.

Mary Jane laughed at her tone.

—Really, she said archly, he is very attentive.

—He has been laid on here like the gas, said Aunt Kate in the same tone, all during the Christmas.

She laughed herself this time good-humouredly and then added quickly:

—But tell him to come in, Mary Jane, and close the door. I hope to goodness he didn't hear me.

At that moment the hall-door was opened and Mr Browne came in from the doorstep, laughing as if his heart would break. He was dressed in a long green over-coat with mock astrakhan cuffs and collar and wore on his head an oval fur cap. He pointed down the snow-covered quay from where the sound of shrill prolonged whistling was borne in.

—Teddy will have all the cabs in Dublin out, he said.

Gabriel advanced from the little pantry behind the office, struggling into his overcoat and looking round the hall, said:

—Gretta not down yet?

—She's getting on her things, Gabriel, said Aunt Kate.

—Who's playing up there? asked Gabriel.

—Nobody. They're all gone.

—O no, Aunt Kate, said Mary Jane. Bartell D'Arcy and Miss O'Callaghan aren't gone yet.

—Someone is strumming at the piano, anyhow, said Gabriel.

Mary Jane glanced at Gabriel and Mr Browne and said with a shiver:

—It makes me feel cold to look at you two gentlemen muffled up like that. I wouldn't like to face your journey home at this hour.

—I'd like nothing better this minute, said Mr Browne stoutly, than a rattling fine walk in the country or a fast drive with a good spanking goer between the shafts.

—We used to have a very good horse and trap at home, said Aunt Julia sadly.

—The never-to-be-forgotten Johnny, said Mary Jane, laughing.

Aunt Kate and Gabriel laughed too.

—Why, what was wonderful about Johnny? asked Mr Browne.

—The late lamented Patrick Morkan, our grandfather, that is, explained Gabriel, commonly known in his later years as the old gentleman, was a glue-boiler.

—O, now, Gabriel, said Aunt Kate, laughing, he had a starch mill.

—Well, glue or starch, said Gabriel, the old gentleman had a horse by the name of Johnny. And Johnny used to work in the old gentleman's mill, walking round and round in order to drive the mill. That was all very well; but now comes the tragic part about Johnny. One fine day the old gentleman thought he'd like to drive out with the quality to a military review in the park.

—The Lord have mercy on his soul, said Aunt Kate compassionately.

—Amen, said Gabriel. So the old gentleman, as I said, harnessed Johnny and put on his very best tall hat and his very best stock collar and drove out in grand style from his ancestral mansion somewhere near Back Lane, I think.

Everyone laughed, even Mrs Malins, at Gabriel's manner and Aunt Kate said:

—O now, Gabriel, he didn't live in Back Lane, really. Only the mill was there.

—Out from the mansion of his forefathers, continued Gabriel, he drove with Johnny. And everything went on beautifully until Johnny came in sight of King Billy's statue:[40] and whether he fell in love with the horse King Billy sits on or whether he thought he was back again in the mill, anyhow he began to walk round the statue.

Gabriel paced in a circle round the hall in his goloshes amid the laughter of the others.

—Round and round he went, said Gabriel, and the old gentleman, who was a very pompous old gentleman, was highly indignant. *Go on, sir! What do you mean, sir? Johnny! Johnny! Most extraordinary conduct! Can't understand the horse!*

The peals of laughter which followed Gabriel's imitation of the incident were interrupted by a resounding knock at the hall-door. Mary Jane ran to open it and let in Freddy Malins. Freddy Malins, with his hat well back on his head and his shoulders humped with cold, was puffing and steaming after his exertions.

—I could only get one cab, he said.

—O, we'll find another along the quay, said Gabriel.

—Yes, said Aunt Kate. Better not keep Mrs Malins standing in the draught.

Mrs Malins was helped down the front steps by her son and Mr Browne and, after many manoeuvres, hoisted into the cab. Freddy Malins clambered in after her and spent a long time settling her on the seat, Mr Browne helping him with advice. At last she was settled comfortably and Freddy Malins invited Mr Browne into the cab. There was a good deal of confused talk, and then Mr Browne got into the cab. The cabman settled his rug over his knees, and bent down for the address. The confusion grew greater and the cabman was directed differently by Freddy Malins and Mr Browne, each of whom had his head out through a window of the cab. The difficulty was to know where to drop Mr Browne along the route and Aunt Kate, Aunt Julia and Mary Jane helped the discussion from the doorstep with cross-directions and contradictions and abundance of laughter. As for Freddy Malins he was speechless with laughter. He popped his head in and out of the window every moment, to the great danger of his hat, and told his mother how the discussion was progressing till at last Mr Browne shouted to the bewildered cabman above the din of everybody's laughter:

—Do you know Trinity College?

—Yes, sir, said the cabman.

—Well, drive bang up against Trinity College gates, said Mr Browne, and then we'll tell you where to go. You understand now?

—Yes, sir, said the cabman.

—Make like a bird for Trinity College.

—Right, sir, cried the cabman.

The horse was whipped up and the cab rattled off along the quay amid a chorus of laughter and adieus.

---

40. Statue of William of Orange, who defeated the Irish Catholic forces in the Battle of the Boyne in 1690, which stood in College Green in front of Trinity College in the heart of Dublin. It was seen as a symbol of British imperial oppression.

Gabriel had not gone to the door with the others. He was in a dark part of the hall gazing up the staircase, a woman was standing near the top of the first flight, in the shadow also. He could not see her face but he could see the terracotta and salmonpink panels of her skirt which the shadow made appear black and white. It was his wife. She was leaning on the banisters, listening to something. Gabriel was surprised at her stillness and strained his ear to listen also. But he could hear little save the noise of laughter and dispute on the front steps, a few chords struck on the piano and a few notes of a man's voice singing.

He stood still in the gloom of the hall, trying to catch the air that the voice was singing and gazing up at his wife. There was grace and mystery in her attitude as if she were a symbol of something. He asked himself what is a woman standing on the stairs in the shadow, listening to distant music, a symbol of. If he were a painter he would paint her in that attitude. Her blue felt hat would show off the bronze of her hair against the darkness and the dark panels of her skirt would show off the light ones. *Distant Music* he would call the picture if he were a painter.

The hall-door was closed; and Aunt Kate, Aunt Julia and Mary Jane came down the hall, still laughing.

—Well, isn't Freddy terrible? said Mary Jane. He's really terrible.

Gabriel said nothing but pointed up the stairs towards where his wife was standing. Now that the hall-door was closed the voice and the piano could be heard more clearly. Gabriel held up his hand for them to be silent. The song seemed to be in the old Irish tonality and the singer seemed uncertain both of his words and of his voice. The voice, made plaintive by distance and by the singer's hoarseness, faintly illuminated the cadence of the air with words expressing grief:

> O, the rain falls on my heavy locks
> And the dew wets my skin,
> My babe lies cold . . .

—O, exclaimed Mary Jane. It's Bartell D'Arcy singing and he wouldn't sing all the night. O, I'll get him to sing a song before he goes.

—O do, Mary Jane, said Aunt Kate.

Mary Jane brushed past the others and ran to the staircase but before she reached it the singing stopped and the piano was closed abruptly.

—O, what a pity! she cried. Is he coming down, Gretta?

Gabriel heard his wife answer yes and saw her come down towards them. A few steps behind her were Mr Bartell D'Arcy and Miss O'Callaghan.

—O, Mr D'Arcy, cried Mary Jane, it's downright mean of you to break off like that when we were all in raptures listening to you.

—I have been at him all the evening, said Miss O'Callaghan, and Mrs Conroy too and he told us he had a dreadful cold and couldn't sing.

—O, Mr D'Arcy, said Aunt Kate, now that was a great fib to tell.

—Can't you see that I'm as hoarse as a crow? said Mr D'Arcy roughly.

He went into the pantry hastily and put on his overcoat. The others, taken aback by his rude speech, could find nothing to say. Aunt Kate wrinkled her brows and made signs to the others to drop the subject. Mr D'Arcy stood swathing his neck carefully and frowning.

—It's the weather, said Aunt Julia, after a pause.

—Yes, everybody has colds, said Aunt Kate readily, everybody.

—They say, said Mary Jane, we haven't had snow like it for thirty years; and I read this morning in the newspapers that the snow is general all over Ireland.

—I love the look of snow, said Aunt Julia sadly.

—So do I, said Miss O'Callaghan. I think Christmas is never really Christmas unless we have the snow on the ground.

—But poor Mr D'Arcy doesn't like the snow, said Aunt Kate, smiling.

Mr D'Arcy came from the pantry, full swathed and buttoned, and in a repentant tone told them the history of his cold. Everyone gave him advice and said it was a great pity and urged him to be very careful of his throat in the night air. Gabriel watched his wife who did not join in the conversation. She was standing right under the dusty fanlight and the flame of the gas lit up the rich bronze of her hair which he had seen her drying at the fire a few days before. She was in the same attitude and seemed unaware of the talk about her. At last she turned towards them and Gabriel saw that there was colour on her cheeks and that her eyes were shining. A sudden tide of joy went leaping out of his heart.

—Mr D'Arcy, she said, what is the name of that song you were singing?

—It's called *The Lass of Aughrim*, said Mr D'Arcy, but I couldn't remember it properly. Why? Do you know it?

—*The Lass of Aughrim*, she repeated. I couldn't think of the name.

—It's a very nice air, said Mary Jane. I'm sorry you were not in voice to-night.

—Now, Mary Jane, said Aunt Kate, don't annoy Mr D'Arcy. I won't have him annoyed.

Seeing that all were ready to start she shepherded them to the door where good-night was said:

—Well, good-night, Aunt Kate, and thanks for the pleasant evening.

—Good-night, Gabriel. Good-night, Gretta!

—Good-night, Aunt Kate, and thanks ever so much. Good-night, Aunt Julia.

—O, good-night, Gretta, I didn't see you.

—Good-night, Mr D'Arcy. Good-night, Miss O'Callaghan.

—Good-night, Miss Morkan.

—Good-night, again.

—Good-night, all. Safe home.

—Good-night. Good-night.

The morning was still dark. A dull yellow light brooded over the houses and the river; and the sky seemed to be descending. It was slushy underfoot; and only streaks and patches of snow lay on the roofs, on the parapets of the quay and on the area railings. The lamps were still burning redly in the murky air and, across the river, the palace of the Four Courts[41] stood out menacingly against the heavy sky.

She was walking on before him with Mr Bartell D'Arcy, her shoes in a brown parcel tucked under one arm and her hands holding her skirt up from the slush. She had no longer any grace of attitude but Gabriel's eyes were still bright with happiness. The blood went bounding along his veins; and the thoughts went rioting through his brain, proud, joyful, tender, valorous.

She was walking on before him so lightly and so erect that he longed to run after her noiselessly, catch her by the shoulders and say something foolish and affectionate into her ear. She seemed to him so frail that he longed to defend her against something and then to be alone with her. Moments of their secret life together burst like stars upon his memory. A heliotrope envelope was lying beside his breakfast-cup and he was caressing it with his hand. Birds were twittering in the ivy and the sunny web of the

---

41. The Irish law courts.

curtain was shimmering along the floor: he could not eat for happiness. They were standing on the crowded platform and he was placing a ticket inside the warm palm of her glove. He was standing with her in the cold, looking in through a grated window at a man making bottles in a roaring furnace. It was very cold. Her face, fragrant in the cold air, was quite close to his; and suddenly she called out to the man at the furnace:

—Is the fire hot, sir?

But the man could not hear her with the noise of the furnace. It was just as well. He might have answered rudely.

A wave of yet more tender joy escaped from his heart and went coursing in warm flood along his arteries. Like the tender fires of stars moments of their life together, that no one knew of or would ever know of, broke upon and illumined his memory. He longed to recall to her those moments, to make her forget the years of their dull existence together and remember only their moments of ecstasy. For the years, he felt, had not quenched his soul or hers. Their children, his writing, her household cares had not quenched all their souls' tender fire. In one letter that he had written to her then he had said: *Why is it that words like these seem to me so dull and cold? Is it because there is no word tender enough to be your name?*

Like distant music these words that he had written years before were borne towards him from the past. He longed to be alone with her. When the others had gone away, when he and she were in their room in the hotel, then they would be alone together. He would call her softly:

—Gretta!

Perhaps she would not hear at once: she would be undressing. Then something in his voice would strike her. She would turn and look at him. . . .

At the corner of Winetavern Street they met a cab. He was glad of its rattling noise as it saved him from conversation. She was looking out of the window and seemed tired. The others spoke only a few words, pointing out some building or street. The horse galloped along wearily under the murky morning sky, dragging his old rattling box after his heels, and Gabriel was again in a cab with her, galloping to catch the boat, galloping to their honeymoon.

As the cab drove across O'Connell Bridge Miss O'Callaghan said:

—They say you never cross O'Connell Bridge without seeing a white horse.

—I see a white man this time, said Gabriel.

—Where? asked Mr Bartell D'Arcy.

Gabriel pointed to the statue, on which lay patches of snow. Then he nodded familiarly to it and waved his hand.

—Good-night, Dan,[42] he said gaily.

When the cab drew up before the hotel Gabriel jumped out and, in spite of Mr Bartell D'Arcy's protest, paid the driver. He gave the man a shilling over his fare. The man saluted and said:

—A prosperous New Year to you, sir.

—The same to you, said Gabriel cordially.

She leaned for a moment on his arm in getting out of the cab and while standing at the curbstone, bidding the others good-night. She leaned lightly on his arm, as lightly as when she had danced with him a few hours before. He had felt proud and happy then, happy that she was his, proud of her grace and wifely carriage. But now, after the kindling again of so many memories, the first touch of her body,

42. A statue of Daniel O'Connell, 19th-century nationalist leader, stands at the south end of Sackville Street (now called O'Connell Street).

musical and strange and perfumed, sent through him a keen pang of lust. Under cover of her silence he pressed her arm closely to his side; and, as they stood at the hotel door, he felt that they had escaped from their lives and duties, escaped from home and friends and run away together with wild and radiant hearts to a new adventure.

An old man was dozing in a great hooded chair in the hall. He lit a candle in the office and went before them to the stairs. They followed him in silence, their feet falling in soft thuds on the thickly carpeted stairs. She mounted the stairs behind the porter, her head bowed in the ascent, her frail shoulders curved as with a burden, her skirt girt tightly about her. He could have flung his arms about her hips and held her still for his arms were trembling with desire to seize her and only the stress of his nails against the palms of his hands held the wild impulse of his body in check. The porter halted on the stairs to settle his guttering candle. They halted too on the steps below him. In the silence Gabriel could hear the falling of the molten wax into the tray and the thumping of his own heart against his ribs.

The porter led them along a corridor and opened a door. Then he set his unstable candle down on a toilet-table and asked at what hour they were to be called in the morning.

—Eight, said Gabriel.

The porter pointed to the tap of the electric-light and began a muttered apology but Gabriel cut him short.

—We don't want any light. We have light enough from the street. And I say, he added, pointing to the candle, you might remove that handsome article, like a good man.

The porter took up his candle again, but slowly for he was surprised by such a novel idea. Then he mumbled good-night and went out. Gabriel shot the lock to.

A ghostly light from the street lamp lay in a long shaft from one window to the door. Gabriel threw his overcoat and hat on a couch and crossed the room towards the window. He looked down into the street in order that his emotion might calm a little. Then he turned and leaned against a chest of drawers with his back to the light. She had taken off her hat and cloak and was standing before a large swinging mirror, unhooking her waist. Gabriel paused for a few moments, watching her, and then said:

—Gretta!

She turned away from the mirror slowly and walked along the shaft of light towards him. Her face looked so serious and weary that the words would not pass Gabriel's lips. No, it was not the moment yet.

—You looked tired, he said.

—I am a little, she answered.

—You don't feel ill or weak?

—No, tired: that's all.

She went on to the window and stood there, looking out. Gabriel waited again and then, fearing that diffidence was about to conquer him, he said abruptly:

—By the way, Gretta!

—What is it?

—You know that poor fellow Malins? he said quickly.

—Yes. What about him?

—Well, poor fellow, he's a decent sort of chap after all, continued Gabriel in a false voice. He gave me back that sovereign I lent him and I didn't expect it really. It's a pity he wouldn't keep away from that Browne, because he's not a bad fellow at heart.

He was trembling now with annoyance. Why did she seem so abstracted? He did not know how he could begin. Was she annoyed, too, about something? If she would only turn to him or come to him of her own accord! To take her as she was would be brutal. No, he must see some ardour in her eyes first. He longed to be master of her strange mood.

—When did you lend him the pound? she asked, after a pause.

Gabriel strove to restrain himself from breaking out into brutal language about the sottish Malins and his pound. He longed to cry to her from his soul, to crush her body against his, to overmaster her. But he said:

—O, at Christmas, when he opened that little Christmas-card shop in Henry Street.

He was in such a fever of rage and desire that he did not hear her come from the window. She stood before him for an instant, looking at him strangely. Then, suddenly raising herself on tiptoe and resting her hands lightly on his shoulders, she kissed him.

—You are a very generous person, Gabriel, she said.

Gabriel, trembling with delight at her sudden kiss and at the quaintness of her phrase, put his hands on her hair and began smoothing it back, scarcely touching it with his fingers. The washing had made it fine and brilliant. His heart was brimming over with happiness. Just when he was wishing for it she had come to him of her own accord. Perhaps her thoughts had been running with his. Perhaps she had felt the impetuous desire that was in him and then the yielding mood had come upon her. Now that she had fallen to him so easily he wondered why he had been so diffident.

He stood, holding her head between his hands. Then, slipping one arm swiftly about her body and drawing her towards him, he said softly:

—Gretta dear, what are you thinking about?

She did not answer nor yield wholly to his arm. He said again, softly:

—Tell me what it is, Gretta. I think I know what is the matter. Do I know?

She did not answer at once. Then she said in an outburst of tears:

—O, I am thinking about that song, *The Lass of Aughrim*.

She broke loose from him and ran to the bed and, throwing her arms across the bed-rail, hid her face. Gabriel stood stock-still for a moment in astonishment and then followed her. As he passed in the way of the cheval-glass he caught sight of himself in full length, his broad, well-filled shirt-front, the face whose expression always puzzled him when he saw it in a mirror and his glimmering gilt-rimmed eyeglasses. He halted a few paces from her and said:

—What about the song? Why does that make you cry?

She raised her head from her arms and dried her eyes with the back of her hand like a child. A kinder note than he had intended went into his voice.

—Why, Gretta? he asked.

—I am thinking about a person long ago who used to sing that song.

—And who was the person long ago? asked Gabriel, smiling.

—It was a person I used to know in Galway when I was living with my grandmother, she said.

The smile passed away from Gabriel's face. A dull anger began to gather again at the back of his mind and the dull fires of his lust began to glow angrily in his veins.

—Someone you were in love with? he asked ironically.

—It was a young boy I used to know, she answered, named Michael Furey. He used to sing that song, *The Lass of Aughrim*. He was very delicate.

Gabriel was silent. He did not wish her to think that he was interested in this delicate boy.

—I can see him so plainly, she said after a moment. Such eyes as he had: big dark eyes! And such an expression in them—an expression!

—O then, you were in love with him? said Gabriel.

—I used to go out walking with him, she said, when I was in Galway.

A thought flew across Gabriel's mind.

—Perhaps that was why you wanted to go to Galway with that Ivors girl? he said coldly.

She looked at him and asked in surprise:

—What for?

Her eyes made Gabriel feel awkward. He shrugged his shoulders and said:

—How do I know? To see him perhaps.

She looked away from him along the shaft of light towards the window in silence.

—He is dead, she said at length. He died when he was only seventeen. Isn't it a terrible thing to die so young as that?

—What was he? asked Gabriel, still ironically.

—He was in the gasworks, she said.

Gabriel felt humiliated by the failure of his irony and by the evocation of this figure from the dead, a boy in the gasworks. While he had been full of memories of their secret life together, full of tenderness and joy and desire, she had been comparing him in her mind with another. A shameful consciousness of his own person assailed him. He saw himself as a ludicrous figure, acting as a pennyboy[43] for his aunts, a nervous well-meaning sentimentalist, orating to vulgarians and idealising his own clownish lusts, the pitiable fatuous fellow he had caught a glimpse of in the mirror. Instinctively he turned his back more to the light lest she might see the shame that burned upon his forehead.

He tried to keep up his tone of cold interrogation but his voice when he spoke was humble and indifferent.

—I suppose you were in love with this Michael Furey, Gretta, he said.

—I was great with him at that time, she said.

Her voice was veiled and sad. Gabriel, feeling now how vain it would be to try to lead her whither he had purposed, caressed one of her hands and said, also sadly:

—And what did he die of so young, Gretta? Consumption, was it?

—I think he died for me, she answered.[44]

A vague terror seized Gabriel at this answer as if, at that hour when he had hoped to triumph, some impalpable and vindictive being was coming against him, gathering forces against him in its vague world. But he shook himself free of it with an effort of reason and continued to caress her hand. He did not question her again for he felt that she would tell him of herself. Her hand was warm and moist: it did not respond to his touch but he continued to caress it just as he had caressed her first letter to him that spring morning.

—It was in the winter, she said, about the beginning of the winter when I was going to leave my grandmother's and come up here to the convent. And he was ill at the time in his lodgings in Galway and wouldn't be let out and his people in Oughterard[45] were written to. He was in decline, they said, or something like that. I never knew rightly.

She paused for a moment and sighed.

—Poor fellow, she said. He was very fond of me and he was such a gentle boy. We used to go out together, walking, you know, Gabriel, like the way they do in the

43. Errand boy.
44. Gretta here echoes the words of Yeats's Cathleen ní Houlihan: "Singing I am about a man I knew one time, yellow-haired Donough that was hanged in Galway. . . . He died for love of me: many a man has died for love of me." The play was first performed in Dublin on 2 April 1902.
45. A small village in Western Ireland.

country. He was going to study singing only for his health. He had a very good voice, poor Michael Furey.

—Well; and then? asked Gabriel.

—And then when it came to the time for me to leave Galway and come up to the convent he was much worse and I wouldn't be let see him so I wrote a letter saying I was going up to Dublin and would be back in the summer and hoping he would be better then.

She paused for a moment to get her voice under control and then went on:

—Then the night before I left I was in my grandmother's house in Nuns' Island, packing up, and I heard gravel thrown up against the window. The window was so wet I couldn't see so I ran downstairs as I was and slipped out the back into the garden and there was the poor fellow at the end of the garden, shivering.

—And did you not tell him to go back? asked Gabriel.

—I implored him to go home at once and told him he would get his death in the rain. But he said he did not want to live. I can see his eyes as well as well! He was standing at the end of the wall where there was a tree.

—And did he go home? asked Gabriel.

—Yes, he went home. And when I was only a week in the convent he died and he was buried in Oughterard where his people came from. O, the day I heard that, that he was dead!

She stopped, choking with sobs, and, overcome by emotion, flung herself face downward on the bed, sobbing in the quilt. Gabriel held her hand for a moment longer, irresolutely, and then, shy of intruding on her grief, let it fall gently and walked quietly to the window.

She was fast asleep.

Gabriel, leaning on his elbow, looked for a few moments unresentfully on her tangled hair and half-open mouth, listening to her deep-drawn breath. So she had had that romance in her life: a man had died for her sake. It hardly pained him now to think how poor a part he, her husband, had played in her life. He watched her while she slept as though he and she had never lived together as man and wife. His curious eyes rested long upon her face and on her hair: and, as he thought of what she must have been then, in that time of her first girlish beauty, a strange friendly pity for her entered his soul. He did not like to say even to himself that her face was no longer beautiful but he knew that it was no longer the face for which Michael Furey had braved death.

Perhaps she had not told him all the story. His eyes moved to the chair over which she had thrown some of her clothes. A petticoat string dangled to the floor. One boot stood upright, its limp upper fallen down: the fellow of it lay upon its side. He wondered at his riot of emotions of an hour before. From what had it proceeded? From his aunt's supper, from his own foolish speech, from the wine and dancing, the merry-making when saying good-night in the hall, the pleasure of the walk along the river in the snow. Poor Aunt Julia! She, too, would soon be a shade with the shade of Patrick Morkan and his horse. He had caught that haggard look upon her face for a moment when she was singing *Arrayed for the Bridal*. Soon, perhaps, he would be sitting in that same drawing-room, dressed in black, his silk hat on his knees. The blinds would be drawn down and Aunt Kate would be sitting beside him, crying and blowing her nose and telling him how Julia had died. He would cast about in his mind for some words that might console her, and would find only lame and useless ones. Yes, yes: that would happen very soon.

The air of the room chilled his shoulders. He stretched himself cautiously along under the sheets and lay down beside his wife. One by one they were all becoming shades. Better pass boldly into that other world, in the full glory of some passion, than fade and wither dismally with age. He thought of how she who lay beside him had locked in her heart for so many years that image of her lover's eyes when he had told her that he did not wish to live.

Generous tears filled Gabriel's eyes. He had never felt like that himself towards any woman but he knew that such a feeling must be love. The tears gathered more thickly in his eyes and in the partial darkness he imagined he saw the form of a young man standing under a dripping tree. Other forms were near. His soul had approached that region where dwell the vast hosts of the dead. He was conscious of, but could not apprehend, their wayward and flickering existence. His own identity was fading out into a grey impalpable world: the solid world itself which these dead had one time reared and lived in was dissolving and dwindling.

A few light taps upon the pane made him turn to the window. It had begun to snow again. He watched sleepily the flakes, silver and dark, falling obliquely against the lamplight. The time had come for him to set out on his journey westward. Yes, the newspapers were right: snow was general all over Ireland. It was falling on every part of the dark central plain, on the treeless hills, falling softly upon the Bog of Allen and, farther westward, softly falling into the dark mutinous Shannon waves.[46] It was falling, too, upon every part of the lonely churchyard on the hill where Michael Furey lay buried. It lay thickly drifted on the crooked crosses and head-stones, on the spears of the little gate, on the barren thorns. His soul swooned slowly as he heard the snow falling faintly through the universe and faintly falling, like the descent of their last end, upon all the living and the dead.

T. S. Eliot
1888–1965

The Love Song of J. Alfred Prufrock

S'io credessi che mia risposta fosse
a persona che mai tornasse al mondo,
questa fiamma staria senza più scosse.
Ma per ciò che giammai di questo fondo
non tornò vivo alcun, s'i'odo il vero,
senza tema d'infamia ti rispondo.[1]

Let us go then, you and I,
When the evening is spread out against the sky
Like a patient etherised upon a table;
Let us go, through certain half-deserted streets,
5   The muttering retreats
Of restless nights in one-night cheap hotels
And sawdust restaurants with oyster-shells:
Streets that follow like a tedious argument

46. Where Ireland's longest river, the Shannon, empties into the sea.
1. From Dante's *Inferno* (27.61–66). Dante asks one of the damned souls for its name, and it replies: "If I thought my answer were for one who could return to the world, I would not reply, but as none ever did return alive from this depth, without fear of infamy I answer thee."

Of insidious intent
10   To lead you to an overwhelming question . . .
Oh, do not ask, "What is it?"
Let us go and make our visit.

In the room the women come and go
Talking of Michelangelo.

15   The yellow fog that rubs its back upon the window-panes,
The yellow smoke that rubs its muzzle on the window-panes,
Licked its tongue into the corners of the evening,
Lingered upon the pools that stand in drains,
Let fall upon its back the soot that falls from chimneys,
20   Slipped by the terrace, made a sudden leap,
And seeing that it was a soft October night,
Curled once about the house, and fell asleep.

And indeed there will be time
For the yellow smoke that slides along the street
25   Rubbing its back upon the window-panes;
There will be time, there will be time
To prepare a face to meet the faces that you meet;
There will be time to murder and create,
And time for all the works and days of hands
30   That lift and drop a question on your plate;
Time for you and time for me,
And time yet for a hundred indecisions,
And for a hundred visions and revisions,
Before the taking of a toast and tea.

35   In the room the women come and go
Talking of Michelangelo.

And indeed there will be time
To wonder, "Do I dare?" and, "Do I dare?"
Time to turn back and descend the stair,
40   With a bald spot in the middle of my hair—
(They will say: "How his hair is growing thin!")
My morning coat, my collar mounting firmly to the chin,
My necktie rich and modest, but asserted by a simple pin—
(They will say: "But how his arms and legs are thin!")
45   Do I dare
Disturb the universe?
In a minute there is time
For decisions and revisions which a minute will reverse.

For I have known them all already, known them all—
50   Have known the evenings, mornings, afternoons,
I have measured out my life with coffee spoons;
I know the voices dying with a dying fall
Beneath the music from a farther room.
    So how should I presume?

55   And I have known the eyes already, known them all—
      The eyes that fix you in a formulated phrase,
      And when I am formulated, sprawling on a pin,
      When I am pinned and wriggling on the wall,
      Then how should I begin
60   To spit out all the butt-ends of my days and ways?
          And how should I presume?

      And I have known the arms already, known them all—
      Arms that are braceleted and white and bare
      (But in the lamplight, downed with light brown hair!)
65   Is it perfume from a dress
      That makes me so digress?
      Arms that lie along a table, or wrap about a shawl.
          And should I then presume?
          And how should I begin?
                    . . .
70   Shall I say, I have gone at dusk through narrow streets
      And watched the smoke that rises from the pipes
      Of lonely men in shirt-sleeves, leaning out of windows? . . .

      I should have been a pair of ragged claws
      Scuttling across the floors of silent seas.
                    . . .
75   And the afternoon, the evening, sleeps so peacefully!
      Smoothed by long fingers,
      Asleep . . . tired . . . or it malingers,
      Stretched on the floor, here beside you and me.
      Should I, after tea and cakes and ices,
80   Have the strength to force the moment to its crisis?
      But though I have wept and fasted, wept and prayed,
      Though I have seen my head (grown slightly bald) brought
          in upon a platter,[2]
      I am no prophet—and here's no great matter;
      I have seen the moment of my greatness flicker,
85   And I have seen the eternal Footman hold my coat, and snicker,
      And in short, I was afraid.

      And would it have been worth it, after all,
      After the cups, the marmalade, the tea,
      Among the porcelain, among some talk of you and me,
90   Would it have been worth while,
      To have bitten off the matter with a smile,
      To have squeezed the universe into a ball
      To roll it towards some overwhelming question,
      To say: "I am Lazarus, come from the dead,
95   Come back to tell you all, I shall tell you all"[3]—
      If one, settling a pillow by her head,

---

2. Cf. Matthew 14. John the Baptist was beheaded by
Herod and his head was brought to his wife, Herodias, on
a platter.

3. Cf. John 11. Jesus raised Lazarus from the grave after
he had been dead four days.

Should say: "That is not what I meant at all.
That is not it, at all."

And would it have been worth it, after all,
100   Would it have been worth while,
After the sunsets and the dooryards and the sprinkled streets,
After the novels, after the teacups, after the skirts that trail
    along the floor—
And this, and so much more?—
It is impossible to say just what I mean!
105   But as if a magic lantern[4] threw the nerves in patterns on a
    screen:
Would it have been worth while
If one, settling a pillow or throwing off a shawl,
And turning toward the window, should say:
    "That is not it at all,
110   That is not what I meant, at all."
        . . .

No! I am not Prince Hamlet, nor was meant to be;
Am an attendant lord, one that will do
To swell a progress, start a scene or two,
Advise the prince; no doubt, an easy tool,
115   Deferential, glad to be of use,
Politic, cautious, and meticulous;
Full of high sentence, but a bit obtuse;
At times, indeed, almost ridiculous—
Almost, at times, the Fool.

120   I grow old . . . I grow old . . .
I shall wear the bottoms of my trousers rolled.

Shall I part my hair behind? Do I dare to eat a peach?
I shall wear white flannel trousers, and walk upon the beach.
I have heard the mermaids singing, each to each.

125   I do not think that they will sing to me.

I have seen them riding seaward on the waves
Combing the white hair of the waves blown back
When the wind blows the water white and black.

We have lingered in the chambers of the sea
130   By sea-girls wreathed with seaweed red and brown
Till human voices wake us, and we drown.

---

4. A device that employs a candle to project images, rather like a slide projector.

Virginia Woolf
1882–1941

from A Room of One's Own

from Chapter 3

It would have been impossible, completely and entirely, for any woman to have written the plays of Shakespeare in the age of Shakespeare. Let me imagine, since facts are so hard to come by, what would have happened had Shakespeare had a wonderfully gifted sister, called Judith, let us say. Shakespeare himself went, very probably—his mother was an heiress—to the grammar school, where he may have learnt Latin—Ovid, Virgil, and Horace—and the elements of grammar and logic. He was, it is well known, a wild boy who poached rabbits, perhaps shot a deer, and had, rather sooner than he should have done, to marry a woman in the neighbourhood, who bore him a child rather quicker than was right. That escapade sent him to seek his fortune in London. He had, it seemed, a taste for the theatre; he began by holding horses at the stage door. Very soon he got work in the theatre, became a successful actor, and lived at the hub of the universe, meeting everybody, knowing everybody, practising his art on the boards, exercising his wits in the streets, and even getting access to the palace of the queen. Meanwhile his extraordinarily gifted sister, let us suppose, remained at home. She was as adventurous, as imaginative, as agog to see the world as he was. But she was not sent to school. She had no chance of learning grammar and logic, let alone of reading Horace and Virgil. She picked up a book now and then, one of her brother's perhaps, and read a few pages. But then her parents came in and told her to mend the stockings or mind the stew and not moon about with books and papers. They would have spoken sharply but kindly, for they were substantial people who knew the conditions of life for a woman and loved their daughter—indeed, more likely than not she was the apple of her father's eye. Perhaps she scribbled some pages up in an apple loft on the sly, but was careful to hide them or set fire to them. Soon, however, before she was out of her teens, she was to be betrothed to the son of a neighbouring wool-stapler. She cried out that marriage was hateful to her, and for that she was severely beaten by her father. Then he ceased to scold her. He begged her instead not to hurt him, not to shame him in this matter of her marriage. He would give her a chain of beads or a fine petticoat, he said; and there were tears in his eyes. How could she disobey him? How could she break his heart? The force of her own gift alone drove her to it. She made up a small parcel of her belongings, let herself down by a rope one summer's night and took the road to London. She was not seventeen. The birds that sang in the hedge were not more musical than she was. She had the quickest fancy, a gift like her brother's, for the tune of words. Like him, she had a taste for the theatre. She stood at the stage door; she wanted to act, she said. Men laughed in her face. The manager—a fat, loose-lipped man—guffawed. He bellowed something about poodles dancing and women acting—no woman, he said, could possibly be an actress. He hinted—you can imagine what. She could get no training in her craft. Could she even seek her dinner in a tavern or roam the streets at midnight? Yet her genius was for fiction and lusted to feed abundantly upon the lives of men and women and the study of their ways. At last—for she was very young, oddly like Shakespeare the poet in her face, with the same grey eyes and rounded brows—at last Nick Greene the actor-manager took pity on her; she found herself with child by that gentleman and so—who shall measure the heat and violence of the poet's heart when caught and tangled in a woman's body?—killed herself one winter's night and lies buried at some cross-roads where the omnibuses now stop outside the Elephant and Castle.[1]

That, more or less, is how the story would run, I think, if a woman in Shakespeare's day had had Shakespeare's genius. But for my part, I agree with the deceased bishop, if such he was—it is unthinkable that any woman in Shakespeare's day should have had Shakespeare's genius. For genius like Shakespeare's is not born among labouring, uneducated, servile people. It was not born in England among the Saxons and the Britons. It is not born today among the working classes. How, then, could it have been born among women whose work began, according to Professor Trevelyan,[2] almost before they were out of the nursery, who were forced to it by their parents and held to it by all the power of law and custom? Yet genius of a sort must have existed among women as it must have existed among the working classes. Now and again an Emily Brontë or a Robert Burns blazes out and proves its presence. But certainly it never got itself on to paper. When, however, one reads of a witch being ducked, of a woman possessed by devils, of a wise woman selling herbs, or even of a very remarkable man who had a mother, then I think we are on the track of a lost novelist, a suppressed poet, of some mute and inglorious Jane Austen, some Emily Brontë who dashed her brains out on the moor or mopped and mowed about the highways crazed with the torture that her gift had put her to. Indeed, I would venture to guess that Anon, who wrote so many poems without signing them, was often a woman. It was a woman Edward Fitzgerald,[3] I think, suggested who made the ballads and the folk-songs, crooning them to her children, beguiling her spinning with them, or the length of the winter's night.

This may be true or it may be false—who can say?—but what is true in it, so it seemed to me, reviewing the story of Shakespeare's sister as I had made it, is that any woman born with a great gift in the sixteenth century would certainly have gone crazed, shot herself, or ended her days in some lonely cottage outside the village, half witch, half wizard, feared and mocked at. For it needs little skill in psychology to be sure that a highly gifted girl who had tried to use her gift for poetry would have been so thwarted and hindered by other people, so tortured and pulled asunder by her own contrary instincts, that she must have lost her health and sanity to a certainty. No girl could have walked to London and stood at a stage door and forced her way into the presence of actor-managers without doing herself a violence and suffering an anguish which may have been irrational—for chastity may be a fetish invented by certain societies for unknown reasons—but were none the less inevitable. Chastity had then, it has even now, a religious importance in a woman's life, and has so wrapped itself round with nerves and instincts that to cut it free and bring it to the light of day demands courage of the rarest. To have lived a free life in London in the sixteenth century would have meant for a woman who was poet and playwright a nervous stress and dilemma which might well have killed her. Had she survived,

---

1. A tavern on the outskirts of South London.   3. Poet and translator (1809–1883).
2. George Trevelyan (1876–1962), historian.

whatever she had written would have been twisted and deformed, issuing from a strained and morbid imagination. And undoubtedly, I thought, looking at the shelf where there are no plays by women, her work would have gone unsigned. That refuge she would have sought certainly. It was the relic of the sense of chastity that dictated anonymity to women even so late as the nineteenth century. Currer Bell, George Eliot, George Sand,[4] all the victims of inner strife as their writings prove, sought ineffectively to veil themselves by using the name of a man. Thus they did homage to the convention, which if not implanted by the other sex was liberally encouraged by them (the chief glory of a woman is not to be talked of, said Pericles, himself a much-talked-of man), that publicity in women is detestable.[5] Anonymity runs in their blood. The desire to be veiled still possesses them. They are not even now as concerned about the health of their fame as men are, and, speaking generally, will pass a tombstone or a signpost without feeling an irresistible desire to cut their names on it, as Alf, Bert or Chas. must do in obedience to their instinct, which murmurs if it sees a fine woman go by, or even a dog, Ce chien est à moi [that dog is mine]. And, of course, it may not be a dog, I thought, remembering Parliament Square, the Sieges Allee[6] and other avenues; it may be a piece of land or a man with curly black hair. It is one of the great advantages of being a woman that one can pass even a very fine negress without wishing to make an Englishwoman of her.

That woman, then, who was born with a gift of poetry in the sixteenth century, was an unhappy woman, a woman at strife against herself. All the conditions of her life, all her own instincts, were hostile to the state of mind which is needed to set free whatever is in the brain. * * * There would always have been that assertion—you cannot do this, you are incapable of doing that—to protest against, to overcome. Probably for a novelist this germ is no longer of much effect; for there have been women novelists of merit. But for painters it must still have some sting in it; and for musicians, I imagine, is even now active and poisonous in the extreme. The woman composer stands where the actress stood in the time of Shakespeare. Nick Greene, I thought, remembering the story I had made about Shakespeare's sister, said that a woman acting put him in mind of a dog dancing. Johnson repeated the phrase two hundred years later of women preaching.[7] And here, I said, opening a book about music, we have the very words used again in this year of grace, 1928, of women who try to write music. "Of Mlle. Germaine Tailleferre one can only repeat Dr. Johnson's dictum concerning a woman preacher, transposed into terms of music. 'Sir, a woman's composing is like a dog's walking on his hind legs. It is not done well, but you are surprised to find it done at all.'"[8] So accurately does history repeat itself.

Thus, I concluded, shutting Mr Oscar Browning's life and pushing away the rest, it is fairly evident that even in the nineteenth century a woman was not encouraged to be an artist. On the contrary, she was snubbed, slapped, lectured and exhorted. Her mind must have been strained and her vitality lowered by the need of opposing this, of disproving that. For here again we come within range of that very interesting and obscure masculine complex which has had so much influence upon the woman's

---

4. Currer Bell, pen name of Charlotte Brontë; George Eliot, pen name of Mary Ann Evans; George Sand, pen name of Amandine Aurore Lucille Dupin (1804–1876).
5. The Athenian statesman Pericles was reported by the historian Thucydides to have said, "That woman is most praiseworthy whose name is least bandied about on men's lips, whether for praise or dispraise."

6. Victory Road, a thoroughfare in Berlin.
7. Samuel Johnson (1709–1784), poet and man of letters.
8. *A Survey of Contemporary Music*, Cecil Gray, page 246 [Woolf's note].

movement; that deep-seated desire, not so much that she shall be inferior as that he shall be superior, which plants him wherever one looks, not only in front of the arts, but barring the way to politics too, even when the risk to himself seems infinitesimal and the suppliant humble and devoted. Even Lady Bessborough, I remembered, with all her passion for politics, must humbly bow herself and write to Lord Granville Leveson-Gower:[9] ". . . notwithstanding all my violence in politics and talking so much on that subject, I perfectly agree with you that no woman has any business to meddle with that or any other serious business, farther than giving her opinion (if she is ask'd)." And so she goes on to spend her enthusiasm where it meets with no obstacle whatsoever upon that immensely important subject, Lord Granville's maiden speech in the House of Commons. The spectacle is certainly a strange one, I thought. The history of men's opposition to women's emancipation is more interesting perhaps than the story of that emancipation itself. An amusing book might be made of it if some young student at Girton or Newnham would collect examples and deduce a theory— but she would need thick gloves on her hands, and bars to protect her of solid gold.

But what is amusing now, I recollected, shutting Lady Bessborough, had to be taken in desperate earnest once. Opinions that one now pastes in a book labelled cock-a-doodle-dum and keeps for reading to select audiences on summer nights once drew tears, I can assure you. Among your grandmothers and great-grandmothers there were many that wept their eyes out. Florence Nightingale shrieked aloud in her agony.[10] Moreover, it is all very well for you, who have got yourselves to college and enjoy sitting-rooms—or is it only bed-sitting-rooms?—of your own to say that genius should disregard such opinions; that genius should be above caring what is said of it. Unfortunately, it is precisely the men or women of genius who mind most what is said of them. Remember Keats. Remember the words he had cut on his tombstone. Think of Tennyson; think—but I need hardly multiply instances of the undeniable, if very unfortunate, fact that it is the nature of the artist to mind excessively what is said about him. Literature is strewn with the wreckage of men who have minded beyond reason the opinions of others.

And this susceptibility of theirs is doubly unfortunate, I thought, returning again to my original enquiry into what state of mind is most propitious for creative work, because the mind of an artist, in order to achieve the prodigious effort of freeing whole and entire the work that is in him, must be incandescent, like Shakespeare's mind, I conjectured, looking at the book which lay open at *Antony and Cleopatra*. There must be no obstacle in it, no foreign matter unconsumed.

For though we say that we know nothing about Shakespeare's state of mind, even as we say that, we are saying something about Shakespeare's state of mind. The reason perhaps why we know so little of Shakespeare—compared with Donne or Ben Jonson or Milton—is that his grudges and spites and antipathies are hidden from us. We are not held up by some "revelation" which reminds us of the writer. All desire to protest, to preach, to proclaim an injury, to pay off a score, to make the world the witness of some hardship or grievance was fired out of him and consumed. Therefore his poetry flows from him free and unimpeded. If ever a human being got his work expressed completely, it was Shakespeare. If ever a mind was incandescent, unimpeded, I thought, turning again to the bookcase, it was Shakespeare's mind.

9. Lady Bessborough (1761–1821), correspondent of the British statesman Lord Granville.

10. See *Cassandra*, by Florence Nightingale, printed in *The Cause*, by R. Strachey [Woolf's note].

Katherine Mansfield
1888–1923

The Daughters of the Late Colonel

1

The week after was one of the busiest weeks of their lives. Even when they went to bed it was only their bodies that lay down and rested; their minds went on, thinking things out, talking things over, wondering, deciding, trying to remember where . . .

Constantia lay like a statue, her hands by her sides, her feet just overlapping each other, the sheet up to her chin. She stared at the ceiling.

"Do you think father would mind if we gave his top-hat to the porter?"

"The porter?" snapped Josephine. "Why ever the porter? What a very extraordinary idea!"

"Because," said Constantia slowly, "he must often have to go to funerals. And I noticed at—at the cemetery that he only had a bowler." She paused. "I thought then how very much he'd appreciate a top-hat. We ought to give him a present, too. He was always very nice to father."

"But," cried Josephine, flouncing on her pillow and staring across the dark at Constantia, "father's head!" And suddenly, for one awful moment, she nearly giggled. Not, of course, that she felt in the least like giggling. It must have been habit. Years ago, when they had stayed awake at night talking, their beds had simply heaved. And now the porter's head, disappearing, popped out, like a candle, under father's hat. . . . The giggle mounted, mounted; she clenched her hands; she fought it down; she frowned fiercely at the dark and said "Remember" terribly sternly.

"We can decide to-morrow," she sighed.

Constantia had noticed nothing; she sighed.

"Do you think we ought to have our dressing-gowns dyed as well?"

"Black?" almost shrieked Josephine.

"Well, what else?" said Constantia. "I was thinking—it doesn't seem quite sincere, in a way, to wear black out of doors and when we're fully dressed, and then when we're at home—"

"But nobody sees us," said Josephine. She gave the bedclothes such a twitch that both her feet became uncovered, and she had to creep up the pillows to get them well under again.

"Kate does," said Constantia. "And the postman very well might."

Josephine thought of her dark-red slippers, which matched her dressing-gown, and of Constantia's favourite indefinite green ones which went with hers. Black! Two black dressing-gowns and two pairs of black woolly slippers, creeping off to the bathroom like black cats.

"I don't think it's absolutely necessary," said she.

Silence. Then Constantia said, "We shall have to post the papers with the notice in them to-morrow to catch the Ceylon mail. . . . How many letters have we had up till now?"

"Twenty-three."

Josephine had replied to them all, and twenty-three times when she came to "We miss our dear father so much" she had broken down and had to use her handkerchief, and on some of them even to soak up a very light-blue tear with an edge of blotting-paper. Strange! She couldn't have put it on—but twenty-three times. Even now, though, when she said over to herself sadly. "We miss our dear father so much" she could have cried if she'd wanted to.

"Have you got enough stamps?" came from Constantia.

"Oh, how can I tell?" said Josephine crossly. "What's the good of asking me that now?"

"I was just wondering," said Constantia mildly.

Silence again. There came a little rustle, a scurry, a hop.

"A mouse," said Constantia.

"It can't be a mouse because there aren't any crumbs," said Josephine.

"But it doesn't know there aren't," said Constantia.

A spasm of pity squeezed her heart. Poor little thing! She wished she'd left a tiny piece of biscuit on the dressing-table. It was awful to think of it not finding anything. What would it do?

"I can't think how they manage to live at all," she said slowly.

"Who?" demanded Josephine.

And Constantia said more loudly than she meant to, "Mice."

Josephine was furious. "Oh, what nonsense, Con!" she said. "What have mice got to do with it? You're asleep."

"I don't think I am," said Constantia. She shut her eyes to make sure. She was.

Josephine arched her spine, pulled up her knees, folded her arms so that her fists came under her ears, and pressed her cheek hard against the pillow.

2

Another thing which complicated matters was they had Nurse Andrews staying on with them that week. It was their own fault; they had asked her. It was Josephine's idea. On the morning—well, on the last morning, when the doctor had gone, Josephine had said to Constantia, "Don't you think it would be rather nice if we asked Nurse Andrews to stay on for a week as our guest?"

"Very nice," said Constantia.

"I thought," went on Josephine quickly, "I should just say this afternoon, after I've paid her, 'My sister and I would be very pleased, after all you've done for us, Nurse Andrews, if you would stay on for a week as our guest.' I'd have to put that in about being our guest in case—"

"Oh, but she could hardly expect to be paid!" cried Constantia.

"One never knows," said Josephine sagely.

Nurse Andrews had, of course, jumped at the idea. But it was a bother. It meant they had to have regular sit-down meals at the proper times, whereas if they'd been alone they could just have asked Kate if she wouldn't have minded bringing them a tray wherever they were. And meal-times now that the strain was over were rather a trial.

Nurse Andrews was simply fearful about butter. Really they couldn't help feeling that about butter, at least, she took advantage of their kindness. And she had that maddening habit of asking for just an inch more bread to finish what she had on her plate, and then, at the last mouthful, absent-mindedly—of course it wasn't absent-mindedly—taking another helping. Josephine got very red when this happened, and she fastened her small, beadlike eyes on the tablecloth as if she saw a minute strange insect creeping through the web of it. But Constantia's long, pale face lengthened and set, and she gazed away—away—far over the desert, to where that line of camels unwound like a thread of wool. . . .

"When I was with Lady Tukes," said Nurse Andrews, "she had such a dainty little contrayvance for the buttah. It was a silvah Cupid balanced on the—on the bordah of a glass dish, holding a tayny fork. And when you wanted some buttah you simply pressed his foot and he bent down and speared you a piece. It was quite a gayme."

Josephine could hardly bear that. But "I think those things are very extravagant" was all she said.

"But whey?" asked Nurse Andrews, beaming through her eye-glasses. "No one, surely, would take more buttah than one wanted—would one?"

"Ring, Con," cried Josephine. She couldn't trust herself to reply.

And proud young Kate, the enchanted princess, came in to see what the old tabbies wanted now. She snatched away their plates of mock something or other and slapped down a white, terrified blancmange.

"Jam, please, Kate," said Josephine kindly.

Kate knelt and burst open the sideboard, lifted the lid of the jam-pot, saw it was empty, put it on the table, and stalked off.

"I'm afraid," said Nurse Andrews a moment later, "there isn't any."

"Oh, what a bother!" said Josephine. She bit her lip. "What had we better do?"

Constantia looked dubious. "We can't disturb Kate again," she said softly.

Nurse Andrews waited, smiling at them both. Her eyes wandered, spying at everything behind her eye-glasses. Constantia in despair went back to her camels. Josephine frowned heavily—concentrated. If it hadn't been for this idiotic woman she and Con would, of course, have eaten their blancmange without. Suddenly the idea came.

"I know," she said. "Marmalade. There's some marmalade in the sideboard. Get it, Con."

"I hope," laughed Nurse Andrews, and her laugh was like a spoon tinkling against a medicine-glass—"I hope it's not very bittah marmalayde."

3

But, after all, it was not long now, and then she'd be gone for good. And there was no getting over the fact that she had been very kind to father. She had nursed him day and night at the end. Indeed, both Constantia and Josephine felt privately she had rather overdone the not leaving him at the very last. For when they had gone in to say good-bye Nurse Andrews had sat beside his bed the whole time, holding his wrist and pretending to look at her watch. It couldn't have been necessary. It was so tactless, too. Supposing father had wanted to say something—something private to them. Not that he had. Oh, far from it! He lay there, purple, a dark, angry purple in the face, and never even looked at them when they came in. Then, as they were standing there, wondering what to do, he had suddenly opened one eye. Oh, what a difference it would have made, what a difference to their memory of him, how much easier to tell people about it, if he had only opened both! But no—one eye only. It glared at them a moment and then . . . went out.

4

It had made it very awkward for them when Mr Farolles, of St John's, called the same afternoon.

"The end was quite peaceful, I trust?" were the first words he said as he glided towards them through the dark drawing-room.

"Quite," said Josephine faintly. They both hung their heads. Both of them felt certain that eye wasn't at all a peaceful eye.

"Won't you sit down?" said Josephine.

"Thank you, Miss Pinner," said Mr Farolles gratefully. He folded his coat-tails and began to lower himself into father's armchair, but just as he touched it he almost sprang up and slid into the next chair instead.

He coughed. Josephine clasped her hands; Constantia looked vague.

"I want you to feel, Miss Pinner," said Mr Farolles, "and you, Miss Constantia, that I'm trying to be helpful. I want to be helpful to you both, if you will let me. These are the times," said Mr Farolles, very simply and earnestly, "when God means us to be helpful to one another."

"Thank you very much, Mr Farolles," said Josephine and Constantia.

"Not at all," said Mr Farolles gently. He drew his kid gloves through his fingers and leaned forward. "And if either of you would like a little Communion, either or both of you, here *and* now, you have only to tell me. A little Communion is often very help—a great comfort," he added tenderly.

But the idea of a little Communion terrified them. What! In the drawing-room by themselves—with no—no altar or anything! The piano would be much too high, thought Constantia, and Mr Farolles could not possibly lean over it with the chalice. And Kate would be sure to come bursting in and interrupt them, thought Josephine. And supposing the bell rang in the middle? It might be somebody important—about their mourning. Would they get up reverently and go out, or would they have to wait . . . in torture?

"Perhaps you will send round a note by your good Kate if you would care for it later," said Mr Farolles.

"Oh yes, thank you very much!" they both said.

Mr Farolles got up and took his black straw hat from the round table.

"And about the funeral," he said softly. "I may arrange that—as your dear father's old friend and yours, Miss Pinner—and Miss Constantia?"

Josephine and Constantia got up too.

"I should like it to be quite simple," said Josephine firmly, "and not too expensive. At the same time, I should like—"

"A good one that will last," thought dreamy Constantia, as if Josephine were buying a nightgown. But of course Josephine didn't say that. "One suitable to our father's position." She was very nervous.

"I'll run round to our good friend Mr Knight," said Mr Farolles soothingly. "I will ask him to come and see you. I am sure you will find him very helpful indeed."

5

Well, at any rate, all that part of it was over, though neither of them could possibly believe that father was never coming back. Josephine had had a moment of absolute terror at the cemetery, while the coffin was lowered, to think that she and Constantia had done this thing without asking his permission. What would father say when he found out? For he was bound to find out sooner or later. He always did. "Buried. You two girls had me *buried*!" She heard his stick thumping. Oh, what would they say? What possible excuse could they make? It sounded such an appalling heartless thing to do. Such a wicked advantage to take of a person because he happened to be helpless at the moment. The other people seemed to treat it all as a matter of course. They were strangers; they couldn't be expected to understand that father was the very last person for such a thing to happen to. No, the entire blame for it all would fall on her and Constantia. And the expense, she thought, stepping into the tight-buttoned cab. When she had to show him the bills. What would he say then?

She heard him absolutely roaring, "And do you expect me to pay for this gim-crack excursion of yours?"

"Oh," groaned poor Josephine aloud, "we shouldn't have done it, Con!"

And Constantia, pale as a lemon in all that blackness, said in a frightened whisper, "Done what, Jug?"

"Let them bu-bury father like that," said Josephine, breaking down and crying into her new, queer-smelling mourning handkerchief.

"But what else could we have done?" asked Constantia wonderingly. "We couldn't have kept him, Jug—we couldn't have kept him unburied. At any rate, not in a flat that size."

Josephine blew her nose; the cab was dreadfully stuffy.

"I don't know," she said forlornly. "It is all so dreadful. I feel we ought to have tried to, just for a time at least. To make perfectly sure. One thing's certain"—and her tears sprang out again—"father will never forgive us for this—never!"

6

Father would never forgive them. That was what they felt more than ever when, two mornings later, they went into his room to go through his things. They had discussed it quite calmly. It was even down on Josephine's list of things to be done. *Go through father's things and settle about them.* But that was a very different matter from saying after breakfast:

"Well, are you ready, Con?"

"Yes, Jug—when you are."

"Then I think we'd better get it over."

It was dark in the hall. It had been a rule for years never to disturb father in the morning, whatever happened. And now they were going to open the door without knocking even. . . . Constantia's eyes were enormous at the idea; Josephine felt weak in the knees.

"You—you go first," she gasped, pushing Constantia.

But Constantia said, as she always had said on those occasions, "No, Jug, that's not fair. You're eldest."

Josephine was just going to say—what at other times she wouldn't have owned to for the world—what she kept for her very last weapon, "But you're tallest," when they noticed that the kitchen door was open, and there stood Kate. . . .

"Very stiff," said Josephine, grasping the door-handle and doing her best to turn it. As if anything ever deceived Kate!

It couldn't be helped. That girl was . . . Then the door was shut behind them, but—but they weren't in father's room at all. They might have suddenly walked through the wall by mistake into a different flat altogether. Was the door just behind them? They were too frightened to look. Josephine knew that if it was it was holding itself tight shut; Constantia felt that, like the doors in dreams, it hadn't any handle at all. It was the coldness which made it so awful. Or the whiteness—which? Everything was covered. The blinds were down, a cloth hung over the mirror, a sheet hid the bed; a huge fan of white paper filled the fireplace. Constantia timidly put out her hand; she almost expected a snowflake to fall. Josephine felt a queer tingling in her nose, as if her nose was freezing. Then a cab klop-klopped over the cobbles below, and the quiet seemed to shake into little pieces.

"I had better pull up a blind," said Josephine bravely.

"Yes, it might be a good idea," whispered Constantia.

They only gave the blind a touch, but it flew up and the cord flew after, rolling round the blindstick, and the little tassel tapped as if trying to get free. That was too much for Constantia.

"Don't you think—don't you think we might put it off for another day?" she whispered.

"Why?" snapped Josephine, feeling, as usual, much better now that she knew for certain that Constantia was terrified. "It's got to be done. But I do wish you wouldn't whisper, Con."

"I didn't know I was whispering," whispered Constantia.

"And why do you keep on staring at the bed?" said Josephine, raising her voice almost defiantly. "There's nothing *on* the bed."

"Oh, Jug, don't say so!" said poor Connie. "At any rate, not so loudly."

Josephine felt herself that she had gone too far. She took a wide swerve over to the chest of drawers, put out her hand, but quickly drew it back again.

"Connie!" she gasped, and she wheeled round and leaned with her back against the chest of drawers.

"Oh, Jug—what?"

Josephine could only glare. She had the most extraordinary feeling that she had just escaped something simply awful. But how could she explain to Constantia that father was in the chest of drawers? He was in the top drawer with his handkerchiefs and neckties, or in the next with his shirts and pyjamas, or in the lowest of all with his suits. He was watching there, hidden away—just behind the door-handle—ready to spring.

She pulled a funny old-fashioned face at Constantia, just as she used to in the old days when she was going to cry.

"I can't open," she nearly wailed.

"No, don't, Jug," whispered Constantia earnestly. "It's much better not to. Don't let's open anything. At any rate, not for a long time."

"But—but it seems so weak," said Josephine, breaking down.

"But why not be weak for once, Jug?" argued Constantia, whispering quite fierce-ly. "If it is weak." And her pale stare flew from the locked writing-table—so safe—to the huge glittering wardrobe, and she began to breathe in a queer, panting way. "Why shouldn't we be weak for once in our lives, Jug? It's quite excusable. Let's be weak—be weak, Jug. It's much nicer to be weak than to be strong."

And then she did one of those amazingly bold things that she'd done about twice before in their lives; she marched over to the wardrobe, turned the key, and took it out of the lock. Took it out of the lock and held it up to Josephine, showing Josephine by her extraordinary smile that she knew what she'd done, she'd risked deliberately father being in there among his overcoats.

If the huge wardrobe had lurched forward, had crashed down on Constantia, Josephine wouldn't have been surprised. On the contrary, she would have thought it the only suitable thing to happen. But nothing happened. Only the room seemed quieter than ever, and bigger flakes of cold air fell on Josephine's shoulders and knees. She began to shiver.

"Come, Jug," said Constantia, still with that awful callous smile, and Josephine followed just as she had that last time, when Constantia had pushed Benny into the round pond.

7

But the strain told on them when they were back in the dining-room. They sat down, very shaky, and looked at each other.

"I don't feel I can settle to anything," said Josephine, "until I've had something. Do you think we could ask Kate for two cups of hot water?"

"I really don't see why we shouldn't," said Constantia carefully. She was quite normal again. "I won't ring. I'll go to the kitchen door and ask her."

"Yes, do," said Josephine, sinking down into a chair. "Tell her, just two cups, Con, nothing else—on a tray."

"She needn't even put the jug on, need she?" said Constantia, as though Kate might very well complain if the jug had been there.

"Oh no, certainly not! The jug's not at all necessary. She can pour it direct out of the kettle," cried Josephine, feeling that would be a labour-saving indeed.

Their cold lips quivered at the greenish brims. Josephine curved her small red hands round the cup; Constantia sat up and blew on the wavy stream, making it flutter from one side to the other.

"Speaking of Benny," said Josephine.

And though Benny hadn't been mentioned Constantia immediately looked as though he had.

"He'll expect us to send him something of father's, of course. But it's so difficult to know what to send to Ceylon."

"You mean things get unstuck so on the voyage," murmured Constantia.

"No, lost," said Josephine sharply. "You know there's no post. Only runners."

Both paused to watch a black man in white linen drawers running through the pale fields for dear life, with a large brown-paper parcel in his hands. Josephine's black man was tiny; he scurried along glistening like an ant. But there was something blind and tireless about Constantia's tall, thin fellow, which made him, she decided, a very unpleasant person indeed. . . . On the veranda, dressed all in white and wearing a cork helmet, stood Benny. His right hand shook up and down, as father's did when he was impatient. And behind him, not in the least interested, sat Hilda, the unknown sister-in-law. She swung in a cane rocker and flicked over the leaves of the *Tatler*.

"I think his watch would be the most suitable present," said Josephine.

Constantia looked up; she seemed surprised.

"Oh, would you trust a gold watch to a native?"

"But of course I'd disguise it," said Josephine. "No one would know it was a watch." She liked the idea of having to make a parcel such a curious shape that no one could possibly guess what it was. She even thought for a moment of hiding the watch in a narrow cardboard corset-box that she'd kept by her for a long time, waiting for it to come in for something. It was such beautiful firm cardboard. But, no, it wouldn't be appropriate for this occasion. It had lettering on it: *Medium Women's 28. Extra Firm Busks*. It would be almost too much of a surprise for Benny to open that and find father's watch inside.

"And of course it isn't as though it would be going—ticking, I mean," said Constantia, who was still thinking of the native love of jewellery. "At least," she added, "it would be very strange if after all that time it was."

8

Josephine made no reply. She had flown off on one of her tangents. She had suddenly thought of Cyril. Wasn't it more usual for the only grandson to have the watch? And then dear Cyril was so appreciative, and a gold watch meant so much to a young man. Benny, in all probability, had quite got out of the habit of watches; men so seldom wore waistcoats in those hot climates. Whereas Cyril in London wore them from year's end to year's end. And it would be so nice for her and Constantia, when he came to tea, to know it was there. "I see you've got on grandfather's watch, Cyril." It would be somehow so satisfactory.

Dear boy! What a blow his sweet, sympathetic little note had been! Of course they quite understood; but it was most unfortunate.

"It would have been such a point, having him," said Josephine.

"And he would have enjoyed it so," said Constantia, not thinking what she was saying.

However, as soon as he got back he was coming to tea with his aunties. Cyril to tea was one of their rare treats.

"Now, Cyril, you mustn't be frightened of our cakes. Your Auntie Con and I bought them at Buszard's this morning. We know what a man's appetite is. So don't be ashamed of making a good tea."

Josephine cut recklessly into the rich dark cake that stood for her winter gloves or the soling and heeling of Constantia's only respectable shoes. But Cyril was most unmanlike in appetite.

"I say, Aunt Josephine, I simply can't. I've only just had lunch, you know."

"Oh, Cyril, that can't be true! It's after four," cried Josephine. Constantia sat with her knife poised over the chocolate-roll.

"It is, all the same," said Cyril. "I had to meet a man at Victoria, and he kept me hanging about till . . . there was only time to get lunch and to come on here. And he gave me—phew"—Cyril put his hand to his forehead—"a terrific blow-out," he said.

It was disappointing—to-day of all days. But still he couldn't be expected to know.

"But you'll have a meringue, won't you, Cyril?" said Aunt Josephine. "These meringues were bought specially for you. Your dear father was so fond of them. We were sure you are, too."

"I *am*, Aunt Josephine," cried Cyril ardently. "Do you mind if I take half to begin with?"

"Not at all, dear boy; but we mustn't let you off with that."

"Is your dear father still so fond of meringues?" asked Auntie Con gently. She winced faintly as she broke through the shell of hers.

"Well, I don't quite know, Auntie Con," said Cyril breezily. At that they both looked up.

"Don't know?" almost snapped Josephine. "Don't know a thing like that about your own father, Cyril?"

"Surely," said Auntie Con softly.

Cyril tried to laugh it off. "Oh, well," he said, "it's such a long time since—" He faltered. He stopped. Their faces were too much for him.

"Even *so*," said Josephine.

And Auntie Con looked.

Cyril put down his teacup. "Wait a bit," he cried. "Wait a bit, Aunt Josephine. What am I thinking of?"

He looked up. They were beginning to brighten. Cyril slapped his knee.

"Of course," he said, "it was meringues. How could I have forgotten? Yes, Aunt Josephine, you're perfectly right. Father's most frightfully keen on meringues."

They didn't only beam. Aunt Josephine went scarlet with pleasure; Auntie Con gave a deep, deep sigh.

"And now, Cyril, you must come and see father," said Josephine. "He knows you were coming to-day."

"Right," said Cyril, very firmly and heartily. He got up from his chair; suddenly he glanced at the clock.

"I say, Auntie Con, isn't your clock a bit slow? I've got to meet a man at—at Paddington just after five. I'm afraid I shan't be able to stay very long with grandfather."

"Oh, he won't expect you to stay *very* long!" said Aunt Josephine.

Constantia was still gazing at the clock. She couldn't make up her mind if it was fast or slow. It was one or the other, she felt almost certain of that. At any rate, it had been.

Cyril still lingered. "Aren't you coming along, Auntie Con?"

"Of course," said Josephine, "we shall all go. Come on, Con."

9

They knocked at the door, and Cyril followed his aunts into grandfather's hot, sweetish room.

"Come on," said Grandfather Pinner. "Don't hang about. What is it? What've you been up to?"

He was sitting in front of a roaring fire, clasping his stick. He had a thick rug over his knees. On his lap there lay a beautiful pale yellow silk handkerchief.

"It's Cyril, father," said Josephine shyly. And she took Cyril's hand and led him forward.

"Good afternoon, grandfather," said Cyril, trying to take his hand out of Aunt Josephine's. Grandfather Pinner shot his eyes at Cyril in the way he was famous for. Where was Auntie Con? She stood on the other side of Aunt Josephine; her long arms hung down in front of her; her hands were clasped. She never took her eyes off grandfather.

"Well," said Grandfather Pinner, beginning to thump, "what have you got to tell me?"

What had he, what had he got to tell him? Cyril felt himself smiling like a perfect imbecile. The room was stifling, too.

But Aunt Josephine came to his rescue. She cried brightly, "Cyril says his father is still very fond of meringues, father dear."

"Eh?" said Grandfather Pinner, curving his hand like a purple meringue-shell over one ear.

Josephine repeated, "Cyril says his father is still very fond of meringues."

"Can't hear," said old Colonel Pinner. And he waved Josephine away with his stick, then pointed with his stick to Cyril. "Tell me what she's trying to say," he said.

(My God!) "Must I?" said Cyril, blushing and staring at Aunt Josephine.

"Do, dear," she smiled. "It will please him so much."

"Come on, out with it!" cried Colonel Pinner testily, beginning to thump again.

And Cyril leaned forward and yelled, "Father's still very fond of meringues."

At that Grandfather Pinner jumped as though he had been shot.

"Don't shout!" he cried. "What's the matter with the boy? *Meringues*! What about 'em?"

"Oh, Aunt Josephine, must we go on?" groaned Cyril desperately.

"It's quite all right, dear boy," said Aunt Josephine, as though he and she were at the dentist's together. "He'll understand in a minute." And she whispered to Cyril, "He's getting a bit deaf, you know." Then she leaned forward and really bawled at Grandfather Pinner, "Cyril only wanted to tell you, father dear, that *his* father is still very fond of meringues."

Colonel Pinner heard that time, heard and brooded, looking Cyril up and down.

"What an esstrordinary thing!" said old Grandfather Pinner. "What an esstrordinary thing to come all this way here to tell me!"

And Cyril felt it *was*.

"Yes, I shall send Cyril the watch," said Josephine.

"That would be very nice," said Constantia. "I seem to remember last time he came there was some little trouble about the time."

10

They were interrupted by Kate bursting through the door in her usual fashion, as though she had discovered some secret panel in the wall.

"Fried or boiled?" asked the bold voice.

Fried or boiled? Josephine and Constantia were quite bewildered for the moment. They could hardly take it in.

"Fried or boiled what, Kate?" asked Josephine, trying to begin to concentrate. Kate gave a loud sniff. "Fish."

"Well, why didn't you say so immediately?" Josephine reproached her gently. "How could you expect us to understand, Kate? There are a great many things in this world, you know, which are fried or boiled." And after such a display of courage she said quite brightly to Constantia, "Which do you prefer, Con?"

"I think it might be nice to have it fried," said Constantia. "On the other hand, of course boiled fish is very nice. I think I prefer both equally well . . . Unless you . . . In that case—"

"I shall fry it," said Kate, and she bounced back, leaving their door open and slamming the door of her kitchen.

Josephine gazed at Constantia; she raised her pale eyebrows until they rippled away into her pale hair. She got up. She said in a very lofty, imposing way, "Do you mind following me into the drawing-room, Constantia? I've something of great importance to discuss with you."

For it was always to the drawing-room they retired when they wanted to talk over Kate.

Josephine closed the door meaningly. "Sit down, Constantia," she said, still very grand. She might have been receiving Constantia for the first time. And Con looked round vaguely for a chair, as though she felt indeed quite a stranger.

"Now the question is," said Josephine, bending forward, "whether we shall keep her or not."

"That is the question," agreed Constantia.

"And this time," said Josephine firmly, "we must come to a definite decision."

Constantia looked for a moment as though she might begin going over all the other times, but she pulled herself together and said, "Yes, Jug."

"You see, Con," explained Josephine, "everything is so changed now." Constantia looked up quickly. "I mean," went on Josephine, "we're not dependent on Kate as we were." And she blushed faintly. "There's not father to cook for."

"That is perfectly true," agreed Constantia. "Father certainly doesn't want any cooking now, whatever else—

"Josephine broke in sharply. "You're not sleepy, are you, Con?"

"Sleepy, Jug?" Constantia was wide-eyed.

"Well, concentrate more," said Josephine sharply, and she returned to the subject. "What it comes to is, if we did"—and this she barely breathed, glancing at the door—"give Kate notice"—she raised her voice again—"we could manage our own food."

"Why not?" cried Constantia. She couldn't help smiling. The idea was so exciting. She clasped her hands. What should we live on, Jug?"

"Oh, eggs in various forms!" said Jug, lofty again. "And, besides, there are all the cooked foods."

"But I've always heard," said Constantia, "they are considered so very expensive."

"Not if one buys them in moderation," said Josephine. But she tore herself away from this fascinating bypath and dragged Constantia after her.

"What we've got to decide now, however, is whether we really do trust Kate or not."

Constantia leaned back. Her flat little laugh flew from her lips.

"Isn't it curious, Jug," said she, "that just on this one subject I've never been able to quite make up my mind?"

11

She never had. The whole difficulty was to prove anything. How did one prove things, how could one? Suppose Kate had stood in front of her and deliberately made a face. Mightn't she very well have been in pain? Wasn't it impossible, at any rate, to ask Kate if she was making a face at her? If Kate answered "No"—and of course she would say "No"—what a position! How undignified! Then again Constantia suspected, she was almost certain that Kate went to her chest of drawers when she and Josephine were out, not to take things but to spy. Many times she had come back to find her amethyst cross in the most unlikely places, under her lace ties or on top of her evening Bertha. More than once she had laid a trap for Kate. She had arranged things in a special order and then called Josephine to witness.

"You see, Jug?"

"Quite, Con."

"Now we shall be able to tell."

But, oh dear, when she did go to look, she was as far off from a proof as ever! If anything was displaced, it might so very well have happened as she closed the drawer; a jolt might have done it so easily.

"You come, Jug, and decide. I really can't. It's too difficult."

But after a pause and a long glare Josephine would sigh, "Now you've put the doubt into my mind, Con, I'm sure I can't tell myself."

"Well, we can't postpone it again," said Josephine. "If we postpone it this time—"

12

But at that moment in the street below a barrel-organ struck up. Josephine and Constantia sprang to their feet together.

"Run, Con," said Josephine. "Run quickly. There's sixpence on the—"

Then they remembered. It didn't matter. They would never have to stop the organ-grinder again. Never again would she and Constantia be told to make that monkey take his noise somewhere else. Never would sound that loud, strange bellow when father thought they were not hurrying enough. The organ-grinder might play there all day and the stick would not thump.

> It never will thump again,
> It never will thump again,

played the barrel-organ.

What was Constantia thinking? She had such a strange smile; she looked different. She couldn't be going to cry.

"Jug, Jug," said Constantia softly, pressing her hands together. "Do you know what day it is? It's Saturday. It's a week to-day, a whole week."

> A week since father died,
> A week since father died,

cried the barrel-organ. And Josephine, too, forgot to be practical and sensible; she smiled faintly, strangely. On the Indian carpet there fell a square of sunlight, pale red; it came and went and came—and stayed, deepened—until it shone almost golden.

"The sun's out," said Josephine, as though it really mattered.

A perfect fountain of bubbling notes shook from the barrel-organ, round, bright notes, carelessly scattered.

Constantia lifted her big, cold hands as if to catch them, and then her hands fell again. She walked over to the mantelpiece to her favourite Buddha. And the stone and gilt image, whose smile always gave her such a queer feeling, almost a pain and yet a pleasant pain, seemed to-day to be more than smiling. He knew something; he had a secret. "I know something that you don't know," said her Buddha. Oh, what was it, what could it be? And yet she had always felt there was . . . something.

The sunlight pressed through the windows, thieved its way in, flashed its light over the furniture and the photographs. Josephine watched it. When it came to mother's photograph, the enlargement over the piano, it lingered as though puzzled to find so little remained of mother, except the earrings shaped like tiny pagodas and a black feather boa. Why did the photographs of dead people always fade so? wondered Josephine. As soon as a person was dead their photograph died too. But, of course, this one of mother was very old. It was thirty-five years old. Josephine remembered standing on a chair and pointing out that feather boa to Constantia and telling her that it was a snake that had killed their mother in Ceylon. . . . Would everything have been different if mother hadn't died? She didn't see why. Aunt Florence had lived with them until they had left school, and they had moved three times and had their yearly holiday and . . . and there'd been changes of servants, of course.

Some little sparrows, young sparrows they sounded, chirped on the window-ledge. *Yeep-eyeep-yeep.* But Josephine felt they were not sparrows, not on the window-ledge. It was inside her, that queer little crying noise. *Yeep-eyeep-yeep.* Ah, what was it crying, so weak and forlorn?

If mother had lived, might they have married? But there had been nobody for them to marry. There had been father's Anglo-Indian friends before he quarreled with them. But after that she and Constantia never met a single man except clergymen. How did one meet men? Or even if they'd met them, how could they have got to know men well enough to be more than strangers? One read of people having adventures, being followed, and so on. But nobody had ever followed Constantia and her. Oh yes, there had been one year at Eastbourne a mysterious man at their boarding-house who had put a note on the jug of hot water outside their bedroom door! But by the time Connie had found it the steam had made the writing too faint to read; they couldn't even make out to which of them it was addressed. And he had left next day. And that was all. The rest had been looking after father, and at the same time keeping out of father's way. But now? But now? The thieving sun touched Josephine gently. She lifted her face. She was drawn over to the window by gentle beams. . . .

Until the barrel-organ stopped playing Constantia stayed before the Buddha, wondering, but not as usual, not vaguely. This time her wonder was like longing. She remembered the times she had come in here, crept out of bed in her nightgown when the moon was full, and lain on the floor with her arms outstretched, as though she was crucified. Why? The big, pale moon had made her do it. The horrible dancing figures on the carved screen had leered at her and she hadn't minded. She remembered too how, whenever they were at the seaside, she had gone off by herself and got as close to the sea as she could, and sung something, something she had made up, while she gazed all over that restless water. There had been this other life, running out, bringing things home in bags, getting things on approval, discussing them with Jug, and taking them back to get more things on approval, and arranging father's trays and trying not to annoy father. But it all seemed to have happened in a kind of tunnel. It wasn't real. It was only when she came out of the tunnel into the moonlight or by the sea or into a thunderstorm that she really felt herself. What did it mean? What was it she was always wanting? What did it all lead to? Now? Now?

She turned away from the Buddha with one of her vague gestures. She went over to where Josephine was standing. She wanted to say something to Josephine, something frightfully important, about—about the future and what . . .

"Don't you think perhaps—" she began.

But Josephine interrupted her. "I was wondering if now—" she murmured. They stopped; they waited for each other.

"Go on, Con," said Josephine.

"No, no, Jug; after you," said Constantia.

"No, say what you were going to say. You began," said Josephine.

"I . . . I'd rather hear what you were going to say first," said Constantia.

"Don't be absurd, Con."

"Really, Jug."

"Connie!"

"Oh, Jug!"

A pause. Then Constantia said faintly, "I can't say what I was going to say, Jug, because I've forgotten what it was . . . that I was going to say."

Josephine was silent for a moment. She stared at a big cloud where the sun had been. Then she replied shortly, "I've forgotten too."

D. H. Lawrence
1885–1930

Odour of Chrysanthemums
1

The small locomotive engine Number 4, came clanking, stumbling down from Selston[1] with seven full wagons. It appeared round the corner with loud threats of speed, but the colt that it startled from among the gorse,[2] which still flickered indistinctly in the raw afternoon, out-distanced it at a canter. A woman, walking up the railway line to Underwood,[3] drew back into the hedge, held her basket aside, and watched the footplate of the engine advancing. The trucks thumped heavily past, one by one, with slow inevitable movement, as she stood insignificantly trapped between the jolting black wagons and the hedge; then they curved away towards the coppice where the withered oak leaves dropped noiselessly, while the birds, pulling at the scarlet hips beside the track, made off into the dusk that had already crept into the spinney.[4] In the open, the smoke from the engine sank and cleaved to the rough grass. The fields were dreary and forsaken, and in the marshy strip that led to the whimsey, a reedy pit-pond, the fowls had already abandoned their run among the alders, to roost in the tarred fowl-house. The pit-bank loomed up beyond the pond, flames like red sores licking its ashy sides, in the afternoon's stagnant light. Just beyond rose the tapering chimneys and the clumsy black headstocks of Brinsley Colliery. The two wheels were spinning fast up against the sky, and the winding engine rapped out its little spasms. The miners were being turned up.

The engine whistled as it came into the wide bay of railway lines beside the colliery, where rows of trucks stood in harbour.

Miners, single, trailing and in groups, passed like shadows diverging home. At the edge of the ribbed level of sidings squat a low cottage, three steps down from the cinder track. A large bony vine clutched at the house, as if to claw down the tiled roof. Round the bricked yard grew a few wintry primroses. Beyond, the long garden sloped down to a bushcovered brook course. There were some twiggy apple trees, winter-crack trees, and ragged cabbages. Beside the path hung dishevelled pink chrysanthemums, like pink cloths hung on bushes. A woman came stooping out of the felt-covered fowl-house, half-way down the garden. She closed and padlocked the door, then drew herself erect, having brushed some bits from her white apron.

She was a tall woman of imperious mien, handsome, with definite black eyebrows. Her smooth black hair was parted exactly. For a few moments she stood steadily watching the miners as they passed along the railway: then she turned towards the brook course. Her face was calm and set, her mouth was closed with disillusionment. After a moment she called:

"John!" There was no answer. She waited, and then said distinctly:

"Where are you?"

1. Mining village in Nottinghamshire, central England.
2. Wild, yellow-flowered shrub.

3. Small village in central England.
4. A small thicket.

"Here!" replied a child's sulky voice from among the bushes. The woman looked piercingly through the dusk.

"Are you at that brook?" she asked sternly.

For answer the child showed himself before the raspberrycanes that rose like whips. He was a small, sturdy boy of five. He stood quite still, defiantly.

"Oh!" said the mother, conciliated. "I thought you were down at that wet brook—and you remember what I told you——"

The boy did not move or answer.

"Come, come on in," she said more gently, "it's getting dark. There's your grandfather's engine coming down the line!"

The lad advanced slowly, with resentful, taciturn movement. He was dressed in trousers and waistcoat of cloth that was too thick and hard for the size of the garments. They were evidently cut down from a man's clothes.

As they went slowly towards the house he tore at the ragged wisps of chrysanthemums and dropped the petals in handfuls among the path.

"Don't do that—it does look nasty," said his mother. He refrained, and she, suddenly pitiful, broke off a twig with three or four wan flowers and held them against her face. When mother and son reached the yard her hand hesitated, and instead of laying the flower aside, she pushed it in her apron-band. The mother and son stood at the foot of the three steps looking across the bay of lines at the passing home of the miners. The trundle of the small train was imminent. Suddenly the engine loomed past the house and came to a stop opposite the gate.

The engine-driver, a short man with round grey beard, leaned out of the cab high above the woman.

"Have you got a cup of tea?" he said in a cheery, hearty fashion.

It was her father. She went in, saying she would mash.[5] Directly, she returned.

"I didn't come to see you on Sunday," began the little greybearded man.

"I didn't expect you," said his daughter.

The engine-driver winced; then, reassuming his cheery, airy manner, he said:

"Oh, have you heard then? Well, and what do you think——?"

"I think it is soon enough," she replied.

At her brief censure the little man made an impatient gesture, and said coaxingly, yet with dangerous coldness:

"Well, what's a man to do? It's no sort of life for a man of my years, to sit at my own hearth like a stranger. And if I'm going to marry again it may as well be soon as late—what does it matter to anybody?"

The woman did not reply, but turned and went into the house. The man in the engine-cab stood assertive, till she returned with a cup of tea and a piece of bread and butter on a plate. She went up the steps and stood near the footplate of the hissing engine.

"You needn't 'a' brought me bread an' butter," said her father. "But a cup of tea"—he sipped appreciatively—"it's very nice." He sipped for a moment or two, then: "I hear as Walter's got another bout on," he said.

"When hasn't he?" said the woman bitterly.

"I heerd tell of him in the 'Lord Nelson' braggin' as he was going to spend that b—— afore he went: half a sovereign that was."

"When?" asked the woman.

<hr>

5. Separate tea from the leaves.

"A' Sat'day night—I know that's true."

"Very likely," she laughed bitterly. "He gives me twenty-three shillings."

"Aye, it's a nice thing, when a man can do nothing with his money but make a beast of himself!" said the grey-whiskered man. The woman turned her head away. Her father swallowed the last of his tea and handed her the cup.

"Aye," he sighed, wiping his mouth. "It's a settler, it is——"

He put his hand on the lever. The little engine strained and groaned, and the train rumbled towards the crossing. The woman again looked across the metals. Darkness was settling over the spaces of the railway and trucks: the miners, in grey sombre groups, were still passing home. The winding engine pulsed hurriedly, with brief pauses. Elizabeth Bates looked at the dreary flow of men, then she went indoors. Her husband did not come.

The kitchen was small and full of firelight; red coals piled glowing up the chimney mouth. All the life of the room seemed in the white, warm hearth and the steel fender reflecting the red fire. The cloth was laid for tea; cups glinted in the shadows. At the back, where the lowest stairs protruded into the room, the boy sat struggling with a knife and a piece of white wood. He was almost hidden in the shadow. It was half-past four. They had but to await the father's coming to begin tea. As the mother watched her son's sullen little struggle with the wood, she saw herself in his silence and pertinacity; she saw the father in her child's indifference to all but himself. She (seemed to be) occupied by her husband. He had probably gone past his home, slunk past his own door, to drink before he came in, while his dinner spoiled and wasted in waiting. She glanced at the clock, then took the potatoes to strain them in the yard. The garden and fields beyond the brook were closed in uncertain darkness. When she rose with the saucepan, leaving the drain steaming into the night behind her, she saw the yellow lamps were lit along the high road that went up the hill away beyond the space of the railway lines and the field.

Then again she watched the men trooping home, fewer now and fewer.

Indoors the fire was sinking and the room was dark red. The woman put her saucepan on the hob, and set a batter-pudding near the mouth of the oven. Then she stood unmoving. Directly, gratefully, came quick young steps to the door. Someone hung on the latch a moment, then a little girl entered and began pulling off her outdoor things, dragging a mass of curls, just ripening from gold to brown, over her eyes with her hat.

Her mother chid her for coming late from school, and said she would have to keep her at home the dark winter days.

"Why, mother, it's hardly a bit dark yet. The lamp's not lighted, and my father's not home."

"No, he isn't. But it's a quarter to five! Did you see anything of him?"

The child became serious. She looked at her mother with large, wistful blue eyes.

"No, mother, I've never seen him. Why? Has he come up an' gone past, to Old Brinsley? He hasn't, mother, 'cos I never saw him."

"He'd watch that," said the mother bitterly, "he'd take care as you didn't see him. But you may depend upon it, he's seated in the 'Prince o' Wales.' He wouldn't be this late."

The girl looked at her mother piteously.

"Let's have our teas, mother, should we?" said she.

The mother called John to table. She opened the door once more and looked out across the darkness of the lines. All was deserted: she could not hear the winding-engines.

"Perhaps," she said to herself, "he's stopped to get some ripping[6] done."

They sat down to tea. John, at the end of the table near the door, was almost lost in the darkness. Their faces were hidden from each other. The girl crouched against the fender slowly moving a thick piece of bread before the fire. The lad, his face a dusky mark on the shadow, sat watching her who was transfigured in the red glow.

"I do think it's beautiful to look in the fire," said the child.

"Do you?" said her mother. "Why?"

"It's so red, and full of little caves—and it feels so nice, and you can fair smell it."

"It'll want mending directly," replied her mother, "and then if your father comes he'll carry on and say there never is a fire when a man comes home sweating from the pit. A public-house[7] is always warm enough."

There was silence till the boy said complainingly: "Make haste, our Annie."

"Well, I am doing! I can't make the fire do it no faster, can I?"

"She keeps wafflin' it about so's to make 'er slow," grumbled the boy.

"Don't have such an evil imagination, child," replied the mother.

Soon the room was busy in the darkness with the crisp sound of crunching. The mother ate very little. She drank her tea determinedly, and sat thinking. When she rose her anger was evident in the stern unbending of her head. She looked at the pudding in the fender, and broke out:

"It is a scandalous thing as a man can't even come home to his dinner! If it's crozzled up to a cinder I don't see why I should care. Past his very door he goes to get to a public-house, and here I sit with his dinner waiting for him——"

She went out. As she dropped piece after piece of coal on the red fire, the shadows fell on the walls, till the room was almost in total darkness.

"I canna see," grumbled the invisible John. In spite of herself, the mother laughed.

"You know the way to your mouth," she said. She set the dust-pan outside the door. When she came again like a shadow on the hearth, the lad repeated, complaining sulkily:

"I canna see."

"Good gracious!" cried the mother irritably, "you're as bad as your father if it's a bit dusk!"

Nevertheless, she took a paper spill from a sheaf on the mantelpiece and proceeded to light the lamp that hung from the ceiling in the middle of the room. As she reached up, her figure displayed itself just rounding with maternity.

"Oh, mother——!" exclaimed the girl.

"What?" said the woman, suspended in the act of putting the lamp-glass over the flame. The copper reflector shone handsomely on her, as she stood with uplifted arm, turning to face her daughter.

"You've got a flower in your apron!" said the child, in a little rapture at this unusual event.

"Goodness me!" exclaimed the woman, relieved. "One would think the house was afire." She replaced the glass and waited a moment before turning up the wick. A pale shadow was seen floating vaguely on the floor.

"Let me smell!" said the child, still rapturously, coming forward and putting her face to her mother's waist.

"Go along, silly!" said the mother, turning up the lamp. The light revealed their suspense so that the woman felt it almost unbearable. Annie was still bending at her waist. Irritably, the mother took the flowers out from her apron-band.

6. Tearing a vein of coal from the earth.   7. Pub; tavern.

"Oh, mother—don't take them out!" Annie cried, catching her hand and trying to replace the sprig.

"Such nonsense!" said the mother, turning away. The child put the pale chrysanthemums to her lips, murmuring:

"Don't they smell beautiful!"

Her mother gave a short laugh.

"No," she said, "not to me. It was chrysanthemums when I married him, and chrysanthemums when you were born, and the first time they ever brought him home drunk, he'd got brown chrysanthemums in his button-hole."

She looked at the children. Their eyes and their parted lips were wondering. The mother sat rocking in silence for some time. Then she looked at the clock.

"Twenty minutes to six!" In a tone of fine bitter carelessness she continued: "Eh, he'll not come now till they bring him. There he'll stick! But he needn't come rolling in here in his pit-dirt, for I won't wash him. He can lie on the floor——Eh, what a fool I've been, what a fool! And this is what I came here for, to this dirty hole, rats and all, for him to slink past his very door. Twice last week—he's begun now——"

She silenced herself, and rose to clear the table.

While for an hour or more the children played, subduedly intent, fertile of imagination, united in fear of the mother's wrath, and in dread of their father's home-coming, Mrs. Bates sat in her rocking-chair making a 'singlet' of thick cream-coloured flannel, which gave a dull wounded sound as she tore off the grey edge. She worked at her sewing with energy, listening to the children, and her anger wearied itself, lay down to rest, opening its eyes from time to time and steadily watching, its ears raised to listen. Sometimes even her anger quailed and shrank, and the mother suspended her sewing, tracing the footsteps that thudded along the sleepers outside; she would lift her head sharply to bid the children 'hush', but she recovered herself in time, and the footsteps went past the gate, and the children were not flung out of their play-world.

But at last Annie sighed, and gave in. She glanced at her wagon of slippers, and loathed the game. She turned plaintively to her mother.

"Mother!"—but she was inarticulate.

John crept out like a frog from under the sofa. His mother glanced up.

"Yes," she said, "just look at those shirt-sleeves!"

The boy held them out to survey them, saying nothing. Then somebody called in a hoarse voice away down the line, and suspense bristled in the room, till two people had gone by outside, talking.

"It is time for bed," said the mother.

"My father hasn't come," wailed Annie plaintively. But her mother was primed with courage.

"Never mind. They'll bring him when he does come—like a log." She meant there would be no scene. "And he may sleep on the floor till he wakes himself. I know he'll not go to work to-morrow after this!"

The children had their hands and faces wiped with a flannel. They were very quiet. When they had put on their night-dresses, they said their prayers, the boy mumbling. The mother looked down at them, at the brown silken bush of intertwining curls in the nape of the girl's neck, at the little black head of the lad, and her heart burst with anger at their father, who caused all three such distress. The children hid their faces in her skirts for comfort.

When Mrs. Bates came down, the room was strangely empty, with a tension of expectancy. She took up her sewing and stitched for some time without raising her head. Meantime her anger was tinged with fear.

2

The clock struck eight and she rose suddenly, dropping her sewing on her chair. She went to the stair-foot door, opened it, listening. Then she went out, locking the door behind her.

Something scuffled in the yard, and she started, though she knew it was only the rats with which the place was over-run. The night was very dark. In the great bay of railway lines, bulked with trucks, there was no trace of light, only away back she could see a few yellow lamps at the pit-top, and the red smear of the burning pit-bank on the night. She hurried along the edge of the track, then, crossing the converging lines, came to the stile by the white gates, whence she emerged on the road. Then the fear which had led her shrank. People were walking up to New Brinsley; she saw the lights in the houses; twenty yards farther on were the broad windows of the 'Prince of Wales', very warm and bright, and the loud voices of men could be heard distinctly. What a fool she had been to imagine that anything had happened to him! He was merely drinking over there at the 'Prince of Wales'. She faltered. She had never yet been to fetch him, and she never would go. So she continued her walk towards the long straggling line of houses, standing back on the highway. She entered a passage between the dwellings.

"Mr. Rigley?—Yes! Did you want him? No, he's not in at this minute."

The raw-boned woman leaned forward from her dark scullery and peered at the other, upon whom fell a dim light through the blind of the kitchen window.

"Is it Mrs. Bates?" she asked in a tone tinged with respect.

"Yes. I wondered if your Master was at home. Mine hasn't come yet."

" 'Asn't 'e! Oh, Jack's been 'ome an' 'ad 'is dinner an' gone out. 'E's just gone for 'alf an hour afore bed-time. Did you call at the 'Prince of Wales'?"

"No——"

"No, you didn't like——! It's not very nice." The other woman was indulgent. There was an awkward pause. "Jack never said nothink about—about your Master," she said.

"No!—I expect he's stuck in there!"

Elizabeth Bates said this bitterly, and with recklessness. She knew that the woman across the yard was standing at her door listening, but she did not care. As she turned:

"Stop a minute! I'll just go an' ask Jack if 'e knows anythink," said Mrs. Rigley.

"Oh no—I wouldn't like to put——!"

"Yes, I will, if you'll just step inside an' see as th' childer doesn't come downstairs and set theirselves afire."

Elizabeth Bates, murmuring a remonstrance,[8] stepped inside. The other woman apologised for the state of the room.

The kitchen needed apology. There were little frocks and trousers and childish undergarments on the squab and on the floor, and a litter of playthings everywhere. On the black American cloth of the table were pieces of bread and cake, crusts, slops, and a teapot with cold tea.

"Eh, ours is just as bad," said Elizabeth Bates, looking at the woman, not at the house. Mrs. Rigley put a shawl over her head and hurried out, saying:

"I shanna be a minute."

---

8. Protestation or objection.

The other sat, noting with faint disapproval the general untidiness of the room. Then she fell to counting the shoes of various sizes scattered over the floor. There were twelve. She sighed and said to herself: "No wonder!"—glancing at the litter. There came the scratching of two pairs of feet on the yard, and the Rigleys entered. Elizabeth Bates rose. Rigley was a big man, with very large bones. His head looked particularly bony. Across his temple was a blue scar, caused by a wound got in the pit, a wound in which the coal-dust remained blue like tattooing.

" 'Asna 'e come whoam yit?" asked the man, without any form of greeting, but with deference and sympathy. "I couldna say wheer he is—'e's non ower theer!"—he jerked his head to signify the 'Prince of Wales'.

" 'E's 'appen⁹ gone up to th' 'Yew'," said Mrs. Rigley.

There was another pause. Rigley had evidently something to get off his mind: "Ah left 'im finishin' a stint,"¹⁰ he began. "Loose-all 'ad bin gone about ten minutes when we com'n away, an' I shouted: 'Are ter comin', Walt?' an' 'e said: 'Go on, Ah shanna be but a'ef a minnit,' so we com'n ter th' bottom, me an' Bowers, thinkin' as 'e wor just behint, an' 'ud come up i' th' next bantle¹¹——"

He stood perplexed, as if answering a charge of deserting his mate. Elizabeth Bates, now again certain of disaster, hastened to reassure him:

"I expect 'e's gone up to th' 'Yew Tree', as you say. It's not the first time. I've fretted myself into a fever before now. He'll come home when they carry him."

"Ay, isn't it too bad!" deplored the other woman.

"I'll just step up to Dick's an' see if 'e *is* theer," offered the man, afraid of appearing alarmed, afraid of taking liberties.

"Oh, I wouldn't think of bothering you that far," said Elizabeth Bates, with emphasis, but he knew she was glad of his offer.

As they stumbled up the entry, Elizabeth Bates heard Rigley's wife run across the yard and open her neighbour's door. At this, suddenly all the blood in her body seemed to switch away from her heart.

"Mind!" warned Rigley. "Ah've said many a time as Ah'd fill up them ruts in this entry, sumb'dy 'll be breakin' their legs yit."

She recovered herself and walked quickly along with the miner.

"I don't like leaving the children in bed, and nobody in the house," she said.

"No, you dunna!" he replied courteously. They were soon at the gate of the cottage.

"Well, I shanna be many minnits, Dunna you be frettin' now, 'e'll be all right," said the butty.¹²

"Thank you very much, Mr. Rigley," she replied.

"You're welcome!" he stammered, moving away. "I shanna be many minnits."

The house was quiet. Elizabeth Bates took off her hat and shawl, and rolled back the rug. When she had finished, she sat down. It was a few minutes past nine. She was startled by the rapid chuff of the winding-engine at the pit, and the sharp whirr of the brakes on the rope as it descended. Again she felt the painful sweep of her blood, and she put her hand to her side, saying aloud: "Good gracious!—it's only the nine o'clock deputy going down," rebuking herself.

She sat still, listening. Half an hour of this, and she was wearied out.

---

9. Perhaps, maybe.
10. Amount of work to be done.

11. Carload.
12. Fellow coal miner.

"What am I working myself up like this for?" she said pitiably to herself, "I s'll only be doing myself some damage."

She took out her sewing again.

At a quarter to ten there were footsteps. One person! She watched for the door to open. It was an elderly woman, in a black bonnet and a black woollen shawl—his mother. She was about sixty years old, pale, with blue eyes, and her face all wrinkled and lamentable. She shut the door and turned to her daughter-in-law peevishly.

"Eh, Lizzie, whatever shall we do, whatever shall we do!" she cried.

Elizabeth drew back a little, sharply.

"What is it, mother?" she said.

The elder woman seated herself on the sofa.

"I don't know, child, I can't tell you!"—she shook her head slowly. Elizabeth sat watching her, anxious and vexed.

"I don't know," replied the grandmother, sighing very deeply. "There's no end to my troubles, there isn't. The things I've gone through, I'm sure it's enough——!" She wept without wiping her eyes, the tears running.

"But, mother," interrupted Elizabeth, "what do you mean? What is it?"

The grandmother slowly wiped her eyes. The fountains of her tears were stopped by Elizabeth's directness. She wiped her eyes slowly.

"Poor child! Eh, you poor thing!" she moaned. "I don't know what we're going to do, I don't—and you as you are—it's a thing, it is indeed!"

Elizabeth waited.

"Is he dead?" she asked, and at the words her heart swung violently, though she felt a slight flush of shame at the ultimate extravagance of the question. Her words sufficiently frightened the old lady, almost brought her to herself.

"Don't say so, Elizabeth! We'll hope it's not as bad as that; no, may the Lord spare us that, Elizabeth. Jack Rigley came just as I was sittin' down to a glass afore going to bed, an' 'e said: ''Appen you'll go down th' line, Mrs. Bates. Walt's had an accident. 'Appen you'll go an' sit wi' 'er till we can get him home.' I hadn't time to ask him a word afore he was gone. An' I put my bonnet on an' come straight down, Lizzie. I thought to myself: 'Eh, that poor blessed child, if anybody should come an' tell her of a sudden, there's no knowin' what'll 'appen to 'er.' You mustn't let it upset you, Lizzie—or you know what to expect. How long is it, six months—or is it five, Lizzie? Ay!"—the old woman shook her head—"time slips on, it slips on! Ay!"

Elizabeth's thoughts were busy elsewhere. If he was killed—would she be able to manage on the little pension and what she could earn?—she counted up rapidly. If he was hurt—they wouldn't take him to the hospital—how tiresome he would be to nurse!—but perhaps she'd be able to get him away from the drink and his hateful ways. She would—while he was ill. The tears offered to come to her eyes at the picture. But what sentimental luxury was this she was beginning? She turned to consider the children. At any rate she was absolutely necessary for them. They were her business.

"Ay!" repeated the old woman, "it seems but a week or two since he brought me his first wages. Ay—he was a good lad, Elizabeth, he was, in his way. I don't know why he got to be such a trouble, I don't. He was a happy lad at home, only full of spirits. But there's no mistake he's been a handful of trouble, he has! I hope the Lord'll spare him to mend his ways. I hope so, I hope so. You've had a sight o' trouble with him, Elizabeth, you have indeed. But he was a jolly enough lad wi' me, he was, I can assure you. I don't know how it is . . . ."

The old woman continued to muse aloud, a monotonous irritating sound, while Elizabeth thought concentratedly, startled once, when she heard the winding-engine chuff quickly, and the brakes skirr with a shriek. Then she heard the engine more slowly, and the brakes made no sound. The old woman did not notice. Elizabeth waited in suspense. The mother-in-law talked, with lapses into silence.

"But he wasn't your son, Lizzie, an' it makes a difference. Whatever he was, I remember him when he was little, an' I learned to understand him and to make allowances. You've got to make allowances for them——"

It was half-past ten, and the old woman was saying: "But it's trouble from beginning to end; you're never too old for trouble, never too old for that——" when the gate banged back, and there were heavy feet on the steps.

"I'll go, Lizzie, let me go," cried the old woman, rising. But Elizabeth was at the door. It was a man in pit-clothes.

"They're bringin' 'im, Missis," he said. Elizabeth's heart halted a moment. Then it surged on again, almost suffocating her.

"Is he—is it bad?" she asked.

The man turned away, looking at the darkness:

"The doctor says 'e'd been dead hours. 'E saw 'im i' th' lamp-cabin."

The old woman, who stood just behind Elizabeth, dropped into a chair, and folded her hands, crying: "Oh, my boy, my boy!"

"Hush!" said Elizabeth, with a sharp twitch of a frown. "Be still, mother, don't waken th' children: I wouldn't have them down for anything!"

The old woman moaned softly, rocking herself. The man was drawing away. Elizabeth took a step forward.

"How was it?" she asked.

"Well, I couldn't say for sure," the man replied, very ill at ease. " 'E wor finishin' a stint an' th' butties 'ad gone, an' a lot o' stuff come down atop 'n 'im."

"And crushed him?" cried the widow, with a shudder.

"No," said the man, "it fell at th' back of 'im. 'E wor under th' face, an' it niver touched 'im. It shut 'im in. It seems 'e wor smothered."

Elizabeth shrank back. She heard the old woman behind her cry:

"What?—what did 'e say it was?"

The man replied, more loudly: "'E wor smothered!"

Then the old woman wailed aloud, and this relieved Elizabeth.

"Oh, mother," she said, putting her hand on the old woman, "don't waken th' children, don't waken th' children."

She wept a little, unknowing, while the old mother rocked herself and moaned. Elizabeth remembered that they were bringing him home, and she must be ready. "They'll lay him in the parlour," she said to herself, standing a moment pale and perplexed.

Then she lighted a candle and went into the tiny room. The air was cold and damp, but she could not make a fire, there was no fireplace. She set down the candle and looked round. The candlelight glittered on the lustre-glasses, on the two vases that held some of the pink chrysanthemums, and on the dark mahogany. There was a cold, deathly smell of chrysanthemums in the room. Elizabeth stood looking at the flowers. She turned away, and calculated whether there would be room to lay him on the floor, between the couch and the chiffonier.[13] She pushed the chairs aside. There

13. Chest of drawers.

would be room to lay him down and to step round him. Then she fetched the old red tablecloth, and another old cloth, spreading them down to save her bit of carpet. She shivered on leaving the parlour; so, from the dresser drawer she took a clean shirt and put it at the fire to air. All the time her mother-in-law was rocking herself in the chair and moaning.

"You'll have to move from there, mother," said Elizabeth. "They'll be bringing him in. Come in the rocker."

The old mother rose mechanically, and seated herself by the fire, continuing to lament. Elizabeth went into the pantry for another candle, and there, in the little pent-house under the naked tiles, she heard them coming. She stood still in the pantry doorway, listening. She heard them pass the end of the house, and come awkwardly down the three steps, a jumble of shuffling footsteps and muttering voices. The old woman was silent. The men were in the yard.

Then Elizabeth heard Matthews, the manager of the pit, say: "You go in first, Jim. Mind!"

The door came open, and the two women saw a collier backing into the room, holding one end of a stretcher, on which they could see the nailed pit-boots of the dead man. The two carriers halted, the man at the head stooping to the lintel of the door.

"Wheer will you have him?" asked the manager, a short, white-bearded man.

Elizabeth roused herself and came from the pantry carrying the unlighted candle.

"In the parlour," she said.

"In there, Jim!" pointed the manager, and the carriers backed round into the tiny room. The coat with which they had covered the body fell off as they awkwardly turned through the two doorways, and the women saw their man, naked to the waist, lying stripped for work. The old woman began to moan in a low voice of horror.

"Lay th' stretcher at th' side," snapped the manager, "an' put 'im on th' cloths. Mind now, mind! Look you now——!"

One of the men had knocked off a vase of chrysanthemums. He stared awkwardly, then they set down the stretcher. Elizabeth did not look at her husband. As soon as she could get in the room, she went and picked up the broken vase and the flowers.

"Wait a minute!" she said.

The three men waited in silence while she mopped up the water with a duster.

"Eh, what a job, what a job, to be sure!" the manager was saying, rubbing his brow with trouble and perplexity. "Never knew such a thing in my life, never! He'd no busines to ha' been left. I never knew such a thing in my life! Fell over him clean as a whistle, an' shut him in. Not four foot of space, there wasn't—yet it scarce bruised him."

He looked down at the dead man, lying prone, half naked, all grimed with coal-dust.

"''Sphyxiated', the doctor said. It is the most terrible job I've ever known. Seems as if it was done o' purpose. Clean over him, an' shut 'im in, like a mouse-trap"—he made a sharp, descending gesture with his hand.

The colliers standing by jerked aside their heads in hopeless comment.

The horror of the thing bristled upon them all.

Then they heard the girl's voice upstairs calling shrilly: "Mother, mother—who is it? Mother, who is it?"

Elizabeth hurried to the foot of the stairs and opened the door:

"Go to sleep!" she commanded sharply. "What are you shouting about? Go to sleep at once—there's nothing—"

Then she began to mount the stairs. They could hear her on the boards, and on the plaster floor of the little bedroom. They could hear her distinctly:

"What's the matter now?—what's the matter with you, silly thing?"—her voice was much agitated, with an unreal gentleness.

"I thought it was some men come," said the plaintive voice of the child. "Has he come?"

"Yes, they've brought him. There's nothing to make a fuss about. Go to sleep now, like a good child."

They could hear her voice in the bedroom, they waited whilst she covered the children under the bedclothes.

"Is he drunk?" asked the girl, timidly, faintly.

"No! No—he's not! He—he's asleep."

"Is he asleep downstairs?"

"Yes—and don't make a noise."

There was silence for a moment, then the men heard the frightened child again: "What's that noise?"

"It's nothing, I tell you, what are you bothering for?"

The noise was the grandmother moaning. She was oblivious of everything, sitting on her chair rocking and moaning The manager put his hand on her arm and bade her "Sh—sh!!"

The old woman opened her eyes and looked at him. She was shocked by this interruption, and seemed to wonder.

"What time is it?" the plaintive thin voice of the child, sinking back unhappily into sleep, asked this last question.

"Ten o'clock," answered the mother more softly. Then she must have bent down and kissed the children.

Matthews beckoned to the men to come away. They put on their caps and took up the stretcher. Stepping over the body, they tiptoed out of the house. None of them spoke till they were far from the wakeful children.

When Elizabeth came down she found her mother alone on the parlour floor, leaning over the dead man, the tears dropping on him.

"We must lay him out," the wife said. She put on the kettle, then returning knelt at the feet, and began to unfasten the knotted leather laces. The room was clammy and dim with only one candle, so that she had to bend her face almost to the floor. At last she got off the heavy boots and put them away.

"You must help me now," she whispered to the old woman. Together they stripped the man.

When they arose, saw him lying in the naïve dignity of death, the women stood arrested in fear and respect. For a few moments they remained still, looking down, the old mother whimpering. Elizabeth felt countermanded.[14] She saw him, how utterly inviolable he lay in himself. She had nothing to do with him. She could not accept it. Stooping, she laid her hand on him, in claim. He was still warm, for the mine was hot where he had died. His mother had his face between her hands, and was murmuring incoherently. The old tears fell in succession as drops from wet leaves; the mother was not weeping, merely her tears flowed. Elizabeth embraced the body of her husband,

14. Overruled, contradicted.

with cheek and lips. She seemed to be listening, inquiring, trying to get some connection. But she could not. She was driven away. He was impregnable.

She rose, went into the kitchen, where she poured warm water into a bowl, brought soap and flannel and a soft towel.

"I must wash him," she said.

Then the old mother rose stiffly, and watched Elizabeth as she carefully washed his face, carefully brushing the big blond moustache from his mouth with the flannel. She was afraid with a bottomless fear, so she ministered to him. The old woman, jealous, said:

"Let me wipe him!"—and she kneeled on the other side drying slowly as Elizabeth washed, her big black bonnet sometimes brushing the dark head of her daughter-in-law. They worked thus in silence for a long time. They never forgot it was death, and the touch of the man's dead body gave them strange emotions, different in each of the women; a great dread possessed them both, the mother felt the lie was given to her womb, she was denied; the wife felt the utter isolation of the human soul, the child within her was a weight apart from her.

At last it was finished. He was a man of handsome body, and his face showed no traces of drink. He was blond, full-fleshed, with fine limbs. But he was dead.

"Bless him," whispered his mother, looking always at his face, and speaking out of sheer terror. "Dear lad—bless him!" She spoke in a faint, sibilant ecstasy of fear and mother love.

Elizabeth sank down again to the floor, and put her face against his neck, and trembled and shuddered. But she had to draw away again. He was dead, and her living flesh had no place against his. A great dread and weariness held her: she was so unavailing. Her life was gone like this.

"White as milk he is, clear as a twelve-month baby, bless him, the darling!" the old mother murmured to herself. "Not a mark on him, clear and clean and white, beautiful as ever a child was made," she murmured with pride. Elizabeth kept her face hidden.

"He went peaceful, Lizzie—peaceful as sleep. Isn't he beautiful, the lamb? Ay— he must ha' made his peace, Lizzie. 'Appen he made it all right, Lizzie, shut in there. He'd have time. He wouldn't look like this if he hadn't made his peace. The lamb, the dear lamb. Eh, but he had a hearty laugh. I loved to hear it. He had the heartiest laugh, Lizzie, as a lad——"

Elizabeth looked up. The man's mouth was fallen back, slightly open under the cover of the moustache. The eyes, half shut, did not show glazed in the obscurity. Life with its smoky burning gone from him, had left him apart and utterly alien to her. And she knew what a stranger he was to her. In her womb was ice of fear, because of this separate stranger with whom she had been living as one flesh. Was this what it all meant—utter, intact separateness, obscured by heat of living? In dread she turned her face away. The fact was too deadly. There had been nothing between them, and yet they had come together, exchanging their nakedness repeatedly. Each time he had taken her, they had been two isolated beings, far apart as now. He was no more responsible than she. The child was like ice in her womb. For as she looked at the dead man, her mind, cold and detached, said clearly: "Who am I? What have I been doing? I have been fighting a husband who did not exist. He existed all the time. What wrong have I done? What was that I have been living with? There lies the reality, this man." And her soul died in her for fear: she knew she had never seen him, he had never seen her, they had met in the dark and had fought in the dark, not knowing whom they met nor whom they fought. And now she saw, and turned silent in seeing. For she had been wrong. She had said he was something he was not; she had felt familiar with him. Whereas he was apart all the while, living as she never lived, feeling as she never felt.

In fear and shame she looked at his naked body, that she had known falsely. And he was the father of her children. Her soul was torn from her body and stood apart. She looked at his naked body and was ashamed, as if she had denied it. After all, it was itself. It seemed awful to her. She looked at his face, and she turned her own face to the wall. For his look was other than hers, his way was not her way. She had denied him what he was—she saw it now. She had refused him as himself. And this had been her life, and his life. She was grateful to death, which restored the truth. And she knew she was not dead.

And all the while her heart was bursting with grief and pity for him. What had he suffered? What stretch of horror for this helpless man! She was rigid with agony. She had not been able to help him. He had been cruelly injured, this naked man, this other being, and she could make no reparation. There were the children—but the children belonged to life. This dead man had nothing to do with them. He and she were only channels through which life had flowed to issue in the children. She was a mother—but how awful she knew it now to have been a wife. And he, dead now, how awful he must have felt it to be a husband. She felt that in the next world he would be a stranger to her. If they met there, in the beyond, they would only be ashamed of what had been before. The children had come, for some mysterious reason, out of both of them. But the children did not unite them. Now he was dead, she knew how eternally he was apart from her, how eternally he had nothing more to do with her. She saw this episode of her life closed. They had denied each other in life. Now he had withdrawn. An anguish came over her. It was finished then: it had become hopeless between them long before he died. Yet he had been her husband. But how little!

"Have you got his shirt, 'Lizabeth?"

Elizabeth turned without answering, though she strove to weep and behave as her mother-in-law expected. But she could not, she was silenced. She went into the kitchen and returned with the garment.

"It is aired," she said, grasping the cotton shirt here and there to try. She was almost ashamed to handle him; what right had she or anyone to lay hands on him; but her touch was humble on his body. It was hard work to clothe him. He was so heavy and inert. A terrible dread gripped her all the while: that he could be so heavy and utterly inert, unresponsive, apart. The horror of the distance between them was almost too much for her—it was so infinite a gap she must look across.

At last it was finished. They covered him with a sheet and left him lying, with his face bound. And she fastened the door of the little parlour, lest the children should see what was lying there. Then, with peace sunk heavy on her heart, she went about making tidy the kitchen. She knew she submitted to life, which was her immediate master. But from death, her ultimate master, she winced with fear and shame.

W. H. Auden
1907–1973

Musée des Beaux Arts[1]

About suffering they were never wrong,
The Old Masters: how well they understood
Its human position; how it takes place
While someone else is eating or opening a window or just walking dully along;
5   How, when the aged are reverently, passionately waiting
For the miraculous birth, there always must be
Children who did not specially want it to happen, skating
On a pond at the edge of the wood:
They never forgot
10   That even the dreadful martyrdom must run its course
Anyhow in a corner, some untidy spot
Where the dogs go on with their doggy life and the torturer's horse
Scratches its innocent behind on a tree.

In Brueghel's *Icarus*, for instance: how everything turns away
15   Quite leisurely from the disaster; the ploughman may
Have heard the splash, the forsaken cry,
But for him it was not an important failure; the sun shone
As it had to on the white legs disappearing into the green
Water; and the expensive delicate ship that must have seen
20   Something amazing, a boy falling out of the sky,
Had somewhere to get to and sailed calmly on.

1938   1940

---

1. The Musées Royaux des Beaux-Arts in Brussels contain a collection of paintings by the Flemish painter Pieter Brueghel (1525–1569) that includes *The Fall of Icarus*; Brueghel is famous for his acute observation of ordinary life. A figure from Greek mythology, Icarus had wings of wax and feathers but flew too close to the sun, which melted the wax and caused him to fall into the sea.

George Orwell
1903–1950

Shooting an Elephant

In Moulmein, in Lower Burma,[1] I was hated by large numbers of people—the only time in my life that I have been important enough for this to happen to me. I was sub-divisional police officer of the town, and in an aimless, petty kind of way anti-European feeling was very bitter. No one had the guts to raise a riot, but if a European woman went through the bazaars alone somebody would probably spit betel[2] juice over her dress. As a police officer I was an obvious target and was baited whenever it seemed safe to do so. When a nimble Burman tripped me up on the football field and the referee (another Burman) looked the other way, the crowd yelled with hideous laughter. This happened more than once. In the end the sneering yellow faces of young men that met me everywhere, the insults hooted after me when I was at a safe distance, got badly on my nerves. The young Buddhist priests were the worst of all. There were several thousands of them in the town and none of them seemed to have anything to do except stand on street corners and jeer at Europeans.

All this was perplexing and upsetting. For at that time I had already made up my mind that imperialism was an evil thing and the sooner I chucked up my job and got out of it the better. Theoretically—and secretly, of course—I was all for the Burmese and all against their oppressors, the British. As for the job I was doing, I hated it more bitterly than I can perhaps make clear. In a job like that you see the dirty work of Empire at close quarters. The wretched prisoners huddling in the stinking cages of the lock-ups, the grey, cowed faces of the long-term convicts, the scarred buttocks of the men who had been flogged with bamboos—all these oppressed me with an intolerable sense of guilt. But I could get nothing into perspective. I was young and ill-educated and I had had to think out my problems in the utter silence that is imposed on every Englishman in the East. I did not even know that the British Empire is dying, still less did I know that it is a great deal better than the younger empires that are going to supplant it. All I knew was that I was stuck between my hatred of the empire I served and my rage against the evil-spirited little beasts who tried to make my job impossible. With one part of my mind I thought of the British Raj[3] as an unbreakable tyranny, as something clamped down, *in saecula saeculorum*,[4] upon the will of prostrate peoples; with another part I thought that the greatest joy in the world would be to drive a bayonet into a Buddhist priest's guts. Feelings like these are the normal by-products of imperialism; ask any Anglo-Indian official, if you can catch him off duty.

One day something happened which in a roundabout way was enlightening. It was a tiny incident in itself, but it gave me a better glimpse than I had had before of the real nature of imperialism—the real motives for which despotic governments act. Early one morning the sub-inspector at a police station the other end of the town rang me up on the phone and said that an elephant was ravaging the bazaar. Would I please come and do something about it? I did not know what I could do, but I wanted

---

1. Republic in southeast Asia, bordered by Bangladesh, India, China, Laos, and Thailand.
2. An East Indian pepper plant, the leaves of which are chewed.
3. "Rule" (Hindi).
4. Forever and ever (Latin).

to see what was happening and I got on to a pony and started out. I took my rifle, an old 44 Winchester and much too small to kill an elephant, but I thought the noise might be useful in *terrorem*.[5] Various Burmans stopped me on the way and told me about the elephant's doings. It was not, of course, a wild elephant, but a tame one which had gone "must".[6] It had been chained up as tame elephants always are when their attack of "must" is due, but on the previous night it had broken its chain and escaped. Its mahout,[7] the only person who could manage it when it was in that state, had set out in pursuit, but he had taken the wrong direction and was now twelve hours' journey away, and in the morning the elephant had suddenly reappeared in the town. The Burmese population had no weapons and were quite helpless against it. It had already destroyed somebody's bamboo hut, killed a cow and raided some fruit-stalls and devoured the stock; also it had met the municipal rubbish van, and, when the driver jumped out and took to his heels, had turned the van over and inflicted violence upon it.

The Burmese sub-inspector and some Indian constables were waiting for me in the quarter where the elephant had been seen. It was a very poor quarter, a labyrinth of squalid bamboo huts, thatched with palm-leaf, winding all over a steep hillside. I remember that it was a cloudy stuffy morning at the beginning of the rains. We began questioning the people as to where the elephant had gone, and, as usual, failed to get any definite information. That is invariably the case in the East; a story always sounds clear enough at a distance, but the nearer you get to the scene of events the vaguer it becomes. Some of the people said that the elephant had gone in one direction, some said that he had gone in another, some professed not even to have heard of any elephant. I had almost made up my mind that the whole story was a pack of lies, when we heard yells a little distance away. There was a loud, scandalised cry of "Go away, child! Go away this instant!" and an old woman with a switch in her hand came round the corner of a hut, violently shooing away a crowd of naked children. Some more women followed, clicking their tongues and exclaiming; evidently there was something there that the children ought not to have seen. I rounded the hut and saw a man's dead body sprawling in the mud. He was an Indian, a black Dravidian[8] coolie,[9] almost naked, and he could not have been dead many minutes. The people said that the elephant had come suddenly upon him round the corner of the hut, caught him with its trunk, put its foot on his back and ground him into the earth. This was the rainy season and the ground was soft, and his face had scored a trench a foot deep and a couple of yards long. He was lying on his belly with arms crucified and head sharply twisted to one side. His face was coated with mud, the eyes wide open, the teeth bared and grinning with an expression of unendurable agony. (Never tell me, by the way, that the dead look peaceful. Most of the corpses I have seen looked devilish.) The friction of the great beast's foot had stripped the skin from his back as neatly as one skins a rabbit. As soon as I saw the dead man I sent an orderly to a friend's house nearby to borrow an elephant rifle. I had already sent back the pony, not wanting it to go mad with fright and throw me if it smelled the elephant.

The orderly came back in a few minutes with a rifle and five cartridges, and meanwhile some Burmans had arrived and told us that the elephant was in the paddy fields below, only a few hundred yards away. As I started forward practically

5. To frighten it (Latin).
6. A period of heightened aggressiveness and sexual activity in male elephants, during which violent frenzies occur.
7. Elephant driver (Hindi).
8. Native of southeast India or Sri Lanka.
9. A derogatory term for an unskilled Asian laborer.

the whole population of the quarter flocked out of their houses and followed me. They had seen the rifle and were all shouting excitedly that I was going to shoot the elephant. They had not shown much interest in the elephant when he was merely ravaging their homes, but it was different now that he was going to be shot. It was a bit of fun to them, as it would be to an English crowd; besides, they wanted the meat. It made me vaguely uneasy. I had no intention of shooting the elephant—I had merely sent for the rifle to defend myself if necessary—and it is always unnerving to have a crowd following you. I marched down the hill, looking and feeling a fool, with the rifle over my shoulder and an ever-growing army of people jostling at my heels. At the bottom, when you got away from the huts, there was a metalled road and beyond that a miry waste of paddy fields a thousand yards across, not yet ploughed but soggy from the first rains and dotted with coarse grass. The elephant was standing eighty yards from the road, his left side towards us. He took not the slightest notice of the crowd's approach. He was tearing up bunches of grass, beating them against his knees to clean them and stuffing them into his mouth.

I had halted on the road. As soon as I saw the elephant I knew with perfect certainty that I ought not to shoot him. It is a serious matter to shoot a working elephant—it is comparable to destroying a huge and costly piece of machinery—and obviously one ought not to do it if it can possibly be avoided. And at that distance, peacefully eating, the elephant looked no more dangerous than a cow. I thought then and I think now that his attack of "must" was already passing off; in which case he would merely wander harmlessly about until the mahout came back and caught him. Moreover, I did not in the least want to shoot him. I decided that I would watch him for a little while to make sure that he did not turn savage again, and then go home.

But at that moment I glanced round at the crowd that had followed me. It was an immense crowd, two thousand at the least and growing every minute. It blocked the road for a long distance on either side. I looked at the sea of yellow faces above the garish clothes—faces all happy and excited over this bit of fun, all certain that the elephant was going to be shot. They were watching me as they would watch a conjuror about to perform a trick. They did not like me, but with the magical rifle in my hands I was momentarily worth watching. And suddenly I realised that I should have to shoot the elephant after all. The people expected it of me and I had got to do it; I could feel their two thousand wills pressing me forward, irresistibly. And it was at this moment, as I stood there with the rifle in my hands, that I first grasped the hollowness, the futility of the white man's dominion in the East. Here was I, the white man with his gun, standing in front of the unarmed native crowd—seemingly the leading actor of the piece; but in reality I was only an absurd puppet pushed to and fro by the will of those yellow faces behind. I perceived in this moment that when the white man turns tyrant it is his own freedom that he destroys. He becomes a sort of hollow, posing dummy, the conventionalised figure of a sahib.[10] For it is the condition of his rule that he shall spend his life in trying to impress the "natives" and so in every crisis he has got to do what the "natives" expect of him. He wears a mask, and his face grows to fit it. I had got to shoot the elephant. I had committed myself to doing it when I sent for the rifle. A sahib has got to act like a sahib; he has got to appear resolute, to know his own mind and do definite things. To come all that way, rifle in hand, with two thousand people marching at my heels, and then to trail feebly away, having done nothing—no, that was impossible. The crowd would laugh at me. And my whole life, every white man's life in the East, was one long struggle not to be laughed at.

10. White gentleman (Urdu).

But I did not want to shoot the elephant. I watched him beating his bunch of grass against his knees, with that preoccupied grandmotherly air that elephants have. It seemed to me that it would be murder to shoot him. At that age I was not squeamish about killing animals, but I had never shot an elephant and never wanted to. (Somehow it always seems worse to kill a *large* animal.) Besides, there was the beast's owner to be considered. Alive, the elephant was worth at least a hundred pounds; dead, he would only be worth the value of his tusks—five pounds, possibly. But I had got to act quickly. I turned to some experienced-looking Burmans who had been there when we arrived, and asked them how the elephant had been behaving. They all said the same thing: he took no notice of you if you left him alone, but he might charge if you went too close to him.

It was perfectly clear to me what I ought to do. I ought to walk up to within, say, twenty-five yards of the elephant and test his behaviour. If he charged I could shoot, if he took no notice of me it would be safe to leave him until the mahout came back. But also I knew that I was going to do no such thing. I was a poor shot with a rifle and the ground was soft mud into which one would sink at every step. If the elephant charged and I missed him, I should have about as much chance as a toad under a steam-roller. But even then I was not thinking particularly of my own skin, only the watchful yellow faces behind. For at that moment, with the crowd watching me, I was not afraid in the ordinary sense, as I would have been if I had been alone. A white man mustn't be frightened in front of "natives"; and so, in general, he isn't frightened. The sole thought in my mind was that if anything went wrong those two thousand Burmans would see me pursued, caught, trampled on and reduced to a grinning corpse like that Indian up the hill. And if that happened it was quite probable that some of them would laugh. That would never do. There was only one alternative. I shoved the cartridges into the magazine and lay down on the road to get a better aim.

The crowd grew very still, and a deep, low, happy sigh, as of people who see the theatre curtain go up at last, breathed from innumerable throats. They were going to have their bit of fun after all. The rifle was a beautiful German thing with cross-hair sights. I did not then know that in shooting an elephant one should shoot to cut an imaginary bar running from ear-hole to ear-hole. I ought therefore, as the elephant was sideways on, to have aimed straight at his ear-hole; actually I aimed several inches in front of this, thinking the brain would be further forward.

When I pulled the trigger I did not hear the bang or feel the kick—one never does when a shot goes home—but I heard the devilish roar of glee that went up from the crowd. In that instant, in too short a time, one would have thought, even for the bullet to get there, a mysterious, terrible change had come over the elephant. He neither stirred nor fell, but every line of his body had altered. He looked suddenly stricken, shrunken, immensely old, as though the frightful impact of the bullet had paralysed him without knocking him down. At last, after what seemed a long time—it might have been five seconds, I dare say—he sagged flabbily to his knees. His mouth slobbered. An enormous senility seemed to have settled upon him. One could have imagined him thousands of years old. I fired again into the same spot. At the second shot he did not collapse but climbed with desperate slowness to his feet and stood weakly upright, with legs sagging and head drooping. I fired a third time. That was the shot that did for him. You could see the agony of it jolt his whole body and knock the last remnant of strength from his legs. But in falling he seemed for a moment to rise, for as his hind legs collapsed beneath him he seemed to tower upwards like a huge rock toppling, his trunk reaching skyward like a tree. He trumpeted, for the first and only time. And then down he came, his belly towards me, with a crash that seemed to shake the ground even where I lay.

I got up. The Burmans were already racing past me across the mud. It was obvious that the elephant would never rise again, but he was not dead. He was breathing very rhythmically with long rattling gasps, his great mound of a side painfully rising and falling. His mouth was wide open—I could see far down into caverns of pale pink throat. I waited a long time for him to die, but his breathing did not weaken. Finally I fired my two remaining shots into the spot where I thought his heart must be. The thick blood welled out of him like red velvet, but still he did not die. His body did not even jerk when the shots hit him, the tortured breathing continued without a pause. He was dying, very slowly and in great agony, but in some world remote from me where not even a bullet could damage him further. I felt that I had got to put an end to that dreadful noise. It seemed dreadful to see the great beast lying there, powerless to move and yet powerless to die, and not even to be able to finish him. I sent back for my small rifle and poured shot after shot into his heart and down his throat. They seemed to make no impression. The tortured gasps continued as steadily as the ticking of a clock.

In the end I could not stand it any longer and went away. I heard later that it took him half an hour to die. Burmans were arriving with dahs[11] and baskets even before I left, and I was told they had stripped his body almost to the bones by the afternoon.

Afterwards, of course, there were endless discussions about the shooting of the elephant. The owner was furious, but he was only an Indian and could do nothing. Besides, legally I had done the right thing, for a mad elephant has to be killed, like a mad dog, if its owner fails to control it. Among the Europeans opinion was divided. The older men said I was right, the younger men said it was a damn shame to shoot an elephant for killing a coolie, because an elephant was worth more than any damn Coringhee[12] coolie. And afterwards I was very glad that the coolie had been killed; it put me legally in the right and it gave me a sufficient pretext for shooting the elephant. I often wondered whether any of the others grasped that I had done it solely to avoid looking a fool.

---

11. Large knives.   12. Burmese place-name.

Dylan Thomas
1914–1953

The Force That Through the Green Fuse Drives the Flower

The force that through the green fuse drives the flower
Drives my green age; that blasts the roots of trees
Is my destroyer.
And I am dumb to tell the crooked rose
5   My youth is bent by the same wintry fever.

The force that drives the water through the rocks
Drives my red blood; that dries the mouthing streams
Turns mine to wax.
And I am dumb to mouth unto my veins
10   How at the mountain spring the same mouth sucks.

The hand that whirls the water in the pool
Stirs the quicksand; that ropes the blowing wind
Hauls my shroud sail.
And I am dumb to tell the hanging man
15   How of my clay is made the hangman's lime.

The lips of time leech to the fountain head;
Love drips and gathers, but the fallen blood
Shall calm her sores.
And I am dumb to tell a weather's wind
20   How time has ticked a heaven round the stars.

And I am dumb to tell the lover's tomb
How at my sheet goes the same crooked worm.

1933

Do Not Go Gentle into That Good Night

Do not go gentle into that good night,
Old age should burn and rave at close of day;
Rage, rage against the dying of the light.

Though wise men at their end know dark is right,
5   Because their words had forked no lightning they
Do not go gentle into that good night.

Good men, the last wave by, crying how bright
Their frail deeds might have danced in a green bay,
Rage, rage against the dying of the light.

10   Wild men who caught and sang the sun in flight,
And learn, too late, they grieved it on its way,
Do not go gentle into that good night.

Grave men, near death, who see with blinding sight
Blind eyes could blaze like meteors and be gay,
15   Rage, rage against the dying of the light.

And you, my father, there on the sad height,
Curse, bless, me now with your fierce tears, I pray.
Do not go gentle into that good night.
Rage, rage against the dying of the light.

1951

Philip Larkin
1922–1985

MCMXIV[1]

Those long uneven lines
Standing as patiently
As if they were stretched outside
The Oval or Villa Park,
5   The crowns of hats, the sun
On moustached archaic faces
Grinning as if it were all
An August Bank Holiday lark;

And the shut shops, the bleached
10   Established names on the sunblinds,
The farthings and sovereigns,
And dark-clothed children at play
Called after kings and queens,
The tin advertisements
15   For cocoa and twist, and the pubs
Wide open all day;

And the countryside not caring:
The place-names all hazed over
With flowering grasses, and fields
20   Shadowing Domesday[2] lines
Under wheat's restless silence;
The differently-dressed servants
With tiny rooms in huge houses,
The dust behind limousines;

25   Never such innocence,
Never before or since,
As changed itself to past
Without a word—the men
Leaving the gardens tidy,
30   The thousands of marriages
Lasting a little while longer:
Never such innocence again.

1960   1964

---

1. 1914, in the style of a monument to the war dead.   value, and ownership of lands in England.
2. The Domesday Book is the medieval record of the extent,

Seamus Heaney
b. 1939

The Singer's House

When they said *Carrickfergus*[1] I could hear
the frosty echo of saltminers' picks.
I imagined it, chambered and glinting,
a township built of light.

5   What do we say any more
to conjure the salt of our earth?
So much comes and is gone
that should be crystal and kept,

and amicable weathers
10   that bring up the grain of things,
their tang of season and store,
are all the packing we'll get.

So I say to myself *Gweebarra*[2]
and its music hits off the place
15   like water hitting off granite.
I see the glittering sound

framed in your window,
knives and forks set on oilcloth[3],
and the seals' heads, suddenly outlined,
20   scanning everything.

People here used to believe
that drowned souls lived in the seals.
At spring tides they might change shape.
They loved music and swam in for a singer

25   who might stand at the end of summer
in the mouth of a whitewashed turf-shed,
his shoulder to the jamb, his song
a rowboat far out in evening.

When I came here first you were always singing,
30   a hint of the clip of the pick
in your winnowing climb and attack.
Raise it again, man. We still believe what we hear.

---

1. Seaport just north of Belfast on the northeast coast of Ireland.
2. Bay in County Donegal, in the northwest of Ireland.
3. Stiff, waterproof cloth often used as tablecloth.

Postscript

And some time make the time to drive out west
Into County Clare,[1] along the Flaggy Shore,
In September or October, when the wind
And the light are working off each other
5   So that the ocean on one side is wild
With foam and glitter, and inland among stones
The surface of a slate-grey lake is lit
By the earthed lightning of a flock of swans,
Their feathers roughed and ruffling, white on white,
10   Their fully grown headstrong-looking heads
Tucked or cresting or busy underwater.
Useless to think you'll park and capture it
More thoroughly. You are neither here nor there,
A hurry through which known and strange things pass
15   As big soft buffetings come at the car sideways
And catch the heart off guard and blow it open.

Ted Hughes

Hawk Roosting

I sit in the top of the wood, my eyes closed.
Inaction, no falsifying dream
Between my hooked head and hooked feet:
Or in sleep rehearse perfect kills and eat.

The convenience of the high trees!
The air's buoyancy and the sun's ray
Are of advantage to me;
And the earth's face upward for my inspection.

My feet are locked upon the rough bark.
It took the whole of Creation
To produce my foot, my each feather:
Now I hold Creation in my foot

Or fly up, and revolve it all slowly—
I kill where I please because it is all mine.
There is no sophistry in my body:
My manners are tearing off heads—

The allotment of death.
For the one path of my flight is direct
Through the bones of the living.
No arguments assert my right:

The sun is behind me.
Nothing has changed since I began.
My eye has permitted no change.
I am going to keep things like this.

1. County in west Ireland.

Eavan Boland

b. 1944

The Pomegranate

The only legend I have ever loved is
The story of a daughter lost in hell.
And found and rescued there.
Love and blackmail are the gist of it.
5   Ceres and Persephone the names.
And the best thing about the legend is
I can enter it anywhere. And have.
As a child in exile in
A city of fogs and strange consonants,
10   I read it first and at first I was
An exiled child in the crackling dusk of
The underworld, the stars blighted. Later
I walked out in a summer twilight
Searching for my daughter at bedtime.
15   When she came running I was ready
To make any bargain to keep her.
I carried her back past whitebeams.
And wasps and honey-scented buddleias.
But I was Ceres then and I knew
20   Winter was in store for every leaf
On every tree on that road.
Was inescapable for each one we passed.
And for me.
It is winter
25   And the stars are hidden.
I climb the stairs and stand where I can see
My child asleep beside her teen magazines,
Her can of Coke, her plate of uncut fruit.
The pomegranate! How did I forget it?
30   She could have come home and been safe
And ended the story and all
Our heartbroken searching but she reached
Out a hand and plucked a pomegranate.[1]
She put out her hand and pulled down
35   The French sound for apple and
The noise of stone and the proof
That even in the place of death,
At the heart of legend, in the midst
Of rocks full of unshed tears
40   Ready to be diamonds by the time
The story was told, a child can be

---

1. In the classical myth, Persephone would have emerged from the underworld unharmed except for the fact that she broke a command to bring nothing back: by plucking a pomegranate, she became liable to death. The next lines recall the derivation of the term "pomegranate" from Old French *pomme granade*, "seeded apple."

Hungry. I could warn her. There is still a chance.
The rain is cold. The road is flint-coloured.
The suburb has cars and cable television.
45   The veiled stars are above ground.
It is another world. But what else
Can a mother give her daughter but such
Beautiful rifts in time?
If I defer the grief I will diminish the gift.
50   The legend must be hers as well as mine.
She will enter it. As I have.
She will wake up. She will hold
The papery, flushed skin in her hand.
And to her lips. I will say nothing.

Derek Walcott

b. 1930

A Far Cry from Africa

A wind is ruffling the tawny pelt
Of Africa. Kikuyu,[1] quick as flies,
Batten° upon the bloodstreams of the veldt.°   *fasten / open country*
Corpses are scattered through a paradise.
5   Only the worm, colonel of carrion, cries:
  "Waste no compassion on these separate dead!"
Statistics justify and scholars seize
The salients of colonial policy.
What is that to the white child hacked in bed?
10   To savages, expendable as Jews?

Threshed out by beaters, the long rushes break
In a white dust of ibises[2] whose cries
Have wheeled since civilization's dawn
From the parched river or beast-teeming plain.
15   The violence of beast on beast is read
As natural law, but upright man
Seeks his divinity by inflicting pain.
Delirious as these worried beasts, his wars
Dance to the tightened carcass of a drum,
20   While he calls courage still that native dread
Of the white peace contracted by the dead.

Again brutish necessity wipes its hands
Upon the napkin of a dirty cause, again
A waste of our compassion, as with Spain,
25   The gorilla wrestles with the superman.
I who am poisoned with the blood of both,
Where shall I turn, divided to the vein?

---

1. Indigenous people of Kenya.   2. Wading birds resembling storks.

I who have cursed
The drunken officer of British rule, how choose
30   Between this Africa and the English tongue I love?
Betray them both, or give back what they give?
How can I face such slaughter and be cool?
How can I turn from Africa and live?

52

I heard them marching the leaf-wet roads of my head,
the sucked vowels of a syntax trampled to mud,
a division of dictions, one troop black, barefooted,
the other in redcoats bright as their sovereign's blood;
5   their feet scuffled like rain, the bare soles with the shod.
One fought for a queen, the other was chained in her service,
but both, in bitterness, travelled the same road.
Our occupation and the Army of Occupation
are born enemies, but what mortar can size
10   the broken stones of the barracks of Brimstone Hill
to the gaping brick of Belfast? Have we changed sides
to the moustached sergeants and the horsy gentry
because we serve English, like a two-headed sentry
guarding its borders? No language is neutral;
15   the green oak of English is a murmurous cathedral
where some took umbrage,[1] some peace, but every shade, all,
helped widen its shadow. I used to haunt the arches
of the British barracks of Vigie[2]. There were leaves there,
bright, rotting like revers or epaulettes[3], and the stenches
20   of history and piss. Leaves piled like the dropped aitches
of soldiers from rival shires, from the brimstone trenches
of Agincourt to the gas of the Somme.[4] On Poppy Day[5]
our schools bought red paper flowers. They were for Flanders.[6]
I saw Hotspur cursing the smoke through which a popinjay
25   minced from the battle. Those raging commanders
from Thersites to Percy,[7] their rant is our model.
I pinned the poppy to my blazer. It bled like a vowel.

1. In two senses: offence, shade.
2. Vigie Beach near Castries, Saint Lucia.
3. Turned-up edges of ornamental shoulder pieces worn on uniforms.
4. French sites of important battles in 1415 and in World War I.
5. Veterans Day.
6. Scene of a disastrous World War I offensive—"the battle of the mud"—in which the British lost 324,000 soldiers.
7. The headstrong Sir Henry Percy (1364–1403) became known as "Hotspur"; he serves as rival to Prince Hal in Shakespeare's *Henry IV*. Thersites accuses Achilles of cowardice in Homer's *Iliad*.

INDEX

Alfred, Lord Tennyson, 227
Argument of His Book, The, 126
Arnold, Matthew, 272
Auden, W.H., 452
Aurora Leigh, 225–27

Barbauld, Anna Letitia, 178
Bede, 20
Beowulf, 5–19
Blake, William, 179
Boland, Eavan, 462
Boswell, James, 176
Browning, Elizabeth Barrett, 224
Browning, Robert, 235
Burns, Robert, 188
Byron, George Gordon, Lord, 206

Canterbury Tales, 44–50
Carroll, Lewis, 276
Charge of the Light Brigade, The, 233–34
Chaucer, Geoffrey, 41
Childe Harold's Pilgrimage, 207–8
"Childe Roland to the Dark Tower Came," 238–41
Chimney Sweeper, The, 181
Coleridge, Samuel Taylor, 198
Composed upon Westminster Bridge, Sept. 3, 1802, 195
Conrad, Joseph, 317
Convergence of the Twain, The, 388–89
Crown of Sonnets Dedicated to Love, A., 125

Daughters of the Late Colonel, The, 426–38
Dead, The, 392–418
Delight in Disorder, 126
Diary, The, 138–42
Dickens, Charles, 221
Dictionary of the English Language, A, 172–76
Dombey and Son, 221–22
Don Juan, 209–12
Donne, John, 123
Do Not Go Gentle into That Good Night, 458–59
Dover Beach, 272
Doyle, Sir Arthur Conan, 257

Ecclesiastical History of the English People, An, 20–22
Elegy Written in a Country Churchyard, 168–71
Eliot, T.S., 418
Elizabeth I, 58
Equiano, Olaudah, 185

Essay on Criticism, An, 164–65

Faerie Queene, The, 52–58
Far Cry from Africa, A, 463–64
52, 464
Fly, The, 182
Force That Through Green Fuse Drives the Flower, The, 458

Gaskell, Elizabeth, 242
Geoffrey of Monmouth, 27
God's Grandeur, 275
Good Morrow, The, 123
Gordon, George. See Byron, George Gordon, Lord
Gransmere Journals, The, 196–97
Gray, Thomas, 168
Gulliver's Travels, 144–63

Hard Times, 222–23
Hardy, Thomas, 388
Hawk Roosting, 461
Heaney, Seamus, 460
Heart of Darkness, 317–20
Herrick, Robert, 126
Hesperides, 126–27
History of the Kings of Britain, 27–28
Holy Sonnets, 124–25
Hopkins, Gerard Manley, 275
How Soon Hath Time, 128
Hughes, Ted, 461
Humpty Dumpty on Jabberwocky, 277–78

Importance of Being Earnest, The, 278–317
In Memoriam A.H.H., 232–33
Interesting Narrative of the Life of Olaudah Equiano, The, 185–86
It is a beauteous Evening, 195
I wandered lonely as a cloud, 195–96

Jabberwocky, 276–77
Johnson, Samuel, 172
Jonson, Ben, 122
Joyce, James, 392

Keats, John, 218
Kubla Khan, 205–6

Lady of Shalott, The, 227–31
Lake Isle of Innisfree, The, 390
Lamb, The, 180
Larkin, Philip, 459
Lawrence, D.H., 439

Life of Samuel Johnson, LL.D., The, 176–78
Lines Written a Few Miles above Tintern Abbey, 190–94
Lines Written in Early Spring, 190
Love Among the Ruins, 236–38
Love Song of J. Alfred Prufrock, The, 418–21

Mansfield, Katherine, 426
Marlow, Christopher, 60
Marvell, Andrew, 127
Mary, Lady Chudleigh, 142
MCMXIV, 459
Metres of Boethius's Consolation of Philosophy, The, 59
Milton, John, 128
Mouse's Petition to Dr. Priestley, The, 178–79
Musée des Beaux Arts, 452
My heart leaps up, 196
My Last Duchess, 235–36

"No, Thank You, John," 273–74
Nymph's Reply to the Shepherd, The, 63

Ode to a Nightingale, 219–21
Ode to the West Wind, 213–15
Odour of Chrysanthemums, 439–51
On First Looking into Chapman's Homer, 218
On My First Son, 122
On Something, That Walks Somewhere, 122
On the Departure Platform, 388
Orwell, George, 453
Our Society at Cranford, 242–56
Ozymandias, 212–13

Paradise Lost, 129–37
Passionate Shepherd to His Love, The, 60
Pepys, Samuel, 138
Pied Beauty, 276
Poison Tree, A, 184
Pomegranate, The, 462–63
Pope, Alexander, 164
Postscript, 461
Promises Like Pie-Crust, 274
Psalm 13, 58–59
Pygmalion, 321–87

Raleigh, Sir Walter, 63
Rape of the Lock, The, 166–68
Red, Red Rose, A, 189
Rime of the Ancient Mariner, The, 198–205

Room of One's Own, A, 422–25
Rossetti, Christina, 273

Sailing to Byzantium, 391
Scandal in Bohemia, A, 257–71
Shakespeare, William, 65
Shaw, Bernard, 321
Shelley, Percy Bysshe, 212
She walks in beauty, 206
Shooting an Elephant, 453–57
Singer's House, The, 460
Sir Gawain and the Green Knight, 29–40
Songs
    "She dwelt among th' untrodden ways," 194
    When I am dead, my dearest, 273
Songs of Innocence and of Experience, 180–84
Song to Celia, 122–23
Sonnets from the Portuguese, 224

Sonnets (Shakespeare), 65–66
Spenser, Edmund, 51
Swift, Jonathan, 143

Thomas, Dylan, 458
To a Mouse, 188–89
To a Sky-Lark, 215–17
To His Coy Mistress, 127–28
To the Ladies, 142
To the Virgins, to Make Much of Time, 126–27
Tragical History of Dr. Faustus, The, 60–62
Twelfth Night; or, What You Will, 66–121
Tyger, The, 183

Valediction: Forbidding Mourning, A., 123–24
Vindication of the Rights of Woman, A, 187–88

Walcott, Derek, 463
Wanderer, The, 23–25
When I Consider How My Light Is Spent, 129
When I have fears, 218
Wilde, Oscar, 278
Wild Swans at Coole, The, 390–91
Windhover, The, 275
Wollstonecraft, Mary, 187
Woolf, Virginia, 422
Wordsworth, Dorothy, 196
Wordsworth, William, 190
World is too much with us, The, 194
Wroth, Lady Mary, 125

Yeats, William Butler, 390

Color Plate 1 First page of the Gospel of Matthew, from the *Lindisfarne Gospels*, c. 698. This illustrated gospel book was made on the "holy island" of Lindisfarne off the coast of Northumberland, partly in honor of St. Cuthbert, who had died there 11 years earlier and whose cult was fast developing at the time. The manuscript reflects an extraordinary flowering of artistic production during these years, and the meeting of world cultures that occurred in Northumbrian monastic life: Mediterranean Latin language and imagery, Celtic interlace, and Germanic animal motifs. In the 10th century an Anglo-Saxon translation was added in the margins and between the lines. *(By permission of The British Library, Cott. Nero. D.IV f.27.)*

Color Plate 2 Gold buckle, from the Sutton Hoo ship-burial, c. 625–630. Fragments of a remarkably preserved ship-burial, probably for an Anglo-Saxon king, were discovered among other burial mounds at Sutton Hoo, in Suffolk, England, in 1939. The burial mound contained numerous coins and 41 objects in gold, among them this magnificent buckle. Stylized animal heads (including two dragons in the circle at bottom) invite comparison with the powerful animal imagery in *Beowulf.* Other objects in the ship include two silver spoons inscribed "Saul" and "Paul," signs of the mixing of pagan practices and Christian influences in this era. *(Copyright The British Museum.)*

Color Plate 3 The Ardagh Chalice, c. 9th century. This greatest surviving piece of medieval Celtic metalwork was found near the site of an ancient fort at Ardagh, in County Limerick in the southwest of Ireland. Measuring 9.5 inches across and 7 inches tall, the chalice was probably used for wine on great holidays like Easter, when laypeople took Communion. In the 7th century, the learned Irish monk Adamnan had described the chalice of the Last Supper as a silver cup with two opposite handles. The Ardagh Chalice is very similar. It is made of silver alloy, magnificently decorated with gilt and enamel. Its elaborate interlace decoration uses a wide range of Celtic motifs, including fearsomely toothed animal heads. In a band running around the entire bowl are the names of the 12 apostles, further linking its liturgical role to the Last Supper. *(National Museum of Ireland.)*

Color Plate 4 Map of England, from Matthew Paris's *Historia Major*, mid-13th century. A monk of St. Albans, Matthew Paris wrote a monumental *History of England*, of which two illustrated copies in his own hand survive. Matthew's richly detailed map of England, including counties and major towns, illustrates the geographical knowledge of his day. It further suggests how alert he was to the ethnic divisions that still crossed his island and to the settlements and invasions, both mythic and actual, that had given rise to them. His inscription near the depiction of Hadrian's Wall, for example, informs us that the wall "once divided the English and the Picts." Recalling the claim that the original Britons were Trojan refugees, he writes about Wales (left center): "The people of this region are descended from the followers of Brutus." The story of Arthur's conception may have led Paris to identify Tintagel ("Tintaiol," lower left). Matthew also links geography and racial character, as in his comment on northern Scotland (top center): "A mountainous, woody region producing an uncivilized people." *(By permission of The British Library, Cott. Claud. D.IV f.12v.)*

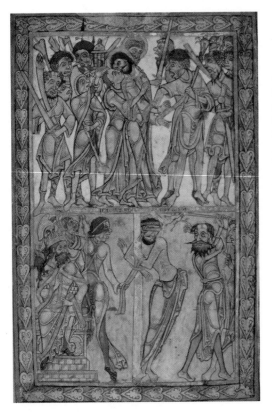

Color Plate 5 *Passion Scenes,* from the *Winchester Psalter,* 1150–1160. A series of full-page miniatures of crucial scenes from the Bible precedes the Psalter texts of this manuscript. The page reproduced here depicts scenes of the betrayal and flagellation of Christ. The vividly drawn images show the clinging drapery and exaggerated expressions typical of the manuscript; equally exaggerated are the African and Semitic features of some of the tormentors, associating them with peoples who were exotic or reviled in 12th-century England. Some of the original richness of color of this manuscript has been lost through damp, but also because blue pigment has been scraped off, presumably for reuse—a sign of how costly was the making of such manuscripts. *(By permission of The British Library, Cott. Nero. C.IV f.21.)*

Color Plate 6 *King Arthur and His Knights,* from a manuscript of the *Prose Lancelot,* late 13th century. This miniature appears in a manuscript of French prose Arthurian romances, which were also widely known in England. Here, King Arthur asks his knights to tell about their adventures on the quest for the Holy Grail. *(Beinecke Rare Book and Manuscript Library, Yale University.)*

Color Plate 7 *Annunciation to the Shepherds* (top) and *Nativity Scene* (bottom), from *The Holkham Bible Picture Book*, c. 1325–1330. This vividly illustrated manuscript depicts episodes from the Bible, adding events from later Christian legends. Crowded scenes are vigorous and full of gesture; they may reflect contact with liturgical drama and look forward to vernacular enactments such as the *Second Play of the Shepherds*. Short rhyming narratives above each picture mix up the major languages of early 14th-century England. At first the shepherds cannot understand the angel's Latin "*Gloria in excelsis*"; in Anglo-French they say "Glum? Glo? That means nothing. Let's go there, we'll understand better." At the scene of the Nativity, below, Middle English breaks in and "Songen alle with one stevene [voice]," though the shepherds can now sing famous Latin hymns: "*Gloria in excelsis deo*" and "*Te deum laudamus*." Both the images and French and Middle English text mediate between the learned clerical class and the wealthy lay people who were the manuscript's intended audience. *(By permission of The British Library, Add. 18850 f.257v.)*

Color Plate 8 *Richard II with His Regalia*, 1394–1395. Richard himself commissioned this splendid life-size and unusually lifelike portrait soon after the death of his beloved first wife, Anne of Bohemia. It was probably mounted at the back of the King's private pew at Westminster Abbey in London, but it also may suggest his wish to be perpetually near Anne, who was entombed nearby. At the same time, the throne, crown, orb, and scepter are all signs of Richard's sense of kingship and secular authority. *(Copyright: Dean and Chapter of Westminster.)*

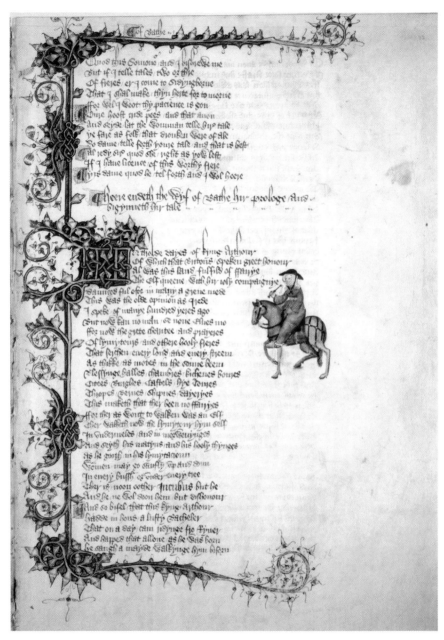

Color Plate 9 Opening page of *The Wife of Bath's Tale,* from the Ellesmere manuscript of Chaucer's *Canterbury Tales*, 1405–1410. One of the two earliest surviving manuscripts of the *Tales,* it was owned for centuries by the Egerton family, who became Earls of Ellesmere in the nineteenth century. The Ellesmere Chaucer was probably made in London, by then the center of book production in England. Its elaborate decoration and illustration are all the more striking, given how few Middle English texts received such treatment. The portrait of the Wife of Bath is positioned to highlight the beginning of her tale. Her red clothing, whip, and large hat follow details of her description in the *General Prologue* of the *Tales,* and her own words in the prologue to her tale. The grandeur of the treatment of text and decoration in this manuscript—clearly meant both for display and reading—reflect the speed with which Chaucer became a "canonical" author in the years after his death in 1400, and perhaps the wish of wealthy patrons to associate themselves and their interests with his work. It is partly the same wish that ultimately led the American railroad tycoon Henry E. Huntington to buy the manuscript in 1917 and leave it to his library in San Marino, California. *(This item is reproduced by permission of The Huntington Library, San Marina, California. EL26C9F72r.)*

Color Plate 10 *Anne, Duchess of Bedford, Kneeling Before the Virgin Mary and Saint Anne*, from the *Bedford Hours*, early 15th century. A book of hours was a prayerbook used by laypeople for private devotion. The *Bedford Hours* was produced in a Paris workshop for the Duke of Bedford, a brother of Henry V, and his wife, Anne of Burgundy. Here, Saint Anne is shown teaching her daughter, the Virgin Mary, to read; another book lies open on a lectern in front of the kneeling Anne of Burgundy. *(By permission of The British Library, Add. 18850 f.257v.)*

Color Plate 11 John Martin, *The Bard*, 1817. "Ruin seize thee, ruthless King!" According to the legend retold in Thomas Gray's 1757 ode *The Bard*, in the thirteenth century Edward I attempted to stamp out Welsh resistance to English power by ordering the court poets, bards, put to death. John Martin's large canvas captures the sublime moment at which the last bard denounced the invading monarch before leaping into the River Conway below. *(Tyne and Wear Museums.)*

Color Plate 12   Thomas Gainsborough (1727–1788), *Mrs. Mary Robinson ("Perdita")*. Gainsborough was one of the most fashionable portraitists of his day, surpassed only by his rival Sir Joshua Reynolds. His elegant depiction of the actress and poet Mary Robinson is witness to her social triumph. The locket in Robinson's hand reveals a portrait of the Prince of Wales, whose infatuation with her was the cause of her first celebrity. *(By kind permission of the trustees of the Wallace Collection.)*

Color Plate 13   Thomas Phillips (1770–1845), *George Gordon Byron, 6th Baron Byron,* (c. 1835, replicated by Thomas Phillips from an 1813 original). Byron himself was the premier model for the "Byronic hero." He wrote to his mother in 1809, full of admiration for Albanian dress: "the most magnificent in the world, consisting of a long <u>white</u> <u>kilt</u>, old worked cloak, crimson velvet gold laced jacket & waistcoat, silver mounted pistols & daggars." He purchased some outfits for himself: "the only expensive articles in this country they cost 50 guineas each & have so much gold they would cost in England two hundred." *(By courtesy of The National Portrait Gallery, London.)*

Color Plate 14 *Portrait of Olaudah Equiano*, late-18th century. This handsome portrait vividly attests Equiano's rise from kidnapped slave to British respectability. *(Royal Albert Memorial Museum, Exeter, Devon, UK/Bridgeman Art Library.)*

Color Plate 15 Joseph Mallord William Turner (British 1775–1851), *Slave Ship (Slavers Throwing Overboard the Dead and Dying, Typhoon Coming On)*, 1840. Turner depicts a notorious incident that galvanized the abolition movement. In 1781 the captain of the slave ship *Zong* ordered 133 weak and diseased slaves ejected into shark-infested waters, planning to collect on a policy that held the insurer liable for cargo jettisoned in order to salvage the remainder. In 1783 Olaudah Equiano brought the incident to the attention of the abolition movement; the resulting trial (which debated not the captain's criminal liability but the insurer's financial liability), presided over by Lord Mansfield, sided with the captain. (*Oil on canvas, 90.8 x 122.6 cm [35 3/4 x 48 1/4 in.]. Henry Lillie Pierce Fund. Courtesy, Museum of Fine Arts, Boston.*)

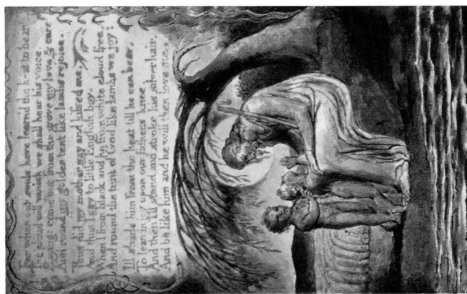

Color Plates 16 and 17 William Blake, two versions of the second plate of *The Little Black Boy*, from *Songs of Innocence*. As can be seen here, Blake sometimes tints the black boy's skin as light as the English boy's (near left); in others, he colors them differently (far left). While the heavenly scene portrays both boys sheltered by the tree and welcomed by Christ, it also puts the black boy outside the inner circle formed by the curve of Christ's body and the praying English boy. The black boy is not part of this configuration of prayer, but rather a witness to it, stroking the hair of the English boy, who has no regard for him. *(Fitzwilliam Museum, University of Cambridge, UK/Bridgeman Art Library.)*

Color Plate 18 (far left)   William Blake, *The Tyger*, from *Songs of Experience*. In some copies, Blake colors the tyger in lurid tones; in others, the tyger is colored in pastels. Strangely, the unmenacing, sideways image of the tyger not only fails to display the "fearful symmetry" that alarms the poem's speaker, but also seems no cause for the horrified tone of address. *(Fitzwilliam Museum, University of Cambridge, UK/Bridgeman Art Library.)*

Color Plate 19 (near left)   William Blake, *The Sick Rose*, from *Songs of Experience*. The sickness of the rosebush is conveyed not only by its trailing on the ground but also by several particulars: the encircling thorns; the quite visible worm wrapped around the naked body emerging (in joy? in pain?) from the rose; the caterpillars devouring the leaves; a second naked body constricted by a snakelike worm. *(Fitzwilliam Museum, University of Cambridge, UK/Bridgeman Art Library.)*

Color Plate 20   Joseph Wright, *An Iron Forge Viewed from Without*, 1773. Derby was a center of the Industrial Revolution, and Wright (1734–1797), a native, gained fame for his treatment of scientific and industrial subjects. He was particularly renowned for his handling of artificial light, and the dramatic contrast of fire and dark in this painting illustrates the romantic effects that could be drawn from technology. The contrast between the lurid forge and the picturesque background also suggests the contemporary spread of manufacture into peaceful landscapes. *(Hermitage, St. Petersburg, Russia/Bridgeman Art Library.)*